THE
CRANE
LOG

American Authors Log Series

Philip Gerard Holthaus
GENERAL EDITOR

THE
CRANE
LOG

A Documentary Life of Stephen Crane
1871–1900

STANLEY WERTHEIM

PAUL SORRENTINO

G.K. HALL & CO.
An Imprint of Macmillan Publishing Company
New York

Maxwell Macmillan Canada
Toronto

Maxwell Macmillan International
New York Oxford Singapore Sydney

G.K. Hall & Co.
An Imprint of Macmillan Publishing Company
866 Third Avenue
New York, NY 10022

Maxwell Macmillan Canada, Inc.
1200 Eglington Avenue East
Suite 200
Don Mills, Ontario M3C 3N1

Macmillan Publishing Company is part of the Maxwell Communications Group
of Companies.

Library of Congress Catalog Card Number: 93–8872

Printed in the United States of America

printing number
1 2 3 4 5 6 7 8 9 10

Library of Congress Cataloging-in-Publication Data
Wertheim, Stanley.
    The Crane log : a documentary life of Stephen Crane, 1871–1900 /
Stanley Wertheim and Paul Sorrentino.
        p. cm. — (American authors log series)
    Includes bibliographical references (p.) and index.
    ISBN 0–8161–7292–7
    1. Crane, Stephen, 1871–1900—Biography. 2. Authors,
American—19th century—Biography. I. Sorrentino, Paul.
II. Title. III. Series.
PS1449.C85Z982   1993
813'.4—dc20   93–8872
[B]   CIP

The paper used in this publication meets the minimum requirements of American
National Standard for Information Sciences —Permanence of Paper for Printed
Library Materials. ANSI Z39.48–1984. ∞™

For Mary and for Peg

Contents

CONTENTS

General Editor's Preface

Malcolm Lowry wrote that "fame like a drunkard consumes the life of the soul." Certainly, early fame probably did Stephen Crane more harm than good. The brilliant achievement of *The Red Badge of Courage*, published when Crane was just twenty-three years old, an achievement that was so obvious that even mediocre critics recognized that Crane had a unique genius, and an achievement that made Crane an overnight literary celebrity, created critical and public expectations that thereafter caused Crane to squander his genius and destroy his health while trying to live up to his reputation as a man who could capture the true essence of war. *The Red Badge* was an imaginative creation, but the public, the critics, and eventually even Crane himself seemed to think it would be bettered only if he immersed himself in actual wartime experiences and then transmuted these experiences into literary gold. In truth, although his adventures as a reporter in the Southwest and Mexico, and as a war correspondent assigned to a filibustering expedition to Cuba in 1896, Greece during the Greco-Turkish War in 1897, and Cuba again during the Spanish-American War did produce occasional examples of inspired writing, his best work after *The Red Badge* rarely had anything to do with warfare, and might well have been written had he pursued a less strenuous life.

Do the major events of an author's life shape his literary work, and eventually his literary reputation, or does the eventual reputation of an author's works shape the interpretation of his known life events and their effect on his works? Many of the world's greatest authors have died in relative obscurity because no one recognized their genius when they were alive or thought to record their conversation, thoughts, and life events. Is not Shakespeare the object of so much interpretation at least in part because the richness of the works and the paucity of information about the author's life encourage maximum fields of interpretation? Crane was recognized as a person of note after the publication of *The Red Badge*, but he died so young—not yet twenty-nine—that none of his contemporary admirers had the opportunity to interview him extensively and neither Crane himself nor anyone else had bothered to record the truly significant events in his life. In a very real sense, a kind of biographical "hole" concerning Crane encouraged speculations and myths about the life that impacted the works and their critical reputation.

His first biographer, Thomas Beer, whose biography was published in 1923, almost a quarter century after Crane's death, envisioned Crane as a kind of ideal embodiment of genius, and went so far as to invent key people in the story of Crane's life, to suppress information about Crane's sex life and his relationship with Cora Crane, to fabricate incidents that exemplified the "true artist" through Crane, and to quote from nonexistent letters from Crane to other correspondents and from other correspondents to Crane to provide "documentation" for his interpretation of Crane's life and work. But Beer's biography, despite its fabrications and misrepresentations, was taken as the truth by subsequent literary historians, and critics of Crane's works. Thus what in many ways was a totally false record of Crane's life was used to interpret Crane's works, thereby leading to a skewed evaluation of his artistic achievement.

His second major biographer, John Berryman, who published his biography in 1950, had the advantage of drawing on another quarter century of Crane scholarship, but he superimposed his own idiosyncratic psychoanalytic interpretation involving mother fixation on Crane's life and literary achievement. And Crane's third major biographer, R. W. Stallman, who created a biography much more in keeping with our current ideas about objectivity, published in 1968, still carried over many of the inaccuracies and myths from Beer and Berryman, with the result that this faulty record of events when used by biographical-minded critics also led to misinterpretation of Crane's works.

Stanley Wertheim and Paul Sorrentino, who have already demonstrated their high standards of scholarly investigation in their jointly edited *The Correspondence of Stephen Crane* (Columbia University Press, 1988) and a host of Crane-related articles, are two scholars who have not only made themselves familiar with the works of Crane, the history of Crane criticism and scholarship, and all the evidence concerning the facts of Crane's life and career, they have devoted years of search and questioning to adding to our knowledge of the true facts of Crane's life and refuting the myths and misrepresentations that have grown up over the decades since Crane's death. In *The Crane Log* Wertheim and Sorrentino attempt to provide a truthful record—based on documented fact, not opinion, conjecture, speculation, wish fulfillment, or myth—of all the known events in the life of

Stephen Crane. This record should serve as the foundation for all subsequent Crane biography, biographical criticism, and literary interpretation.

Jay Leyda deserves our thanks for recognizing that students of American literature needed an exact record of the lives of our country's greatest authors, and for creating such a model record in his *Melville Log*. Inspired by Leyda's effort, we at G. K. Hall Reference have already published Dwight Thomas and David K. Jackson's *The Poe Log* and Raymond R. Borst's *The Thoreau Log*. It is our hope that eventually we will be able to commission and publish a series of logs to record in detail the lives of all of America's greatest authors, men and women, white and black, and that our log series will win recognition as a key resource for American literary studies. Meanwhile, we welcome the latest additon to our log family, Stanley Wertheim and Paul Sorrentino's *The Crane Log*.

PHILIP GERARD HOLTHAUS

Illustrations

ILLUSTRATIONS

ILLUSTRATIONS

Introduction

Reviewing a recently published critical evaluation of Stephen Crane's achievement, Edwin H. Cady commented that "his biography presents so many enigmas, despite his celebrity, that no adequate 'Life' is presently feasible."[1] Cady's intrinsic supposition that the present biographies of Crane are inadequate is not misplaced. As an experimenter in impressionistic prose, a novelist, and a cultural historian of the 1890s, Crane's first biographer, Thomas Beer, had a fortunate empathy with the mind and temperament of his subject. From the beginning, however, critics complained that his book was not an objective factual biography but a verbal mood painting created by a literary pointillist, an inconsecutive accretion of incidents and images lacking in focus and detailed reporting. In Vincent Starrett's often quoted (and often misquoted) assessment, the book is essentially "a study of the times, in strong light; and across that light moves a somewhat inconspicuous shadow called Stephen Crane."[2] John Berryman's densely written *Stephen Crane* (1950) in the American Men of Letters series did little to clarify the details of Crane's life. Although more focused on Crane's personality and art than Beer, Berryman adds little factual information and superimposes a pseudo psychoanalytic reading on his subject that tendentiously attempts to identify patterns of sexual imagery and episodes in Crane's work and incidents in his life with the neurotic fixation on the mother image described in Freud's essay, "A Special Type of Choice of Object Made by Men." Later short biographies of Crane by James B. Colvert (1984) and Christopher Benfey (1992) offer useful summaries, but R. W. Stallman's massive compendium of fact and fallacy, *Stephen Crane: A Biography* (1968; rev. ed. 1973), has by default become generally accepted as the authoritative life. The book incorporates a wealth of primary and secondary material unknown or unavailable to Beer and Berryman: letters, memoirs, tales, sketches, and poems, much of which Stallman brought to light in previous publications. Nevertheless, the narrative is clogged by extended summaries of minor creative writing and travel and war correspondence, and it is sporadically documented and replete with inaccuracies. Reviewers lamented that Stallman had not penetrated into the paradoxes and mysteries of Crane's personality.

Indeed, Crane's proverbial elusiveness has been distended by recent revelations that Beer fabricated many of the letters and incidents that have been the foundation of what has passed for the facts of Crane's life, his literary career, and his critical stances.[3] From the beginning, suspicions were voiced that Beer's *Stephen Crane: A Study in American Letters* (1923) was in essence a work of fiction. Mark Van Doren reviewed it as "a realistic novel. . . . If the book is indeed a novel, and it reads like one from the first page to the last, it is the sort which Crane might have written about himself had he had the inclination and had he known as much about himself as his biographer does."[4] Subsequent biographers of Crane have all expressed their apprehension of Beer's essential unreliability, the pattern of distortion and obfuscation inherent in his colorful, impressionistic style. Nevertheless, they have usually given his unsubstantiated accounts of events and relationships equal authority with those for which independent documentation is available, and they have not distinguished between letters by or about Stephen and Cora Crane whose only source is Beer's biography and his articles and those for which originals are extant or other verification can be made.

Only one of Beer's published Crane letters has come to light, a will sent to his brother William on 29 November 1896[5] that had in part been previously published by Max Herzberg in the *Newark Evening News* and of which Herzberg lent Beer a typescript, which he never returned.[6] There is no parallel in American literary history to the disappearance for 70 years of some 60 letters by a prominent writer to 30 or 40 correspondents.[7] Furthermore, there are no letters to Beer in his extensive correspondence preserved in Yale University's Sterling Library from any of the recipients other than William of the Crane letters quoted in *Stephen Crane: A Study in American Letters.* These facts have more or less been ignored by Crane's biographers, although they have long been aware of them. In consequence of Beer's obfuscations, fabrications, and deceptions, *The Crane Log* excludes letters, accounts of incidents and persons, and chronology that cannot be verified or paralleled outside of his writings. Our understanding of Crane's life, his literary career, and the interrelationships between his art and life is considerably challenged by these proscriptions.

A number of characters hitherto notable in Crane biography as important to the background of his works will not be found in the *Log.* Among these are Olive Brett, who in 1883 "came upon Stephen Crane digging her small nephew from the sands at Ocean Grove and was told that Johnny was a corpse foolishly planted by the burial squad while he still had a canteen full of whisky on him and that Stephen was his provident comrade retrieving supplies" and who later, as Mrs. Armstrong, lent Crane the volumes of *Battles and Leaders of the Civil War* that formed much of the background of *The Red Badge of Courage*;[8] Helen Trent, ostensibly Crane's first serious romantic attachment, whose beautiful arms inspired his poem "Should the wide world roll away"; Edward Grover, the 16-year-old boy Crane is said to have found sobbing on a sidewalk in San Antonio's Alamo Plaza and funded his return home, later advising him in a letter not to "'rush out into the red universe any more'" (p. 116); the nameless farmer who guided a lost and bewildered Crane to his brother Edmund's house in Lake View, New Jersey, and who became the model for the man with the cheery voice in *The Red Badge* (p. 92); Thomas McCumber, described as a genial barfly who Richard Harding Davis fought after he claimed in Delmonico's that "Crane was dying of nameless and disgusting diseases and everybody knew it" (p. 202); Keenan, a refugee from the Bowery who in a Mexican boardinghouse "told Crane a tale of shooting down some Mexicans who tried to drive his sheep from a waterhole" (p. 116), giving him the basis for the plot of "A Man and Some Others"; the Mexican guide Miguel Itorbide and the bandit Ramon Colorado, supposedly real-life characters with whom Crane experienced adventures that became the autobiographical framework of his story "One Dash—Horses" (pp. 116–117); and Willis Clarke, Beer's fictional alter ego, whose notes for a Crane biography, including those of extensive interviews with Crane, Beer quotes at length in four chapters of his book.

Some often-quoted apothegms will also not be found in the *Log*. There is no evidence external to Beer that Crane described his mother as hurt "'that any of us should be slipping from Grace and giving up eternal damnation or salvation or those things. You could argue just as well with a wave'" (pp. 49–50); that he wrote a Miss Catherine Harris a letter in November 1896 in which he maintained that in "An Experiment in Misery" he "'tried to make plain that the root of Bowery life is a sort of cowardice. Perhaps I mean a lack of ambition or to willingly be knocked flat and accept the licking'" (p. 140); that he told someone at a dinner party given by Mrs. Edward Garnett "'that I got my artistic education on the Bowery'" (p. 167); or that he told Willis Clarke "'I'm just a dry twig on the edge of the bonfire'" (p. 233).

A number of Beer's accounts of experiences in Crane's obscure early life are equally suspect: that in infancy at Ocean Grove Crane "saw the waves from the beach and had an atrocious dream of black riders on black horses charging at him from the long surf up the shore and so woke screaming night after night" (p. 39); that a few years later in Asbury Park "he saw a white girl stabbed by her negro lover on the edge of a roadmaker's camp" (p. 48); that while a student at Syracuse he was offered a place on a professional baseball team (p. 58); and that *Maggie* was produced by a firm of religious and medical printers who grossly overcharged for the job (pp. 90–91). Another canard extrapolated from Beer by all Crane's subsequent biographers to date is that on returning to the United States from England in April 1898 he attempted to enlist in the navy and was rejected for physical deficiencies. Documentary evidence confirms that Crane was en route to Cuba as a correspondent, which is indicated on his passport, that he had signed an agreement to write articles on the war for Blackwood before leaving London, and that he contracted to report for the *World* within a day or two of his arrival in New York.

Probably spurious as well and not quoted in the *Log* are Crane's frequent negative judgments of literary contemporaries found in Beer's biography but virtually absent from his extant letters or conversations recorded in reminiscences: *A Connecticut Yankee in King Arthur's Court* was as "'inappropriate as a drunken bride'" (p. 93), and "a baby could have improved the end of 'Huckleberry Finn'!" (p. 113); Tolstoy's *War and Peace* was too long—"He could have done the whole business in one third of the time and made it just as wonderful. It goes on and on like Texas'"(p. 143); *Anna Karenina* was also too long because Tolstoy "'has to stop and preach'" (p. 157); a "lesser fellow named Flaubert . . . had written a novel much too long called Salammbô" that was "a firework which failed to explode," but it "was better writing than the English could do" (p. 55); Zola "is a sincere writer but—is he much good? He hangs one thing to another and his story goes along but I find him pretty tiresome" (p. 148); Frederic's *The Damnation of Theron Ware* "'could have been written a darned lot better'" (p. 150); Walter Besant would be "'forgotten in twenty years'"; most of Robert Louis Stevenson's work was "'insincere'" (p. 231).

To compensate for the repudiation of Beer's apocrypha, *The Crane Log* incorporates and synthesizes a good deal of material unknown to previous biographers or only partly and inadequately utilized by them. Much of Crane's shadowy childhood is highlighted by information about the activities of members of his immediate family gleaned from the microfilm newspaper files of Port Jervis and Asbury Park. Especially important are the sermons, debates, public writings, and family letters of his father, the Reverend Jonathan Townley Crane, and the fervent temperance and other social work of his mother,

Helen Peck Crane; the reminiscences of his brothers Edmund and Wilbur, and the social and professional activities of two other brothers, William and Townley; and a rediscovered transcription by John Berryman of a diary of Jonathan Townley Crane encompassing Stephen's early years and a diary kept by his sister Agnes Elizabeth in much the same period of time. In addition, a new reminiscence by Carl F. Price emphasizes the close relationship between Stephen and Agnes and recounts anecdotes about Crane's camping experience and fraternity life. Significant corrections to previous accounts of Crane's childhood emerge from these sources, such as the fact that he began formal schooling at the normal age of six and not eight and that after his father died in February 1881 he most likely remained in the care of Edmund, who was teaching school in Sussex County, New Jersey, and did not move to Roseville with the rest of the family. A presentiment of his later stubborn independence is shown in his dropping out of Pennington Seminary and refusing to return because a teacher had charged him with lying.

Investigations by Michael Robertson and the research notes assembled by Melvin H. Schoberlin for his unfinished Crane biography "Flagon of Despair" supplement known sources and afford new details of Crane's brief sojourns at Lafayette College and Syracuse University, his hitherto little-explored social life as a student, and the circumstances of his abrupt departures from these institutions. Schoberlin's plausible attribution to Crane of a newspaper sketch, "Where 'De Gang' Hears the Band Play," and the recollections of a fellow student that Crane and his friends frequented a music hall where "pretty girls sang and danced on the stage daringly clad in low neck waists and skirts just above the knees" as well as visiting often another flat in Syracuse's tenderloin district inhabited by "Madge and her friends"[9] provide supporting evidence for a Syracuse origin of *Maggie*. The Schoberlin collection and contemporary newspaper accounts also offer new details and insights into Crane's relationships with Lily Brandon Munroe and Amy Leslie and his involvement in the Dora Clark incident. A previously unpublished reminiscence by W. W. Carroll illuminates the autobiographical background of "An Experiment in Misery."

Subsequent milestones in Crane's life were his early years in New York City, his journey through the West and Mexico for the Bacheller newspaper syndicate, the publication and reception of *The Black Riders* and *The Red Badge of Courage*, the Dora Clark affair, which added notoriety to his newly acquired fame, the wreck of the *Commodore*, Crane's reporting of the Greco-Turkish War of 1897 and the Cuban War, and his years in England with their important literary relationships, short-lived triumphs, decline in popularity, and struggle for survival. These are illuminated by an interweaving of excerpts from his works, letters from and to him, representative newspaper and magazine reviews of his books, many of them previously unknown, and important reminiscences by friends and literary confreres hitherto undiscovered. Crane's life and literary career are reconstructed through the use of contemporary sources to the extent that this can be accomplished.

First publication of works published in Crane's lifetime is noted. The vague and faulty chronology of previous biographers is refined and corrected through the use of primary sources whenever these are available. A much greater degree of precision in correlation of time and place is attained, and a number of small but notable shifts result. For example, Crane's trip to eastern Pennsylvania to report conditions in the coal mines for S. S. McClure's newspaper syndicate and *McClure's Magazine* occurred in mid-May and not in June 1894, and the experiences with the First Marine Battalion at Guantánamo Bay that Crane reported in his early correspondence for the *New York World* took place on 10–12 June 1898 and not on 7–9 June. The detailed documentation of the *Log* should provide an ordered and accurate record that, along with Crane's recently published correspondence, offers basic support for the much-needed definitive biography.

Entries in the *Log* are arranged chronologically, interrupted by a minimal amount of editorial commentary to reconcile discrepancies or to explain scholarly controversies surrounding particular events. Chapters correspond to significant periods in Crane's life and begin with a summary of the most important events. The list of sources following the text identifies citations. Brief identifications of persons appearing in the *Log* are made in the text. Added information about prominent individuals, when available, may be found in the Biographical Notes preceding the text. Each entry begins with a date based on existing evidence. A date in brackets can be supported only by imprecise evidence, logic, or conjecture. Dates verifiable only by month or year appear in appropriate position rather than mechanically at the beginning of a month or year. For example, a monthly magazine was presumably available at the beginning of the month; thus "A Tent in Agony," which appeared in the December 1892 issue of *Cosmopolitan*, was most likely available before 1 December. Crane's important friendship with Corwin K. Linson, however, though it begins at the beginning of 1893, cannot be pinned down more closely than to say they had met by the end of January 1893; thus it appears at the end of that month. Similarly, Crane inscribed his name in a copy of one of Bishop Jesse T. Peck's books, but the inscription cannot be dated more closely than 1881; hence the entry appears at the end of that year. If there are multiple entries for the same date, the date appears once, with the entries under it. If possible, the series of entries is arranged logically, with an attempt to decide what was done earlier in the day and what was done later. In some instances, however, there is no clear sequence. In these instances, excerpts to or from Crane appear first, followed by entries from writers mentioning him; these entries may be followed by Crane's publication on that day and finally by reviews of his work. An entry for a clearly identifiable date and one for a bracketed date are not treated as multiple entries for the same date. Hence, 6 JANUARY and [6 JANUARY] for 1895 are listed separately.

Excerpts from manuscripts are presented as clear text, with no attempt to correct errors or to use *sic* except where it is essential to prevent confusion. This practice is observed despite such idiosyncrasies as Stephen and Cora Crane's eccentric spelling or John Berryman's confusing use of dots, which may indicate an ellipsis or random marks between passages, in his transcription of the Reverend Jonathan Townley Crane's diary. Entries from *The Correspondence of Stephen Crane* and other editions of letters are reproduced as they appear in these editions. In entries from other printed sources such as contemporary newspapers and magazines or from typescripts, we have silently corrected obvious typographical errors. In a few instances we have added *sic* to alert the reader to confusing wording, and at times we have added brackets to clarify the texts. In one or two instances an entry contains wavy brackets that are used in the quoted source to indicate an editorial reconstruction of destroyed or partly illegible text. Titles of newspapers are regularized so that the place of publication is treated as part of the title—such as the *New York World* rather than the New York *World*. Entries that require further identification than is given in the text conclude with an abbreviated citation keyed to the list of sources. When useful, citations include references to particular collections in libraries, such as "NN-Berg Collection" and "NN-Century Collection" in the New York Public Library.

For permission to quote unpublished letters and reminiscences of members of the Crane family, we are grateful to Dr. Robert K. Crane, who has contributed much to our understanding of Crane family history and genealogy.

The University Press of Virginia has granted permission to publish excerpts from their 10-volume edition of *The Works of Stephen Crane* (1969–1976). For detailed information about the publication history of

Crane's writings, we are greatly indebted to the historical introductions to these volumes by J. C. Levenson and the textual introductions and notes by Fredson Bowers.

We should like to thank Columbia University Press for permission to reprint excerpts from our edition of *The Correspondence of Stephen Crane*, 2 vols. (1988).

We are much indebted to the librarians who have aided our research. To the following individuals and their libraries special thanks are due: Kenneth A. Lohf, Bernard Crystal, Ellen Scaruffi, Patrick Lawlor, Rare Book and Manuscript Library, Columbia University; Lucy Cox, Sharon Gotkiewicz, and Anita I. Haney, Carol M. Newman Library, Virginia Polytechnic Institute and State University; Mark F. Weimer, Carolyn Davis, Diane Cooter, George Arents Research Library, Syracuse University; Warren Platt, New York Public Library; Richard C. Fyffe, University of Connecticut; Dr. Iain G. Brown, National Library of Scotland; Susan Halmi, Centenary College; Ted Zaragoza, Methodist Library, Drew University.

Peter Osborne, III, Executive Director of the Minisink Valley Historical Society, provided valuable information about the life of the Crane family in Port Jervis and its environs. We should also like to thank William G. Clark, Jr., for information about the Sussex County census and Mrs. Walter Von Ignatius, who called our attention to a clipping about the *Pike County Puzzle* in the *Port Jervis Union*.

We are especially grateful to Philip G. Holthaus, general editor of the American Authors Log Series, for his careful review of our manuscript.

The administrations of William Paterson College and Virginia Polytechnic Institute and State University generously granted research time and travel funds.

Notes

1. *Nineteenth-Century Literature* 45 (1990): 395.

2. "Stephen Crane: Notes Biographical and Bibliographical," *Colophon* 2 (September 1931): Part 7.

3. See Stanley Wertheim and Paul Sorrentino, "Thomas Beer: The Clay Feet of Stephen Crane Biography," *American Literary Realism 1870–1910* 22 (Spring 1990): 2–16; John Clendenning, "Thomas Beer's Stephen Crane: The Eye of His Imagination," *Prose Studies* 14 (1991): 68–80; Christopher Benfey, *The Double Life of Stephen Crane* (New York: Knopf, 1992), 7–8. Clendenning concludes that "except for a few snippets, the letters that Beer published in his biography and afterwards were forgeries. It seems

most likely that he did not alter or destroy Crane's letters: he wrote them" (p. 69). Benfey characterizes Beer's biography as "a tissue of lies, a forgery through and through" (p. 8).

4. *Nation* 16 January 1924: 66.

5. *The Correspondence of Stephen Crane*, ed. Stanley Wertheim and Paul Sorrentino (New York: Columbia University Press, 1988) No. 285.

6. Also never returned, although Garnett pleaded with Beer to do so, were the only original Crane letter known to be in Beer's possession, a note inviting Edward Garnett to lunch that Beer did not use in his biography (*Correspondence*, No. 342), and three letters from Cora to Garnett (*Correspondence*, Nos. 442, 445, 449), one of which (No. 442) he quotes. Garnett lent these letters to Beer when he went to England early in 1923 to complete his research. These are now in the Beinecke Library at Yale. It is significant that Beer's excerpts from the typescript of Crane's letter to William and from Cora's letter to Garnett are precise. There are no drafts or revisions as with his spurious Crane letters.

7. To explain this anomaly, Stallman at one point hypothesized that Beer "destroyed all the Crane letters quoted in his book" (*Stephen Crane: A Biography* [New York: Braziller, 1968], viii), an improbable surmise since it seems most unlikely that the many recipients of Crane letters who presumably lent them to Beer would not complain about the destruction of their valuable literary property.

8. Thomas Beer, *Stephen Crane: A Study in American Letters* (New York: Knopf, 1923), 46, 98. Subsequent page references are indicated in the text.

9. William McMahon, "Steve Crane Told to 'Stick to Poems' After 'Bangup' Piano Recital at Party," *Syracuse Post Standard* 20 February 1955: 13.

Biographical Notes on Persons Mentioned in the Text

HENRY MILLS ALDEN (1836–1919) In 1863 Alden accepted an assignment to assist Alfred H. Guernsey in writing *Harper's Pictorial History of the Great Rebellion*. This began a connection with Harper and Brothers that continued for over 50 years. Alden was managing editor of *Harper's Weekly* from 1863 to 1869 and editor of *Harper's Magazine* from 1869 until his death. Under his editorship it became the most widely circulated magazine in the United States.

EBEN ALEXANDER (1851–1911) Educated at Yale, Alexander taught ancient languages there for 13 years. In 1886 he was appointed professor of Greek at the University of North Carolina. During the years 1893 to 1897 he served as envoy extraordinary and minister plenipotentiary to Greece, Rumania, and Serbia. Following his government service, he returned to his university position.

IRVING BACHELLER (1859–1950) After graduating from St. Lawrence University, Bacheller worked for a time on a hotel-trade journal before joining the staff of the *Brooklyn Daily Times*. In 1884, with James W. Johnson, he formed a press syndicate to supply special articles to newspapers and magazines. Besides Stephen Crane, Bacheller introduced Arthur Conan Doyle and Rudyard Kipling to the American reading public. He also supplied material by other contemporary writers, notably Joseph Conrad, Hamlin Garland, and Anthony Hope. In 1896 Bacheller sold his syndicate to John Brisben Walker, the owner of *Cosmopolitan*. From 1898 to 1900 he was Sunday editor of the *New York World*. Bacheller wrote many short stories, poems, and essays and more than 30 novels, the most popular of which, *Eben Holden*, sold almost 1,000,000 copies.

MARK BARR (1871–1950) Born in Pennsylvania but a British subject, Barr became assistant editor of *Electrical World* in 1891. In 1895 he received a degree in physics and mathematics at London University. He was a frequent contributor to professional journals in these fields. His special interest was in early electronic calculating machinery.

ROBERT BARR (1850–1912) Born in Glasgow, Scotland, Barr emigrated to Canada with his family at age five. He joined the editorial staff of the *Detroit Free Press* in 1876, writing under the name "Luke Sharp." In

1881 Barr went to England and with Jerome K. Jerome established the popular monthly magazine the *Idler*, which he edited until his death. The first English publication of *The O'Ruddy* was as a serial in the *Idler*. Barr was the author of many romantic and historical novels, notably *From Whose Bourne* (1893), *Tekla: A Romance of Love and War* (1898), and *The Watermead Affair* (1906).

JOHN D. BARRY (1866–1942) Born and educated in Boston, Barry graduated from Harvard in 1888. For some time he served as drama critic for *Harper's Weekly* and later *Collier's*. He was an instructor in the American Academy of Dramatic Arts and the author of novels. In later years he was a columnist, writing on art, literature, and social questions for San Francisco newspapers.

JOHN F. BASS (1866–1931) Bass graduated from Harvard College in 1891 and from Harvard Law School three years later. During the Greek-Turkish War he was a correspondent for the *New York Times*. In 1898 he covered the Spanish-American War from Manila for *Harper's Weekly*. He also served as a correspondent in the Boxer insurrection in China, the Russian-Japanese War, and World War I.

CHARLES BECKER (1870–1915) Like Crane, Becker grew up in Sullivan County, New York. He came to New York City in his late teens, worked at a number of odd jobs, and in November 1893 was sworn in as a police officer, having saved up the $250 Tammany Hall then extorted from police candidates. Becker was assigned to the 29th Precinct, where he worked under Inspector Alexander "Clubber" Williams, the man who gave the Tenderloin its name. The Tenderloin, an area lying roughly between 23d and 42d streets and Fourth and Seventh avenues, was the entertainment district of the city and consequently afforded the greatest opportunities for corruption and graft. Becker thrived in this environment. He was promoted to sergeant in 1907 and a year or two later, when department ranks were reorganized, he automatically became a lieutenant. In 1912 he was involved in a conspiracy to murder his gambling partner, Herman Rosenthal, who was shot to death in front of the Hotel Metropole on 43d Street near Broadway. Becker became the first policeman to die in the electric chair at Sing Sing Prison. The incident is immortalized by F. Scott Fitzgerald in *The Great Gatsby* (1925) when Meyer Wolfsheim reminisces about the shooting of Rosenthal. "Four of them were electrocuted," Nick Carraway recalls. "Five," replies Wolfsheim, "with Becker."

CURTIS BROWN (1866–1945) Brown began his editorial career on the staff of the *Buffalo Express*. From 1894 to 1898, he was Sunday editor of the *New York Press*, and from 1898 he was London representative for a number of American newspapers. He established his literary agency, Curtis Brown, Ltd., in London and New York and served as president of the London branch. He also founded and headed the International Publishing Bureau.

ABRAHAM CAHAN (1860–1951) Born in what is now Lithuania, the son of a Hebrew teacher, Cahan educated himself largely by self-study and graduated from the Vilna Teacher's Institute in 1881, an accredited government schoolmaster. He emigrated to the United States in 1882 and became a labor agitator, helping to organize the first Jewish tailors' union and the Jewish cloak makers' union. In 1890 Cahan became editor of the weekly *Arbeiter Zeitung*, the organ of the United Hebrew Trades. In 1896 he published *Yekl: A Tale of the New York Ghetto*, the first authentic immigrant novel. It was praised by Howells as an important milestone of literary realism. This book was a forerunner of Cahan's masterful epic of the Jewish immigrant experience, *The Rise of David Levinsky* (1917). For many years Cahan was the editor of the *Jewish Daily Forward*, a socialist newspaper written largely in Yiddish that became a national institution.

WILLA CATHER (1873–1947) Born in Virginia, Cather is best remembered for her depictions of Nebraska, where she spent her youth. She was especially concerned with the transforming impact of a postpioneer environment upon emigrants from older, more stable European societies. Beginning with her junior year at the University of Nebraska, Cather supported herself as a writer for the *Nebraska State Journal* and after graduation as an editor and journalist in Pittsburgh. For five years, during which she produced a book of poems, *April Twilights* (1903), she taught high school English and Latin. Her first collection of stories was *The Troll Garden* (1905). In 1906 Cather moved to New York City,

where she was for a time an editor of *McClure's Magazine. O Pioneers!* (1913) marked her first extended use of Nebraska materials and anticipated *My Ántonia* (1918). *The Professor's House* (1925), partly set in the Southwest, another favorite Cather locale, looked forward to *Death Comes for the Archbishop* (1927), considered by Cather to be her best novel. In later years Cather turned to historical fiction, notably *Shadows on the Rock* (1931) and *Sapphira and the Slave Girl* (1940).

LADY RANDOLPH CHURCHILL (1854–1921) Born in Brooklyn, the daughter of financier Leonard Jerome, owner of the *New York Times*, Jennie Jerome married Lord Henry Randolph Spencer Churchill, second son of the Duke of Marlborough in 1874. They would become the parents of the future prime minister, Winston Spencer Churchill. Jennie's older sister, Clara, married Moreton Frewen, later the owner of Brede Place. Another sister, Leonie, married John Leslie and became mother of the writer Sir Shane Leslie. Lord Randolph died in 1895, and in 1900 Jennie married George Cornwallis-West, 20 years her junior. She launched her elaborate miscellany, the *Anglo-Saxon Review*, in which Crane's "War Memories" appeared, in 1899. The periodical was short-lived, ending publication for financial reasons in 1902 after 10 issues. Through her association with the Society of American Women in London, of which Cora Crane was an honorary member, Lady Churchill was instrumental in raising funds to outfit a hospital ship, the *Maine*, during the Boer War, a gesture signifying the unity of English and American women.

JOSEPH CONRAD (1857–1924) Born in what was then Russian Poland, Józef Teodor Konrad Korzeniowski spent his early life at sea and until the age of 20 was almost entirely ignorant of English. From 1874 he served in the French mercantile marine, at one time running contraband to Spanish royalists. *Nostromo* (1904) and *The Arrow of Gold* (1919) draw on these experiences. From 1878 to 1894 he served aboard English ships, rising through the officers' ranks to become a ship's master in 1886, the year he became a British subject. During 1887 and 1888 Conrad sailed the Malay Archipelago and in the next year cruised the regions of the Congo described in "Heart of Darkness" and "An Outpost of Progress." He left the merchant marine service in January 1894 to establish himself as an author. His first novel, *Almayer's Folly*, appeared in 1895. The next year Conrad married Jessie George, daughter of a bookseller; they had two sons. His second novel, *An Outcast of the Islands*, was published in 1896, and *The Nigger of the "Narcissus"* ran serially in the *New Review* during the latter half of 1897. Two later novels, *The Secret Agent* (1907) and *Under Western Eyes* (1911), drew on his memories of Russia. *Chance* (1914) brought Conrad into prominence, giving him tardy recognition and securing his previously precarious financial future.

COPELAND & DAY At Number 69 Cornhill Street in Boston during the six years between 1893 and 1899, Herbert Copeland and Fred Holland Day produced printed books that attempted to emulate the achievements in fine printing of private presses in England, such as Kelmscott, Ashendene, and Doves, that grew out of the Arts and Crafts movement of the 1880s. Copeland was a member of the staff of the *Youth's Companion,* and a number of Copeland & Day books came from contributors to the magazine, among them John Banister Tabb and Louise Imogen Guiney. Day was the financial and artistic leader of the firm. He was a bibliophile, especially devoted to the poetry of Keats. Copeland & Day were American publishers for *The Yellow Book.* The firm printed 108 titles before its dissolution in 1899. Among the more notable books are Oscar Wilde's *Salome* (1894), with illustrations by Aubrey Beardsley, Bliss Carman and Richard Hovey's *Songs from Vagabondia* (1894), Stephen Crane's *The Black Riders* (1895), and Elizabeth Barrett Browning's *Songs from the Portuguese* (1896).

CORA CRANE (1865–1910) Cora Howorth, known also by her married names of Murphy and Stewart, was 31 years old, the estranged wife of the son of an English baronet, and the madam of a Jacksonville house of assignation that she operated under the name of "Cora Taylor," when Crane met her at her place of business, the Hotel de Dream, in late 1896. A few months after the wreck of the *Commodore,* Crane and Cora traveled to Greece together to cover the Greek-Turkish War. Cora sent back dispatches to the *New York Journal* under the name of "Imogene Carter." Afterward the two lived together, first at Ravensbrook, Oxted, Surrey, and then at Brede Place, Northiam, Sussex, as "Mr. and Mrs. Stephen Crane." About a year after Crane's death Cora returned to Jacksonville and borrowed money from friends and from bankers to erect a brothel known as the Court and an annex at Pablo, a seaside suburb of Jacksonville, that she called Palmetto Beach. In 1905 she bigamously married Hammond Mc-Neil. In 1907 he fatally shot a man he believed to be her lover, and she fled to England to avoid testifying at his trial. She was welcomed back by the Conrads and the Wellses but Henry James snubbed her. Cora operated the Court until her death and was buried as "Cora Crane."

JONATHAN TOWNLEY CRANE (1819–1880) Stephen Crane's father was converted from the Presbyterian to the Methodist faith at the age of 18. On graduation from the College of New Jersey (Princeton), he prepared for the ministry, was licensed as a local preacher in 1844, and was admitted to the New Jersey Conference in 1846. On 8 January 1848 he married Mary Helen Peck of Wilkes-Barre, Pennsylvania, daughter of the Reverend George Peck. They had 14 children, of whom Stephen was the last. In 1849 Jonathan Townley Crane became principal of the Conference Seminary at Pennington, New Jersey. In 1858 he returned to the pastorate as minister of churches in Jersey City; Haverstraw, New York; Newark and Morristown, New Jersey. For eight years he was a church administrator, serving as presiding elder of the Newark district (1868–

1872) and the Elizabeth district (1872–1876). He was subsequently pastor of the Cross Street Church in Paterson and, from 1878 until his death, pastor of Drew Methodist Church in Port Jervis, New York.

Jonathan Townley Crane was author of numerous essays in the *Methodist Quarterly Review* and the *Christian Advocate* (New York). A number of his books, notably *An Essay on Dancing* (1849), *Popular Amusements* (1869), and *Arts of Intoxication: The Aim and the Results* (1870) deplored venial sins such as dancing; reading trashy novels; playing cards, billiards, or chess; and drinking alcoholic beverages. Other books such as *Holiness the Birthright of All God's Children* (1874) and *Methodism and Its Methods* (1876) dealt with theological questions.

JONATHAN TOWNLEY CRANE, JR. (1852–1908) Always called "Townley" (pronounced "Toonley") by his brothers, he was three-times married and, like Stephen, took an early interest in journalism. In 1874 he worked as a reporter for a Newark, New Jersey, newspaper. In 1880 he began operating a summer news agency for the *New York Tribune* and the Associated Press and in 1883 served briefly as the editor of the *Asbury Park Shore Press*. Because of his voracity in finding items of interest for his *Tribune* column, he became known as the "Shore Fiend." Though eccentric, Townley developed a reputation as a valued reporter, covering important stories and speaking to organizations on the nature of newspaper work; in 1884 he was elected secretary of the

New York Press Club. During the summer months from 1888 to 1892 Stephen helped him by gathering society gossip for the news agency and reporting local events from Asbury Park, Ocean Grove, and other places along the New Jersey coast. In 1892 a controversial article written by Stephen probably led to his and Townley's dismissal from the *Tribune* staff, and a few months later Townley became the associate editor of the *Shore Press*. In the late 1890s he lived with his brother and sister-in-law, Wilbur and Martha, in Binghamton, New York, but died indigent in the local hospital.

WILBUR FISKE CRANE (1859–1918) Stephen's brother Wilbur was born in Jersey City and attended Centenary Collegiate Institute in Hackettstown, New Jersey, along with his brothers Edmund and Luther and his sister Agnes. In 1881 he enrolled as a medical student at the College of Physicians and Surgeons (Columbia University), which he attended until 1886 without graduating. For a time, as did Stephen, he worked in his brother Townley's news agency in Asbury Park, reporting shore news for the *New York Tribune*. In 1888 he married Martha R. Kellogg, a servant in the Port Jervis home of his brother William. This marriage estranged some members of the Crane family from him. Wilbur's first child, Helen R. Crane, published a memoir of Stephen's family life in the *American Mercury* in January 1934 that further infuriated her relatives. In 1897 or 1898 Wilbur and Martha Crane moved to Binghamton, New York. Wilbur's eccentric brother Townley lived with them there during the last

few years of his life. Some time after Wilbur's wife left him for another man in 1907, taking their four children with her, he moved away from Binghamton. In 1915 he settled in a small town in Georgia, where he lived until his death.

WILLIAM HOWE CRANE (1854–1926) Paterfamilias of the Crane family after the death of his father, Stephen's brother William Howe attended New York University and the Albany Law School, from which he graduated in 1880. He practiced law in Port Jervis, New York, establishing his own firm in 1882. In 1889, with relatives and friends, he formed the Hartwood Park Association, which in January 1893 incorporated as the Hartwood Club. William Howe was elected its first president, a position he held until 1902. This hunting and fishing preserve served as the setting for Stephen's Sullivan County sketches. In 1890, with his wife and five daughters, William Howe moved into the house on East Main Street in Port Jervis where Stephen often visited and wrote. He was prominent in community life, serving as district clerk of the Board of Education, treasurer of the Port Jervis Water Works, and, for one year, special judge for Orange County. For the remainder of his life, he was known as "Judge Crane." In later years he practiced law in New York City and retired to California.

JAMES CREELMAN (1859–1915) Creelman joined the staff of the *New York Herald* as an 18-year-old cub reporter. He quickly gained a reputation for his innovative reporting and interviews with colorful figures. In

1889 he went to Europe as the *Herald's* special correspondent and served as editor of the London edition and later as editor of the Paris edition. In 1894 he covered the Sino-Japanese War for Pulitzer's *New York World*, and in 1896 he reported for the *World* from Cuba. Later that year he left the *World* for Hearst's *New York Journal*. He served as *Journal* correspondent in the Greek-Turkish and Cuban wars and was wounded leading a charge of American troops at El Caney on 1 July 1898. Creelman rejoined the *World* in 1900. From 1906 to 1910 he served as special correspondent for the *New York Times*.

ACTON DAVIES (1870–1928) Born in Quebec, Davies came to New York in 1897. He worked as a free-lance reporter until 1893 when he became drama critic for the *New York Evening Sun*. In 1898 he was a war correspondent for the *New York Sun* in Cuba and Puerto Rico and, like Crane, was with the marines in the landing at Guantánamo Bay. Davies was a frequent contributor to magazines.

RICHARD HARDING DAVIS (1864–1916) Davis was one of the most popular romantic novel and short story writers of his generation. His early literary career was guided by his father, Lemuel C. Davis, an influential journalist, and his mother, Rebecca Harding Davis, an innovative fiction writer. Davis served a journalistic apprenticeship in New York City and focused on slum environments and characters in his stories; unlike Crane, however, he avoided the more sordid aspects of urban life. He was propelled into fame when his short story "Gallagher" appeared in the August 1890 issue of *Scribner's Magazine*. In contrast, his Van Bibber stories presented a light-hearted portrayal of life in New York society. Between 1897 and 1916 Davis traveled widely as a journalist. He served as war correspondent of the *Times* of London and the *New York Herald* in the Greek-Turkish, Spanish-American, South African, and Russian-Japanese wars. In books such as *The Cuban and Puerto Rican Campaigns* (1898) and *With Both Armies in South Africa* (1900), he established himself as the hero of his own romantic adventures, an image already depicted in the protagonist of his best-known work of fiction, *Soldiers of Fortune* (1897).

HENRY D. DAVRAY (1874–1944) Davray was an ardent worker for Anglo-French relations. From 1898 he edited books by foreign authors published by the *Mercure de France*. He was a frequent contributor to French, Swiss, Belgian, and Italian newspapers and periodicals. Davray translated into French books by H. G. Wells, Arnold Bennett, Rudyard Kipling, and Joseph Conrad. His translation of *The Red Badge of Courage* (with Francis Vielé-Griffin) under the title of *La conquête du courage* (1911) was uninspired and is sometimes said to be responsible for Crane's lack of reputation in France.

ELISHA JAY EDWARDS (1847–?) From the time he graduated from Yale in 1870, Edwards was a journalist. He was Washington correspondent for the *New York Sun* (1880–1884) and editor of the *New York Evening Sun* (1887–1889). In 1889 he began to write a column over the signature "Holland" for the *Philadelphia Press, Chicago Inter-Ocean,* and *Cincinnati Inquirer.*

DAVID ERICSON (1870–?) One of the "Indians" who roomed with Crane in the old Art Students' League building, Ericson was born in Sweden and studied painting in New York with William M. Chase and later with Whistler in Paris. He won a medal for the work he exhibited at the St. Louis Exposition in 1904. Ericson was best known for his murals of American historical subjects.

BENJAMIN ORANGE FLOWER (1858–1918) Flower was a social reformer and editor whose *Arena* magazine served as a leading voice for progressive sentiments in the last decade of the nineteenth century. In its editorials and columns, the *Arena* decried the concentration of wealth in the hands of the few. Flower himself wrote some 1,000 book reviews, 200 articles, and hundreds of editorials. The *Arena* also published creative literature that exposed social evils. The magazine was founded in Boston in 1889 and at one point reached a circulation of 35,000. Among the reforms sought by Flower were strict child-labor laws, suffrage for women, and prohibition of liquor. The *Arena* ceased publication in 1909. Flower subsequently edited two other magazines: *Twentieth-Century Magazine* (1909–1911), similar in outlook to the *Arena,* and the *Menace,* which was virulently anti-Catholic.

FORD MADOX FORD (1873–1939) Born Ford Hermann Hueffer, Ford anglicized his name in 1919, partly as a reaction to World War I and partly for reasons connected with his complicated marital affairs. Ford wrote more than 60 books, including a number of lively but factually unreliable autobiographies. Some of his works were written in collaboration with Joseph Conrad. Ford launched the *English Review* in 1908. Among the contributors to this magazine were Conrad, William James, W. H. Hudson, John Galsworthy, T. S. Eliot, and Robert Frost. After the war Ford founded the *Transatlantic Review* in Paris, to which James Joyce and Ernest Hemingway contributed. Ford's best novels were a series centered on England and the war whose protagonist was Christopher Tietjens. These are *Some Do Not* (1924), *No More Parades* (1925), *A Man Could Stand Up* (1926), and *The Last Post* (1928).

HAROLD FREDERIC (1856–1898) Frederic began his career in journalism as a writer and editor for local newspapers in his native city of Utica, New York. In 1884 he became London correspondent of the *New York Times* and for many years his weekly columns were featured on the front page of the Sunday edition. His first novel, *Seth Brother's Wife* (1887), was set in the Mohawk Valley, as was his second novel, *The Lawton Girl* (1890). In 1891 Frederic moved his wife and four children to a new home outside London and established a second household in the city with Kate Lyon, an American woman with whom he had three more children. The third of Frederic's novels of contemporary upstate New York, *The Damnation of Theron Ware* (1896), a searching character study and trenchant social satire, sustains his reputation today. In his last years Frederic lived with Kate Lyon and their children at Homefield, a large house in Surrey. *Gloria Mundi* (1898) and *The Market Place* (1899) are set in England. These books were popularized by the notoriety surrounding Frederic's death while under the care of a Christian Science practitioner and Kate Lyon's subsequent trial for manslaughter, which ended in acquittal.

MORETON FREWEN (1853–1924) The son of a wealthy Sussex squire, Frewen had the private education of an English gentleman and took a degree at Cambridge. Throughout his life he was an inveterate traveler, engaging in many speculative and often unsuccessful ranching and mining enterprises in the United States, Canada, and Kenya. In 1881 he married Clara Jerome, elder sister of Lady Randolph Churchill, and for a time settled with her on his enormous ranch in Wyoming. He also owned homes in London and in County Cork, Ireland. Frewen bought Brede Place from his brother Edward and in 1898, while Stephen was in Cuba, rented it to Stephen and Cora Crane for £40 a year on the condition that they continue restorations. Active in politics, Frewen championed bimetallism, the theory that currency should adopt a double standard of gold and silver in fixed ratio. He was elected to the House of Commons in 1910 and surrendered his seat in 1914.

HAMLIN GARLAND (1860–1940) Garland is best remembered for his early reform journalism and realistic fiction. His childhood was spent on subsistence farms in Wisconsin, Iowa, and the Dakota Territory. At the age of 24 he went east to Boston, where he spent 12 hours a day in the public library reading the works of Darwin, Herbert Spencer, and Eugene Veron. Garland returned to Iowa and Dakota in the summer of 1887. He was angered by the life of drudgery and cultural impoverishment led by farm people, and this inspired him to write the grim stories of *Main-Travelled Roads* (1891) and its companion volume, *Prairie Folks* (1893). These books and the social and aesthetic essays gathered together in *Crumbling Idols* (1894) were infused with Garland's conception of realism, the replacing of theoretical knowledge with visual experience, which he called *veritism*, a term adopted from his reading of Veron. Garland's assertion of the superiority of realistic fiction over romance and his praise for local color and impressionism greatly influenced Stephen Crane. Garland's best novel, *Rose of Dutcher's Coolly* (1895), deals with a Wisconsin farm girl who overcomes her background to graduate from the state university and make a career for herself in Chicago. Garland himself moved to Chicago in 1894 and, desiring popularity and a better income, turned to writing historical romances set in the Rocky Mountains. In later years he wrote many reminiscences and family memoirs. He became very conservative, but *A Son of the Middle Border* (1917), the first of an autobiographical trilogy, was praised by reviewers as a moving account of his youth and his struggles to establish himself as a realistic writer and militant reformer.

EDWARD GARNETT (1868–1937) Son of the celebrated Dr. Richard Garnett who succeeded his own father as Keeper of Printed Books in the British Museum, and husband of Constance Garnett, renowned for her translations into English of the nineteenth-century Russian novelists, Edward Garnett was overshadowed much of his life by the greater fame of his father and his wife. Garnett was a critic, essayist, and novelist. He advised and helped to publicize Joseph Conrad, John Galsworthy, and D. H. Lawrence. He also acted as literary adviser to the publishing firms of Fisher Unwin, Heinemann, and Jonathan Cape. Garnett's essays in the *Academy* and in his collection of literary essays, *Friday Nights* (1922) offer rich insights into the English literary world of his time.

RICHARD WATSON GILDER (1844–1909) Through his long tenure as managing editor and then editor of *Century Monthly Magazine*, Gilder became one of the most influential figures in the American literary world during the last two decades of the nineteenth century. Under Gilder's direction, the *Century* featured American writers. Gilder excerpted a number of Mark Twain's novels, including *Huckleberry Finn*, some chapters of which appeared between December 1884 and Febru-

ary 1885. William Dean Howells's *A Modern Instance* (1882) and *The Rise of Silas Lapham* (1885) also ran as serials in the *Century*. Stephen Crane learned the factual background for the Battle of Chancellorsville from a highly successful series of recollections of the Civil War by participants that appeared serially in the *Century* from 1884 to 1887 under the general title of "Battles and Leaders of the Civil War" and was published subsequently in four volumes by the Century Publishing Company. In later years Gilder became more identified with the prudishness and sentimental literature of the genteel tradition, but he was occasionally daring. He serialized Jack London's *The Sea-Wolf* (1904) and in the early 1900s provided space for young poets such as Edward Arlington Robinson. Gilder also published slim volumes of his own poetry throughout his lifetime.

FREDERICK C. GORDON (1856–1924) Somewhat older than the other "Indians" who roomed with Crane in the old Art Students' League building, Gordon was born in Canada and studied at the League and at the Julian and Colarossi Academies in Paris. He began his work in Toronto in 1882 and came to the United States in 1886. He drew illustrations for *Century Magazine* and was a book illustrator and designer. He also painted portraits and landscapes and served as mayor of Mountainside, New Jersey.

NELSON GREENE (1869–1956) Greene was one of several young artists and illustrators, among them Frederick C. Gordon, Edward S. Hamilton, R. G.

Vosburgh, and David Ericson, with whom Crane shared quarters in the old Art Students' League building on East 23d Street at various times during the years 1893–1895. After Greene's relationship with this group ended, he spent three years in Buffalo as an illustrator for the *Courier* and later the *Sunday Express*. He returned to New York City in 1898 and free-lanced. Intermittently from 1905 to 1922 Greene was an advertising artist for United Cigar Stores. He did illustrations for *Puck* in 1914–1915 and was a political cartoonist during World War I. He later became an historian of New York State, notable for his *History of the Mohawk Valley* (1925) and the five-volume *History of the Valley of the Hudson* (1931).

JAMES H. HARE (1856–1946) "Jimmy" Hare was the son of an English camera manufacturer. In 1889 he came to the United States to accept a position as a technical adviser to a New York City camera-supplies firm, but after a year he quit to produce his own handmade cameras. He became a photographer for the *Illustrated American* and a free-lance contributor to newspapers and magazines. In the spring of 1898 he went to Cuba as a photographer for *Collier's Weekly*. With Sylvester Scovel, he made a daring trip into the interior to interview the rebel leader General Máximo Gómez. He later covered events leading to the siege of Santiago and photographed the battles of San Juan Hill and El Caney. In the early years of the twentieth century *Collier's* sent Hare to report revolutions in Haiti, Venezuela, Panama, and Mexico, and the Russian-Japanese War. He covered World War I for *Leslie's Weekly*.

KARL EDWIN HARRIMAN (1875–1935) Harriman entered newspaper work in 1895 as a reporter for the *Detroit Journal*. During 1898–1899 he wrote daily editorials for the *Detroit Free Press*, and in the spring of 1899 the *Free Press* sent him to England as a correspondent. He was subsequently editor of the *Red Book*, the *Blue Book*, and the *Green Book* magazines. Harriman was the author of a number of novels and published short stories and articles in various magazines.

WILLIAM RANDOLPH HEARST (1863–1951) Born into wealth, Hearst began his journalistic career as owner of the *San Francisco Examiner*, a newspaper his father, a United States senator, had purchased in 1880 to forward his political career. In 1895 Hearst bought the *New York Journal* and began a circulation battle with Joseph Pulitzer's *New York World* that created the style known as "yellow journalism." During the Spanish-American War the *Journal* and the *World* achieved circulations over one million on some days, marking the first time in American history such numbers had been achieved by a newspaper. After the war Hearst became involved in politics. He ran unsuccessfully several times for the governorship of New York. He served two terms in Congress (1903–1907), but this was his only political success. For the remainder of his career Hearst devoted himself to building a media empire that included ownership of one and sometimes two newspapers in many major American cities. He also owned magazines such as *Cosmopolitan, Good Housekeeping,* and *Harper's Bazaar.* To this he added the International News Service, King Features, and broadcasting and motion-picture companies.

WILLIAM HEINEMANN (1863–1920) Heinemann set up as a publisher in London without any previous experience. Having an international perspective, he made available to the British public for the first time direct English translations of Dostoevsky, Turgenev, and Tolstoy. Besides works by Crane, he also published books by R. L. Stevenson, Henry James, Joseph Conrad, George Moore, and many others. He is credited with "discovering" John Galsworthy, Max Beerbohm, and Somerset Maugham.

JOHN NORTHERN HILLIARD (1872–1935) Largely self-educated, Hilliard lived on a ranch as a boy and came to journalism early as a reporter for the *Chicago Press* and the *Chicago Herald* from 1889 to 1895. From 1895 to 1911 Hilliard was successively literary editor, drama critic, and editorial writer for the *Rochester Post Express.* He contributed for many years to newspapers and magazines in Chicago, New York, Boston, and St. Louis, and he was the author of books of poetry and fiction. He wrote several books on magic and in later years was the advance man for the American illusionist Howard Thurston.

RIPLEY HITCHCOCK (1857–1918) Born James Ripley Wellman Hitchcock, he joined the staff of the *New York Tri-*bune as an art critic in 1882, following graduation from Harvard, postgraduate study in art and philosophy, and a year spent as a medical student. He was the author of a number of books on art, such as *Etching in America* (1886), *Madonnas by Old Masters* (1888), and *Some American Painters in Water Colors* (1890). Hitchcock traveled widely for eight years as a *Tribune* correspondent and in 1890 left the newspaper to become literary adviser for the publishing house of D. Appleton and Company. He edited and wrote introductions for many Appleton books. In 1906 he became literary adviser and director for Harper and Brothers, a position he held until his death.

WILLIAM DEAN HOWELLS (1837–1920) Howells was regarded as the foremost American man of letters in the late nineteenth and early twentieth centuries. He wrote over 40 novels and short story collections as well as plays, poetry, travel books, and literary reminiscences. He was also a leading critic and editor. From the onset of his career, Howells was a proponent of realism, and his best novels, such as *A Modern Instance* (1882), *The Rise of Silas Lapham* (1885), *Indian Summer* (1886), and *A Hazard of New Fortunes* (1889), exemplify his devotion to verisimilitude.

In 1860 Howells traveled from his native Ohio to Boston where he met Nathaniel Hawthorne, Ralph W. Emerson, and Henry David Thoreau, and to New York where he met Walt Whitman. He waited out the Civil War as American consul in Venice. Howells returned to the United

States to take up the assistant editorship of the *Atlantic Monthly* and in 1871 became editor in chief, a position he held for 10 years. In 1886 Howells launched a monthly series of essays called "The Editor's Study" in *Harper's Magazine*, which, along with the serial publication of *Indian Summer* in the magazine, initiated a long association with Harper and Brothers, who became his publishers. The economic and social unrest of the 1880s moved Howells away from social complacency. He embodied his vision of an ideal society in his utopian romances, *A Traveler from Altruria* (1894) and *Through the Eye of the Needle* (1907). At the turn of the century, Howells revived the prestigious "The Editor's Easy Chair" in *Harper's*, writing monthly essays until shortly before his death.

ELBERT HUBBARD (1856–1915) Little is verifiable about the fantastic variety of working experiences Hubbard claimed to have had before he moved to Buffalo, New York, where for some 15 years he was a salesman for a soap manufacturer. In 1892 he retired from business and, after a brief experience as an adult undergraduate at Harvard, traveled to England where he fell under the influence of William Morris. On his return, Hubbard went to work for B. O. Flower's Arena Publishing Company in Boston, which published his first two novels. In 1895, inspired by Morris's Kelmscott Press, he founded the Roycroft Shop in East Aurora, a suburb of Buffalo. In the same year, the first issue of *The Philistine* appeared. It was to be the most successful little magazine of the 1890s. In 1908 Hubbard initiated another periodical, the *Fra*, which was discontinued two years after his death. Hubbard's most spectacular piece of writing, *A Message to Garcia*, appeared initially in the March 1899 *Philistine*. It was a preachment from the Gospel of Work that was widely reprinted by American corporations. Another successful venture of the Roycrofters was Hubbard's series of *Little Journeys*. Issued monthly from January 1895 when the pamphlet on George Eliot appeared, they reached an aggregate of 170 by 1917. In May 1915 Hubbard died when the liner *Lusitania* was torpedoed and sank.

RUPERT HUGHES (1872–1956) Hughes graduated from Adelbert College (now Case-Western Reserve University) in 1892 and received an M.A. from the same university in 1894. He established himself in the publishing world while working as an assistant editor of *Godey's Magazine, Current Literature*, and the *Criterion*. His articles in these magazines often appeared over the name "Chelifer." Intending to become an English professor, Hughes earned an M.A. at Yale in 1899, but his interest in the theater drew him back to New York City. In May 1901 Hughes began editorial work in London where his first play, *The Wooden Wedding*, was produced in 1902. Over the next 20 years he wrote more than a dozen plays. Hughes also wrote short stories, many of which were turned into film scripts. By 1923 he was living in Hollywood where he built a mansion inspired by illustrations from an edition of *Arabian Nights*. Throughout the 1920s and 1930s he wrote and directed films.

His enduring reputation rests on the culmination of a lifelong interest, his three-volume biography of George Washington.

JAMES GIBBONS HUNEKER (1860–1921) Huneker studied piano at the Conservatorie in Paris. His first published work was a column of musical commentary in the *Musical Courier* of New York. In 1900, having gained experience on other newspapers, Huneker became music critic of the *New York Sun* and, later, drama critic. Between 1902 and 1917 he wrote more about art and literature than music. In later years he was music critic for a number of New York newspapers and a respected commentator on other arts. His autobiography, *Steeplejack* (1920), offers scintillant insights into the artistic world of his time. Other important works are Ivory Apes and Peacocks (1915) and Painted Veils (1920), a novel intended only for private circulation.

HENRY JAMES (1843–1916) Born in New York City, the son of Henry James, Sr., and the younger brother of William James, Henry James, Jr., was schooled to lead a life of cosmopolitan leisure. From the age of 12 he accompanied his family on extended trips back and forth across the Atlantic, a pattern that became habitual until he settled permanently in Europe. Many of James's earlier works such as *Roderick Hudson* (1876), *The American* (1877), *Daisy Miller* (1879), and *The Portrait of a Lady* (1881) reflect his concern with questions of national identity. His interests in national contrasts gradually lessened, and the settings and char-

acters of *The Princess Casamassima* (1886), published 10 years after he had established permanent residence in London, are entirely European. James's novels failed to win him popular success, and the plays he wrote in the 1890s were even less well accepted.

During the late 1880s and early 1890s James wrote a number of short novels, notably *The Aspern Papers* (1888), *The Lesson of the Master* (1892), and *The Real Thing* (1893), that won him the enduring esteem of discerning readers. From 1898 to 1903 he lived at Lamb House in Rye. Here he was especially prolific, to some extent because he had developed the habit of dictation. During this period he produced the three great novels now often considered the epitome of his art: *The Wings of the Dove* (1902), *The Ambassadors* (1903), and *The Golden Bowl* (1904). In his last years James traveled in the United States, assembled an edition of his novels and tales, and wrote reminiscences. In 1915, as an act of protest against America's failure to enter the war, he became a British subject.

WILLIS FLETCHER JOHNSON (1857–1931) A member of the editorial staff of the *New York Tribune* since 1880, Johnson was day editor from 1887 to 1894. He remained an editorial writer for the *Tribune* until 1917, when he became literary editor, a position he held until 1920. Johnson was also a contributing editor of the *North American Review* and a lecturer on foreign relations at a number of schools and colleges.

FREDERIC M. LAWRENCE Although their parents had been well acquainted in Port Jervis, Stephen Crane and Frederic M. Lawrence did not know each other until they met as Delta Upsilon fraternity brothers at Syracuse University in January 1891. That August and for five summers afterward, Crane joined Lawrence and a number of other friends at a campsite in Milford, Pike County, Pennsylvania, on land owned by the Lawrence family. In the fall Lawrence went to New York City to attend medical school. During the autumn and winter of 1892–1893 Crane and Lawrence roomed together; with a number of medical students, they shared a boarding house on Avenue A which they named the Pendennis Club. Here Crane made the final revision of *Maggie: A Girl of the Streets.*

"AMY LESLIE" (1855?–1939) Born in Idaho to Albert Waring West and Katie (Webb) West, Lillie West achieved considerable fame as a light opera soprano. Following the death of her son Francis in 1889, she left the stage and began a career in journalism as "Amy Leslie." She also at various times apparently used the surnames "Huntington" and "Traphagen." In 1901 she married her second husband, wild-animal impresario Frank Buck, then only 20 years old. They were divorced in 1916. For 40 years Amy Leslie was drama critic of the *Chicago Daily News.* She retired in 1930. She was author of *Amy Leslie at the Fair* (1893), an account of the World's Columbian Exposition, and *Some Players* (1899), a collection of sketches of actors and actresses reprinted from the *Chicago Daily News.*

CORWIN KNAPP LINSON (1864–1959) Linson was born in Brooklyn and spent his childhood there and in Albion, New York. He studied in Paris at the Julian Académie and the École des Beaux Arts, where he was a pupil of Jean Gérôme and Jean Paul Laurens. He was a portrait painter and an illustrator for the *Century, Scribner's Magazine,* and *Cosmopolitan.* After the period of his association with Crane, Linson covered the first modern Olympic Games in Greece for *Scribner's* in 1896 and won a bronze medal for his depictions. McClure's sent him to accompany the Barnum and Bailey Circus to sketch animals. He spent two years in Palestine drawing illustrations for John Watson's *Life of the Master* (1901). His paintings were exhibited at the Pan-American Exhibition of 1901, the St. Louis Exhibition of 1904, and the National Academy of Design and other museums.

SAMUEL S. McCLURE (1857–1949) Born in Ireland, S. S. McClure, as he was generally known, emigrated to the United States with his family at the age of nine. He grew up in northwestern Indiana and graduated in 1882 from Knox College in Galesburg, Illinois. After an apprenticeship in magazine publishing, he launched McClure's Syndicate in 1884, bringing fiction and nonfiction by distinguished British and American writers to a widespread public. In 1893, with John S. Phillips, McClure founded *McClure's Magazine,* which featured personality profiles lavishly illustrated with photographs, fiction, and scientific news. By 1900 the circulation of *McClure's* was 400,000, and it became a leading publication in the muckraking movement. The McClure organization also established a book publishing company. McClure surrendered control of his magazine in 1911. Much of the rest of his life was devoted to lecturing and writing political philosophy.

BURR McINTOSH (1862–1942) A prominent actor at the turn of the century, McIntosh created the role of Taffy in *Trilby* and appeared in many Broadway plays. In 1898 he went to Cuba for *Leslie's Weekly* as a correspondent and photographer to report the siege of Santiago. Yellow fever caused him to return to the United States, but in 1905 he went as official photographer on Secretary of War Taft's trip to the Philippines. In 1909 McIntosh toured the country, playing the leading role in *The Gentleman from Mississippi*. He left the stage in 1910 and went to California where he founded his own movie company.

EDWARD MARSHALL (1869?–1933) Marshall became Sunday editor of the *New York Press* in 1888 and was notable for his crusade to improve tenement housing. He was foreign correspondent and Sunday editor of the *New York World* during 1897–1898, and in 1898 went to Cuba for the *New York Journal*. He was wounded at the battle of Las Guásimas.

"LILY" BRANDON MUNROE Born in Brooklyn, Alice Augusta Brandon (nicknamed Lily) received her early education in London and returned to the United States at the age of 11. She married Hersey Munroe, an employee of the U.S. Geological Survey in 1891; they had one child born in 1893. At the time of her relationship with Crane, Lily was neither divorced nor separated from her husband, but he was frequently away on business trips and they were estranged. Crane gave Lily the manuscript of *Maggie* in 1894 or 1895. It was presumably destroyed by her jealous husband. The Munroes were divorced in 1897 and in 1901 Lily married George Smillie, chief engraver of the Bureau of Engravings and Printings. They also had one son, Frederick B. Smillie, born in 1904.

FRANK NORRIS (1870–1902) Eclectically educated in San Francisco private schools, the Julian Académie in Paris where he studied painting, and the University of California at Berkeley, Norris turned to realistic fiction in a writing class at Harvard taught by Professor Lewis E. Gates in 1894–1895. In 1895 he traveled to South Africa as a correspondent for the *San Francisco Chronicle*. From 1896 to 1898 he wrote short stories, book reviews, articles, and parodies for the *Wave*, a San Francisco weekly magazine. His first published novel, *Moran of the Lady Letty* (1898), was serialized in the *Wave*. Norris went to New York to work for *McClure's Magazine*. McClure, who became publisher of Norris's books, sent him to Cuba to report the Spanish-American War, in the course of which he met Crane, Richard Harding Davis, and Frederic Remington. *McTeague: A Story of San Francisco* (1899) is Norris's earliest extended venture into a complex fictional mode that interweaves realistic, naturalistic, and melodramatically romantic elements. *Vandover and the Brute* (1914) was probably completed by 1900. *The Octopus* (1901) was intended as the first volume of a trilogy centered on the production, distribution, and consumption of Western wheat. The flow of wheat eastward is the background of the second volume, *The Pit* (1903), but before the serialization of this novel was concluded, Norris died of appendicitis, and the third volume, "The Wolf," was never written.

FRANK NOXON (1872–1945) While a student at Syracuse University, Noxon was a reporter for the *Syracuse Herald* and a Delta Upsilon fraternity brother of Stephen Crane. He was drama critic for the *Boston Record* from 1893 to 1900 and managing editor of several other Providence and Boston newspapers until 1905. For most of his subsequent career Noxon was secretary of the Railway Business Association. He was active in the Presbyterian church and wrote several books on the subjects of religion and government.

WALTER HINES PAGE (1855–1918) After two or three false starts, Page chose journalism as his profession. He worked for a number of newspapers, including the *New York World*, until in 1895 he became literary adviser and associate editor of the *Atlantic Monthly*; three years later he succeeded to the editorship. In 1899 he became a partner in the new publishing house of Doubleday, Page & Company, and in the following year he founded the *World's Work*, a magazine of politics and practical affairs that he edited

until 1913. In this year he became United States ambassador to Great Britain.

RALPH D. PAINE (1871–1925) Paine began his career as a journalist in Jacksonville, Florida, where his father was a clergyman. In 1890 he entered Yale College, paying for his education by reporting athletic news for a newspaper syndicate. He was a member of the crew and the football squad. On graduation Paine joined the staff of the *Philadelphia Press* and served as their correspondent during the Cuban War and the Boxer Rebellion. In 1902 the *New York Herald* placed him in charge of a successful journalistic campaign against the beef trust. After a brief stint as managing editor of the *New York Telegraph*, Paine gave up journalism and pursued a prolific career as an historian of the sea and a writer of fiction. In 1917 he was a special observer with the Allied fleet. His autobiography, *Roads of Adventure* (1922), vividly chronicles his experiences in three wars.

GEORGE PECK (1797–1876) Stephen Crane's maternal grandfather was an active Methodist minister for over 50 years and had an important part in shaping the governance of his church. He became editor of the *Methodist Quarterly Review* in 1840 and eight years later became editor of the *Christian Advocate* (New York). After retiring from this position, he served as pastor and presiding elder in the Methodist church's Wyoming Conference, Pennsylvania. The year after his retirement, he published his autobiography, *The Life and Times of Reverend George*

Peck, D. D. (1874). He had previously published a number of polemical and historical works, including *The Scripture Doctrine of Christian Perfection, Stated and Defended* (1842), *Our Country: Its Trial and Its Triumph* (1865), and *Wyoming: Its History, Stirring Incidents, and Romantic Adventures* (1858).

JESSE TRUESDELL PECK (1811–1883) Crane's maternal great-uncle was one of six brothers who became Methodist ministers. At a meeting of the General Conference in 1844, Peck made a speech on the slavery question that brought him into prominence in the church. In 1848 he became president of Dickinson College in Carlisle, Pennsylvania, a position he held until 1852. For much of the remainder of his career he served as pastor and presiding elder of churches and conferences in California and New York State. At the General Conference of 1872 he was elected bishop. During the remaining 11 years of his life he presided at 83 conferences in the United States and in Europe. Among his books are *The Central Idea of Christianity* (1856) and *The History of the Great Republic Considered from a Christian Standpoint* (1868). He wrote numerous tracts and pamphlets and contributed to Methodist periodicals.

JOHN S. PHILLIPS (1861–1949) With his Knox College classmate, S. S. McClure, Phillips launched *McClure's Magazine* in 1893. While McClure traveled gathering ideas and soliciting contributions, Phillips ran the home office. In 1900 he became head of the publishing firm of McClure, Phillips and Company. The journalistic staff Phillips brought together and trained for *McClure's*, including Ida M. Tarbell, Ray Stannard Baker, and Lincoln Steffens, began an investigative series on political, corporate, and union corruption in 1903, which made the magazine important in the muckraking movement. In 1906 Phillips broke with McClure and, along with Tarbell, Baker, and Steffens, purchased the *American Magazine.* In 1911 the group sold its interests to the Crowell Publishing Company. Phillips resigned in 1915 but continued as advisory editor until 1938.

JAMES B. PINKER (1864?–1922) Pinker was a London literary agent who represented many English authors and American authors living in England, among them Henry James, Stephen Crane, Joseph Conrad, John Galsworthy, and Compton Mackenzie. He traveled frequently to the United States on their behalf and died in New York City on one of his business trips.

JOSEPH PULITZER (1847–1911) As publisher of the *New York World*, Pulitzer became an important voice for progressive social movements. He was born in Hungary and came to the United States in 1864. Collecting a bounty for enlisting, he served for less than one year with a New York regiment. After the war Pulitzer went to St. Louis where he read law and was admitted to the bar. In 1869 he was elected as a Republican to the Missouri legislature. In 1878 Pulitzer purchased the *St. Louis Dispatch* and combined it with the *Post* to create the *St. Louis Post-Dispatch.* In 1883 he assumed ownership of the marginal *New York World* and through a combination of sensationalism in news reporting and a crusading editorial page he rapidly increased its circulation. During the Spanish-American War Pulitzer was drawn into jingoistic competition with Hearst's *New York Journal*, which greatly increased the circulation of both newspapers. Pulitzer's will left funds to establish a school of journalism at Columbia University and to endow the Pulitzer Prizes.

PAUL REVERE REYNOLDS (1864–1944) Reynolds studied psychology and philosophy at Harvard under William James. He began working as a literary agent in New York in 1892, offering books to other publishers on behalf of the English firm of Cassell and its American branch. Reynolds founded his own literary agency in 1893. Among his clients were Stephen Crane, George Bernard Shaw, Arnold Bennett, John Galsworthy, Joseph Conrad, and Leo Tolstoy.

JACOB RIIS (1849–1914) A Danish immigrant to the United States, Riis spent his career as a journalist-photographer exposing the working and living conditions of slum dwellers and child laborers in New York City. From 1877 to 1899 Riis was a reporter for the *New York Tribune* and the *New York Evening Sun*. His investigative journalism on poverty and crime made him familiar with the city's poorest neighborhoods. Riis's books—*How the Other Half Lives* (1890), *Children of the Poor* (1892), *Out of Mulberry Street* (1898), and *Children of the Tenements* (1903)—

anticipated the writings of the muckrakers.

THEODORE ROOSEVELT (1858–1919) An early interest in American history turned Roosevelt to authorship, beginning with the publication of *The Naval War of 1812* (1882). His devotion to heroic action and literary narrative is exemplified in *The Winning of the West* (1889–1896) and *The Strenuous Life* (1900). Roosevelt's political career began with three terms in the New York State Assembly (1882–1884). When a reform mayor of New York City organized a nonpolitical administration in 1895, Roosevelt became president of the board of police commissioners. He held this position for two years until President McKinley appointed him assistant secretary of the navy. In the spring of 1898, with Leonard Wood, Roosevelt recruited a volunteer cavalry regiment and secured its inclusion in the expeditionary force mobilizing in Tampa for the invasion of Cuba. The Rough Riders, necessarily dismounted, captured Kettle Hill in the fighting on the San Juan Heights on 1 July 1898. After Wood was promoted to brigadier general, Roosevelt became colonel of the regiment. In 1899 Roosevelt became governor of New York. He was elected vice president of the United States in 1900 and, following the assassination of President McKinley, became the 26th president. He served until 1909.

SYLVESTER SCOVEL (1869–1905) Henry Sylvester Scovel had little experience as a journalist when he was appointed correspondent for the *Pittsburgh Dispatch* and the *New York Herald* to cover the growing insurrection in Cuba. He was arrested by the Spanish authorities in Havana in 1896 and after escaping from prison was hired by the *New York World*. Returning to Cuba, he lived with the insurgents for 11 months. In 1897 he was again captured by the Spaniards and released after the United States government exerted pressure to secure his freedom. The *World* sent him to cover the Greek-Turkish conflict, but shortly before the outbreak of war between Cuba and Spain he was recalled and once more sent back to Cuba. His career as a correspondent ended when during an altercation at the ceremonies marking the surrender of Santiago, he struck General Shafter.

FREDERICK A. STOKES (1857–1939) After graduation from Yale in 1879, Stokes went to New York City to learn publishing. He was a partner in various ventures and in 1887 established a firm with his brother which he continued as the Frederick A. Stokes Company after the partnership broke up three years later. Stokes published Anthony Hope and Marie Corelli and is credited with discovering Edna Ferber and Louis Bromfield. His firm leaned toward the popular and maintained a large list of children's books. From 1898 to 1901 Stokes edited his own periodical, the *Pocket Magazine*.

EDWARD LIVINGSTON TRUDEAU (1848–1915) A graduate of the College of Physicians and Surgeons (Columbia University), Trudeau developed tuberculosis early in his career as a physician and moved to the Adirondacks. In 1884 he established the Adirondack Cottage Sanitorium, later the Trudeau Sanitorium, which he headed for 30 years. In 1904 he became president of what was later called the National Tuberculosis Association and in 1910 president of the Congress of American Physicians and Surgeons.

H. G. WELLS (1866–1946) Herbert George Wells was born into an impoverished home in Bromley, Kent, and received a desultory education until he entered the Normal School of Science (later Royal College) at South Kensington. For a brief time after graduation he was a tutor, but he soon turned to writing. *The Time Machine* (1895) was the first of a series of science-fantasy novels alternating with such general interest fictions as *The Wheels of Chance* (1896) and *Love and Mr. Lewisham* (1900). Wells moved restlessly from one social movement to another, envisioning a perfectible society through religion in *Mr. Britling Sees It Through* (1916) or through scientific progress in *The World of William Clissoid* (1926). He also wrote encyclopedic treatises such as his ambitious *An Outline of History* (1920). Wells's considerable abilities as a novelist were increasingly subordinated to theories of scientific progress and education. His two-volume *An Experiment in Autobiography* (1934) is a lively commentary on his times. In a lifetime of assiduous authorship, he produced more than 100 books.

(GEORGE) POST WHEELER (1869–1956) Often called America's first career diplomat, Wheeler's background was similar to Crane's in that his father was a Methodist minister and his mother an evangelist for the Women's Christian Temperance Union. Wheeler was extensively educated at Princeton, the University of Pennsylvania, and the Sorbonne. In 1895 he became editor of the *New York Press*. He began his diplomatic career in 1906 as second secretary of the American embassy in Tokyo. He subsequently held diplomatic posts in the embassies at St. Petersburg, Rome, Stockholm, London, Madrid, and Rio de Janeiro. At his retirement in 1934, he was minister to Albania. Throughout his diplomatic career, Wheeler continued to write. He published Russian folk tales, biblical stories, and Japanese legends. With his wife, Hallie Ermine Rives, Wheeler wrote a joint autobiography, *Dome of Many-Coloured Glass* (1955).

HERBERT P. WILLIAMS (1871-?) Williams graduated from Harvard in 1892 and studied for an additional year at Harvard Law School. From 1895 to 1903 he was literary editor of the *Boston Herald*, and from 1903 to 1906 he was head of the literature department at the Macmillan Company.

GEORGE WYNDHAM (1863–1913) Educated at Eton and Sandhurst, Wyndham joined the Coldstream Guards in 1883; he served through the Suakin campaign of 1885. He was private secretary to Arthur Balfour and in 1889 was elected to the House of Commons. In 1892 the Conservatives went into opposition, and for the next five years Wyndham devoted himself mainly to literature. He wrote for the Heinemann house organ, the *New Review*, edited by William Ernest Henley, and he edited a collection of Shakespeare's poetry. In the autumn of 1899 Wyndham was appointed parliamentary undersecretary in the War Office. In 1900 he became chief secretary for Ireland.

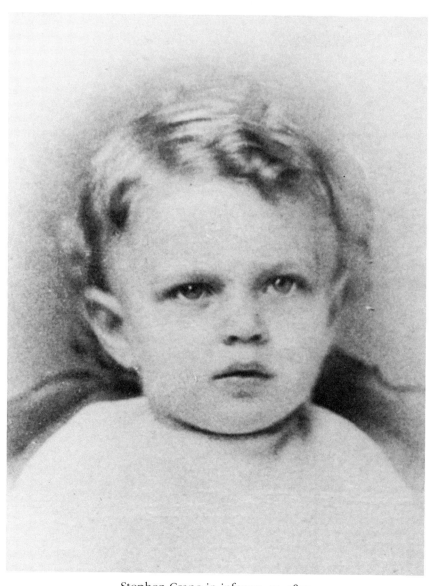

Stephen Crane in infancy, ca. 1873
(Syracuse University)

CHAPTER ONE

Northern New Jersey, Port Jervis, and Asbury Park

1871–1887

Stephen Crane is born at 14 Mulberry Place, Newark, New Jersey, on 1 November 1871, the 14th and last child of Jonathan Townley Crane, presiding elder of Methodist churches in the Newark district (1868–1872) and the Elizabeth district (1872–1876), and Mary Helen (Peck) Crane, daughter of a clergyman and niece of Methodist bishop Jesse Truesdell Peck. Only 8 of the 13 children who preceded Stephen are alive at the time of his birth. His Revolutionary War namesake (1709–1780) had served two terms as a delegate from New Jersey to the Continental Congress in Philadelphia. Both Dr. and Mrs. Crane are active in temperance work. The family moves in the spring of 1874 to Bloomington, New Jersey, and then in April 1876 to Paterson, where Dr. Crane becomes pastor of the Cross Street Church. Stephen receives his primary education from his sister Agnes Elizabeth, 15 years his senior. In April 1878 Dr. Crane becomes pastor of Drew Methodist Church in Port Jervis, New York, a post he holds until his death on 16 February 1880. Stephen enrolls in public school in September 1878. After a short residence in Roseville following the death of the father, the family returns to Port Jervis. In June 1883 the mother and her younger children move to Asbury Park, a resort town on the New Jersey coast, where Agnes resumes the teaching career she had begun in Port Jervis. Stephen's brother Townley operates a summer news agency in Asbury Park for the *New York Tribune* and the Associated Press. Another brother William Howe remains in Port Jervis, where he practices law. Agnes dies in June 1884 at the age of 28. Crane writes his first known story, "Uncle Jake and the Bell Handle," in 1885. From the fall of 1885 until the fall of 1887 he attends Pennington Seminary (Pennington, New Jersey), where his father had been principal (1849–1858), but he leaves without graduating.

Mary Helen Peck Crane
(Syracuse University)

*

1871

*

I NOVEMBER. The Reverend Jonathan Townley Crane writes in his diary: "This morning at 5.30' our fourteenth child was born. We call him Stephen, the name of the ancestor of the Elizabethtown Cranes, who was one of the Company of 'Associates' who settled at E. town

Jonathan Townley Crane
(Syracuse University)

in 1665: also of S. Crane of Revolutionary times, who was prominent in patriotic labors and counsels for 15 years" (Gullason 1972, 20).

1871. From the reminiscences of Wilbur F. Crane: "He was the youngest of mother's children, and with his blue eyes and light curls with just a glint of gold in them, he was a beautiful baby" (WFC).

George Peck, D. D.
(Robert K. Crane)

*

1872

*

16 APRIL. Jonathan Townley Crane writes to his father-in-law: "the baby grows finely & seems uncommonly strong." Mary Helen Crane adds: "Our precious baby has begun to go out in his carriage and enjoys it much when the weather is pleasant" (ViU).

5 JULY. From the diary of Jonathan Townley Crane: "Went to the Campground [at Denville, New Jersey], and found my family well, and the infant [Stephen], especially, much improved by the change from the city to the woods" (Gullason 1972, 20).

1 NOVEMBER. From the diary of Jonathan Townley Crane: "Went to Ocean Grove Camp Ground for the first time to choose a lot" (Gullason 1972, 20).

CA. 1872. As presiding elder, Jonathan Townley Crane preaches in the church of the Reverend Louis Burgess in Kingwood, New Jersey:

Bishop Jesse T. Peck
(Robert K. Crane)

"When Crane rose in the pulpit and announced his text, Burgess pulled his coat-tails and said: 'Brother Crane, you preached from this text here once before.' The elder replied: 'Well, we have another barrel load along with us, and we'll see what we can do with another text.' Whereupon he launched into quite a different sermon and held his audience spell-bound as he delivered his message with tenderness and with real eloquence" (Price, 866).

*

1873

*

30 JUNE. Mrs. Crane's brother, Wilbur F. Peck, an alcoholic who had dropped out of New York University and could not hold a job, signs a temperance pledge in Newark with his father and Jonathan Townley Crane as witnesses to abstain from the use of alcoholic beverages for three years (Benfey 1992, 34–35).

Stephen Crane's birthplace, 14 Mulberry Place,
Newark, NJ
(Syracuse University)

16 SEPTEMBER. Jonathan Townley Crane writes to his father-in-law:

The baby is fat & flourishing. He has been pulling at me within ten minutes, saying that he "want to yite to ganma,"—which extraordinary specimen of English you will be able to comprehend. . . . Ed. & Lu. go to the Public School. Will went to day to the New York University, was examined & admitted. He does not like the looks of things much. He says that he is about the oldest boy of the Freshman Class & he almost rebels against the idea of spending even a year among them. I try to comfort him by saying that as soon as it becomes possible, he shall go to Middletown, but he thinks this rather cold comfort. . . . we have a Swedish woman, with a child about as old as Stevy. . . . My wife brings me one of Stevie's letters to his *Ganma*, to inclose to her. I suppose that he will expect her to reply in regard to every topic introduced. (ViU)

20 OCTOBER. Jonathan Townley Crane notes in his diary: "Stephen is so sick that we are anxious about him" (Gullason 1972, 21).

[1873]. From the recollections of Edmund B. Crane: "He was bright and very teachable. After he learned to talk I amused myself by having him pronounce five and six syllable words. After a few laughable failures, he would accomplish a correct pronunciation by spelling the word after me syllable by syllable, resolving them into their sound elements. This was great fun for us children. Stevie also enjoyed it" (EBC).

Cora Crane records in her notebook that Stephen's "greatest play as infant boy buttons which he would call soldiers & would manuevre his armies—never picked up buttons after play" (*Works*, 10: 345).

Mrs. George Crane recalls, "He loved to play at soldiers from his early childhood. Most of his playthings were in the form of toy soldiers, guns, and the like" (Mrs. GC).

*

1874

*

1 JANUARY. From the diary of Jonathan Townley Crane: "Spent the day at home, reading Wesley, Foster, Peck, and others, on the Subject of Entire Sanctification. Wrote to Dr. Geo. Peck. The state is scriptural, but the theory of the work does seem to me, at this juncture, unsatisfactory. If I read aright, all the exhortations, all the promises, refer to truly regenerated persons as they are. No one of the writers named but is constantly running the one state into the other, first distinguishing the two states and then confounding them" (Gullason 1972, 21).

29 MAY. Jonathan Townley Crane offers literary advice to Wilbur F. Peck: "In regard to the poetry which you mention, & a specimen of which you send, I can form no definite idea from the little extract. The last stanza is good. The others depend so much on what precedes, that I do not get the run of things. I am not able to judge of the house, by the small brick exhibited. Your theme, the 'Argument of Love,' is certainly a popular one, judging by the style of the numberless weeklies, & monthlies, which are filled with it. I certainly see no harm in your spending your leisure hours thus; & good may come out of it. Go ahead with your 'Argument'" (ViU).

[MAY]. From Cora Crane's notes for a proposed biography of Stephen: "When first he spoke called himself 'Tevie' one day when 2 1/2 yrs of age some one asked him his name while his eyes fairly danced he said: 'nome Pe-pop-ty' no one ever knew where he got it from; he evidently made it up—His sister Nellie used to call him by this name when he grew up" (*Works*, 10: 343).

15 JULY. From the diary of Jonathan Townley Crane: "In the afternoon, married, in my own house, Joseph Harley, and Emily L. Cooke, of Newark. Dr. G. Peck at the same time baptized our youngest child, Stephen, who was born Nov. 1, 1871" (Gullason 1972, 22).

10 AUGUST. Stephen accompanies his parents and Agnes to a Methodist revival meeting at Camp Tabor, the Methodist camp-meeting ground he had helped to establish near Denville, New Jersey: "'The preacher stamped and raised his clenched hand to his head, and dashed it down, and, in a voice of thunder, gave a terrific description of the final conflagration. "O, sinner, sinner," thundered the preacher, "are you determined to take hell by storm? Are your bones iron, and your flesh brass, that you plunge headlong into the lake of fire?" There was an unbroken roar of fervent supplication, while the awful voice of the preacher resounded above this tempest of prayer.' Stevie was frightened; he clung to his sister's skirt, and wept" (Schoberlin II, 8).

23 AUGUST. From the diary of Agnes Elizabeth Crane: "Went to S. S. [Sunday school] taking Stevie. Meant to have gone to church at night but John was sick" (Sorrentino 1986, 125).

1874. Edmund B. Crane recalls: "When [Stephen] was about three years old, an older brother, Townley, was a cub reporter on one of the Newark dailies, either the Courier, or Advertiser, and when writing his stories at home would often call on his Mother for the correct spelling of a word. Stevie was making weird marks on a paper with a lead pencil one day and in the exact tone of one, absorbed in composition, and coming to the surface only for a moment for needed information, called to his mother, 'Ma, how do you spell "O"?,' this happening to be a letter he had just become acquainted with" (EBC).

Jonathan Townley Crane publishes *Holiness the Birthright of All God's Children*: "He that believeth not is condemned; he that believeth is saved." Until the moment that the penitent passes from

8

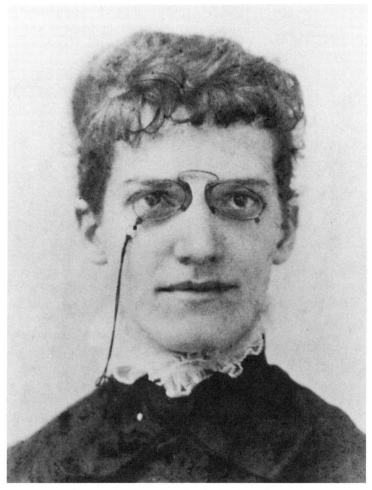

Agnes Elizabeth Crane
(Syracuse University)

unbelief to belief, his condition is "one of inexpressible evil. He is guilty, condemned, corrupt, helpless, the wrath of God resting on him, and hell waiting his coming, with its eternal darkness and despair" (JTC, 9). [Dr. Crane's book was written in opposition to the Holiness Movement in the Methodist church, which demanded a return to "'the primitive simplicity and power of Christianity'" and called for a second experience of conversion known as "'entire sanctifica-

9

tion.'" Jonathan Townley Crane's hostility to this conservative trend was probably responsible for the loss of his administrative position and return to the itinerant ministry (Benfey 1990, 33).]

[1874]. Cora Crane recalls: "Stephen tought himself to read befor 4 yrs of age. Could read well at that age" (*Works*, 10: 343).

*

1875

*

3 JANUARY. From the diary of Agnes Elizabeth Crane: "First. I want to, *must*, be a better Christian. That is my first aim. I want to be unostentatious but whole-souled in this if the rest has to go. 'Ich dien.' Second. I want to be a lady in the fullest sens{e} of the word. My motto for this 'Noblesse oblige.' And then. Oh dear me, I want a classical & scienti{fic} educ{ation,} a thorough knowledge of the best literature, to {know} how to draw and paint and *write*" (Sorrentino 1986, 127).

SUMMER. Edmund B. Crane recalls:

We often took Stevie bathing with us in the Raritan river about half a mile above the bridge [between Bloomington and Bound Brook, New Jersey]. There was a smooth, sandy bar extending from the south bank across the river, very shallow near shore and growing deeper toward the middle of the river. Stevie would wade around in the shallows watched by one of us. Wading breast deep in water he would stretch out his arms and waving his hands, would achieve what he called "fimming." He started to "fim" to Wee-wee, (Willie), my next older brother, who was farther out in the river. As the depth gradually increased the water came up to his chin, then to his mouth, and then his eyes, but he kept steadily on, and, I plucked him out, gasping but unscared, just as his yellow hair was going under. We boys were naturally delighted with his grit. (EBC)

Wilbur F. Crane recalls: "The family watchdog was a large New-foundland named Solomon, and it was a common thing for Solomon to swim the Raritan river when we were bathing, with Stephen lying along his back, holding on to his collar" (WFC).

1876

*

SPRING. Dr. Crane publishes *Methodism and Its Methods.* He reviews the development of the church and examines major problems of the episcopal structure, the itinerant ministry, and the system of presiding elders. He concludes that prosperity is the greatest obstacle the church must overcome to avoid stagnation.

5 APRIL. Jonathan Townley Crane writes in his diary: ". . . appointed to the Cross Street Church, Paterson" (Wertheim 1993, 37). The Cranes take up residence at 25 Hotel Street in Paterson.

9 APRIL. SUNDAY. From the diary of the Reverend Jonathan Townley Crane: "Preached . . . Evergreen . . 'God bless our new Pastor' . . I am pleased w. the cordial spirit . . & hope for good" (Wertheim 1993, 37).

22 MAY. The Crane family attends the funeral of Dr. George Peck in Scranton, Pennsylvania (Diary of Jonathan Townley Crane, Wertheim 1993, 38).

19 JULY. From the diary of Jonathan Townley Crane: "Warm still. Will, Aggie, Ed, & Stevie started this morning for Ocean Grove" (Wertheim 1993, 39).

23 AUGUST. Dr. Crane writes in his diary: "Mrs Peck, Aggie & Stephen arrived from O.G." (Wertheim 1993, 39).

19 SEPTEMBER. From Jonathan Crane's diary: "William began in Soph. year at the New York University. Ed. is at Mr. Walters' School. Wilbur & Lu. not well enough to go to school" (Wertheim 1993, 39).

21 OCTOBER. Jonathan Crane writes in his diary: "Ministerial meeting . . (some &) myself, declared our belief in a universal atonement . . We did not so much argue as simply state our positions w. all good humor. I confess that I was surprised to find the most repulsive features of old style Calvinism advanced w. scarce an apology for their deformities. Mr. Clark declared that he does not believe in the doctrine of free agency" (Wertheim 1993, 40).

31 OCTOBER. Jonathan Crane records in his diary that his wife, her mother, and Stephen departed in the morning for Kingston, Pennsylvania, where the family owns shares of coal lands (Wertheim 1993, 40).

13 NOVEMBER. Jonathan Crane records in his diary that Stephen came home from Kingston (Wertheim 1993, 40).

1876. Cora Crane recounts that Stephen was "delicate & precocious—read as did William Morris at four years of age only he read Fennimore Cooper novels" (*Works*, 10: 345).

*

1877

*

JANUARY. The Reverend Jonathan Townley Crane conducts a revival in Paterson.

3 FEBRUARY. From the diary of Jonathan Townley Crane: ". . Much encouragement in my work. I find everybody approachable on the subject of religion, almost; ready to confess his need of Christ. Still, thus far, no wave of power has come sweeping all before it, as we sometimes see. Perhaps it will, if we hold on our way, doing our duty & leaving the event to God" (Wertheim 1993, 41).

5 JULY. Dr. Crane records in his diary that his wife and some of the children, including Stephen, left this morning for Camp Tabor (Wertheim 1993, 43).

*

1878

*

27 MARCH. The presiding elder of the Newark Conference of the Methodist Episcopal Church decides that the Cross Street Church should reduce its operating expenses by engaging a pastor whose salary is lower than that of Jonathan Townley Crane. He reluctantly resigns (Diary of Jonathan Townley Crane, Wertheim 1993, 43).

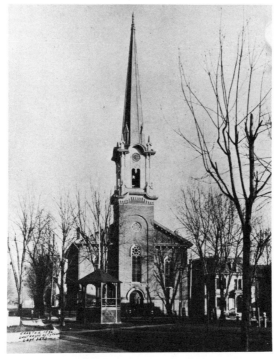

Drew Methodist Church, Port Jervis, NY
(Wertheim Collection)

6 APRIL. Jonathan Townley Crane takes up his new duties as pastor of Drew Methodist Church in Port Jervis (*Port Jervis Evening Gazette,* 9 April).

18 APRIL. Jonathan Townley Crane writes in his diary: "At 3 o'c. married my son, J. T. Crane, Jun. to Miss Fannie G. McCauley . . The whole family then set out for our new house" (Wertheim 1993, 43). The *Port Jervis Evening Gazette* (20 April) reports that the wedding was conducted in Paterson, and "on the same evening the newly-married pair arrived in this village and are here at present. Mr. Crane is a resident of Jersey City and is connected with the New York *Tribune* being on the regular corps of reporters. His wife will remain with his parents in this village during the summer."

18 MAY. Mrs. Crane lectures upon the effects of alcohol:

The lecture by Mrs. Crane, wife of the Rev. J. T. Crane of this village, delivered at the free reading-room last Saturday evening, was listened to by a large audience. The room was filled to its utmost capacity, and it is estimated that well over 100 persons were unable to gain admittance. Her subject was "The effects of alcohol upon the organs and tissues of the body." Illustrations in crayon, executed by herself and daughter, showed the effect of introducing liquor into the system, advanced stages being represented by different drawings. The process of fermentation and distillation of alcohol, as well as the effects of the same as a beverage was treated with, the object being to enlighten her hearers on the sad and inevitable result which follows the continued use of liquor. The lecture was the most convincing and practical effort yet listened to. Mrs. Crane intends speaking on "The effects of alcohol upon the nerves and brain" on Saturday evening of this week. (*Port Jervis Evening Gazette*, 21 May)

25 MAY. At the temperance meeting in the free reading room, Mrs. Crane demonstrates the effect of alcohol upon the brain

by breaking into a glass the white of an egg, upon which was poured a small quantity of the liquid. The result was the albumen of the egg became transformed into a solid mass, much resembling the state of being cooked. Her remarks were also diversified by reading from medical works, the results of research by eminent practitioners, wherein it was shown that alcohol introduced into the system was alcohol when it was discharged from the system, no change in its condition taking place during its circulation. Mrs. Crane is a practical, common-sense talker, and her efforts to demonstrate to the intemperate the folly of their course, proves her to have made intemperance and its terrible consequences a close study. (*Port Jervis Evening Gazette*, 28 May)

[The long-standing passion of Mary Helen Crane and her husband for the temperance cause was not misplaced in Port Jervis. An article from the *Philadelphia Ledger* (reprinted in the *Port Jervis Evening Gazette*, 15 March 1879) identifies Port Jervis as "in Orange County, 88 miles from New York, and on the line of the Erie Railroad. It is on the Delaware River, and near the junction of the three states—New York, New Jersey, and Pennsylvania. The population—numbering nearly 10,000—is composed mainly of persons engaged in the railroad shops, or employed upon the road. About two years ago there were over eighty drinking saloons in the place, and it is said that much distress was occasioned by so large a number." There were two large temperance groups in Port Jervis: the WCTU headed by Mrs. Crane and the Christian Temperance Union, whose president was Dr. Charles M. Lawrence, father of Stephen's later fraternity brother and friend, Frederic Lawrence. Shortly after their arrival in Port Jervis, Dr. and Mrs. Crane began holding temperance meetings to convince people to take the pledge; local newspapers frequently reported these meetings: "Judging from the tone of the temperance people, and especially of this Women's Temperance Union, there is to be no let up in the fight until, as they say, the last liquor shop is closed, and Port Jervis is redeemed from the great curse of dram drinking" (*Port Jervis Tri-States Union*, 21 May).]

26 MAY. Mrs. Crane's lecture in the Methodist church is "on the false religions of India, taking for her special subject the Hindu representations of the goddess *Kali*, the female Satan of the Hindu mythology" (*Port Jervis Evening Gazette*, 25 May).

Dr. and Mrs. Crane organize "a Sunday school among the colored people." Mrs. Crane is elected the superintendent; her son Luther, the librarian (*Port Jervis Tri-States Union*, 30 May 1879; Copy, NSyU).

9 JUNE. At a children's day festival in the Methodist church, Dr. Crane delivers a sermon on "Life as a Journey," in which he depicts "the great difficulties through which the young mind passes before it is properly moulded and prepared to meet the world in its many phases of sin and folly" (*Port Jervis Evening Gazette*, 11 June).

13 JUNE. Mrs. Crane lectures on "China and Its People" in the Drew Methodist Church. The presentation is "illustrated with curiosities and children dressed in the costume of the literary class or Chinese gentlemen, the little-footed woman or lady and the cooley or laboring man" (*Port Jervis Evening Gazette*, 8 June; Copy, NSyU). The admission charge of 10¢ is used to raise money for the parsonage.

JULY. WYOMING, PENNSYLVANIA. Post Wheeler recalls that before the age of seven Crane was already smoking Sweet Caporal cigarettes and drinking beer. At the centenary commemoration of the British and Indian attack on Forty Fort in July 1778 (George Peck had published a history of Wyoming [1858], and Crane would write three posthumously published stories about the Wyoming massacre), Stephen bought a mug of beer from a street vendor and consumed it before the eyes of the astonished eight-year-old Wheeler, who afterwards exclaimed, "'Stevie' . . . 'how'd you dast do it?' 'Pshaw!' said Stevie. 'Beer ain't nothing at all.' Then he added, defensively but emphatically, 'How was I going to

Stephen Crane on the New Jersey Coast,
ca. 1879
(Syracuse University)

know what it tasted like less'n I tasted it? How you going to know about things at all less'n you *do* 'em?'" (Wheeler and Rives, 22).

AUGUST. The Crane family builds a summer camp in the dense forest near the falls of the Mongaup River in Sullivan County. Agnes satirically christens the shack they live in "Saint's Rest" and later makes it the setting of her short story, "Laurel Camp, and What Came of It" (*Frank Leslie's Illustrated Newspaper*, 2 July 1887). According to Agnes's school friend Josephine Baldwin, "Saint's Rest" was "usually overcrowded by so large a family. Agnes slept directly under the hammock that nightly held the slumbering Stephen. One night the hammock broke and Stephen landed in full length on top of his sister. Luckily for her, he was slight in weight, but still she bemoaned the misfortune that 'his bones were not sufficiently upholstered to make it anything but an unpleasant experience'" (Price, 867).

2 SEPTEMBER. Jonathan Townley Crane writes in his diary: "Stevie began his public school education today. Lu began at the Mountain House School" (Wertheim 1993, 43).

The Mountain House School, Port Jervis
(Minisink Valley Historical Society)

[Stephen's health was fragile, and his school attendance was at first irregular. Three of Crane's biographers assert that he did not begin school until he was eight years old (Beer 1923, 40; Stallman 1973, 7; Benfey 1992, 40), but this is incorrect. According to Melvin H. Schoberlin's undocumented account, he was not regularly enrolled in school until 5 January 1880, when "he reluctantly forfeited his freedom and trudged tremulously across the Canal [the Delaware and Hudson Canal] and among the snowballs of two warring artilleries, to be devoured by the avaricious doors of the Mountain House School. He was assigned to a seat in the first grade. He shriveled his body contritely to appear less conspicuous among the cohort of five- and six-year-old babies who eyed the tall miscreant and tittered" (Schoberlin III, 20). Evidently, Stephen had been forced to drop out of the Main Street school because of poor health and reenrolled in the school attended by his brother Luther.]

10 SEPTEMBER. The *Port Jervis Tri-States Union* reports that William Howe Crane "is now at Holly Springs, Miss, to which place he went some days ago as teacher in the State Normal school in that place. As

the yellow fever is very bad at that place there is considerable anxiety for Mr. Crane."

21 SEPTEMBER. The *Evening Gazette* comments that "the New Jersey newspapers state that Mrs. Nellie Van Nortwick, daughter of the Rev. Dr. Crane of this village, was thrown from her wagon in Morris County last week and severely injured. The facts are that the lady was thrown from her carriage, but her injuries were very trifling."

22 SEPTEMBER. At the Drew Methodist Church, Dr. Crane delivers a philosophical discourse on the nature of Truth and singles out "six truths which do not admit of doubt," one of which supports the compatibility of Genesis with Darwinism: "There can be no beginning without a beginner. The development theory of Darwin, Huxley and the rest is not an infidel theory. They refer to the starting point, and tell us how the process went on, but without . . . a mighty hand to set the engineery in motion, how could the process commence? . . . . My reasonings end with the utterance with which Genesis commences: 'In the beginning, God'" (*Port Jervis Tri-States Union*, 27 September; Copy, NSyU). A series of letters to two local newspapers defends and criticizes Dr. Crane's scientific analysis (*Port Jervis Tri-States Union*, 22 and 25 October; Copy, NSyU).

24 SEPTEMBER. Mrs. Crane leaves Port Jervis to attend the three-day state convention of the Women's Christian Temperance Union in Geneva, New York (*Port Jervis Evening Gazette*).

1 OCTOBER. Dr. Crane predicts the ultimate destruction of the world since "the sun and the fixed stars, which are also suns, are expending an inconceivable amount of force in the production of light and heat. Science sees no way in which these central fires are replenished. The inevitable conclusion to which scientific reasoning comes is that the sun is slowly wasting away, as a source of light and heat, and in the lapse of ages must totally lose its power. This diminution of light and heat will affect the earth and in the course of time destroy all animal and vegetable life here" (*Port Jervis Evening Gazette*).

10 OCTOBER. Dr. Crane lectures on astronomy at the Drew Methodist Church (*Port Jervis Evening Gazette*; Copy, NSyU).

11 OCTOBER. Mrs. Crane is elected president of the WCTU of Port Jervis (*Port Jervis Evening Gazette*, 15 October).

15 OCTOBER. The *Port Jervis Evening Gazette* announces that "The Rev. Dr. Crane will deliver his lecture on astronomy Thursday evening of this week [17 October]. Special subjects: Eclipses, comets, shooting stars and aerolites. Hour, 7:30. Admission, 10 cents for adults, five cents for children."

16 OCTOBER. Jonathan Townley Crane writes in his diary: "Stevie has been sick today" (Wertheim 1993, 44).

5 NOVEMBER. The *Port Jervis Evening Gazette* reports that Mrs. Crane has been chosen to represent her congressional district at the national meeting of the WCTU in Baltimore.

16 NOVEMBER. The *Port Jervis Evening Gazette* announces that on 20 November Mrs. Crane will lecture to the Good Templars of Carpenters Point on the effects of alcohol on blood and the stomach (Copy, NSyU).

21 NOVEMBER. A concert at the Drew Methodist Church given by the "colored people" of the Mission Sunday School raises $35. Mrs. Crane thanks the church and "the press of Port Jervis which has rendered us valuable assistance" (*Port Jervis Tri-States Union*, 26 November; Copy, NSyU).

14 DECEMBER. A package of silks, velvets, and an ostrich plume are stolen from Mrs. Crane while she is riding a local train (*Port Jervis Evening Gazette*, 17 December; Copy, NSyU).

*

1879

*

6 JANUARY. Mrs. Crane and four other women organize an industrial school for "colored women and children. . . . The design of this movement is in some cases to supply the lack of early training and in others to supplement the work of the day school by instruction in the use of the needle" (*Port Jervis Tri-States Union*, 30 May; Copy, NSyU).

10 JANUARY. Dr. Crane lectures in the Presbyterian church "at length on the growing tendency of the people for reading trashy literature."

He speaks "strongly against the reading of story papers of the more ordinary class, claiming that the taste for such literature would grow upon the readers until their wants would not be satiated with anything but high tragedies. . . . He endeavored to impress upon the minds of the mothers present that it was their duty to their children to supply them with suitable reading, to the end that as they progressed and became older their minds would be so trained that the low, sensational trash would be odious to them, and as the demand for such publications becomes less[,] so also would the supply decrease" (*Port Jervis Evening Gazette*, 11 January).

18 FEBRUARY. The *Port Jervis Tri-States Union* reports that Luther Crane has become secretary of the Young People's Temperance Union (Copy, NSyU).

18 MARCH. *The Port Jervis Evening Gazette* lists Stephen Crane on the honor roll of Miss E. Reeves's room in the Main Street School.

30 MAY. Mrs. Crane and her co-workers in the Drew Mission and Industrial School are commended in a report "of the year's work just finished" for their efforts "to better the condition of our colored population" (*Port Jervis Tri-States Union*; Copy, NSyU).

15 JUNE. Dr. Crane preaches against the Darwinians, toward whom he had shown a compromising spirit in a lecture the previous September: "The question of the origin of things has produced 'a multitude of dreams,' the wildest of which is evolution—a dream of a few modern scientists and others who know little of science but are ever on the watch for something to set against the bible" (*Port Jervis Evening Gazette*, 17 June). In his 29 June sermon, Dr. Crane denounces the corollary doctrine of determinism, which "teaches us that every man, whether we choose to call him virtuous or vicious, is what he is by virtue of an inexorable law. Each individual man is only one little wheel in the universal enginery, which is driven by blind, resistless, external force, unknown and unknowable. . . . From such follies and insanities which destroy the very foundations of moral obligation and strip humanity of every immortal hope and every ennobling attribute, may the God of eternal truth in his infinite mercy deliver us" (*Port Jervis Evening Gazette*, 1 July).

18 JUNE. Agnes Crane wins two awards at Centenary Collegiate Institute (of which her father was a founder) in Hackettstown, New

Jersey: the complete works of Shakespeare for the best English essay and Macaulay's *History of England* for the best German exam. "Miss Crane being a Junior, it shows that she is not an ordinary scholar" (*Port Jervis Tri-States Union*, 24 June; Copy, NSyU).

8 AUGUST. Jonathan Townley Crane records in his diary: ". . Letter from my wife at Harwood [Hartwood, a hamlet 15 miles north of Port Jervis where the Cranes sometimes vacationed], this evening. Stevie is not well" (Wertheim 1993, 44).

9 AUGUST. From Jonathan Townley Crane's diary: "I hear, this morning, that S. is better . . . My wife came down in the evening train for medicine for Stevie, & returned at 8:20" (Wertheim 1993, 44).

11 AUGUST. Jonathan Townley Crane writes in his diary: "Letter . . : Stevie is 'very much better'" (Wertheim 1993, 44).

AUGUST. Stephen's life is imperiled when he is bitten by a poisonous snake near "Saint's Rest." His brother Wilbur performs emergency surgery, and a doctor at Forestburgh cauterizes the wound (Schoberlin III, 18).

24 SEPTEMBER. Jonathan Townley Crane records in his diary: "Will left us . . for the Law School at Albany, where he hopes to graduate next May" (Wertheim 1993, 45).

8 OCTOBER. Jonathan Townley Crane records in his diary: "Began to try my ideas down on paper, in regard to a very interesting, but difficult subject, the original state of man, his fall, &c." (Wertheim 1993, 45).

14 OCTOBER. From the diary of Jonathan Townley Crane: "Wrote on *Depravity*, reaching 30th page" (Wertheim 1993, 45).

17 NOVEMBER. Jonathan Townley Crane writes his daughter Agnes: "Stevie is well, and is getting some flesh on his bones, but is not at school" (Copy, NSyU).

DECEMBER. Crane writes his first surviving poem:

I'd Rather Have—

Last Christmas they gave me a sweater,
And a nice warm suit of wool,

But I'd rather be cold and have a dog,
To watch when I come from school.

Father gave me a bicycle,
But that isn't much of a treat,
Unless you have a dog at your heels
Racing away down the street

They bought me a camping outfit,
But a bonfire by a log
Is all the outfit I would ask,
If I only had a dog.

They seem to think a little dog
Is a killer of all earth's joys;
But oh, that "pesky little dog"
Means hours of joy to the boys.
(*Works*, 10: frontispiece)

CA. 1879. Mrs. Crane was so casual in her housekeeping habits "that when she came under that scrutiny which the ladies of the congregation sometimes delight in lavishing upon a minister's wife, she suffered much open criticism and was finally informed that she ought to stay at home and take care of her large family, instead of making so many speeches" (Price, 867).

*

1880

*

8 FEBRUARY. SUNDAY. From the diary of Jonathan Townley Crane: "Preached from John 1.47, 'a Christian indeed' . . . (at night) Preached against the 'Liberals' . . . so long that we omitted the prayer meeting" (Wertheim 1993, 48).

16 FEBRUARY. Jonathan Townley Crane dies suddenly at the age of 60 in his Port Jervis parsonage on East Broome Street. According to the next day's issue of the *Port Jervis Evening Gazette*,

At about 10:30 [A.M.] he had gone up stairs to write, when he was attacked with pains in his chest. He came down and Mrs. Crane placed mustard plasters upon the chest and feet. A dose of brandy was administered, and afterward a dose of morphine. The pains still increasing a physician was sent for, but before his arrival Mr. Crane was attacked with a spasm and died about half an hour after the first attack of pain. Paralysis of the heart is attributed as the cause of death. Mr. Crane had been in apparent health up to the hour of his fatal illness. The evening previous he had preached to an unusually large congregation on the theme announced in Saturday's papers: "What infidelity must do before it can destroy the Christian religion." He preached with his accustomed vigor, and Monday morning set about his labors as usual, preparing a discourse which it had been announced he would deliver at the free reading-room that evening. The only children at home were the two youngest, Luther and Stephen, and Mr. J. T. Crane, junior, of the New York *Tribune*, who, with his wife, arrived in town Saturday evening on a brief visit and was to return to duty Monday evening.

[LATE FEBRUARY]. Mrs. Crane and her younger children are required to leave the parsonage. Edmund, Wilbur, and Luther drop out of Centenary Collegiate Institute (*A Record of the Alumni of Centenary Collegiate Institute: 1874–1934*). Family affairs are "unsettled for several months," and Mrs. Crane moves temporarily to Roseville, near Newark (EBC), but Stephen probably remains in the care of his brother Edmund in Sussex County, New Jersey. A census taken on 9 and 11 June in Sandyston Township, Sussex County, lists Stephen, 8 years old, and Edmund B. Crane, 22 years old, as boarders in the home of H. W. Van Sycle and his wife and four sons. Edmund's occupation is given as schoolteacher (*Sussex County Census*, 21 [1880], 12). The Van Sycle (sometimes spelled "Van Sickle") family was related by marriage to the Cranes.

8 APRIL. The *Port Jervis Daily Union* reports that Edmund B. Crane is teaching school at Centreville in Sussex County, New Jersey.

MAY. William Howe Crane is graduated from the Albany Law School and admitted to the bar of the town of Deerpark (Allerton, 3).

MID-JUNE. After a three-month's residence in Roseville, Mrs. Crane returns to Port Jervis. Shortly afterward the family settles with William in a home at 21 Brooklyn Street in the "Brooklyn" neighborhood of Port Jervis, on the far side of the Delaware and Hudson Canal (*Middletown and Port Jervis Directory for 1882–1883*).

17 JUNE. Agnes graduates as class valedictorian from Centenary Collegiate Institute (*Commencement Program, Centenary Collegiate Institute, 1880*).

SUMMER. ASBURY PARK. Townley Crane assumes charge of the Long Branch departments of the *New York Tribune* and the Associated Press (Copy of announcement, NySU).

11 NOVEMBER. FORT LEE, NEW JERSEY. Agnes E. Crane writes in her diary:

> Some wiseacre has said that no one ever writes a journal but with the idea that some one will read it after him and be impressed, I suppose, with the lively character revealed thereby. However that may be with mankind in general, I feel convinced that no such illusion now possesses me and guides my pen. That I am twenty five years old, and no longer a sentimental girl in her teens, ought to effectually banish such a suspicion. It is only that my vexations seem at times too great to be borne in silence. I feel that I *must* express them and to whom can I? Coming from such an oyster-like family there are few to whom I can speak freely and I have learned, too, that people will talk to me with great vivacity about their own troubles but grow inattentive when a reciprocal confidation—ever so slight, is attempted. (Sorrentino 1986, 128)

*

1881

*

20 MAY. In a debate at the Young Men's Literary Society William Howe Crane argues against the proposition "That the intellect of woman is as great as that of man" (*Port Jervis Evening Gazette*, 21 May).

1881. Stephen inscribes his name in a copy of Bishop Jesse T. Peck's hortatory tract, *What Must I Do to Be Saved?* (1858): "You must go alone to the bar of God. You must answer for your own life of guilt, and you yourself must, if finally impenitent, obey the terrific words, 'Depart ye cursed, into everlasting fire.' You alone must suffer for your own obstinate rebellion" (34). He also signed and dated two other books in this year: Daniel T. Atwood's *Atwood's Country and Suburban Houses* (1871) and James Dixon's *Personal Narrative of a Tour Through a Part of the United States and Canada* (1850) (NNC).

*

1882

*

3 MARCH. William Howe Crane delivers a lecture to the Young Men's Literary Society on the subject of "The Mississippi Pig": "He

William Howe Crane
(Robert K. Crane)

related some amusing stories of the pig's place in social life, gave graphic accounts of its struggles through life with its natural enemies, the negro and the dog, on to its final entombment in the form of bacon or sausage in the stomach of man, or if blessed with a natural death and left as carrion in the field is gathered to its fathers and buried in the maw of the buzzard, the scavenger of the South" (*Port Jervis Evening Gazette*, 4 March).

7 MARCH. William Howe Crane, the Republican candidate for the office of town clerk of Deerpark Township, loses the election (*Port Jervis Evening Gazette*, 8 March).

Farnum Building, corner of Pike and Hammond Streets,
Port Jervis, NY. Site of William Howe Crane's law office
(Minisink Valley Historical Society)

1 APRIL. William Howe Crane establishes his law practice in the
Farnum Building on the corner of Pike and Hammond streets in Port
Jervis (*Port Jervis Evening Gazette*). He becomes prominent in community life, serving as district clerk of the Board of Education, treasurer of the Port Jervis Water Works, and, for one year, special judge
for Orange County.

20 NOVEMBER. The *Order of Business* record book of the Port Jervis
schools reveals behavior problems in the classroom of Agnes Crane,
who is teaching at the Mountain House School. The superintendent
makes special mention that "In Miss Crane's room . . . there was a
hard set of boys that were not properly controlled; the room was in
trouble and likely to become worse" (Gullason 1977, 235).

Pike Street, Port Jervis, NY
(Minisink Valley Historical Society)

18 DECEMBER. Agnes submits her resignation as a teacher at the Mountain House School but withdraws it at the request of the Board of Education (Gullason 1977, 235).

26 DECEMBER. The Port Jervis Board of Education accepts Agnes Crane's resignation (Gullason 1977, 235).

*

1883

*

13 JANUARY. Agnes publishes the first of four unsigned sentimental stories, "A Victorious Defeat," in *Frank Leslie's Illustrated Newspaper* (Gullason 1986, 73n4).

19 JANUARY. At the conclusion of a debate in the Young Men's Literary Society on the resolution that "the civil law is inadequate to the suppression of polygamy in Utah," the judges vote with the affirmative supported by William Howe Crane while the audience decides in the negative. The society is reorganized as the Young People's Liter-

ary Union, making women eligible for membership, a change that the *Evening Gazette* feels comes none too soon since "there is a certain boyishness in the society that should by all means be eliminated. During the exercises the audience was frequently disturbed by the snapping of beans across the room, and one of the members after the close had a snow ball thrown down the back of his neck. These performances should cease at once, and the most stringent measures used to suppress them. Then the society needs the active co-operation of some live lady members, who by their presence and interest will diversify the order of exercises and add very materially to the pleasure and entertainment of the members" (*Port Jervis Evening Gazette*, 20 January).

2 FEBRUARY. William Howe Crane is elected president of the Young People's Social and Literary Union (*Port Jervis Daily Union*, 3 February).

6 MARCH. William Howe Crane, Republican candidate for the office of town clerk, again loses the election (*Port Jervis Daily Union*, 7 March).

3 APRIL. The *Jersey City Evening Journal* reports a bizarre incident involving Wilbur F. Crane, who is attending medical school. In searching an ice-filled barrel on the roof of the building where Wilbur lives, neighbors discovered "a human foot . . . a female pelvis and other portions of a body. . . . The remains were evidently those of a woman about 45 years of age." During a police interrogation, Wilbur said he had brought the body from the College of Physicians and Surgeons in New York City. "He did not know the name of the subject or what parties had possession of the other portions of the body. He explained that he wished to mount the skeleton and intended to boil the subject on the roof by means of an oil stove. He said that he would have completed the work long ago had it not been for a sudden cold snap that froze the barrel solid. Chief Murphy asked him if he had not procured the subject from a near by cemetery, but Crane stated that he could prove the truth of his assertions. He was then released, after showing his college credentials. . . . He does not appear to be at all disturbed by his actions."

Wilbur writes to the county physician:

> I am a student in the College of Physicians and Surgeons and reside at No. 303 Eighth street, Jersey City. I had part of the skeleton of a woman from the pelvis down, which had been all dissected excepting a portion of the foot, which I was macerating in a barrel on the roof of my resi-

dence. The barrel was interviewed [sic] by an old lady from the next house, who sent Police Captain Edmonson to interview me. After a council of war, the Chief of Police and City Physician Morris being present, the remains were confiscated and sent to the morgue. The bones were brought by me from the college about two months ago, and would have been prepared before this had I not been prevented, first by their freezing and later by sickness. I would like to have my bones returned to me if it can be consistently done. (*Jersey City Evening Journal*)

The physician agreed that the bones should be returned.

4 APRIL. The county physician returns the bones to Wilbur (*Port Jervis Daily Union*).

5 APRIL. The *Port Jervis Daily Union* reports that Agnes Crane and another local girl scored highest in the examination given for applicants for teaching positions in the Paterson public schools the previous week.

6 APRIL. The *Port Jervis Evening Gazette* reports that Agnes Crane is applying for a teaching position in Paterson. The paper adds that Agnes "was a teacher in our public schools here. She proved herself a thoroughly competent teacher in every respect and should never have been allowed to resign."

3 MAY. The *Port Jervis Evening Gazette* announces a meeting to be held the next evening at the Literary Union in which there will be "a critical discussion of the character of George Washington reviewed from the historical, political, sentimental, pathetic, humorous, intellectual and moral standpoint." William Howe Crane is to be one of the participants. The *Daily Union* of 5 May reports that William spoke of the sentimental aspect of Washington's character.

17 MAY. Bishop Jesse T. Peck dies of pneumonia in Syracuse (*Port Jervis Daily Union*, 19 May).

19 MAY. William Howe Crane is a participant in a debate at the Literary Union on the question of whether "British rule in India has been a benefit to the people of that country" (*Port Jervis Daily Union*).

30 JUNE. J. Townley Crane is listed on the masthead as the editor of the *Asbury Park Shore Press*.

JUNE. Mary Helen Crane moves her family to 508 Fourth Avenue, Asbury Park. William Howe Crane remains in Port Jervis, moving into his own home at 270 Main Street (*Middletown and Port Jervis Directory for 1884–1885*).

28 JULY. Townley's name is dropped from the masthead as editor of the *Shore Press*.

30 JULY. As "Librarian pro-tem" of the Port Jervis District Library, William Howe Crane announces that the library will be open only two evenings of the week during the summer (*Port Jervis Daily Union*).

29 SEPTEMBER. Mrs. Crane becomes president of the WCTU of Asbury Park and Ocean Grove and is reelected annually until her resignation in January 1891. She "is a lady in every way qualified for the position; having gained a wide experience and rich fund of knowledge in the various departments of Christian and temperance work, in which she has been engaged for several years past, as Secretary of the New York Branch of the Women's Foreign Missionary Society, and as vice-president of the Women's Temperance Union, of New Jersey, and in several other offices requiring judgment and mental ability. She has purchased a residence in Asbury Park, corner Grand and Fourth avenue, and with a part of her family will remain here permanently" (*Asbury Park Shore Press*, 8 December). Her credentials, according to a correspondent for the WCTU, are "her varied experience as a prominent minister's wife, her intelligence and culture, and marked administrative ability" (*Asbury Park Journal*, 8 December). She lectures frequently on the debilitating effects of alcohol.

SEPTEMBER. Stephen enrolls in the sixth grade at the Asbury Park School. Agnes takes a teaching position in the intermediate school. Three years after her death in 1884, the *Daily Press* describes her as one of the area's "most efficient school teachers" (*Asbury Park Daily Press*, 6 July 1887).

20 OCTOBER. Agnes Crane's story "How It Happened" appears in *Frank Leslie's Illustrated Newspaper* (Gullason 1986, 73n4).

26 NOVEMBER. Townley Crane's wife, Fannie, dies in Asbury Park at the age of 29 of Bright's disease. A childhood playmate of Townley, she and her husband were married in 1878; they had two children, both of whom died (*Asbury Park Shore Press*, 1 December).

I DECEMBER. "Owing to the increased illness and subsequent death of Mrs. J. Townley Crane, Miss Agnes Crane, teacher of C class, intermediate department of our school, has not been in school this week" (*Asbury Park Journal*).

8 DECEMBER. Mrs. Crane holds a "juvenile temperance meeting" in the afternoon and in the evening discusses "Water versus Alcohol," the first in a series of semi-monthly public lectures "for the better understanding of the prohibition question and for the instruction of the people in the nature and effects of alcohol upon the human system" (*Asbury Park Shore Press*).

CA. 1883. Agnes "used to say of herself: 'Mother has hope that her ugly duckling may turn out a swan.' Her face was as solemn as that of anyone who ever lived; but her alert mind, her spirit of fun, and her radiant personality made her most companionable. And she was Stephen Crane's good angel, brightening his boyhood as an older sister can sometimes do" (Price, 867).

*

1884

*

[The panic of 1884 precipitates strikes in the Pennsylvania coal mines, reducing the dividends from Mary Helen Crane's inherited coal shares. She rents her home in Asbury Park to summer visitors. Money is found for Wilbur to continue his medical education, but his thesis on typhoid fever is twice rejected and he fails to maintain an adequate grade average. In 1886, after five years in medical school, he leaves without completing his degree (annual catalogues of the College of Physicians and Surgeons, Columbia University, 1881–1886). Much of the responsibility of the household descends upon Agnes, despite her teaching load and her own failing health. A playmate of Stephen's recalls that "his mother was small, a bright, round, active woman, bird-like in movement, an ardent temperance lecturer. You could not be a temperance worker then and be much at home. His sister Agnes taught public school, a tall, kindly, graceful, brown-eyed young woman of magnetic charm, a sweet nature. She mothered the family, but the brood was too much for her. Steve was just grown out of 'knee pants'; small, under-nourished, coming home from school or play, maybe skating on the lake, to find no supper. He would then range the neighborhood for food and companionship, telling tales to the children of the various mothers—mine was one—who often sewed on his buttons" (Anonymous, undated transcription sent to Melvin H. Schoberlin by Corwin K. Linson, NSyU).]

15 MARCH. In the *Ocean Grove Record*, Mrs. Crane deplores "the growing taste for worldly amusements which keeps the young from the house of God, dissipating religious convictions and makes the commands of God of no effect. In this category we may count card playing, dancing and theatre going. These frivolous amusements have little to recommend them. They are good as devices to 'kill time,' which means to waste the precious hours given us for holier uses" (Gullason 1972, 36).

22 MARCH. In a letter printed in the *Shore Press* Townley denies that he has written dispatches slandering Asbury Park and has circulated them through the Associated Press, for which he is the Long Branch agent.

APRIL. Declining health compels Agnes Crane to resign her teaching position in the Asbury Park School (Gullason 1977, 236).

17 MAY. Agnes's story "The Result of an Experiment" appears in *Frank Leslie's Illustrated Newspaper* (Gullason 1986, 73n4).

10 JUNE. Agnes Elizabeth Crane dies of cerebrospinal meningitis in the home of her brother Edmund at Rutherford, New Jersey.

LATE JUNE. The Asbury Park Board of Education adopts the following preamble and resolution:

> "Whereas, we have received with profound sorrow the painful intelligence of the death of Miss Agnes Crane, of the Asbury Park public school; and,
> "Whereas, it seems just and proper for this Board to give public expression to our high appreciation of her amiable character and her invaluable services as a teacher; be it
> "*Resolved*, that in the death of Miss Crane this community has lost a member who adorned it with many rare graces of character, the cause of education a sincere, zealous, and devoted friend, and the school with which she was connected a faithful and efficient teacher, to whose tireless industry, skill and tact it owes much of its high degree of excellence.
> "Resolved, that we tender to her special and related friends the assurance of our earnest sympathy and condolence." (*Asbury Park Journal*, 28 June)

28 JUNE. Luther almost dies from an accidental overdose of laudanum taken to relieve diarrhea and cramps. "Not being accustomed to the drug he took too much, and in a short time was discovered unconscious at his home on Fourth avenue. Dr. Mitchell was summoned, and after five hours of hard work, assisted by Capt. Baker and others, succeeded in restoring him. Fifteen minutes delay in calling the physician would have cost the young man his life" (*Asbury Park Evening Journal,* 30 June; Copy, NSyU).

EARLY NOVEMBER. Mary Helen Crane attends the WCTU Convention in St. Louis as the Asbury Park delegate (*Asbury Park Shore Press,* 1 November).

13 NOVEMBER. Townley Crane acts as a chaperon for the Knights of the Quill in Freehold, New Jersey (*Asbury Park Shore Press,* 15 November).

EARLY DECEMBER. Townley Crane is elected recording secretary of the New York Press Club (*Asbury Park Shore Press,* 6 December).

*

1885

*

[*Van Horn's Directory of Asbury Park for* 1885 lists the following addresses and occupations of the Cranes: Luther P., "reporter, Fourth avenue, E Emory st"; J. Townley, "correspondent NY Associated Press, Fourth ave"; Wilbur F., "Fourth avenue, E Emory"; M. Helen, "Arbutus Cottage, Fourth ave, E Emory st" (p. 5). Arbutus Cottage was located at 605 East Fourth Avenue. *Smith's Directory of Asbury Park* lists Mrs. Crane's "occupation" as widow and that of Wilbur as student.]

13 MARCH. Townley Crane "is at last 'home again,' after a long siege at the Wainwright trial at Toms River. Mr. Crane represented the *Tribune* and the Associated Press." In a column titled "Richard's Rambling Reflections," "Richard" comments that Townley "is a good fellow, but some of his ideas are certainly original—for a man. His latest is a 'crazy' quilt, which he was showing to some of his friends, myself among the number, the other day. It was pretty, and Townley seemed

proud of it. But when somebody offered to bet it never would be finished, Mr. Crane didn't want to 'take 'em up.' I guess he knows something about the fate of the average crazy quilt" (*Asbury Park Shore Press*).

8–9 APRIL. Mary Helen Crane attends the New Jersey WCTU Convention in Salem as a delegate from Asbury Park and Ocean Grove (*Asbury Park Shore Press*, 10 April).

14 SEPTEMBER. Crane enrolls in Pennington Seminary, Pennington, New Jersey, for the fall term of 1885. His father had been principal of Pennington, a boarding school sponsored by the Methodist Episcopal Church, from 1849 to 1858. A major function of the school is to train young men for the ministry. Discipline at the school reflects a "'rigid, yet mild and parental' tone." Students are required to attend two religious services in the chapel daily and either the Methodist or Presbyterian church services in town on Sundays. Smoking, drinking, gambling, and frequenting places of entertainment are forbidden. Yet the school has a familial environment and a good athletic program (Gullason 1968a, 530–531, 534–535, 537–538).

*

1886

*

8 FEBRUARY. Crane registers at Pennington Seminary for the winter term, which started on 4 January (Gullason 1968a, 531).

11 MARCH. The *Asbury Park Shore Press* reports that "Mrs. M. Helen Crane, who has been very ill for several months, is now suffering from a temporary aberration of the mind, and is in a critical condition."

13 MARCH. The *Asbury Park Journal* reports that Mrs. Crane "has been extremely ill for some time, and though her mind is yet feeble it is hoped with returning strength her mental troubles will disappear."

5 APRIL. Crane registers for the spring term at Pennington Seminary (Gullason 1968a, 531).

Pennington Seminary
(Robert K. Crane)

6 SEPTEMBER. Crane returns to Pennington Seminary for the fall term (Gullason 1968a, 531).

21 SEPTEMBER. In New York City Cora Ethel Howorth marries Thomas Vinton Murphy, son of the former collector of the Port of New York in the Grant administration. They take up residence in the Gedney house on Broadway and 40th Street in the heart of the theater district (Friedmann 1989, 5).

[Prior to her marriage, Cora Howorth had been the mistress of Jerome Stivers, son of New York's leading carriage manufacturer and a notorious man about town. During their four-year cohabitation Cora served as hostess of the London Club, a gambling house in the Tenderloin (Friedmann 1989, 3).]

26 SEPTEMBER. Luther Crane, who had become a flagman on the Erie Railroad line, falls beneath the wheels of a moving train and is killed (*Asbury Park Journal*, 2 October).

26 NOVEMBER. Mary Helen Crane is elected permanent president of the newly formed WCTU of Asbury Park (*Asbury Park Journal*, 27 November).

*

1887

*

11 JANUARY. Crane registers for the winter term at Pennington Seminary (Gullason 1968a, 531).

LATE MARCH. After the death of her first husband, Stephen's oldest sister, Mary Helen Van Nortwick ("Nellie"), later Mrs. Philip M. Murray-Hamilton of Philadelphia, establishes an art school in the family's Fourth Avenue home. "She is an accomplished artist and has been teaching drawing, painting, etc., in Newark for some years. She proposes to take pupils in these branches of art here, and we think her services will soon be in demand, as her work is unusually excellent" (*Asbury Park Journal*, 26 March).

4 APRIL. Crane registers for the spring term at Pennington Seminary (Gullason 1968a, 531).

27 APRIL. Stephen's oldest brother, George Peck Crane, marries Lizzie Archer in Jersey City (*Asbury Park Tribune*, Copy, NSyU).

MAY. Townley Crane is "elected an honorary member of the Veteran Zouaves, of Elizabeth" (*Asbury Park Journal*, 21 May).

22 JUNE. Jeff Graves, a pseudonym for Frank M. Taylor of the *Daily Press*, writes: "I understand that J. Townley Crane is writing a series of articles for the New York *Evening Sun* on Jersey dogs. If Mr. Crane is ever called upon to write on Jersey hogs and will call on me, I can give him some data that may prove of value in the preparation of his article. Some newspapers have an office cat you know, Mr. Crane, but I know one where they have a different species of animal" (*Asbury Park Daily Press*).

28 JUNE. The *New York Times, Tribune,* and *Sun* contain an article, probably written by Townley Crane, reporting a meeting at the African Methodist Church in West Asbury Park to protest remarks by James A. Bradley "in reference to the obnoxious manners of certain classes on the beach plaza." Bradley had referred "to the way the beach seats and plaza are monopolized by the colored help of the hotels and cottages."

The Crane family house at 508 4th Avenue, Asbury
Park, NJ; known as Arbutus Cottage
(Syracuse University)

29 JUNE. The *Asbury Park Tribune* reports that "Master Stephen
Crane has returned home from Pennington Seminary where he has
been studying for the past two years, and will spend his vacation at
his mother's pleasant home on 4th Avenue."

2 JULY. Agnes Crane's last posthumous story, "Laurel Camp, and
What Came of It," is published in *Frank Leslie's Illustrated Newspaper*
(Gullason 1986, 73n4).

12 JULY. The *Philadelphia Press* prints "Asbury's New Move."
[Schoberlin (IV, 22–23) identifies the item as being Crane's initial
appearance in print on the basis of its idiosyncrasies of style, ironic
point of view, and colloquial expressions. (At another point in his
biography, Schoberlin refers to an earlier unlocated piece, "The Summer Tramp," in an Asbury Park newspaper, the *Daily Spray*, 20 June
1887). "Asbury's New Move" concerns a pair of young lovers whose
flirtations on the beach at Asbury Park are interrupted by a puritanical
Superintendent Snedeker: "Nearly everybody on the beach near the
bathing ground had been amused during the half hour preceding the
Superintendent's unwelcome appearance by a pair of those tender
seaside doves who have been so numerous at Asbury Park. They
were partly protected from the sun's rays by a very loud-striped para-

sol, but shielded from the gaze of the beach throng by nothing. There they sat, or rather reclined, upon the half-dry sand, and the whole world was but a myth to them."]

23 JULY. During the seventeenth annual meeting of the New Jersey State Dental Society, held in Asbury Park, the *Daily Press* jokingly refers to Townley as a dentist: "Photographer Hill's photograph of the members of the Dental Society is unusually good for a large group picture. Among the local dentists whose handsome faces loom up in the throng are Dr. I. G. Burton, J. Townley Crane and Fred J. Long. It's a Long Crane that don't get left" (*Asbury Park Daily Press*).

17 AUGUST. In a photo of the presidents of the National League of Baseball, who are meeting in Asbury Park, "The well-known features of J. Townley Crane, the well-known journalist, form a part of the group. Mr. Crane is the League historian" (*Asbury Park Daily Press*).

24 AUGUST. "J. Townley Crane is preparing an article for the New York *Evening Sun* on the babies of Asbury Park and Long Branch. It is an interesting subject, and Mr. Crane's facile pen will make it more so" (*Asbury Park Daily Press*).

SUMMER. Mrs. Crane reports the sessions of the Seaside Summer School of Pedagogy at Avon-by-the-Sea for the *New York Tribune*. The *Asbury Park Journal* (13 August) reports that "much of the prominence that has been given the meetings in the daily papers is due to her attention."

5 SEPTEMBER. Crane returns to Pennington Seminary for the fall term; this is his last term at the school (Gullason 1968a, 531).

7 SEPTEMBER. The *Asbury Park Tribune* reports that "Stephen Crane, after spending the summer at the Grove, returned to Pennington Seminary last week."

BETWEEN 25 AND 30 SEPTEMBER. Mrs. Mary Helen Van Nortwick takes "first premium in the Art Department of the State Fair . . . for a plush-framed placque with a cat's head painted upon it. It is now on exhibition in the window of Schneider's store on Main street" (*Asbury Park Journal*, 1 October).

14 NOVEMBER. Mrs. Crane leaves for Nashville to attend the National Convention of the WCTU (*Asbury Park Tribune*, 16 November).

1887

LATE NOVEMBER-EARLY DECEMBER. Stephen abruptly leaves Pennington Seminary. Wilbur F. Crane recalls:

Stephen's most marked characteristic was his absolute truthfulness. He was in many minor scrapes but no consideration of consequences would induce him to lie out of them, and the imputation that he was a liar, made the imputer *non persona grata* with Stephen forever thereafter.

While at Pennington seminary some hazing was done which one of the professors charged to Stephen. He denied any knowledge of it, and when the professor told him he lied, Stephen went to his room, packed his trunk and went home to Asbury Park where he told his story, adding that "as the Professor called me a liar there was not room in Pennington for us both, so I came home." Nothing would induce him to return to the seminary. (WFC)

7 DECEMBER. Mrs. Crane returns to Asbury Park from the WCTU convention in Nashville (*Asbury Park Tribune*, 14 December).

23 DECEMBER. Mrs. Crane writes to the Reverend Arthur M. Flack, principal of Claverack College and Hudson River Institute, who had often visited the Seaside Summer School of Pedagogy at Avon-by-the-Sea, inquiring for terms of tuition and room and board for children of Methodist ministers. The word *Claverack* is a Dutch corruption of "Clover Reach," a phrase that describes the miles of clover in the vicinity (Thomas W. Lamont, *My Boyhood in a Parsonage* [New York: 1946], p. 1). Claverack is a coeducational preparatory school and junior college with a military training battalion for boys composed of four companies and a color guard. "Colonel" Flack is commander of the battalion. Mrs. George Crane, one of Stephen's sisters-in-law, recalls: "His fondness for everything military induced his mother to send him to the Claverack Military Academy. While a student there he kept up his interest in athletics and became fond of horses. He had a pony of his own and spent much time riding it" (Mrs. GC).

26 DECEMBER. The Reverend A. H. Flack replies to Mrs. Crane: "Should you place your son under our care we would do our best to give him a thorough college praparation [*sic*] and at the same time make for him a pleasant Christian school home" (Photocopy, OU).

31 DECEMBER. A. H. Flack writes to Mary Helen Crane: "We note what you say with regard to room-mate and course of study for your son and will carry out your instructions carefully" (Photocopy, OU).

Claverack College and Hudson River Institute
(Wertheim Collection)

CHAPTER TWO

Claverack, Lafayette College, and Syracuse University

1888–1891

Crane transfers to Claverack College and Hudson River Institute in January 1888 at the age of 16 motivated primarily by his interest in the military training program. At Claverack he has his most intense period of exposure to the classics and to nineteenth-century English and American literature and rises rapidly in the ranks of the student battalion, being gazetted captain in the June 1890 issue of the school's magazine, *Vidette*. In the summer months from 1888 through 1892 he helps his brother Townley, who operates a news-reporting agency in Asbury Park for the *New York Tribune* and the Associated Press. He leaves Claverack before completing the program and in the fall of 1890 enrolls as a freshman in the mining-engineering program at Lafayette College, Easton, Pennsylvania. At Lafayette Crane plays baseball and joins Delta Upsilon fraternity. Excessive absence from classes leads to academic deficiencies, and he transfers in January 1891 to Syracuse University where he is entitled to a scholarship as grandnephew of one of the founders, Bishop Jesse Truesdell Peck. At Syracuse he rooms in the Delta Upsilon house but devotes much of his time to baseball rather than study and wins local acclaim as catcher and sometimes shortstop of the varsity baseball team. Crane publishes sketches in the *University Herald* and works as a stringer for the *New York Tribune*. At the end of the spring semester he leaves Syracuse voluntarily. During the summer he continues to report shore news for the *Tribune* and writes feature articles for the *New York Herald*. In the fall he intensifies his explorations of the New York City slum world.

*

1888

*

4 JANUARY. Crane registers at Claverack College and Hudson River Institute as a student in the Classical Department, as distinguished

from the Academic and Commercial departments, but he later transfers to the Academic Department. Claverack's Classical graduates had often been accepted into the junior year at Yale, Syracuse, Cornell, or Wesleyan, but, according to Crane's schoolmate Harvey Wickham, "the high reputation once enjoyed by the school was wholly in the past, and no longer survived save among the uninformed. . . . The college, in fact, had become all absorbed in the Hudson River Institute—a mere boarding-school, quartered like an octopus in the college dormitories, taught by the college faculty and drawing much of its patronage from parents cursed with backward or semi-incorrigible offspring" (Wickham, 291).

7 JANUARY. The *Asbury Park Journal* reports that "Mr. Stephen Crane has entered the Hudson River Military Institute, at Claverack, N.Y., preparatory to a college course."

The *Asbury Park Journal* reports that Townley Crane "desires us to say that as he has heard reports to the effect that he was the author of the recent false report concerning a scarlet fever epidemic here which appeared in the *New York Tribune*, he wishes to state that he was sick in bed at the time and knew nothing whatever about it until he read it in the paper two days afterward."

19 JANUARY. Mrs. Crane offers "a very fraternal welcome address" and a brief presentation on "'Press Work' and its influences" at the January meeting of the WCTU of Monmouth County in Ocean Grove (*Asbury Park Journal*, 21 January).

28 JANUARY. Mrs. Crane "will give [on 31 January] a practical illustration—by means of a small distillery apparatus—of the presence of alcohol in many things in common use" (*Asbury Park Journal*).

27 MARCH. Crane inscribes himself "S. T. Crane/New York City" in the autograph album of a friend, E. L. Gray, Jr. (*C*, 31). Cora Crane later recalls: "When at Claverick he was ashamed of being only boy without middle name so called himself Stephen D̲. Crane" (*Works*, 10: 344). More likely, as Edith Crane wrote to Melvin H. Schoberlin, "Stephen Crane may as an adolescent thought he might as well have the middle name of 'Townley'—T—the same as so many others" (Edith Crane to Melvin H. Schoberlin, n.d., NSyU).

12 APRIL. The Reverend A. H. Flack writes to Mary Helen Crane, who has apparently objected to the high cost of Stephen's education

at Claverack, that the courses he is taking require quite a number of books and that the only superfluous item on the bill is a baseball for 67 cents: "His last report is better than the one before it and is high in all classes except grammar. Punctuality is low—That should not be—I will stir him up on it and it will be well for you to call his attention to that point also." In a postscript he adds, "We will excuse him from declaiming but dont like to do so" (Photocopy, OU). [Crane retained an indifference toward formal grammar, and his dislike for public speaking is amusingly depicted in his Whilomville story "Making an Orator."]

15 JUNE. Mrs. Crane delivers "a temperance lecture in the Baptist Church, at Manasquan, Friday evening." She is "greeted by a large audience" (*Asbury Park Daily Press*, 18 June).

19 JUNE. Stephen "is home for the summer. He is a student at Claverack (N.Y.) College, and wears the stripes of a corporal on his natty uniform" (*Asbury Park Daily Press*).

Townley Crane, "who has been in bad health all winter, was able to walk a few blocks on Saturday. His illness has left him very weak" (*Asbury Park Daily Journal*).

"Mrs. M. Helen Crane has so enlarged and beautified Arbutus Cottage, on Fourth avenue, that it is now one of the finest cottages in the Park. It is rented this season to Commodore Louis C. Sartori, of the United States Navy, who is a resident of Philadelphia. The Commodore won his title by many years of faithful service to his country. His mother and several accomplished nieces are with him" (*Asbury Park Daily Press*).

BETWEEN 20 AND 23 JUNE. "Mr. J. Townley Crane, of the Associated Press, while on his way home from the *Daily Press* office early one morning last week, was accosted by a negro who tried to grab his watch. Mr. Crane struck at him with his right hand and then with his left. The left hand not being tightly closed the blow broke the bone back of the knuckle of the little finger. The hand is now badly swollen" (*Asbury Park Daily Press*, 25 June).

LATE JUNE. Frances E. Willard, national president of the WCTU, is a guest in the Crane home (*Asbury Park Tribune*, 4 July; Copy, NSyU).

2 JULY. "You all know Townley Crane, don't you? He wears a *very* handsome new suit of summer clothes. It is a pleasure to thus see the material prosperity of our friends" (*Asbury Park Daily Press*).

JULY. Stephen becomes Townley's assistant in reporting about the New Jersey shore from his office in Asbury Park's Lake Avenue Hotel. Townley, known as the "Shore Fiend" because of his voracity in searching out items of interest for his *Tribune* column, "On the New Jersey Coast," was, according to Post Wheeler, "Middle-aged, sandy-haired and baldish, thick set. He wore incredible clothes and even in hot weather a long tweed overcoat sadly in need of cleaning. I do not think he ever wore a shirt. Instead a colored muffler was wound around his neck, pinned close and tucked in. Teeth yellow and un-cared for. A physical derelict" (Post Wheeler to Melvin H. Schoberlin, 25 December 1947, NSyU).

26 AUGUST. The satiric tone of an account of a camp meeting "love feast" in Ocean Grove (published in the *New York Tribune*, 27 August) suggests Crane's authorship: "Dr. Stokes asked the people to shake hands in token of brotherly love, which they did with shouts and tears. Four Christian Chinamen sent up a written testimony that they 'loved Jesus better and better every day'" (*Works*, 8: 531).

29 AUGUST. Mrs. Crane leads "the mothers' meeting in the Tabernacle. Her topic was: 'Overcome'" (*Asbury Park Daily Press*, 30 August).

10 SEPTEMBER. Crane registers for the fall term at Claverack (Pratt 1939a, 461–462).

21 SEPTEMBER. The Reverend A. H. Flack writes to Mary Helen Crane: "One of our regulations is that students shall not have horses—The livery is connected with the hotel and we do not wish that the students shall have any business there at all—On that account I would not favor the horse-back riding—Stephen is very much interested in base ball and tennis and seems to take all the exercise he has time for out of study hours in that way" (Photocopy, OU).

SEPTEMBER. Mary Helen Van Nortwick wins "a premium" at the New Jersey State Fair for her "painting of a King Charles spaniel, from life" (*Asbury Park Journal*, 29 September).

FALL. CLAVERACK. Crane is promoted to cadet sergeant in Company B. He befriends Armistead Borland. "'I was only a kid of fourteen,'" Borland has written, "'and "Steve" was my hero and ideal. I must have been somewhat of a nuisance to him always hanging around—sometimes when I was not wanted. I tried to copy him in every way and

Cadet Company B, Claverack College, ca. 1889. Crane
stands second from left. Armistead Borland
stands second from right
(Syracuse University)

learned many things, not all for the good of my immortal soul—the
rudiments of the great American game of poker and something more
than the rudiments of the ways of a man with a maid'" (Schoberlin V,
17).

[1888–1889]. A schoolmate recalls:

Although Crane was not an all around student, yet he was far in advance of his fellow students in his knowledge of History and Literature.
He preferred these subjects and always seemed glad to enter the Regents
examination in them as he was sure of passing with a fine marque. If he
passed in Mathematics or Science, it would be by some power other than
Crane. He was a voracious reader of all the nineteenth century English
writers and reveled in the classics of Greece and Rome. Plutarch's lives
was his constant companion and even at this age he was familiar with the
English and American poets. He would frequently quote from Tennysons
"In Memoriam" and Bryant's "Thanatopsis." (Reminiscence written on or
about 20 March 1930 included in a letter from A. Lincoln Travis to Mansfield J. French, NSyU)

Officers and non-commissioned officers of the Cadet
Corps at Claverack College, 1889. Crane is seated third
from left in the second row
(*Newark Museum*)

*

1889

*

2 JANUARY. The *New Jersey Tribune and Advertiser* prints Mrs.
Crane's humorous dialect story "How Jonathan Saved the Ash Barrel"
under the nom de plume "Jerusha Ann Stubbs." Another story,
"Thanksgiving or Christmas. *Which?*" appeared, probably a short time
earlier, under the by-line of Mrs. M. Helen Crane in the *Monmouth
Tribune*, a temperance newspaper published in Asbury Park. The
latter story contains a character named Jerusha Ann Jarvis, whom
Mrs. Crane may have featured in other works of fiction (Gullason
1986, 71).

26 JANUARY. LONDON. Having divorced Thomas Vinton Murphy,
Cora Howorth marries Captain Donald William Stewart, son of the
former British commander in chief in India. The couple take up residence at his father's house in fashionable South Kensington
(Friedmann 1989, 8).

13 MARCH. Mrs. Crane speaks on "the causes that led her to devote the late years of her life to the crusade against rum, and the reason for the women banding together" at a meeting to unify the WCTU of Monmouth County (*Asbury Park Journal*, 16 March).

4 APRIL. Crane inscribes himself "Stephen T. Crane/N.Y.C." in Armistead Borland's autograph album (*C*, 33).

9 JULY. Mrs. Crane "delivers a carefully prepared address" at the state WCTU meeting in Ocean Grove on the role that newspapers should play in furthering the causes of the WCTU and the YMCA (*Asbury Park Daily Press*, 10 July). This lecture and one the following week to the Sunday School Assembly on the importance of teaching temperance to children in the Sunday schools are reported in the *Tribune* on 10 and 18 July (Elconin, 276n5), probably by Townley.

30 AUGUST. Mrs. Crane is listed as one of the "ladies and gentlemen at the reporters' table in the Auditorium" whose work has "elicited much praise and been copied by the papers throughout the country." She is "the pleasant-faced little lady seldom absent from her seat" and "is a regular writer for the Associated Press and the New York *Tribune*" (*Asbury Park Daily Press*).

9 SEPTEMBER. Crane registers for the fall term at Claverack (Pratt 1939a, 462).

14 SEPTEMBER. The *Asbury Park Journal* announces that Mary Helen Van Nortwick will open on 23 September an art studio at 516 Cookman Avenue "for pupils or those who desire assistance in procuring materials, or oil or water color drawings."

30 OCTOBER. William Howe Crane and a group of relatives and friends form the Hartwood Park Association, assembling numerous separate parcels of land, some of which enclose lakes, into a preserve for hunting, fishing, and the enjoyment of outdoor life (Campbell, 31–32).

1889. Borland recalls that at Claverack Crane was "'a congenital introvert, and his intimacy with other men was out of character and went only so far as was necessary to give the appearance of normal behavior. . . . He had no intimates and was not *popular* and didn't want to be; he would have scorned the idea of popularity. . . . He was extremely irregular in his habits—a law unto himself, indifferent[!] to the opinions of others who might be critical of him, reserved and more or less difficult to approach. He was slow to anger but became viciously ungovernable when aroused'" (Schoberlin V, 9). This impression of Crane is confirmed by Harvey Wickham's recollection that "it was his pose in those days to take little interest in anything save poker and baseball, and even in speaking of these great matters there was in his manner a suggestion of *noblesse oblige*. Undoubtedly he felt himself peculiar, an oyster beneath whose lips there was already an irritating grain of some foreign substance. Not altogether welcome, either. . . . He wanted to be a democrat and yet a dictator. Hence that contradiction, self-depreciation coupled with arrogance, which has puzzled so many" (Wickham, 293).

Vincent Starrett reports an interview with Earl Reeves [the name is given as "Reeves" by Wickham and "Reeve" by Borland], Crane's roommate at Claverack, and, according to Wickham, "the richest boy in school," in which Reeves recalls that "Stephen rose mornings at the last possible minute for drill, hurled himself into socks, shoes and trousers, and from the waist up wore usually only his uniform jacket. Also: at church or chapel there was an organ that required pumping, and Crane used to volunteer for this job, which kept him reasonably busy and made it unnecessary for him to sit out front and listen to the sermon" (*SCraneN* 2 [Fall 1967]: 4).

Crane carries on flirtations with two girls at Claverack, Harriet Mattison and Jennie Pierce. In a March 1896 letter to another schoolmate, Viola Allen, he fondly recollects: "Alas, Jennie Pierce. You must remember that I was in love with her, madly, in the headlong way of seventeen. Jennie was clever. With only half an effort she made my life so very miserable" (*C*, 212).

*

1890

*

FEBRUARY. Crane contributes his first signed publication, a bland two-column sketch on the exploits of the explorer Henry M. Stanley, to the *Vidette*. He attributes Stanley's success to his "indomitable will and faith in a Supreme Power, who guided him through the forests and valleys of the great continent" (*Works*, 8: 566–567).

21 FEBRUARY. At the prize drill on Friday afternoon that inaugurates the commemoration of Washington's birthday at Claverack, the prize is awarded to Company C, of which Crane is first lieutenant. General John B. Van Petten is one of the judges (Pratt 1939b, 2).

[Van Petten is the professor of elocution and history at Claverack (1885–1900). He had been chaplain of the 34th New York Volunteers, a regiment that had been forced into flight at the Battle of Antietam on 17 September 1862. Henry Fleming's fictional regiment in *The Red Badge of Courage* is the 304th New York. On 19 September 1864 Van Petten, who at this time was lieutenant colonel of the 160th New York Volunteers, witnessed large parts of a Union division—not his own—fleeing in terror from a Confederate infantry charge. Van Petten was severely wounded in this engagement (O'Donnell, 200–201).]

MARCH. The "Battalion Notes" column of *Vidette* lists Crane's promotion to "Adjutant–1st Lieutenant" (Stallman 1972, 237).

[SPRING]. Harvey Wickham recalls: "When I arrived at Claverack he was already a first lieutenant, with enough of the true officer in him to have a perfectly hen-like attitude toward the rank and file. Well do I remember the anguish I caused him by dropping my gun during a prize drill! . . . 'Idiot! Imbecile!' stormed Crane when it was over. 'You were fairly decent up to the last minute. And then to drop your gun! Such a thing was never heard of. Do you think *order arms* means to drop your gun?'" (Wickham, 294).

MAY. A baseball item in the May issue of *Vidette*, perhaps authored by Crane, states tersely: "Crane, catcher, was tendered the office of captain, but declining, Jones, 1st base, was elected captain" (*Works*, 8: 568).

16 MAY. The *Asbury Park Shore Press* commends Crane on his *Vidette* article about Henry M. Stanley and reports that he "will leave Claverack at the close of the present term, as he expects to take a college scientific course."

JUNE. The "Battalion Notes" column of *Vidette*, written by Crane, records, "1st Lieut. Crane, promoted to Captain." Crane reports that "During the past few months the battalion has done exceedingly good work. The captains, by hard work and persevering efforts, have gotten their companies so that they can give a very good exhibition drill. Memorial Day the battalion proceeded in line to the cemetery, and there, after a brief religious exercise, the soldiers' graves were covered with flowers" (Wertheim 1976a, 80).

15 JUNE. Crane writes his schoolmate Odell Hathaway from Asbury Park: "I am home with lots of friends, yet, longing for some of my old companions at Old Claverack. I am smoking a cigar after a 10.00 AM breakfast of roast pigeon and gooseberries yet I wish to God I was puffing on a cigarette butt after a 7.00 AM breakfast of dried-beef and oat meal at H. R. I." (*C*, 34).

26 JUNE. Townley Crane, "the most experienced newspaper reporter on the New Jersey coast," marries Anna Jeffreys Bradford in New York City. "The bride traces her ancestry back to Lord Jeffreys, Lord Chief Justice of England under Charles II" (*Asbury Park Daily Press*, 27 June. The marriage is also reported in the *Asbury Park Daily Journal*, 27 June, and the *Asbury Park Journal*, 5 July).

30 JUNE. A wedding reception for Mr. and Mrs. Townley Crane elicits "the telegraphic congratulations of Governor Leon Abbett, and letters bearing good wishes from General and Mrs. Clinton B. Fisk, State Senator Thompson, Mr. John C. Hennessy, ex-president of the New York *Press*, and many other friends" (*Asbury Park Daily Press*, 2 July).

25 JULY. The Reverend H. C. Hovey delivers a lecture at Avon-by-the-Sea entitled "Mazes and Marvels of Mammoth Cave." Crane writes a brief account of Hovey's explorations in "Across the Covered Pit," unpublished in his lifetime.

28 JULY. Crane reports on activities at the Seaside Assembly, Avon's "Summer Schools by the Surf," in the *New York Tribune*.

2 AUGUST. In the *New York Tribune* Townley Crane defends the Ocean Grove Camp Meeting Association against charges of puritanism, although "The by-laws absolutely prohibit dancing, card-playing or any such diversions as are prohibited by the general rules of the Methodist Episcopal Church, the buying and selling or drinking of spirituous liquors, excepting in cases of extreme necessity, and the sale of tobacco in any form. The strict observance of the Christian sabbath is rigidly insisted upon. The gates of the association are closed at midnight Saturdays and not opened until Monday morning at an early hour, excepting an inmate of the ground dies, when the undertaker is allowed to drive his wagon through the gates and remove the body to his warehouse."

4 AUGUST. Crane's report in the *Tribune* headlined "Avon's School by the Sea" contains a paragraph about the tenor Albert Thies, who had performed at the Seaside Assembly in July. He expands this into an article, "The King's Favor," published later in the Syracuse *University Herald* for May 1891.

8 AUGUST. The *Asbury Park Shore Press* calls Townley's *Tribune* article on Ocean Grove "an excellently written production."

13 AUGUST. OCEAN GROVE. The Alumni Association of Pennington Seminary holds a reunion and banquet for alumni and students. Mrs. Crane, an honored guest, gives a toast to the "Press." Although with "few exceptions the gathering was composed of young people," Stephen does not attend (*Asbury Park Daily Press*, 14 August).

15 AUGUST. Townley Crane lectures at the Seaside Assembly in Avon on "'Newspaper Work and Workers.' Mr. Crane has been for some years on the staff of the *New York Tribune*. He is also the agent of the New York Associated Press for this section of the State. His personal experiences in such cases as the illness and death of President Garfield, the Rahway mystery, the lynching of Mingo Jack, the famous pine-tree needle murder, and the Hudson tunnel disaster, must certainly be interesting" (*Asbury Park Shore Press*). The next day the *Shore Press* reports that Townley "described his own experiences in newspaper life, and spoke of the work of collecting news from all parts of the world. The lecture was listened to by an appreciative audience" (*Asbury Park Shore Press*, 16 August). Because of his successful lecture, Townley is "invited to continue his remarks next week" and to speak in Plainfield and at Albert College (*Asbury Park Daily Journal*, 16 August).

AUGUST. "The latest publication from the pen of Mrs. Helen Peck Crane, the president of the WCTU of the Park, is a brief account of 'Elim,' the oldest cottage in Ocean Grove. The leaflet is valuable in that it gives in a condensed form the history of that interesting place" (*Asbury Park Daily Press*, 29 August).

12 SEPTEMBER. Crane enrolls as a mining engineering student in the Pardee Scientific Department at Lafayette College. He rooms in No. 170, East Hall. Cora Crane later explains that Stephen was dissuaded from returning to Claverack in the fall and pursuing a military career by his brother William: "Wanted to go to West Point—Will said no war in your life time & persuaded him to give it up" (*Works*, 10: 345).

East Hall, Lafayette College, Easton PA. Crane roomed
in No. 170
(Wertheim Collection)

[The *Fifty-Ninth Annual Catalogue of Lafayette College, for the Year* 1890–1891 stipulates that "'in addition to the systematic and thorough study of the Word of God in all classes, special attention will be given to the harmony of Science with Revealed Religion.'" Even the required course on "'Human Physiology'" in the Physical Culture program gives "'special consideration . . . to the bearing of the facts and principles upon Natural Theology'" (Sloane, 104).]

18 SEPTEMBER. Crane pledges Delta Upsilon fraternity. With 19 members it is the largest fraternity on campus; but there is no chapter house and meetings are held in rented rooms above a drugstore in downtown Easton (Robertson, 6).

19 SEPTEMBER. Mrs. Crane is elected as one of two delegates from the Monmouth County WCTU to attend the national WCTU convention in Atlanta in November (*Asbury Park Journal*, 27 September).

[SEPTEMBER]. Hazing of freshman students by the sophomores is a notorious tradition at Lafayette College. Colonel Ernest G. Smith of the class of 1894 recalls a raid on East Hall:

52

1890

In a rear room of that even then somewhat unsavory structure, Steve Crane occupied a single room. No response followed the dire commands of Sophomore gangsters seeking admission and the door was forced. An oil lamp burning in the room I [sic] indicated plainly to the attacking force and to a fringe of already hazed Freshmen on the outskirts the figure of Crane backed into a corner with a revolver in hand. He was ghastly white as I recall and extremely nervous. There was no time to escape what might have proved a real tragedy until Crane unexpectedly seemed to wilt limply in place and the loaded revolver dropped harmlessly to the floor. I have often thought since, particularly while reading his "Red Badge of Courage," an autographed copy of which he long afterwards sent me, how the imagination ofttimes outruns performances of the flesh. Of the incident he never afterwards spoke, as I recall. (E. G. Smith, 6)

LATE SEPTEMBER–OCTOBER. Crane participates in the "banner scrap," a fall tradition at Lafayette in which freshmen suspend a banner above ground in the angle of a building and sophomores armed with paper bags filled with flour throw them at the freshmen and then rush them in an attempt to seize the banner (Robertson, 6–7). To Odell Hathaway and other former Claverack schoolmates, Crane writes: "I send you a piece of the banner we took away from the Sophemores [sic] last week. It dont look like much does it? Only an old rag, ain't it? But just remember I got a *black and blue nose*, a barked shin, skin off my hands and a lame shoulder, in the row you can appreciate it. So, keep it, and when you look at it think of me scraping [sic] about twice a week over some old rag that says 'Fresh '94' on it" (C, 35).

8 OCTOBER. Already one of the 34 freshmen members of the Washington Literary Society, Crane is invited to join the rival Franklin Literary Society. "The two societies were the first extracurricular organizations on campus and originally had many of the characteristics of fraternities: freshman rush, secret meetings, and intergroup rivalry. Even after the first fraternities were established on campus in 1853, the literary societies remained popular. Both societies occupied lavishly decorated headquarters in Pardee Hall and sponsored frequent lectures and debates. They also offered libraries of current books, an important asset at a time when the college library was a room in South College, where almost all the books were confined to locked cases" (Robertson, 4).

22 OCTOBER. ATLANTIC CITY, N.J. Mrs. Crane, "Superintendent of Press Work," speaks at the annual convention of the New Jersey WCTU on "the excellent work done by newspapers during the year," noting "that one-fifth of them publish temperance matter" (*Asbury Park Journal*, 8 November).

[OCTOBER]. William Howe Crane and his wife, Cornelia Zearfoss Crane, move their growing family (they have five daughters) to a large house at 19 East Main Street, Port Jervis, where Stephen often visits and writes during the next five years (Copy, Certificate of Indenture, 1 October 1890, between Edward A. and Anna M. Brown and Cornelia Crane, Minisink Valley Historical Society).

OCTOBER–NOVEMBER. The *Delta Upsilon Quarterly* of Lafayette College (November 1890) records: "The freshman class numbers over a hundred, of whom four have become Delta U'S." Crane is listed among the four (C. Jones, 82).

7 NOVEMBER. The *Asbury Park Shore Press* reports that Townley's wife is very ill with "congestion of the brain."

The *Shore Press* reports that William Howe Crane, who has switched his political allegiance to the Democrats, has been elected a judge in Orange County, New York.

[NOVEMBER]. Crane writes to a Claverack College schoolmate: "The fellows here raise more hell than any college in the country, yet I have still left a big slice of my heart up among the pumpkin seeds and farmers of Columbia Co." (C, 35). On the reverse of a photograph of Claverack, he writes ambivalently, "A place around which tender (?) memories cling" (NSyU).

2 DECEMBER. Crane inscribes his name in a copy of Frances L. Mace's *Under Pine and Palm* (1888) (Kibler, 222).

14 DECEMBER. PERTH AMBOY, N.J. Mrs. Crane lectures on "'The Price of a Boy'. . . . This lecture is very highly spoken of in its bearing on temperance work" (*Asbury Park Journal*, 20 December).

[Crane remained at Lafayette through the first semester, ending in December. He belonged to an eating club called the Campus Club and played intramural baseball. He received grades in four out of seven courses: 60 in algebra; 88 in French; 92 in elocution; and zero in theme writing, themes at Lafayette being on technical subjects assigned by the engineering faculty (Pratt 1939a, 468). Excessive absence probably prevented his being graded in the other courses. After the Christmas holidays Crane returned briefly to Lafayette, although the semester was over. Despite his academic deficiencies, he was not asked to leave the college. He was dissatisfied with the mining-engineering curriculum at Lafayette and transferred to Syracuse Uni-

Syracuse University baseball team. Crane is seated
in the middle of the first row
(*Syracuse University*)

versity with the approval of his mother, who believed that as the
grandnephew of Jesse T. Peck, one of the founders and chairman of
the first board of trustees of that Methodist institution, he was entitled
to a scholarship. The minutes of the faculty of Lafayette College record: "It was voted that a paper be given to S. Crane, Fresh., stating
that he had been here, matriculated, left without censure, and, that no
objections are made to being received at another college" (President
John Macracken to Edna Crane Sidbury, 15 April 1926, NSyU). Later, in
a letter to a journalist, Crane succinctly summarized his college career: "I went to Lafayette College but did not graduate. I found
mining-engineering not at all to my taste. I preferred base-ball. Later
I attended Syracuse University where I attempted to study literature
but found base ball again much more to my taste. At Lafayette I
joined the Delta Upsilon Fraternity" (*C,* 166–167).

The 1894 issue of *Melange,* the yearbook of the Lafayette College
junior class, published in 1893, contains an article entitled "Our

Departed" in which Crane is contrasted with a classmate who had the same surname:

> Funny fowls were these two Cranes,
> Steve had wit and Dwight had brains,
> Dwight was short and Steve was tall,
> One had grit, the other gall.

The inversion of characteristics is probably college humor. Crane was considered sententious and withdrawn by his fraternity brothers at Syracuse. A friend, Clarence Peaslee, correctly described him as "under the average height" (Crane was approximately 5'8") and "very gritty" (Peaslee, 27).]

*

1891

*

6 JANUARY. Crane enrolls as a non-degree candidate in the College of Liberal Arts at Syracuse University (C. Jones, 82). After a short stay with the Widow Peck, he rooms in the Delta Upsilon fraternity house with Clarence N. Goodwin, a freshman from Washington, D.C. Peaslee remembers the characteristic disorder of the room: "The floor was literally covered with loose sheets of paper, books, football shoes, newspaper clippings, canvas trousers and jackets, baseball masks and bats, running trunks, chest-protectors and other athletic and literary sundries. The table was running over with books and papers and scribblings, together with pipes and tobacco cans, and the walls were hung with pictures, trophies, signs and pen-drawings. Certainly the occupant was nothing unless athletic and literary" (Peaslee, 27). Crane's favorite room in the fraternity house is a den constructed by some of the brothers. As Frederic M. Lawrence describes it, "the top of the house was surmounted by an old, unfinished cupola, and we were struck by its possibilities. At vast expense we laid in a stock of thick paper and tacked it to the protruding beams, and from various odd sources we procured an ancient if not antique rug and several odd bits of furniture. Each of us managed to add a Turkish pipe to his already large equipment, and soon we were lounging around the floor in true oriental fashion, talking for long hours of science, art, literature and of course our own lives. If the set courses of the university were contributing little to our education, we were doing a lot for ourselves" (Lawrence, 4).

Delta Upsilon fraternity house
(Syracuse University)

9 JANUARY. Crane writes to his Claverack schoolmate Odell Hathaway that "there are certainly some dam pretty girls here, praised be to God. . . . [This is a] dandy city at least and I expect to see some fun here" (*C*, 36).

EARLY JANUARY. Mrs. Crane resigns as president of the WCTU of Asbury Park. Her "health has made it necessary for her to spend the remainder of the winter elsewhere" (*Asbury Park Journal,* 10 January).

13 JANUARY. Crane inscribes his name in a copy of the fourth edition of Bertha M. Gardiner's *The French Revolution, 1789–1795* (1889) (Kibler, 218).

20 JANUARY. The faculty minutes of Lafayette College record that Crane withdrew "without censure" (Robertson, 8).

30 JANUARY. As his contribution to Delta Upsilon's literary program, Crane reads a jejune anti-imperialist sketch, probably "A Foreign Policy, in Three Glimpses" (*Works*, 8: 574–578). His fraternity brother Frank W. Noxon is impressed by the "exquisite legibility" of the manuscript: "This astonished me in a daily newspaper reporter such as Crane had already been. He replied that from the outset of his writing he had kept in mind the compositor, whose earnings depended upon the amount he could set, and this in turn upon the time it took to read the copy" (Noxon, 4).

[JANUARY]. "One day the steward of the [Delta Upsilon] club-house, a senior, shouted forth: 'I want a freeshie to turn grindstone for the kitchen knives. Come on, Crane.' Whereupon he retorted, quite red in the face, that he never had and never would turn grindstone for anybody" (Price, 867).

2 FEBRUARY. The *Syracusan* announces that "The baseball team begins training in the Alhambra today and all candidates for the team are required to be present every afternoon—Crane, the old catcher of the Lafayette College team, has entered the University and will make a good addition to the team."

16 FEBRUARY. The *University Herald* reports that "'94— Stephen Crane has been quite ill during the past week."

[FEBRUARY–MARCH]. According to Mansfield J. French, a pitcher on the baseball team,

When George Shepherd, manager of the baseball team for the year 1891, issued the call for candidates to report, Stephen must have been among the first to arrive as he obtained a fairly respectable and well-matched uniform. The uniforms in those days consisted of a miscellaneous lot of clothes purchased at second hand from the Syracuse Stars, the local professional ball team, and it was a case of "first come, first served" in the assignment of garments. However, the choice did not extend to hose. "Steve," like the others of us, wore what he chose. He should have worn white stockings of the heavy ribbed kind but of necessity he wore black of a fine knit that made his slender legs look like pipe stems. He was of a sallow complexion, his skin, hair and eyes appeared to be all of one dull and lifeless hue. That is, his eye balls were of the same deep cream tint but the iris was of a cold, bluish gray color. His hair never would stay combed and parted; even after a "washup" following a game there were bound to be stray locks hanging down at the forehead and a bristly bunch at the end of the part in the back. Crane was very quick and active on his feet, his body was slender, his shoulders somewhat drooping, his chest not robust and his knees inclined somewhat to knock together. He was about five feet six inches in height and did not weigh over one hundred and twenty-five pounds. He played ball with a fiendish glee. Usually of a quiet and taciturn mien, on the ball field he was constantly in motion, was free of speech, wantonly profane at times and indulged in biting sarcasms when a teammate made a poor play, but generous in praise of a good play. He was first tried out as a catcher and proved to be, in his ability to hold the ball, the best candidate for that position. His throwing arm was weak, however, and although he threw with the whole body, he was unable to line the ball down to second base in acceptable form. He would not stand on his two feet and snap the ball down to the base. It was necessary for him to throw off his mask, cap and protector, give a hop and skip and throw with a complete body swing. The strain upon the ligaments of his shoulder would, at times, cause him to double up with pain. (French, 3)

EARLY SPRING. Crane frequents the bookshop of Thomas W. Durston in Syracuse. He reads *Anna Karenina* and *War and Peace*. Durston, a Goethe enthusiast, introduces him to *Faust*, and at this time Crane also probably encounters Charles L. Eastlake's translation of Goethe's *Farbenlehre*, which deals with the symbolic nature of color. He later tells Frank W. Noxon "that a passage in Goethe analyzed the effect which the several colors have upon the human mind. Upon Crane this had made a profound impression and he had utilized the idea to produce his effects" (Noxon, 6).

Crane argues a point in the classroom with Chancellor Charles N. Sims: "The Professor sought to silence him by an appeal to the Bible: 'Tut, tut—what does St. Paul say, Mr. Crane, what does St. Paul say?' testily asked the old Professor. 'I know what St. Paul says,' was the answer, 'but I disagree with St. Paul'" (Hubbard, 676).

Another professor chastises him: "Crane, you'll never amount to anything. Why don't you let up on writing and pay a little more attention to conic sections?" (Herford, 413)

APRIL. The middle trimester ends at Syracuse University. Crane has taken only one course, English literature. He takes no courses in the third trimester but remains in residence.

[In a letter to Townley Crane (18 November 1899), Chancellor James R. Day maintains: "No credit marks of scholarship appear opposite his name on our books" (Copy, NSyU). But on 2 August 1900 Professor Frank Smalley writes to Cora Crane: "He was not inclined to be very studious and I find he has credit in only one subject and in that he has our highest mark, of course that study is English literature" (Cady and Wells, 57). The discrepancy results from the fact that a "+" symbol follows the date of course completion (3/91) on Crane's record. The university gave no grades at this time, but on some records there are "one + and two +'s following dates of completion, with absolutely no indication either in the record or catalogue of the meaning" (Edwin D. Smith, Registrar, to John S. Mayfield, 1 April 1969, NSyU). As a result of Smalley's misinterpretation of the "+" symbol following the date of "91" on Crane's record, some scholars have erroneously concluded that the official records indicate only one grade, an "A (91+) in English literature" (C. Jones, 83). Early in 1895 Crane writes to John Northern Hilliard: "I did little work at school, but confined my abilities, such as they were, to the diamond. Not that I disliked books, but the cut-and-dried curriculum of the college did not appeal to me. Humanity was a much more interesting study. When I ought to have been at recitations I was studying faces on the streets, and when I ought to have been studying my next day's lessons I was watching the trains roll in and out of the Central Station. So, you see, I had, first of all, to recover from college" (*C,* 99).]

MAY. Crane burns an inscription in the east wall of the Delta Upsilon cupola:

> Sunset—1891—May
> Steph Crane

"The King's Favor" appears in the *University Herald.*

The Onondagan of '92 (published by the junior class) names Crane as secretary and treasurer of the Claverack College and Hudson River Institute Alumni Association and captain of the Delta Upsilon Cricket Club. In the section entitled "Grinds" Crane's name appears among the freshmen followed by lines from a poem entitled "On a Tear" by the English poet and banker Samuel Rogers:

> Sweet drop of pure and pearly light,
> In thee the rays of virtue shine,
> More calmly clear, more mildly bright
> Than any gem that gilds the mine.
> (Mayfield 1968, 8)

4 MAY. The *Syracusan* reports that on the baseball field "Crane plays a good game behind the bat, but he is weak in throwing to second" (C. Jones, 83).

8 MAY. Crane gives a literary report at a meeting of the Delta Upsilon fraternity (C. Jones, 83).

11 MAY. The *University News* editorializes that "the weak spot on the team is evidently at short, though Crane plays that position much better than Wright" (C. Jones, 83).

24 MAY. The *Syracuse News* reports that in the baseball game between Syracuse University and the Syracuse Stars Crane "was applauded for good work behind the bat" (C. Jones, 83).

JUNE. In the *Arena* editor B. O. Flower exposes the deplorable circumstances of the working girl in the city. Most blameworthy, according to Flower, are the owners of tenements and sweatshops: "A soulless landlord, the slave master who pays only starvation wages, and disease, the natural complement of the wretched squalor permitted by the one and the slow starvation necessarily incident to the prices paid by the other" (Wertheim 1970, vi).

1 JUNE. Crane's tall tale "Great Bugs in Onondaga" appears simultaneously in the *Syracuse Daily Standard* and the *New York Tribune.* Its source is a news item in the *Syracuse Sunday Herald* on 24 May about caterpillars delaying a train in Minnesota. The *Standard* version of Crane's spoof carries added introductory and concluding paragraphs. The initial paragraph describes the story as told by a man who "acted as well as talked strangely, and was evidently suffering from alcoholism," who relates that a horde of "strange insects of immense proportions, some of them lying perfectly still, huddled in bunches, and some of them playing a sort of leapfrog over their fellows' backs," swarmed along a stretch of railroad track between Jamesville and Syracuse, bringing a train to a halt.

2 JUNE. The *New York Tribune* and the *Syracuse Daily Journal* extend Crane's *jeu d'esprit* with a tongue-in-cheek "apology," probably written by Willis Fletcher Johnson, the day editor of the *Tribune,* who was an alumnus of Pennington and a friend of the Crane family (Mayfield 1963, 23). Johnson concludes that if the state entomologist expects to serve another term, "he must board a monster of steel and iron, hurry to Syracuse and report on this new bug."

[This spring Crane sketches out a camping story featuring a large black mastiff named Jack and a bathetic and somewhat anti-Semitic scenario for a playlet entitled "Greed Rampant." Noxon alludes to a first draft of *Maggie*, written in the Delta Upsilon house and based on Crane's interviews with prostitutes in the Syracuse police court and his explorations of the shabby tenement districts of the city as a reporter for the *Tribune*. Thomas E. Martin describes Crane's fascination with the underbelly of Syracuse society: "College studies did not appeal to him and most any night he could be found lurking about the police court watching the prisoners being brought in for minor offenses. Crime seemed to hold a great fascination for him and his curiosity frequently led him into contacts with the lower strata of city civilization. He gloried in talking with shambling figures who lurked in dark door-ways on deserted slum streets, and his love for adventure constantly kept his feet on the illy-lighted thoroughfares honeycombing the city" (Martin, 1–2).

Henry Phillips, who lived in the Delta Upsilon house and edited the *University Herald*, also argues that Crane was writing *Maggie* at Syracuse. Phillips recalls "the reading of some of that original manuscript which was saturated with obscenity and profanity," and another friend recalls boisterous social occasions in a music hall on North Salina Street where "pretty girls sang and danced on the stage daringly clad in low neck waists and skirts just above the knees" and a party with "Madge and her friends who lived in the Florence flats located near the junction of South Salina Street and West Onondaga" (Sorrentino 1985, 182). Another fraternity brother, Frederic M. Lawrence, who roomed with Crane in the fall of 1892, is convinced that he did not begin the composition of *Maggie* until then, after he and Lawrence had explored the New York City slums (Lawrence, 6). Nevertheless, Schoberlin's convincing attribution to Crane of "Where 'De Gang' Hears the Band Play" (*New York Herald*, 5 July) with its Tompkins Square setting, Bowery dialect mixed with standard English, sharp delineation of immigrant groups, "'tough girl' and her 'tough brother'" named Maggie and Jimmy respectively, and Maggie's factory employment indicates that Crane was already revising an earlier version of *Maggie*.

> Hard featured is the "tough youth." Hard mannered is the tough girl. She abounds on the east side. Down around Tompkins square she and her striped jersey are particularly prevalent. There are *musicales* in Tompkins square these hot summer nights—band concerts they are called—and great is the rejoicing thereabouts each season at the advent of the band.
>
> This particular tough girl's name was Maggie. Her intimates call her "Mag." And Mag goes.

After supper last Wednesday in the apartments of her parents in a Stanton street tenement house Mag announced to her brother:—

"Say, Jimmy, I'm going to the band play to-night an' I want de watch."

"Oh, you do, do you! Well, now, I'm just goin' out meself to-night an' I need de ticker mor'n I need a dollar. So you don't get it, see?"

"Don't be fresh, Jimmy, you know it's me own watch, an' you said you'd give it me back last week. Give it me now or you don't get it again."

"Again! Rats! I don't need to get it again. I got it now."

A cloud of suspicion settled in the narrow strip between Mag's bang and her eyebrows.

"Say, Jim, give it to me straight. Have you soaked that watch? If you have, I'll tell dad."

"Soakin' nothin'. You'r always thinking people are soakin' things. If the band loses the air to-night you'll think they've hocked it. An', say, if I catch you doin' the walk to-night with that dude mash I'll spoil his face, see? You'r getting too lifted, anyway, since ye got in de factory."]

12 JUNE. Crane attends his last Delta Upsilon chapter meeting (C. Jones, 84). Shortly afterward he leaves Syracuse University.

MID–JUNE. Crane joins Frederic M. Lawrence and two other Port Jervis friends, Louis E. Carr, Jr., and Louis C. Senger, Jr., on a camping trip in Sullivan County. He returns to Asbury Park late in the month to report the arrival of the summer throng:

OCEAN GROVE, June 28 (Special).—Great train-loads of pleasure-seekers and religious worshippers are arriving at the huge double railway station of Ocean Grove and Asbury Park. The beach, the avenues and the shaded lawns are once more covered with the bright-hued garments of the summer throng. The "old timers," evading the crowds of hackmen, take leisurely routes to their hotels, and gaze at the improvements and new buildings of the twin cities; the newcomer falls a victim to the rapacity of the hackmen because of his great astonishment at the vast length of platform, the huge pile of trunks, the wide roadways and the wriggling, howling mass of humanity which declares itself ready to take him to "any hotel or cottage" at a moderate charge. Having escaped with the connivance of one of these weary toilers after the dollar of the summer traveller, he forgets the turmoil of the station as he rides through the high Main-st. gates and obtains a view of a long, quiet avenue, shaded by waving maples, with a vision of blue sea in the distance. (*New York Tribune*, 29 June; *Works*, 8: 546)

10 JULY. AVON-BY-THE-SEA. Crane develops his satiric perspective by describing the activities of summer visitors "On the Banks of Shark River": "Parties from the hotels go on long pedestrian tours along the

banks of Shark River, and create havoc among the blithesome crabs and the festive oysters. Sketching parties from the Art School of the Seaside Assembly also love the banks of the river, and they can be seen on fine afternoons painting industriously, while their white umbrellas keep off the rays of the sun and give the party the appearance of a bunch of extraordinary mushrooms" (*New York Tribune*, 11 July; Works, 8: 548–549).

ASBURY PARK. "J. Townley, the well-known man-about-town, appeared on the streets about midnight with a blooming button-hole bouquet. This was to light his homeward steps in case the electric lights should again go on a midnight strike" (Asbury Park Daily Press, 11 July).

19 JULY. An unsigned article in the *New York Times*, "Biology at Avon-by-the-Sea," may have been authored by Crane. "Tent Life at Ocean Grove," attributed to him by Melvin H. Schoberlin, appears in the *New York Herald* (Gullason 1986, 73–87).

[JULY]. ASBURY PARK. Crane shows Willis Fletcher Johnson two of his Sullivan County sketches. Johnson also remembers seeing an early draft of *Maggie* at this time (Johnson, 289), but Crane may not have shown him this until the next summer.

11–25 AUGUST. Hamlin Garland presents a series entitled "Lecture Studies in American Literature and Expressive Art" at the Seaside Assembly in Avon (Pizer 1960, 77).

17 AUGUST. Crane covers "Professor" Garland's discussion of William Dean Howells, one of a series of lectures delivered by Garland during July and August in an American literature course at Avon's Seaside Assembly:

> He said: "No man stands for a more vital principle than does Mr. Howells. He stands for modern-spirit, sympathy and truth. He believes in the progress of ideals, the relative in art. His definition of idealism cannot be improved upon, 'the truthful treatment of material.' He does not insist upon any special material, but only that the novelist be true to himself and to things as he sees them. It is absurd to call him photographic. The photograph is false in perspective, in light and shade, in focus. When a photograph can depict atmosphere and sound, the comparison will have some meaning, and then it will not be used as a reproach. Mr. Howells' work has deepened in insight and widened in sympathy from the first. His canvas has grown large, and has thickened with figures. Between *Their Wedding Journey* and *A Hazard of New Fortunes* there is an immense distance. *A Modern Instance* is the greatest, most rigidly artistic

novel ever written by an American, and ranks with the great novels of the world. *A Hazard of New Fortunes* is the greatest, sanest, truest study of a city in fiction." (*New York Tribune*, 18 August; *Works*, 8: 507–508)

OCEAN GROVE. The Alumni Association of Pennington Seminary holds its second reunion and banquet for alumni and students; Stephen does not attend. Willis Fletcher Johnson, Mrs. Crane, and Townley Crane are among the honored guests. Before toasting "Pennington and the Press," Townley is introduced as "'a baby of Pennington Seminary, and the best known newspaper man on the New Jersey coast.' 'Townley' said he'd been waiting to get a chance to speak in the Grove. He forebore giving the location of the room in the Seminary where he was born for fear 'the boys and girls would carry off all the woodwork for canes and breastpins,' referred to Dr. Stokes' attacks on the newspaper men, and exampled a case where the reporter occasionally exaggerates" (*Asbury Park Daily Press*, 18 August).

MID-AUGUST. Crane joins Lawrence, Carr, and Senger at a campsite "in the wilds" of Pike County, Pennsylvania. Lawrence recalls that "Crane loved this life, and his health was magnificent. As the month wore on, exposure to the sun gave his skin a copper color almost like that of an American Indian, and it formed a strange contrast to his still light hair. So great was the success of this camp that for several subsequent summers we made similar incursions into Pike County" (Lawrence, 4).

26 AUGUST. "J. Townley Crane, the hustling and wide-awake correspondent of the Associated Press, *Sun* and *Tribune*, has been appointed press agent of the Monmouth County Fair Society. Townley is posted in this kind of work, and it is certain that he will be a valuable adjunct to the staff of officers. He will be pleased to meet all newspaper men" (*Asbury Park Daily Press*). The *Asbury Park Daily Journal* reports that Townley has also been made "the press agent of the Drummond Driving Park Association and the Monmouth County Fair Society."

16 SEPTEMBER. Townley's wife, Anna, is taken to the "Trenton Asylum . . . as a private patient upon a certificate signed by Drs. Mitchell and Wilbur. Mrs. Crane is violently insane from a relapse of the grippe" (*Asbury Park Journal*, 19 September).

30 SEPTEMBER. Crane inscribes the register of the Hartwood Park Association:

Shortly after dusk this evening a flock of Cranes flew upon the property of the Association and alighted near the clubhouse. The mother bird had considerable difficulty in keeping her children quiet and in making them retire for the night. There were in the flock:

Mrs. Helen Peck Crane,	Asbury Park, N.J.
J. Townley Crane,	" " "
William Howe Crane,	Port Jervis, N.Y.
E. B. Crane,	Lake View, N.J.
Stephen Crane,	Asbury Park, N.J.

2 OCTOBER. Crane notes in the Hartwood Park Association register: "Mother Crane caught seven fine pickerel to her own satisfaction and the astonishment of her brood. The next day she caught three more nice fish in less than an hour."

FALL. Crane makes incursions into the slums of New York's Lower East Side. He lives with his brother Edmund in Lake View, a suburb of Paterson, New Jersey.

LAST WEEK OF OCTOBER. Anna Crane "has had a second attack of paralysis, and lies in a precarious condition at the Asylum in Trenton, where she was placed for treatment for mental troubles" (*Asbury Park Journal*, 31 October).

16 NOVEMBER. Townley's second wife, Anna Jeffreys Bradford Crane, dies (*Asbury Park Shore Press*, 20 November).

28 NOVEMBER. The *Asbury Park Journal* notes that Townley, "who had but lately come" from his mother's "sick room," denies her reported death at Paterson on 25 November. "Mrs. Crane attended the National W.C.T.U. Convention at Boston and took a severe cold. In addition to this a carbuncle on the neck has greatly prostrated her, so that she is in a critical condition. News of the recent death of her daughter-in-law, which reached her after she had been confined to her bed, produced great depression and distress of mind, which it is hoped good nursing and the best medical skill will in time relieve."

DECEMBER. Edgar Fawcett's essay in the *Arena*, "The Woes of the New York Working-Girl," denounces the indifference of civic institutions and churches to girls "starving, slaving, coughing up blood, dragging themselves from dirty vermin-thronged beds at five in the morning, being blackguarded and beaten by drunken parents, being tempted by rakes whose very lust seems a heaven of refuge to them" (Wertheim 1970, vi–vii).

7 DECEMBER. Mrs. Crane dies in Paterson at the age of 68. Stephen makes Edmund his guardian.

Price, 50 Cents

MAGGIE

A Girl of the Streets

(A STORY OF NEW YORK)

By

JOHNSTON SMITH

Copyrighted

Maggie: A Girl of the Streets. Privately published (1893)
(© 1991 Sotheby's, Inc.)

CHAPTER THREE

New York City

1892–1894

Unsuccessful at finding regular employment as a journalist on Park Row, Crane intensifies his exploration of the tenement districts of Manhattan, gathering background material for a final revision of *Maggie*. A number of the Sullivan County sketches and an East Side vignette, "The Broken-Down Van," appear in the *New York Tribune*. The *Tribune's* columns are closed to Crane shortly after his article "Parades and Entertainments" (21 August 1892) offends the Junior Order of United American Mechanics. After a brief stint with the *Newark Daily Advertiser* Crane returns to New York in late October and moves into a rooming house inhabited by a group of medical students on Avenue A near 57th Street in Manhattan. Here he revises *Maggie*, which he publishes privately in early 1893 under the pseudonym of "Johnston Smith." In late spring or early summer Crane begins the composition of *The Red Badge of Courage*. That spring and into the following winter he takes up desultory residence in various Manhattan studios and tenements, relieved by extended stays in his brother Edmund's Lake View, New Jersey, home. *George's Mother*, begun in the spring of 1893, is completed in November. From the spring of 1894 into the following winter, Crane writes Sunday feature articles on street life in New York for the *New York Press*. In August, as he does each summer through 1896, he camps with Frederic M. Lawrence, Louis E. Carr, Jr., and Louis C. Senger, Jr., at Twin Lakes near Milford in Pike County, Pennsylvania. In the fall he negotiates with the Boston publisher Copeland & Day over *The Black Riders*, and he retrieves the manuscript of *The Red Badge* from S. S. McClure, who had held it for almost half a year. The novel is serialized by the Bacheller syndicate, appearing in December 1894 in an abridged and truncated form in the *Philadelphia Press*, the *New York Press*, and a number of other newspapers.

*

1892

*

4 JANUARY. A sketch in the *New York Herald* editorially entitled "Youse Want 'Petey,' Youse Do" is probably written by Crane. It deals with three young boys at the bar of the Jefferson Market Police Court charged with breaking into a street stand on lower Broadway and stealing several brushes and a can of corn.

> The juvenile prisoners were Nathan Alstrumpt, seven years old, of No. 181 South Fifth avenue; Solomon Cashman, seven years old, of No. 507 Broome street, and Joseph Chriller, thirteen years old, of No. 41 Thompson street.
> "Yer see," said little Alstrumpt, the leader of the gang, to Justice Divver, "we was doin' notten but playen tag in der street when a blokie wat's called 'Petey' come along and says, 'Hi, fellers, lets go a swipen.' We went wid him—see? Youse wants 'Petey,' youse do. He did der swipen—not me nor de kids. "
> "Who's Petey?" asked Justice Divver.
> "Why he's 'Petey' Larkin, a mug wot lives in Thompson street," said the little reprobate.
> The boys were committed to the care of Mr. Gerry's society.

14 JANUARY. Mrs. Crane's will is probated. William and Edmund are named executors. William is named trustee of Mrs. Crane's shares of coal lands in Luzerne County, Pennsylvania, the income from which is to be divided among the living children. Funds not to exceed $300 a year are set aside for Stephen's support and education until he completes a four-year college course. The family library is to remain undivided until Stephen reaches the age of 21, when he may select one-fourth of the books (Gullason 1968c, 232–234).

16 FEBRUARY. Crane writes a revealing letter to Armistead Borland, who lives in Norfolk, Virginia: "So you lack females of the white persuasion, do you? How unfortunate! And how extraordinary! I never thought that the world could come to such a pass that you would lack females, Thomas! You indeed must be in a God forsaken country. Just read these next few lines in a whisper:—I—I think black is quite good—if—if its yellow and young" (*C*, 44).

21 FEBRUARY. "The Last of the Mohicans," datelined Hartwood, 15 February, appears in the *New York Tribune*, the first in a series of

unsigned Sullivan County sketches and tales published in Sunday issues of the *Tribune* through July. The sketch contrasts the noble savage of Cooper's *The Last of the Mohicans* with what the residents claim was "the real and only authentic last of the Mohicans," a drunken derelict who was "a demoralized, dilapidated inhabitant of Sullivan County. . . . He was a veritable 'poor Indian.' He dragged through his wretched life in helpless misery" (*New York Tribune*, 21 February; *Works*, 8: 199–201). Crane's familiarity with this legend helps to explain the sobriquet "Indians" he later applied to the ragged, impoverished illustrators among whom he lived in the old Art Students' League building (although the term may have been in common use since Crane's artist friend Corwin Knapp Linson also employs it in his memoirs) and to the hordes of American journalists and curiosity seekers who sought him out in England, at Ravensbrook and Brede Place, and overstayed their welcome.

28 FEBRUARY. "Hunting Wild Hogs," a Sullivan County sketch, appears in the Sunday *Tribune*.

MARCH. Stephen and William Howe Crane are listed in *The Hartwood Park Association Record* as visitors to the clubhouse in March.

3 APRIL. "The Last Panther" in the Sunday *Tribune* recounts legends of panther hunters in Sullivan County.

1 MAY. In the *Tribune*, Crane describes some of the adventures of Tom Quick, a renowned Sullivan County Indian slayer, under the headline "Not Much of a Hero." He concludes that if the adventures attributed to Quick are true, he was "a man whose hands were stained with unoffending blood, purely and simply a murderer" (*Works*, 8: 215). Another hunting sketch, "Sullivan County Bears," is also printed in this issue of the *Tribune*.

8 MAY. "The Way in Sullivan County," in the Sunday *Tribune*, recalls famous tall tales of hunting experiences.

17 MAY. Stephen and William Howe Crane register at the Hartwood Club (*Hartwood Park Association Record*).

2 JUNE. A black man is brutally lynched in Port Jervis. A mob yanks Robert Lewis, who had purportedly raped Lena McMahon, out of a wagon taking him to jail in the custody of policemen and drags him

up Sussex Street to East Main Street, where he is twice hanged in a maple tree in front of the Reformed church opposite the home of William Howe Crane (*New York Tribune*, 4 June). William is foremost among several men in the crowd of about 2,000 who vainly attempt to prevent the lynching.

Lily Brandon Munroe and her husband, Hersey Munroe
(Syracuse University)

8 JUNE. At the inquest into the lynching, Judge Crane offers a detailed account of his actions in the events of the evening. According to the *Port Jervis Evening Gazette*,

The first witness called was Judge W. H. Crane. He stated that he saw and heard something of the lynching of Bob Lewis Thursday evening last. . . . He was at home in the house and his work girl came home and told him a "nigger" was going to be hung on their front tree. He slipped on some clothing and went out and the mob was in front of Fowler's. I saw a man or boy climb the tree on which the negro was hung and he threw the rope over a limb. Just as I reached the crowd the body was going up. The negro's hands were tied and his elbows were crooked. I went through the crowd between those who had hold of the rope and the tree. I took hold of the rope and shouted "let go of that rope!" They eased up a little and the body commenced to descend. Again I shouted and gave a jerk on the rope and it came loose in my hands and the negro fell into the gutter on his back. I pulled the rope down from the tree and loosened the noose from his neck and took it off. As I straightened up I saw Officer Yaples. Said to him, "have you a revolver?" He said "yes." I said to him "protect that man." He drew his revolver and said, "I will if they kill me."

The crowd commenced to press in on us and I took a stand directly across the negro's head.

Heard Yaples threaten to shoot if anyone touched the man and I heard people say if he shot that they would shoot too. Different people commenced to light matches and hold them close to the negro's face. I could see that he was alive. He was gasping for breath and his whole body was quivering. His face was covered with blood and I did not recognize him as Bob Lewis there or at any other time. At this point I saw Dr. Illman bending over the negro and I asked him if he would take charge of him if we could get him away. He said "yes, the man is all right if we can get him to the hospital." At this point Raymond Carr struck a match and held it down to the negro's face, and said "you have got the right man boys, that is Bob Lewis, I know him." My right hand was hanging by my side and I tapped him several times to keep quiet. He said, "———, he ought to be hung," and the crowd then took up the cry, "hang him!" "don't let the doctor touch him! hang all the niggers!" I was standing then by the left shoulder of the negro, and a man dove down in front of me and attempted to put a rope around the negro's neck. He shoved me aside, I jerked the rope away from him. Then there ensued a scuffle for the rope. The next I saw of it, it was over the branch of the tree again. I sprang to the tree and caught hold of the rope and tried to pull it down but there were too many at the other end. Just then some one caught hold of me and jerked me back. I turned and saw Dr. Illman. He said there is no use, Judge, we will only get hurt. The crowd gave a great surge and I flew out into the middle of the street. I turned toward the tree again but there was a dense body of men about it. The negro was hanging. I turned away and went home.

26 JUNE. Under the headline "A Reminiscence of Indian War" in the *New York Tribune*, Crane recounts the slaughter of Sullivan County militia men by a detachment of British troops and Indians during the Revolution.

LATE JUNE. ASBURY PARK. Crane meets Lily Brandon Munroe, the wife of Hersey Munroe, a geologist with homes in New York and Washington. She is staying with her mother-in-law and younger sister in a suite in the Lake Avenue Hotel, where Townley has his press bureau. Crane and Lily begin a summer romance. According to notes made by Ames Williams, who interviewed Lily after she had become Mrs. George F. Smillie:

> Crane was not a handsome man, but had remarkable almond-shaped gray eyes. He appeared to be frail and had a hacking cough even at that time. He smoked incessantly and usually had a cigarette dangling from his lower lip, but he drank very little. He was abjectly poor and undernourished—ate little and seemed to resent others eating heartily. He was indifferent to dress. At times he would use his cuffs for making notes.
>
> Crane was rather prudish and would comment on the bathing suits worn by the women. Lily Brandon, as a result, has never been swimming in her life. Steve did not care for dancing, although he danced several times with Lily. Lily had a good voice and would attract a group of admirers when she sang; Crane discouraged this practice.
>
> Lily and Steve spent happy hours riding the merry-go-round and pulling the rings, going to Day's for ice cream (Crane never ate any and Lily felt guilty about squandering his meager income), walking the board walk and observing people. Steve particularly enjoyed watching the surf with Lily and told her that whenever she saw the ocean she would think of him. . . . Crane hated the gossiping porch-sitters at the hotels (who were probably devoting some of their attention to his reputation) and delighted in shocking them.
>
> Steve was very much in love with Lily and she with him, but he seemed to have no concrete plans for the future and was melancholy and anxious in that respect. He was a troubled spirit seeking happiness which always seemed beyond reach. She believed him to have a degree of feminine intuition—he once told her that he would not live long. All he wanted was a few years of real happiness. Crane begged Lily to elope with him and she considered the proposal seriously before declining. Her family was wealthy and not too eager for a marriage between the two, and strangely enough, his family was also opposed. Crane appeared to have little use for his family except his mother of whom he was very fond. (NSyU)

1 JULY. Crane reports the gathering of Methodist religious crusaders at Ocean Grove: "The sombre-hued gentlemen who congregate at this place in summer are arriving in solemn procession, with black valises in their hands and rebukes to frivolity in their eyes. They greet each other with quiet enthusiasm and immediately set about holding meetings" (*New York Tribune*, 2 July; *Works*, 8: 508).

3 JULY. In a *Tribune* report datelined 2 July Crane describes the horde of summer visitors in "Crowding into Asbury Park."

The *Tribune* publishes "Four Men in a Cave," the first in a group of phantasmagoric Sullivan County camping stories involving a "tall man" modeled on Louis C. Senger, Jr., "a pudgy man" for whom Frederic M. Lawrence was the prototype, a "little man" based on Crane himself, and a "quiet man" whose characteristics were shared by Crane and Louis E. Carr, Jr.

10 JULY. "Travels in New York: The Broken-Down Van," Crane's impressionistic montage of a downtown street blocked by a huge furniture van with a broken wheel, appears in the *Tribune*. In the same issue is an unsigned review of Zola's *La Débâcle*, stressing that

> [i]n making his witnesses private soldiers or non-commissioned officers, he has clearly taken a leap from Tolstoy's "Peace and War," though no suspicion of plagiarism attaches to him. The plan is indeed a good one, his purpose being to show what the experiences and sufferings of the rank-and-file really were and particularly to explain the demoralization of the French army. The scene opens in a camp of raw recruits near Mulhausen. The men are still full of the blind confidence which was expressed in the popular cry, "To the Rhine!" Yet nobody knew the plans of the generals, and they did not appear very clear about them themselves. Then came rumors of encounters, victories, defeats. Next came a confused series of marches, first in advance, then in retreat. From day to day the soldiers became more bewildered and irritated. The rumor spread that they were being hurried along away from the Prussians, who seemed to be advancing everywhere. The heavy marching began to demoralize the young troops. (Colvert 1956, 99–100)

The *Tribune* prints "The Octopush," a Sullivan County story.

17 JULY. The Sullivan County story "A Ghoul's Accountant" appears in the *Tribune*. This issue also contains a lengthy account of summer amusements in Asbury Park headed "Joys of Seaside Life."

18 JULY. The *Asbury Park Daily Journal* reports that Townley Crane "has a curious stool made from a section of a whale's backbone. The whale was killed on Long Island several years ago by fishermen, and the carcass left on the beach to be covered by sand. Last winter's storms uncovered the skeleton, and one of the grandchildren of a man who helped harpoon the whale had this relic made and presented to Mr. Crane. It stands on the piazza of Lake Avenue Hotel."

20 JULY. Jacob A. Riis, author of *How the Other Half Lives* (1890), lectures on the plight of tenement dwellers at Avon-by-the-Sea. Crane reports Riis's lecture in the *Tribune* on 24 July.

24 JULY. Another Sullivan County story, "The Black Dog," appears in the *Tribune*. Crane also comments upon "Summer Dwellers at Asbury Park and Their Doings" in this issue under the series heading, "On the New Jersey Coast." A hunting sketch, "Two Men and a Bear," appears in the same issue.

31 JULY. The *Tribune* prints "Killing His Bear," a Sullivan County story.

7 AUGUST. Crane's humorous sketch, "The Captain," appears in the *Tribune*. It centers on a group of young people taking a day's outing on a catboat commanded by an aging volunteer fireman. The women are a composite portrait of Lily Brandon Munroe. When the young woman from New York becomes drenched by spray, she loosens her hair:

> "How do I look, Captain," she asks, putting her elbows on her knees and laying a hand on each cheek so that she can lean forward and look into his face with dark, flashing and tantalizing eyes.
> "Look like the gypsies that camps in the woods back of our house," he says, carefully measuring his words.
> "They're pretty, aren't they?" asks the "smart young man" from nowhere.
> "Well," answers the captain-fireman cautiously, "they're wild, you know." (*Works*, 8: 13)

14 AUGUST. In "On the Boardwalk" (datelined 13 August), Crane satirizes the middle-class visitor to Asbury Park, "with a good watch-chain and a business suit of clothes, a wife and about three children," the "'summer girl,'" and, above all, "'Founder'" James A. Bradley, the town's principal property owner and leading citizen, whose zeal in supporting puritanical restrictions on dress and behavior infuriates

Crane: "'Founder' Bradley has lots of sport with his ocean front and boardwalk. It amuses him and he likes it. It warms his heart to see the thousands of people tramping over his boards, helter-skeltering in his sand and diving into that ocean of the Lord's which is adjacent to the beach of James A. Bradley" (*New York Tribune*, 14 August; *Works*, 8: 516–517, 517, 518–519).

[14 AUGUST]. Arthur Oliver recalls that he and Crane were sitting on the beach at Asbury Park discussing the difficulty of rendering experience convincingly through language:

> "Somehow I can't get down to the real thing," I said. "I know I have something unusual to tell, but I get all tangled up with different notions of how it ought to be told."
> "Stevie" scooped up a handful of sand and tossed it to the brisk sea breeze.
> "Treat your notions like that," he said. "Forget what you think about it and tell how you feel about it. Make the other fellow realize you are just as human as he is. That's the big secret of story-telling. Away with literary fads and canons. Be yourself!" (Oliver, 454–455)

15 AUGUST. "Along the Shark River," datelined from Avon on 14 August, is printed in the *Tribune*.

17 AUGUST. The Junior Order of United American Mechanics (JOUAM) of New Jersey holds its annual "American Day" parade in Asbury Park. Townley is apparently away at a funeral and Stephen covers the parade.

21 AUGUST. Crane's account of the JOUAM parade appears in the *Tribune*:

> Asbury Park creates nothing. It does not make; it merely amuses. There is a factory where nightshirts are manufactured, but it is some miles from town. This is a resort of wealth and leisure, of women and considerable wine. The throng along the line of march was composed of summer gowns, lace parasols, tennis trousers, straw hats and indifferent smiles. The procession was composed of men, bronzed, slope-shouldered, uncouth and begrimed with dust. Their clothes fitted them illy, for the most part, and they had no ideas of marching. They merely plodded along, not seeming quite to understand, stolid, unconcerned and, in a certain sense, dignified—a pace and a bearing emblematic of their lives. They smiled occasionally and from time to time greeted friends in the crowd on the sidewalk. Such an assemblage of the spraddle-legged men of the middle

class, whose hands were bent and shoulders stooped from delving and constructing, had never appeared to an Asbury Park summer crowd, and the latter was vaguely amused. (*Works*, 8: 521–522)

22 AUGUST. In an *Asbury Park Daily Press* article headlined "Asbury Park as a News Centre," Townley Crane comments that "there are some people here who claim that the correspondents have no right to say anything about the town excepting in the way of praise and when articles are published that they do not like they are very bitter in remarks about the writers. I have been terribly blackguarded by persons that took exception to articles that have been published in some of the papers that I write for and yet I had nothing to do with the ones that were declared objectionable . . . . I have been reviled like a pickpocket over an alleged Associated Press dispatch that was never seen by any person in the employ of the great news gathering corporation until it was published." He concludes sententiously, "When the editors are not suited with their reporters' work they discharge them" (Gullason 1972, 38–39).

The third annual reunion banquet of the Seaside Alumni Association of Pennington Seminary is held, with Townley Crane giving a toast to "'The Press'" (*Asbury Park Daily Press*, 23 August). Whether Stephen attends is unknown.

23 AUGUST. The JOUAM protests

the uncalled-for and un-American criticism published in The Tribune on Sunday, August 21, in regard to the annual outing of the order at Asbury Park, on Wednesday, August 17. . . . In the strictest sense, we are a national organization, but we do not recognize any party. Our main objects are to restrict immigration, and to protect the public schools of the United States and to prevent sectarian interference therein. We also demand that the Holy Bible be read in our public schools, not to teach sectarianism but to inculcate its teachings. We are bound together to protect Americans in business and shield them from the depressing effect of foreign competition. We are not a labor organization, nor are we a military company, drilled to parade in public and be applauded for our fine appearance and precision; but we were appreciated for our Americanism and we were applauded for it. (*New York Tribune*, 24 August)

24 AUGUST. The *Tribune* appends an apology to the JOUAM protest for "a bit of random correspondence, passed inadvertently by the copy editor."

[Crane's article angered the *Tribune*'s owner, Whitelaw Reid, who was the Republican vice-presidential nominee. Hamlin Garland, John

D. Barry, and Arthur Oliver maintain that Crane was dismissed by the *Tribune*, Oliver stating that Post Wheeler told him "'Townley Crane was fired by mail and Stevie by wire!'" (Oliver, 458). This is denied by Willis Fletcher Johnson (Johnson, 290), but nothing of Crane's appeared in the *Tribune* after 1892, and the paper became Crane's nemesis, seizing upon every opportunity to revile him for the remainder of his career.]

Townley Crane is among the local journalists honored at a banquet given by the owners of a local hotel. During the toasts Townley, "Chauncey M. Depew's rival in the post-prandial oratory, attempted to tell 'Why People Drink Water,' and said that it might be because they stayed at Asbury Park" (*Asbury Park Daily Press*, 25 August).

25 AUGUST. On the stationery of the New Jersey Coast News Bureau, of which Townley is manager and he is secretary, Crane writes to the manager of the American Press Association projecting a trip to the South and the West in the fall and offering to write feature articles from these areas (*C*, 45).

The *Asbury Park Daily Journal* reports on the JOUAM incident:

The *New York Tribune* is either unfortunate in its selection of a correspondent at Asbury Park or else its night editor, or day editor, or "copy" editor, whichever may be the title of the man who passes upon such slanderous articles, lacks sense and decency, and the ability to distinguish between news matter and studied insult.

The article of last Sunday which spoke of the Junior Mechanics' parade as "the most ungainly, uncut and uncarved procession that ever raised clouds of dust on sun beaten streets," and called the paraders "an assemblage of spraddle legged men of the middle class," has raised more dust than was ever known in Asbury Park's streets by wind or a marching army. The Junior Mechanics have very properly resented this gross affront, and the *Tribune* apologizes humbly for its "copy" editor and his crime of allowing this bit of "random correspondence" to have a place in the columns of a respectable newspaper.

This is the second time within a year that the *Tribune* has been compelled to make amends for untruthful and scandalous statements about matters and men in Asbury Park. The editor in chief should either secure a new "copy" editor who knows enough to cut random lies and personal spite out of windy specials of the correspondents, or make a change in the men who send such stuff and thus relieve the "copy" editor from the imputation that he is a booby, or is only too anxious for an opportunity to vent his spleen against Asbury Park.

It is said that the *Tribune's* regular letter-writer, J. Townley Crane, was engaged on something else last week, and delegated the task of writing up the usual Sunday gabble to another. This young man has a hankering for razzle-dazzle style, and has a great future before him if, like the good, he fails to die young. He thought it smart to sneer at the Juniors for their personal appearance and marching, and the "copy" editor of the *Tribune* made the same sad mistake. The article was in bad taste, unworthy a reputable reporter, and still more discreditable to a newspaper with the standing of the *New York Tribune*.

LATE AUGUST. Hamlin Garland returns to Asbury Park, and he and Crane play baseball and discuss literature together. Crane shows Willis Fletcher Johnson and Garland a penultimate draft of *Maggie*. In his faulty recollections, Garland remembers reading *Maggie* only in book form, but at this time he gives Crane a letter of recommendation to Richard Watson Gilder, editor of *Century Magazine*: "Dear Gilder: I want you to read a *great* M.S. of Stephen Crane's making. I think him an astonishing fellow. And have advised him to bring the M.S. to you." After a revision of *Maggie* in the fall, Crane pencils across the bottom of the note, "This is not the MS spoken of. This is a different one" (NNC). Post Wheeler recalls that Garland sent Gilder the manuscript (Wheeler and Rives, 100).

29 AUGUST. The first part of Crane's report on the activities of the Seaside Assembly appears in the *Tribune*, datelined 28 August from Avon.

31 AUGUST. The *Asbury Park Daily Press* quotes from Townley Crane's "Snap Shots at Seaside Follies": "They stood together at the gate. The moon was low, the night was late. He vowed that he would learn his fate or not go home till morning. Her face was fair, her eye was bright. She was so sweet, the little sprite, he couldn't help but clasp her tight—without a word of warning the fond paternal foot irate propelled him through the garden gate—ah, sad regret! He learned his fate. He did go home ere morning."

6 SEPTEMBER. Crane concludes his report on the summer season of "The Seaside Assembly's Work at Avon" in the *Tribune*.

11 SEPTEMBER. Under the headline "The Seaside Hotel Hop," Crane reports a typical Saturday night resort hotel dance in the *Tribune*.

SEPTEMBER–OCTOBER. Crane reports for the *Newark Advertiser*. Schoberlin identifies six articles in the *Advertiser* between 3 October and 2 November that he believes are by Crane (Schoberlin VIII, 42), but these are uncertain attributions.

LATE OCTOBER. Crane moves into a rooming house at 1064 Avenue A (formerly Eastern Boulevard) in Manhattan inhabited by a group of medical students; they sardonically christen the place "The Pendennis Club." He shares a room with Frederic M. Lawrence overlooking the East River and Blackwell's Island, and he begins a thorough revision of *Maggie.* Senger "read Maggie from chapter to chapter in a house over on the far east side, where he lived with a crowd of irresponsibles" (Louis C. Senger to Hamlin Garland, 9 October 1900, CLSU). Frederic Lawrence recalls:

> At that time our library, as I recall it, consisted of Voltaire's *Candide,* a collection of short stories by de Maupassant and one of Zola's books, I think it was *Pot Bouille.* The forceful naturalism of the French school had its profound effect. The narrow cross-streets around us were filled with squalid habitations whose denizens almost filled the roadways, and here was material hitherto little used. Crane observed it all with keen and sympathetic, if detached vision. To a certain extent he could enter into an understanding of this submerged populace, and he made it his task to peer beneath the surface. One day he came in, his usually somber face alight, and queried abruptly: "Did you ever see a stone-fight?" When I replied in the negative, he launched into a glowing description of one that he had just seen. A little later that same day the description had been set down on paper, and the first chapter of *Maggie* was written. As the story, a sordid tale of life in the tenements and the under-world took shape in Crane's mind, he became enthusiastic, I with him, and we sallied forth into the mean streets and dangerous neighborhoods in search of the local color that would give life to the great work. (Lawrence, 6–7)

FALL. William Howe Crane recalls: "My brother, Edmund, told the following. . . . When Stephen was gathering his impression of the Bowery, he said to my brother, who was employed on Beekman St. 'Ed, if ever I come into your place and ask for a nickle, don't give me more than that.' A few days later, Stephen slouched into the place, dressed shabbily and looking hungry and forlorn and asked for a nickel which Ed., without a word, handed to him. There was no further conversation" (William Howe Crane to Thomas Beer, 21 November 1922. Beer Papers).

5 NOVEMBER. The *Asbury Park Journal* reports that Townley Crane has become associate editor of the *Asbury Park Shore Press.*

EARLY NOVEMBER. Jacob Riis publishes *Children of the Poor,* a sequel to *How the Other Half Lives,* which deals with the degenerative effects of the tenements, sweatshops, saloons, and gangs upon the young people of the slums. He emphasizes that "the entire absence of privacy in their homes and the foul contact of the sweaters' shops, where men and women work side by side from morning till night, scarcely half clad in the hot summer weather, does for the girls what the street completes in the boy" (Wertheim 1970, vii).

NOVEMBER. Garland's article "The West in Literature" emphasizes that "art, after all, is an individual thing. A man must first be true to himself. The advice I give to my pupils who are ambitious to write is the essence of veritism: 'Write of those things of which you know most, and for which you care most. By so doing you will be true to yourself, true to your locality, and true to your time'" (Wertheim 1970, iv).

DECEMBER. The publication of the Sullivan County story "A Tent in Agony" in *Cosmopolitan* marks Crane's first appearance in a popular magazine.

23 DECEMBER. The Syracuse *University Herald* prints Crane's Sullivan County story "The Cry of a Huckleberry Pudding."

[Other Sullivan County stories probably written in 1892, including "The Holler Tree," "An Explosion of Seven Babies," and "The Mesmeric Mountain," remain unpublished in Crane's lifetime.]

WINTER, 1892–1893. Crane brings the manuscript of *Maggie* with Garland's letter of recommendation to Richard Watson Gilder, who rejects it for publication in the *Century*. Willis Fletcher Johnson recalls sending Crane to Ripley Hitchcock and maintains that Hitchcock hesitated to recommend the acceptance of *Maggie* by Appleton (Johnson, 289). But Hitchcock does not mention Crane's entering the Appleton office until December 1894 (Hitchcock, v).

*

1893

*

EARLY JANUARY. William Howe Crane buys Stephen's and Wilbur's one-seventh shares in their mother's Asbury Park house (Gullason 1968c, 234).

14 JANUARY. The Hartwood Park Association is incorporated as the Hartwood Club, with William Howe Crane as its first president (Campbell, 31).

19 JANUARY. The Library of Congress receives Crane's copyright application for *Maggie*, the typewritten title page reading simply, "A Girl of the Streets,/A Story of New York./—By—/Stephen Crane." The name "Maggie" is added later, perhaps at William's suggestion (*C*, 47n1).

24 JANUARY. Stephen sells William his shares in the coal mine at Kingston, Pennsylvania (Katz 1968, 7). This, added to the money received from the sale of Mrs. Crane's Asbury Park home, provides him with the means to have *Maggie* privately printed.

[JANUARY]. Louis Senger introduces Crane to his cousin, the painter Corwin Knapp Linson, who has a studio on the southwest corner of Broadway and 30th Street.

[Linson witnessed and shared Crane's poverty in the winter of 1893 and preserved a humorous poem referring to that period written on "A wrinkled and yellowed page . . . whose smoothed creases betray its rescue from an intended oblivion," at the top of which Crane penciled, "I'd sell my steps to the grave at ten cents per foot, if t'were but honestie" (Linson 1958, 13):

Ah, haggard purse, why ope thy mouth
Like a greedy urchin
I have nought wherewith to feed thee
Thy wan cheeks have ne'er been puffed
Thou knowest not the fill of pride
Why then gape at me
In fashion of a wronged one
Thou do smilest wanly
And reproachest me with thine empty stomach
Thou knowest I'd sell my steps to the grave
If t'were but honestie
Ha, leer not so,
Name me no names of wrongs committed with thee
No ghost can lay hand on thee and me
We've been too thin to do sin
What, liar? When thou wast filled of gold, didst I riot?
And give thee no time to eat?
No, thou brown devil, thou stuffed now with lies as with wealth,
The one gone to let in the other. (*Poems*, 130)]

"Party at the Pendennis Club," 1064 Avenue A
in Manhattan, 18 March 1893, to celebrate
the publication of *Maggie*. Crane is seated
with banjo; on his left is Lucius L. Button
(Syracuse University)

LATE FEBRUARY–EARLY MARCH. *Maggie: A Girl of the Streets* appears under the pseudonym of "Johnston Smith," printed, according to Lawrence, at "a little printing shop on lower Sixth Avenue whose sign we had often noticed" (Lawrence, 9). The origin of the nom de plume is in dispute. Post Wheeler recalls proposing it to Crane as a joke (Wheeler and Rives, 100). Lawrence reports that Crane wished to disguise the authorship of a book that would offend his prudish relatives, and the jest consisted in elevating the plebian "John Smith" into a more aristocratic pseudonym (9). According to Willis Fletcher Johnson, Crane chose the two most common surnames in the New York City directory and whimsically added a "t" to the first (Johnson, 289). Crane told Corwin K. Linson that "The alias was a mere chance. 'Commonest name I could think of. I had an editor friend named Johnson, and put in the "t," and no one could find me in the mob of Smiths'" (Linson 1958, 21).

William Dean Howells
(NYPL Picture Collection)

EARLY MARCH. At the suggestion of Hamlin Garland, Crane sends a copy of *Maggie* to William Dean Howells. Later in the month, also with Garland's encouragement, he sends copies to Brander Matthews, Julius Chambers, John D. Barry, and others.

13 MARCH. *Maggie* is reviewed in the *Port Jervis Union*, the earliest known review of a Crane work: "The evident object of the writer is to show the tremendous influence of environment on the human character and destiny. Maggie, the heroine, or central figure of the tale, grows up under surroundings which repress all good impulses, stunt the moral growth and render it inevitable that she should become what she eventually did, a creature of the streets. The pathos of her sad story will be deeply felt by all susceptible persons who read the book" (Gullason 1968b, 301).

18 MARCH. The weekly humor magazine *Truth* contains "Why Did the Young Clerk Swear?," Crane's parodic satire of spurious eroticism in French naturalistic fiction.

Photographic study by Corwin Knapp
Linson for his oil painting of Crane, 1894
(Barrett Collection,
University of Virginia)

A party at the Pendennis Club celebrates the publication of *Maggie.*
John Henry Dick, "electing himself a Committee for the Advancement
and Preservation of *Maggie,* greeted each guest with a determined
expression, a hammer upraised significantly in one hand, and a *Maggie* clutched conspicuously in the other. The success of *Maggie* was
toasted, drunk to, and drunk; although Linson recalls that after the
first hour the ostensible purpose of the party was forgotten, and
mustard-yellow piles lay unheeded. Inventive minds kept improving
the punch, Stevie strummed his banjo, and the 'wild Indians' sang
increasingly loud with decreasing harmony. Mrs. Creegan [the land-
lady] was patient until midnight; then she ascended in wrapper,
braids, and cap. She roared with dragon-like fervor for quiet. She was
in the habit, she said pointedly, of renting her rooms to *gentlemen* not
animals. Stevie poked his head through a crack in the door, waving
his hands frantically behind his back for silence. 'The animals apolo-
gize,' he said, 'and will immediately return to their cages'; but to the
menagerie he whispered: 'Cheese it, for God's sake! She'll throw me

Corwin Knapp Linson's oil painting
of Stephen Crane, 1894
(Barrett Collection, University of Virginia)

out if you Indians don't die. We owe her a month's rent as it is'"
(Schoberlin IX, 30–31; see Linson 1958, 27).

22 MARCH. John D. Barry, assistant editor of the *Forum*, writes to Crane:

> Thank you very much for sending me your book. It reached me on
> my return after an absence of several days from the city. Otherwise, I
> should have acknowledged it sooner. I have read it with the deepest
> interest. It is pitilessly real and it produced its effect upon me—the
> effect, I presume, that you wished to produce, a kind of horror. To be
> frank with you, I doubt if such literature is good: it closely approaches
> the morbid and the morbid is always dangerous. Such a theme as
> yours, in my judgment, ought not to be treated so brutally—pardon the
> word—as you have treated it: you have painted too black a picture,
> with no light whatever to your shade. I know one might say that the
> truth was black and that you tried to describe it just as it was; but, one
> ought always to bear in mind that literature is an art, that effect, the
> effect upon the reader, must always be kept in view by the artist and
> as soon as that effect approaches the morbid, the unhealthful, the art
> becomes diseased. It is the taint in the peach. I really believe that the
> lesson of your story is good, but I believe, too, that you have driven
> that lesson too hard. There must be moderation even in well-doing;
> excess of enthusiasm in reform is apt to be dangerous. The mere
> brooding upon evil conditions, especially those concerned with the
> relation of the sexes, is the most dangerous and the most sentimental
> of all brooding, and I don't think that it often moves to action, to actual
> reform work. This, it seems to me, is just the kind of brooding your
> book inspires. I presume you want to make people think about the
> horrible things you describe. But of what avail is their thought unless
> it leads them to work? It would be better for them not to think about
> these things at all—if thinking ends as it began, for in itself it is un-
> pleasant and in its tendency unhealthful. (*C*, 49–50)

Garland and Howells meet for lunch and discuss *Maggie* (Pizer
1960, 78–79).

[LATE MARCH]. Crane begins a draft of *George's Mother* on the reverse side of a manuscript leaf of "The Holler Tree" but lays it aside
until May 1894.

28 MARCH. Crane sends a plaintive letter to Howells, asking why he
has received no response to the copy of *Maggie* he sent him. (*C*, 51).

28 OR 29 MARCH. Howells replies that he has not yet had the opportunity to read the book (*C*, 52).

[MARCH]. Crane inscribes a copy of *Maggie* to Lucius L. Button, one of the medical students of the Pendennis Club (*C*, 52). Copies with almost identical inscriptions are sent to Hamlin Garland and other friends and to a few crusading reformers who ignore the book:

Stephen Crane
to Budgon.
It is inevitable that you be great{ly}
shocked by this book but continue, plea{se,}
with all possible courage, to the end. For, {it}
tries to show that environment is a tremend{ous}
thing in the world and frequently shapes liv{es}   .
regardless. If one proves that theory, one makes room {in}
Heaven for all sorts of souls, notably an occasional
street girl, who are not confidently expected to be
there by many excellent people.
It is probable that the reader of this small thi{ng}
may consider the author to be a bad man, bu{t,}
obviously, that is a matter of small consequence to
                              The Au{thor}

MARCH–APRIL. Crane spends hours lounging in Corwin Knapp Linson's studio, poring over old copies of the *Century Magazine* in which the series "Battles and Leaders of the Civil War," which included graphic accounts of the Battle of Chancellorsville and the series by Warren Lee Goss entitled "Recollections of a Private," had run from November 1884 through November 1887. He tells Linson: "'I wonder that some of those fellows don't tell how they *felt* in those scraps. They spout enough of what they *did*, but they're as emotionless as rocks'" (Linson 1903, 19).

LATE MARCH–APRIL. At the Pendennis Club, Crane composes his Asbury Park escape fantasy, "The Pace of Youth" (Linson 1958, 28–29).

APRIL. Hamlin Garland in his *Arena* essay on "The Future of Fiction" opines that "The novel of the slums must be written by one who has played there as a child, and taken part in all its amusements; not out of curiosity, but out of pleasure seeking. It cannot be done from above nor from the outside. It must be done out of a full heart and without seeking for effect" (Garland 1893a, 521).

[Garland is probably thinking of Crane because in his June review of *Maggie* he incorrectly states that "it is written by one who has lived the life. The young author, Stephen Crane, is a native of the city, and has grown up in the very scenes he describes."]

EARLY APRIL. Wearing a suit borrowed from his friend John Northern Hilliard, Crane visits Howells in his home at 40 West 59th Street, New York City. At this time, or perhaps on a later visit, Howells reads some of Emily Dickinson's poems to him, and Crane is deeply impressed (Barry, 148).

Crane writes to Lily Brandon Munroe:

> Well, at least, I've done something. I wrote a book. Up to the present time, I think I can say I am glad I did it. Hamlin Garland was the first to over-whelm me with all manner of extraordinary language. The book has made me a powerful friend in W. D. Howells. B. O. Flower of the "*Arena*" has practically offered me the benefits of his publishing company for all that I may in future write. Albert Shaw of the "Review of Reviews" wrote me congratulations this morning and to-morrow I dine with the editor of the "Forum."
>
> So I think I can say that if I "watch out", I'm almost a success. And "such a boy, too", they say. (*C*, 55)

[EARLY APRIL]. Thomas Beer relates that one afternoon Crane was lounging in the studio of the artist William Dallgren, watching Dallgren sketch drama critic Acton Davies, "when Davies tossed him Emile Zola's 'Le Débâcle' [*sic*], in a translation. Davies was a round youth who doted on Zola and when Crane slung the book aside he was annoyed.

> 'I suppose you could have done it better?'
> 'Certainly,' said Crane." (Beer 1923, 97–98)

[Ripley Hitchcock in his preface to the 1900 memorial issue of *The Red Badge* mentions that *La Débâcle* possibly influenced Crane's war novel and that one cannot "verify the tale that its origin was the challenge of an artist friend uttered in response to Mr. Crane's criticism of a battle story which he had just read" (vi). Hitchcock does not refer to Dallgren or Davies, and the source for his story was most likely Kenneth Herford's recently published article "Young Blood—Stephen Crane":

> On a winter afternoon about six years ago a boy of twenty-two lolled upon a divan in the New York studio of an artist friend. While the artist painted, the boy read the stories in the current number of an American magazine. Finishing the last, he tossed the periodical aside, and, picking up a guitar, twanged the strings idly. He was thinking.
> "Huh!" he exclaimed disgustedly.
> "What's the matter, Steve?" asked the artist, turning from his easel.

"I've just read a battle story in that magazine," was the reply, "and I was thinking I could write a better one myself."

"Why don't you, then?" The artist dabbed a little spot of paint on his canvas and stepped back to observe the effect.

The boy was silent for a moment, then suddenly he exclaimed, "By jove! I believe I will. Good-by." And he was off. (Herford, 413)

Beer's story was based on the accounts of Hitchcock and Herford. Whether Dallgren and Davies were actors in the events recounted is problematical.]

8 APRIL. Crane writes to Howells asking for a recommendation to Edwin L. Godkin, editor of the *New York Evening Post*. Howells replies on the same day, advising Crane to show Godkin a letter from Howells to Crane that praised *Maggie* (*C*, 53–54).

MID-APRIL. The Pendennis Club disbands. Crane follows his landlady to another boardinghouse at 136 West 15th Street. On occasion he shares a loft with artists and illustrators still remaining in the building on East 23d Street recently abandoned by the Art Students' League.

JUNE. Hamlin Garland reviews *Maggie*, but even his praise for the novelette's realism is tempered by distaste for the unrelenting pessimism of Crane's perspective since for Garland realism should ultimately be melioristic:

His book is the most truthful and unhackneyed study of the slums I have yet read, fragment though it is. It is pictorial, graphic, terrible in its directness. It has no conventional phrases. It gives the dialect of the slums as I have never before seen it written—crisp, direct, terse. It is another locality finding voice.

It is important because it voices the blind rebellion of Rum Alley and Devil's Row. It creates the atmosphere of the jungles, where vice festers and crime passes gloomily by, where outlawed human nature rebels against God and man.

The story fails of rounded completeness. It is only a fragment. It is typical only of the worst elements of the alley. The author should delineate the families living on the next street, who live lives of heroic purity and hopeless hardship. (Garland 1893b, xi–xii)

[JUNE]. Crane begins to write the trial manuscript of *The Red Badge of Courage*. He tells Louis Senger, "'I deliberately started in to do a pot-boiler . . . something that would take the boarding-school element—you know the kind. Well, I got interested in the thing in spite of myself, and I couldn't, I couldn't. I *had* to do it my own way'" (Louis C. Senger to Hamlin Garland, 9 October 1900, CLSU).

MID-JUNE. Crane lives in Edmund's Lake View home while working on *The Red Badge of Courage*.

LATE JUNE. NEW YORK CITY. Crane shows Linson two of his "Tommie" stories, "An Ominous Baby" and "A Great Mistake," based upon the Tommie of *Maggie* who died in infancy, and asks him to draw illustrations for them (Linson 1958, 39). A third "Tommie" story, "A Dark Brown Dog," is written shortly after this but remains unpublished in Crane's lifetime.

Linson draws illustrations for Crane's farcical sketch, "The Reluctant Voyagers," but the manuscript is retained by "a responsible magazine" for six months and then returned for minor revisions. Upon resubmission, Linson's drawings are lost (Linson 1958, 18–20). The sketch itself did not appear until 1900.

3 JULY. *Truth* prints "At Clancy's Wake," a burlesque playlet.

JULY-EARLY SEPTEMBER. Crane continues to work on the manuscript of *The Red Badge* in Lake View (Linson 1958, 42). About one third of the way through the novel he abandons his trial draft and begins a final inscription. Edmund B. Crane recalls:

His day began at noon when he arose and ate breakfast when my wife and the little girls ate lunch. The afternoons he spent coaching the boys of the neighborhood in football tactics. From this he gained exercise in the open air, and much amusement. The evenings were spent around the piano singing, or socially at some friend's house. When the family retired, Stephen went to the garret, where he worked and slept, and wrote far into the night, if composition was going smoothly. As soon as the story began to take shape he read it to me as the finished parts grew. He told me he did not want my literary opinion, only to know if I liked the story. That was pretty good from a kid fourteen years my junior. I liked the story. When, listening to the reading of the story, I ventured to suggest the substitution of a word that would give the meaning intended better than the word he used, he would consider the matter and then decide, oftener against than for the suggestion. He had the confidence of genius. (EBC, 3)

20 JULY. Townley Crane marries his third wife, Elizabeth Richards of New York City (*Asbury Park Daily Press*, 27 July).

7 SEPTEMBER. A cyclone strikes Port Jervis, destroying Drew Methodist Church: "The greatest damage was to the Methodist Episcopal church which faces the west on Orange Square, and lay directly in the path of the storm. The wind hit it squarely in the face and blew the tall steeple over on the roof which was carried down with it into the interior of the church, where it lies a mass of rubbish. The church is almost a total wreck" (*Port Jervis Evening Gazette*, 8 September). The church is rebuilt in 1894.

MID-SEPTEMBER–OCTOBER. Crane moves into the old Art Students' League building at 143–147 East 23d Street. Here he shares a large studio with William W. Carroll, Nelson Greene, and R. G. Vosburgh. Other artist friends such as Frederick Gordon and David Ericson have separate studios in the building. In his notebook Crane describes the interior of the building as "a place of slumberous corridors rambling in puzzling turns and curves. The large studios rear their brown rafters over scenes of lonely quiet. Gradually the tinkers, the tailors, and the plumbers who have captured the ground floor are creeping toward those dim ateliers above them. One by one the besieged artists give up the struggle and the time is not far distant when the conquest of the tinkers, the tailors and the plumbers will be complete. . . . In the top-most and remotest studio there is an old beam which bears this line from Emerson in half-obliterated chalk marks: 'Congratulate yourselves if you have done something strange and extravagant and broken the monotony of a decorous age.' It is a memory of the old days" (*Notebook*, 8–9, 15–16). The Emerson quotation is apparently apocryphal. Frederick Gordon describes life in the building:

> There were three street entrances, and it had been remodeled and twisted about so much at various times, to suit the growing needs of the League, that it took an expert pilot to guide a stranger through its mysteries. The upper floors were filled with artists, musicians and writers, young men and women, decent people all, who were glad of the low rents and really congenial atmosphere. The landlord was an artist, and as considerate of our financial difficulties as he could be in reason. Our life there was free, gay, hard working—and *decent*. I had one of the biggest studios, and naturally people gathered there a good deal. Smoking, talking, and sometimes a little cards. There was no money going—no one had any—but I remember some game that required the loser to go out and fetch a can of beer. Once he failed to come back, and a search party with lamps (the hall lights went out at 11) found him comfortable on a remote stairway, but the can was empty! He explained that he had lost himself in the labyrinth, but was not worrying so long as the beer lasted.

And there you see the sum of Crane's sins while he was with me—so far as I know. (Frederick C. Gordon to Thomas Beer, 25 May 1923, CtY)

AUTUMN–SPRING 1894. Crane lives in the Art Students' League building, working on his poems and the final manuscript of *The Red Badge of Courage*. Nelson Greene recalls that "Crane's literary idols were De Maupassant first (in English) and Zola. I think he also considerably admired Tolstoi—but De Maupassant was his favorite as a literary technician. However, he liked anyone who favored his impressionistic new approach to fictional composition" (Greene, 3). According to R. G. Vosburgh,

For seven or eight months, from one autumn until the following summer, the four men lived together. It was during that time that *The Red Badge of Courage* was written. At the time he came to live in the studio, Crane was reading over the descriptive articles on the Civil War published in the *Century*. War and fighting were always deeply interesting to him. The football articles in the newspapers were an especial pleasure. "Ah!" he would say after reading one of them, "that's great. That's bully! That's like war!". . . .

The articles in the *Century*, then, were full of interest and fascination for Crane, and when he moved to the studio on Twenty-third street he borrowed the magazines and took them with him to read and study. All of his knowledge of the war and of the country depicted in *The Red Badge of Courage* was gathered from those articles and from the study of maps of that region. . . .

Crane spent his afternoons and evenings studying the war and discussing his stories. Every incident and phase of character in *The Red Badge of Courage* was discussed and argued fully and completely before being incorporated into the story. . . .

In his work he always tried for individuality. His daring phrases and short, intense descriptions pleased him greatly. They were studied out with much care, and after they had been trimmed and turned and changed to the final form, he would repeat them aloud and dwell on them lovingly. Impressionism was his faith. Impressionism, he said, was truth, and no man could be great who was not an impressionist, for greatness consisted in knowing truth. (Vosburgh, 26–27)

David Ericson remembers:

We were all poor struggling for means of existence. He was at that time writing "The Red Badge of Courage." I remember one time when he was lying in a hammock of his saying "That is great!" It shocked me for the moment. I thought how conceited he is. But when he read me the passage, I realized at once how wonderfully real it was, and said that the writer had that advantage over us painters in that he could make his men talk, walk and think. Where as a painter can only depict a man in one position at a time. He seemed very pleased with this compliment. . . . I can remember so well how when he came down from the country he would come in and put his little hand bag down in the middle of the Studio floor, sit down on a little sketching stool, pull out his pad, pen, and a bottle of ink, and begin to write with only a few words of greetings. I do not remember that he ever erased or changed anything. His writing was clean and round with a ring around his periods. He wrote slowly. It amazed me how he could keep the story in mind while he was slowly forming the letters. This I thought the most extra-ordinary thing I had ever seen. I do not think that any one ever noticed it. I felt an awe for him when I saw how naturally his imagination worked through his hand as though he really lived in another world. It seemed as though his concentration of ideas of what he had seen, and heard with a certain artistic perception enabled him to draw his characters so vividly. (*L*, 341–342)

4 NOVEMBER. *Truth* publishes Crane's parody of popular melodrama, "Some Hints for Play-Makers."

LATE DECEMBER. Garland takes an apartment at 107 West 105th Street with his brother Franklin, an actor appearing in James A. Herne's successful melodrama *Shore Acres*, which begins its New York run on 30 October and on Christmas Day moves to Daly's theater near 29th Street. Crane makes several visits to the Harlem apartment (Pizer 1960, 80).

WINTER. From the Art Students' League building, Crane writes an anguished love letter to Lily Brandon Munroe: "Your face is a torturing thing, appearing to me always, with the lines and the smile that I love,—before me always this indelible picture of you with it's fragrance of past joys and it's persistent utterance of the present griefs which are to me tragic, because they say they are engraven for life. It is beyond me to free myself from the thrall of my love for you; it comes always between me and what I would enjoy in life—always—like an ominous sentence—the words of the parrot on the death-ship: 'We are all damned'" (*C*, 57).

*

1894

*

2 JANUARY. Garland sends Crane to S. S. McClure to return some manuscripts and adds a recommendation: "If you have any work for

Mr. Crane talk things over with him and for Mercy Sake! Dont keep him *standing* for an hour, as he did before, out in your pen for culprits" (ViU).

JANUARY–MARCH. In an intense period of creative activity, Crane composes most of the poems of *The Black Riders* (*Works*, 10: 190).

7 FEBRUARY. Crane's earliest known fable, "How the Ocean Was Formed," is printed in the humorous weekly, *Puck.*

MID-FEBRUARY. Crane brings some of his poems to Linson, now living in a studio on West 22d Street near Sixth Avenue. They include "There was a man who lived a life of fire," "The ocean said to me once," "There was a crimson clash of war," and "In Heaven." Linson recalls:

> There by the flaring gaslight of an evening of mid-February, I was at work on a drawing when a rap on the door was followed by the entrance of Steve. Between his snow-flecked derby and his tightly buttoned ulster there hovered a sphinx-like smile. He shook the clinging snow from his hat and from the depths of his coat drew some sheets of foolscap and held them hesitatingly.
> "What do you think I have been doing, CK?"
> When a question is unanswerable one merely waits. Responding to my inquiring gaze, he laid the sheets on my drawing as if to say, "That, just now, is of minor importance." I read the topmost script.. . . . I became conscious of an uneasy waiting—then a swift challenge. "What do you think?"
> "I haven't had time to think! I'm seeing pictures."
> "What do you mean?"
> "Just what I said. They make me see pictures. How did you think of them?"
> A finger passed across his forehead, "They came, and I wrote them, that's all." . . . I confessed that their newness of form, their disregard of the usual puzzled me—"but that's their value, after all, Steve. I'm glad they're not Whitman. I thought at first they might be." He laughed.
> "That's all right, CK. If you can see them like that it's all I want." And he broke into a little chant. (Linson 1958, 48–50)

26 FEBRUARY. MONDAY. A blizzard engulfs New York City, covering the streets with almost a foot and a half of snow. The *New York Times* (27 February) compares it with the blizzard of 1888. The *Tribune* (27 February) reports that the storm, which began after midnight

Sunday and lasted for 30 hours, was accompanied by winds of 40 miles an hour much of the time. Crane spends part of the night in the Bowery.

27 FEBRUARY. Corwin Knapp Linson recalls:

> One morning early, after a blizzardy night, I found him in bed [at the Art Students' League building]. He looked haggard. He was alone, the others being presumably in pursuit of the art editors.
>
> Pulling a manuscript from mysterious seclusion, he tossed it to me. It was the sketch, The Men in the Storm, suggested by Mr. Garland. He had been all night at it, out in the storm in line with the hungry men, studying them; then inside, writing it.
>
> This was the period of his tramp studies, written for a press syndicate. He disappeared from view for days, and was suddenly dug up looking as if he had lived in a grave. All this time he had inhabited the tramp lodging-houses nights, and camped on the down-town park benches days. With grim delight he related how an old acquaintance had passed him a foot away, as he sat with a genuine hobo in front of the City Hall, and how the police had eyed his borrowed rags askance, or indicated with official hand that another bench needed dusting. (Linson 1903, 19–20)

EARLY MARCH. Crane and his friend W. W. Carroll, who later became a Methodist minister, leave the Art Students' League building costumed as tramps to explore the Bowery. Carroll recalls:

> Garland and Howells got him an assignment with the Bacheller & Johnson syndicate to cover the "bum lodging houses" of New York. At Crane's invitation, I went with him on this dreary round. We went as hoboes with about thirty cents each, endured much misery for four days and three nights, and landed finally at Corwin Knapp Linson's studio, where we dozed and rested after being served with some stout punch and some real food. In the 5, 7, or 10c beds, Stephen Crane slept like a healthy baby while I struggled with a myriad host that did murder sleep. His stories of these days and nights were strings of words that made one see flaring gas jets and dark interiors, where one could smell crude disinfectants mingled with exhalations from many human bodies. He made much of a little round-headed, pot-bellied man, who cried out in nightmares with a shrill treble voice. A Bowery sign "*Delectable Coffee 1c*," the elaborate arrangements of the Charity Organization Society to circumvent and defeat any hungry person's efforts to eat, and the directness and efficiency of the saloons in filling us up with hot soup and cold beer—these things delighted Stephen Crane. The saloon men were good to us, especially at Steve Brodie's. We saw Steve himself, acting as his own bouncer, handling "repeaters" in his daily bread and soup line.

We were posing dejectedly at a saloon entrance, when a big raw-boned Howard Pyle type of pirate panhandled us for the price of a meal. We reproved him sadly. He looked us up and down and said, "Yous lads look like yous were in hard luck, but yous are woikin' some game." He went away—and he came back. He said, "Wot are yous lads doing? Wots yer lay? Yous have got me guessin'. Tell me, wots de game?" We told him. We knocked around with him and watched him panhandle promising passerby [sic]. He steered us into some sleeping places. Finally he got so friendly he became a nuisance, and we shook him. (Carroll, 2–3)

BETWEEN 10 AND 15 MARCH. Crane brings some of his poems to Hamlin Garland's 105th Street apartment. They include "God fashioned the ship of the world carefully." Garland remembers:

> I read this with delight and amazement. I rushed through the others, some thirty in all, with growing wonder. I could not believe they were the work of the pale, reticent boy moving restlessly about the room.
> "Have you any more?" I asked.
> "I've got five or six all in a little row up here," he quaintly replied, pointing to his temple. "That's the way they come—in little rows, all made up, ready to be put down on paper."
> "When did you write these?"
> "Oh! I've been writing five or six every day. I wrote nine yesterday. I wanted to write some more last night, but those 'Indians' wouldn't let me do it. They howled over the other verses so loud they nearly cracked my ears. You see, we all live in a box together and I've no place to write, except right in the general squabble. They think my lines are funny. They make a circus of me." (Garland 1900, 16)

Garland gives Crane a letter recommending the poems to William Dean Howells, and within the next day or two Crane brings the poems to Howells, who attempts to interest Henry Mills Alden, editor of *Harper's Magazine*, in them.

[Garland's naive acceptance of Crane's assertion that his poems were simply unconscious projections, composed without effort, was a consequence of his strong interest in psychical phenomena. He was a contributor to the *Psychical Review* and future president of the American Psychical Association (*Poems*, xxiii).]

18 MARCH. William Dean Howells writes to Crane: "I could not persuade Mr. Alden to be of my thinking about your poems. I wish you had given them more form, for these things so striking would have found a public ready made for them; as it is they will have to make one" (*C*, 62).

1894

MARCH–APRIL. Crane writes to Lily Brandon Munroe: "You know, when I left you, I renounced the clever school in literature. It seemed to me that there must be something more in life than to sit and cudgel one's brains for clever and witty expedients. So I developed all alone a little creed of art which I thought was a good one. Later I discovered that my creed was identical with the one of Howells and Garland and in this way I became involved in the beautiful war between those who say that art is man's substitute for nature and we are the most successful in art when we approach the nearest to nature and truth, and those who say— well, I don't know what they say. They don't, they can't say much but they fight villianously and keep Garland and I out of the big magazines. Howells, of course, is too powerful for them" (*C*, 63).

EARLY APRIL. Crane completes the inscription of the final holograph manuscript of *The Red Badge of Courage*. He moves out of the Art Students' League building into a flat of his own at 111 West 33d Street. Here he makes a preliminary revision of *The Red Badge* manuscript, altering every name not in direct address to epithets in the first 38 pages, so that Fleming becomes "the youth"; Conklin, first "the excited soldier" and then "the tall soldier"; and Wilson, "the young private" and "the blatant young soldier" but later "the loud young soldier" (Bowers 1975, 194).

Crane shows some of his poems to John D. Barry, who sends them to Copeland & Day (Garland 1930, 200).

14 APRIL. SATURDAY EVENING. Barry reads a selection of Crane's poems before the Uncut Leaves Society in the small ballroom at Sherry's. Mrs. Frances Hodgson Burnett is the guest of honor. According to Barry, Crane was "too modest" to read the poems himself; "in fact, the poet made the assertion that he would 'rather die than do it'" (*New York Tribune*, 16 April).

15 APRIL. Edward Marshall interviews Howells, "Greatest Living American Writer," in the *New York Press*: "Mary E. Wilkins, Mark Twain, Sarah Orne Jewett, Hamlin Garland and George W. Cable are probably the most strikingly American writers we have to-day. There is another whom I have great hopes of. His name is Stephen Crane, and he is very young, but he promises splendid things. He has written one novel so far—'Maggie.' I think that as a study of East Side life in New York 'Maggie' is a remarkable book. There is so much realism of a certain kind in it that unfits it for general reading, but once in a way [*sic*] it will do to tell the truth as completely as 'Maggie' does."

[A somewhat different version of this interview is published simultaneously as "A Great American Writer" in the *Philadelphia Press.*]

The *New York Press* prints excerpts from *Maggie* and evaluates the novelette: "There is unquestionably truth in it; the kind of truth that no American has ever had the courage (or is it bravado?) to put between book covers before. It is a question if such brutalities are wholly acceptable in literature. Perhaps, as Mr. Howells says, they will be before long. Perhaps there will always be certain phases of life which we will not want to have woven with entire realism into our reading matter."

17 APRIL. Garland writes to Crane: "You'll find me at home any morning at 12. I'd like to know how things are going with you. I am going West on the 25*th*" (*C,* 65).

18 APRIL. Crane replies to Garland, making no mention of his war novel: "I have not been up to see you because of various strange conditions—notably, my toes are coming through one shoe and I have not been going out into society as much as I might. I hope you have heard about the Uncut Leaves affair. I tried to get tickets up to you but I couldn't succeed. I mail you last Sunday's *Press*. I've moved now—live in a flat. People can come to see me now. They come in shools and say that I am a great writer. Counting five that are sold, four that are unsold, and six that are mapped out, I have fifteen short stories in my head and out of it. They'll make a book" (*C,* 65).

[Wilbur's daughter Helen describes Crane's disheveled appearance on his casual visits to his Port Jervis relatives at this time: "He never had a clean shirt . . . and most of the time his toes were coming through his shoes 'most lamentably,' as he expressed it. His old gray ulster would have made quite a satisfactory stable-mop, but was scarcely good for anything else. His hands were finely textured and small, but they were always stained with cigarette yellow, and his hair—that was sailing in the general direction of the last wind" (HRC, 25). Describing the reaction of Crane's relatives to his bohemian life, John Northern Hilliard comments:

> I suppose that they are not particularly enamored of the way he looked at life and lived it, though it is difficult to think this in this age. But they were ministerial folk. Crane lived the life of the bohemian in those days—a bit too feverishly, perhaps, for his own good, that is to say for his physical health. He drank and he smoked and like Robert Louis Stevenson he had a hankering after the women. He took up with many a drab, and was not overly particular as to her age, race or color. Many a time I

have heard him say that he would have to go out and get a nigger wench "to change his luck." Time and time again he would bring a lady from the streets to his room. He had no eye for women of his own class or station. He preferred the other kind. I can understand this. Women of his own class could have given him nothing. In the slums he got life. He got the real thing, and that was what he was always looking for—the real, naked facts of life. And in seeking them, in living them, he was tolerant and absolutely unashamed. (John Northern Hilliard to Thomas Beer, 1 February 1922, CtY)]

21 APRIL. "A Night at the Millionaire's Club" appears in *Truth*.

21 OR 22 APRIL. Crane calls on Garland with the first part of the manuscript of *The Red Badge of Courage*, probably entitled "Private Fleming/His various battles" at this time, although Garland later remembers the manuscript as being untitled (Garland 1900, 17). After browsing through the manuscript, Garland comments:

"Crane, I daren't tell you how much I value this thing—at least not now. But wait! Here's only part of the manuscript. Where's the rest of it?"
Again he grinned, sourly, with a characteristic droop of his head. "In hock."
"To whom?"
"Typewriter."
"How much do you owe him or her?"
"Fifteen dollars."
Plainly this was no joking matter to him, but my brother and I were much amused by his tragic tone. At last I said, "I'll loan you the fifteen dollars if you'll bring me the remainder of the manuscript to-morrow."
"I'll do it," he said as if he were joining me in some heroic enterprise, and away he went in high spirits. (Garland 1930, 197)

22 APRIL. "An Experiment in Misery," based on Crane's experiences in the Bowery with W. W. Carroll, appears in the *New York Press*. The sketch contains a framework that opens with two men regarding a tramp:

"I wonder how he feels," said one, reflectively. "I suppose he is homeless, friendless, and has, at the most, only a few cents in his pocket. And if this is so, I wonder how he feels."

And concludes:

"Well," said the friend, "did you discover his point of view?"
"I don't know that I did," replied the young man; "but at any rate I think mine has undergone a considerable alteration."

Crane dropped the framework introduction and conclusion and revised the beginning when the sketch was included in the Heinemann edition of *The Open Boat* (1898).

Garland writes Crane congratulating him on "An Experiment in Misery" and advising him that his brother Franklin will meet him at the stage door of Daly's theater the next evening to lend him $15 (*C, 66*).

The *Philadelphia Press* publishes a commentary on *Maggie* by Elisha J. Edwards ("Holland"), a *New York Press* reporter who had occasionally provided Crane with a place to sleep in his room on West 27th Street during the peripatetic years of 1892–1893.

> The realism of Mr. Crane as it is done in that book is certainly cold, awful, brutal realism, and it reveals a power which when the author has learned of experience and has disciplined his artistic sense may give us something that may be compared to Tolstoi with respect to art as well as realism. But it is possible to tell a story of realism quite as suggestive and not so shocking as that one told in Mr. Crane's book, and it is a realism in which he had an unconscious part.
>
> Stephen Crane was not long ago in a certain office in New York where the tools are those of literature and journalism. The cases upon the walls contain dusty and dog-eared manuscripts. The desks were littered in charming confusion with proof slips, sheets of copy daubed here and there with the carelessly thrown, unwiped pen. Cigarette stubs were on the floor and a dismal bell over an editor's desk jingled with the peremptory resonance of a call from the composing room beyond.
>
> Stephen Crane stood in the middle of that room as odd and plaintive appearing a specimen of eager humanity as had ever been there. He seemed to have withered so that all the vitality of his body was concentrated in his head. He was a slender, sad-eyed slip of a youth, looking around the room with yearning glances of his eyes as though he would like to find a place where he could deposit the manuscript. He looked like one who had been fed for months on crackers and milk, as very likely was the fact, since he had starved himself in order to get together money enough to publish at his own expense, every publisher having rejected it, the very book which Mr. Howells has praised.
>
> At last turning to a man of authority who sat before a desk and who did not even look up when Crane spoke to him, the youth said in a voice in which there was the note of despair: "Well, I am going to chuck the whole thing," and he pulled a listless hand out of his pocket and let it deliver an impulsive gesture, as though he was casting something away from him.
>
> "What do you mean by that?" said the busy man.
>
> "Oh, I have worked two years, living with tramps in the tenements on the East Side so that I could get to know those people as they are, and

what is the use? In all that time I have received only $25 for my work. I can't starve even to carry on this work, and I'm going home to my brother in New Jersey and perhaps learn the boot and shoe trade."

"I am sorry," said the busy man, and then Crane wheeled about and walked away with the set of a man in whose blood there was not a particle of the vitality which comes from good beef or mutton. He went out and strolled down Broadway, far more miserable than any of the sorry creatures whom he has been studying because he was conscious of his misery. He had failed in an ambition, whereas they had no ambition.

A friendly hand was laid upon his shoulder and he started as though it was the clutch of a policeman. Then he saw that there was greeting in the touch and the smile.

"Crane," said his friend, "what do you think? William D. Howells has read your book, and he says it's great."

"Eh?" said the youth, and it seemed to the friend as though a sort of blur came over his eyes.

"I say that Howells has read your book, and he compares you with Tolstoi, and he is going to say so in print." It came upon that half-starved youth with such sudden force that he received it like a blow. If he had been told that Howells had condemned the book he might have heaved a sigh. He seemed dazed. He looked around like a man who did not know where he was. He gulped something down his throat, grinned like a woman in hysterics, and then went off to take up his vocation again.

The story must have impressed Howells only because of the brutal force of the blunt description which the author revealed. It is faithful; no newspaper man in New York, no one who is familiar with the life of the tenements, can deny the accuracy of the picture, but it is awful, just as life there is awful. And the wonder is that having gone so far in his realism Crane did not dare to go—as Tolstoi did and as Victor Hugo once did in his "Les Miserables"—clear over the line. Quite as realistic pictures, however, have been occasionally painted by some of the reporters for the newspapers, but they have done it without any sense of art or vocation, but simply as an incident in the reporting of some great tragedy or other important happening in those parts of the city. (LaFrance, 198–200)

[Parallel to a clipping of this article pasted in his scrapbook, Crane wrote, "This is a fake—not only a fake but a wretched, unartistic fake written by a very stupid man. But it was a great benefit" (NNC).]

23 APRIL. Crane redeems the second half of the *Red Badge of Courage* manuscript from the typist.

24 APRIL. Crane returns to Garland's apartment with the second half of the manuscript of *The Red Badge*. Garland reads the manuscript and makes penciled corrections and word substitutions on some

pages. Especially, he questions Crane's insistent use of dialect (Bowers 1975, 193–196).

25 APRIL. Garland leaves for Chicago, not to return to the East until December 1895 (Pizer 1960, 82).

[LATE APRIL]. Crane completes his revision of *The Red Badge of Courage* manuscript. He standardizes references to Wilson as "the loud soldier" and to Conklin as "the tall soldier," makes some stylistic changes, and, following Garland's suggestion, recasts the use of dialect in early chapters for Conklin and Wilson and partly for Fleming's mother to normal usage. In later chapters, having apparently changed his mind, he retains the original dialect for Conklin and Wilson, altering only Fleming's speech (Bowers 1975, 197). Probably at this time he inscribes the final title, "The Red Badge of Courage/An Episode of the American Civil War." Shortly after the completion of the manuscript, Crane offers it to S. S. McClure for publication in the McClure Newspaper Features Syndicate or in *McClure's Magazine*, which had been established in June 1893. Having overextended himself with his magazine venture and suffering financially in the current recession, McClure keeps his option open by declining to commit himself either to accept or reject the novel.

[Whether Crane at this time removed the original chapter 12 from the manuscript and made the other extensive deletions at the conclusions of chapters 7, 10, and the original chapter 15 containing Henry Fleming's interior monologues rationalizing his cowardice and rebellions against the universal order, as argued by Fredson Bowers (1975, 199–203), Donald Pizer (1979, 77–81), and James Colvert (1990, 248–249), or whether these changes were mandated by Appleton editor Ripley Hitchcock in the spring of 1895, after Crane returned from his trip to the West and Mexico, as argued by Henry Binder (11–23; 42n7) and Hershel Parker (35–41), is problematical and remains a matter of scholarly debate. In part, the controversy rests on the question of whether the manuscript Crane revised under Hitchcock's direction was the holograph or a carbon of the typescript made for the Bacheller syndicate's serialization of the novel. Binder and Parker maintain that the second group of deletions—which removed material that is still intact in the manuscript, primarily in the original chapters 16 and 25, but does not appear in the Appleton first edition—was also made in the spring of 1895 from a new typescript prepared for Appleton.

Hitchcock, however, accepted *The Red Badge* for publication by Appleton after reading clippings of the newspaper serialization that Crane sent him (Hitchcock, vi); Bowers points out that the deleted chapter endings do not appear in the newspaper version, which was derived from the Bacheller typescript, and that there is no evidence that Hitchcock ever saw the holograph. Bowers concludes that "the deleted chapter endings were thus initiated solely by Crane and represent his last intention before he ordered the pre-Hitchcock final typescript and carbon. . . . Every piece of evidence indicates that the manuscript was not touched in any way after the typescript and its carbon were made from it except to abstract a few pages of a battle scene for separate magazine publication. A recent edition of the *Red Badge* trumpeting the reprinting of these repetitious chapter endings as the restoration of Crane's true intention from Hitchcock's requested deletion is just plain wrong. The evidence of the manuscript clearly shows that it was Crane who on his own initiative deleted them and wisely so" (Bowers 1989, 102).]

29 APRIL. The *New York Press* prints "An Experiment in Luxury," a fictional counterpart to "An Experiment in Misery."

[APRIL–MAY]. James Gibbons Huneker recalls:

> One night in April or May of 1894, I ran into Crane on Broadway and we started over to the Everett House together. I'd been at a theater with [Edgar] Saltus and was in evening dress. In the Square, a kid came up and begged from us. I was drunk enough to give him a quarter. He followed along and I saw that he was really soliciting. Crane was damned innocent about everything but women and didn't see what the boy's game was. We got to the Everett House and we could see that the kid was painted. He was very handsome—looked like a Rossetti angel—big violet eyes— probably full of belladonna—Crane was disgusted. Thought he'd vomit. Then he got interested. He took the kid in and fed him supper. Got him to talk. The kid had syphilis, of course—most of that type do—and wanted money to have himself treated. Crane rang up Irving Bacheller and borrowed fifty dollars.
>
> He pumped a mass of details out of the boy whose name was something like Coolan and began a novel about a boy prostitute. I made him read A Rebours which he didn't like very much. Thought it stilted. This novel began with a scene in a railroad station. Probably the best passage of prose that Crane ever wrote. Boy from the country running off to see New York. He read the thing to Garland who was horrified and begged him to stop. I don't know that he ever finished the book. He was going to call it "Flowers of Asphalt." (Beer Papers)

[Although in his reminiscences Bacheller condensed his initial meetings with Crane, it is unlikely that they were closely acquainted

Edmund Crane's house on the Mill Pond,
Hartwood, New York
(Minisink Valley Historical Society)

at this time and even more unlikely, given Crane's poverty, that he could or would have borrowed $50 to give to a stranger. Huneker told Vincent Starrett that "Flowers in Asphalt" was begun in October 1898 and that it was to be "longer than anything he had done" (Starrett 1923, 10), but Crane was in Havana at this time, and, as John Berryman has suggested, no longer innocent of New York street life (Berryman, 88n). If Crane did begin this novel, it is uncertain whether the title was to be "Flowers of Asphalt" or "Flowers in Asphalt."]

MAY. "An Ominous Baby" appears in the *Arena*. The same issue includes a commentary on the story probably written by Benjamin Orange Flower, the radical editor of the *Arena*, which draws attention to the story "as a social study. The little chap who had acquired the engine and who refused the gamin the pleasure of even playing with it for a few moments, places the toy behind him the moment there is danger. The 'divine right' of property, as practically held by modern plutocracy, finds a striking expression in the involuntary action of the little aristocrat, who risks a thrashing by placing himself between the toy and danger. When he grows older he will probably become wiser in the way of the world and employ others to be bomb protectors; that is, if times do not change. But I believe they will change. The conscience of the nation is waking, and conscience, when aroused, is more powerful than avarice" (Gullason 1971, 298).

1 MAY. Elisha J. Edwards writes a syndicated piece describing the 14 April reading of Crane's poems before the Uncut Leaves Society:

There was another surprise for this company of cultured litterateurs when several of the poems of Stephen Crane were read by Mr. Barry. People asked, "Who is Stephen Crane?" but there were some in that company who knew that in a recent article Mr. Howells had praised Crane's work as he has praised the work of no new man for many years, and that Mr. Howells would give his formal approval by way of introductory note to the volume of poems of this young man which is soon to be published.

Mr. Barry read the poems with delightful elocution, suggesting their perfect rhythmical quality, although they are not arranged in metrical form. If the opinion of those who heard the poems is a just one, they are likely to suggest high talent when they are published.

Stephen Crane is a New York lad, for he is scarcely more than a lad, who plunged into the miseries of tenement life in New York and associated with the tramps and the outcasts for many months so that he might see them as they are and paint them thus. Mr. Howells has said that in the single book which Mr. Crane has written he has revealed a power of realism, a capacity to paint with almost brutal force and directness, which suggests much of the power of Tolstoi. (*SCraneN* 1 [Spring (for Summer) 1967]: 2–3)

8 MAY. Garland writes from Chicago: "What is the state of things? Did McClures finally take that war story for serial rights?" (*C*, 68).

William Howe Crane's house, 19 East Main Street,
Port Jervis, New York
(*Minisink Valley Historical Society*)

9 MAY. Crane writes to Garland that he is "writing another novel which is a bird," a reference to *George's Mother*. If this is a reply to Garland's letter of 8 May, Crane's statement "when anything happens I'll keep you informed" is his only response to Garland's question about McClure's acceptance of *The Red Badge*. He adds: "I have got the poetic spout so that I can turn it on or off. I wrote a decoration day thing for the *Press* which aroused them to enthusiasm. They said, in about a minute though, that I was firing over the heads of the soldiers" (*C*, 68, 69). This is probably an allusion to the sardonic "Veterans' Ranks Thinner by a Year," which appeared in the *New York Press* on 31 May 1894 in the guise of an eyewitness report of the Decoration Day parade (Gullason 1957, 157–158). There is an untitled manuscript of a sentimental Decoration Day tribute, prefaced by the poem "A soldier, young in years, young in ambitions" (*Works*, 8: 587–590) in the Columbia University Crane collection, but it can be in no way described as "firing over the heads of the soldiers."

MID-MAY. Edmund B. Crane moves to a house on the mill pond in Hartwood, New York, near the Hartwood Club, where he is custodian of a 3,600 acre tract of land known as the Clapham property that William Howe Crane obtained for his legal services to the club. Crane becomes a frequent boarder (EBC, 3–4).

17 MAY. NEW YORK. Crane inscribes a copy of *Maggie* to L. S. Linson, brother of Corwin Knapp Linson (*C*, 69).

Crane and C. K. Linson arrive in Port Jervis in the evening and spend the night at William Howe Crane's home on East Main Street. The *Port Jervis Union* (18 May) reports: "Mr. Stephen Crane, of New York city, whose novel 'Maggie' has given its author considerable literary celebrity, and whose magazine articles have many readers in this village, was in town over night, as the guest of his brother, Mr. W. H. Crane. He started for Scranton this noon, where he goes to obtain material for an article in McClure's magazine on the coal fields of that region. He was accompanied by Mr. C. K. Linson, the well known artist, who will furnish the illustrations for the article."

18–19 MAY. PENNSYLVANIA. After two descents into one of the Dunmore mines, Crane writes a draft of his article at the house of the painter John Willard Raught in Dunmore (Linson 1958, 67). The draft reveals that McClure deleted material from the printed text that he considered overly critical of business interests. Crane had concluded that "If all men who stand uselessly and for their own extraordinary profit between the miner and the consumer were annually doomed to a certain period of danger and darkness in the mines, they might at least comprehend the misery and bitterness of men who toil for existence at these hopelessly grim tasks" (*Works*, 8: 607).

[20 MAY]. Crane and Linson return to Port Jervis.

20 MAY. The *New York Press* prints "Billy Atkins Went to Omaha," a humorous study of tramp life on the rails. Crane's own title for the article is "An Excursion Ticket" (*Works*, 8: 784–785).

BETWEEN 22 AND 25 MAY. PORT JERVIS. Crane completes and revises "In the Depths of a Coal Mine" at William's house.

26 MAY. The *Port Jervis Union* reports: "Mr. Stephen Crane, the novelist and magazinist, started for New York today after a brief sojourn in this village. During his stay here, Mr. Crane worked up the material gathered in his trip to the coal regions into an article which will presently make its appearance in McClure's Magazine with illustrations by Mr. C. K. Linson, who . . . is a relative of Mr. Lewis Senger of this place. A good deal of the product of Mr. Crane's literary activity will appear in print within the next few months. A New York publishing firm have purchased the copyright in a war story written by him, while a Boston firm will presently bring out a volume of his poetry in all the glories of rich binding, heavy paper, fine type and wide margins."

29 MAY. The *Port Jervis Union* reports: "Dr. Fred Lawrence, who graduated at Hahnemann Medical college, two weeks ago, and is now a full fledged medico, is spending a few days in town before locating in practice at Philadelphia, where, in addition to his private practice he will perform the duties of assistant physician in the department of nervous diseases at the Hahnemann Hospital, under Dr. Clarence Bartlett."

10 JUNE. "Sailing Day Scenes" appears in the *New York Press*.

14 JUNE. The *Port Jervis Union* announces that "Mr. Stephen Crane, returned here from New York city today. He will spend the summer season in Port Jervis." For the next six weeks, Crane lounges in the homes of his brothers William and Wilbur and in Edmund B. Crane's house on the mill pond at Hartwood. His newly acquired Bowery demeanor shocks his staid and proper relatives. Helen R. Crane recalls:

My mother and my aunts never got quite used to the idea that he might suddenly interrupt a dinner conversation which was running along smoothly on croup or hats to inquire earnestly if any of the guests had ever seen a Chinaman murdered in Mott Street. Nor did they feel any happier when he called attention to his black eye and explained how he had got it in a grand fight on the Bowery.

It was impossible for him to be a social lion, because he simply could not understand small talk. He could spend hours with Mike Flanagan who drove a beer-truck on the East Side, for Mike's life was so foreign to his own world that all its details were colorful, and he could talk all night with Theodore Roosevelt, Hamlin Garland, or William Dean Howells about the virtues of the Single-Tax or the genius of Flaubert, but when it came to the inanities of ordinary gossip, he was sunk. And he did not get along with young people, the boys and girls of his own age. They thought he was cracked and he thought they were stupid. (HRC, 26)

8 JULY. The *New York Press* prints "Mr. Binks' Day Off: A Study of a Clerk's Holiday."

22 JULY. SUNDAY. "In the Depths of a Coal Mine" is syndicated by McClure in a number of newspapers under different headlines. Crane is disgusted by the cuts. According to Linson, "When Stephen read his article in type, he grunted and tossed it aside. 'The birds didn't want the truth after all. Why the hell did they send me up there then? Do they want the public to think the coal mines gilded ball-rooms with the miners eating ice-cream in boiled shirt-fronts?'" (Linson 1958, 70).

30 JULY. Crane, accompanied by Frederic Lawrence, Wickham Young, and others, leaves Port Jervis for Twin Lakes in Pike County, Pennsylvania, seven miles from Milford, for a month-long camping trip on land owned by Edgar Wells and his brothers, who are neighbors of the Lawrences in Port Jervis. The trip is organized by Mrs. Lawrence to celebrate the completion of Frederic's internship and staff appointment at the Hahnemann Medical College in Philadelphia (*Port Jervis Union*, 31 July). They christen their camp "Camp Interlaken" to distinguish it from the nearby encampment of Edgar Wells and his family.

AUGUST. "In the Depths of a Coal Mine" appears in *McClure's Magazine* with Linson's illustrations. Despite McClure's excisions, the article still contains strong social criticism cast in Crane's ironic style. Writing about the young boys whose task it is to separate the slate from the coal, Crane comments:

The slate-pickers, all through this region, are yet at the spanking period. One continually wonders about their mothers and if there are any schoolhouses. But as for them, they are not concerned. When they get time off, they go out on the culm-heap and play base-ball, or fight with boys from other breakers, or among themselves, according to the opportunities. And before them always is the hope of one day getting to be door-boys down in the mines and, later, mule-boys. And yet later laborers and helpers. Finally when they have grown to be great big men they may become miners, real miners, and go down and get "squeezed," or perhaps escape to a shattered old man's estate with a mere "miner's asthma." They are very ambitious. (*Works*, 8: 592)

[23 AUGUST]. PIKE COUNTY, PENNSYLVANIA. Crane writes to Copeland & Day from camp at Twin Lakes: "I would like to hear from you concerning my poetry. I wish to have my out-bring all under way by early fall and I have not heard from you in some time. I am in the dark in regard to your intentions" (*C*, 72).

28 AUGUST. Crane and his friends leave Twin Lakes. On the return trip they kill a rattlesnake. According to the *Port Jervis Union* (29 August):

It had been the ambition of the camp to kill a rattlesnake and do other proper Pike County things. Disappointment was escaped by a narrow margin. As the last section of the last contingent got within two miles of Parker's Glen on their return, a large black rattlesnake happily tried to cross the road within plain view. He seemed as large as a water main and was rattling like a trolley car. Mr. Crane ran forward heaving stones as he ran and owing to his being a base ball expert, he missed with each stone. He procured a little stick however in time to keep the snake from escaping into the stone wall, and a second later Mr. Senger arrived with an enormous bludgeon. There is no more to be said. They tossed up for the skin. Today they are filling the souls of the Middletown people with grief by writing long and eloquent accounts of it.

29 AUGUST. PORT JERVIS. Crane, with Senger's cooperation (Katz, 1983a), writes *The Pike County Puzzle*, a four-page humorous mock newspaper based on their camping experiences and the return trip. It is dated 28 August and privately printed by the staff of the *Port Jervis Union*. Crane's intellectualism was apparently a subject of satire to his friends: "PORT JERVIS, N.Y. Aug. 14.—As Stephen Crane was traversing the little rope ladder that ascends the right hand side of the

cloud-capped pinnacle of his thoughts, he fell and was grievously injured."

7 SEPTEMBER. Crane arrives in Hartwood and writes to Odell Hathaway regretting that he did not respond to Hathaway's letter because it was difficult to write from camp (*C*, 73).

The *Port Jervis Union* comments on the publication of *The Pike County Puzzle*:

A very handsomely printed and cleverly edited publication entitled the "Pike County Puzzle" has just made its appearance. It is intended for the special edification of the party of campers who recently went to Twin Lakes (dubbed Camp Interlaken by the party) under the chaperonage of Mrs. C. M. Lawrence of this place and Mrs. W. T. Hulse of Middletown and of which Dr. F. M. Lawrence, Ray Tubbs, L. C. Senger and Stephen Crane were distinguished members. The "Puzzle" from beginning to end is the product of the prolific genius Mr. Crane and all that it contains, including editorials, advertisements, telegraphic dispatches, reading notices and puffs, were written by him.

The sole responsibility as well as the sole credit of the achievement therefore belongs to him.

The satiric genius of the editor has been unrestrained by any consideration for persons and the personal characteristics of the members of the camp, their foibles, failings and follies have been burlesqued with a free hand. The editor has clearly aimed to be clever, amusing, funny, satirical, ironical and witty at the expense of his associates (not even sparing himself) and has succeeded in producing a clever burlesque. Much of the contents of this surprisingly witty publication is made up of personal allusions to the members of the camp, and the incidents of camp life and can be fully understood and enjoyed by them alone. The merit of the performance consists largely in the fact that personal characteristics have been faithfully reproduced and that the jokes are all founded on actual occurrences. The author has been true to the school of literature of which he is a distinguished ornament.

The "Puzzle" was printed in this office and is a credible illustration of the resources of our job department and the skill and good taste of our job printer, Mr. William Wade.

9 SEPTEMBER. HARTWOOD. Crane writes an angry letter to Copeland & Day:

Dear sirs:—We disagree on a multitude of points. In the first place I should absolutely refuse to have my poems printed without many of those which you just as absolutely mark "No." It seems to me that you cut all the ethical sense out of the book. All the anarchy, perhaps. It is the anarchy which I particularly insist upon. From the poems which you keep you could produce what might be termed a "nice little volume of verse by Stephen Crane" but for me there would be no satisfaction. The ones which refer to God, I believe you condemn altogether. I am obliged to have them in when my book is printed. There are some which I believe unworthy of print. These I herewith enclose. As for the others, I cannot give them up—in the book.

In the second matter, you wish I would write a few score more. It is utterly impossible to me. We would be obliged to come to an agreement upon those that are written.

If my position is impossible to you, I would not be offended at the sending of all the retained lines to the enclosed address. I beg to express my indebtedness to you and remain

Yours sincerely
Stephen Crane
(*C*, 73–74)

15 SEPTEMBER. The *Port Jervis Union* reports: "Mr. Stephen Crane left town today for New York city. He expects some important assignments from magazines and reviews to supply them with articles."

[27 SEPTEMBER]. NEW YORK CITY. Crane writes to Copeland & Day accepting a royalty of 10 percent for his poems. "As for the title I am inclined toward: 'The Black Riders and other lines,' referring to that one beginning 'Black riders rode forth,' etc." This poem is an early version of "Black riders came from the sea." He concludes, "I am indebted to you for your tolerance of my literary prejudices" (*C*, 74–75).

LATE SEPTEMBER. Crane shows Howells a copy of the manuscript of *The Black Riders*.

OCTOBER. The *Arena* contains "The Men in the Storm," based on Crane's experiences in the Bowery during the blizzard on the night of 26 February. In the same issue, the editor comments: "Mr. Stephen Crane's little story is a powerful bit of literature. This young writer belonging to the new school is likely to achieve in his own field something like the success Hamlin Garland has attained in his."

2 OCTOBER. William Dean Howells writes to Crane about his poems: "These things are too orphic for me. It is a pity for you to do them, for you can do things solid and real, so superbly. . . . I do not think a merciful Providence meant the 'prose-poem' to last" (*C*, 75).

EARLY OCTOBER. Crane moves back into the Art Students' League building on East 23d Street.

14 OCTOBER. In "Coney Island's Failing Days" (*New York Press*), Crane gently satirizes his own determinism and nihilism in the character of "'a very great philosopher,'" who, watching three young men enjoying themselves, reflects upon "'the purposes of the inexorable universe which plans to amuse us occasionally to keep us from the rebellion of suicide. . . . The insertion of a mild quantity of the egotism of sin into the minds of these young men causes them to wildly enjoy themselves. It is necessary to encourage them, you see, at this early day. After all, it is only great philosophers who have the wisdom to be utterly miserable'" (*Works*, 8: 324, 326–327).

MID-OCTOBER. At the suggestion of Edward Marshall, Crane brings Irving Bacheller the manuscript of the *Red Badge* for publication in his new newspaper syndicate, which is to begin service on 29 October. Bacheller recalls:

> He brought with him a bundle of manuscript. He spoke of it modestly. There was in his words no touch of the hopeful enthusiasm with which I presume he had once regarded it. No doubt it had come back to him from the "satraps" of the great magazines. They had chilled his ardor, if he ever had any, over the immortal thing he had accomplished. This is about what he said:
>
> "Mr. Howells and Hamlin Garland have read this stuff and they think it's good. I wish you'd read it and whether you wish to use the story or not, I'd be glad to have your frank opinion of it."
>
> The manuscript was a bit soiled from much handling. It had not been typed. It was in the clearly legible and rather handsome script of the author. I took it home with me that evening. My wife and I spent more than half the night reading it aloud to each other. We got far along in the story, thrilled by its power and vividness. In the morning I sent for Crane and made an arrangement with him to use about fifty thousand of his magic words as a serial. I had no place for a story of that length, but I decided to take the chance of putting it out in instalments far beyond the length of those permitted by my contracts. It was an experiment based on the hope that my judgment would swing my editors into line. They agreed with me. (Bacheller 1928, 277–278)

19 OCTOBER. Copeland & Day write to Crane offering to publish his poems with certain omissions. They list seven that they believe would be "*far* better left unprinted" but are willing to include all but three

(*C*, 76). Crane apparently agrees to the omission of all seven, for none of them appears in *The Black Riders*. Two of these poems, "To the maiden" and "There was a man with tongue of wood," are included in *War Is Kind*.

28 OCTOBER. Crane's interview with William Dean Howells is syndicated by S. S. McClure in a number of newspapers, the galley proof headlined "Howells Fears the Realists Must Wait." Howells's remarks about the distorting prevalence of the theme of romantic love in the popular novel seem to anticipate *George's Mother*. "'Somebody touched the universal heart with the fascinating theme—the relation of man to maid—and, for many years, it was as if no other relation could be recognized in fiction. Here and there an author raised his voice, but not loudly. I like to see the novelists treating some of the other important things in life—the relation of mother and son, of husband and wife, in fact all these things that we live in continually. The other can be but fragmentary'" (*Works*, 8: 637–638).

The *New York Press* prints Crane's humorous sketch "In a Park Row Restaurant" and "Stories Told by an Artist," a fictional account of bohemian life in the old Art Students' League building. Crane later revised material from these two stories and used it in *The Third Violet* (1897). Some of the same characters appear in "The Silver Pageant," which was also composed at this time but published posthumously.

[30 OCTOBER]. Crane sends to Copeland & Day a revised version of "Black riders came from the sea" (*C*, 77).

31 OCTOBER. Copeland & Day respond to Crane's letter of the previous day. They intend to publish *The Black Riders* in a format "more severely classic than any book ever yet issued in America" (*C*, 77).

11 NOVEMBER. Datelined Asbury Park, 9 November, Crane's short report of spectral legends, "Ghosts on the New Jersey Coast," appears in the *New York Press*.

14 NOVEMBER. Crane inscribes a copy of *Maggie* to his artist friend James Moser:

> To Jim Moser from Stephen Crane.
> May his smile blossom like
> an electric light for many
> years. May his genial words

string together like amber
beads for many more years.
And may he not die before
he gets "good and ready."

Gordon's Studio, New York.
Nov 14, 1894
(*C*, 78–79).

15 NOVEMBER. Crane writes to Hamlin Garland:

My dear friend: So much of my row with the world has to be silence and endurance that sometimes I wear the appearance of having forgotten my best friends, those to whom I am indebted for everything. As a matter of fact, I have just crawled out of the fifty-third ditch into which I have been cast and I now feel that I can write you a letter that wont make you ill. McClure was a Beast about the war-novel and that has been the thing that put me in one of the ditches. He kept it for six months until I was near mad. Oh, yes, he was going to use it but—Finally I took it to Bacheller's. They use it in January in a shortened form. I have just completed a New York book [*George's Mother*] that leaves Maggie at the post. It is my best thing. Since you are not here, I am going to see if Mr Howells will not read it. I am still working for the *Press*. (*C*, 79)

25 NOVEMBER. Crane's fictional "Realistic Pen Picture" of a fire "on one of the shadowy side streets, west of Sixth avenue" is printed in the *New York Press* under the headline "When Every One Is Panic Stricken."

[LATE NOVEMBER]. Crane composes his Bowery vignette, "A Desertion," not published until November 1900.

[NOVEMBER]. Crane borrows $15 from John Henry Dick to pay for a revised typescript of *The Red Badge* that Bacheller can cut up for serialization (*C*, 80).

2 DECEMBER. The *New York Press* prints Crane's study in human isolation, "When Man Falls, a Crowd Gathers," describing the indifference of a noisy group of men to the plight of an Italian immigrant who falls into an epileptic fit on an East Side street.

3–8 DECEMBER. An abridged and truncated version of *The Red Badge of Courage* is syndicated by Bacheller in the *Philadelphia Press* and in at least six other newspapers throughout the country, the *San Francisco Examiner* printing the novel in three intermittent installments in July (*Works*, 2: 249–252; Monteiro and Eppard, 74).

7 DECEMBER. The lead item on the editorial page of the *Philadelphia Press* promotes *The Red Badge*: "If you have not been reading 'The Red Badge of Courage,' by Stephen Crane, the story which has been running in 'The Press' for three or four days, you have been missing one of the best war stories going. Stephen Crane is a new name now and unknown, but everybody will be talking about him if he goes on as he has begun in this staving [*sic*] story" (LaFrance, 196).

8 DECEMBER. Writing as "Holland" in the *Philadelphia Press*, Elisha J. Edwards comments upon the previous day's editorial. A hasty reading of the manuscript of *The Red Badge* in the spring of 1893 had greatly impressed him:

> Here was a young man not born until long after the war days had closed, who nevertheless, by power of imagination, by a capacity intuitively to understand the impulses which prevailed in war days, had been able to write a story perhaps the most graphic and truthful in its suggestion of some of the phases of that epoch which has ever appeared in print.
>
> If Mr. Crane is careful, is true to his best impulses, follows his intuitions and pays no heed to those who write this or that about American fiction, he is quite likely to gain recognition before very long as the most powerful of American tellers of tales. (LaFrance, 201–202)

9 DECEMBER. The syndicated version of *The Red Badge* appears in the *New York Press*. Curtis Brown recalls:

> On the winter Sunday morning of the appearance of "The Red Badge of Courage," pitilessly compressed into seven columns, I went to the office for the reason that many a hard-and-fast newspaper man goes to his office on his day off—because his desk and the morning mail mysteriously draw him—and on emerging, met Stephen on that bitter, wind-swept, acute corner of Park Row and Beekman Street where the Potter Building stands, and within which the *Press* was housed. He was without an overcoat, but his face, thin and white, lit up when he saw me. He threw his arms around me and said: "Oh, *do* you think it was good?" Fortunately I could guess what he meant, and said: "It's great."
>
> "God bless you," said he, and hurried on to anywhere in the sleet. (*C.* Brown, 222–223)

"The Duel That Was Not Fought" appears in the *New York Press*.

10 DECEMBER. Crane writes to Copeland & Day for news about the production of *The Black Riders*. He has apparently misinterpreted their reference to the "severely classic" form in which they intend to bring out the book of poetry to refer to the elaborate black-letter fonts of William Morris: "I have grown somewhat frightened at the idea of old English type since some of my recent encounters with it have made me think I was working out a puzzle. Please reassure me on this point and tell me what you can of the day of publication" (*C*, 80).

BEFORE 15 DECEMBER. PHILADELPHIA. Bacheller brings Crane to meet Talcott Williams, editor of the *Philadelphia Press*. "We presented ourselves," Bacheller relates, "at Mr. Williams' sanctum. Word flew from cellar to roof that the great Stephen Crane was in the office. Editors, reporters, compositors, proof-readers crowded around him shaking his hand. It was a revelation of the commanding power of genius" (Bacheller 1928, 278–279).

PHILADELPHIA. From the Continental Hotel Crane writes to Linson that he has given his address to Bacheller, who will soon ask Linson to lend him the portrait of Crane that Linson has recently painted (*C*, 83).

15 DECEMBER. Crane responds testily to a suggestion from Copeland & Day that he has not answered their letters. He agrees to "the classic form" of the sample of *The Black Riders* sent to him. "It is however paragraphed wrong. There should be none. As to punctuation, any uniform method will suit me" (*C*, 81).

16 OR 17 DECEMBER. Crane visits Ripley Hitchcock, literary adviser of D. Appleton and Company, bringing with him two newspaper stories as examples of his work. According to Hitchcock, "The impression made by the stories was so strong that Mr. Crane was asked if he had a story long enough for publication in book form. He replied hesitatingly that he had written one rather long story, which was appearing in a Philadelphia newspaper, and 'some of the boys in the office seemed to like it.' He was asked to send the story at once, and presently there appeared a package of newspaper cuttings containing The Red Badge of Courage, which was promptly accepted for publication" (Hitchcock, v–vi).

18 DECEMBER. Crane sends a copy of the serialized *The Red Badge of Courage* to Ripley Hitchcock (*C*, 81).

21 DECEMBER. In the *Musical News* Crane reviews the career of the soprano Louise Gerard, whom he had met with her husband, Albert Thiess, at Avon-by-the-Sea in the summer of 1890.

22 DECEMBER. Crane writes a jocular letter to Post Wheeler (*C*, 82).

THE BLACK RIDERS AND
OTHER LINES BY STE-
PHEN CRANE

BOSTON COPELAND AND DAY MDCCCXCV

Front panel of Copeland and Day's prospectus for *The Black Riders*
(Wertheim Collection)

CHAPTER FOUR

The West and Mexico, New York City

January 1895–November 1896

In late January, after a number of delays, Crane departs on an extensive tour of the West and Mexico to write feature articles for the Bacheller syndicate. He stays briefly in Saint Louis before continuing on to Nebraska. After a brief stop in Lincoln, he journeys to the central area of the state, which had suffered a searing drought the previous summer followed by an exceptionally hard winter. Here he experiences the blizzard so vividly described in "The Blue Hotel." Leaving Nebraska in mid-February, Crane passes through Hot Springs, Arkansas, en route to New Orleans, where Ripley Hitchcock sends a manuscript of *The Red Badge of Courage* for him to correct. While in New Orleans he writes sketches about the performance of the French Opera company and the Mardi Gras. From Galveston, Texas, he journeys into Mexico through Laredo and Neuvo Laredo and on to Mexico City. Crane spends some two months in Mexico City and the Mexican hinterlands, during which time he writes a number of colorful but unfocused and disconnected sketches of Mexican life. Copeland & Day publish *The Black Riders* in early May, and in the middle of the month Crane returns to New York. June and July are spent in the city with frequent trips to Port Jervis and Hartwood. In August Crane once again camps in Pike County, Pennsylvania. At Hartwood in the fall, he writes *The Third Violet*. *The Red Badge of Courage* is published by Appleton in late September, and in December Crane is feted by the Society of the Philistines in Buffalo.

The success of *The Red Badge of Courage* in England in the first months of 1896 projects Crane into a fame he finds more difficult to cope with than his early struggles. He is panicked by the adulation of admirers and fearful that the war stories he is writing are unequal in quality to the novel. When McClure proposes a series of articles on Civil War battlefields, Crane makes a hurried trip to Virginia, but having little interest in becoming a Civil War historian, he declines the project. A trip to Washington in March to gather material for a political novel also proves fruitless. By the beginning of April he is again in New York working as a free-lance journalist. In the next few months he contributes over 20 articles to the Bacheller and McClure syndicates and the *New York Journal*. He becomes a member of the Author's Club and the Sons of the American Revolution. *George's Mother* is published in May, and an expurgated version of *Maggie* appears in June. During the summer at Hartwood, Crane writes short stories based on his Western trip. In September he accepts an assignment from the *New York Journal* to write a series of feature articles on life in the Tenderloin, and his explorations among the demimonde lead to his encounter with Dora Clark and Patrolman Charles Becker. Crane becomes *persona non grata* with the New York police by appearing in court to defend Dora Clark. The widespread publicity attendant on this case devastates his reputation, already tarnished by rumors that he is an alcoholic and a drug addict. Realizing that his career as an investigative journalist in New York is over, Crane accepts an offer from the Bacheller syndicate to go to Cuba to report on the rebellion there. Before he leaves for Florida *The Third Violet* is syndicated by McClure and *The Little Regiment* is published by Appleton.

*

1895

*

JANUARY. In the *University Herald* (Syracuse), John W. Sadler notes, "'The Red Badge of Courage' is the title of a new novel by Stephen Crane, ex '94. The story has attracted considerable attention and Mr. Crane is looked upon as one of the most promising young writers before the public by such an able critic as William D. Howells."

1 JANUARY. "A Christmas Dinner Won in Battle" appears in the *Plumbers' Trade Journal, Gas, Steam and Hot Water Fitters' Review*.

2 JANUARY. Crane writes to Copeland & Day urging them to hurry proofs for *The Black Riders* since he intends to start for the West soon. He also asks "if some manner of announcement card can be printed which I can send to my friends" (*C*, 87).

"The Merry-Go-Round," a variant version of "The Pace of Youth," is published in the *Sketch*, a London weekly (Morace 1978, 147). This is Crane's first periodical appearance in England.

[6 JANUARY]. Crane sends to Copeland & Day a copy of Elisha J. Edwards's *Philadelphia Press* review of the syndicated *Red Badge* and points out that another review suitable for publicity and advertising

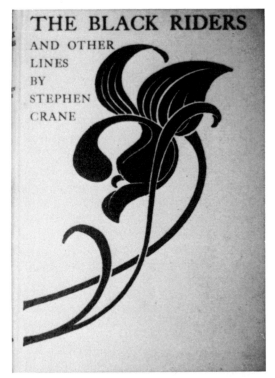

Front cover of *The Black Riders,* 1895
(Wertheim Collection)

might be Garland's *Arena* notice of *Maggie.* He comments: "I have a good many notices but none of them are particular. Most of them call me a prominent youth" (*C,* 88).

6 JANUARY. The *New York Press* prints Crane's sketch "A Lovely Jag in a Crowded Car."

EARLY JANUARY. Crane meets Nellie Crouse, a prim, thoroughly conventional young woman from Akron, Ohio, at a tea given by Lucius Button in his New York City apartment for his Akron friends.

[10 JANUARY]. Crane asks Copeland & Day to include a dedication in the book, "*To Hamlin Garland.*" He also asks the publisher to send "an exact rendering of the words of the cover" for the designer, Frederick Gordon (*C,* 88).

13 JANUARY. In the *New York Press* Crane relates a legend of spectral visitation on the New Jersey coast, "The Ghostly Sphinx of Metedeconk."

14 JANUARY. Crane writes to Copeland & Day: "I start for the west on a very long and circuitous newspaper trip on the last day of this week. I end ultimately in the City of Mexico. I will probably not return before the book is issued." He again requests information for the designer about the dimensions of the book and the lettering of the cover (*C*, 93).

17–18 JANUARY. "The Pace of Youth" is syndicated in two parts in various American newspapers by Bacheller.

18 JANUARY. Crane informs Copeland & Day that his trip has been delayed for 10 days. He adds: "The artist wishes to know what you mean by the phrase: 'Both sides the same.' in relation to the book cover" (*C*, 94).

[28 JANUARY]. Crane begins his westward journey.

30 JANUARY. SAINT LOUIS. Crane gives Copeland & Day forwarding addresses in Lincoln and New Orleans and again inquires about a prospectus for *The Black Riders* (*C*, 94).

[30 JANUARY]. Crane writes to Ripley Hitchcock giving him forwarding addresses in Lincoln and New Orleans: "Any news of the war story will be grateful to me. If you had not read the story, I would wish you to hear the Philadelphia Press staff speak of it. When I was there some days ago, I was amazed to hear the way in which they talked of it" (*C*, 95).

[31 JANUARY]. Crane writes a playful note to Lucius Button from Saint Louis: "Hello, Budge, I am en route to kill Indians" (*C*, 96).

1 FEBRUARY. Crane arrives in Lincoln, Nebraska, to cover a story very much in the news, the drought and wind storms of the previous summer, having caused destitution and starvation in the extremely cold winter of 1894–1895. The *Nebraska State Journal* (2 February) reports: "Stephen Crane, representing a large syndicate of newspapers of national reputation and influence, arrived in Lincoln last evening, drawn to the state by the distressing special dispatches sent out of Omaha to advertise the drouth [a series of 15 articles in the *Omaha*

World Record (14–31 December, 1894) by Robert B. Pettie on "The Land of the Drouth"]. Mr. Crane's papers have asked him to get the truth, whether his articles are sensational or not, and for that reason his investigation will doubtless be welcomed by the business interests of Nebraska" (Slote, 193). Later in the evening, Crane meets Willa Cather, who in December had copy edited *The Red Badge* for the *State Journal*, in the newspaper's office.

4 FEBRUARY. Frederick C. Gordon sends Copeland & Day a cover design for *The Black Riders*, commenting that "The orchid, with its strange habits, extraordinary forms and curious properties, seemed to me the most appropriate floral motive ['motif'], an idea in which Mr. Crane concurred before he left New York"(*C*, 89n2).

4–5 FEBRUARY. Crane travels west into the drought area of Nebraska.

6–8 FEBRUARY. DAWSON COUNTY, NEBRASKA. Crane is in the area of Eddyville in the north central part of the state when a 24-hour storm begins. Snow is light but a fierce wind blows. At Kearny, a possible model for the Fort Romper of "The Blue Hotel," the wind velocity reaches 60 miles per hour on 7 February, and the temperature range is 14 to 18 degrees below zero on the three days that Crane spends in the region (Slote, 196). Crane views the storm from his unheated hotel room: "Over the wide white expanses of prairie, the icy winds from the north shriek, whirling high sheets of snow and enveloping the house in white clouds of it. The tempest forces fine stinging flakes between the rattling sashes of the window that fronts the storm. The air has remained gloomy the entire day. From other windows can be seen the snowflakes fleeing into the south, traversing as level a line as bullets, speeding like the wind" (*Works*, 8: 415).

9 OR 10 FEBRUARY. Crane returns to Lincoln. He interviews Governor Holcomb and writes his dispatch, "Nebraska's Bitter Fight for Life," describing the windstorms of the previous summer, the drought, and the blizzards in the western portion of the state. In response to the question "How did you get along?" a farmer in Lincoln County who has received no aid responds, "Don't git along, stranger. Who the hell told you I did get along?" (*Works*, 8: 418).

EARLY FEBRUARY. Appleton and Company accept *The Red Badge of Courage* for publication. Crane asks Hitchcock to forward the manuscript to him in New Orleans. "The Ms could be corrected by me there in short order. I shall have to reflect upon the title" (*C*, 97).

[12 FEBRUARY]. Crane writes to Clarence Loomis Peaslee: "As far as myself and my own meagre success are concerned, I began the war with no talent, but an ardent admiration and desire. I had to build up. I always want to be unmistakable. That to my mind is good writing. There is a great deal of labor connected with literature. I think that is the hardest thing about it. There is nothing to respect in art, save one's own opinion of it" (*C*, 97).

13 FEBRUARY. LINCOLN. Late in the evening Willa Cather and Crane converse in the *State Journal* office. In an obituary tribute written under one of her established pseudonyms, "Henry Nicklemann," Cather provides a dramatized account of the conversation:

> I had come back from the theatre and was in the *Journal* office writing a notice of the play [*The Passport*]. It was eleven o'clock when Crane came in. He had expected his money to arrive on the night mail and it had not done so, and he was out of sorts and deeply despondent. He sat down on the ledge of the open window that faced on the street, and when I had finished my notice I went over and took a chair beside him. Quite without invitation on my part, Crane began to talk, began to curse his trade from the first throb of creative desire in a boy to the finished work of the master. . . . In all his long tirade, Crane never raised his voice; he spoke slowly and monotonously and even calmly, but I have never known so bitter a heart in any man as he revealed to me that night. It was an arraignment of the wages of life, an invocation to the ministers of hate. . . . He gave me to understand that he led a double literary life; writing in the first place the matter that pleased himself, and doing it very slowly; in the second place, any sort of stuff that would sell. And he remarked that his poor was just as bad as it could possibly be. He realized he said, that his limitations were absolutely impassable. "What I can't do, I can't do at all, and I can't acquire it. I only hold one trump." . . . The thing that most interested me was what he said about his slow method of composition. He declared that there was little money in story-writing at best, and practically none in it for him, because of the time it took him to work up his detail. Other men, he said, could sit down and write up an experience while the physical effect of it, so to speak, was still upon them, and yesterday's impressions made to-day's "copy." But when he came in from the streets to write up what he had seen there, his faculties were benumbed, and he sat twirling his pencil and hunting for words like a schoolboy. . . . He declared that his imagination was hide-bound; it was there, but it pulled hard. After he got a notion for a story, months passed before he could get any sort of personal contact with it, or feel any potency to handle it. "The detail of a thing has to filter through my blood, and then it comes out like a native product, but it takes forever," he remarked. (Cather 1900, 234–235)

14 FEBRUARY. The *State Journal* announces Crane's departure from Lincoln: "Mr. Stephen Crane of the New York Press and the Bacheller & Johnson syndicate has finished his work in Nebraska and will next visit New Orleans, the southwest and Mexico in search of picturesque material for special articles. It so happened that he was out in Dawson County at the time of the blizzard and he felt that he had the material for a thrilling story. When he returned to civilization and found that he could have met a meaner blizzard at about the same date if he had remained in New York, his disgust was copious enough to fill a furniture van" (Slote, 195).

15 FEBRUARY. Crane stops briefly in Hot Springs, Arkansas.

[16 FEBRUARY]. Crane arrives in New Orleans and rooms for a few days in a boardinghouse.

19 FEBRUARY. Crane writes to Corwin Knapp Linson in mock French and German:

> Mon ami Linson: Friedweller die schonënberger je suis dans New Orleans. Cracked ice dans Nebraska, terra del fuego dans New Orleans. Table d'hotes sur le balconies just like spring. A la mode whiskers on the citizens en masse, merci, of the vintage de 1712.
> Frequented I all the time here again l'etoile de Virginitie sur St Louis Street. Sic semper tyrannis! Mardi gras tres grande but it not does until next Tuesday begin. Spiel! Senger to me one letter wrote filled with abuse. Ce matin I write un article sur le railways du South which were all made in hell.
> This boarding-house est le terrible Francais: I have learned to ask for the vinegar at the table but otherwise I shall perhaps to Heaven go through starvation. (*C*, 98)

20 FEBRUARY. Crane moves to the Hotel Royal. He writes to Hitchcock asking him to send the manuscript of *The Red Badge* to him in New Orleans, care of Marion Baker, the Sunday editor of the *Times-Democrat* (*C*, 98).

In the evening Crane sees a performance by the French Opera Company of Jacques Halevy's *La Juive* and on Sunday evening, 24 February, or Thursday afternoon, 28 February, *La Fille de Madame Angot* (Katz 1970, xvii). He later describes the activity of the company in an article, "Grand Opera in New Orleans."

24 FEBRUARY. "Nebraska's Bitter Fight for Life," the first of Crane's Western sketches, is given wide distribution by the Bacheller syndicate.

25 FEBRUARY. Hitchcock sends the manuscript of *The Red Badge* to Crane by express mail (*C*, 99n1).

Frederick Gordon writes to Copeland & Day suggesting that their designer adapt his cover drawing to their own requirements since they were not entirely satisfied with it (*C*, 89n2).

26 FEBRUARY. Crane witnesses the Mardi Gras procession on Canal Street in New Orleans.

EARLY MARCH. Copeland & Day issue the notice for *The Black Riders* requested by Crane: "MESSRS. COPELAND AND DAY announce for early publication THE BLACK RIDERS, AND OTHER LINES, by STEPHEN CRANE. Five hundred copies, small octavo, printed in capitals throughout, on the same paper as this announcement, $1.00. With fifty copies additional, printed in green ink on Japan paper, $3.00." Below this announcement are excerpts from Hamlin Garland's *Arena* review of *Maggie* and, on the opposite page, the first printing of *The Black Riders*, XXVIII, "'Truth,' said a traveller."

3 MARCH. Bacheller syndicates Crane's travel sketch, "Seen at Hot Springs."

5 MARCH. Crane arrives in Galveston at 9: 00 A.M. He registers at the Tremont Hotel and spends the day in separate drinking bouts with the mayor of the city and the managing editor of the *Galveston Daily News*. The next day he writes to James Moser: "My struggle through that day was a distinctly homeric one. To my honor be it said that I didn't mention the managing editor to the mayor nor the mayor to the managing editor, but withstood both assaults with good manners and tranquility. If any man hereafter says I can't hold liquor, he lies. I am a liquor holder from Holdersville. . . . Galveston is a great town I think, and all heavy wit aside I am deeply indebted to you for introducing me to such a royal good fellow as Sam Penland" (Catalogue 38, James Cummins, Bookseller, New York City).

7 MARCH. The *Galveston Daily News* welcomes Crane to the city (Katz 1970, xviii). He is extended the privileges of the Aziola Club for 10 days (Admission card, NNC). Crane concludes that Galveston is lacking in distinction and labors to complete a dispatch that he does not send. Nevertheless, "Galveston, Texas, in 1895"(*Works*, 8: 474–479) reveals that, as in San Antonio, he is impressed by the rapid modern-

ization or Easternization of the West that underlies the ironic themes of "The Blue Hotel"and "The Bride Comes to Yellow Sky."

8 MARCH. Crane advises Hitchcock that he returned the manuscript of *The Red Badge* from New Orleans. Sardonically, he adds: "I made a great number of small corrections. As to the name I am unable to see what to do with it unless the word 'Red' is cut out perhaps. That would shorten it" (*C*, 100).

9 MARCH. GALVESTON. Crane writes to Copeland & Day to tell them that he likes the brochure for *The Black Riders* (*C*, 100).

12 MARCH. Crane arrives in San Antonio. He writes a humorous letter from the Mahncke Hotel, jesting with Button about "a most intolerable duffer" from Button's hometown, Akron, Ohio, whom he had met in New Orleans. He tells Button, "I am off for Mexico tonight," but his departure is delayed (*C*, 100–101).

13–16 MARCH. Crane tours San Antonio, admiring both its modern and historical districts. In a dispatch not published until 1899 he describes events leading to the Battle of the Alamo, commenting upon the "strange inverted courage" of a man who declines to die with his comrades (*Works*, 8: 472).

15 MARCH. NEW YORK CITY. The *New York Times*, under the headline "Stewart Suit Dismissed," reports that Donald William Stewart has unsuccessfully attempted to collect damages from Ferris S. Thompson, grandson of the founder of the Chase National Bank, for alienating the affections of his wife, Cora:

> An end was made yesterday to a suit that promised a sensational trial. The plaintiff in the suit was Donald Stewart, who sought to recover $50,000 damages from Ferris S. Thompson, the young millionaire, for alienating the affections of Mrs. Stewart, generally known in this city, Paris, and London as "Lady" Stewart. . . . Ferris Thompson on the death of his father was left about $5,000,000, much of which he is said to have scattered far and wide. He made several trips to Europe with "Lady" Stewart, and made her presents of many valuable articles, including a house in this city and numerous horses and carriages. While he was in Paris with the woman some time ago, it is said that he left her for an actress, and his former companion stabbed him in the arm. His mother then went on to France and brought her son home.

17 MARCH. Crane leaves San Antonio by train to Laredo (Railway passenger ticket, NNC).

[19 MARCH]. Crane arrives in Mexico City and registers in the Hotel Iturbide.

21 MARCH. JACKSONVILLE. Cora E. Taylor leases a boardinghouse at the corner of Jefferson and Ashley Streets known as the Hotel de Dreme, after its owner, Ethel Dreme (Friedmann 1989, 10).

22 MARCH. The Bacheller syndicate sends Crane another check for expenses (*C*, 102).

24 MARCH. "Grand Opera in New Orleans" is syndicated by Bacheller.

25 MARCH. Samuel M. Penland writes to James Moser from Galveston: "The quiet demeanor and unobtrusive manner of Mr. Stephen Crane together with his impressive countenance made him a special mark of interest to several of my friends to whom I had the pleasure of introducing him. His stay with us was altogether agreeable from our point of view and we anticipate with great interest his expected return from the City of Mexico" (Catalogue 38, James Cummins, Bookseller, New York City).

30 MARCH. Crane writes to Wickham Young that he is planning to ascend Popocatepetl (*C*, 102).

APRIL–MAY. Crane observes street life in Mexico City and makes forays into the surrounding countryside gathering background material for his dispatches and such later stories as "One Dash—Horses," "The Wise Men," "The Five White Mice," and "A Man and Some Others." In an untitled sketch unpublished in his lifetime Crane observes the squalor and impassivity of the Mexican lower classes and contrasts them with American slum dwellers: "The people of the slums of our own cities fill a man with awe. That vast army with its countless faces immovably cynical, that vast army that silently confronts eternal defeat, it makes one afraid. One listens for the first thunder of the rebellion, the moment when this silence shall be broken by a roar of war. Meanwhile one fears this class, their numbers, their wickedness, their might—even their laughter. There is a vast national respect for them. They have it in their power to become terrible. And their silence suggests everything" (*Works*, 8: 436).

MAY. In the *Bookman* Harry Thurston Peck calls Crane

the Aubrey Beardsley of poetry. When one first takes up his little book of verse and notes the quite too Beardsleyesque splash of black upon its staring white boards, and then on opening it discovers that the "lines" are printed wholly in capitals, and that they are unrhymed and destitute of what most poets regard as rhythm, the general impression is of a writer who is bidding for renown wholly on the basis of his eccentricity. But just as Mr. Beardsley with all his absurdities is none the less a master of black and white, so Mr. Crane is a true poet whose verse, long after the eccentricity of its form has worn off, fascinates us and forbids us to lay the volume down until the last line has been read. Even in the most fantastic of his conceits there are readily to be found a thought and a meaning. In fact, if Walt Whitman had been caught young and subjected to aesthetic influences, it is likely that he would have mellowed his barbaric yawp to some such note as that which sounds in the poems that are now before us.

An article on Crane's achievements and aspirations in the *Bookman,* accompanied by a reproduction of a black-and-white sketch of him by David Ericson, observes that "Stephen Crane is not yet twenty-four years old, but competent critics aver that his command of the English language is such as to raise the highest hopes for his future career. The impression he makes on his literary co-workers is that he is a young man of almost unlimited resource. The realism of his *Maggie*—a story that might have taken greater hold on the public than even *Chimmie Fadden,* had the publishers been less timid—is of that daring and terrible directness which in its iconoclasm is the very characteristic of rugged undisciplined strength in a youth of genius." *The Red Badge of Courage* is forthcoming from Appleton, and "among other manuscripts which are now in the publishers' hands is one entitled *A Woman Without Weapons* [an early title for *George's Mother*]. It is a story of New York life, like *Maggie,* but its scenes are laid on the borderland of the slums, and not down in the Devil's Row and Rum Alley."

1 MAY. BOSTON. Copeland & Day send Crane three copies of *The Black Riders* (*C,* 103).

3 MAY. Deposit copy of *The Black Riders* is made in the Library of Congress.

11 MAY. Publication of *The Black Riders* is announced in *Publishers' Weekly.* Five hundred copies of the trade edition are issued, with an adaptation of Gordon's orchid design on the front and rear covers.

There is also a printing of 50 copies in green ink on Japan paper with a special binding, a few of these bound in white vellum stamped in gold. The poems are printed entirely in capitals. The distinctive design of the book is to elicit almost as much comment from reviewers as its contents.

The *Chicago Daily Inter-Ocean* comments upon *The Black Riders*: "The most remarkable thing about this neatly printed little volume is the amount of blank paper—six, eight, and ten lines crowd the bulk of the pages. But after reading, you may well be glad that it is so. There is not a line of poetry from the opening to the closing page. Whitman's "Leaves of Grass" were luminous in comparison. Poetic lunacy would be a better name for the book" (Ferrara and Dossett, 168).

15 MAY. Crane leaves Mexico City on his return journey to New York City (Hotel Iturbide invoice for room rental, 14 May, NNC).

17 OR 18 MAY. Crane returns to New York City. He rooms with Nelson Greene at the old Art Students' League building for some two weeks. He meets Greene's model, Gertrude Selene, who becomes the prototype for Florinda in *The Third Violet* (Greene, 10). In Greene's studio he writes one of the Civil War stories of *The Little Regiment*, "A Grey Sleeve" (Wertheim 1976b, 52). "A Mystery of Heroism" is also probably written about this time.

MID-MAY. Crane joins the Lantern (alternatively spelled "Lanthorn" or "Lanthorne") Club organized by a group of young writers and journalists including Post Wheeler, Edward Marshall, Richard Watson Gilder, Irving Bacheller, and Willis Brooks Hawkins. The club is located in a shanty on the roof of an old house on William Street near the Brooklyn Bridge. It is decorated as a ship's cabin with lanterns, and an old ship's lantern hangs outside the door. According to Bacheller, the club's president,

> The shanty on the roof was occupied by an old Dutchman, who gladly gave up possession for the sum of $50. Then the organizers, among whom was Stephen Crane, employed a cook and fitted up the shanty so that it looked like a ship's cabin. There, far above the madding crowd, the "Lanthornes" held high intellectual revels. A luncheon was served every day, and the members let their hair grow long and their minds grow high. Every Saturday night they held a literary banquet. Each week some member of the club was assigned to write a story, and it was read at the dinner. Encomium and favorable criticism were prohibited. After the

The Lantern Club, William Street, New York City
(Syracuse University)

reading of the story the members jumped upon it as hard as they could, pointed out the flaws in it and pooh-poohed it generally, if possible. The highest tribute that a story could receive was complete silence. That was the best any writer ever got. (Bacheller 1901, 33)

19 MAY. Bacheller syndicates a Mexico City sketch under various headlines in which Crane cautions against buying from street vendors, especially those selling opals, who are "particularly seductive. They polish their wares and boil them in oil and do everything to give them a false quality" (*Works*, 8: 443). Crane evidently was taken in by this scam, for shortly after his return he visited Corwin Linson's studio, and "from his pocket he handed me a half dozen or more opals, with the lambent flame of sunsets in their depths. He freely gave me the choice of the lot" (Linson 1958, 88–89).

[Crane himself was not above an occasional fraud, such as padding his expense account. Nelson Greene recalls that shortly after Crane's return from Mexico

> he had been given an expense fund by Bacheller and he was fussed up about an accounting. He had to give his swindle sheet to Bacheller one day and he asked me to go to the [Lantern] Club with him that noon. I went down and we had a good feed but otherwise it was dull. Crane's razor like mind was out of whack with the very obvious fellows there and I noticed how shrewdly he kept himself tuned down to their level.
> The swindle sheet came out and was discussed. Then Crane pulled out a big gun which he said was one of the considerable expense items.
> I blurted out—
> "Why Steve, that's just like Doc Biggs' gun."
> Crane merely said that it was one of his expenses and things went along all right.
> On the way up on the 3rd Ave. L., Crane busted out—
> "You damned fool. Why did you want to try to queer me like that. I borrowed the gun from Doc to pad out my expense account." (Wertheim 1976b, 52)]

22 MAY. "The Voice of the Mountain" is syndicated by Bacheller, but only one newspaper appearance, in the *Nebraska State Journal*, has been observed (*Works*, 8: 794–795). Crane's two other Mexican fables, "How the Donkey Lifted the Hills" (6 June) and "The Victory of the Moon" (24 July), also syndicated by Bacheller, appeared in at least two newspapers, the *Nebraska State Journal* and the *New York Commercial Advertiser* (*Works*, 8: 795–797; Monteiro and Eppard, 74).

26 MAY. NEW YORK CITY. Crane inscribes a copy of *The Black Riders* for Curtis Brown, Sunday editor of the *New York Press* (*C*, 103).

8 JUNE. THE HARTWOOD CLUB. Crane writes to Copeland & Day asking for sales figures on *The Black Riders*. He is pleased that the book is "making some stir" (*C*, 104).

In *Harper's Weekly* William Dean Howells says that the "tough" dialect of E. W. Townsend's Chimmie Fadden stories "had been anticipated by Mr. Stephen Crane in a story called 'Maggie, a Girl of the Streets,' which was printed some years ago, but could not be said to have been published, so wholly did it fail of recognition. There was reason for this in its grim, not to say grimy truth, and in the impossibility to cultured ears of a parlance whose texture is so largely profanity. All its conscience and all its art could not save it, and it will probably remain unknown, but it embodied perhaps the best tough dialect which has yet found its way into print."

9 JUNE. The *New York Tribune* dismisses *The Black Riders* as "so much trash."

11 JUNE. Elbert Hubbard sends Crane the first issue of his monthly little magazine, the *Philistine*, subtitled *A Periodical of Protest*, and asks him for a contribution (*C*, 109). The "protest" is against such editors as Howells of *Harper's*, Gilder of the *Century*, and McClure of *McClure's Magazine* who had become arbiters of literary taste. The *Philistine* is nominally edited from its second issue through January 1896 by Henry Persons Taber. Although Taber insists that the periodical "for seven months was under my editorial direction—mine and no other" ("Chant after Battle," XIV—4. Unpublished manuscript, NSyU), Hubbard's guiding hand is evident from the beginning. Published in East Aurora, New York, the first three issues of the *Philistine* are hand-set and printed by Taber. The June *Philistine* reprints "I saw a man pursuing the horizon" and contains Hubbard's review of *The Black Riders*: "Messrs. Copeland & Day of Boston recently published for Mr. Stephen Crane a book which he called 'The Black Riders.' I don't know why; the riders might have as easily been green or yellow or baby-blue for all the book tells about them, and I think the title 'The Pink Rooters' ["The Pink Roosters"] would have been better, but it doesn't matter."

17 JUNE. Crane signs a contract with D. Appleton and Company to publish *The Red Badge of Courage*. He agrees to a royalty of 10 percent paid annually. No provision is made for foreign rights, and no payments at all are to be made until Appleton's total publication costs are met (InU).

28 JUNE. NEW YORK CITY. Crane inscribes a copy of *The Black Riders* to Gordon Pike (*C*, 110).

[Henry McBride recalls that Crane

dined regularly every night for two or three years with a certain coterie which had managed to incorporate a little bit of France into a dingy but quite clean tenement somewhere in the Thirtieth Streets west of Broadway. This coterie revolved around the Pike brothers, two husky giants built on the style of our modern professional football players. Both I think were architects, and Charley Pike, the elder of the two, had gained a certain prestige among his fellows because Charles Dana Gibson had featured him in drawings illustrating art-student life in Paris, just then published in the *Century Magazine*. Both the Pikes were rollicking, good-natured, social types, always the center of a crowd wherever they were; and not long after their return from abroad—homesick for Paris, the café evenings and the good food—they somehow found two oldish French peasant women and persuaded them to cook a dinner which they guaranteed should be for twelve every night; and if any of the promised twelve customers failed to show up they would be paid for just the same. . . . We ate in the kitchen which was one flight down from the street in the rear with windows giving upon an area-way, the two cooks plumping the dishes hot from the range directly upon our very plates. It was great fun. Who the convives were I don't completely recall. I still remember, in addition to the Pike boys and Stephen Crane, only my two especial friends, Edward S. Hamilton and Gustave Verbeek, but most of the twelve were artists. . . . At the conclusion of dinner the dishes were taken away and the Pike boys and Stephen Crane invariably threw dice for unpretentious stakes. The French hostesses, being French, showed no aversion to calling it an evening and were never in a hurry about shooing us out. (McBride, 46)]

30 JUNE. Crane comments on high prices and poor living conditions in Mexico in a syndicated column, "Free Silver Down in Mexico."

[JUNE]. Crane offers Copeland & Day his Sullivan County stories, which he characterizes as "eight little grotesque tales of the woods which I wrote when I was clever" (*C*, 111).

JUNE–JULY. Crane rooms with Charles J. Pike, Nelson Greene, and other artist and illustrator friends in New York City, making occasional excursions to Port Jervis and Hartwood. His mailing address is the Lantern Club.

JULY. *Munsey's Magazine* condemns the free verse form of *The Black Riders*: "Mr. Crane has thoughts. We are finding fault with him because they are not put into frank prose. Is this poetry?"

The *Philistine* parodies Crane's poetry under the title of "THE SPOTTED SPRINTER":

> After the Manner of Mr. Steamin' Stork.
>
> I saw a man making a fool of himself;
> He was writing a poem,
> Scratch, scratch, scratch, went his pen,
> "Go 'way, Man," says I; "you can't do it."
> He picked up a handful of red devils and

Threw them at my head.
"You infernal liar," he howled,
"I can write poetry with my toes!"
I was disquieted. I turned and
Ran like a Blue Streak for the Horizon,
Yelling Bloody Murder.
When I got there I
Bit a piece out of it
And lay down on my stomach and
Thought.
And breathed hard.

Current Literature quotes Crane's inscription to the Reverend Thomas Dixon, written on a copy of *Maggie* shortly before Crane departed on his Western trip (*C,* 96). Also mentioned is the Bacheller serialization of *The Red Badge* and its forthcoming publication by Appleton. *Current Literature* repeats the announcement in the May *Bookman* that a Crane manuscript entitled "A Woman Without Weapons" is under consideration by a publisher.

[EARLY JULY]. Crane writes to Lily Brandon Munroe in Washington, D.C., that Copeland & Day have agreed to publish his Sullivan County stories but that only she has copies of them. He asks that she send him the copies (*C,* 112).

10 JULY. Crane acknowledges with gratitude his appointment as an honorary member of the Aziola Club in Galveston, Texas (*C,* 112).

MID-JULY. Crane anxiously inquires of Hamlin Garland whether he minds that *The Black Riders* was dedicated to him without his permission (*C,* 113–114).

20 JULY. Elbert Hubbard acknowledges receipt of two poems, "The chatter of a death-demon from a tree-top" and "Each small gleam was a voice." He asks Crane to contribute these poems without pay (*C,* 114–115), demonstrating what Frank Noxon called "the Fra's democratic prejudice against royalties" (Noxon, 9).

21 JULY. Bacheller syndicates Crane's dispatch describing his train ride from San Antonio to Mexico City under various headlines such as "Stephen Crane in Mexico" and "Ancient Capital of Montezuma." The geographical features of this trip are later incorporated into "The Bride Comes to Yellow Sky" and "A Man and Some Others."

LATE JULY. Hubbard writes to Crane making an offer (not fulfilled) to place a full-page advertisement for *The Red Badge* in the September issue of the *Philistine*. He comments on his reaction to Crane's poetry:

> I do not confess to an unqualified liking for your work. When you hand me the book I am grown suddenly blind. It rather appeals to my nerves than to my reason—it gives me a thrill. Your work is of a kind so charged with electricity that it cannot be handled. It is all live wire. It eludes all ordinary criticism and it escapes before one can apply his Harvard Rhetorical Test. What is left? I'll tell you, we can stand off and hoot—if we have columns to fill we can fill them with plain hoot. Your lines show too much individuality to pass by and so we laugh and work the feeble joke. Thank God for the feeble joke! It fills in many an awkward pause. Those Roman soldiers hailed him "King of the Jews!" It was a great joke and the only thing they could think of to say or do. (*C,* 115)

AUGUST. "The chatter of a death-demon from a tree-top" appears in the *Philistine* with a line ("Lift your grey face!") that is deleted when the poem is collected in *War Is Kind* (1899). The *Philistine* quotes the London *Athenaeum,* which calls Crane "the coming Boozy Prophet of America."

Under the title "In the Heat of the Battle," *Current Literature* prints a pre-publication excerpt from *The Red Badge of Courage* containing the battle scene that concludes the fourth chapter of the novel.

[I AUGUST]. Crane returns to the Parker's Glen encampment in Pike County, Pennsylvania.

1–2 AUGUST. "A Mystery of Heroism" is syndicated by Bacheller in various newspapers.

3 AUGUST. PIKE COUNTY. Crane asks Hitchcock to send him page proofs of *The Red Badge* at Parker's Glenn but then adds as an afterthought that he really does not care to see the page proofs (*C,* 116).

9 AUGUST. Crane writes to Willis Brooks Hawkins from Parker's Glen: "I am cruising around the woods in corduroys and feeling great. . . . There are six girls in camp and it is with the greatest difficulty that I think coherently on any other subject" (*C,* 118).

11 AUGUST. In "A Jag of Pulque Is Heavy," syndicated by Bacheller, Crane characterizes the taste of what he considers the Mexican na-

tional drink to be "like—some terrible concoction of bad yeast perhaps. Or maybe some calamity of eggs" (*Works*, 8: 457).

The first parody of "I saw a man pursuing the horizon" appears in the "Men, Women and Books" column of the *New York Recorder*, reprinted from the *Buffalo Express* (Monteiro 1980, 402):

> I saw a meter measuring gas.
> On and on it ran.
> I was disturbed at this,
> Because no gas was being used.
> "It is futile," I said,
> "You can't register"—
> "You lie!" it cried.
> I did.
> It ran on.

18 AUGUST. Crane asks Hawkins, who is editing a magazine, *Brains*, "Devoted to the Art of Advertising," to help him write the advertisement for *The Red Badge* that Hubbard offered to print in the September number of the *Philistine* (*C*, 119).

26 AUGUST. Crane writes to Ripley Hitchcock approving the title page for *The Red Badge* and asking him to write the advertisement for the *Philistine* (*C*, 119).

Elbert Hubbard writes to Crane to tell him that his poem, "The chatter of a death-demon from a tree-top," which appeared in the August issue of the *Philistine*, evoked a great deal of comment and that "Each small gleam was a voice" will appear in the September issue (*C*, 120).

SEPTEMBER. EAST AURORA. Harry P. Taber sets up a printing plant of his own, calling it the Roycroft Printing Shop, after the seventeenth-century English printers Thomas and Samuel Roycroft. Beginning with the fourth (September) issue, the *Philistine* appears in butcher-paper covers because, as its sponsors quipped, "it has meat inside" (Dirlam and Simmons, 24). This issue includes Crane's "Each small gleam was a voice," which is titled "*A Lantern Song*." A parodic poem by Nelson Ayers of the *New Orleans Picayune* debunks Crane's pretensions to poetry and Hubbard's to protest:

> In
> Praising poetry of William Morris
> And Stephen Crane
> Were you poking fun?

I hope 'twas so:
For You must perceive
That those slashed and mangled lines
Do no more resemblance bear
To true poetry
Than hacked and shattered corpse
On battle field
Bears
To a perfect man,
Whose form divinely fair
Fitly enfolds feelings consummate
Against such lines—
And in fact 'gainst all your verse,
I do
Protest.

6 SEPTEMBER. PHILADELPHIA. Crane writes to Willis Brooks Hawkins that he has accepted a position as drama critic for the *Philadelphia Press,* but he plans to return to New York on Tuesday for a dinner at the Lantern Club to which he has invited William Dean Howells (*C,* 121–122).

10 SEPTEMBER. TUESDAY. Crane writes to Willis Brooks Hawkins: "Dear old man: Things fell ker-plunk. Stranded here in Phila. Dont you care! Nice town. Got lots of friends, though, and 23,842 invitations

Front wrapper of *The Philistine,*
September 1895, containing Crane's poem
"Each small gleam was a voice"
(Wertheim Collection)

to dinner of which I have accepted 2. The Press wanted me bad enough but the business manager suddenly said: 'Nit'" (*C*, 122).

18 SEPTEMBER. PHILADELPHIA. Crane writes to Hawkins that he will stay in Philadelphia for the next few days. He is engaged in writing about his "personal troubles in Mexico" (*C*, 123), presumably "One Dash—Horses," a story he told Linson was based upon an actual experience (Linson 1958, 87–88).

25 SEPTEMBER. Elbert Hubbard writes to Lyman Chandler: "You flatter me when you ask me to give you a clue to Mr. Cranes verse; for Sir, nobody understands Mr Crane, he only makes us feel creepy which is all according to his creed—that poetry should impart a *feeling* and not teach a truth. All scripture is mystical and affords various interpretations, so prophecy of the highest order is always a bit boozy" (*SCraneN* 3 [Fall 1968]: 9).

27 SEPTEMBER. Appleton secures English copyright of *The Red Badge* (InU) and applies for American copyright. Deposit is made in the Library of Congress on the same day.

[An Appleton summary of printings stipulates 27 September as the date of publication of *The Red Badge*. There were two, possibly three, Appleton printings in 1895 and as many as 11 more in 1896 (InU).]

OCTOBER. In *Godey's Magazine*, Rupert Hughes, under the pseudonym of "Chelifer," praises the "great humanity and fearless art" in *Maggie* and calls it "the strongest piece of slum writing we have."

The *Philistine* accuses Bliss Carman of having published poems that are "worse than Stephen Crane's, for he at least has a vague idea somewhere, though he rarely does us the favor to express it in a seemly manner."

5 OCTOBER. *Publishers' Weekly* announces publication of *The Red Badge of Courage*.

7 OCTOBER. The *Detroit Free Press* compares Crane's style with that of Victor Hugo. *The Red Badge* "will give you so vivid a picture of the emotions and the horrors of the battlefield that you will pray your eyes may never look upon the reality."

EARLY OCTOBER. NEW YORK CITY. Crane writes two notes to Hawkins from the loft apartment he shares with Post Wheeler at 165 West 23rd

Street (Wheeler and Rives, 99) asking him to organize a poker party. He is moving to Hartwood soon (*C*, 123–124).

[EARLY OCTOBER]. Harry B. Smith recalls:

One afternoon I happened to be in the Hoffman House bar where art lovers used to go to look at Bouguereau's painting, "Satyr and Nymphs," and I found myself standing beside Willis Hawkins, sending himself to an early grave by imbibing a silver fizz. Hawkins I had known as a member of the editorial staff of the Chicago *Daily News*. He had with him a book which he asked me to read. We had lunch together the next day, and he asked:
"What do you think of 'The Red Badge of Courage'?"
I praised the vividness of the battle scenes but diffidently suggested that the author might have read Zola's "Le Débâcle" [*sic*].
"I don't think so," said Hawkins. "I don't believe he reads French."
"Then," I suggested, "he must have been a soldier to be able to describe battle scenes so realistically."
"Oh, no." Hawkins laughed at the idea. "Steve Crane is just a kid. I'm going to his place to play poker this evening. Come on along."
I intimated that I was not ambitious to lose much money at the national indoor game.
"Nobody will lose much," he promised. "It will be something like the games we used to play at the Chicago Press Club to see who would lose if anybody had any money."
That evening Hawkins acted as guide and deputy host. It was after dark and I was a comparative stranger in Gotham; but my impression is that the building to which he conducted me was somewhere in the West Twenties. We went to the top floor, an extensive loft. In one corner was a bedroom partitioned off. The loft contained just about furniture enough for a small poker game. There were some odd things around, Indian blankets and a Mexican saddle. A curious piece of pottery was used as a depository for tobacco ashes. "Some kind of an Aztec damned thing," Crane drawled, when asked what it was. The supply of Pilsener was plentiful. There was no literary pose about Crane. He seemed to be what Hawkins had said—"just a kid"; but thin, pallid, looking like a consumptive. We played cards till two or three o'clock in the morning and, as we started for home, we passed the window of the partitioned bedroom. A girl was asleep in the bed.
"Gosh!" said Crane. "I didn't hear her come in."
There were facetious comments. "Is it *Maggie*?" asked one of the ribald, referring to Crane's story.
"Some of her," said Crane. (H. B. Smith, 177–178)

PHILADELPHIA. Crane inscribes a copy of *The Red Badge of Courage* to Frederic M. Lawrence:

> Stephen Crane
> and
> F. Mortimer Lawrence, M.D.
> Of a friendship that began when books and
> medicine alike were dreams
> and ended—
> This from one to the other (*C*, 124).

8–10 OCTOBER. "A Grey Sleeve" is syndicated in three parts by the Bacheller syndicate in the *Providence News* (Monteiro and Eppard, 74). Other syndicated appearances follow.

13 OCTOBER. An unsigned review by Edward Marshall in the *New York Press* extolls the impressionism of *The Red Badge of Courage*: "At times the description is so vivid as to be almost suffocating. The reader is right down in the midst of it where patriotism is dissolved into its elements and where only a dozen men can be seen, firing blindly and grotesquely into the smoke. This is war from a new point of view, and it seems more real than when seen with an eye only for large movements and general effects." Similarly, the *Philadelphia Press* commends Crane for evolving "from his imagination purely what strikes the reader as a most impressive and accurate record of actual personal experiences." The *New York Tribune*, however, condemns *The Red Badge*, calling it "a chromatic nightmare" that is as "tedious as a funeral march." The *Tribune* particularly deplores the "anti-climaxes, produced by strivings for grotesque effect, the result of which is to make ridiculous some scenes which otherwise would not have been devoid of tragic power." In parting, Crane is warned that "the exaggerated common-places of Tolstoi, the brutal coarseness of Zola, and the reduplicated profanities of Maeterlinck, are not commendable ideals for the student of literary art. Nor is decadent morbidity destined to win a commanding place in literature."

14 OCTOBER. Crane inscribes a copy of *The Red Badge of Courage* to Irving Bacheller (*C*, 125).

MID-OCTOBER. Crane moves to his brother Edmund's house in Hartwood and begins work on *The Third Violet*.

19 OCTOBER. The *New York Times* reviews *The Red Badge*, concluding that "it is as a picture which seems to be extraordinarily true, free

from any suspicion of ideality, defying every accepted tradition of martial glory, that the book commends itself to the reader" but cautions against "some unpleasant affectations of style which the author would do well to correct." The *Chicago Daily Inter-Ocean*, however, finds the novel often lacking in verisimilitude:

> The volume recites an episode of the American Civil War. Its author is evidently a theoretical soldier, and never carried a knapsack or a gun, or heard the roar of battle. The hero of the story is a young man, who had dreamed he was a hero, and made for heroic deeds, who went to war as a raw recruit, and in the midst of a great battle got scared and ran away, but the next day returned, and proved a real hero in many a conquest.
>
> Mr. Crane tells some things well, but he is too profuse, profane, and prolix. He doesn't tell things as a soldier would, and he doesn't see things as a soldier did, and will make the real soldier tired to follow him. He has small conception of the humor and comradeship and spirit of a regiment, or a great army, and leads the reader to believe a regiment of American soldiers is made up of a thousand dull automatons with a great amount of coarseness, if not brutality. Some of his pictures of the horror of battle fields, and especially deserted fields, with dead unburied, are graphic and impressive. It is not an even balanced book, with its pictures overdrawn, often to the surfeit of the reader. (Ferrara and Dossett, 170)

The Red Badge is also reviewed in the San Francisco *Wave* by editor John O'Hara Cosgrave. Frank Norris is a contributor to the *Wave*, which becomes his primary outlet for publication from April 1896 until February 1898. Cosgrave considers Crane's poetry eccentric, "an issue of the aesthetic craze." He finds *The Red Badge* a powerful and promising but undisciplined work (Morace 1975, 164).

20 OCTOBER. The *Brooklyn Daily Eagle* commends *The Red Badge*, commenting insightfully that "the purpose of the book seems to be to show that courage on the battle field is, after all, not a matter of reason, but of instinct and circumstance."

The *St. Paul Globe* believes that "the book is one which both Mr. Howells and Andrew Lang might enjoy. This is equivalent to say that Mr. Crane has performed a feat compared to which the pasturing of the lion and lamb in company is a mere bagatelle."

21 OCTOBER. THE HARTWOOD CLUB. Crane writes to his Middletown friend Wickham W. Young and asks him to vote for his brother William, who is running for surrogate judge of Orange County on the Democratic ticket (*C*, 125–126).

23 OCTOBER. Appleton sells William Heinemann British publication rights to *The Red Badge* for £35 (*SCraneN* 2 [Summer 1968]: 9n1), without arranging for a royalty to the author.

24 OCTOBER. In an unsigned review of *The Black Riders* in the *Nation*, Thomas Wentworth Higginson compares Crane's poetry with that of Walt Whitman and Emily Dickinson but warns that "so marked a new departure rarely leads to further growth. Neither Whitman nor Miss Dickinson ever stepped beyond the circle they first drew."

[24 OCTOBER]. HARTWOOD. Crane writes to Willis Brooks Hawkins:

The brown October woods are simply great. There is a kitten in the stables who walks like Ada Rehan and there is a dog who trims his whiskers like the late President Carnot's whiskers. Gipsey, cousin to Greylight and blood relative of the noble Lynne bel, who lost the Transylvania so capably at Lexington this season—well. Gipsey ran away with me. What can be finer than a fine frosty morning, a runaway horse, and only the still hills to watch. Lord, I do love a crazy horse with just a little pig-skin between him and me. You can push your lifeless old bicycles around the country but a slim-limbed thoroughbred's dauntless spirit is better. Some people take much trouble to break a horse of this or that. I dont. Let him fling himself to the other side of the road because a sumach tassle waves. If your knees are not self-acting enough for that sort of thing, get off and walk. Hartwood scenery is good when viewed swiftly. (*C*, 127)

[William Howe Crane's daughter Edna recalls:

There behind the syringa bush, he was writing "The Third Violet." Our old setter, Chester, is fully described in that book. It would seem impossible that the people of Port Jervis could call back recollections of us children without thinking of Chester. He was a pedigreed English setter, took many blue ribbons in his time, and was our constant companion and protector for ten years. I dare say that Uncle Stephen had him in mind when he insisted to Joseph Conrad that every boy should have a dog. When Chester was a pup, father was teaching him to lie down at the command, "Charge!" One of his brothers began to quote:
"Charge, Chester, charge!
On, Stanley, on!"
Thereupon the dog was named Chester, and when he appears in "The Third Violet," he is called Stanley. He was a dog with a soul, and I am sure has been in heaven these many years. (Sidbury, 249)]

26 OCTOBER. The *Boston Evening Transcript* finds *The Red Badge* to be "a book with a mighty theme." Unlike many other works of Civil

War fiction, "this is not a story but a study. It stands absolutely alone. It forces upon the reader the conviction of what fighting really means, and it is strong with a terrible strength, which has yet not a touch of brutality."

The *Chicago Post* considers "the action of the story throughout . . . splendid and all aglow with color, movement, and vim. The style is as keen and bright as a sword-blade and Kipling has done nothing better in this line. The rank and file has its historian at last."

In *Harper's Weekly* Howells gives an unenthusiastic review to *The Red Badge*. Crane has

> attempted to give a close-at-hand impression of battle as seen by a young volunteer in the civil war, and I cannot say that to my inexperience of battle he has given such a vivid sense of it as one gets from some other authors. The sense of deaf and blind turmoil he does indeed give, but we might get that from fewer pages than Mr. Crane employs to impart it. . . . The dialect employed does not so much convince me; I have not heard people speak with those contractions, though perhaps they do it; and in commending the book I should dwell rather upon the skill shown in evolving from the youth's crude expectations and ambitions a quiet honesty and self-possession manlier and nobler than any heroism he had imagined. There are divinations of motive and experience which cannot fail to strike the critical reader, from time to time; and decidedly on the psychological side the book is worth while as an earnest of the greater things that we may hope from a new talent working upon a high level, not quite clearly as yet, but strenuously.

27 OCTOBER. The *Boston Times* calls *The Red Badge* "the most realistic and ghastly picture of the late war which has ever come to our notice. It brings to mind with pitiless vividness the reality of the war as it appeared to the soldier, but while the scenes have an intense fascination we feel that they might better fade, as they are doing into natural oblivion, than be brought by the literature of today into such dreadful and ghastly light. Such books do not tend toward amicableness between North and South."

29 OCTOBER. Crane writes to Ripley Hitchcock that *The Third Violet* "is working out fine. I have made seven chapters in the rough and they have given me the proper enormous interest in the theme. I have adopted such a 'quick' style for the story that I don't believe it can work out much beyond twenty-five thousand words—perhaps thirty—possibly thirty-five. Can you endure that length?—I mean, should you like the story otherwise, can you use a story that length?"

(*C,* 128). Only a few days previously he had written Hawkins, "I haven't written a line yet. Dont intend to for some time" (*C,* 127).

31 OCTOBER. *The Youth's Companion* asks Crane for a contribution (*C,* 129–130).

NOVEMBER. The *Philistine* comments: "Why Bliss Carman and Stephen Crane do not write for *Lippincott's* has long been a mystery to me. Some of their verse is bad enough. But the secret is out. They have only two names apiece."

Talcott Williams in *Book News* concludes that *The Red Badge* is the best novel that the Civil War has produced. "In its special field, at describing things as they are, there may be a better novel by an American writer, but I know of none and few by any writers."

Nancy H. Banks in the *Bookman* calls *The Red Badge* "a powerful, but morbid book."

1 NOVEMBER. Crane writes to Willis Brooks Hawkins: "There has been an enormous raft of R. B. of C. reviews and Appleton and Co have written me quite a contented letter about the sale of the book. Copeland and Day have written for my New York sketches and Appleton and Co wish to put my new story in their Zeit-Geist series,

Invitation to the Society
of the Philistines dinner
honoring Stephen Crane
(*Wertheim Collection*)

147

Which I leave you alone to pronounce. Devil take me if I give you any assistance" (*C*, 131).

4 NOVEMBER. Hubbard writes to Crane congratulating him on *The Red Badge* and sending an enclosure in his hand (*C*, 132):

East Aurora N.Y. Nov 5, '95
My Dear Mr Crane:
Recognizing your merit as a man and your genius as a poet, and wishing that the world should know you better, the Society of the Philistines tender you a dinner to take place at the Iroquois Hotel in Buffalo in about one month.
As soon as we receive your acceptance stating the date that suits you best we will send out invitations to 200 of the best known writers publishers and newspaper men of the United States and England.
We have already secured transportation for you and we further beg to assure you that you will be our guest as long as you remain here. We believe that aside from the charming friendly intercourse of the occasion that the dinner will be of very great value to your books and will lead to a wider recognition of your talent.
Pray favor us with an early answer giving date that suits you best.
With high esteem, Dear Sir, we are,

Elbert Hubbard
H. P. Taber.
W*m* McIntosh, Mgn Editor Buffalo News
E R White, of the News
A. G. Blythe Buffalo Express.
(*C*, 134–135)

5 NOVEMBER. Crane replies to the *Youth's Companion*, stating that he is much occupied with his novel at the moment but would be glad to write a story for the *Companion* in the future if they would inform him of their "literary platform" (*C*, 133). They mark his letter as "Ans./Nov 9" (Sorrentino 1984, 244).

[6 NOVEMBER.] HARTWOOD. In a letter postmarked 8 November from Port Jervis, Crane writes to Willis Brooks Hawkins about the death of Eugene Field, who had died on 4 November:

I never thought him a western barbarian. I have always believed the western people to be much truer than the eastern people. We in the east are overcome a good deal by a detestable superficial culture which I think is the real barbarism. Culture in it's true sense, I take it, is a comprehension of the man at one's shoulder. It has nothing to do with an adoration

148

for effete jugs and old kettles. This latter is merely an amusement and we live for amusements in the east. Damn the east! I fell in love with the straight out-and-out, sometimes-hideous, often-braggart westerners because I thought them to be the truer men and, by the living piper, we will see in the next fifty years what the west will do. They are serious, those fellows. When they are born they take one big gulp of wind and then they live. . . .

Garland will wring every westerner by the hand and hail him as a frank honest man. I wont. No, sir. But what I contend for is the atmosphere of the west which really is frank and honest and is bound to make eleven honest men for one pessimistic thief. More glory be with them. . . .

My brother William went down in the Democratic wreck [of the 5 November election]. Poor boy. (*C*, 136)

8 NOVEMBER. Crane sends the Philistine invitation to Hawkins with a mock protestation: "My dress suit took to the woods long ago and my 1895 overcoat is not due until 1896. I have not owned a pair of patent leather shoes in three years. Write me at once and tell me how to get out of the thing. Of course I am dead sore but I think if you will invent for me a very decent form of refusal, I will still be happy up here with my woods" (*C*, 135).

10 NOVEMBER. The Philistines issue another formal invitation to Crane, adding to the list of signatories other prominent journalists, including Crane's friends John Northern Hilliard and Walter Blackburn Harte (*C*, 137).

11 NOVEMBER. Hawkins urges Crane to accept the invitation, guaranteeing that "you'll be togged properly for the occasion." On the strength of this assurance, Crane writes Hubbard giving his acceptance but expressing his desire to remain at Hartwood until he has finished *The Third Violet*, "which must end in forty-five more days but I have it over half finished" (*C*, 139, 138).

15 NOVEMBER. Crane sends a formal acceptance to the Society of the Philistines (*C*, 141). Upon receiving Crane's responses, Hubbard prints invitations enclosing the Philistine invitation to Crane of 10 November and Crane's 15 November response, which he sends to authors, journalists, and others who he feels might confer prestige upon a literary event.

THE MEMBERS OF THE SOCIETY
OF THE PHILISTINES
VERY CORDIALLY

REQUEST THE HONOR OF
YOUR PRESENCE
TO MEET
MR. STEPHEN CRANE
AT DINNER
IN EAST AURORA
NEW YORK
THURSDAY EVENING
DECEMBER NINETEENTH
EIGHTEEN HUNDRED
AND
NINETY FIVE

16 NOVEMBER. Hubbard acknowledges Crane's letters of acceptance and assures him: "I feared you might think we were merely contemplating a pleasant meeting and dinner with you. But it is more than this—you represent a 'cause' and we wish in a dignified, public (and at the same time) elegant manner to recognize that cause" (*C*, 142).

18 NOVEMBER. PORT JERVIS. William Howe Crane lectures the Carroll Post of the G. A. R. [Grand Army of the Republic] on the strategy of the Battle of Gettysburg (*Port Jervis Union*, 19 November).

19 NOVEMBER. Crane writes to Hawkins expressing delight that most of the reviews of *The Red Badge* he has received from his clipping bureau are unreservedly favorable. "About six in the patch are roasts. One is a copy of the Tribune's grind. New York, throughout, has treated me worse than any other city. Damn New York." He tells Hawkins that *The Third Violet* is "two-thirds done" (*C*, 144).

20 NOVEMBER. Crane submits his poem "In the night" for publication in the *Chap-Book* (*C*, 146).

25 NOVEMBER. Crane submits his parable "The Judgment of the Sage" for publication in the *Bookman* (*C*, 149).

The *Port Jervis Union* calls *The Red Badge* "An Extraordinary Work" and reflects upon the local significance of the Battle of Chancellorsville: "In view of the fact that the 124th Regiment, recruited from Orange county, bore an honorable and important part in this battle, checking the advance of Stonewall Jackson's impetuous troopers after the extreme right of the Union line had been driven back and

The Red Badge Of Courage

An Episode of the American Civil War

BY

Stephen Crane

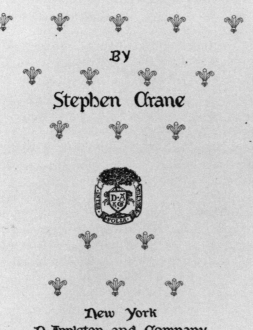

New York
D·Appleton and Company
1895

Title page of the first American edition of
The Red Badge of Courage
(Columbia University)

disorganized by their unexpected onset, the work will have special interest in this locality."

[The men of the 124th New York State Volunteer Regiment, known as the "Orange Blossoms," had their first experience of combat at the Battle of Chancellorsville, and their actions in that conflict roughly correspond to those of Crane's fictional 304th. After Chancellorsville, the 124th was transferred from the Third to the First Division of the Third Corps, and the men then wore the red diamond insignia known as the Kearny patch, devised by General Philip Kearny so that he could recognize the men under his command. Two of these patches that survive today bear the name of Private James Conklin. It was under the impressive monument to the valor of the 124th that still stands in the town park of Port Jervis that Crane interviewed veterans as background for *The Red Badge of Courage* (LaRocca, 108).]

26 NOVEMBER. The first English edition of *The Red Badge of Courage* is published in the Pioneer Series, according to Heinemann records, but the British Library deposit copy is stamped 25 November (*Works*, 2: 248).

In an influential review in the *Pall Mall Gazette*, H. B. Marriott-Watson asserts that *The Red Badge* goes beyond the paintings of Verestschagin in conveying the emotional impact of war. "Mr. Crane . . . has written a remarkable book. His insight and his power of realization amount to genius" (Weatherford, 94).

29 NOVEMBER. Crane writes to Hubbard: "I shall appear promptly in Buffalo on December 19th. The invitation reached me today and it made still greater reason for me to cudgel my brains, as to why you so distinguish me. I shall make a strong effort to appear as a man not altogether unworthy of this. I see that you allowed me liberty in the matter of a speech. There is where you did another clever thing. I would be very bad at a regular speech but I will do my best in some way" (*C*, 150).

30 NOVEMBER. The *Critic* considers *The Red Badge* "true to life, whether it be taken as a literal transcript of a soldier's experience in his first battle, or (as some have fancied) a great parable of the inner battle which every man must fight."

DECEMBER. "A slant of sun on dull brown walls" appears on a front endpaper of the *Philistine*.

4 DECEMBER. Sidney Pawling, William Heinemann's partner, writes to Crane:

> We think so highly of your work—of its actuality—virility & literary distinction that we have been very pleased to take special pains to place it prominently before the British public. I have sent about one hundred gratis copies to the leading literary men of this country, & have personally seen some of the principal London reviewers. I have called Mr. Sheldon's attention to some of the excellent reviews obtained already—Mr. Sheldon represents Messrs. Appleton over here. I hope in the January number of our review "The New Review" to have a special article by the Hon George Wyndham MP on the book—Mr. Wyndham is now secretary to Mr. A. J. Balfour the Leader of our House of Commons, & served as a soldier in Her Majesty's Guards: he has also done very excellent literary work. I think there is no doubt the book will obtain the success it so eminently deserves, & I have thus early made an opportunity to write to you to say how pleased we are to be identified with your work. (*C,* 151)

14 DECEMBER. John Northern Hilliard writes to Crane to advise him that he intends to include him in a series of illustrated articles on American and foreign authors in the *Rochester Union and Advertiser* and asks him to submit a signed photograph and some notes about his life and work (*C,* 153).

MID-DECEMBER. Crane writes to Hawkins expressing trepidation about the Philistine dinner and concern over his lack of adequate clothing: "I bought to-day one full dress shirt and what goes with it. I have a damn fine hat. I have no overcoat save that little gauze one which you may remember. Nor no dress-suit. My brother has—(had)—a pair of patent leathers and I am sleeping with them under my pillow. I've got 'em" (*C,* 154).

15 DECEMBER. Hubbard writes to Crane advising him that the dinner will take place at the Genesee Hotel in Buffalo and that "it will be a very select little affair—only twenty-five—and all men who admire your work and recognize your genius" (*C,* 155).

Crane moves from Hartwood for a few days' visit with his brother William in Port Jervis (*C,* 155).

16 DECEMBER. Hubbard writes to Crane thanking him for sending more poems to the *Philistine*. In a postscript he adds, "I see the papers all over the country are 'chewing' about the Dinner!" (*C,* 156).

17 DECEMBER. Hawkins writes to Crane promising to make up the deficiencies in his wardrobe for the dinner: "I shall express an overcoat to you this afternoon. In Buffalo we will fix up the dress suit question. You bring along your shirt, hat & shoes. I will attend to coat, vest and trousers" (*C,* 156).

18 DECEMBER. The *Sketch* (London) calls *The Red Badge* "a fascinating book" and praises "the almost diabolically clever analysis of character, the sincere sympathy, that never degenerates once into half-contemptuous pity, the amazing—indeed, Zolaesque—minuteness of detail, and the refreshing common sense, that go to lift this book above the level of the romantic war-story."

19 DECEMBER. Crane arrives in Buffalo and registers at the Genesee House. The Philistine dinner in the evening turns into something of a fiasco. According to Frank Noxon,

> there must have been 15 or 20 there, most of us freaks or near-freaks, and on the menu were scriptures by others who couldn't come but admired the guest. Hubbard, still timid, sat at the foot of the table and Taber at the head; Crane on Taber's right; Claude Fayette Bragdon . . . on his left, with me next; and on Crane's right Willis B. Hawkins, editor then of *Brains.* Hawkins borrowed cuff links of me which I never got back.
>
> After dinner Taber rose and began his speech. "Probably," he said, "the most unique—" That was as far as he got. A voice somewhere down toward Hubbard called out "Can 'unique' be compared?" This was the signal. It determined the tone of the festivities. In the best clown and gridiron manner Taber and all the other speakers were guyed and ragged from start to finish. Crane, having the time of his life, was called up, and they had as much fun with him as with the others.
>
> When Crane sat down up rose Claude Bragdon. After 31 years I can still hear the sound of his voice and see the look on his face. "I come here," he said, "to do honor to Stephen Crane, not to ridicule him. I regret to take this step, but I cannot longer remain in the room." The door was on the far side of the table. To get out, Bragdon had to walk around behind Taber and Crane. Hawkins stood and blocked him. "One moment," he said. "I am the oldest man in this room. I know Stephen Crane better than any one else here. I have slept with him, eaten with him, starved with him, ridden with him, swum with him. I know him through and through, every mood. I have taken part in all that has occurred, and he knows I love him and admire him. He knows that you all do. I have come here, like our friend, to do honor to Stephen Crane. I assure you he feels more complimented by the spirit of this meeting than he would have been by all the solemn eulogies that could be pronounced." Crane was nodding his head off. Everybody applauded.

"I am sorry," said Bragdon, "if I have made a mistake. I ask your pardon."

"Pardon is granted you," Hawkins answered, "on one condition."

Bragdon looked up inquiringly.

"That condition," said Hawkins, "is that you turn around and take your seat."

And Bragdon did it. (Noxon, 8–9)

The souvenir menu for the Philistine dinner, "*The Time Has Come*," has on its rear cover the first printing of "I have heard the sunset song of the birches" in capital letters. Among those whose "regrets" are published in the menu are Charles Dudley Warner, Irving Bacheller, Ripley Hitchcock, Amy Leslie, Richard Harding Davis, Hamlin Garland, Bliss Carman, W. D. Howells, S. S. McClure, Daniel Appleton, and Ambrose Bierce, Crane's more distinguished literary acquaintances not wanting to associate themselves with one of Hubbard's promotional schemes by attending the dinner. As McClure expresses it, he prefers to admire the Philistines "from a safe distance." Hitchcock's refusal contains a significant misprint: "I am glad to know that our puppets,/when they prove themselves prophets,/are not without honor in their own/country."

20 DECEMBER. In an unsigned article, "The Philistines at Dinner," William MacIntosh, the editor of the *Buffalo Evening News*, who had attended the dinner, reports in that paper:

Souvenir menu of
the Philistine dinner,
19 December 1895
(*Wertheim Collection*)

The Colonial parlor of the Genesee was the scene of an interesting gathering last evening. The "Society of the Philistines," as the literary men interested in the "periodical of protest" and some of their friends rather ambitiously term themselves, met to do honor to Mr. Stephen Crane, author of "The Black Riders" and some other striking verse, and "The Red Badge of Courage," a book of prose dealing with our civil war which is exciting widespread interest just now. . . . There were 31 in all and every seat was filled. . . .

Mr. Taber presided and acted as toastmaster and Mr. Hubbard from the opposite end of the table made the address of welcome to the special guest of the evening, who sat on Mr. Taber's right. He traced the story of the Philistines, who, he said, had had the worst of it in all times, because a tribe of invaders of their country, who had been slaves in Egypt, "had the pull with the publishers" and the narrative of Palestine told only one side of the story. Later Matthew Arnold, representing the colleges and the culture of England, and having a pretty heavy burden to carry, had bunched all critics and opponents of what he professed in one category and called them all Philistines. He went on to vindicate the apostles of sincerity and personal independence, and closed with an eloquent tribute to the "strong voice now heard in America," the voice of Stephen Crane.

Mr. Crane responded modestly and gracefully, saying he was a working newspaper man who was trying to do what he could "since he had recovered from college" with the machinery which had come into his hands—doing it sincerely, if clumsily, and simply setting forth in his own way his own impressions. The poet made a very good impression. He is a young fellow, 24, with a smooth face and a keen eye and doesn't take himself over-seriously.

[20 DECEMBER]. Crane inscribes a copy of *Maggie* to Elbert Hubbard:

My dear Hubbard: This tawdry thing will make you understand the full import of the words: "it is mor{e}
blessed to give than to recieve." I am very sensible
{o}f the truth of the sentence when I give book of
mine.

I am always
your friend.
Stephen Cran{e} (*C*, 158)

24 DECEMBER. Crane leaves East Aurora for New York, where he spends Christmas (*C*, 158).

26 DECEMBER. Ripley Hitchcock writes to Crane: "Confusion to the printers! I have just received the printed responses to the invitations to your dinner and I find myself set down as referring to our 'pup-

pets.' I used no such word, and I am disgusted." Hitchcock had written "prophets." At the top of this letter Crane writes "Joke on Taber./S. C." (*C*, 158–159).

27 DECEMBER. HARTWOOD. Crane sends Hitchcock the manuscript of *The Third Violet* (*C*, 159).

28 DECEMBER. Crane inscribes a copy of his yet unpublished poem "What says the sea, little shell" to Hubbard's East Aurora neighbor, Dr. A. L. Mitchell (*C*, 160).

In a "London Letter" in the *Critic* datelined 13 December, Arthur Waugh comments:

> A great and deserved success has been made during the last fortnight in London by an American author, in the person of Mr. Stephen Crane, who has hitherto been practically unknown upon this side of the ocean. Now, however, everyone is asking about him; and his "Red Badge of Courage" is being read all over the country. Mr. Crane, moreover, is making no vulgarly popular success: his keen and manly story has won the praise of the best-esteemed critics; and I understand one leading man-of-letters, who is not noted for the excess of his enthusiasm as a rule, has said that he considers "The Red Badge" a very remarkable piece of work in every sense. It is not often that an American novelist "catches on" with British readers, and Mr. Crane's success is the more welcome for its rarity. His next book will be "awaited here with interest," as the current, outworn phrase runs.

29 DECEMBER. The *New York Tribune* vituperatively attacks the Society of the Philistines for tendering Crane a testimonial dinner: "But the Crane dinner redirects attention to the head and front of Philistine offending, the cause of it all, the irrepressible mediocrity which insists upon affronting public intelligence though the heavens cry out for shame. We had thought the 'Philistines' would help to quench the Minor Poet. Instead they give him a dinner and sing his praises to the moon!"

30 DECEMBER. Crane declines a request from John S. Phillips of the McClure syndicate to write a series of sketches about Civil War battlefields (*C*, 160–161).

31 DECEMBER. Crane writes to Curtis Brown that he is "plodding along. I have finished my new novel—"The Third Violet"—and sent it to Appleton and Co., as per request, but I've an idea it won't be

accepted. It's pretty rotten work. I used myself up in the accursed 'Red Badge'"(*C*, 161).

Crane writes the first of his camouflaged love letters to Nellie Crouse, telling her that the sight of an American girl in a new spring gown who resembled her in the town of Puebla had caused him to leave Mexico. He continues in the melodramatic tone characteristic of his letters to her: "The lives of some people are one long apology. Mine was, once, but not now. I go through the world unexplained, I suppose. Perhaps this letter may look like an incomparable insolence. Who knows. Script is an infernally bad vehicle for thoughts. I know that, at least" (*C*, 163).

Crane writes to Hawkins expressing concern about his behavior at the Philistine roast: "I did not drink much but the excitement soon turned everything into a grey haze for me and I am not sure that I came off decently" (*C*, 164).

*

1896

*

JANUARY. The *Philistine* observes that the dinner on 19 December was "a large time, and much good copy was passed off into space that otherwise might have been used to enrich publishers."

The London *Bookman* extols the realism of *The Red Badge of Courage*. In the Heinemann house organ, the *New Review*, George Wyndham, a member of Parliament who had served with distinction in the Coldstream Guards during the Suakin campaign and who would become Parliamentary Undersecretary of War, extravagantly praises *The Red Badge*. Wyndham calls Crane "a great artist" and *The Red Badge* "a masterpiece." Crane's depiction of war is "more complete than Tolstöi's, more true than Zola's," but the novel goes beyond the war story "to recognise all life for a battle and this earth for a vessel lost in space."

The *Bookman* prints Crane's fable, "The Judgment of the Sage."

The *Bauble* parodies "I have heard the sunset song of the birches":

"I have smelled the sunset song of the lobsters—
"A scarlet melody in the chafing dish.
"I have tasted the breast of the canvass-back.
"At nightfall
"The oysters have rushed down me

"With the terrapin.
"These things have I eaten," quoth the gourmet,
"Possessing only mouth and nose.
"But you—
"You put tomato catsup on your salad."

1 JANUARY. HARTWOOD. Crane sends New Year's greetings to William Dean Howells: "Every little time I hear from some friend a kind thing you have said of me, an interest which you have shown in my work. I have been so long conscious of this, that I am grown uncomfortable in not being able to express to you my gratitude and so I sieze the New Year's Day as an opportunity to thank you and tell you how often I think of your kind benevolent life" (*C*, 165).

2 JANUARY. Crane responds to John Northern Hilliard's 14 December 1895 request for autobiographical information:

Occasionally, interested acquaintances have asked me if "Stephen Crane" was a nom de guerre but it is my own name. In childhood, I was bitterly ashamed of it and now when I sometimes see it in print, it strikes me as being the homliest name in created things. The first Stephen Crane to appear in America, arrived in Massachusetts from England in 1635. His son Stephen Crane settled in Connecticut and the Stephen Crane of the third American generation settled in New Jersey on lands that now hold the cities of Newark and Elizabeth. When the troubles with England came, he was president of both Colonial Assemblies that met in New York. Then he was sent by New Jersey to the Continental Congress and he served in that body until just about a week before the Declaration was signed, when the Tories made such trouble in New Jersey that he was obliged to return and serve as speaker in the colony's assembly. He died in the old homestead at Elizabeth when the British troops were marching past to what pappened [sic] to be the defeat at Trenton. His eldest son commanded the 6th New Jersey infantry during the Revolution and ultimately died the ranking Major-general in the regular army from an old wound recieved in the expedition to Quebec. The second son became the ranking commodore in the navy at a time when the title of admiral was unknown. The youngest son, while proceeding to his father's bedside, was captured by some Hessians and upon his refusing to tell the road by which they intended to surprise a certain American out-post, they beat him with their muskets and then having stabbed him with their bayonets, they left him dead in the road. In those old times the family did it's duty.
Upon my mother's side, everybody as soon as he could walk, became a Methodist clergyman—of the old ambling-nag, saddle-bag, exhorting kind. My uncle, Jesse T. Peck, D.D., L.L.D., was a bishop in the Methodist Church. My father was also a clergyman of that church, author of numer-

ous works of theology, an editor of various periodicals of the church. He graduated at Princeton. He was a great, fine, simple mind.

As for myself, I went to Lafayette College but did not graduate. I found mining-engineering not at all to my taste. I preferred base-ball. Later I attended Syracuse University where I attempted to study literature but found base ball again much more to my taste. At Lafayette I joined the Delta Upsilon fraternity.

My first work in fiction was for the *New York Tribune* when I was about eighteen years old. During this time, one story of the series went into the *Cosmopolitan.* Previous to this I had written many articles of many kinds for many newspapers. I began when I was sixteen. At age of twenty I wrote my first novel—*Maggie.* It never really got on the market but it made for me the friendships of W. D. Howells and Hamlin Garland and since that time I have never been conscious for an instant that those friendships have at all diminished. After completing *Maggie* I wrote mainly for the *New York Press* and for the *Arena* magazine. The latter part of my twenty-first year I began *The Red Badge of Courage* and completed it early in my twenty-second year. In my twenty-third year, I wrote *The Black Riders.* On the 1st day of November, 1895, I was precisely 24 years old. Last week I finished my new novel: "The Third Violet." It is a story of life among the younger and poorer artists in New York.

I have only one pride and that is that the English edition of *The Red Badge of Courage* has been recieved with great praise by the English reviewers. I am proud of this simply because the remoter people would seem more just and harder to win.

I live in Hartwood, Sullivan Co., N.Y., on an estate of 3500 acres belonging to my brother and am distinguished for corduroy trousers and briar-wood pipes. My idea of happiness is the saddle of a good-riding horse. (*C*, 166–167)

Crane writes to Elbert Hubbard praising Hubbard's novel, *No Enemy (but Himself)* (*C*, 168–169).

3–4 JANUARY. Crane's Mexican adventure story, "One Dash—Horses," is syndicated in two parts by Bacheller in a number of American newspapers.

4 JANUARY. The London *Saturday Review* comments that it will review *The Red Badge* fully next week but wishes to call its readers' attention to the novel as "the most realistic description ever published of modern war."

Crane asks Linson to forward to him at Hartwood the poetry manuscripts he has left in Linson's studio as well as the contracts for *The Red Badge of Courage* and *The Black Riders* (*C*, 169).

1896

6 JANUARY. Crane writes to Nellie Crouse, sending her a newspaper clipping of "A Grey Sleeve." He comments: "I observe that you think it wretched to go through life unexplained. Not at all. You have no idea how it simplifies matters. But in your case I make humble concession and I am prepared to explain anything at all which I can find power to do" (*C*, 171).

Ripley Hitchcock writes to Crane accepting *The Third Violet* for publication by Appleton and suggesting some revisions:

> I wish you were here in the city for I should like to talk over the story with you. I should make any suggestions with the greatest diffidence, for your pictures of summer life and contrasting types and your glimpses of studio life are so singularly vivid and clear. I have found myself wishing that Hawker and Hollended were a trifle less slangy in their conversation, and that the young lady who plays the part of the heroine was a little more distinct. You will pardon these comments I am sure, for I think you know my appreciation of your work and the value that I set upon the original flavor of your writing. Sometime, perhaps, we can talk the matter over. It will probably not be desirable to publish before March or April so that there will be plenty of time for the proof reading. I will let you know as soon as the style of the book is settled. (*C*, 174)

[7 JANUARY]. Crane writes to Willis Brooks Hawkins noting that he is writing another war story, "The Little Regiment," for *McClure's Magazine*. He is pleased by Ripley Hitchcock's plans to give a dinner in his honor at the Author's Club: "By the way, you ought to see the effect of such things upon my family. Aint they swelled up, though! Gee! I simply cant go around and see 'em near enough. It's great. I am no longer a black sheep but a star" (*C*, 175).

9 JANUARY. Crane writes to John S. Phillips agreeing to go to Fredericksburg to research the site of what he calls "the most dramatic battle of the war" for the series of historical pieces on major Civil War battles requested by the McClure syndicate (*C*, 177).

11 JANUARY. In an unsigned review, probably written by Sidney Brooks, the *Saturday Review* (London) opines that Zola in *La Débâcle* "has done some excellent literary work, but work not so convincing as Kipling's, and work certainly far inferior to Mr. Stephen Crane's, whose picture of the effect of actual fighting on a raw regiment is simply unapproached in intimate knowledge and sustained imaginative strength. . . . Whether Mr. Crane has had personal experience of

the scenes he depicts we cannot say from external evidence; but the extremely vivid touches of detail convince us that he has. Certainly if his book were altogether a work of the imagination, unbased on personal experience, his realism would be nothing short of a miracle." The *National Observer* calls the book "clever, original, and striking." The *Speaker* comments that the novel has "the rare and distinctive merit of originality. . . . A book like this, with its vivid picture of the realities of war, and of the way in which the heroic strife affects the individual combatants, is more likely to cool the blood of the Jingo, on whichever side of the Atlantic he may be found, than a hundred sermons or tracts from the Peace Society."

In the *Literary World* John D. Barry chides his countrymen for being slow to recognize Crane's literary merit: "I cannot think of the case of another American writer who was accepted as a man of consequence in England before winning marked recognition in his own country, and I doubt if Mr. Crane's recent experience has a precedent."

12 JANUARY. Crane writes to Nellie Crouse:

> For my own part, I am minded to die in my thirty-fifth year. I think that is all I care to stand. I dont like to make wise remarks on the aspect of life but I will say that it doesn't strike me as particularly worth the trouble. The final wall of the wise man's thought however is Human Kindness of course. If the road of disappointment, grief, pessimism, is followed far enough, it will arrive there. Pessimism itself is only a little, little way, and moreover it is ridiculously cheap. The cynical mind is an uneducated thing. Therefore do I strive to be as kind and as just as may be to those about me and in my meagre success at it, I find the solitary pleasure of life. (*C*, 180)

In the evening Crane leaves Hartwood for New York City to confer with S. S. McClure about the proposed battle sketches and *The Little Regiment* stories and with Ripley Hitchcock about *The Third Violet*.

AFTER 13 JANUARY. Crane travels to northern Virginia to study the Civil War battlefields.

BEFORE 24 JANUARY. Crane returns to New York City.

24 JANUARY. Crane attends a dinner at the Lantern Club; he is toasted by Irving Bacheller.

25 JANUARY. In *Harper's Weekly* Howells criticizes the "unbroken pha-
lanxes of small capitals" and the free verse form of *The Black Riders.*

Crane visits the offices of Appleton and Company and reads English reviews of *The Black Riders* and *The Red Badge of Courage* (*C,*
187). Probably on this visit an agreement is reached for Appleton to
reissue *Maggie* in a revised form.

26 JANUARY. Under the headline "Stephen Crane's Triumph," Harold
Frederic reports in the *New York Times* on the success of *The Red
Badge* in England:

> The first one [Henry James] who mentioned in my hearing that this "Red
> Badge" was well worth reading happened to be a person whose literary
> admirations serve me generally as warnings what to avoid, and I remem-
> bered the title languidly, from that standpoint of self-protection. A little
> later others began to speak of it. All at once, every bookish person had it
> at his tongue's end. It was clearly a book to read, and I read it. Even as I
> did so, reviews burst forth in a dozen different quarters, hailing it as
> extraordinary. . . . and it is evident that for the next few months it is to be
> more talked about than anything else in current literature. It seems almost
> equally certain that it will be kept alive, as one of the deathless books
> which must be read by everybody who desires to be, or seem, a connois-
> seur of modern fiction.

Crane returns to Hartwood; he responds to a letter from Nellie Crouse
that had been forwarded to him in New York. Here, as in his other
letters to her, he engages in considerable posturing in his efforts to impress a prim and thoroughly conventional middle western beauty:

> Most people consider me successful. At least, they seem to so think. But
> upon my soul I have lost all appetite for victory, as victory is defined by
> the mob. I will be glad if I can feel on my death-bed that my life has been
> just and kind according to my ability and that every particle of my little
> ridiculous stock of eloquence and wisdom has been applied for the ben-
> efit of my kind. From this moment to that deathbed may be a short time
> or a long one but at any rate it means a life of labor and sorrow. I do not
> confront it blithely. I confront it with desperate resolution. There is not
> even much hope in my attitude. I do not even expect to do good. But I
> expect to make a sincere, desperate, lonely battle to remain true to my
> conception of my life and the way it should be lived, and if this plan
> accomplish anything, it shall be accomplished. It is not a fine prospect. I
> only speak of it to people in whose opinions I have faith. No woman has
> heard it until now.
> When I speak of a battle I do not mean want, and those similar spectres.

Hartwood
Sullivan Co., N. Y.
January 27th.

Dear Mr Heineman:

I have just read Mr George Wyndham's review and I feel glad to be able to write you that I think it a very wonderful thing. Of course it is difficult for me to speak of The Red Badge of Courage as I wrote it when I was between twenty-one and twenty-two years of age and have lost sense of it's being of any value. Still I am conscious that Mr Wyndham has reproduced in a large measure my own hopeful thoughts of the book when it was still for the most part in my head. As near as a man can do it, he convinces me that the thing is in some

Stephen Crane to William Heinemann, 27 January 1896
(Newark Museum)

ways an artistic success. As far as I know he is the one writer to arouse in me the joyful hope that perhaps the book is good. I wish you would extend to him a serious expression of my gratitude and appreciation. If it were not my own work that was under discussion I would give you many ~~the~~ reasons for my ~~think-~~ ing ~~the~~ the article in The New Review a very remarkable essay.

Yours sincerely
Stephen Crane

P.S.: If you would care to send me two or three copies of The New Review, of January, I would be very glad. I ~~trouble~~ you only because ~~being~~ at Hartwood it would be im-mensely difficult to otherwise get them.

I mean myself and the inherent indolence and cowardice which is the lot of all men. I mean, also, applause. Last summer I was getting very ably laughed at for a certain book called The Black Riders. When I was at my publishers yesterday I read long extracts from English newspapers. I got an armful of letters from people who declared that The Black Riders was—etc, etc,—and then for the first time in my life I began to be afraid, afraid that I would grow content with myself, afraid that willy-nilly I would be satisfied with the little, little things I have done. For the first time I saw the majestic forces which are arrayed against man's true success—not the world—the world is silly, changeable, any of it's decisions can be reversed—but man's own colossal impulses more strong than chains, and I percieved that the fight was not going to be with the world but with myself. I had fought the world and had not bended nor moved an inch but this other battle—it is to last on up through the years to my grave and only on that day am I to know if the word Victory will look well upon lips of mine. (*C*, 186–187)

William Dean Howells congratulates Crane on his English triumphs but adds that he will "remain true to my first love, 'Maggie.' That is better than all the Black Riders and Red Badges" (*C*, 188).

27 JANUARY. Crane responds to Howells's letter of congratulation and expresses the hope that success will not deter him "from what I believe to be the pursuit of truth" (*C*, 192).

Crane expresses remorse for having neglected Hawkins in New York. "But oh you dont know how that damned city tore my heart out by the roots and flung it under the heels of it's noise. Indeed it did. I couldnt breathe in that accursed tumult." He mails to him the manuscript of *The Red Badge* as a compensatory gift (*C*, 189, 189n1).

Crane writes to William Heinemann expressing his gratification over George Wyndham's perceptive review of *The Red Badge* in the *New Review* (*C*, 190).

Crane writes to Ripley Hitchcock:

Dear Mr. Hitchcock: I fear that when I meet you again I shall feel abashed. As a matter of truth, New York has so completely muddled me on this last visit that I shant venture again very soon. I had grown used to being called a damned ass but this sudden new admiration of my friends has made a gibbering idiot of me. I shall stick to my hills.
I think it is as well to go ahead with The Third Violet. People may just as well discover now that the high dramatic key of The Red Badge cannot be sustained. You know what I mean. I dont think The Red Badge to be any great shakes but then the very theme of it gives it an intensity that the writer cant reach every day. The Third Violet is a quiet little story but then

it is serious work and I should say let it go. If my health and my balance remains to me, I think I will be capable of doing work that will dwarf both books. (*C*, 191)

Crane writes to S. S. McClure that he is "getting the Fredericksburg row into shape," a reference to "The Little Regiment." McClure has evidently already accepted "Three Miraculous Soldiers." He concludes, "By the way I would like to go to the scene of the next great Street-car strike. I feel I could do something then to dwarf the Red Badge, which I do not think is very great shakes" (*C*, 192–193).

28 JANUARY. Crane sends a manuscript or typescript of "The Veteran" to S. S. McClure (*C*, 194).

[LATE JANUARY]. Crane writes a letter intended for publication to John Northern Hilliard:

When I was the mark for every humorist in the country I went ahead, and now, when I am the mark for only 50 per cent of the humorists of the country, I go ahead, for I understand that a man is born into the world with his own pair of eyes and he is not at all responsible for his quality of personal honesty. To keep close to my honesty is my supreme ambition. There is a sublime egotism in talking of honesty. I, however, do not say that I am honest. I merely say that I am as nearly honest as a weak mental machinery will allow. This aim in life struck me as being the only thing worth while. A man is sure to fail at it, but there is something in the failure. (*C*, 195–196)

FEBRUARY. "One Dash—Horses" is given first English publication in the *New Review* under the title "Horses," the word "dash" being an American sporting term for a race run in a single heat. Crane himself makes the same deletion in a table of contents he prepares for the English edition of *The Open Boat* (NNC). "What says the sea, little shell" appears in the *Philistine*, "Do not weep, maiden, for war is kind" appears in the *Bookman*, which also contains a parody of Crane's poetry that Hayden Carruth had sent to the Philistines:

> "I saw a man reading an invitation.
> Anon he chortled like a bull-frog—
> Like a billy-be-dasted bull-frog.
> It was a dinner invitation,
> Which accounted for the chortle.
> 'They will have Grub,' quoth the
> Man.
> 'Better yet, Grape Juice; I will go!'

The red chortle died on his white lips.
His ashy hand shot into his black
Pocket.
A gray wail burst from his parched,
Brown throat
Like the scarlet yowl of a yellow
Tom Cat—
The man didn't have the price!
Which accounted for the wail.
I left him cursing the Railroad
Company, with great, jagged,
Crimson curses."

The *Bookman* reports that the Philistine dinner was "a very hilarious affair, at which [Crane] made a speech, a regular Black Rider poem that scintillated with flashes of wit, to the merriment of all. 'Since he had recovered from College,' he had thrown off the sophomoric yoke, and was doing what he could to give the world the best that he had. 'I will write what is in me,' said he, 'and it will be enough to follow with obedience the promptings of that inspiration, if it be worthy of so dignified a name.' In introducing the guest of honour, Mr. Elbert Hubbard spoke of the 'strong voice now heard in America, the voice of Stephen Crane.'"

In the *Philistine* Elbert Hubbard comments that "a whole half column of heavy criticism is levelled against the Philistines by the New York *Tribune* because, as alleged, they 'lauded Stephen Crane to the Skies' at the recent Square Meal. I don't think it's necessary to defend Mr. Crane against the Serious Critic, but one thing may be said in his favor by way of contrast: he knows a joke at sight."

In the *Atlantic Monthly* Mark Antony De Wolfe Howe finds *The Black Riders* "generally rebellious and modern in the extreme, occasionally blasphemous to a degree which even cleverness will not reconcile to a liberal taste. . . . Many of the lines are intentionally amusing, and the satiric note sometimes serves to mollify the profanity. The parable form into which many of the fragments are cast gives them half their effectiveness. The audacity of their conception, suggesting a mind not without kinship to Emily Dickinson's, supplies the rest."

1 FEBRUARY. William M. Payne in the *Dial* notes that "'The Red Badge of Courage' is a book that has been getting a good deal of belated praise within the past few weeks, but we cannot admit that much of it is deserved."

2 FEBRUARY. Crane writes to Hitchcock that he is revising *Maggie* for publication by Appleton. He expresses his delight with Frederic's letter in the *Times* and adds, "I see also that they are beginning to charge me with having played base ball. I am rather more proud of my base ball ability than of some other things" (*C*, 196).

[BETWEEN 4 AND 6 FEBRUARY]. Crane writes to Hitchcock that he is continuing his revision of *Maggie* according to Hitchcock's recommendations and has "dispensed with a goodly number of damns." He asks for an advance of $100 so that he can buy from Elbert Hubbard a gelding (mistakenly called a mare by Crane), to which he had taken a fancy while visiting East Aurora in December 1895. "The price will go up each week, almost, until spring and I am crazy to get her now" (*C*, 197).

8 FEBRUARY. In an article in the *Rochester Union and Advertiser* entitled "The Hideousness of War: Stephen Crane and The Red Badge," John Northern Hilliard calls Crane "a Verestchagin in print, this young man who has revealed the utter hideousness of warfare as no writer has yet done, not even the microscopic Zola in his realistic and sanguinary descriptions of carnage." Hilliard summarizes Crane's career. He paraphrases and reproduces portions of the letter Crane sent to him on 2 January without using quotation marks.

10 FEBRUARY. Crane writes to Hitchcock thanking him for approving his request for an advance on *Maggie* that will enable him to buy Hubbard's saddle horse. He will submit sections of *Maggie* as he revises them, having "carefully plugged at the words which hurt. Seems to me the book wears quite a new aspect from very slight omissions," but he reminds Hitchcock that *Maggie* is very short, suggesting that significant excisions might compromise the integrity of the novelette (*C*, 200).

[Crane's revisions of *Maggie* continued into early March and were more than "very slight," although Crane did not rewrite the novel but marked up a copy of the 1893 edition, which then served as revised text for the 1896 version. A great deal of profanity and many blasphemous epithets were excised; an editor probably turned the remaining "damns" and "hells" into the elliptical form of "d——n" and "h——l" or "h——ll." (Appleton house styling was certainly responsible for British orthography in words like "honour" and "valour.") References to God or "Gawd" were eliminated. Grammar and style were improved and verbal excesses tempered. The most significant change was made at the end of chapter 17, the symbolically compressed chapter that dramatizes Maggie's decline and suicide or murder. Maggie no longer solicits the last two men she meets, and the paragraph describing the "huge fat man in torn and greasy garments" was removed. The first sentence of the final paragraph, "At their feet the river appeared a deathly black hue," referring to the feet of Maggie and the fat man, is replaced by "At the feet of the tall buildings appeared the deathly black hue of the river," a reference to the tall buildings of the final block described in what now becomes the previous paragraph.]

11 FEBRUARY. Crane writes a self-conscious response to Nellie Crouse, who has written him that she can like "the man with the high aims and things" in her soul but not in her heart. He condemns the social lion and affirms, "I swear by the real aristocrat. The man whose forefathers were men of courage, sympathy and wisdom, is usually one who will stand the strain whatever it may be. He is like a thorough-bred horse. His nerves may be high and he will do a lot of jumping often but in the crises he settles down and becomes the most reliable and enduring of created things" (*C,* 201).

13 FEBRUARY. Crane writes to Hubbard agreeing to pay $60 for "Peanuts" rather than the $100 he had told Hitchcock the horse would cost (*C,* 204).

15 FEBRUARY. Crane writes a short autobiographical summary for the editor of the *Critic.* He mentions that he is completing "The Little Regiment" for *McClure's Magazine,* "which represents my work at it's best I think and is positively my last thing dealing with battle" (*C,* 205).

Crane sends Hitchcock the first six chapters of the revised *Maggie* (*C,* 206).

John Barrow Allen in the London *Academy* condemns *The Red Badge.* "The author, in quaint, bantering style, describes some military operations, and presents us with a running analysis of a young soldier's varying emotions during the course of the campaign. It must be confessed that the narrative soon becomes tiresome. A serio-comic effect seems to be intended throughout, and Mr. Crane is no doubt highly gifted with that grotesqueness of fancy which is peculiarly a Transatlantic production; but the humour is scarcely of a sort to be appreciated by readers on this side, and not a few of them will lay the book down before getting half way through."

16 FEBRUARY. Bacheller syndicates Crane's eyewitness account, "The Fete of Mardi Gras."

17 FEBRUARY. Crane sends a copy of *The Black Riders* to William Heinemann. He mentions that the revised *Maggie* will probably be his next publication: "*Maggie* was born into a world of enemies three years ago but I have toned it somewhat at the request of the Appletons. . . . Kipling carried it in his pocket to England once—I have heard. Sort of a private view for some friends. For my own part, I hate the book" (*C*, 206–207).

21 FEBRUARY. "Stephen Crane, Hartwood" registers at the Hartwood Club. On the line below his registration is that of Kate Douglas Wiggin, popular writer of children's books (*Hartwood Park Association Record*).

22 FEBRUARY. The *Critic* announces the forthcoming Appleton publication of *Maggie* and comments on the 1893 paperbound edition, claiming that the novelette, like Edward Waterman Townsend's *Chimmie Fadden* (1895), is coarse but not immoral.

23 FEBRUARY. In the *New York World* Jeannette Gilder disparagingly reviews Crane's career. *Maggie* and Crane's journalism illustrate that "He did not spend much time at school, which probably accounts for his grammatical lapses and for many faults of style." *The Black Riders* "had better be forgotten," but *The Red Badge* shows Crane's promise as a prose writer: "If he turns his back upon the Muse and gives himself time to write prose he will make a mark that it will be hard to erase."

28 FEBRUARY. The *Times* of London concludes that *The Red Badge* reveals "more talent than taste. The inflated style of the descriptions is monotonously irritating, and we are struck by the marvelous dexterity with which the author avoids the use of plain English words." Crane's attention to detail distinguishes him as "the Rudyard Kipling of the American Army," but "We ask if there were no gentlemen among the raw levies of the Northern army, for here we see nothing of the educated students of West Point."

29 FEBRUARY. William Dean Howells writes to Ripley Hitchcock expressing his willingness to nominate Crane for membership in the Author's Club (NNC).

[BEFORE 1 MARCH]. Harry P. Taber and a number of associates propose to purchase the *Philistine* from Hubbard and to establish a new publishing firm. Taber and Eugene White meet with Crane at the Hotel Imperial in New York, and he impulsively promises them one of his forthcoming books, probably *The Little Regiment*, but when they return to East Aurora, Hubbard reneges on his decision to sell the *Philistine*, and the publishing venture is abandoned.

MARCH. The *Philistine* contains Crane's "A Great Mistake," another story about the babe "Tommie," who in *Maggie* dies in infancy. "In the night" appears in the Chicago *Chap-Book*, entitled *"Verses."*

Hubbard's essay "As to Stephen Crane" appears in the *Lotos*. Hubbard asserts that Crane is an untutored genius who caused Howells to exclaim, "'This man has sprung into life full-armed.'" Hubbard finds no false note in Crane's fiction, but he has reservations about *The Black Riders*. He concludes that if Crane "never produces another thing, he has done enough to save the fag-end of the century from literary disgrace; and look you, friends, that is no small matter!"

Quoting Crane's poem "In the desert," the *Bookman* comments that "when we remember all the bitterness of Mr. Hardy's pessimism, his keen, remorseless sense of the ironies of life, the passionate insurgence of his heart against nature's injustice, and the revolt of his soul against this sad, mad world, which seems to have reached a climax in this last work of his, we think irresistibly of a certain passage in Stephen Crane's *Lines* which might serve some purpose if pinned to the title-page of *Jude the Obscure*."

1 MARCH. NEW YORK. Crane writes a letter to Nellie Crouse that he does not complete, complaining about the strain of being lionized in New York: "You know what I mean. That disgraceful Red Badge is doing so very well that my importance has widened and everybody sits down and calmly waits to see me be a chump" (*C*, 207). Apparently, shortly afterward he receives a letter from her advising him that she is about to become engaged, which casts him into despair, and he continues his letter, again leaving it unfinished: "If there is a joy of living I cant find it. The future? The future is blue with obligations— new trials—conflicts. It was a rare old wine the gods brewed for mortals. Flagons of despair—" (*C*, 208).

The *Lotus* comments that "Stephen Crane need depend no longer on a stray poem or a prismatic flash of pen for his reputation. The author of the 'Black Riders' and 'The Red Badge of Courage' has been dined by the Philistines and has been the butt of the sparkling wit of some of our best litterateurs, who do not understand his poetry any

Nellie Crouse, 1896
(Syracuse University)

more than they understand the hieroglyphics on the monolith in Central Park. These same critics can have no such fear of his last book, 'The Red Badge of Courage,' which is free from the obscurity of much of his poetry, and so full of the fire of genius that it promises to be the novel of the hour in the English market."

2 MARCH. Walter Hines Page, associate editor of the *Atlantic Monthly*, asks Crane for a contribution. He sends "An Indiana Campaign" and asks Hitchcock to forward the manuscript of *The Third Violet* to Page (*C*, 210, 210n2).

[2 MARCH]. Crane responds to a letter from an admirer, Daisy D. Hill: "Of course your letter appeals to me. It is the expression of a vibratory sensitive young mind reaching out for an ideal. But then I cannot for a moment allow you to assume that I am properly an ideal. Ye Gods! I am clay—very common uninteresting clay. I am a good deal of a rascal, sometimes a bore, often dishonest. When I look at myself I know that only by dint of knowing nothing of me are you enabled to formulate me in your mind as something of a heroic figure. If you could once scan me you would be forever dumb" (*C*, 209).

BEFORE 6 MARCH. Crane goes to Washington to study the political life of the city in preparation for a novel to be published by S. S. McClure. He resides at the Cosmos Club.

6 MARCH. Crane deposits $175 with the American Security and Trust Company in Washington (Stephen Crane's Bank Book; also used for addresses, etc. [1896], NNC). Hubbard writes to Crane to warn him that Taber and his associates are impecunious: "My friends have started the Opposition Co. But bless my soul they are none of them business men and none have capital. I hear you are going to give them Ms for a book, but look you Stephen! they never can or will pay you a dollar for it" (*C*, 210).

7 MARCH. The *Critic* summarizes Crane's career and prints for the first time the retouched photograph of him by F. H. King.

15 MARCH. WASHINGTON. From the Cosmos Club Crane writes a letter to Hawkins apologizing for having neglected him in New York because of his entanglement with a woman, probably Amy Leslie, drama critic of the *Chicago Daily News*, whom he had met in 1895. He also writes Hitchcock and apologizes for his eccentric behavior: "After all, I cannot help vanishing and disappearing and dissolving. It

is my foremost trait. But I hope you will forgive me and treat me as if you still could think me a pretty decent sort of chap." He asks Hitchcock to send him "the edited Maggie," referring, as in his letter of 15 February, either to proof or to corrected printer's copy, of the revised *Maggie* (*C*, 212–213).

Bacheller syndicates a shortened version of "Three Miraculous Soldiers" and Crane's lampoon of the Poe school of mystery and horror, "A Tale of Mere Chance," which appears also in the March issue of the *English Illustrated Magazine*. In a circular sent to newspapers carrying the tale, Bacheller presents a sketch of Crane's career, concluding: "Mr. Crane is one of the founders of 'The Sign o' the Lanthorn,' a unique literary club in a historic building on William street, New York, the great attractions being 'two fine old fire-places and good company.' He is still an enthusiastic member; and among the many honors heaped upon him of late, none, probably, have been more acceptable than the invitation to be the guest of this club at a complimentary dinner to be given early in April" (*Chicago Tribune; Works*, 8: 800).

An article by Professor Charles K. Gaines in the *Philadelphia Press*, "Rise to Fame of Stephen Crane," emphasizes the two strains in Crane's heritage, the soldier and the clergyman, that had contributed to the thematic background of *The Red Badge*. Gaines had interviewed Crane at the Lantern Club, and his remarks about the significance of Crane's ancestry echo those that Crane himself had made in his 2 January letter to John Northern Hilliard.

16 MARCH. The *Dial* announces spring publication of "Dan Emmonds, a story, by Stephen Crane (Edward Arnold.)."

18 MARCH. WASHINGTON. Crane concludes the letter to Nellie Crouse that he began in New York on 1 March; it is the last time he writes to her: "Really, by this time I should have recovered enough to be able to write you a sane letter, but I cannot—my pen is dead. I am simply a man struggling with a life that is no more than a mouthful of dust to him" (*C*, 208).

21 MARCH. Crane accepts membership in the Author's Club (*C*, 214).

23 MARCH. Crane writes to Hitchcock from the Cosmos Club that he is revising *Maggie* and that he is studying the political life of Washington: "I have been already in a number of the senatorial interiors. But I want to know all the congressmen in the shop. I want to know Quay of Pennsylvania. I want to know those long-whiskered devils

from the west. So whenever you see a chance to send me headlong at one of them, do so" (*C,* 214).

24 MARCH. Crane writes to Irving Bacheller, asking him to thank Charles K. Gaines for his article in the *Philadelphia Press*. Crane is especially pleased that Gaines "didnt try to appear as wise as all-hell. I suppose the American critic's first anxiety is to impress the reader with the fact that he knows everything. No doubt there are many of them that do know everything but then the positive tone grows exasperating at last" (*C,* 215).

25 MARCH. Crane deposits $25 with the American Security and Trust Company in Washington (Stephen Crane's Bank Book; also used for addresses, etc. [1896], NNC).

26 MARCH. Crane writes to Ripley Hitchcock:

> I have not told you that I am beset—quite—with publishers of various degrees who wish—or seem to wish—to get my books and who make me various offers. Some of them are little firms but I think nearly every representative American house has made overtures of some kind to me as well as five or six London firms. I have not thought it worth while to talk much about it and in fact this letter contains the first mention of it, I believe. I have not considered at all the plan of playing one house against another but have held that the house of Appleton would allow me all the benefits I deserved. Without vanity I may say that I dont care a snap for money until I put my hand in my pocket and find none there. If I make ill terms now there may come a period of reflection and so I expect you to deal with me precisely as if I was going to write a *great* book ten years from now and might wreak a terrible vengeance on you by giving it to the other fellow. And so we understand each other.
>
> As for Edward Arnold, his American manager is an old school-mate and ten-year's friend of mine and he conducted such a campaign against me as is seldom seen. He appealed to my avarice and failing appealed to my humanity. Once I thought he was about to get "The Little Regiment," when you stepped in and saved it. Finally I thought of a satirical sketch of mine—an old thing, strong in satire but rather easy writing—called Dan Emmonds—and I gave it to him.
>
> You know of course that my mind is just and most open but perhaps in this case I violated certain business courtesies. But, before God, when these people get their fingers in my hair, it is a wonder that I escape with all my clothes. My only chance is to keep away from them. (*C,* 217)

[A 10-page typescript of an uncompleted sketch entitled "Dan Emmonds," which remained unpublished until 1963, is preserved at

NNC. Because of a significant number of notices, before and after the publication of *George's Mother*, that Edward Arnold intended to publish a novel entitled "Dan Emmonds" (or "Dan Emmons"), including an announcement in the August 1896 Arnold catalogue that *Dan Emmonds* will be published in the fall, George Monteiro concludes that the extant sketch dates from Crane's English period, some time after late 1897, while the "Dan Emmonds" manuscript, now presumably lost, which Crane gave to Edward Arnold in March 1896 was novel length (Monteiro 1969a, 35–36). Fredson Bowers advances the more likely hypothesis that the typescript at NNC is a transcription Cora Crane had professionally made of a "satirical sketch," as Crane referred to it, which represents all that was written of the opening pages of a novel Crane began and abandoned in March 1896 (*Works*, 10: 292–295). What Crane gave Edward Arnold to publish was *George's Mother*. In doing this he violated business conventions but did nothing unethical since Appleton contracts did not bind an author to submit subsequent books to them.]

LATE MARCH. Crane submits "An Episode of War" for publication in the *Youth's Companion*. He stipulates that "it was written for you" (*C*, 220); but although the *Companion* bought the story, the editors apparently found it unsuitable for publication in their family magazine and sold the English rights to the *Gentlewoman*, where the story was first published in the December 1899 issue. "An Episode of War" finally appeared in the 16 March 1916 issue of the *Youth's Companion* (Sorrentino 1984, 244–245).

30 MARCH. Crane writes to Hitchcock that he has given up thoughts of writing a political novel: "You may see me back in New York for good by the end of this week. These men pose so hard that it would take a double-barreled shotgun to disclose their inward feelings and I despair of knowing them" (*C*, 218).

APRIL. Crane's poem "To the maiden" appears in the *Philistine*.

[2 APRIL]. Crane returns to New York City. He moves back into the studio apartment he shares with Post Wheeler at 165 West 23d Street, near Amy Leslie, who lives at 121 West 27th Street (Stephen Crane's Bank Book; also used for addresses, etc. [1896], NNC). He writes to Hitchcock that he is writing a preface to *Maggie*. "The proofs make me ill. Let somebody go over them—if you think best—and watch for bad grammatical form & bad spelling. I am too jaded with Maggie to be able to see it" (*C*, 224).

4 APRIL. Crane applies for membership in the District of Columbia Society of the Sons of the American Revolution (*C,* 505n1). His application is approved on 9 April and officially registered on 11 May (National Society of the Sons of the American Revolution, Lexington, Kentucky).

7 APRIL. The Lantern Club hosts a dinner for Crane. Among the guests are William Dean Howells, Ripley Hitchcock, and Francis F. Brown, editor of the Chicago *Dial.* Crane is introduced by Irving Bacheller, president of the club, and makes a brief address (*New York Tribune,* 8 April). Howells is the principal speaker:

> Mr. Howells spoke of the future of American literature, which he thought was bright. He said that he had critically compared the works of Miss Jewett and Miss Wilkins with the productions of the famous authors of other countries, and that the American stories did not suffer by the comparison. Mr. Crane had taken the right course in looking at and describing men and things as they are. Things had come to such a pass that the American public and the critics undervalued the productions of American authors.
>
> It was an error to say that the American public would not accept anything that had not received the approval of the English, as the success of Mr. Crane showed. It was a further mistake to think that any American who was well received by the English would be welcomed in this country, as many Americans whose works are prized in England are unknown here. To Mr. Hamlin Garland Mr. Howells gave the credit for "discovering" Mr. Crane, so far as he was discovered by any one but himself. Mr. Howells was applauded at the conclusion of his remarks.
>
> Mr. John Swinton took an opposite view of the situation. He declared that over every American writer hangs the fear of the editorial blue pencil, and that not until men dare to be themselves and not the echoes of others can the country hope for a literature that will compare favorably with that of England and France. (*New York Sun,* 8 April)

Walter Hines Page rejects "An Indiana Campaign" and *The Third Violet* for publication in the *Atlantic Monthly* (*C,* 225–226).

12 APRIL. The *New York Press* announces that "Stephen Crane has come back to town from Hartwood, Sullivan County, and is going to stay here several months, taking things easy, chiefly, and, incidentally, writing a thousand words or so a week on a story that he has on hand. Somebody has wanted to know how in the world this original young man conceived so vivid an idea of battle as is put forth in 'The Red Badge of Courage.' He has answered the question for him-

self in the April Bookbuyer in this characteristic fashion: 'I have never been in a battle, of course, and believe that I got my sense of the rage of conflict on the football field.'"

Bacheller syndicates "A Freight Car Incident," a Hemingwayesque Western confrontation story.

14 APRIL. Crane inscribes a copy of his photograph taken at the Prince Studio in Washington to Post Wheeler (*C*, 227).

16 APRIL. In a letter to the *Dial* dated 11 April, Alexander C. McClurg, a Chicago bookseller and publisher who had enlisted in the Union army as a private and emerged as a decorated brigadier general, having fought at Perryville, Stone River, Chickamauga, Missionary Ridge, and Atlanta, condemns what he calls "The Red Badge of Hysteria." McClurg mistakenly believes that the novel was first published in England and reprinted in the United States only after it had received the plaudits of English reviewers contemptuous of American culture and of American military prowess:

Under such circumstances we cannot doubt that "The Red Badge of Courage" would be just such a book as the English would grow enthusiastic over, and we cannot wonder that the redoubtable "Saturday Review" greeted it with the highest encomiums, and declared it to be the actual experiences of a veteran of our War, when it was really the vain imaginings of a young man born long since that war, a piece of intended realism based entirely on unreality. The book is a vicious satire upon American soldiers and American armies. The hero of the book (if such he can be called—"the youth" the author styles him) is an ignorant and stupid country lad, who, without a spark of patriotic feeling, or even of soldierly ambition, has enlisted in the army from no definite motive that the reader can discover, unless it be because other boys are doing so; and the whole book, in which there is absolutely no story, is occupied with giving what are supposed to be his emotions and his actions in the first two days of battle. His poor weak intellect, if indeed he has any, seems to be at once and entirely overthrown by the din and movement of the field, and he acts throughout like a madman. Under the influence of mere excitement, for he does not even appear to be frightened, he first rushes madly to the rear in a crazy panic, and afterwards plunges forward to the rescue of the colors under exactly the same influences. In neither case has reason or any intelligent motive any influence on his action. He is throughout an idiot or a maniac, and betrays no trace of the reasoning being. No thrill of patriotic devotion to cause or country ever moves his breast, and not even an emotion of manly courage. Even a wound which he finally gets from a comrade who strikes him on the head with his musket to get rid of him; and this is the only "Red Badge of Courage" (!) which we discover in the book. A number of other characters come in to fill out the two hundred and thirty-three pages of the book,— such as "the loud soldier," "the tall soldier," "the tattered soldier," etc., but not one of them betrays any more sense, self-possession, or courage than does "the youth." On the field all is chaos and confusion. "The young lieutenant," "the mounted officer," even "the general," are all utterly demented beings, raving and talking alike in an unintelligible and hitherto unheard-of jargon, rushing about in a very delirium of madness. No intelligent orders are given; no intelligent movements are made. There is no evidence of drill, none of discipline. There is a constant senseless and profane babbling going on, such as one could hear nowhere but in a madhouse. Nowhere are seen the quiet, manly, self-respecting, and patriotic men, influenced by the highest sense of duty, who in reality fought our battles.

23 APRIL. Paul M. Paine's parody of *The Red Badge*, "The Blue Blotch of Cowardice. An Incident of the Pursuit of the Insurgents, with Profuse Apologies to Mr. Stephen Crane," appears in *Life*. The parody, which alludes to the developing struggle between the Spaniards and Cuban insurgents, begins:

> Above, the sun hung like a custard pie in a burnt blanket. A Spanish cavalier, muttering mild green curses, stood near. He was stewing the last dish of leeks which his mother had given him before he left home. From a clump of sordid trees two miles off came the happy cackling of muskets.
> "There will be death to-day," said the youth. "Dark-brown death." At this point [the] cavalier's chameleon curse turned to a light yellow, owing to the proximity of a pot of Spanish mustard. (Hagemann 1968, 356–357)

24 APRIL. Referring to ridicule in the press of *The Black Riders* and the Philistine dinner, Howells writes Hitchcock: "I hope Crane, who has not let praise spoil him, will not let blame. He seems such a good boy, and has lots in him in spite of both" (Howells, 126).

29 APRIL. Crane inscribes a photograph to "Kid," Amy Leslie's sister, Sadie Siesfeld (*C*, 228).

MAY. Under the heading "A Remarkable First Success," *Demorest's Family Magazine* prints a letter from Crane:

> I have heard a great deal about genius lately, but genius is a very vague word; and as far as I am concerned I do not think it has been rightly used. Whatever success I have had has been the result simply of imagination coupled with great application and concentration. It has been a theory of mine ever since I began to write, which was eight years ago, when I was

sixteen, that the most artistic and the most enduring literature was that which reflected life accurately. Therefore I have tried to observe closely, and to set down what I have seen in the simplest and most concise way. I have been very careful not to let any theories or pet ideas of my own be seen in my writing. Preaching is fatal to art in literature. I try to give to readers a slice out of life; and if there is any moral or lesson in it I do not point it out. I let the reader find it for himself. As Emerson said, "There should be a long logic beneath the story, but it should be kept carefully out of sight."

Before "The Red Badge of Courage" was published I often found it difficult to make both ends meet. The book was written during this period. It was an effort born of pain, and I believe that this was beneficial to it as a piece of literature. It seems a pity that this should be so,—that art should be a child of suffering; and yet such seems to be the case. Of course there are fine writers who have good incomes and live comfortably and contentedly; but if the conditions of their lives were harder, I believe that their work would be better.

Personally, I like my little book of poems, "The Black Riders," better than I do "The Red Badge of Courage." The reason is, I suppose, that the former is the more ambitious effort. In it I aim to give my ideas of life as a whole, so far as I know it, and the latter is a mere episode,—an amplification. Now that I have reached the goal for which I have been working ever since I began to write, I suppose I ought to be contented; but I am not. I was happier in the old days when I was always dreaming of the thing I have now attained. I am disappointed with success. Like many things we strive for, it proves when obtained to be an empty and a fleeting joy. (*C,* 230–231)

Five Crane poems appear in the *Bookman* under the title "Legends": "A man builded a bugle for the storms to blow," "When the suicide arrived at the sky," "A Man said: 'Thou tree!,'" "A warrior stood upon a peak and defied the stars," and "Oh, a rare old wine ye brewed for me."

A Souvenir and a Medley, the first of three issues of Elbert Hubbard's *Roycroft Quarterly,* reprints Hubbard's essay on Crane from the *Lotos* (March 1896) under the title "As to the Man," seven Crane poems and his Tommie story, "A Great Mistake," from the *Philistine,* and publishes for the first time his playlet, "A Prologue," and a new poem, "Fast rode the knight." The issue also reprints the regrets in the souvenir menu of the Philistine dinner, with a few added, of those who could not attend. The last of these, which did not appear in the original menu, is by a certain Colonel John L. Burleigh: "'It grieves me greatly to think I cannot be with you at the Feed. I was with Crane at Antietam and saw him rush forward, seize two of the enemy and bump their heads together in a way that must have made

The Roycroft Quarterly, May 1896
(*Wertheim Collection*)

them see constellations. When a Rebel General remonstrated with him, Steve, in a red fury, gave him a kick like a purple cow when all at once—but the story is too long to tell now.'"

[Some of Crane's biographers have taken this obvious spoof, wholly in tenor with other jesting regrets in the menu, as an entirely serious, if mistaken, recollection, despite its hyperbolic mockery of Crane's style and the allusion to Gelett Burgess's comic poem, "The Purple Cow" (see Stallman 1973, 181; Levenson 1975, xcii; Benfey 1992, 3). Only John Berryman grouped Burleigh's regrets as among those that "still amuse" (Berryman, 125). Sharon Carruthers, who suspects that Elbert Hubbard may have invented Burleigh, complains that "Berryman did not, unfortunately, state what it was he found humorous about the regret" (Carruthers, 159).]

The *Bookman* announces that Edward Arnold will have

a new novel by Mr. Stephen Crane ready for publication in June, with the probable title *Dan Emmonds*. In this story Mr. Crane returns to the satiric vein of his *Black Riders*. Mr. Thompson, who is Mr. Arnold's representative in America, and Mr. Crane were schoolmates; and a curious circumstance about the renewal of their early association is that Mr. Thompson had lost sight of Mr. Crane since they parted at school, but on the former observing the portrait of Crane in the February *Bookman* he immediately recalled him and hunted him up. Needless to add that a common enthusiasm for the baseball and football field was a closer bond than that usually derived from books. Mr. Edward Arnold arrives in New York as we go to press.

1 MAY. D. Appleton and Company reply to General McClurg in a letter to the *Dial* dated 20 April citing favorable reviews of *The Red Badge* in many American newspapers before its English publication and pointing out that not until the end of November, two months after American publication, did the first reviews appear in England. Nevertheless, following the Appleton disclaimer in this issue of the *Dial*, there is another attack upon *The Red Badge*, by J. L. Onderdonk, who considers the book "realism run mad, rioting in all that is revolting to man's best instincts, and utterly false to nature and to life" and calls attention to the slipshod grammar and typographical errors.

2 MAY. William M. Payne in *Harper's Weekly* congratulates General McClurg for censuring "the monstrous extravagance" of *The Red Badge* and asserts that the praise received by the novel has been "a most extraordinary aberration of critical judgment on the part of writers who should have known better, both in England and the United States."

3 MAY. The *Newark Sunday Call* contains Crane's letter to the editor, dated 29 April, in which he retraces the background of his family in New Jersey. He concludes, "I am about as much of a Jerseyman as you can find" (*C*, 227).

The *New York Press* carries an announcement, similar in wording to that in the May *Bookman*, that Edward Arnold will publish a novel entitled *Dan Emmonds* in June.

6 MAY. Crane fills out a preliminary application form for membership in the National Society of the Sons of the American Revolution

(NSyU), having already applied on 4 April for membership in the District of Columbia chapter of the SAR.

10 MAY. Crane inscribes a copy of the 1893 *Maggie* to his artist friend Charles J. Pike (*C*, 233).

11 MAY. Appleton grants English and colonial publication rights for *Maggie* and *The Little Regiment and Other Stories* to William Heinemann for 15 percent of the retail price of copies sold and an advance of £30 for each book (InU).

13 MAY. Appleton issues a contract for *Maggie*. Crane is to receive 15 percent of the retail price (Memorandum, InU).

15 MAY. Edward Arnold applies for copyright of *George's Mother*.

16 MAY. In the *Dial* Sidney Brooks, who may have written the review of *The Red Badge* in the London *Saturday Review* (11 January), calls General McClurg's letter "a compound of misjudged patriotism and bad criticism."

17 MAY. One of Crane's most graphic Sunday newspaper features, "Opiums's Varied Dreams," is widely syndicated by McClure. The piece describes opium smokers, their smoking equipment, and opium dens in Chinatown and the Tenderloin. Crane empathetically characterizes the people of the Tenderloin as "they who are at once supersensitive and hopeless, the people who think more upon death and the mysteries of life, the chances of the hereafter, than any other class, educated or uneducated. Opium holds out to them its lie, and they embrace it eagerly, expecting to find a definition of peace, but they awake to find the formidable difficulties of life grown more formidable. And if the pipe should happen to ruin their lives they cling the more closely to it because then it stands between them and thought" (*Works*, 8: 370).

19 MAY. Hubbard writes to Crane: "I have Col Higginsons Ms on 'The Red Badge.' It is very choice and exceedingly sympathetic. He makes the point that the book is not written from the patriotic broadness of the great General McClurg but from that of Henry Fleming, and as such is true to life" (*C*, 234).

22 MAY. In the *New York Journal* Percival Pollard, editor of the Chicago *Echo*, attacks *The Red Badge* as a crude imitation of Ambrose Bierce.

23 AND 25 MAY. Bacheller syndicates "An Indiana Campaign," usually in two parts, in various newspapers.

25 MAY. Ambrose Bierce writes to Percival Pollard: "That was a pleasant reminder of your continued existence that you gave me in the Journal, and my sense of it is lively. I valued it, I really believe, more for its just censure of the Crane freak than for its too kindly praise of me. I have been hoping some one still in the business of reading (I have not myself looked into a book for months) would take the trouble to say something of that kind about that Crane person's work" (NN-Berg Collection).

26 MAY. Crane signs a contract with Appleton for *The Little Regiment*. He is to receive a royalty of 15 percent (InU).

28 MAY. An article by J. Herbert Welch, "The Personality and Work of Stephen Crane," in *Leslie's Weekly*, contains a letter by Crane giving an account of his career and his conception of literary realism: "I decided that the nearer a writer gets to life the greater he becomes as an artist, and most of my prose writings have been toward the goal partially described by that misunderstood and abused word, realism. Tolstoï is the writer I admire most of all."

Appleton applies for copyright of *Maggie: A Girl of the Streets*.

29 MAY. PORT JERVIS. On the letterhead of his lawyer brother William, Crane asks Copeland & Day for a financial settlement on *The Black Riders*.

Copyright deposit of *George's Mother* is made in the Library of Congress.

31 MAY. The *New York Times* considers verisimilitude, its "vivid and terrible accuracy," the best feature of *Maggie*. Crane is a master of slum dialect, and his depiction of Manhattan low life, if somber and repellent, is nonetheless true. The *New York Tribune*, however, is unrelenting in its condemnation of the novelette:

> Mr. Stephen Crane in "Maggie" studies New York tenement-house life with the pretense of aggressive realism. He puts on paper the grossness and brutality which are commonly encountered only through actual contact with the most besotted classes. Oaths, drunkenness, rags, stained walls, cut heads, black eyes, broken chairs, delirious howlings, the flat staleness of a police report are his properties. . . . He has no charm of style, no touch of humor, no hint of imagination. His story is one of

unrelieved dulness in which the characters interest neither by their words
nor acts, are depraved without being either thrilling or amusing, are dirty
without being picturesque. . . . The book shocks by the mere fact of its
monotonous and stupid roughness. To read its pages is like standing
before a loafer to be sworn at and have one's face slapped twice a minute
for half an hour.

JUNE. "The Little Regiment" appears in *McClure's Magazine* and in
England in *Chapman's Magazine*.

The *Bookman* states that "Stephen Crane's forthcoming novel, *Dan
Emmonds*, which was announced for publication in June, will not be
ready until the autumn. Mr. Edward Arnold will publish immediately,
however, a new story by Mr. Crane entitled *George's Mother*. Mr. W.
D. Howells has expressed the opinion that this story is altogether the
best bit of work Mr. Crane has yet done."

1 JUNE. The *Lotus* reports that "Stephen Crane is now in the woods
near East Aurora caging blue air, and I predict that with a sympathetic
sky and a red background, the effect of those approaching Lines will
be unparalleled."

The *New York Commercial Advertiser* commends Crane for his objectivity in *Maggie*; the novelette "is free of maudlin sentiment."

3 JUNE. Deposit copy of *Maggie* is made in the Library of Congress.

5 JUNE. Edward Arnold publishes the English edition of *George's
Mother* (BAL).

6 JUNE. Publication of *George's Mother* is advertised in *Publishers'
Weekly*.

7 JUNE. The *Brooklyn Daily Eagle* considers *George's Mother* nothing
more than a potboiler: "It is simply a succession of dull and uninteresting
events. The book means nothing. The writer has simply described certain common enough incidents in the life of the tenement districts,
which do not possess any striking significance." The *St. Louis Globe
Democrat* concludes that "the portrayal of the ignorant old woman's
love for her child is in keeping with Mr. Crane's artistic sense, but what
he would have us admire, in the character of 'George,' as he limns it, is
a problem, for a more coarse, vicious, unmannerly and unfilial brute one
could hardly rake out of the slums of New York. Mr. Crane must not
depend too much on the deftness of his pen in analyzing human
thought and emotions. At least, let him choose for subjects characters

with some pleasing attributes, and not drunken brutes, who abuse their patient mothers to their death" (Ferrara and Dossett, 173).

8 JUNE. Heinemann deposits an advance copy of the American edition of *Maggie*, with the title page a cancellans bearing his imprint, in the British Museum.

13 JUNE. In a column announcing the "Summer Plans of Authors," the *Critic* notes that Crane will spend the summer at Hartwood: He "does not expect to do any literary work this summer—in fact he will do nothing but rest. His brother's estate covers some 3000 acres; and as Mr. Crane prefers horseback riding to any other form of exercise, he can do it all within his brother's gates, and not feel that any pent-up Utica contracts his powers."

Publishers' Weekly advertises publication of *Maggie*.

The *Critic* commends Crane for avoiding rhetoric and denunciation in *Maggie* and *George's Mother*:

> It is such an easy trick of art, and such a convenience to good people who want a definite object of attack, to throw all the blame for our social disorder upon some particular class—the monopolists, the rum-sellers, the politicians, the clergy,—that it is little wonder that such is the course usually pursued by writers who take their themes from the slums. But their books are bad art, and only add to the muddle they profess to depict. Mr. Crane is not yet a skilled artist: he indulges too frequently in needless repetition, and is not always as careful as he should be about the construction of his sentences. But he knows the essential thing in his line of work is to focus the vital facts in a given field of observation, without distortion; and this he succeeds in doing.

14 JUNE. Bacheller syndicates "The Snake," a woodland sketch with a setting resembling Sullivan County.

The *Boston Courier* considers *George's Mother* a portrayal of "simple, coarse, home life, drawn by a master hand." Like *The Red Badge*, the novelette deals with battles, "the universal warring of humankind against its fellows and its vices. It deals with the strifes that the present generation beholds and comrades with. It is only the common everyday tale of the poor, low life of a young man that falls, and of a plain, loving mother who beholds this ruin, and cannot survive the shame of it. But the weaving of it into the web of narration is done by the skillful hand of an artisan whose threads are whole and sound. What if the plane is low? There is something to learn."

21 JUNE. The *New York Times* praises the verisimilitude of *George's Mother.* "Mr. Crane is giving ample proof that scenes of war are not the only ones he can describe with an artist's hand."

25 JUNE. *Town Topics* quips: "I can recall no tale that approaches *Maggie* in the illustration of drunkenness, promiscuous pugilism, joyless and repellent dialogue, and noise. Of course, I like it. Mr. Howells has educated me in realism, and I hope I know a good thing in that line when I see it."

27 JUNE. The *Boston Beacon* asserts that *Maggie*

unfolds a picture that in its sordidness and pathos amounts to a positive revelation. No reasonable person could think of reading the story of Maggie for entertainment, but those who are not afraid to face the realities of existence, and who are willing to look upon humanity at its worst, will find the book a source of edification, if not of pleasure. Mr. Crane seems to be the first of American novelists to go into the slums of a great city with the intent of telling the truth and the whole truth, instead of seeking for humorous or romantic "material." He has drawn a picture that takes hold upon the mind and that in its strenuous fidelity is filled with a potent meaning.

The *Spectator* contends that *The Red Badge* has been admired for the wrong reason by English reviewers. It has been "praised as a novel; we are inclined to praise it chiefly as an interesting and painful essay in pathology. . . . It convinces; one feels that not otherwise than as he describes did such a man fall wounded and another lie in the grasp of corruption. But when we are asked to say that a specialised record of morbid introspection and an exact description of physical horrors is good art we demur; there *is* art in *The Red Badge of Courage*—an infelicitous title by the way—but the general effect which it leaves behind it is not artistic."

28 JUNE. The *Boston Courier* asserts that in *Maggie* "the story of Darkest America has been told in the most realistic way by Stephen Crane. In all the work he has ventured upon, he has rendered the seamy side of modern existence, the real life of the slums, with a force and actuality of description that has not been equalled by any depiction of low life."

[JUNE–JULY. HARTWOOD]. Crane writes "The Wise Men," "The Five White Mice," and "A Man and Some Others" (Levenson 1970, xli).

JULY. In the *Philistine*, Thomas Wentworth Higginson, who had commanded a black regiment during the Civil War, defends the verisimilitude of *The Red Badge* as "A Bit of War Photography":

> No one except Tolstoy, within my knowledge, has brought out the daily life of war so well; it may be said of these sentences, in Emerson's phrase, "Cut these and they bleed." The breathlessness, the hurry, the confusion, the seeming aimlessness, as of a whole family of disturbed ants running to and fro, yet somehow accomplishing something at last; all these aspects, which might seem the most elementary and the easiest to depict, are yet the surest to be omitted, not merely by the novelists, but by the regimental histories themselves. . . . Yet this very point of view, strange to say, has been called a defect. Remember that he is telling the tale, not of a commanding general, but of a common soldier—a pawn in the game; a man who sees only what is going on immediately around him, and, for the most part, has the key to nothing beyond. This he himself knows well at the time. Afterward, perhaps, when the affair is discussed at the camp-fire, and his view compared with what others say, it begins to take shape, often mixed with all sorts of errors; and when it has reached the Grand Army Post and been talked over afterward for thirty years, the narrator has not a doubt of it all. It is now a perfectly ordered affair, a neat and well arranged game of chess, often with himself as a leading figure. That is the result of too much perspective. The wonder is that this young writer, who had no way of getting at it all except the gossip—printed or written—of these very old soldiers, should be able to go behind them all, and give an account of their life, not only more vivid than they themselves have ever given, but more accurate. It really seems a touch of that marvelous intuitive quality which for want of a better name we call genius.

In the *Bookman* Harry Thurston Peck disparages *George's Mother* as a warmed-over potboiler from the period in which Crane wrote *Maggie*: "This is sorry stuff. Even if it were well done, it is not worth the doing; and it is not well done. There is absolutely no reason why it should have been done at all. The whole thing is simply an incoherent fragment, told with no purpose and fraught with no interest." The *Book Buyer* maintains that *Maggie* "is written as pitilessly as *L'Assommoir*, and deserves praise, in a degree, for the same literary qualities," but in *George's Mother*, "the subject seems more suitable for drawing in shades of grey, while Mr. Crane's brushes are full of red and yellow paint."

The *Lotus* quips: "It is rumored that Mr. Elbert Hubbard, self-appointed manager of Stephen Crane, will return to America sooner than he expected, owing to the unfavorable criticism which "George's Mother" is receiving from the press. He will give another banquet for his protege, after which the publishers will put this highly colored story of New York slum life in its twentieth edition. Mr. Hubbard is getting local color for his forthcoming introduction to the book of Deuteronomy in Scotland."

2 JULY. In an unsigned review in the *Nation*, A. G. Sedgwick condemns Crane's impressionistic style and naturalistic perspective in *The Red Badge, Maggie*, and *George's Mother*:

> Mr. Crane has not learnt the secret that carnage is itself eloquent, and does not need epithets to make it so. What is a "crimson roar"? Do soldier's hear crimson roars, or do they hear simply roars? If this way of getting expression out of language is allowable, why not extend it to the other senses, and have not only crimson sounds, but purple smells, prehensile views, adhesive music? Color in language is just now a fashionable affectation; Mr. Crane's originality does not lie in falling into it. "George's Mother" is the story of a degenerate drunkard who breaks his mother's heart; "Maggie" is a story of the Bowery in the dialect of "Chimmie Fadden."
>
> Taking all three stories together, we should classify Mr. Crane as a rather promising writer of the animalistic school. His types are mainly human beings of the order which makes us regret the power of literature to portray them. Not merely are they low, but there is little that is interesting in them. We resent the sense that we must at certain points resemble them. Even the old mother is not made pathetic in a human way; her son disgusts us so that we have small power of sympathy with her left. Maggie it is impossible to weep over. We can feel only that it is a pity that the gutter is so dirty, and turn in another direction. In short, Mr. Crane's art is to us very depressing. Of course, there is always the crushing reply that one who does not love art for the sake of art is a poor devil, not worth writing for. But we do not; we do not even love literature for its own sake.

Robert Bridges in *Life* commends *George's Mother* for its verisimilitude: "There is a similar verity about *George* himself, although he painfully suggests the awful warnings of hundreds of temperance tracts of a very sloppy kind" (Hagemann 1968, 349).

4 JULY. In "Stephen Crane's Stories of Life in the Slums," an unsigned article in the San Francisco weekly the *Wave*, previously attributed to Frank Norris but probably written by John O'Hara Cosgrave, editor of the *Wave* (McElrath 1988, 87–90), praises the impressionistic style of *Maggie* but finds *George's Mother* less pretentious and more

unified and expresses reservations about the depth of Crane's depictions of character:

> I think that the charm of his style lies chiefly in his habit and aptitude for making phrases—short, terse epigrams struck off in the heat of composition, sparks merely, that cast a momentary gleam of light upon whole phases of life. . . . But though these stories make interesting reading, the reader is apt to feel that the author is writing, as it were, from the outside. There is a certain lack of sympathy apparent. Mr. Crane does not seem to *know* his people. You are tempted to wonder if he has ever studied them as closely as he might have done. He does not seem to me to have gotten down *into* their life and to have written from what he saw around him. His people are types, not characters; his scenes and incidents are not particularized. It is as if Mr. Crane had merely used the "machinery" and "business" of slum life to develop certain traits or to portray certain emotions and passions that might happen anywhere. With him it is the broader, vaguer, *human* interest that is the main thing, not the smaller details of a particular phase of life.

In the *Illustrated London News*, Clement Shorter points out that "most of the unfavourable criticism of Mr. Stephen Crane's 'Red Badge of Courage' have come from his own country. Here its merits have been fully recognised. It may be of interest, however, that General Sir Evelyn Wood—than whom a braver man never lived—has expressed the opinion that Mr. Crane's work is quite the finest thing in that line that has ever been done, and that the intuitions of the boy who has never seen war are worth far more than the experiences of any writer known to him, even though he may have been in the thick of the fiercest battle."

5 JULY. McClure syndicates Crane's "New York's Bicycle Speedway," a Sunday feature article on bicycling activities along Western Boulevard from Columbus Circle to the Hudson River.

8 JULY. Crane writes to Herbert P. Williams, expressing approval of the proof text of the interview Williams had with him to be published in the *Illustrated American* (*C,* 240).

11 JULY. In the *Illustrated American* Edward Bright, like a number of other reviewers, assumes that *Maggie* was composed after *The Red Badge* and that Crane's talents are "in a process of degeneration." Bright also echoes other reviewers in acknowledging that while *Maggie* is based on observation of the life of the slums, lurid melodrama undermines its realism: "To change the form of expression, he might

MR. CRANE AS A LITERARY ARTIST.

A FEW days ago I called on the author of "The Red
Badge of Courage." When in New York Stephen
Crane lives alone in an enormous room at the top
of a house near the heart of the city, in the shopping district. The furniture of the room is curiously typical of
the man; a tinted wall is relieved at intervals by war trophies and by impressionistic landscapes. The latter might
have been painted in any state in the Union; the feeling
for color is what you observe; the locality is nothing
worthy of remark. The small bookshelf contains batches
of gray manuscript and potential literature in the form of
stationery. One of the two chairs stands between the
window and a writing-table at which a club might dine.
An ink-bottle, a pen and a pad of paper occupy dots in the
vast green expanse. A sofa stretches itself near the window and tries to fill space. No crowded comfort is here—
no luxury of ornament—no literature, classic or periodical;
nothing but the man and his mind.

During our long talk Mr. Crane proved himself frank,
open, natural and completely devoid of affectation. It
was the simplicity of the man who "sees things flat." He
knows his mind without being self-conscious. He is
hampered by nothing; the traditions of the past—the sensationalism and the subjectivity of the present he neither
imitates nor criticises. He merely writes what he pleases,
that is, what seems to him true; you are privileged to like
it; he is your good friend if you don't. It has been said
that he describes everything in terms of color; perhaps he
would call his position "red independence." After five
minutes in his company you will see colors everywhere,
even if you did not see them before.

"Why, no," he said, in answer to a question, "I do
not find that short stories are utterly different in character
from other fiction. It seems to me that short stories are
the easiest things we write."

Three years ago, when Mr. Crane had just attained his
majority, he wrote a story
of war. He had never seen
a battle, of course, and he
does not know how he came
to choose a war theme. Perhaps it is in the blood; his
ancestors were soldiers; Mr.
Crane himself, though a
small man, made a reputa-
tion at Rochester University
for successfully resisting attempts at browbeating on
the part of the captain of a
visiting team; he rejoices in
a fight (vide "Maggie");
and he says himself that he
gained his knowledge of the
sensations of his hero from
the football field and elsewhere.

His method, he told me, is to get away by himself and
think over things. "Then comes a longing for you don't
know what; sorrow, too, and heart-hunger." He mixes
it all up. Then he begins to write. The first chapter is
immaterial; but, once written, it determines the rest of
the book. He grinds it out, chapter by chapter, never
knowing the end, but forcing himself to follow "that
fearful logical conclusion;" writing what his knowledge

of human nature tells him would be the inescapable outcome of those characters placed in those circumstances.

Loving color, he early learned to note it in everything.
He learned landscape more than surveying while in college. His observation, cultivated on natural objects,
served him well in cities. He knows human nature very
well in many of its moods; but of the artificial life of society
he knows and cares to know nothing. His manners show
it. He has reverted to the unconventional. If he cared
to make an impression I suppose he would adopt those
formalities which many people consider essential to good
breeding. It would be a failure.

But we are getting away from the writer. Here we find
an artist who will not play for applause. Mr. Crane has
too much good sense, too deep a regard for what he sees,
too much determination to describe things clearly, no matter what the medium, to care overmuch for the reader's
praise.

"Oh, of course," he said, "I should be glad if everybody, Canadians, Feejees, Hottentots, wild men of Borneo,
would buy 'The Red Badge'—four copies of it—but they
won't: so what's the use of thinking of the reader? If
what you write is worthy, somebody will find it out some
time. Meanwhile that is not one of the problems that interests me." It is Mr. Crane's contention that any one
can describe any sensation if he uses his experience, because suggestion creates so many sensations. "Didn't
you ever see through whole years of friendship in the face
of a man you met on the street?" But in spite of a vivid
imagination that can conjure up almost anything, he does
not think to trust the imagination of any one who reads.
He puts everything so plainly that you can't help understanding it as he meant it.

"Trust their imaginations? Why, they haven't got
any! They are used to having everything detailed for
them. Our imaginations are defunct for lack of use, like
our noses. So whether I say a thing or suggest it, I try
to put it in the most forcible way."

Singular declaration, this, for a man whose books appeal
chiefly to men of powerful imagination.

He usually draws his pictures in four sentences like
thumb-nail strokes. He has never tried to paint, which
he says is fortunate because it would not have been a success. It is fortunate for another reason. Verestschagin
has painted the most wonderful pictures of war ever seen.
How do his pictures compare with Crane's? Chiefly in
three ways:

Verestschagin has lived everything that he has ever
painted; his works are highly finished—complete in every
detail; and he points a moral. On the other hand Mr.
Crane wrote "The Red Badge" from pure power of the
imagination to conjure up scenes and sensations; his
descriptions tell parts of the landscape and suggest the
rest, and he merely states a problem in its barrenness, re-
lying for effect on truth and vividness.

Something in Verestschagin's "All Quiet at Shipka,"
and in his picture showing the Czar comfortably seated on
a knoll while 18,000 Russians are being slaughtered before
the redoubts opposite, is a rebuke to existing conditions.
Tolstoï, too, writes with an obvious purpose. These three
men are alike in this: they see things in their nakedness.
It is curious to note that Verestschagin and Crane both
have that feeling for the right *kind* of the right color (the
right quality of sunlight, for instance). Mr. Crane is not
inferior to either Russian in point of truth; but while he
has accentuated the individual, Tolstoï and Verestschagin
continually preach the insignificance of the unit.

HERBERT P. WILLIAMS.

BOOKS RECEIVED.

"Vera Vorontzoff," by Sonja Kovalevsky, translated by Anna von Rydeng-
svärd.—Lamson, Wolffe & Co., Boston.
"German-American Gymnastics," by W. A. Stecher.—Lee & Shepard, Boston.
"French Method," by François Berger.—F. Berger, Paris.
"Fairy Tales," by Mabel Fuller Blodgett.—Lamson, Wolffe & Co., Boston.
"A Bad Penny," by John T. Wheelwright.—Lamson, Wolffe & Co., Boston.

Profile of Crane in *The Illustrated American*, 18 July 1896
(*Wertheim Collection*)

be likened to an artist who knows how to draw but cannot paint. He has 'laid in' an admirable sketch, which raises one's hopes high for the success of the finished picture. But the moment he begins to lay on his colors it is evident that he is a caricaturist, not an artist; and to make matters worse, he is a caricaturist without humor."

12 JULY. The reviewer for the *New York Press*, probably Edward Marshall, concludes that while *Maggie* evokes empathy, *George's Mother* provides little more than sociological information. "It is the clearest and most intelligent study of a life that thousands of young men live that we remember to have seen. But it isn't good fiction, for the reader feels no particular personal interest in either George or his mother; and its author can retort, 'Who said it was fiction?' much as he responded when some critic asserted that his famous 'Lines' were not poetry."

13 JULY. Howells writes to Hitchcock that he has written nearly 3000 words about *Maggie* and *George's Mother* for the *New York World*. He adds: "I like Crane's Maggie better than ever, and I believe in him thoroughly. I'm not afraid of his spoiling. But he's necessarily in his own hands" (Howells, 129–130).

14 JULY. "Waiting for George," excerpts from the first three chapters of *George's Mother*, appears in *Book News* (Monteiro and Eppard, 74).

[MID-JULY]. Crane inscribes a copy of *George's Mother* to Hamlin Garland:

> To Hamlin Garland
> Of the great honest West
> From Stephen Crane
> of the false East.
>
> New York City
> July, 1896.

With the inscribed book Crane leaves a note at Garland's hotel asking him to join him and Theodore Roosevelt for dinner at the Lantern Club that evening (*C,* 242, 242n1).

16 JULY. Crane writes to Daniel Appleton assuring him that he will not again breach business courtesies as he did with *George's Mother* and that he has written Edward Arnold that he will honor the arrange-

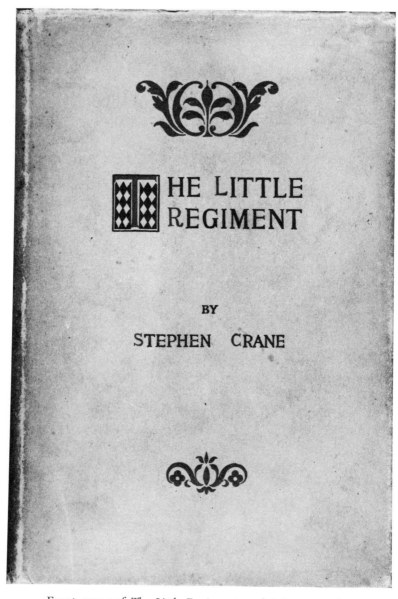

Front cover of *The Little Regiment and Other Episodes of the American Civil War*, D. Appleton and Company, 1896
(© 1991 Sotheby's, Inc)

ment Appleton made with Heinemann concerning English publication rights to *The Little Regiment* and *The Third Violet* (*C*, 240).

18 JULY. Herbert P. Williams's interview, "Mr. Crane as a Literary Artist," appears in the *Illustrated American*. Williams describes Crane's studio at 165 West 23d Street as

> an enormous room at the top of a house near the heart of the city, in the shopping district. The furniture of the room is curiously typical of the man; a tinted wall is relieved at intervals by war trophies and by impressionistic landscapes. The latter might have been painted in any state in the Union; the feeling for color is what you observe; the locality is nothing worthy of remark. The small bookshelf contains batches of gray manuscript and potential literature in the form of stationery. One of the two chairs stands between the window and a writing-table at which a club might dine. An ink-bottle, a pen and a pad of paper occupy dots in the vast green expanse. A sofa stretches itself near the window and tries to fill space. No crowded comfort is here—no luxury of ornament—no literature, classic or periodical; nothing but the man and his mind.

Crane tells Williams that

> he does not know how he came to choose a war theme. Perhaps it is in the blood; his ancestors were soldiers . . . and he says himself that he gained his knowledge of the sensations of his hero from the football field and elsewhere.
>
> His method, he told me, is to get away by himself and think over things. "Then comes a longing for you don't know what; sorrow, too, and heart-hunger." He mixes it all up. Then he begins to write. The first chapter is immaterial; but, once written, it determines the rest of the book. He grinds it out, chapter by chapter, never knowing the end, but forcing himself to follow "that fearful logical conclusion"; writing what his knowledge of human nature tells him would be the inescapable outcome of those characters placed in those circumstances.

Crane tells Williams that he does not trust the imaginations of readers:

> "Trust their imaginations? Why, they haven't got any! They are used to having everything detailed for them. Our imaginations are defunct for lack of use, like our noses. So whether I say a thing or suggest it, I try to put it in the most forcible way."

Williams draws perceptive parallels between Crane's work and Verestschagin's paintings and Tolstoy's fiction:

These three men are alike in this: they see things in their nakedness. It is curious to note that Verestschagin and Crane both have feeling for the right *kind* of the right color (the right quality of sunlight, for instance). Mr Crane is not inferior to either Russian in point of truth; but while he has accented the individual, Tolstoï and Verestschagin continually preach the insignificance of the unit.

20 JULY. Theodore Roosevelt, as president of the Board of Police Commissioners, writes to Crane agreeing to be interviewed. He adds, "I have much to discuss with you about 'Madge'" (*C*, 241).

22 JULY. Amy Leslie's column, "Books and Builders," in the *Chicago Daily News* combines a personal note on Crane with comparisons between *Maggie* and two other slum novels, George Moore's *Esther Waters* (1894) and Samuel Rutherford Crockett's *Cleg Kelly: Arab of the City* (1896):

> One New Year there reached me a slip of paper squirming under the autograph of Stephen Crane in which the author of "The Black Riders" and other beatitudes beguiled himself and me with two characteristic sentences. One is "My dear Indian, did you really like the stuff?" and the other is "A long flaming '96 to you!" Crane could not wish a body happy new year in the humor of any other being; it had to be long and flaming or broad and purple or wide and scarlet for Stephen.
> His "Maggie" is put into dashing robes by Appleton and is perhaps as vehement and realistic a sketch of *l'enfant du pavé* as any presented to end-of-race literature. It is a hopeless brutalizing of truth, but it is truth, and while it is as a reeking young breath against Moore's or Crockett's slum masterpieces "Maggie" is the impressionistic defiled by vivid naturalism, and that is almost a discovery. Crockett's "Cleg Kelly" is in some respects the greatest work of melodramatic romance ever drawn from the slums. But it is a ponderous parade of horrors full of probable impossibilities and picturesque vice with tangent revolutions and the usual Crockett extravagance of fancy. In Crane's "Maggie" and Crockett's "Cleg Kelly" almost identical situations furnish the motives for the two stories. Crockett leads his faithful out of Sodom with a suggestion of the pillar of fire and flaming sword, but Crane skillfully lets his sinners sink and sink until the torture of their degradation is venomous and blinding. Of the two Crane's is truer and all art pulses in its sodden realism, but Crockett's story will outlive "Maggie." (Monteiro 1981–82, 147–148)

Howells writes to Garland: "What a boom Crane has had! Have you read George's Mother? Mrs Howells thinks it the best of all.— He's a good boy, with lots of outcome" (Howells, 130).

Amy Leslie
(Syracuse University)

25 JULY. The *New York Press* maintains that Ambrose Bierce, speaking of Percival Pollard, remarked that Pollard had "'dragged to upper day two worse writers than Stephen Crane. . . . I had thought there could be only two worse writers than Stephen Crane, namely, two Stephen Cranes.'" Yet, shortly after the publication of *The Red Badge*, Bierce had commented to Robert Davis, "this young man . . . has the power to feel. He knows nothing of war, yet he is drenched in blood. Most beginners who deal with this subject spatter themselves merely with ink'" (Davis, x).

26 JULY. Theodore Roosevelt writes to Anna Roosevelt Cowles that he had dined the previous week in New York with a Professor Smith, and also Jacob Riis and Stephen Crane (Roosevelt, 550).

Crane's "In the Broadway Cable Cars," syndicated by McClure as a Sunday feature, describes the bustling life of downtown New York from morning until late evening from the vantage point of the cable cars.

The *Richmond Times* commends Crane's "distinctive realism" in *Maggie*, "but with all admiration for unusual genius, we think his inattention to his grammar is to be regretted."

William Dean Howells compares *Maggie* and *George's Mother* with Abraham Cahan's *Yekl: A Story of the New York Ghetto*, also published by Appleton in 1896, in an article in the *New York World* entitled "New York Low Life in Fiction." His remarks on Crane's novels are almost identical with those made in his introduction to the English edition of *Maggie*, abstracted from this article, which Howells had expected would be published a month earlier (*C*, 241). Although Howells finds Cahan's work essentially humorous, while Crane's is essentially tragic, "both of these writers persuade us that they have told the truth, and that such as conditions have made the people they deal with, we see their people. If we have any quarrel with the result we cannot blame the authors, who have done their duty as artists and for a moment have drawn aside the thick veil of ignorance which parts the comfortable few from the uncomfortable many in this city."

30 JULY. Howells sends Crane a copy of his *World* article and suggests that he visit him at his summer home in Far Rockaway (*C*, 241).

AUGUST. "The Veteran" is published in *McClure's Magazine*.

Munsey's Magazine perceives a continuity from *The Red Badge* to Crane's slum novelettes:

In this, mainly, lies Mr. Crane's art. He has ruthlessly robbed war of its glamour and exposed it for the awful reality that it is, and with equally relentless fidelity he has painted his gloomy picture of life in the city slums. Every soldier knows how true to nature is "The Red Badge," and every mission worker will recognize that "George's Mother" and "Maggie" possess the same virtue. Some of us, perhaps, may prefer to dwell upon the gallantry of battle and the rare instances of humor in the tenements, but a large majority will admire Mr. Crane for his painstaking accuracy, and read his books because their author has taken the trouble to learn his ground before venturing to guide others over it.

2 AUGUST. Crane's "Six Years Afloat," an account of the sighting of a lost 600-foot raft built to transport lumber, is syndicated in a small number of newspapers.

7 AUGUST. Assessing "The Art of Stephen Crane" in the *New York Commercial Advertiser*, Vance Thompson avers that "in spite of his vigor, stress and poignancy, it is not amiss to say that Mr. Crane writes like a woman—a woman Amazonic, unimammiferous, to be sure—rather than a man. The reasoning faculty is not conspicuous in him. By way of compensation he has the faculty, intuitive, feminine, of taking the near and simple view of things, of seeing what is in front of his nose, as Schopenhauer would say. Equally feminine, I think, is the habit of saying something and then looking into it for a meaning."

8 AUGUST. In the *Illustrated American* Edward Bright reports:

It comes to my ear from a trustworthy source that Stephen Crane has completed a series of sketches of New York life which are destined to add a new lustre to the young writer's already enviable popularity. The scene of these tales, I learn, is the metropolitan district familiarly known as the "Tenderloin," and I am the more inclined to credit the rumor since I vividly remember the surprise with which I one night discovered the author of the *Red Badge of Courage* sitting in a well-known restaurant in the small hours of the morning. I felt certain that when my eye fell upon him that there was something "in the air," for when I saw Mr. Crane on a previous occasion he put himself to considerable pains to assure me that he was an inveterate hater of town life, and seldom, if ever, permitted himself the distracting luxury of a visit to Gotham. (Monteiro 1969b, 51)

9 AUGUST. A Sunday feature article syndicated under various titles by McClure, "The Roof Gardens and Gardeners of New York," contrasts the opulence of roof gardens such as Oscar Hammerstein's Olympia on Broadway with those formed by necessity in the slums: "An evening upon a tenement roof with the great golden march of the stars across the sky and Johnnie gone for a pail of beer is not so bad if you have never seen the mountains nor heard, to your heart, the slow sad song of the pines" (*Works*, 8: 381).

The *San Francisco Chronicle* finds *Maggie* "brutal in its frankness" and contends that it illustrates the need for missionary work in America's large cities.

11 AUGUST. William Randolph Hearst cables to Crane, asking what remuneration he requires for a series of sketches about the Tenderloin (*C*, 244).

12 AUGUST. NEW YORK CITY. In the midst of a record heat wave William Jennings Bryan, the Democratic candidate for president, speaks in Madison Square Garden: "The speech was commonplace. When he began Madison Square Garden was crowded to the doors. He had not talked five minutes before the audience began to melt away. When he had talked twenty minutes a majority of the boxes were empty and the galleries were more than half cleared. Even those who remained showed no enthusiasm" (*New York Press*, 13 August). Crane sends Theodore Roosevelt an inscribed copy of *George's Mother* and a typescript of "A Man and Some Others." In a letter to Roosevelt, now lost, he complains about the conduct of the police at the rally (Katz 1983b, 43).

15 AUGUST. Crane responds to Howells's letter of 30 July, apologizing for the delay resulting from his isolation "deep in the woods" at Twin Lakes in Pike County, Pennsylvania, so that he was not aware of Howells's essay in the *World*. He has been reading Cahan's *Yekl* and would like to meet him. Howells replies on the same day and invites Crane to Far Rockaway on Wednesday, 25 August. He gives him Cahan's Manhattan address (*C*, 245–246).

16 AUGUST. William Schuyler, a St. Louis composer, writes to Crane asking permission to use the lyrics of three of his poems that he has set to music (C, 246–247).

McClure syndicates "A Yellow Under-Sized Dog," a humorous sketch about a mongrel who becomes involved in a blasting operation at a construction site in Harlem. "Asbury Park as Seen by Stephen Crane," another satiric foray against Founder James A. Bradley, appears in the *New York Journal.*

17 AUGUST. Crane inscribes an 1896 issue of *The Red Badge of Courage* to Howells, but he mistakenly dates it 1895 and never sends the inscribed book to him. On the second front flyleaf Crane transcribes his poem, "Do not weep, maiden, for war is kind" (*C*, 247–248):

> To W. D. Howells this small and
> belated book as a token of the ven-
> eration and gratitude of Stephen Crane

for many things he has learned
of the common man and, above
all, for a certain re-adjustment of his point of view victoriously
concluded some time in 1892.

August 17, 1895.

18 AUGUST. Theodore Roosevelt replies to Crane's letter:

I am much obliged to you for "George's Mother" with your own autograph on the front. I shall keep it with your other books. Some day I shall
try to get you to write your autograph in my "Red Badge of Courage", for
much though I like your other books, I think I like that book the best.
Some day I want you to write another story of the frontiersman and the
Mexican Greaser in which the frontiersman shall come out on top; it is
more normal that way! I wish I could have seen Hamlin Garland, but I am
leaving in a few days for a three weeks trip to the West.
This evening I shall be around at the Madison Square Garden to see
exactly what the Police do. They have a very difficult task with a crowd
like that, because they have to be exceedingly good humored with the
crowd, and they also have to please the Managers of the meeting who
know nothing about crowds, and yet they have to control twenty thousand people. I will say one thing for them at the Bryan meeting; we have
not had a single complaint of clubbing or brutality from any man claiming
to have suffered; the Managers of the meeting and the Manager of the
Garden have both written us in the warmest terms. (C, 249)

21 AUGUST. HARTWOOD. Crane accepts Howells's invitation to visit
him in Far Rockaway on the 25th (C, 250).

Despite Roosevelt's disclaimer, Crane publicly criticizes the behavior of the New York police at the Bryan rally, but he does so in an
obscure place in the first of a series of three articles headed "From the
Metropolis" in the *Port Jervis Evening Gazette*:

The wretched mismanagement which marked the police arrangements
at the recent Bryan and Sewall notification at Madison Square Garden has
occasioned a great deal of unfavorable comment, finding an echo in the
columns of the daily press. The brutality and unnecessary harshness with
which the large crowd was handled would have been inexcusable at any
time, and on the evening in question it was simply shameful. Such blundering as was painfully in evidence on the night of the 12 inst. would not
have been possible under the Byrnes regime, and that fact is another
reminder that what we have gained in official honesty through administrative reforms is more than counter-balanced by the effects of official
incapacity and inexperience. (Katz 1983b, 44)

23 AUGUST. "Stephen Crane[,] New York" registers at the Hartwood Club, unaccompanied by other members of his family (*Hartwood Park Association Record*).

24 AUGUST. Walter Blackburn Harte writes to Crane, asking for a short story to be published in his monthly little magazine, the *Lotus* (*C*, 251).

28 AUGUST. In an article "From the Metropolis" in the *Port Jervis Evening Gazette* entitled "What an Observant Correspondent Sees Worth Noting," Crane once again attacks Roosevelt's police administration, this time for using the blue laws to harass shopkeepers. He also criticizes the police harassment of prostitutes, referring to the recent arrest of Ruby Young, better known by her street names of Dora Wilkins and Dora Clark, a known streetwalker, by officer Rosenberg in the Tenderloin district of the city: "It is to be hoped that an example will be made of the policeman who arrested an unoffending and innocent woman on 6th avenue the other night. This is a form of outrage that has become very frequent of late, and the disgrace and exemplary punishment of some of the official brutes would have a beneficial effect in serving as a warning to over zealous policemen" (Katz 1983b, 47).

29 AUGUST. Crane inscribes a copy of the 1893 *Maggie* for a book collector, Paul Lemperly (*C*, 252):

> "And the wealth of the few
> shall be built upon the
> patience of the poor."
> Prophecy not made in B C 1090
> Stephen Crane
>
> New York
> Aug 29, 1896

30 AUGUST. Bacheller syndicates "A Detail," a vignette about an encounter between a tiny old lady and two well-dressed young girls amid the bustle of Sixth Avenue.

SEPTEMBER. In *Godey's Magazine* Rupert Hughes, writing as "Chelifer," criticizes Crane's impressionistic techniques and faulty grammar, but reiterates his admiration for *Maggie*: "In our issue of November [October], 1895, we praised it as the strongest representative of American slum-fiction. It has the inevitableness of a Greek tragedy, and the reader that grants to the fate of Euripides's fanciful 'Medea,' an import and significance he refuses to see in the predestined ugliness of the end of this well-meaning 'Maggie,' has an outlook on life that is too literary to be true. Indeed, he has misread his classics, if the woes of their creatures leave him uneducated into sympathy with the miseries of the miserables of his own town."

Based upon an interview with him, E. St. Elmo Lewis describes Crane's writing habits in *Book News*. He writes "when he 'has the fit on him,' so to speak. In the quiet of solitary rambles he 'gets close to things and thinks.' Then he goes home and writes, with the whole story in his head, always knowing the end from the beginning, playing no tricks as he goes with his characters, springing no surprises wantonly, but working out with relentless logic what to him is the inevitable ending of the tale. Once finished . . . there is no word added or subtracted. The story is put aside, and for that time that phrase of human nature is interpreted."

5 SEPTEMBER. In a *Saturday Review* (London) essay on "The New American Novelists," perhaps written by H. G. Wells, *George's Mother* is distinguished for its "immense vigour and sympathy. But the story must be read for its power to be understood, quotation fails for the simple reason that it is a bare story and nothing beyond. There are no purple passages, no decorations, no digressions." Crane is described as a disciple of Tolstoy "in the extraordinary use in narrative of sustained descriptions of the mental states of his characters. Great lengths of story are told in a kind of monologue in the third person. Mr. Crane outdoes his master in this direction in the present book almost as much as in 'The Red Badge of Courage.'"

6 SEPTEMBER. William Schuyler again writes to Crane, advising him that he has set more of his poems to music and intends to publish a collection of six of them (*C*, 252–253). A group of five poems is published the next year as *Song's from Stephen Crane's* Black Riders: *Music by William Schuyler* (St. Louis: Thiebes-Stierlin Music Co., 1897).

8 SEPTEMBER. Crane writes to Belle Walker, giving her tongue-in-cheek advice to delete a detail in the manuscript of a short story she has sent him: "Frankly I do not consider your sketch to be very good but even if you do me the honor to value my opinion, this need not discourage you for I can remember when I wrote just as badly as you do now. Furthermore there are many men, far our superiors who once wrote just as badly as I do today and no doubt as badly as you" (*C*, 253).

9 SEPTEMBER. Crane writes to Paul Revere Reynolds, one of the first American literary agents, to whom he had been introduced by Irving Bacheller earlier in the year, asking him to sell "A Man and Some Others." He asks for at least $350 with £25 more for English rights. Crane cautions him not to approach Bacheller or McClure, probably because in giving the story to Reynolds to sell he is breaking his prior commitments to them (*C,* 254).

The last of Crane's New York City columns in the *Port Jervis Evening Gazette,* "An Interesting Letter from Our Correspondent," deals with the disappearance of the old-fashioned campaign banners, unsanitary conditions at summer resorts, and the opening of a Wanamaker store. Crane again indirectly attacks Roosevelt by criticizing police enforcement of the Raines law passed in 1896, which prohibited the sale of liquor on Sunday except by a hotel having at least 10 bedrooms, the effect of which was to drive neighborhood saloons out of business and foster the establishment of brothels (Katz 1983b, 42).

10 SEPTEMBER. H. R. Huxton, an editorial assistant to William Randolph Hearst, writes to Crane a letter marked "Confidential":

> I managed to catch Mr. Hurst on a stairway for a moment this afternoon and spoke to him about your doing novelettes based upon real incidents of New York life. He said to go ahead and that he would decide afterwards whether to use them in the Sunday or in one of the daily editions. I am sure that if you read the police news in next Sunday and Monday mornings' papers and go to Jefferson Market Police Court on Monday morning, you will get the material for a good Tenderloin story to start with. I suppose that if you are going there on Monday you would be glad to have a reporter, who knows the ropes, meet you there. (*C,* 255)

11 SEPTEMBER. Reynolds thanks Crane for asking him to market "A Man and Some Others" and advises him that he has submitted the story to a New York newspaper and will get in touch with a London literary agent about it (*C,* 256). The story does not appear in an English magazine.

Maggie: A Child of the Streets is published by Heinemann (Bruccoli and Katz, 279). The book is prefaced with "An Appreciation" by William Dean Howells, abstracted from his 26 July *New York World* article, which does not appear in the American edition. Howells finds in *Maggie* "that quality of fatal necessity which dominates Greek tragedy." He also praises *George's Mother* for dealing with persons "absolutely average" with compassion but not pity.

13 SEPTEMBER. Huxton, Hearst's editorial assistant, advises Crane that a reporter familiar with the police court and the Tenderloin will meet him at Shanley's bar near 42d street at 8:45 the next day, Monday morning (*C*, 257).

14 SEPTEMBER. In the morning Crane sits beside Magistrate Cornell at the Jefferson Market Police Court to observe "the machinery of justice in full operation. The novelist felt, however, that he had seen but a kaleidoscopic view of the characters who passed rapidly before the judicial gaze of the presiding Magistrate. He must know more of that throng of unfortunates; he must study the police court victims in their haunts" (*New York Journal*, 20 September). One of the cases he observes provides the impetus for "An Eloquence of Grief," published as one of the "Midnight Sketches" in the English edition of *The Open Boat* (1898).

15 SEPTEMBER. In the evening Crane meets two chorus girls, by appointment, in "a Turkish Smoking Parlor" on West 29th Street. Some time before midnight they proceed to the Broadway Garden between 31st and 32d streets, where he interviews them. They are joined by Dora Clark. The Broadway Garden is a notorious resort of prostitutes. An investigative reporter visiting a few months later finds that "from midnight until daylight the place was crowded with rum-befuddled patrons. The men were about all very young, while the women were mostly outcasts. These women go in without escorts, but rarely leave alone" (*New York World*, 20 January 1897).

In an article dated 15 September, *Book News* (October) announces that "Mr. Stephen Crane sails for England this month for a brief stay, returning probably a short time before the holidays. This will interrupt his work on his new novel 'Dan Emmons,' and will probably postpone its publication until spring. . . . A few chapters of 'Dan Emmons' have been written and they give promise of something quite unlike any of Mr. Crane's former work. Dan is an Irish boy, and the story as far as written deals with life in New York city."

16 SEPTEMBER. At 2:00 A.M. Crane leaves the Broadway Garden with the two chorus girls and Dora Clark. As he returns from having escorted one of the girls to a trolley car across the street, patrolman Charles Becker of the 19th Precinct arrests Dora Clark and the other girl on the corner of 31st and Broadway for soliciting and also threatens to arrest Crane when he attempts to interfere. The chorus girl is

released after Crane confirms her claim that she is his wife. She and Crane follow Becker to the 19th Precinct station house, where Dora Clark is charged. Crane escorts the chorus girl home and, after reflecting upon his position, returns to the precinct house, where, against the advice of Sergeant McDermott, he makes a statement confirming Dora Clark's innocence and promises to return the next morning (Fryckstedt, 141–146). In the evening Crane makes a statement to the New York newspapers:

> As to the girl's character I know nothing. I only know that while with me she acted respectably, and that the policeman's charge was false. She certainly did not look dissipated, and she was very neatly and prettily dressed. I noticed, too, that she was still neat in court, even after the hours of imprisonment.
>
> The policeman roughly threatened to arrest me, when I told him that the girl had done no wrong. He arrested the other girl, too, but let her go when she went into hysterics at the police station. I was strongly advised by Sergeant McDermott not to try to help her, for I seemed a respectable sort of man, he said, and it would injure me. I well knew I was risking a reputation that I have worked hard to build. But . . . she was a woman and unjustly accused, and I did what was my duty as a man. I realized that if a man should stand tamely by, in such a case, our wives and sisters would be at the mercy of any ruffian who disgraces the uniform. The policeman flatly lied, and if the girl will have him prosecuted for perjury I will gladly support her. (*New York Journal,* 17 September)

17 SEPTEMBER. The *New York Sun,* the *New York Times,* and the *New York Journal* report the arrest of Dora Clark and Crane's testimony at the hearing before Magistrate Cornell. According to the *Sun,*

> Dora Clark, who gave her age as 21, and her address as 137 East Eighty-first street, was charged in Jefferson Market Court yesterday with soliciting on the street. The complainant against the woman was Ward Man Becker of the West Thirtieth street station. When the case was called, Becker said that while standing in the entrance to the Grand Hotel, about 2 o'clock yesterday morning, he saw the woman come out of a café on the west side of Broadway, between Thirty-first and Thirty-second streets, and walk south. Near Thirty-first street, Becker said that the woman solicited two men, and afterward joined a man and a woman who were standing on the corner. After watching all the woman's movements, Becker said he walked across the street, placed her under arrest, and warned her companions not to associate with her, as they would only compromise themselves and perhaps be arrested.

Dora Clark responded to Becker by complaining to Magistrate Cornell that she had been harassed by the police of the 19th Precinct and arrested four times since she rebuffed Patrolman Rosenberg, who had a few weeks earlier accosted her on a poorly lighted section of Broadway. "I told him to go along about his business, adding that I wanted nothing to do with negroes. The man is very dark, and I really supposed him to be a negro. He arrested me, and then I recognized my mistake." Since then she had been unjustly arrested by Rosenberg's partner, Patrolman Martin Conway, and twice subsequently by other 19th Precinct patrolmen. "This morning two friends, a man and woman, and myself came out of the Broadway Garden and walked to the corner of Thirty-first street. While the man was handing the woman into a cable car I stood on the corner, I spoke to no one." She does not deny Magistrate Cornell's charge that she is an habitue of the Tenderloin, which is tantamount to admitting to being a prostitute. At this point Crane interrupted the proceedings:

> I was the man whom this woman spoke of as being with her and a companion when they came out of the Broadway Garden this morning. I am studying the life of the Tenderloin for the purpose of getting material for some sketches. I was in the resort mentioned and was introduced to this woman. So far as I know, I had never seen her before. I left the place with the prisoner and one other woman and walked with them to Thirty-first street, where I put one of them on a Broadway car, leaving this woman standing at the corner. I could see the prisoner all the while, and I am positive that she spoke to no one.

On the basis of Crane's testimony, the magistrate discharged Dora Clark.

19 SEPTEMBER. Publication of the first English edition of *Maggie* is announced in the *Publishers' Circular.* There is no record of a British Museum deposit of the English edition.

20 SEPTEMBER. Crane's "Adventures of a Novelist," recounting the arrest of Dora Clark and his own part in the police proceedings, appears in the *New York Journal.* Crane characterizes himself as "a reluctant laggard witness" and a simpleton for having become involved in the affair, and in a fragmentary draft for the article he muses upon the "inopportune arrival of a moral obligation." Nevertheless, he concludes that when confronted with an injustice a man must reject "the united wisdom of the world," which urges him to "'have a conscience for the daytime, but it is idiocy for a man to have a con-

science at 2:30 in the morning, in the case of an arrested prostitute'" (*Works*, 8: 656–661).

21 SEPTEMBER. The *Chicago Dispatch* quips that "Stephen Crane is respectfully informed that association with women in scarlet is not necessarily a 'Red Badge of Courage.'"

26 SEPTEMBER. The "three young exponents of so-called realism in fiction"—Garland, Crane, and Abraham Cahan—are guests of honor at the Lantern Club's first dinner of the season. Garland speaks of the literary culture of Chicago and the West while Cahan recounts his background as an aspiring Jewish writer in Russia. Crane reads a story in manuscript, "which was duly criticized, as the manner of the club is" (*New York Press*, 27 September).

28 SEPTEMBER. Richard Harding Davis writes to his brother, Charles Belmont Davis, noting that "Stephen Crane seems to me to have written the last word as far as battles or fighting is concerned in the Red Badge of Courage" (Osborn, 53).

30 SEPTEMBER. A letter to the editor of the *New York World* headed "Stephen Crane and His 'Type'" ridicules Crane's quixotic defense of Dora Clark:

> To the Editor:
> I wish to say a few words in behalf of Dora Clark, and would inform Detective Harley (or whatever his name is) that Miss Clark showed excellent taste in the selection of her company. Not every young lady can have for an escort a distinguished literary gentleman. Miss Clark was simply returning from a place of amusement in company with two persons when she was arrested. These persons were musical and literary people. What if the hour was late? Not all the talk of Becker and Harley or the rest of the policemen can affect Miss Clark or her noble and heroic defender, Mr. Crane, in the minds of good people.
> F. S. (Clipping, NNC)

OCTOBER. "I explain the silvered passing of a ship at night" is published in the *Bookman* under the title "LINES."

The London *Bookman* concludes that in *Maggie* "Mr. Crane surpasses nearly all his models of the sternly realistic school, who fail so often in their finer, their more beautiful portraits. New York life— nearly at its lowest, surely—is the material of the book, and the material is used by a daring and a relentless hand. But Mr. Crane has reticence and sympathy, and these, as much as his astonishing cleverness, have given him the high rank he holds already in America and England."

The *Lotus* contains "A Little Study of Stephen Crane" by Jonathan Penn, who satirically attributes Crane's success to contemporary fascination with the irrational and bizarre in literary language:

An apprenticeship on a certain New York newspaper, which has made a profound study of revising and reorganizing the body of the language so as to bring it within the comprehension of the largest circulation on earth, completed Mr. Crane's preparation for his momentous career in "poster" literature. A period of effort and introspection revealed to him a certain strain of vague illogic in his mental constitution, which he realized at once could either ruin or make him. Too many strive to overcome such a defect, when they have enough power of self-criticism to detect it. When they succeed, they are reduced to the common crowd of writers who respect the language and are careful and painstaking, but unremarkable. It is the mark of genius to recognize in one's mental constitution a strong vein of illogic. If it is given full swing, it results in the most startling presentations of all the ideas and observations within one's ken. This perception, with perfect satisfaction in it as originality of mind, releases the imagination, so that it plays the very deuce with language, and easily commands attention. It is to literature what the spectacular is to the mechanic-made drama. A rhetorical exuberance, with certain knotty predilections, is an ordinary accompaniment of an uncertain acquaintance with one's mother tongue.

1 OCTOBER. "In the Tenderloin: A Duel Between an Alarm Clock and a Suicidal Purpose," the first of two short stories involving Swift Doyer, appears in *Town Topics*.

2 OCTOBER. Paul Revere Reynolds submits "A Man and Some Others" to Clarence C. Buel for publication in the *Century Magazine*. He emphasizes that the story is "one of great strength, and dealing as it does with western life on the plains, I think it would attract wide attention" and asks $500 for English and American rights" (NN-Century Collection).

The *Boston Traveler* editorializes that "Stevie Crane seems to have gotten into warm water by his valiant defence of a young woman in police court at New York. The chances are that the youthful literary prodigy was on a genuine 'lark,' and, when his companion was apprehended, invented the tale about searching for book material. That is simply the way it looks to a cold and unprejudiced world" (Stallman and Hagemann 1966, 231).

[2 OCTOBER]. Dora Clark prefers charges of false arrest against Becker, Conway, and other police officers who had arrested her under similar circumstances. Crane determines to testify in her behalf as a witness against Becker (Fryckstedt, 151).

4 OCTOBER. At 3:00 A.M. Becker brutally assaults Dora Clark in the presence of witnesses for having brought charges against him:

> Dora Clark in her new charge says: "I was standing on the corner of Sixth avenue and Twenty-eighth street early last Sunday morning talking to a group of cabmen, when Becker came along dressed in citizen's clothes. He walked straight up to me and said: 'So you made charges against me did you?' At the same time using profane language.
>
> "'You're a loafer to talk that way,' I replied, whereupon he seized me by the throat, kicked me and knocked me down. I got up and he threw me down again. The bystanders then interfered and Becker went." (*New York Journal*, 8 October)

7 OCTOBER. Appleton applies for copyright of *The Little Regiment*.

[EARLY OCTOBER]. Crane flees the pressure of publicity by escaping briefly to Philadelphia, where he visits Frederic L. Lawrence, but he maintains confidence in Police Commissioner Roosevelt's objectivity, and he sends a telegram to Roosevelt, telling him that he will return to New York to give testimony at Becker's trial (Lawrence, 17).

10 OCTOBER. *Harper's Weekly* comments that

> Commissioner Roosevelt and other high authorities of the police force are sceptical of the accuracy of Mr. Stephen Crane's observation in the case of that young woman who he thought had been wrongfully arrested. All the reports of the case give the reader the impression that a tendency to light conduct actually existed in the young woman, and that the only question was whether the policeman had observed this tendency at one of the moments of its acute development or not. Of course the existence of the tendency, which is practically admitted, is a point in favor of the force, and one which the Commissioner is not the man to suffer to be overlooked. He has expressed a wish for further testimony from Mr. Crane. (Fryckstedt, 152)

[Roosevelt told Hamlin Garland that he had tried to shield Crane from press coverage, but Crane had insisted upon testifying (Garland 1930, 203). Jimmy Hare recalls that in September 1902, when he was on a train with President Roosevelt and one of his secretaries, George B. Cortelyou, Roosevelt scanned the title page of a copy of the newly published *Wounds in the Rain,* which Cortelyou had brought along, and said:

> "You knew this fellow Crane rather well, didn't you, Jimmy?"
>
> "Yes, sir, very well indeed."
>
> Again the Roosevelt teeth clicked decisively.
>
> "I remember him distinctly myself. When I was Police Commissioner of New York I once got him out of serious trouble."
>
> "Oh, yes," said Jimmy slowly. "I recall the occasion. It was while he was collecting data for his book, 'Maggie: A Girl of the Streets.'"
>
> "Nonsense!" retorted Roosevelt vigorously, careless that Jimmy had come to his feet with a face anything but pale as paper. "He wasn't gathering any data! He was a man of bad character and he was simply consorting with loose women."
>
> Bristling at every whisker, a hundred pounds of human dynamite exploded.
>
> "That is absolutely not so!" flared a man who defended his friends. "Nothing could be farther from the truth!"
>
> Roosevelt stared, and Cortelyou gasped. Admittedly, it was no way to talk to the President of the United States, even if the incumbent himself happened to be a two-fisted wielder of words. Jimmy knew instantly he had been guilty of a lapse in good taste; he forced down his choler and spoke more calmly.
>
> "I'm sorry," he said, a trifle too shortly to be convincing. "You see, I happen to know the story behind that incident. My friend, Crane, was merely taking the part of an unfortunate young woman who was being hounded by the police; that was the whole reason for his getting into a scrape with the law."
>
> Roosevelt was still staring, but a fiery gleam that had lighted his eyes now died away. He nodded understandingly.
>
> "All right, Jimmy," he said. "Have it your own way." (Carnes, 128–129)]

11 OCTOBER. The *New York Journal* reports that the police of the Tenderloin precinct have attempted to frighten Crane by telling him that "they are prepared to swear that he led a fast life among the women of the Tenderloin, and that he would be prosecuted on the charge of maintaining an opium joint in his rooms if he testified in Dora Clark's behalf against Becker. Another rumor was that Crane had left town in order to avoid being subpoenaed in the case." Crane responds that his address is on file with a lawyer, and that the opium layout in his room, a souvenir of his article, "Opium's Varied Dreams," is tacked to a plaque on a wall in his room.

15 OCTOBER. The hearing into Dora Clark's charges against Conway and Becker finally begins at 9 P.M. following a number of other cases and does not end until 2:38 A.M. It is the longest trial ever held at police headquarters (*New York Journal,* 17 October). The hearing officer is Frederick D. Grant, son of the late president. Crane, who had arrived at police headquarters at 3:00 P.M., waits for almost 10 hours before being called to testify at 1:55 A.M. Becker's attorney, Louis D. Grant, puts Crane through a severe cross-examination, focusing upon his alleged opium smoking and frequenting of Tenderloin brothels. According to the *New York World* (16 October),

> Lawyer Grant then took another tack. He asked the witness whether he knew a woman named Sadie or Amy Huntington. It was presumed that Lawyer Grant had reference to Sadie Traphagen, who was the friend of Annie Goodwin, the cigarette girl, who was a victim of Dr. McConigal. It will be remembered, as the Goodwin case was widely published at the time, that the girl was a victim of malpractice.
>
> Whether Amy Huntington was really Sadie Traphagen was not developed.
>
> "Did you ever smoke opium with this Sadie or Amy in a house at 121 West Twenty-seventh street?" asked Lawyer Grant.
>
> "I deny that," said Mr. Crane.
>
> "On the ground that it would tend to degrade or incriminate you?"
>
> "Well—yes," hesitatingly. (Stallman and Hagemann 1966, 250)

Under questioning Crane concedes that "in the summer he had visited at 121 West 27th st. He refused to say whether or not he was acquainted with Sadie or Amy Huntington. He denied that he had smoked opium in the house in question (*New York News,* 16 October).

[Sadie Traphagen was the chief witness in the fall 1890 manslaughter trial of Dr. Henry G. McGonegal, a notorious abortionist, in New York City's Court of General Sessions. McGonegal had caused the death of Sadie's roommate, Annie Goodwin. Although Sadie and Annie ostensibly were both "cigarette makers," McGonegal's attorney frequently implied that both women were really prostitutes, an imputation that the prosecutor did not deny (*New York Evening Sun,* 30 September 1890). Two years after the trial when McGonegal, having exhausted his appeals, was finally committed to 14 years in Sing Sing Prison, the *New York Times* (30 November 1892) commented that Sadie Traphagen had "figured in the police courts on several occasions" since the death of Annie Goodwin.

121 West 27th Street was the address of Amy Leslie, who had a sister named Sadie. The house was located in the middle of a block notori-

ous for its streetwalkers and houses of prostitution and had "a reputation redolent of opium" (*New York Press,* 17 October 1896). Amy Leslie's obituary in the *Chicago Daily News* (5 July 1939) and the reminiscences of her second husband, Frank Buck (*All in a Lifetime* [with Ferrin Fraser. New York: McBride, 1941], p. 55) indicate that she was born as Lillie (or Lily) West, but a family friend states categorically that "John Traphagen had daughters named Amy and Sadie . . . also called 'Kid'" and that "Amy Leslie *was* Amy Traphagen" (Mrs. Charles M. Haltom to John S. Van E. Kohn, 28 September 1975, CtU). Copies of Amy Traphagen's vaccination certificate and an insurance policy in her name, as well as items pertaining to her father, John Traphagen, are among Amy Leslie's papers (Copies, Wertheim Collection), although, paradoxically, they suggest that Amy Traphagen would have been 21 years old in 1896, considerably younger than Amy Leslie, whose age is variously given. Her *New York Times* obituary quotes her physician, who estimates her age as approximately 90 (4 July 1939). The *Chicago Daily News* obituary states that she was born in October 1855, making her 83 years old at death, but her entries in *Who's Who in America* give her date of birth as 1860. By the least of these estimates, she was 11 years older than Crane; more likely, she was 16 years older than he. Nevertheless, it is probable that at times Amy Leslie assumed the identity of Amy Traphagen.]

16 OCTOBER. The police court exonerates Becker, concluding that although he was probably overzealous, he had made an honest mistake in the course of duty (Logan, 110).

17 OCTOBER. The *Brooklyn Daily Eagle* editorially protests what it considers to have been the trial of Stephen Crane by the New York Police Commission:

> The latitude allowed to lawyers to worry, confuse, bully and insult citizens in this land is one of the surest evidences that it is a free country. . . . Mr. Crane collects bric-a-brac, and among the odds and ends in his flat are an opium pipe and lamp. From this circumstance the lawyer tried to prove that he was an opium smoker. . . . And the remarkable thing about it all is that before a board that has the public welfare in its keeping, the reputation of private citizens is permitted to be assailed without comment or protest, while so much is done to shield one of a body of men that collectively was lately shown [by the Lexow Committee report of 1895] to be one of the most corrupt, brutal, incompetent organizations in the world.

18 OCTOBER. Crane's "Hats, Shirts, and Spurs in Mexico" is syndicated by Bacheller.

The *New York Journal* protests "A Police Outrage on a Gallant Gentleman":

The action of the police authorities in the matter of the charges of Dora Clark (or Ruby Young) [Dora Clark's real name] against patrolman Becker has been simply outrageous. The theory upon which the case was tried before the proper tribunal plainly was that the woman was of the lower half world, and that therefore any accusation made by her against a policeman must be discredited if possible. The police felt that the woman's position in the community gave him the whip hand, and they proceeded with the evident intention of driving her to the wall. . . . If Dora Clark was guilty of soliciting, Patrolman Becker's act was justifiable; if she was innocent, his act was an offense against his uniform and deserved punishment. The testimony of eye witnesses was required, and testimony to the effect that she was innocent was offered by a reputable man, who in the pursuit of his calling as a novelist was engaged in the study of life in New York's darkest centre, and was in the company of the woman for that purpose. Mr. Stephen Crane acted the part of a man in declining to abandon Dora Clark to the tender mercies of the police out of fear that his own reputation might be besmirched. He confessed that he expected to be assailed, and his expectation was well founded. Mr. Crane has been haled before a Police Commissioner and subjected to questioning which was an outrage without qualification, and which that Commissioner should never have permitted. The only point that was fairly open to dispute was the novelist's credibility as a witness, and no testimony whatever was submitted on that point. Whether Mr. Crane had previously known Dora Clark, whether he had ever been acquainted with other women of the "Tenderloin" district, had nothing to do with the case, because such acquaintance does not necessarily make a man a liar.

The assault on Mr. Crane's private life was part of a deliberate and despicable scheme of police intimidation, of which any voluntary witness in a trial for police outrage may become a victim.

20 OCTOBER. Through Reynolds, Crane attempts to circumvent his obligation to the McClure syndicate by selling serial rights to *The Third Violet* independently to the *New York World*. Ernest O. Chamberlin of the *World* replies:

The first installments of the Crane story are received and being put into type.

I had supposed from the circular you presented on your first visit that we were dealing with the McClure Syndicate.

It seems from your note accompanying the copy that this affair is with you personally.

Under the circumstances you will pardon me for asking for assurance of your authority to sell the story.

We wish to advertise it extensively before publication and want to be sure of our ground first. (Chamberlin to Reynolds, ViU)

22 OCTOBER. The *Pall Mall Gazette* complains that in *Maggie* Crane "has, like so many of his compatriots, either not the slightest notion of how to tell a story, or a supreme contempt for the art of storytelling. In either case he deserves a kindly lesson, which he might obtain from any one of the great masters of fiction in English or other tongues. . . . He has shown us before that he is a very skillful analyst of certain strong moods, and drunkenness, rage, and jealousy are here set forth in all their undeserved nakedness. It is by no means a pleasant story, but it is a strong one and a true one, and impresses one still more with the talents which Mr. Crane possesses at present in a somewhat crude condition."

24 OCTOBER. Richard Watson Gilder, editor of the *Century*, writes to Reynolds, thanking Crane for having removed a hackneyed "crown of thorns" from "A Man and Some Others." He is, however, still concerned with another word, which the *Century* rendered as "B'G—" when the story was published:

You may think me over anxious, but I am particularly sorry he did not change that "B'Gawd." It is difficult to know what to do with swearing in fiction. When it appears in print it has an offensiveness beyond that of the actual word; and it is never true or "realistic" because, if the actual oaths were printed just as the swearer swears it would be as unendurable among men as among gods.

I am a sincere well-wisher of the author, and I am anxious that this story should not attract unfavorable criticism in any details; so I particularly ask him through yourself to omit that expression, for his sake as well as yours. (Allen, 49)

Reynolds replies on the same day: "I have your letter of to-day about Mr. Crane's story. I will communicate with him and see if he is willing that you should change the word that you object to. Of course you know how sensitive authors are about their literary children, and how much they dislike making any changes in them. I will see what I can do and let you know" (NN-Century Collection).

The *Athenaeum* asserts that *Maggie* "will make a powerful impression on those who are not repelled by the strange oaths in which the story is for the most part told. . . . The telling of the tale is so strong that it produces on the reader an impression of absolute truthfulness, and yet, we are convinced, it is not true to life. Such a case as described may, indeed, be met with; but far more usual would be either the moral destruction of the girl by her mother's influence at an early age, or, on the other hand, the development of a harder type, helped along by the extreme of kindness to one another of the very poor."

25 OCTOBER. "The 'Tenderloin' as It Really Is," a grouping of anecdotes illustrating that "the Tenderloin is more than a place. It is an emotion," appears in the *New York Journal*. In its Sunday magazine section the *New York World* prints "The Devil's Acre," a chilling description of the death chamber at Sing Sing with its sleekly varnished electric chair and the graveyard of the convicts on a hill overlooking the Hudson.

McClure syndication of *The Third Violet* begins in several newspapers; the serial runs through mid-November.

In the *New York World* Jeannette Gilder contends that *The Little Regiment* is as superior to *Maggie* and *George's Mother* "as it is possible to imagine. There are tricks of style that show the same hand to have written these stories and the two above mentioned, as well as 'The Red Badge of Courage,' for Mr. Crane is fond of awkward sentences, and he often labors painfully for eccentricity of expression, but at the same time he shows in this book that he can tell a good story when he does not try too hard. . . . I may say in passing that it is not a little remarkable that Mr. Crane should write so much better of the life that he knows nothing of than of the life with which he is familiar."

29 OCTOBER. The *New York Tribune* delights in Crane's notoriety, explaining that his transient fame was merely an illustration of the English predilection for literary fads:

Soon or late most literary mysteries get themselves explained. One of the biggest of recent times has just been exploded, and it ought to make some people feel very small, now that they see how deceived they were. It is the mystery of Stephen Crane. That industrious and ambitious young writer had his books circulated in London, and London went mad over them. Thoughtful people wondered what was the matter. They could not solve the puzzle. Now comes the English publisher of this surprising novelist, and explains everything. He advertises the "works" of Mr. Crane, and describes the latter as "The Genius of 1896." Does not that tear away the veil? Once a year at least, sometimes twice, London must have its "genius." For a while it had Mr. Wilde. He lasted longer than London wanted him to. So the reputations have been restricted to a brief period. Mr. Hichens was permitted to be talked about for a year or so on the strength of his "Green Carnation." Mrs. Caffyn sailed along for a time on a bubble so iridescent that when her husband wrote anything it was advertised as "by the husband of the author of 'The Yellow Aster.'" When Mr. Crane turned up with his "Red Badge of Courage" (it is curious, this passion of the English for colors), there was a void that ached for him. He filled it, this "genius of 1896." It will be interesting to see who takes his place.

30 OCTOBER. Robert Finley of the McClure syndicate writes Reynolds, asking him to make sure that the *New York World* does not publish the final installment of *The Third Violet* before 14 November because "earlier publication of this instalment by the World would bring our whole syndicate down on our heads" (ViU).

Deposit of The *Little Regiment* is made by Appleton in the Library of Congress. Heinemann deposits a copy of the advance Appleton sheets with a Heinemann title page in the British Museum.

31 OCTOBER. CAMBRIDGE. Crane makes his debut as a sports writer, reporting the football game between Harvard and the Carlisle Indian School. His narration, "Harvard against the Carlisle Indians," appears in the Sunday edition of the *New York Journal* the next day.

A "New York Letter" by John D. Barry in the *Literary World* states that "Mr. Stephen Crane has abandoned the trip to England which he had planned to take this autumn. The novel which he began some time ago is not yet completed, and will not appear this year."

In the *Illustrated American* Edward Bright writes: "I have been asked to express my opinion of Mr. Stephen Crane's recent police court adventure, but after thinking the matter over I have concluded to keep my opinion to myself. I may say this much, however, that Mr. Crane made a great error, in my judgment, in flying into print to justify his conduct. I should have been much better pleased, and have been much more disposed to consider his motives disinterested, had he allowed the episode to pass by unnoticed" (Monteiro 1969b, 52).

Dora Clark is again arrested on Sixth Avenue between 31st and 32d streets at 9:30 P.M. after a brawl with another Tenderloin prostitute named Mary Kane and prefers charges against her in Jefferson Market Court the next morning. Both women are fined by the magistrate (*Rochester Times*, 3 November).

1 NOVEMBER. According to a suit later filed by Amy Leslie, she gives Crane $800 to deposit in a bank for her. Instead he deposits it in his own name (*New York Times*, 4 January 1898).

The *New York Journal* prints a second Tenderloin study, headed "In the 'Tenderloin,'" in its Sunday American magazine section.

4 NOVEMBER. Serialization of *The Third Violet* begins in the *New York World* to run through 14 November.

5 NOVEMBER. Crane deposits $600, presumably derived from Amy Leslie, to his own account with William Clarke & Sons, Bankers in the *Tribune* building. By 25 November $776.50 is deposited in his name (Wm. Clarke & Sons bankbook, NhD).

7 NOVEMBER. Crane is once more in Cambridge reporting the Harvard-Princeton football game. His article, "How Princeton Met Harvard at Cambridge," appears in the Sunday edition of the *Journal* the following day.

The *Little Regiment* is listed as "just ready" in *Publishers' Weekly.*

The San Francisco *Wave* deplores the sensationalism of the *New York Journal*, which it considers "positively the worst newspaper we can recall. . . . One of the 'features' of the 'Journal,' which the editor has advertised with a sound of trumpets, is Stephen Crane's 'The Tenderloin as It Is.' It is immaterial who wrote the article. Stephen Crane's name, notwithstanding, it is the veriest filth. We have yet to see even the 'Police Gazette' descend to such depths" (McElrath 1993, 12).

8 NOVEMBER. The *New York Journal*, celebrating its first year of publication, carries in facsimile "A Birthday Word from Novelist Stephen Crane," along with congratulatory notes from other prominent contributors (*C,* 258).

9 NOVEMBER. Reviewing *The Little Regiment* for *Town Topics,* George Parsons Lathrop finds "real types and typical realities, and there are well worked up bits of human nature that show appreciative insight and sympathetic intuition."

10 NOVEMBER. Reynolds writes to Gilder: "Unless I am very much mistaken, and I don't think I am, you received the proofs back from Mr. Crane. You wished him to modify one sentence where he had used the word 'gawd'. I have been trying to see Mr. Crane for the last week, but we have missed each other. I have now written to him about the matter and will let you know what he says." In a note he adds that Robert Underwood Johnson, associate editor of the *Century,* "certainly had the corrected proofs" (NN-Century Collection).

12 NOVEMBER. In the *Daily Tatler* John D. Barry defends *George's Mother* against detractors. He directs attention to "the intense humanity of the story," which never descends into mawkishness, and he is one of the first critics to compare Crane's literary style to impressionist painting. He says that the description of George and his mother going to a prayer meeting together is

> a unique example of impressionism in literature, as wonderful as a picture by Claude Monet. For the matter of that the whole book is the work of a master of literary impressionism.
>
> Whatever Mr. Crane may be in *The Red Badge of Courage*, he is not a realist in *George's Mother*. The little mother is real, but the son stands for a class, not an individual. Mr. Crane's conversation I don't believe in for a moment, nor do I believe that life is exactly as he depicts it, any more than I think the pictures of the impressionists are like the life they see. But the impressionists think they see what they describe, and that is enough. In *George's Mother* Mr. Crane has written a great book, and I shall be amazed if it does not have a revival.

13 NOVEMBER. Robert Finley writes to Reynolds: "Your letter to the effect that you have received $150 for us from the Evening World, in payment for the New York rights to the Stephen Crane serial received. According to our arrangement with you, you are to take $25 out of this sum as your commission for placing this serial" (ViU).

Heinemann deposits copy of the first English edition of *The Black Riders* in the British Museum.

14 NOVEMBER. The *Publishers' Circular* advertises the first Heinemann edition of *The Black Riders*.

21 NOVEMBER. NEW YORK. Crane applies for a passport and gives his address as the Bacheller syndicate (Copy, CtU).

25 NOVEMBER. Crane writes a check for $500 to Hawkins as "Agent" (NhD).

[26 OR 27 NOVEMBER]. Crane asks Harry Thompson to send him a copy of *George's Mother* if Edward Arnold has any available. He is leaving for Florida that day or in the morning at the latest (*C*, 259).

Stephen Crane in Jacksonville, dressed as a war
correspondent and posing on a livery stable horse,
8 December 1896
(Syracuse University)

CHAPTER FIVE

Florida and Greece
November 1896–May 1897

Shortly after arriving in Jacksonville Crane begins a relationship with Cora Howorth Murphy Stewart, the 31-year-old madam of one of the city's finest houses of assignation, which she operates under the name of Cora Taylor. Crane frequents the Jacksonville waterfront attempting to secure a means of passage to Cuba. On New Year's Eve he sails on the filibustering steamship *Commodore*, which has been cleared by the Treasury Department to carry men and munitions to the Cuban rebels. After a mysterious explosion in its boiler room the *Commodore* founders off the coast of Florida, and Crane and three members of the crew battle heavy seas for almost 30 hours in a 10-foot dinghy until it capsizes in the surf on the beach at Daytona. Out of this experience grows his most famous short story, "The Open Boat."

Following a brief trip to New York City and Hartwood, Crane returns to Florida and makes a prolonged, but futile, effort to find another ship to take him to Cuba. In March 1897 he returns to New York and signs a contract with Hearst's *New York Journal* to report the impending Greco-Turkish War. Later he negotiates an independent contract with the McClure syndicate, which sells his dispatches to other American newspapers and to the *Westminster Gazette*. Cora accompanies him to Greece, and together they report the brief 30-day struggle, consisting largely of retreats and rearguard actions on the part of the Greeks at Pharsala, Velestino, and Domoko, and ending in their complete defeat. *The Third Violet* is published in May. After the armistice is signed the Cranes linger for a few days in Athens and then depart for France, where they spend almost two weeks before proceeding to England.

[27 NOVEMBER]. Crane leaves New York for Jacksonville with a retainer of $700 in Spanish gold from the Bacheller syndicate to report the Cuban insurrection (Bacheller 1928, 292–293). He is accompanied by Amy Leslie, who travels with him as far as Washington, D.C.

28 NOVEMBER. SAUSALITO, CALIFORNIA. The Japanese poet Yoni Noguchi writes to Crane: "I love you: I admire you: Would you like

to be my friend—will you not? Is it too much rude to speak out boldly about that? Why, I don't think so! I am Yoni Noguchi, a little Japanese who live at present at pacific Coast, of course you know—. I regret verily much, some uneducated (in poetry) people compares me with you—I don't like such comparison, as perhaps you don't" (*C,* 259).

Crane arrives in Jacksonville and with Sylvester Scovel of the *New York World* and his assistants registers at the St. James Hotel under the name of Samuel Carleton (*Daily Florida Citizen,* 3 December).

LATE NOVEMBER–EARLY DECEMBER. Charles Michelson recalled that, unlike some of the other correspondents gathered in Jacksonville attempting to find means of passage to Cuba, Crane maintained a low profile:

> In the first place he was there on the lurky business of joining a filibustering expedition, that being the usual way of joining the rebel forces, and as Spanish spies were supposed to be as thick about the outfitting ports as German agents were reputed to be twenty years later, the gun-running masters insisted on inconspicuousness. In the second place Crane always disappeared on his arrival at a new town. He dived into the deep waters of society and stayed under. His associates knew where to find him and hailed him forth when the time came, but he never was to be looked for about his hotel or in the bright cafés where the rest of us sunned ourselves during the waiting-time. . . . Night after night Stephen loitered in the back room of a grimy waterfront saloon, partially, doubtless, because it was close to the dock, but largely because there people did not talk to him about his books—book, rather, for *The Red Badge of Courage* was the only one people knew about then.
> This was the period he was supposed to be sunk in debauchery. Actually he was consuming innumerable bottles of beer—I never knew him to take anything stronger—and listening to the talk of oilers, deck hands, sponge fishermen, wharf-rats and dock thieves, and all the rest of the human flotsam that is washed into a port that has the West Indies for a front yard. This was his way of soaking in knowledge of the reactions of the kind of men he loved to write about, and while he was at it he was one of them—a sombre, silent member, contributing no adventure of his own, never flushing his quarry with a word that was not in their vocabulary. (*Work,* 12: xi-xiii)

29 NOVEMBER. SUNDAY. Expecting that a filibustering ship will be available to take him to Cuba the next day, Crane dictates a will that he sends to his lawyer brother, William, whom he appoints as executor of his estate. He divides his assets among his brothers and appoints Howells, Garland, Hawkins, and Hitchcock as his literary ex-

ecutors. He proposes two groups of stories that might be posthumously collected as books: his *New York Press* sketches of city life under the title of "Midnight Sketches" and a group of adventure stories that would include "One Dash—Horses," "The Wise Men," "The Snake," and "A Man and Some Others." In a final reference to the Dora Clark affair, he maintains "that your brother in that case acted like a man of honor and a gentlemen and you need not fear to hold your head up to anybody and defend his name" (*C,* 265–266). Crane also dictates a letter to Amy Leslie and a letter to Hawkins, with whom he has deposited funds to distribute to Amy and, if necessary, to himself. He asks Hawkins to befriend Amy "in what is now really a great trouble" (*C,* 267), implying that she might be pregnant. On the same day he writes another letter to Amy in which he avers that "the few moments on your train at Washington were the most painful of my life and if I live a hundred years I know I can never forget them." In the evening he writes her yet a third letter, "with all the love in the world" (*C,* 268–269).

A Tenderloin story, "Yen-Hock Bill and His Sweetheart," appears in the *New York Journal.*

30 NOVEMBER. C. R. Bisbee, collector of customs at Jacksonville, telegraphs the secretary of the treasury: SYLVESTER S. SCOVEL, WAR CORRESPONDENT OF THE NEW YORK WORLD WISHES TO CLEAR STEAMER COMMODORE IN · A FEW DAYS FOR HAVANA WITHOUT CARGO TO BE USED AS A DISPATCH BOAT IN THE EMPLOY OF SAID PAPER. SHALL I DO SO? (Copy, NSyU).

1 DECEMBER. Hawkins sends Amy Leslie $35 in response to her request for money (NhD).

2 DECEMBER. Three men "whose movements are reported to be very mysterious . . . are being closely watched by Spanish spies. One of them is registered under the name of George H. Brown, although this is for convenience. He is said to be an expert dynamiter, and will do effective work, for the Cuban cause. Another one is Samuel Carlton [sic], who is reported to be an ex-Lieutenant in the army, and who is fully up to war tactics and maneuvers. The third one is H. K. Sheridan, who will handle a melenite gun, it is said" (*Daily Florida Citizen*).

WASHINGTON, D.C. W. E. Curtis, acting secretary of the treasury, responds to the collector of customs in Jacksonville: YOUR TELEGRAM OF 30TH ULTIMO REGARDING STEAMER "COMMODORE" STATES FACTS WHICH THIS DEPARTMENT HAS NO POWER TO CONSIDER, IN CONNECTION WITH APPLICATION FOR

CLEARANCE PAPERS. IF OWNERS OR CHARTERS WISH TO CLEAR STEAMER IN BALLAST FOR HAVANA AND YOU ARE SATISFIED BY AFFIDAVIT OR OTHERWISE THAT THERE IS NO INTENTION TO VIOLATE NEUTRALITY OR NAVIGATION LAWS, PAPERS MAY BE GRANTED (Copy, NSyU).

3 DECEMBER. The *Florida Times-Union* announces that the three filibuster ships, the *Three Friends*, the *Commodore*, and the *Dauntless*, popularly known as "the Cuban navy," are all in the port of Jacksonville, "endeavoring to get clear of the meshes of the law" and that the *Commodore* will sail "either today or tomorrow for Havana, Cuba, direct, if the treasury department will allow Collector Bisbee to grant her clearance papers."

The alleged filibuster will go to Cuba this time as a dispatch boat for the New York World, and will carry the World correspondent, who is registered at the St. James hotel as George H. Brown. The correspondent has called on Collector Bisbee several times, but Collector Bisbee refuses to be interviewed on the subject.

The Commodore has had her hull cleaned, and has been thoroughly overhauled. She has taken on coal and water, and is now lying at the wharf of the Merrill-Stevens Engineering company, taking on provisions purchased from local dealers. Captain Thomas H. Morton, her former commander, is here, and will probably be in command.

The Cubans say that they have nothing to do with this trip of the Commodore, and that as far as they know she will not carry any munitions of war. It would be foolish, they say, to think of sending arms on a steamer that is going direct to Havana.

The Commodore is one of the fastest boats on the South Atlantic coast, and the revenue cutter Boutwell would be left far behind if she attempted to follow her.

The World correspondent is not named Brown, although that is the name he used at the custom-house. He is Sylvester Scovil [*sic*], war correspondent of the World, who was with Maceo, the Cuban general, on the famous march across the island in which Weyler's trocha was broken. He is accompanied by H. K. Sheridan, George A. Pechen and Samuel Carleton, or at least those are the names the gentlemen are passing under, but the latter is believed to be Walter [*sic*] Crane. Both are assistants of Scovil, and are sent by the World to thoroughly cover the field. It is hardly possible that these newspaper men are going to Havana in the Commodore, for, if that was their object, they could go direct by the Plant Steamship Line or the Key West and Miami steamer. They no doubt desire to reach some other part of the island, and have chartered the Commodore to land them, and may use the boat to send dispatches direct from the insurgents' camps to Key West, where they will be forwarded by telegraph.

Cora Crane, probably taken about the time of her
marriage to Captain Donald William Stewart in 1889
and inscribed later to a niece
(Syracuse University)

BEFORE 4 DECEMBER. Crane meets Cora Taylor at her place of business, a house of assignation named the Hotel de Dream (a pun on the name of its former proprietress, Ethel Dreme). She is 31 years old, divorced from her first husband, Thomas Vinton Murphy, and the estranged wife of an English aristocrat, Captain Donald William Stewart, younger son of a baronet (Gilkes 1960, 20–25).

4 DECEMBER. Leroy Fairman, a poker playing friend, sends $95 to Crane under the name Samuel Carleton (NNC). Crane inscribes the copy of *George's Mother* he requested from Harry Thompson to Cora as "an unnamed sweetheart" (*C*, 270) and an unidentified book to her under the initials of her married name, Cora Ethel Stewart:

> To C. E. S.
>
> Brevity is an element
> that enters importantly
> into all pleasures of
> life and this is what
> makes pleasure sad
> and so there is no
> pleasure but only sad-
> ness.
>
> Stephen Crane
> Jacksonville, Fla
> Nov [for December] 4th, 1896. (*C*, 269)

Crane also gives Cora a copy of an American edition of Rudyard Kipling's *The Seven Seas* (1896), which she later inscribes "The first thing my mouse ever gave me was this book" (Kibler, 221).

The *Florida Times-Union* reports that the *Commodore* has not yet cleared customs and not even so intrepid a commander as Captain Thomas H. Morton would risk sailing without legal authority, but the *Daily Florida Citizen* states that the steamer can leave after the captain signs an affidavit saying it is not on a filibustering expedition.

5 DECEMBER. Although the *Daily Florida Citizen* reports that the secretary of the treasury has granted the *Commodore* permission to leave for Cuba, the *Florida Times-Union* says that "it now looks as though the negotiations for the charter of the steamer Commodore by the New York World are off, and that the boat will not go to Cuba as a dispatch boat, but this does not mean that some other boat may not be used for that purpose by Sylvester Scovil [*sic*], the World's corre-

spondent, and his assistants." According to the *Citizen*, Scovel "has other plans under consideration, and one of these is the securing of the fastest possible boat."

6 DECEMBER. The *Florida Times-Union* reports that "there is now every evidence that the deal for the charter of the steamer Commodore by the New York World is off" and that the *World* has "purchased or chartered a fast boat at New York" to take "Sylvester Scovil [*sic*], war correspondent, Walter [*sic*] Crane and the other two assistants of the correspondents . . . to Cuba, but not to Havana, as reported. . . . The real intention is said to be to land two correspondents on the coast of Pinar del Rio to watch the operations in that province while the other two will be landed in the province of Puerto Principe and will join General Gomez' forces."

8 DECEMBER. Captain Morton applies at the customs house for clearance papers to sail the *Commodore* from Jacksonville to Truxillo, British Honduras (*Florida Times-Union*, 9 December).

Sylvester Scovel and his companions, including Crane, don war correspondents' uniforms and are photographed with their equipment on livery stable horses (*Florida Times-Union*, 9 December).

The steamer Commodore, the suspected filibuster, which has been lying in this port since last August, will leave today, but whether she carries Sylvester Scovil [*sic*], the World's war correspondent, to Cuba or not, remains to be seen. (*Florida Times-Union*)

WASHINGTON, D.C. W. E. Curtis again telegraphs C. R. Bisbee in Jacksonville: IS "COMMODORE" CHARTERED BY NEW YORK WORLD FOR TRUXILLO? FOR AFFIDAVIT OF MASTER. INVESTIGATE THOROUGHLY AND REPORT TO DEPARTMENT OBJECT OF PROPOSED VOYAGE. CONSULT U.S. ATTORNEY AND CAPTAIN CUTTER "BOUTWELL." DEPARTMENT WILL INSTRUCT WHEN INFORMED OF FACTS. (Copy, NSyU)

Captain Morton is refused clearance papers. Upon learning of the disposition, he and "the charterers . . . were not all pleased. There was some talk of going out from this port without clearing and applying at some other port for a clearance, but the arrival of the revenue cutter Boutwell and the knowledge that the cruiser Newark was lying off the bar soon put an end to this" (*Florida Times-Union*, 9 December).

9 DECEMBER. JACKSONVILLE. Captain Morton appears before a notary public and swears that he is the master of the *Commodore* and desires

clearance for Truxillo, Honduras. He claims that he will leave Jacksonville without cargo and make no intermediate stop, and also states that "contracts heretofore made with the New York World have been canceled and that the steamer 'Commodore' has no reference or connection whatever with any newspaper" (Copy, NSyU).

The *Florida Times-Union* reports:

> It now appears that the World correspondents have not intended to go to Havana on the Commodore, and that the application for clearance to that port was only a big bluff. The Commodore and her master, Captain Morton, are too well known to the Spaniards to be friends and allies of the Cuban cause to risk taking her inside the harbor of Havana, for once inside it is doubtful if either would be permitted to leave again in a hurry.
>
> In fact, the entire project, as given out by the World men, appears to have been a bluff, and if the Commodore had succeeded in clearing she would no doubt have been back here in a few days. The World men were merely using this steamer as a blind, but now that she is tied up for several days they will no doubt show their hand. The World really has made other arrangements for getting its men to Cuba and the Commodore deal was positively declared off last Saturday.

10 DECEMBER. Bisbee forwards Morton's affidavit to the secretary of the treasury and affirms that he has consulted with the United States district attorney and Captain Kilgore of the Boutwell and there is general agreement that the Commodore might be cleared to sail. He cautions:

> I have no means of ascertaining what may be done by this vessel after she gets clear of American waters,—certain it is that she will not be permitted to carry munitions of war out of this river. She has a crew list of 14, and a passenger list of 5 persons.
>
> On the surface, everything appears correct. The "Newark" might convey her beyond the jurisdiction of the United States the master is anxiously awaiting your decision, and a reply by "wire" would be acceptable. The "Commodore" has been "laid up" in our port for three months.
>
> At the conference had with Captain Kilgore, he expressed himself as believing that the affidavit is in good faith, and that under the circumstances the "Commodore" might be permitted to depart. (Copy, NSyU)

Hawkins sends Amy Leslie another $120, "which was the amount Mr. Fairman said Miss Leslie told him (last evening) she would need today" (NhD).

[11 DECEMBER]. Crane writes a love letter to Amy Leslie: "I think of you, night and day, my own love. Remember me sweetheart even in your dreams" (*C*, 270).

12 DECEMBER. WASHINGTON, D.C. The U. S. Treasury Department clears the *Commodore* for departure to Truxillo, Honduras (Copy, NSyU).

[12 DECEMBER]. Crane begins a letter on Saturday to Amy Leslie to which he appends notations on Sunday and on Monday describing preparations for departure for Cuba. On Monday he adds: "Seems sure that we leave tomorrow. I love you, mine own girl. Be good and wait for me. I love you" (*C*, 271).

13 DECEMBER. The *Three Friends*, carrying munitions and men, sails for Cuba without authorization; Ralph D. Paine and other correspondents are aboard. To mislead local authorities and Spanish spies and to facilitate the departure, the *Commodore* had earlier in the day served as a "dummy filibuster" pretending to prepare for a secret mission by displaying a placard reading "positively no admittance" and by posting a watchman to prevent people from boarding (*Florida Times-Union*, 14, 24, 25 December).

14 DECEMBER. The *Daily Florida Citizen* lists a number of the correspondents waiting in Jacksonville for boats to Cuba and states that "Sylvester Scovel of the New York *World* has been here for several days with Stephen Crane, the novelist, all thirsting for fame and glory on the battlefields of Cuba as non-combatants. Several of these writers have come to Florida, trusting to luck or some chance expedition to reach the scene of their labors."

17 DECEMBER. Hawkins pays Amy Leslie an additional $25 (NhD).

19 DECEMBER. In the *Saturday Review*, H. G. Wells presents an ambivalent evaluation of *Maggie*:

The relative merits of "The Red Badge of Courage" and "Maggie" are open to question. To the present reviewer it seems that in "Maggie" we come nearer to Mr. Crane's individuality. Perhaps where we might expect strength we get merely stress, but one may doubt whether we have not been hasty in assuming Mr. Crane to be a strong man in fiction. Strength and gaudy colour rarely go together; tragic and sombre are well nigh inseparable. One gets the impression from the "Red Badge" that at the end Mr. Crane could scarcely have had a gasp left in him—that he must have been mentally hoarse for weeks after it. But here he works chiefly for pretty effects, for gleams of sunlight on the stagnant puddles he paints. He gets them, a little consciously perhaps, but, to the present reviewer's sense, far more effectively than he gets anger and fear. And he has done his work, one feels, to please himself. His book is a work of art, even if it is not a very great or successful work of art—it ranks above the novel of commerce, if only on that account.

The *Minneapolis Tribune* finds *The Little Regiment* "intensely realistic. In fact, the whole thing seems to be projected on the mental vision as from a stereopticon slide. The stories are fascinating but there is a sameness about them that makes one wish that the writer will not always give us war stories. Perhaps battles cannot be varied in description and preserve their charm. So let us have variety, along some other line if Mr. Crane is to be a permanent favorite."

20 DECEMBER. The *New York Tribune* considers *The Little Regiment* a significant advance over Crane's previous work:

The trouble with "The Red Badge of Courage" was that it took a great deal of mannerism, a great deal of "art," and spread it thin over too large a surface. Then, on the strength of the specious encouragement offered by some of the critics of that book, Mr. Crane brought his vaunted realism to bear upon urban slums, and straightway sank lower than ever in the estimation of cool-headed readers. In "The Little Regiment" he goes far to redeem his literary reputation from reproach. His descriptive taste is still a trifle florid and artificial; he still has too much confidence in the style of word painting which his friends have praised for its color and vividness. The color is forced. The vividness is doubtful. But the broad effect of the sketches gathered together in this little volume is unquestionably voracious and original. Moreover, the situations exploited are picturesque and dramatic. The gentle fun with which the tale of the "Three Miraculous Soldiers" is developed is a stroke which is emphatically creditable to Mr. Crane's imaginative instinct and to his skill as a designer. If he carries a sense of design in his present work, it must also be stated that the present term may be used without any suggestion of hollow artifice in the man. The stories are workmanlike, but they are human, and in the particular narrative to which reference has just been made there is a certain artless verisimilitude which we had thought was quite beyond Mr. Crane. He proves in this book that with a certain concision in his plots and a toning down of his rhetoric he may earn a position of serious import among American writers of fiction.

The *Daily Florida Citizen* notes:

Not a hint of any but the strongest of action appears in this collection of episodes of the American Civil War. They are full of virility and spring, of eager life and intense emotion. They are not without a certain dry humor, but their keynote is necessarily tragedy. Mr. Crane's forceful writing is too well known to need dilation upon; his pen pictures of army scenes are like things alive; one can, as he reads, feel the rush of swift motion in the charge, the dull, vague uneasiness that besets the private waiting, for he knows not what, the keen watchfulness of the scout on duty.

Bacheller syndicates "Stephen Crane in Minetta Lane," an anecdotal history of a crime-ridden Greenwich Village street.

22 DECEMBER. Reynolds writes to Robert Underwood Johnson, associate editor of the *Century*, in reference to another allusion Crane was evidently required to drop from "A Man and Some Others": "I have your letter of Dec. 19th. I must confess that the expression 'British' in the connection you mention does not strike me as especially offensive. I think it was merely a humorous touch. I don't think it is nearly as offensive as many of the references to Americans that you see in English books and English Magazines. However, you may properly say I am not the judge. It is hardly necessary to say that Mr. Crane will not like the excisions in his Ms. He is I believe not in New York at the present, so I cannot communicate with him. I suppose however it is pretty safe to say that an author does not like to see the child of his brain cut or in any way changed" (Copy, NSyU).

24 DECEMBER. Crane telegraphs Hawkins: "leave soon telegraph Frankly amys mental condition. Also send fifty if possible. Will arrange payments from appleton troubled over Amy" (*C,* 272).

28 DECEMBER. Hawkins sends Crane the $50 he requested (NhD).

31 DECEMBER. Amy Leslie receives $25 from Hawkins (NhD).

The *Florida Times-Union* reports that the secretary of the treasury has wired C. R. Bisbee to clear the steamer *Dauntless* for Nuevetas, Cuba, and the *Commodore* for Cienfuegas, Cuba, "both with cargoes of munitions of war":

As soon as the news that the collector had been authorized to clear the Dauntless with a cargo of arms and ammunition for Cuba was heard on the streets the Cubans were jubilant. The Cuban Junta was notified and preparations were at once begun for the shipment of other cargoes from this port.

Paul Rojo, agent of the owner of the steamship Commodore, called at the custom-house in the afternoon and made formal application to clear the Commodore for Cienfuegas, Cuba, with a cargo of arms and ammunition. The collector would not issue the papers until he had communicated with the secretary of the treasury. He at once sent a telegram, and in a short time received a reply from Secretary Carlisle, notifying him that clearance may be granted the Commodore on the same terms as the Dauntless, in accordance with the law, but that the collector must be satisfied that there is no intention to violate the neutrality laws of the United States.

Pedro Solis, the Spanish consul for Florida, protests the clearance of the *Commodore* on the grounds that Spanish law prohibits arms and ammunition "from being landed in any of the ports of Cuba without permission of the authorities of the Spanish Government" and that he believes "the said cargo of arms, ammunition and munitions of war intended to be conveyed by the said steamer 'Commodore' from this port will not be delivered to the port on the Island of Cuba, for which the said steamer or owner of said steamer asks for clearance, and that the said cargo of arms and ammunition, I believe is intended for the use of the insurgents now in rebellion against the lawful government of the Kingdom of Spain" (Copy, NSyU). Although Solis files an official complaint about vessels traveling to Cuba with weapons for the insurgents, he tells the *Florida Times-Union* that he would approve the shipment of war supplies "'just the same as if the cargo were potatoes for the Spanish soldiers. I wish the vessels were larger, for then I would get a larger fee, as my fee is so much per ton, and the greater the tonnage of the vessel the more I receive. I would like to make a fee, as I have not made one here in Jacksonville,' and the consul smiled at the prospect of receiving a fee from the Cubans."

The *Commodore* sails from Jacksonville at approximately 8:00 P.M. with 27 or 28 men and a cargo of supplies and ammunition for the Cuban rebels. The chief items are "203,000 cartridges," "1,000 pounds of giant powder," and "40 bundles of rifles." Crane is aboard "as the representative of a syndicate of Northern newspapers. He will not be employed in the capacity of a newsgatherer, but will write Sunday letters to the papers of New York, Philadelphia, Chicago, Pittsburgh and Boston. He was asked how long he expected to stay in the island, and replied that he could not tell. He shipped as a seaman at a salary of $20 a month" (*Florida Times-Union*, 1, 2, and 4 January 1897). Less than two miles from Jacksonville in a dense fog on the St. John's River, the *Commodore* strikes a sandbar, and, says Crane in his syndicated report of the *Commodore* sinking, "in this ignominious position we were compelled to stay until daybreak" (*New York Press*, 7 January 1897; *Works*, 9: 86).

*

1897

*

JANUARY. Under the title "Ouida's Masterpiece" the *Book Buyer* publishes Crane's appreciation of Marie Louise de la Ramée's two-volume illustrated edition of *Under Two Flags*. Crane contends that Ouida's novel expresses "the old spirit of dauntless deed and sacrifice which is the soul of literature in every age, and we are not growing too tired to listen, although we try to believe so" (*Works*, 8: 678). The *Book Buyer* also reviews *The Little Regiment*, deploring the impressionistic effect that marred *The Red Badge* but finding the book "distinctly less depressing."

The *Philistine* reprints "The Men in the Storm." In his column "Side Talks with the Philistines" Elbert Hubbard comments: "Can you read the sketch in this issue entitled 'The Men in the Storm' and then say that Stephen Crane is not a man of generous sympathies and clear, vivid insight?" In a facetious vein, Hubbard adds: "The Polychrome Bible has been such a success in shedding light on dark places that I understand Stephen Crane has seriously contemplated a polychrome edition of his verse. The fatal objection was Mr. Crane's dislike to the color scheme. He is said to have announced his decision in similar terms to those used by Dean Richmond once when it was proposed to experiment in the painting of some New York Central freight cars. 'You can paint them cars any damn color you like,' said Mr. Richmond, 'so long as you paint 'em red.'"

I JANUARY. At 2:30 A.M. the mate of the *Commodore* boards the revenue cutter *Boutwell* and requests assistance in floating the *Commodore*. At dawn the *Boutwell* attaches a line to the *Commodore* and tows the steamer off the sandbar and some distance down the St. John's River. No examination is made of the damaged hull. At Mayport the *Commodore* is beached again. As Crane describes the incident,

The *Boutwell* was fussing around us in her venerable way, and, upon seeing our predicament, she came again to assist us, but this time with engines reversed the *Commodore* dragged herself away from the grip of the sand and again the *Commodore* headed for the open sea.

The captain of the revenue cutter grew curious. He hailed the *Commodore*: "Are you fellows going to sea to-day?"

Captain Murphy of the *Commodore* called back: "Yes, sir." And then as the whistle of the *Commodore* saluted him Captain Kilgore doffed his cap and said: "Well, gentlemen, I hope you have a pleasant cruise," and this was our last words from shore. (*Works*, 9: 86–87)

At approximately 10:00 P.M. a suspicious leak is discovered in the boiler room, and Captain Murphy starts the pumps, which prove to be defective. The boat comes to a standstill about 16 miles from Mosquito Inlet (*New York Times*, 4 January). When sailors panic, Crane is among the four or five who "soon quieted the excitement and put everybody to work on the pumps and with buckets" (*Florida Times-Union*, 3 January). As the water gains, Crane describes the engine room as resembling "a scene at this time taken from the middle kitchen of hades. In the first place, it was insufferably warm, and the lights burned faintly in a way to cause mystic and grewsome shadows. There was a quantity of soapish sea water swirling and sweeping and swishing among machinery that roared and banged and clattered and steamed, and in the second place, it was a devil of a ways down below" (*Works*, 9: 89).

In the *Fortnightly Review* H. D. Traill questions the realism of *The Red Badge of Courage* and finds *Maggie* and *George's Mother* crude and unconvincing compared to Arthur Morrison's *Tales of Mean Streets* and *A Child of the Jago*.

2 JANUARY. In the early hours of the morning the *Commodore's* boats are lowered. The *New York Press* account for 4 January quotes the steward, Charles B. Montgomery, as stating that "'One of the Cubans got rattled and tried to run out one of the boats before time, and Crane let him have it right from the shoulder, and the man rolled down the leeway, stunned for the moment.'" Three lifeboats leave the vessel and one of them founders; the seven men on the lost boat return to the *Commodore* and build rafts, but the first mate dies when he leaps toward one of the rafts and plunges into the sea. Three men are still on board when the *Commodore* sinks at 7:00 A.M.; three on the improvised rafts also lose their lives. The remaining lifeboats reach shore by noon. Captain Edward Murphy, William Higgins, an oiler, Montgomery, and Crane are the last to leave the ship in a 10-foot dinghy. They drift alongside the *Commodore* until she goes down, and attempt to save the men on the rafts. According to Crane's account,

The colored stoker on the first raft threw us a line and we began to tow. Of course, we perfectly understood the absolute impossibility of any such thing; our dingy was within six inches of the water's edge, there was an enormous sea running, and I knew that under the circumstances a tug-boat would have no light task in moving these rafts. But we tried it, and would have continued to try it indefinitely, but that something critical came to pass. I was at an oar and so faced the rafts. The cook controlled the line. Suddenly the boat began to go backward, and then we saw this negro on the first raft pulling on the line hand over hand and drawing us to him.

He had turned into a demon. He was wild, wild as a tiger. He was crouched on this raft and ready to spring. Every muscle of him seemed to be turned into an elastic spring. His eyes were almost white. His face was the face of a lost man reaching upward, and we knew that the weight of his hand on our gunwale doomed us. The cook let go of the line. (*Works,* 9: 93)

10:00 A.M. Twelve Cubans in a lifeboat commanded by Paul Rojo land about two miles north of the Mosquito Inlet lighthouse, after five or six hours of rowing. Four more Cubans in a second lifeboat commanded by Major Julio Baz land about noon (Day, 194).

4:00 P.M. The dinghy approaches the coast of Florida a few miles south of Daytona. The men attempt to attract the attention of people on shore, only a quarter of a mile away, by flying a flag of distress. Captain Murphy fires his pistol a number of times, but there is no response. Captain Murphy, who had sustained a broken arm aboard the *Commodore*, decides to wait until morning before attempting to beach the dinghy in the heavy surf. Higgins and Crane take turns rowing all night to keep beyond the breakers. By morning the wind and current have carried them north off Daytona Beach (Day, 193–194).

9:00 P.M. Captain Thomas H. Morton writes to Cora Taylor: "I am very sorry that I have no encouraging word to send you. The eleven men who were saved have arrived in town. One of them saw Mr Crane get out of his berth and dress himself with that same non-plussed manner, characteristic of him. He entered the boat containing the 16, which is reported to have swamped. There is conflicting rumors as to the empty boat being washed ashore. Some say it has been washed ashore at Port Orange—others say not. The Operator at New Smyrna tells me that he has it pretty straight that it came in, bottom up. God save Crane if he is still alive" (*C,* 273).

3 JANUARY. SUNDAY. The *Florida Times-Union* reports that "the steamer Commodore, which left here Thursday night with an expedi-

tion for the Cuban insurgents, is now resting on the bottom of the sea, twenty fathoms below the surface, about eighteen miles northeast of Mosquito Inlet."

Sometime between 7:30 and 10:00 A.M. an attempt is made to land the dinghy at Daytona Beach, but it overturns. Crane, Montgomery, and Murphy—the first two wearing life belts (*Boston Daily Globe*, 5 January)—swim and wade ashore, Crane presumably losing the money belt with Bacheller's gold in the surf (Bacheller 1928, 292–293), or, as he later told Bacheller, throwing the gold into the sea before he took to the water (Bacheller 1933, 112), but Higgins drowns. Crane is vague about the cause of his death: "John Kitchell of Daytona came running down the beach, and as he ran the air was filled with clothes. If he had pulled a single lever and undressed, even as the fire horses harness, he could not to me seem to have stripped with more speed. He dashed into the water and grabbed the cook. Then he went after the captain, but the captain sent him to me, and then it was that we saw Billy Higgins lying with his forehead on sand that was clear of the water, and he was dead" (*Works*, 9: 94). Other newspaper accounts of Higgins's death are different and contradictory. According to the *Florida Times-Union* (4 January), Higgins was struck on the head by the dinghy when it overturned in the surf. The *New York Press* (5 January) quotes Captain Murphy as crediting Crane with trying to save Higgins: "'He held up Higgins when the latter got so terribly tired and endeavored to bring him in, but the sailor was so far gone that he could hardly help himself.'" In the *Florida Times-Union* (5 January) Murphy omits any role for Crane: "Higgins tried to swim, but sank. I tried to encourage him, and he made another attempt. The boat went over again, and I saw no more of him until his corpse came up on the beach." The *New York Herald* (4 January) reports: "Higgins had been hurt by falling into the dingy from the Commodore's deck. He was unconscious when landed, and died an hour after reaching Daytona." The *Boston Daily Globe* (4 January) reprints the eyewitness account of the cook, C. B. Montgomery:

> When we all got into the boat he took the stroke oar and manfully pulled. When it became so rough that we could hardly row he started bailing, meanwhile talking as unconcernedly as if on a vessel deck.
> When entering the surf he stood at the prow, trying to pick a clear path. As the boat went over he fell forward, and the heavy oars struck his head, forcing him under. We aided him as he came up, but he begged us to let him go, as each one had all he could attend to. Again, a few minutes later on, the boat drove full tilt on him, forcing him under. As he came up it was seen that he was nearly gone, blood streaming from his hurts. As

soon as he reached land he was taken up and carried tenderly up the beach and every attention paid to him, but of no avail. In half an hour he breathed his last.

Capt. Murphy breathed a sigh as the sailor died, and said, with a tear in his eye, and with a tremble in his tone, "There goes a brave man."

[Montgomery is also quoted in the *Globe* as maintaining that five men rather than four were in the dinghy, but in the *New York Journal* (4 January) he refers to "the four of us." The contradiction, which has long been debated, centers on the number of people aboard the *Commodore*. Although the *Florida Times-Union* lists 28 names on 1 January, evidence in the paper on 4 January suggests that one of the crew quit just before sailing. According to Captain Murphy's account, which various newspapers carried, this crew member was replaced, thus raising the total to 28 again. The log of the *Boutwell*, however, reads "Number persons on board, 27" (Stallman 1972, 550).]

In the afternoon Cora Taylor wires Crane at Daytona: "Telegram received. Thank God your safe have been almost crazy." Later in the afternoon she sends another telegram: "Come by special today never mind overcharges answer and come surely" (*C*, 274, 276). Crane tries to get a "special train" to take him to Jacksonville but fails because no trains run south of St. Augustine on Sunday (*Florida Times-Union*, 4 January).

4 JANUARY. Cora Taylor travels to Daytona and returns to Jacksonville with Crane in the evening. One hundred to two hundred Cubans greet him and other survivors of the *Commodore* at the train station. Captain Murphy "is averse to talking much" about the sinking of the boat because "the Cuban leaders had given him a hint that it would be better to say little," and he denies "the report that the vessel touched on the bar going out" (*Boston Daily Globe*, 5 January). Perhaps in response to telegrams printed earlier in the day in the *Florida Times-Union* from survivors claiming that the *Commodore* was scuttled and that the pumps were tampered with, he calls the charge of treachery "a damned lie." Paul E. F. Rojo, agent for the owners of the boat and commandant of the Cubans on board, claims that Chief Engineer Redigan was drunk, a charge denied by Crane and Montgomery. Montgomery then charges that Rojo "was the first man to leave the vessel after the fires went out and foundering was inevitable" and that he and his associates "saved their baggage, even to their overcoats" (*Florida Times-Union*, 5 January). Crane may have been thinking of Rojo when he later says to Horatio S. Rubens, general counsel of the Cuban Junta, "'He reminded me of George Washington . . . first

in war, first in peace—and first in the lifeboat'" (Rubens, 155). Montgomery also recalls his reason for believing in treachery: "I had good reason to feel uneasy for before leaving a Spaniard, whom I had met in New York, sent word from shore that he wanted to see me. I replied that I could not see him. He came to the ship and begged me not to go, but I told him I was going. He sent word to me five minutes before the ship left: 'My God, Charlie, don't go on that ship. You risk your life.'" Charges of treachery are repeated in the *New York Times* and the *Herald*, but Crane denies any knowledge of sabotage. He telegraphs the *World*, "I am unable to write a thing yet but will later" (*New York World*, 5 January). The *Press* assures its readers that Crane "is not of the sort who are frightened by an experience in a lifeboat. His letters will appear in the Press as soon as they arrive."

Later in the evening Crane inscribes an autograph book for Lillian Barrett, a nine-year-old autograph collector staying at the St. James Hotel: "Stephen Crane, Able Seaman, SS Commodore" (*C*, 276).

5 JANUARY. In the *New York Press*, Captain Murphy extols Crane's heroism:

> That man Crane is the spunkiest fellow out. . . . The sea was so rough that even old sailors got seasick when we struck the open sea after leaving the bar, but Crane behaved like a born sailor. He and I were about the only ones not affected by the big seas which tossed us about. As we went south he sat in the pilot house with me, smoking and telling yarns. When the leak was discovered he was the first man to volunteer aid.
>
> His shoes, new ones, were slippery on the deck, and he took them off and tossed them overboard, saying, with a laugh: "Well, captain, I guess I won't need them if we have to swim." He stood on the deck by me all the while, smoking his cigarette, and aided me greatly when the boats were getting off. When in the dingey he suggested putting up the overcoat for a sail, and he took his turn at the oars or holding up the oar mast.
>
> When we went over I called to him to see that his life preserver was on all right and he replied in his usual tones, saying that he would obey orders. He was under the boat once, but got out in some way. . . . When we were thrown up by the waves, Crane was the first man to stagger up the beach looking for houses. "He's a thoroughbred," concluded the captain, "and a brave man, too, with plenty of grit."

6 JANUARY. Crane telegraphs the *Atlanta Journal*: "Seven of the Commodore's men are now unaccounted for. The ship was probably not scuttled. I will stay in Jacksonville until another expedition starts for Cuba" (*C*, 277).

7 JANUARY. Crane's account of the sinking of the *Commodore* is syndicated by Bacheller and the *New York Press*, which copyrighted the report and seems to have had some control over its distribution (*Works*, 9: 468), under various headlines, appearing in the *New York Press* as "Stephen Crane's Own Story." An unidentified Asbury Park newspaper later reports that a "New York paper wired him an offer of $1000 for 1000 words about the affair. He needed money, as, indeed, was usually the case with him, but he kept faith with the syndicate" (Copy, NSyU).

Hawkins sends another $20 to Amy Leslie, and into mid-March he continues to give her small sums from the fund Crane left with him (NhD).

[EARLY JANUARY]. Crane inscribes an unidentified book to Cora, paraphrasing his poem "I explain the silvered passing of a ship at night" (*C*, 279–280):

> To C. E. S.
> Love comes like the tall
> swift shadow of a ship at
> night. There is for a mom-
> ent, the music of the water's
> turmoil, a bell, perhaps, a
> man's shout, a row of gleam-
> ing yellow lights. Then the
> slow sinking of this mystic
> shape. Then silence and a
> bitter silence—the silence
> of the sea at night.
>
> Stephen Crane

8 JANUARY. Horatio S. Rubens concludes the private inquiry into the sinking of the *Commodore*, and "as far as could be ascertained the blame of the accident was laid to the ignorance of those on board as to the construction of certain portions of the pumps and other machinery." C. B. Montgomery's charge of treachery is refuted, and his claim of cowardice on the part of Cubans during the sinking is met with "violent disavowals" (*Florida Times-Union*, 9 January).

10 JANUARY. The *Florida Times-Union* maintains that Rubens's inquiry has not been concluded and questions the accuracy of blaming faulty equipment and ignorant crew members for the sinking of the *Commodore*. It also challenges the explanation that the accident occurred because of damage to the boat when it got stuck on a sandbar

in the St. John's River. "In short, the investigation grows more inter-esting and one who is supposed to know whereof he speaks was heard to say yesterday that 'there was a big leak somewhere and more than a few of those on board knew of it.' If this is a fact, a recollection of the lost mate, Crane, who was a fervent patriot in the cause of 'Cuba Libre,' will bring the sting of remorse to those cogni-zant of any intention in the sinking of the filibuster."

The *New York World* considers the title story to be the only worth-while piece in *The Little Regiment*, "And even that one seems to be a leftover fragment from the excess of descriptive matter gathered for" *The Red Badge of Courage*. "This is discouraging, for the stories seem to be, not early tentative efforts resurrected for pecuniary profit from the author's celebrity, but late productions concocted in the vein the public may be supposed to expect from Mr. Crane. So viewed they are distinctly a disappointment, artificial, labored, and uninteresting."

11 JANUARY. According to the *Florida Times-Union* (12 January), Crane leaves Jacksonville for Tampa and "will go to Cuba via the Plant steamer Olivette, if he cannot make the trip in any other way." He changes his plans, however, and leaves for New York City.

13 JANUARY. Crane arrives in New York. The *Port Jervis Union* (15 January) reports that "Stephen Crane, whose voyage to Cuba was cut short by the wreck of the filibuster steamer Commodore, returned to New York Wednesday night from Jacksonville. He had nothing to add to his biographic portrayal of the mishap to the expedition which he wrote to the New York Press. 'I am feeling stronger,' he said, 'and after a short rest I shall make new plans for my visit to Cuba.'"

Crane applies for a passport to Cuba, Mexico, and the West Indies, which is issued on 15 January. He describes himself as being 5 feet 8 1/4 inches tall, with gray eyes, light hair, a tawny mustache, and an oval, slightly thin face (Copy, CtU).

14 JANUARY. Two American steamboat inspectors report to the Trea-sury Department that the *Commodore* sank because the engineers misunderstood mechanical problems, but "old steamboat men say there is something very strange about the sinking" (*Florida Times-Union*, 15 January).

[MID-JANUARY–EARLY FEBRUARY]. Crane spends some three weeks in New York, where he completes "The Open Boat." He periodically visits Port Jervis during this period, and probably works on the story at his brother Edmund's house in Hartwood, although Edmund's daughter Edith Crane vigorously denied that Crane ever returned to Hartwood after he first left for Florida (Edith Crane to Thomas Beer, 30 December 1933 and 14 January 1934, CtY). Crane also contracts with S. S. Chamberlain, managing editor of the *New York Journal*, to report the Greco-Turkish War if he cannot reach Cuba.

One evening, near midnight, at the apex of Sixth Avenue and Broadway near 33rd Street, he meets Robert H. Davis, a *Journal* reporter. Davis recalls that as a young prostitute passed them, Crane

detached himself from my side, tossed his cigarette into Greeley Square, placed his left hand upon his heart, removed his hat, and made a most gallant bow. I have never seen a more exquisite gesture of chivalry than this youth sweeping the pavement with his black felt. . . .

"A stranger here?" inquired Crane with the utmost delicacy in his speech as though addressing one lost in a great city.

The girl stood there with her lips parted and a queer expression of indecision on her face. I do not know to this day whether she was lured by the beauty of his eyes and forehead or startled by the weakness of his chin and the poverty of his garb. She caught her breath.

"Well, suppose I am a stranger. Can you show me something?"

"Yes," replied the author of *Maggie*, "I can show you the way out, but if you prefer to remain—" Crane made another gesture with his felt and bowed with an air of magnificent finality.

The girl suddenly found an extra button at the throat of her coat and fastened herself in. The light seemed to go out of Stephen Crane's eyes as though some one had turned down a lamp from within.

"You shouldn't hang out here, kid," said Maggie in a throaty voice. "You look cold. You can't stand it. This fat guy can."

At last I was recognized.

The girl sauntered off utterly indifferent in the direction of Shanley's, Burns's, Delmonico's—

"This is a long cañon," said Crane. "I wonder if there *is* a way out." (Davis, xvii, xviii–xix)

16 JANUARY. In a review of *The Little Regiment*, the *Chicago Record* concludes that

This volume of sketches, rather than stories, was the result of a popular demand following the success of "The Red Badge of Courage." All of the tales bear the marks of hasty and careless work, although they exemplify excellently the Crane method. They are rough sketches of war and carnage done in glaring pigments. There is attempt also at the analysis of the passion of fear, following a suggestion of one of the elements of success in the author's earlier work.

Mr. Crane is not a scientist. His mind does not turn to the abstract. He is above all an impressionist, who now and then transcends in a happy combination of colors, but more by chance than real intention. There is a superficiality about the tales of "The Little Regiment" which is unfortunate. After "The Red Badge of Courage," many marveled at Crane's wonderful insight into nature, and opportunity was offered to prove himself by careful study a master of motives. But in this book the author reveals the rather flimsy foundation upon which this reputation was built.

19 JANUARY. In the early hours of the morning Crane is a guest at the annual French Ball given by the *Cercle Français de l'Harmonie* in Madison Square Garden. The ball begins at 11:00 P.M. the previous evening and is attended by 7,000 people. Upon being asked his impression of it, Crane responds, "'There is the reflection of the light upon the white shirt bosoms of the men. . . . That is about all I can see'" (*New York World*, 20 January). Police Captain Chapman, "the police apostle of purity" who had been Patrolman Becker's superior officer during the Dora Clark affair, is in charge of maintaining order. The presence of Chapman and his men makes "the place look commoner than Tammany Hall during an East Side 'spiel' and [casts] a heavier gloom than the whiskers of Chapman himself" (*New York Journal*, 20 January). When Crane leaves with some friends an attempt is made to arrest him for drunkenness (Schoberlin, XIII–29). The *World* (20 January), however, reports that the ball was decorous and that "there was but one arrest growing out of it, and that was made far from Madison Square Garden."

[Crane may also have been subjected to other police harassment in New York at this time. According to Thomas Beer, whose semifictional biographical accounts are not to be trusted, Crane was accosted leaving a theater with Mrs. William Sonntag, her cousin, the Reverend Patrick Hart, and her son, Henry Sonntag, who ostensibly told Beer the story. Beer places this episode in the first week of December 1898, when Crane was not in the city:

"Mother and Mr. Crane walked out into the lobby ahead of my cousin. As we got out, some man called, 'Oh, there's Stephen Crane!' Two or three men spoke to Mr. Crane. One of them, I think, was Acton Davies. Mr. Crane attracted a good deal of attention. A policeman suddenly shoved through the people, asked if his name was Stephen Crane and then said, 'Come 'round to the station, you drunken bum!' My mother cried out. The fellow turned and yelled at her, 'That will be enough from you, you G— d— French w—!' Nice, was it not? (Mrs. Sonntag was already forty-three, white haired, and supported on crutches owing to spinal trouble. Her lisp suggested an accent.)

"Two or three men tried to interfere. Mr. Crane stood stock still and did not speak. My cousin ended the business, by stepping forward. At sight of a priest's costume the noble cop mumbled something apologetic and fled . . . I was told afterwards that this kind of thing was tried on Mr. Crane two or three times. There was no newspaper notice of this scene, but I was asked about it at school. J. L. Ford was with Mr. Crane, one afternoon, walking up Madison Avenue when another policeman tried the same thing. In other words, someone had sent out word to 'get' Mr. Crane" (Beer 1934, 292).]

21 JANUARY. The *Port Jervis Union* reports: "Stephen Crane arrived in town last night and was a guest of his brother, Judge Crane, over night, returning to New York this morning. Mr. Crane is evidently none the worse for his recent experience in connection with the sinking of the filibustering vessel the 'Commodore' and is in superb health and spirits. He has not relinquished his plan of visiting Cuba and will probably go to that country with the next filibustering expedition which is organized."

FEBRUARY. "A Man and Some Others" appears in the *Century*, with a full-page illustration by Frederic Remington.

The *Philistine* contains a maudlin black-bordered obituary by Elbert Hubbard:

> The last words I wrote about Stephen Crane before his death were words of appreciation. They appear as the first item of "Side Talks" in last month's *Philistine*. I have gibed Stephen Crane and jeered his work, but beneath the banter there was only respect, good will—aye! and affection.
>
> He is dead now—Steve is dead. How he faced death the records do not say; but I know, for I knew the soul of the lad. Within the breast of that pale youth there dwelt a lion's heart. He held his own life and reputation lightly. He sided with the weak, the ignorant, the unfortunate, and his purse and strength and influence were ever given lavishly to those in need. *He died trying to save others.*
>
> So here's to you, Steve Crane, wherever you may be! You were not so very good, but you were as good as I am—and better in many ways—our faults were different, that's all. I don't know where you are, Stevie, but when I die I hope I will face Death as manfully as you did; and I hope too that I shall then go where you are now. And so, Stevie, good-bye and good-bye!

That this is only a spoof is revealed a few pages later in the laconic statement : "LATER: Thanks to Providence and a hen-coop, Steve Crane was not drowned after all—he swam ashore."

6 FEBRUARY. Heinemann publishes *The Little Regiment* in its Pioneer Series (Bruccoli and Katz, 279).

10 FEBRUARY. The *Florida Times-Union* reports that Crane is back in Jacksonville, "having remained very close since his *Commodore* episode. He is on his way to Cuba. He is confident of making the shores of that island before the war is ended, and, if indications are what they seem, it is probable that Mr. Crane will be on the scene of conflict in a very short time writing his Sunday stories for a syndicate of northern papers. He has made a great many friends in Jacksonville, who entertain the best wishes for the future prosperity of the rising novelist."

13 FEBRUARY. The *Publishers' Circular* announces English publication of *The Little Regiment* by Heinemann.

[MID-FEBRUARY]. Ralph D. Paine recalls hearing Crane read to Captain Murphy in a Jacksonville café from the manuscript of "The Open Boat," subtitled upon publication "A Tale Intended to be After the Fact: Being the Experience of Four Men from the Sunk Steamer Commodore." "He stopped reading to say: 'Listen, Ed, I want to have this *right*, from your point of view. How does it sound so far?' 'You've got it, Steve,' said the other man. 'That is just how it happened, and how we felt. Read me some more of it.'" At the conclusion of the reading, "'Do you like it or not, Ed?' asked Stephen Crane. 'It's good, Steve. Poor old Billie! Too bad he had to drown. He was a damn good oiler'" (Paine, 168, 170).

15 FEBRUARY. William Randolph Hearst's yacht, the *Buccaneer*, arrives in Jacksonville. Stephen Crane and Charles Michelson announce they are going to Cuba on the yacht, but Theodore Hilborn, superintendent in charge of Hearst's boating interests, says that they have no authority to make this statement, denies that the yacht will be used as a dispatch boat, and states that it is merely en route to a "pleasure trip" through the West Indies. A local newspaper speculates that Hearst will be coming to town to board his yacht (*Florida Times-Union*, 16 February).

18 FEBRUARY. Crane inscribes a copy of the 1896 *Maggie* to Lyda de Camp, madam of a brothel on Ward Street, popularly known as "the line" in Jacksonville (*C*, 280).

20 FEBRUARY. The *Academy* reviews *The Little Regiment*, acknowledging that "Mr. Crane's peculiar genius is admirably adapted to the exigencies of the short story." Nevertheless, "The awful monotony of his pictures is almost depressing: there is no room for variety of any kind." The *Athenaeum* believes that *The Little Regiment* equals *The Red Badge* and excels *Maggie*. Crane's "extraordinary power of imagination" projects the reader into the scenes of war he describes in a manner "more wonderful than that of Defoe. Mr. Crane's English, when he writes in his own person, is his own, and follows no known rule as to the use and even the meaning of words. It is in dialogue that he is at his strongest, for in this the words are used as the soldiers would have used them."

24 FEBRUARY. Crane wires Hitchcock requesting that payment from the Heinemann editions of *Maggie* and *The Little Regiment* be sent to him—"very important"(C, 280).

The *Florida Times-Union* reports that Crane, Captain Murphy, and Michelson left Jacksonville on the evening of the 22d for the southern part of the state, where they, along with Paine, were to board the *Buccaneer* and sail for Cuba. According to "a statement made by Mr. Crane," Michelson, who had commanded Hearst's dispatch boat *Vamoose*, would soon be assuming command of a yacht that had been in Jacksonville a few days earlier.

Reynolds offers "The Open Boat" to Scribner's Magazine (Allen, 50).

25 FEBRUARY. E. L. Burlingame of *Scribner's* replies to Reynolds expressing interest in "The Open Boat" (Allen, 50).

27 FEBRUARY. The *Spectator* (London) considers *The Little Regiment* an advance over *The Red Badge* because "Alongside of the horrors, the privations, and the discomfort of war he now sets before us the humours, the ironies, and the romance of campaigning."

MARCH. The *Bookman* (London) finds that Crane's power of description in *The Little Regiment* recalls Tolstoy's method of rendering a scene, "which is a translation of the mingled sensations of the mind and body all nervously alert and tingling."

5 MARCH. *Scribner's* accepts "The Open Boat" for $300; Reynolds complains about these terms (Allen, 51).

9 MARCH. Burlingame declines to pay more for "The Open Boat" (Allen, 51), and Reynolds accepts the original terms.

11 MARCH. Crane writes to his brother William: "I have been for over a month among the swamps further south wading miserably to and fro in an attempt to avoid our derned U.S. navy. And it cant be done. I am through trying. I have changed all my plans and am going to Crete" (*C*, 281).

13 MARCH. *The Third Violet* is advertised as forthcoming in *Publishers' Weekly*.

[14–15 MARCH]. Crane returns to New York City. He visits Corwin Knapp Linson, recently returned from covering the first modern Olympic Games in Greece, and asks, "'Willie Hearst is sending me for the war. What I'll do among those Dagoes I don't know. What are they like, CK? How did you chin their lingo?'" (Linson 1958, 99). He also calls on S. S. McClure, and in return for a loan of some $600 or $700 he agrees to give S. S. McClure first option on serial publication of his next stories and first option on his next book, a group of stories centered on "The Open Boat" (Levenson 1970, lxx).

16 MARCH. From the office of the S. S. McClure Company Crane writes William that he is hastily composing another short story inspired by his *Commodore* experience, "Flanagan and His Short Filibustering Adventure": "After all, I do not think I can do anything except come to Port Jervis for about two hours. I am going to sail for Havre on the French line Saturday, and as I am in the middle of a story which I am bound to finish before I leave, my time is most tragically short" (*C*, 281).

17 MARCH. Hawkins disburses a final payment of $12.95 to Amy Leslie. The $500 Crane left with him is now gone in sums sent to Crane and Amy, and he is left with a $4.00 deficit (NhD).

19 MARCH. Crane cannot return to Port Jervis, and Edmund rushes to New York to see him off. As a parting gift Crane gives Edmund a copy of Charles King's *An Army Wife* (*C*, 282).

20 MARCH. Crane sails for Liverpool aboard the Cunard liner *Etruria*. Whether Cora is also aboard or whether she sails separately on another ship a short time later is unclear.

22 MARCH. JACKSONVILLE. A warrant for nonpayment of debts is issued against Cora Taylor, and furniture from the Hotel de Dream is seized as security by the sheriff (*Florida Times-Union,* 23 March).

27 MARCH. The *Etruria* enters the Mersey River, the port of Liverpool, at 5:45 P.M. (*Times* [London], 29 March).

29–30 MARCH. Crane arrives in London. He meets William Heinemann and Sidney Pawling, his partner and editor.

31 MARCH. Richard Harding Davis, who had contracted to report the Greek-Turkish conflict for the *Times* (London), gives a formal luncheon for Crane at the Savoy, which is attended by Harold Frederic, Anthony Hope, and Sir James Barrie (C. B. Davis, 200). After a "'good meeting'" with Crane Davis comments in a letter to his mother, Rebecca Harding Davis, "'He is very modest sturdy and shy. Quiet [*sic*] unlike I imagined'" (Osborn, 53).

1 APRIL. Crane and Richard Harding Davis leave London by train (*London Daily Chronicle,* 2 April). Cora and her companion from the Hotel de Dream, Mrs. Charlotte Ruedy, are in a different compartment. They separate in Paris, Davis proceeding to Florence to visit his brother and Crane continuing on to Marseilles. Earlier in the day Davis had written his family that Crane is accompanied by "'a bi-roxide blonde who seemed to be attending to his luggage for him and whom I did not meet'" (Osborn, 53).

2 APRIL. In his "London Letter" to the *Critic* (17 April), Arthur Waugh comments:

> Mr. Stephen Crane has flitted through London this week on his way to the scene of insurrections in Crete, but his visit was of the briefest. Indeed, it was characterized by extreme and refreshing modesty, being conspicuously free of the tendency to self-advertisement which is so often characteristic of the Novelist's Progress. He reached London early on Monday morning and left it on Thursday afternoon. Within a few hours of his arrival, he naturally made his first calling-place the house of his publisher, Mr. Heinemann, who has worked so hard to push his books in this country. He seems much pleased with the reception of his work in England, and jokingly remarked that he was off to Crete because, having written so much about war, he thought it high time he should see a little fighting. Which proves him a man of humor—an excellent thing in letters.

3 APRIL. Crane sails from Marseilles aboard the *Guadiana,* which leaves port at 5:00 P.M. (Cazemajou, 128). Most likely, he is accompanied by Cora and Mrs. Ruedy (Friedmann 1989, 11–12). On board Crane scrawls a mysterious note: "New York 290/201 [possibly the numbers of his stateroom and Cora's on the *Etruria*]/Took up collection 43 dollars/Captains own money pd to Paris./In Paris, 100 police, commissioner of minister of interior/ Arrested in Marseilles No tickets/Salife Shalife [cancelled]/Sharefe millionaire" (NNC).

The *New York Times* denies that English reviewers "discovered" *The Red Badge of Courage.* "The first edition was entirely exhausted in the United States and a second one was on the market before the book was published in London. The American journals began reviewing it and praising it in October, fully sixty days before there was anything seen of it in England."

4 APRIL. The *Sunday Times* remarks that "a couple of American story writers—Mr. Richard Harding Davis and Mr. Stephen Crane—are both on their way to the seat of the troubles."

7 APRIL. The *Guadiana* changes course and diverts to Suda Bay on the northern coast of Crete to deliver mail to the European fleet—"The Concert of Powers," as Crane called it in a dispatch written later in Athens—which had bombarded and blockaded the Cretan ports. The *Guadiana* reaches Suda Bay at noon and departs three hours later (Wertheim 1983, 9).

8 APRIL. The *Guadiana* arrives at Piraeus, the port of Athens, at 6:00 A.M. (Cazemajou, 128).

9 APRIL. The sultan orders the Turkish commander Edhem Pasha to march against Larisa.

10 APRIL. ATHENS. From the Grand Hotel D'Angleterre Crane writes to his brother William:

> My dear Will: I arrived in Athens three days ago and am going to the frontier shortly. I expect to get a position on the staff of the Crown Prince. Wont that be great? I am so happy over it I can hardly breathe. I shall try—I shall try like blazes to get a decoration out of the thing but that depends on good fortune and is between you and I and God. Athens is not much ruins, you know. It is mostly adobe creations like Mexico although the Acropolis sticks up in the air precisely like it does in the pictures. I was in Crete but saw no fighting. However the exhibition of

foriegn war-ships was great. The reputation of my poor old books had reached a few of the blooming Greeks and that is what has done the Crown Prince business for me. If I get on the staff I shall let you know at once. They say I've got a sure thing. They like Americans very much over here anyhow, or rather they hate all the others and so we have an advantage. It really isnt so much for a foriegner of standing to get on the staff but then it sounds fine and it really is fine too in a way and I am so happy tonight I can hardly remain silent and write I hope and pray that you are all well and that I see you all again. Love to everyone. (*C,* 285)

12 APRIL. The *Philadelphia Public Ledger* briefly summarizes Crane's literary reception in England, with special emphasis on *The Little Regiment*:

Stephen Crane sprang into fame through the appreciation of the English reviewers of his "Red Badge of Courage," with the critic of the *Saturday Review* as pioneer in the discovery of the new writer. The young American's "Maggie" came as a disagreeable surprise to these same literary writers who had gone into such hysterics over Mr. Crane's excellent war sketch. "The Little Regiment," his book of battle scenes, has recently been placed before the London critics, and he of the *Saturday Review* thinks it goes a long way toward rehabilitating the reputation that "Maggie" was in danger of jeopardizing. The *Pall Mall*'s "Irresponsible Reader" is delighted to find that Mr. Crane "has, after his rather unsatisfactory excursion to the slums * * * returned to his true *métier* as a painter of war scenes." This change, according to the *Chronicle,* is "enormously for the better"—for, "with the exception of Tolstoy, no one we know writes as well of war as Mr. Crane. * * * He makes us realize both aspects of it, the noble and the hateful." On the other hand, hear the *Telegraph*: "We have no clue to whether these tales were written prior or subsequent to 'The Red Badge of Courage,' but assuredly they are vastly inferior to that memorable book." The National Observer is skeptical as to the accuracy of that inspiration which in Mr. Crane's war pictures has to take the place of experience. "A Study in Noise" is the heading of the article in which the book is criticized. "Mr. Crane," writes the Observer, "shows to better advantage where his imagination is not lurid with the blaze of battle."

17 APRIL. Turkey declares war on Greece. In a dispatch unpublished in his lifetime Crane describes the exuberance of the crowd in front of the royal palace on Constitution Square in Athens, where "the blare of bugles, the great roaring cheers of recruits mingled with the loud approbation of the populace" (*Works,* 9: 13).

[BETWEEN 17 AND 22 APRIL]. In Athens Crane writes his first published report of the Greco-Turkish War, "An Impression of the 'Concert,'" datelined "On Board French Steamer *Guadiana.*" This dispatch will become the first of a series of "letters" that, after arriving in England, he arranged to write for the McClure syndicate, which sold these Greek war dispatches to other American newspapers and to the *Westminster Gazette* (*Works,* 9: 412).

18 APRIL. Crane sends $100 to Amy Leslie but mails his letter to an address at which she no longer lives; thus she fails to receive it (*C,* 286, 298n1). He leaves Athens for Epirus in the northwest, where Greek guerrillas are harassing Turkish troops near Janina. He witnesses the skirmishing around the town but leaves before the Greek retreat across the Arta river when he receives news of more intensive fighting in Thessaly.

26 APRIL. Under the byline "Imogene Carter" Cora sends her first dispatch from Athens to the *New York Journal,* "War Seen through a Woman's Eyes," but it is not published until 14 May. Some of the phraseology—"amid flowers and tears," "as if death was a wine"— suggests that Crane revised or rewrote this piece:

> To a woman, war is a thing that hits at the heart and at the places around the table. It does not always exist to her mind as a stirring panorama, or at least when it does she is not thinking of battles save in our past tense historic way, which eliminates the sufferings. One cannot, however, be in any part of Greece at this time without coming close to the meaning of war, war in the present tense, war in complete definition. I have seen the volunteers start amid flowers and tears and seen afterward the tears when the flowers were forgotten. I have seen the crowds rave before the palace of the King, appealing to him for permission to sacrifice, as if death was a wine. I have seen the wounded come in hastily and clumsily bandaged, unwashed and wan, with rolling eyes that expressed that vague desire of the human mind in pain for an impossible meadow wherein rest and sleep and peace come suddenly when one lies in the grass. In Athens this is war—the tears of mothers, the cheers of the throng and later the rolling eyes of the wounded. (*Works,* 9: 267)

27 APRIL. Crane returns to Athens. He sends Hawkins another £25 for Amy Leslie, but Hawkins, having been plagued with demands for small amounts by Amy since the previous December, refuses to disburse the money and returns it to him (*C,* 287, 287n1). In Athens there is consternation and rioting in reaction to the news of Greek reverses in Thessaly. Crane's sketch, "The Man in the White Hat," first published as the last of his "With Greek and Turk" series in the *Westminster Gazette* (18 June), depicts a mob in front of the royal palace in

Constitution Square addressed by an orator, a parliamentary deputy who attempts to enter the palace and confront the king but is easily rebuffed when a servant meets him at the door and says "The King does not receive today." Richard Harding Davis (Davis 1903, 202) and John Bass also witness this scene. Bass identifies the deputy as a politician named "Gennadius" (*New York Journal,* 30 April), apparently a satirical reference to the fiery fifteenth-century anti-Unionist Greek monk Gennadius (George Scholarios), who later became patriarch of Constantinople, but Davis does not name him, and Crane describes him only as a man with white hair and a tall hat who asks "Why was Greece shamed? Whose fault was it? He would go to the King—he would speak to the King—now—this instant—and ask him why was Greece shamed?" (*Works,* 9: 71).

28 APRIL. Richard Harding Davis writes to his mother: "'Stephen Crane came in last night having been searching for me all over Albania and to my satisfaction told me he had been in Crete all this time that I have been in Florence. So that he is not a day ahead of me as we start from here together. . . . He has not seen as much as I have for several reasons but then when a man can describe battles as well as he can without seeing them why should he care'" (Osborn, 53–54).

The *Westminster Gazette* announces that Crane will send a series of "letters" describing the Greco-Turkish War.

30 APRIL. The Hearst newspapers syndicate Crane's cable from Athens, headlined in the *New York Journal* as "Stephen Crane Says Greeks Cannot be Curbed." Under the dateline of 29 April Crane outlines his return from Epirus: "The journey from Arta overland to Thessaly requires a longer time than it does to go by the way of Athens, and so I have been fortunate enough to arrive in the capital in time to witness another popular outburst of the Athenians." Crane's enthusiastic version that almost "every man in Athens is arming to go and fight the Turks" is contradicted by other press reports stressing disaffection from the war on the part of the Greek population and the refusal of many men to fight in the war. Crane does not, however, overestimate Greek confidence. "No nation ever had a truer sense of the odds" (*Works,* 9: 14, 15).

Copyright deposit of *The Third Violet* is made in the Library of Congress. British Museum deposit copy is made of the first Heinemann edition of *The Third Violet.*

[30 APRIL]. Crane and Cora, with John Bass, head of the *New York Journal* staff, and Richard Harding Davis, representing the *Times*

(London), as well as other correspondents, leave Athens by steamer at 9:00 P.M. for the scene of combat in Thessaly. Cora's telegram, datelined 29 April under the name Imogene Carter, with dispatches by other correspondents, including Crane, on the front page of the *Journal*, begins "I start to-day for the front of the Greek army to see how the men fight. I learn that even the English nurses have returned from the hospitals of the army because the Turks fire on the Red Cross flag with the same enthusiasm with which they fire on the lines of battle. From this and from other rumors I am quite sure that the *Journal* will have the only woman correspondent within even the sound of the guns" (*Works*, 9: 268). Davis later (16 May) writes to his family: "'I left Athens on the 29th of April. . . . Crane and Bass and I went off together, Crane accompanied by a Lady Stuart [*sic*] who has run away from her husband to follow Crane. She is a commonplace dull woman old enough to have been his mother and with dyed yellow hair. He seems a genius with no responsibilities of any sort to anyone, and I and Bass got shut of them at Velestinos after having had to travel with them for four days. They went to Volo'" (Osborn, 54).

[Cora's diary dates the departure "Left Athens 30th April 1897—steamer to Stylis—Left 9. P.M.—" (*Works*, 9: 272) *contra* Davis's 29 April and the dateline of her own dispatch. While Lillian Gilkes is inclined to accept Davis's dating, as have subsequent biographers, she acknowledges that "if Davis is correct, the various stages of the journey recorded in Cora's notes leave an extra day unaccounted for" (Gilkes 1960, 94n).]

[1 MAY]. The steamer carrying the *Journal* correspondents stops at Chalkis at noon. They transfer to a steamer with the new minister of war on board, arrive in Stylis at 6:00 P.M., and drive in a carriage to Lamia, which they reach at midnight. Cora's sketchy diary continues: "Bunked on Floor wierd Hotel—Cafe—Soldiers—" (*Works*, 9: 272).

2 MAY. Bacheller syndicates Crane's article, "The Filibustering Industry," probably mailed from Greece.

[2 MAY]. The journalists depart by carriage for Domoko at 7:00 A.M., arriving there at 5:00 P.M. Along the route they encounter hordes of Greek civilians fleeing from the advancing Turks. About 7:00 P.M. the party leaves Domoko and drives to Pharsala, where Cora, who has a letter from the United States minister, Eben Alexander (NNC), hopes to interview the crown prince the next day. On the outskirts of Pharsala they are stopped by sentries and separate. Davis and Bass take the route to Velestino; Crane and the other correspondents go to Volo; Cora drives into town to look for a place to sleep and spends the night on a billiard table in a coffeehouse (*Works*, 9: 272–273).

3 MAY. The *Westminster Gazette* publishes Crane's report "An Impression of the 'Concert,'" the first in a series of "letters" entitled "With Greek and Turk."

[3 MAY]. Cora waits in vain at Greek headquarters to interview the crown prince, who is preparing for another hasty departure, having ordered a retreat from Pharsala as he previously did from Larissa. Later in the day she joins Crane in Volo, a seaport village perched above a harbor where English, French, and Italian warships are massed (*Works*, 9: 271, 272).

4 MAY. The Turks launch a major attack upon the Greeks at Velestino, having failed on three attacks on different days to dislodge the center of Colonel Constantine Smolenski's Greek forces. Crane is ill with dysentery, which he perhaps disguises as a toothache (Cora writes in her diary this evening, "mouse ill—8 P.M."), and he and Cora remain in Volo, missing the first day of the second battle of Velestino.

5 MAY. Crane arrives at Velestino at noon on the second day of the battle (*Works*, 9: 19).

Davis, who with John Bass has witnessed the beginning of the offensive against Velestino from Greek infantry trenches, comments in a letter to his family (14 May): "'Crane came up for fifteen minutes and wrote a 1300 word story on that. He was never near the front but dont say I said so. He would have come but he had a toothache which kept him in bed. It was hard luck but on the other hand if he had not had that woman with him he would have been with us and not at Volo and could have seen the show toothache or no toothache'" (Osborn, 54; Lubow, 150). Davis mistakenly recalls seeing Crane at Velestino on 4 May. In a stylized report, "How Novelist Crane Acts on the Battlefield," John Bass describes Crane's conduct with greater empathy:

> At Velestino I was greatly interested to see how the *Journal* correspondent, the well-known novelist Stephen Crane, would act in a real battle. Your correspondent followed him up the steep hill to where the Greek

mountain battery, enveloped in smoke, was dropping shells among the black lines of Turkish infantry in the plain below. Your correspondent sought shelter in a trench and cautiously watched the pale, thin face of the novelist as the latter seated himself on an ammunition box amid a shower of shells and casually lighted a cigarette.

Stephen Crane did not appear surprised, but watched with a quiet expression the quick work of the artillerymen as they loaded, fired and jumped to replace the small cannon overturned by the recoil.

I was curious to know what was passing in his mind, and said:

"Crane, what impresses you most in this affair?"

The author of The Red Badge of Courage lighted another cigarette, pushed back his long hair out of his eyes with his hat and answered quietly:

"Between two great armies battling against each other the interesting thing is the mental attitude of the men. The Greeks I can see and understand, but the Turks seem unreal. They are shadows on the plain—vague figures in black, indications of a mysterious force."

By this time the Greek army was in full retreat.

As the last mountain gun was loaded on the mules Stephen Crane quietly walked down the hill. The Turkish artillery had drawn nearer, and amid the singing bullets and smashing shells the novelist had stopped, picked up a fat waddling puppy and immediately christened it Velestino, the Journal dog. (*New York Journal,* 23 May)

[Later Cora claimed to have rescued the dog, inscribing a photograph, "'Velestino'./Picked up by M⁽ʳ⁾ˢ Stephen Crane in the/midst of the battle of Velestino *Greece*" (Gilkes 1960, 125).]

6 MAY. Crown Prince Constantine once again orders a retreat and the Cranes return to Volo from Velestino. Cora writes her dispatch, datelined 9 May, "Imogene Carter's Pen Picture of the Fighting at Velestino."

The first English edition of *The Third Violet* is listed as published in the *Athenaeum*.

7 MAY. From a *World* dispatch boat approaching the harbor of Stylis, Sylvester Scovel writes to his wife, Frances: "All wires from the front are so full of government news that when I arrived in Athens I found that the Journal men, Julian Ralph, Stephen Crane and Bass, together with Richard Harding Davis, had been at the front for seven days and had not succeeded in getting a telegram back to Athens" (Missouri Historical Society).

8 AND 9 MAY. Crane's humorous article on the English use of the term "bounder" is syndicated by McClure under various headings

such as "New Invasion of Britain." Its earliest dateline, 29 April in the *Chicago Record*, indicates it was sent from Athens to London and then forwarded to the United States to be set up and distributed for publication. Crane's definition of slang in this article is a commentary upon his own much-criticized tendency to employ it: "Good slang is subtle and elusive. If there is a quick equivalent for a phrase it is not good slang, because good slang comes to fill a vacancy" (*Works*, 8: 679).

A reviewer for the *Buffalo Enquirer* writes: "'The Third Violet' comes at a more or less critical period. Many people have looked upon the Post-Red Badge works of the young man as inevitable interludes of genius, tentative gaspings for breath after a supreme effort. They have waited for his second wind, a maturity of judgment, a surety of footing, a wider work of universal interest. Those who still have faith may wait once more, for 'The Third Violet' is a weak sister."

10 MAY. The Cranes flee Volo by ship to Chalkis "when the advance guard of the Turks reached the hill-tops surrounding the town. The decks of every ship in the harbor except the English Red Cross ship were simply packed with women and children. Most of the men of these families were away fighting. Even the little sail boats and fishing smacks carried a heavy quota" (*Works*, 9: 46).

11 MAY. The Hearst newspapers syndicate, with many variations, Crane's account of the second battle of Velestino, sent by courier from Volo to Athens the previous day and headlined in the greater New York edition of the *Journal* as "Crane at Velestino." Crane records the frustration of the Greek army when ordered to retreat in the midst of an apparent victory. Smolenski, who knew that the retreat would sacrifice Volo as well, "bit his fingers and cursed when the order came to retreat. He knew that his army had victory within its grasp. For three days he had been holding the Turks beautifully in check, killing them as fast as they fell upon him. In the middle of intoxication of victory came the orders to fall back. Why?" For Crane, who had previously seen only a few skirmishes, this was his first important battle, and he found it exhilarating: "The roll of musketry was tremendous. From a distance it was like tearing a cloth; nearer, it sounded like rain on a tin roof and close up it was just a long crash after crash. It was a beautiful sound—beautiful as I had never dreamed. It was more impressive than the roar of Niagara and finer than thunder or avalanche—because it had the wonder of human

Stephen Crane in Athens, May 1897. The inscription
is to Sam S. Chamberlain, managing editor
of the *New York Journal*
(Wertheim Collection)

Cora Crane in Athens, May 1897, in the uniform
of a war correspondent
(Syracuse University)

tragedy in it. It was the most beautiful sound of my experience, barring no symphony. The crash of it was ideal." Crane acknowledges that the men who died at Velestino would have taken a different point of view (*Works*, 9: 19–20).

12 MAY. Crane's description of the evacuation of Volo, sent by courier from Chalkis to Athens, is syndicated by Hearst, appearing under the heading of "The Blue Badge of Cowardice" in the *New York Journal*.

[SECOND WEEK IN MAY]. Crane and Cora return to Athens for a period of rest. In the studio of C. Boehringer they have separate cabinet photographs taken (and Crane has one taken with John Bass) sitting on false rocks in the uniforms of war correspondents.

14 MAY. Hearst syndicates a cable by Crane reporting the arrest of George Montgomery, an American graduate of Yale representing the *London Standard*.

15 MAY. *The Third Violet* is listed as published in *Publishers' Weekly* and in the London *Publishers' Circular*.

16 MAY. A few American newspapers carry a McClure syndicated "letter" by Crane that takes a dim view of American correspondents in Greece.

The *New York Tribune* criticizes *The Third Violet* because Crane "has reverted, more or less, to the worst side of his realistic ideal, in other words, to the side where he is not realistic at all in any plausible sense." For the *Brooklyn Daily Eagle* the novel "leaves a distinct impression of dissatisfaction; one feels that the author has undertaken something for which he has no vocation—and the result is weariness and distaste. . . . It is a story that smells of the lamp—something written because there was a demand for a fresh book from a writer in vogue and not because he had any story to tell or any message to convey." Similarly critical, the *Springfield Republican* finds the novel "as inane a story of summer resort flirtations as was ever written," and the *Providence Journal* concludes that not only is *The Third Violet* "a book with badness written large all over it" but also that Crane "so far from being a great writer, is not even a good writer."

17 MAY. Crane and Cora travel north again to observe the Greek resistance at Domoko on a dispatch boat rented by the *New*

York World and placed at their disposal by Sylvester Scovel, but Prince Constantine orders Domoko abandoned and retreats to Thermopylae.

18 MAY. From Bay St. Marina Crane takes a *Journal* dispatch boat to Stylidia, where he watches the abandonment of the town by the rear guard of the Greek army and helps to evacuate civilian refugees before departing for Chalkis: "As we steamed away Smolenski's rear guard also left Stylidia. The beautiful little town, with its streets shaded by May trees and lemons and its ripening gardens, seemed to be putting on its best air, as to bid farewell to its citizens and to receive the Turks" (*Works*, 9: 55). Later in the day, at Chalkis, the Cranes board the *St. Marina*, an ambulance ship returning to Athens crammed with soldiers wounded at Domoko. Crane's dispatch, "War's Horrors," is syndicated by Hearst under various headings on 23 May:

This steamer was formerly used for transporting sheep, but it was taken by the Government for ambulance purposes. It is not a nice place for a well man, but war takes the finical quality out of its victims, and the soldiers do not complain. The ship is not large enough for its dreadful freight. But the men must be moved, and so 800 bleeding soldiers are jammed together in an insufferably hot hole, the light in which is so faint that we cannot distinguish the living from the dead.

Above the vibration of the machinery and the churning of the waves we have listened all night to the cries and groans of those who stopped the Turkish bullets in the trenches. Those who died, and there were not a few, could not be removed, and the corpses lay among the living men, shot through arm, chest, leg or jaw. The soldiers endured it with composure, I thought. Their indifference will never cease to be a marvel to me.

Near the hatch where I can see them is a man shot through the mouth. The bullet passed through both cheeks. He is asleep with his head pillowed on the bosom of a dead comrade. He had been awake for days, doubtless, marching on bread and water, to be finally wounded at Domokos and taken aboard this steamer. He is too weary to mind either his wound or his awful pillow. There is a breeze on the gulf and the ship is rolling, heaving one wounded man against the other. (*Works*, 9: 53–54)

The *New York Tribune* reprints a parody from the *Lewiston* [Maine] *Journal* of what it considers to be Crane's self-centered war correspondence:

I have seen a battle.
I find it is very like what
I wrote up before.
I congratulate myself that
I ever saw a battle.
I am pleased with the sound of war.
I think it is beautiful.
I thought it would be.
I am sure of my nose for battle.
I did not see any war correspondents while
I was watching the battle except
I.

19 MAY. The *St. Marina* docks at Stylis, where the clouds of dust on the highway are all that can be seen of Smolenski's troops retreating toward Thermopylae (*Works*, 9: 54). Crane cables a dispatch from Lamia syndicated by Hearst on 24 May with a delayed dateline as "Greeks Waiting at Thermopylae," which describes the high morale of the Greek troops preparing to defend the pass:

Still backward fall the Greek soldiers. First it was Velestino, then Domokos, next it will be Thermopylae. They have had a hard time of it. Their fiercest fighting has been rewarded, not with victory, but with orders to retreat. . . .

There is a rumor all through the town and the army of an armistice, but the Greeks have no thought that the war is over. . . .

None of the soldiers admits the possibility of losing Thermopylae. Really, the new position is very strong. Although the pass has been widened and much changed since Leonidas' fight, it is still an ideal place to hold an enemy in check and here, if the war goes on according to the rules of the game and the supreme authority lets the Greek army do what is in it to do, the advance of the Turks may be dammed. I would like to write a dispatch telling of a full-blown Greek victory for a change. (*Works*, 9: 57–58)

From Athens, Scovel writes to his wife, Frances:

Stephen Crane is here with Mrs. Stewart. I was afraid that she would ruin him, but really her influence has, so far, been the reverse. He has done such good work since that his publishers and others are increasing their offers for future work.

She went to the front with him; was under artillery fire at Velestino, and was the last non-combatant to leave the place after the battle.

But poor woman, how will it end. She urges him along, but even if he wished to, he cant marry her, as her husband Sir Donald

Stewart, son of the British Commander in Chief of India will not divorce her.

Stephen was very glad to see me and, I to see him. He is true steel. They took my boat off my hands, and went to the front day before yesterday.

I dont know when I shall see them again. If you were here it would be embarrassing if they were here too. Lady Stewart is received by some of the most prominent people and even the Queen may receive her. How's that for the Greeks who are said to be the only moral people in this part of Europe? (Copy, MnU)

20 MAY. ATHENS. An armistice is signed ending the war. Crane inscribes one of his Boehringer photographs to Sam Chamberlain (*C*, 288).

22 MAY. Cora as "Imogene Carter" inscribes a Boehringer photograph to "me old pal Stevie" (*C*, 288).

The *New York Times* reviewer is bored by *The Third Violet*: "People do use bad English and express their thoughts badly. Life is, on the whole, prosy and humdrum and ugly. But why dwell on it? If it were not for the dog and one or two touches of nature in which the sympathy of the poet is betrayed, we should not like '*The Third Violet*' at all." In contrast, the *Academy* is favorably impressed by Crane's ability to transmute the lively imagery and psychological insight found in *The Red Badge* into the domestic sphere. "By this latest product of his genius our impression of Mr. Crane is confirmed: that for psychological insight, for dramatic intensity, and for potency of phrase he is already in the front rank of English and American writers of fiction; and that he possesses a certain separate quality which places him apart." The *Athenaeum* speculates:

In his present book Mr. Crane is more the rival of Mr. Henry James than of Mr. Rudyard Kipling. But he is intensely American, which can hardly be said of Mr. Henry James, and it is possible that if he continues in his present line of writing he may be the author who will introduce the United States to the ordinary English world. We have never come across a book that brought certain sections of American society so perfectly before the reader as does "The Third Violet". . . . Some understanding will really have to be come to between us and the Americans, and our colonists in Australia and elsewhere, as to the English language. If they are going to produce writers who are so certain to be read throughout the English world as Mr. Stephen Crane, our people will have to learn the meaning of many American phrases. There are passages in the present book which will be spoilt for many English readers by the fact that they may be unaware that, across the Atlantic, "bug" means a flying insect. "Snickered" we suppose means *sniggered.* "So long" of course we know to be a salutation on departure; but in England that fact is not generally understood, though it is known in parts and among certain classes. There is one phrase which, with all our admiration for Mr. Crane, we find simply horrible: "mucilaged to their seats," for *glued.*

[LAST WEEK IN MAY]. Stephen and Cora leave Athens, most likely together by ship, for Marseilles. They are accompanied by two Greek servants, Adoni Ptolemy and his twin brother; a woman named "Mathilde," who may have been Cora's companion, Mrs. Charlotte Ruedy; and the dog Velestino. They spend almost two weeks in Paris before crossing the Channel.

[Cora's conjectured separate return to Paris by train westward and the notes Cora made of sights in the Austrian town of Gratz, like her hypothesized eastward overland journey with Stephen to Athens in March (Gilkes 1960, 108, 76–82), apparently belong to an earlier trip to Constantinople in 1892 with a previous lover, Ferris S. Thompson (Friedmann 1990, 264).]

29 MAY. The *Spectator's* reviewer expresses the opinion that in *The Third Violet* Crane has insufficiently subdued "the strenuous accents of his explosive style to the gentler tones naturally associated with such unheroic themes as lawn-tennis and picnics, and the incongruity between matter and manner is, in consequence, rather glaring." Like other reviewers, the *Spectator* finds Hawker's dog Stanley, "one of the most delightful animals we have encountered in recent fiction."

30 MAY. Under the heading "The Dogs of War," the *Journal* prints Crane's humorous account of the dog "Velestino," which had been lost by a boy who brought him from the combat area to Volo and found again by Crane in the possession of the dragoman of an English correspondent at Chalkis.

JUNE. "The Open Boat" receives its only periodical publication in *Scribner's Magazine.*

3 JUNE. The second of McClure's syndicated "letters," "A Fragment of Velestino," appears in the *Westminster Gazette* as part of the "With Greek and Turk" series, with continuations on 4 and 8 June. A foot-

note reads: "Mr. Stephen Crane's letters have by some accident been considerably delayed in transmission, but we make no apology for publishing them three weeks after the events to which they relate, since their literary interest, as impressions of the battlefield, are in no way diminished by the lapse of time—Ed. W. G." (*Works*, 9: 450–51).

The successful man has thrust himself through the ~~paper~~ water of the years
Reeking wet with mistakes, bloody mistakes,
Slimed with victories over the lesser
A figure thankful on the shore of money.
With the bones of fools
He buys silken banners ~~blazing~~ jimmed with his triumphant face
With the skins of wise men
He buys the trivial bows of all
Flesh and marrow contribute a coverlet
A coverlet for his contented slumber
In guiltless ignorance; in ignorant guilt
He delivers his secrets to the riven multitude.
    "Thus I defended: thus I wrought".
Complacent, smiling.
He stands heavily on the dead.
Erect on a pillar of skulls
He declaims his trampling of babes
Protests his murder of widows.
Smirking, fat, dripping,
He makes speech in guiltless ignorance,
~~Innocence~~.
                    Stephen Crane

Dec 5th, 1897.

Manuscript of "The successful man has thrust himself/
Through the water of the years," 5 December 1897
(Columbia University)

CHAPTER SIX

England (Ravensbrook), Cuba, and Puerto Rico

June 1897–December 1898

Crane's early months in England are among the happiest and most productive of his life, although he is increasingly beset by financial exigencies. He makes a number of literary friendships, the most famous of which is with Joseph Conrad, whom he meets in October 1897. He writes his novella "The Monster" and some of his finest short stories, including "The Bride Comes to Yellow Sky," "Death and the Child," and "The Blue Hotel." Nevertheless, he becomes increasingly restless and entertains ideas of foreign correspondence from South Africa, the Sudan, or the Klondike. *The Open Boat and Other Tales of Adventure* is published in mid-April 1898. A few days after Congress passes resolutions recognizing Cuba's independence from Spain, Crane sails from Liverpool to New York and accepts a commission as a war correspondent for Pulitzer's *New York World*. When Spain declares war against the United States, he leaves for Florida to join the scores of correspondents gathered in Key West and Tampa with the army massing to invade Cuba.

Much of May is spent with other correspondents in dispatch boats off the coast of Cuba attempting to garner news of the stalled war from the ships of Admiral William T. Sampson's blockading fleet. In early June Crane participates in the Marine landing at Guantánamo Bay, and he is also present later in the month when General William R. Shafter's troops disembark at Daiquirí and Siboney. He covers the bloody advance toward Las Guásimas and the attack on the San Juan Heights, sending back a large number of dispatches to the *World*. In July a quarrel with members of the *World* editorial staff over his performance as a correspondent, especially concerning a dispatch criticizing the conduct under fire of New York's volunteer 71st Regiment that he did not write, causes Crane's severance from the *World*, and he takes a position with the rival *New York Journal*. In early August the *Journal*'s correspondents are sent to Puerto Rico, but the demoralized Spanish army offers little resistance to the American invasion, and Crane has little to report. After the Protocol of Peace is signed in mid-August, Crane slips into Havana, where he spends more than four months in obscurity writing many of the war stories that make up *Wounds in the Rain* (1900) and the bathetic "Intrigue" series of poems that complete *War Is Kind* (1899). He sends back to the *Journal* a series of bland dispatches centering on the political and social life of Havana. In the third week of December, unable to maintain himself financially after the *Journal* cuts off his expense account and under pressure from Cora, he returns to New York, where he spends only three days before sailing for England.

BEFORE 10 JUNE. Stephen and Cora with their retinue arrive in England. They spend a few days in furnished rooms in Limpsfield, Surrey, before settling, as Mr. and Mrs. Stephen Crane, in Ravensbrook, a plain brick villa found for them by Harold Frederic in the neighboring town of Oxted (Gilkes 1960, 110). Frederic, Edward Garnett, Ford Madox Ford (then known by his given surname of Hueffer), Robert Barr, and Edward Pease, secretary of the Fabian Society, are proximate neighbors in the area of the Romney Marsh, in the environs of London. Further down in Sussex is Henry James in Lamb House at Rye, and just over the line in Essex the Conrads at Ivy Wall cottage.

Adoni Ptolemy remains with the Cranes while his brother becomes a servant in the Pease household. Michael Pease recalls:

> For me, the most remarkable thing about the Cranes was the pair of Greek refugees whom Crane brought back from the war. One came to our house as a domestic—"a butler in shirt sleeves" was Crane's description. My mother repeatedly described him as lazy—but he was a great favourite with me & my younger brother (not [*sic*] doubt he often played with us when he should have been cleaning the silver). At the time Crane visited my parents' house pretty regularly, because he liked to be shaved by the said Greek. My father, who regularly shaved himself before breakfast & who at 91 still does so, I remember commenting unfavourably on Crane's defection from English middle-class standards in this matter! (Michael Pease to Melvin H. Schoberlin, 27 November 1948, ViU)

11 JUNE. In a "London Letter" to the *Critic* (26 June), Arthur Waugh comments: "Mr. Stephen Crane was seen in the Strand yesterday afternoon, and Mr. Richard Harding Davis is also in the neighborhood. Of Mr. Crane's next move there is no certainty, but he will probably 'conclude,' as you say, that nothing pays him like fiction. The unanimity of his reviewers, indeed, must sometimes suggest to him that he merits the envy of the gods. In England nothing succeeds like success. Mr. Crane, one would think, would be the first to confess

that his last little book, 'The Third Violet,' is an absolutely unpretentious piece of work, thrown off as a *parergon*, and yet his critics have been proclaiming it these three weeks as a masterpiece."

14 JUNE. The *San Francisco Argonaut* finds the subject of *The Third Violet* "trivial" and the dialogue "inane."

14–15 JUNE. Crane's interviews with six common soldiers, who universally blame the king and the cowardly crown prince for the precipitous retreats of the Greek army, appear in two parts making the fifth and sixth sections of the "With Greek and Turk" series in the *Westminster Gazette.* At the very end, the *Gazette,* apparently disturbed by the attacks on Queen Victoria's royal relatives and the revolutionary sentiments of some of the soldiers interviewed, rationalizes the bitter views expressed in Crane's dispatch:

> Mr. Stephen Crane's interviews with Greek soldiers after the *débâcle*, of which we publish a further installment this morning, are human documents of immense interest. But they represent not the actual facts so much as a frame of mind. The soldier after a defeat invariably blames his superiors. Even in the thick of the fight, when some order is given which he does not understand, or some hardship, as he thinks, inflicted upon himself which his comrades do not share, he is apt to curse aloud at the stupidity and the idiocy of the commanding officer. That aspect of warfare Mr. Crane himself has pictured for us most vividly in his "Red Badge of Courage." So it is natural that the Greek soldier who is conscious of having done his best should turn and upbraid the King and the Crown Prince. It does not follow that either is to blame, and it is certain that if they are in any respect to blame the burden laid upon them is infinitely heavier than they deserve. But the picture is human and true, and carries its own morals for kings and statesmen who, before going to war, fail to sit down and count up the cost. We are glad to think, however, that since Mr. Crane wrote, a more rational state of opinion has asserted itself in Greece. (*Works*, 9: 461)

18 JUNE. Crane's first known letter from England is an autograph sentiment written on Ravensbrook stationery (Wertheim 1992, 15).

19 JUNE. The *Literary Digest* contends that "There is not a word to be said in favor of *The Third Violet*, whose reason, even for its name, does not appear till we reach the last page."

26 JUNE. Reviewers in the *Critic,* like many other American reviewers, contrast the *Third Violet* unfavorably with *The Red Badge.* One

finds it "inconceivable that even for an experiment in inanity a writer should be willing to follow up a book like '*The Red Badge*' with such a vacuous trifle as '*The Third Violet*.'" Another echoes American resentment of the praise bestowed by such respected English journals as the *Athenaeum* and the *Academy*: "I think that these papers take delight in picking out our most commonplace, vulgar books to praise for their 'Americanism.' They call them 'racy,' and say they are the sort of books American authors should write, instead of those that show cultivation and a decent regard for grammar. What have such barbarians as we to do with literature? Let us describe American life as the English believe it to be—then they will applaud."

[LATE JUNE]. Crane surveys his literary resources, compiling a list of the stories he has written with their designated places of publication or the location of the manuscripts and a word count (NNC). He begins work on "The Monster."

Crane is introduced to Ford Madox Ford by Edward Garnett. Ford is temporarily living in Gracie's cottage, next door to Garnett's home, the Cearne at High Chart near Limpsfield. With characteristic casualness about dates, Ford recalls:

> It was perhaps in 1896—I am never very certain of my dates, but it was about then—that Mr. Garnett brought poor, dear, "Stevie" to call upon me. I was then living a very self-consciously Simple Life at Limpsfield in a newly built cottage of huge lumps of rough stone. These Crane, fresh from the other side of the world, muddledly took to be the remains of an ancient fortification. He put in, I remember, a rose tree beside the immensely thick, oaken front door—for all the world like a king planting a memorial oak!—and looking at an outside fire-place remarked:
> "That's a bully ol' battlement!" (Ford 1921, 106)

In a later reminiscence Ford recalls attending a lecture delivered by Crane at Limpsfield on "flag-wagging, as he called it—Morse signalling by flags" before they actually met. "I remember his standing on an improvised platform in a Fabian drawing-room and looking young, pained, and dictatorial. I avoided being introduced to him" (Ford 1931, 49–50).

[This unlikely recollection—it would have been the only lecture Crane ever gave, and he did not learn about Morse signaling with flags until his combat experiences with the Marines in Cuba—are typical of Ford's treatment of Crane in his prolix, redundant memoirs, what H. G. Wells called his "copious carelessness of reminiscence."

Only Ford among Crane's English friends ever claimed to have called him "Stevie." In *Portraits from Life* (1937) Ford acknowledges that the reticent Crane almost always addressed him as "Mr. Hueffer," and the salutation in Ford's only surviving letter to Crane, written after they had known each other for almost two years, reads very properly, "Dear Mr. Crane" (*C*, 432). Although their relationship was never close or deep, Ford is the originator of many of the proverbial stories about Crane's home life at Ravensbrook and Brede, especially those that emphasize his American gaucherie. At Ravensbrook, Crane loved "to sit about in breeches, leggings, and shirt-sleeves, with a huge Colt strapped to his belt. And he would demonstrate with quite sufficient skill how, on a hot day[,] he could swat a fly on the wall with the bead foresight of his 'gun'" (Ford 1921, 107–108), and at Brede Crane reveled in "a real baronial manor-house on the site of the battle of Hastings, with his wife in medieval dress and with, on the floors of the banqueting-hall, rushes amongst which the innumerable dogs fought for the bones which the guests cast them" (Ford 1937, 26).]

JUNE. Giving only William Heinemann as a return address, Crane writes to his brother Edmund asking him to send the manuscripts of his Western stories "The Wise Men" and "The Five White Mice," which Crane composed at Hartwood (*C*, 292). He does not mention Cora, and not until January 1899 does he give either Edmund or William a home address.

Crane inscribes a copy of *The Third Violet* to Frank Harris, editor of the *Fortnightly* and later the *Saturday Review* and an influential literary figure in the London of the 1890s (*C*, 292):

> Dear Mr Harris: This book
> is even worse than any
> of the others.
> Stephen Crane
>
> London, June, 1897.

Harris inscribes a copy of *Elder Conklin and Other Stories* to Crane (*C*, 292–293n1):

> To Stephen Crane
> from the author.
>
> June '97.

JULY. In *Book News* Harrison S. Morris finds that Crane is out of his element in *The Third Violet*, where "his theme is the flirtation on a hotel porch, terminating in the capture of an heiress. Imagine the panting sentences of *The Red Badge of Courage*, thus degraded, and you have the result."

The London *Bookman* concludes that although *The Third Violet* is a "slighter effort" than *The Red Badge*, "we feel the same directness, the same true reading of the workings of the mind, and the same contempt for conventions and clap-trap sentiment."

2 JULY. Crane writes to Eben Alexander, who has relinquished his post as American minister to Greece, inviting him to visit Ravensbrook on his way home (*C*, 293).

14 JULY. Alexander responds to Crane's invitation, writing that "it would be altogether lovely to drop in and see you and Mrs. Stewart" (*C*, 293), an indication that the Cranes did not represent themselves to him as married while in Greece.

22 JULY. Crane writes to Edmund, commiserating with him on the death of his two-year-old son, a twin, the other one of whom is named Stephen. He concludes, "Expect to hear from me in the Soudan. The S.A. fight is off" (*C*, 294). Hostilities between the Boers and the British in South Africa being suspended, Crane hopes to report the impending clash between the Anglo-Egyptian army in the Sudan and the forces of the Mahdi for an American newspaper, probably the *New York Journal*.

29 JULY. Crane writes to the *London Daily Mail* to arrange English publication for his dispatches from the Sudan (*C*, 295).

31 JULY. The first three sections of "London Impressions" in the English *Saturday Review* contrast the sights and sounds of London and New York City from the point of view of a cab ride and show Crane's concern with the subjectivity of vision:

> The cab finally rolled out of the gas-lit vault into a vast expanse of gloom. This changed to the shadowy lines of a street that was like a passage in a monstrous cave. The lamps winking here and there resembled the little gleams at the caps of the miners. They were not very competent illuminations at best, merely being little pale flares of gas that at their most heroic periods could only display one fact concerning this

tunnel—the fact of general direction. But at any rate I should have liked to have observed the dejection of a search-light if it had been called upon to attempt to bore through this atmosphere. In it each man sat in his own little cylinder of vision, so to speak. It was not so small as a sentry-box nor so large as a circus-tent, but the walls were opaque, and what was passing beyond the dimensions of his cylinder no man knew. (*Works*, 8: 682–683)

AUGUST. *Munsey's Magazine* opines that *The Third Violet* marks a further step in Crane's "progress toward higher literary ideals."

1 AUGUST. Crane's dog "Velestino" dies, and he writes an emotional letter to Sylvester Scovel telling him that the dog will be buried in the Ravensbrook garden wearing a collar Scovel had given as a present (*C*, 295–296).

7 AUGUST. The *Saturday Review* prints the fourth and fifth of the "London Impressions."

14 AUGUST. The last three "London Impressions" appear in the *Saturday Review*. In one of these Crane jestingly speaks of a lift so slow that the "elevator boy" is a man not less than 60 years of age with a streaming white beard.

15 AUGUST. The first of a series of unsigned "European Letters" contributed by "Imogene Carter" appears in the *New York Press*, most likely a collaborative effort in which Crane played a part. Like others in the series, this letter is a miscellany of unrelated subjects, appealing primarily to feminine interests and ranging over a visit to Europe by the king of Siam, the dangers of using petroleum hair wash, the gardens of Buckingham Palace, and the hats and bonnets supplied by the Maison Virot of Paris.

19 AUGUST. Stephen and Cora are injured in a carriage accident while driving to visit Harold Frederic on his birthday at Homefield, Kenley, where Frederic had established a second household, apart from his legal wife and children, with Kate Lyon, by whom he had an additional three children. The Cranes spend a week at Kenley recuperating, after which they join Kate and Frederic for a three-week vacation in Ireland in the tiny fishing village of Ahakista, at Dunmanus Bay, where Frederic has a house lent to him by a wealthy admirer (Gilkes 1969, 36). Here Crane finishes "The Monster" and gathers material for his "Irish Notes" and his sketch "A Fishing Village."

22 AUGUST. Another "European Letter" on diverse topics appears in the *New York Press*.

28 AUGUST. "Flanagan and His Short Filibustering Adventure" is printed in the *Illustrated London News*. The story is not published in the United States until October in *McClure's Magazine*.

29 AUGUST. A "European Letter" in the *New York Press* contains a detailed description of a Turkish harem that Cora visited on her trip to Constantinople with Ferris Thompson.

9 SEPTEMBER. From County Cork, Crane writes to Edmund describing his carriage accident and disclosing that he has completed "The Monster." He asks Edmund to forward any manuscripts still at Hartwood, especially "an ms devoted to the adventures of a certain Irishman," referring to the uncompleted voyage fantasy, "Dan Emmonds." He concludes, "My address will continue to be at Heineman's" (*C*, 296–297).

[12 SEPTEMBER]. From Ireland Crane writes a deceptive letter to Amy Leslie, avoiding any mention of Cora and giving William Heinemann rather than Ravensbrook as his address, as he does in his letters to his brothers at this time:

> My dear Amy: I am sorry to have you write to me in the way that you did because I will always be willing to do anything in the world for you to help you and see that you do not suffer. I never intended to treat you badly and if I did appear to do so, it was more by fate or chance than from any desire of mine. You do not say anything about recieving the $100. I sent you from Greece through Willis. Did you get it? Let me know through Heineman. I am over here in the south of Ireland getting well from a carriage accident. It will be sometime before I get well. I had to leave off work and borrow some money to come here. I was doing very decently in London and would have sent you more money before now if it were not for the accident. As soon as I can I will send some to you if only it is a little at a time.
>
> You know better than to believe those lies about me. You know full well what kind of a man I am. As soon as I get home I shall want to know who told you them.
>
> Keep up heart, Amy. Trust me and it will all turn out right. Go and see Willis and let him always know your address. When you write and tell me that he is still in town and that you got that hundred all right I will rake up more. Dont think too badly of me, dear. Wait, have patience and I will see you through straight. Dont believe anything you hear of me and dont doubt my faith and my honesty. (*C*, 297–298)

18 SEPTEMBER. An article in the Wave (San Francisco), "Crane in London: The American Novelist Investigating England with a Microscope," is signed "Justin Sturgis," a frequent pseudonym for Frank Norris but one also used by other Wave editors including John O'Hara Cosgrave (McElrath 1988, 20, 140). The Wave ridicules Crane's dwelling upon minutiae in his "London Impressions," remarking that Crane's depiction of a lift in his hotel that ran so slowly the elevator boy became an old man between trips resembles his method of development in these sketches: "Mr. Crane has started in with his descriptions at the railway depot. The best that I can wish for him is that he may live long enough to reach his hotel. . . . Mr. Crane observes and observes and observes—always through a microscope; to him life is a play seen through reversed opera glasses. On his wonderful way from the depot a horse falls down. This is an event, a horrible formless catastrophe. Out with the microscope; everything stops; what else matters now?"

19 SEPTEMBER. RAVENSBROOK. Crane writes to an editor, E. Leslie Gilliams, that his "terms for a story of between five and ten thousand words is $500. This does not include the English rights" (C, 299).

[This estimate quoted by Crane to Gilliams would be in accord with an often-repeated recollection by Ford that one evening at Ravensbrook Crane came home from London greatly elated "because his agent, Mr. Pinker, had given him a contract to sign which guaranteed him £20 per thousand words for everything that he chose to write and had advanced him a sum of money sufficient to pay his Oxted debts. So he could get away from Oxted" (Ford 1921, 109). Pinker did not offer to become Crane's English literary agent until late August 1898, and this incident could have occurred only in January 1899, after Crane returned from Cuba and before the move to Brede Place in February. Following the success of The Red Badge, Crane occasionally demanded such amounts from quality magazines for his stories, but he seldom received more than five cents a word and in his English years considerably less than that (Stronks 1963, 340–349).]

A short satirical piece about the Afridis of northern India, "How the Afridis Made a Ziarat," appears in the New York Press.

22 SEPTEMBER. Amy Leslie writes to Hawkins: "Would you kindly call on me as I would like to see you on a little matter concerning Steve I got a letter from Steve stating he sent me one hundred in care of you would you kindly come and see me at your earliest convenience as I need the money very badly and Steve is waiting to hear from me about it before he will write again" (NhD).

26 SEPTEMBER. A "European Letter" apparently written by Cora that appears in the *New York Press* contains an advance endorsement for Harold Frederic's *Gloria Mundi*:

> Mr. Harold Frederic, one of the small group of American novelists who prefer to live in England, has just finished his new book. It has yet no name but I can say that Mr. Frederic has departed from his American working ground and has written a book which deals solely with English people. It is the story of the young inheritor of a Dukedom in the north of England and follows the English life most wonderfully for the work of a writer who is so typically American in all his other books and in all his manners. Every one who has read the manuscript is joyful and enthusiastic over it. "Strawberry Leaves" may be the title. (*Works*, 8: 711)

27 SEPTEMBER. Amy Leslie again writes to Hawkins: "I received a letter from Steve he is in Ireland. he says he sent you one hundred dollars for me from Greece. I am in Cincinnati at present but expect to be in New York in about eleven days when I will call at your office for the money in the mean time please keep same for me" (NhD). Since Hawkins does not reply, she visits his office several times in an effort to collect the money. Failing to find him, she interprets his behavior as embezzlement and turns the matter over to her attorney, George D. Mabon (Katz 1964–1965, 59–60).

[SEPTEMBER]. Crane writes "The Bride Comes to Yellow Sky." He sends this story and "The Monster" to S. S. McClure in New York, probably through Robert McClure, the publisher's younger brother and London representative, as partial payment or collateral for the loan made to him by McClure in March (Levenson 1970, lxxvi).

3 OCTOBER. A "European Letter" in the *New York Press* is concerned with the affairs of various European royal families and other topics.

10 OCTOBER. A final "European Letter" appears in the *New York Press*.

[14 OCTOBER]. Joseph Conrad writes to Edward Garnett: "I shall go to town tomorrow to meet P[awling] and Crane. I *do* admire him. I shan't have to pretend" (Karl and Davies, 1: 396).

15 OCTOBER. Crane and Conrad meet in London at a luncheon arranged by Sidney Pawling (Karl, 431). Conrad had read *The Red Badge*, and Crane had shown interest in meeting the author of *The Nigger of the "Narcissus*," then beginning its run in Heinemann's *New*

Joseph Conrad
(NYPL Picture Collection)

Review (Conrad 1923, 2–3). Conrad recalls that after the lunch ended at 4:00 P.M. when Pawling left, he and Crane tramped through London together:

We certainly paid no heed to direction. The first thing I noticed were the Green Park railings, when to my remark that he had seen no war before he went to Greece Crane made answer: "No. But the 'Red Badge' is all right." I assured him that I never had doubted it; and, since the title of the work had been pronounced for the first time, feeling I must do something to show I had read it, I said shyly: "I like your General." He knew at once what I was alluding to but said not a word. Nothing could have been more tramp-like than our silent pacing, elbow to elbow, till, after we had left Hyde Park Corner behind us, Crane uttered with his quiet earnestness, the words: "I like your young man—I can just see him." . . . I kept my head sufficiently to guess what was coming and to send a warning telegram to my wife in our Essex home. Crane then was, I believe, staying temporarily in London. But he seemed to have no care in the world; and so we resumed our tramping—east and north and south again, steering through uncharted mazes the streets, forgetting to think of dinner but taking a rest here and there, till we found ourselves, standing in the middle of Piccadilly Circus, blinking at the lights like two authentic night-birds. By that time we had been (in Tottenham Court Road) joined by Balzac. How he came in I have no idea. Crane was not given to literary curiosities of that kind. Somebody he knew, or something he had read, must have attracted lately his attention to Balzac. And now suddenly at ten o'clock in the evening he demanded insistently to be told in particular detail all about the Comédie Humaine, its contents, its scope, its plan, and its general significance, together with a critical description of Balzac's style. I told him hastily that it was just black on white; and for the rest, I said, he would have to wait till we got across to Monico and had eaten some supper. I hoped he would forget Balzac and his Comédie. But not a bit of it; and I had no option but to hold forth over the remnants of a meal, in the rush of hundreds of waiters and the clatter of tons of crockery, caring not what I said (for what could Stephen want with Balzac), in the comfortable assurance that the Monstrous Shade, even if led by some strange caprice to haunt the long room of Monico's, did not know enough English to understand a single word I said. I wonder what Crane made of it all. He did not look bored, and it was eleven o'clock before we parted at the foot of that monumentally heavy abode of frivolity, the Pavilion, with just a hand-shake and a good night—no more—without making any arrangements for meeting again, as though we had lived in the same town from childhood and were sure to run across each other next day. (Conrad 1923, 11–12; 16–17)

17 OCTOBER. Cora Crane writes to Sylvester Scovel, who is prospecting for gold in Alaska, relating details of life at Ravensbrook and mentioning that Crane is working hard on his novel about the Greco-Turkish War, *Active Service*: "The conservatory has been made anew and is now full of beautiful flowers. And slowly but surely we are furnishing—getting old oak and that sort of thing. The Greeks are still faithful and happy—I have tried an English housemaid with them but it dont go—so I am still chef-housemaid-housekeeper-etc. but I like it and we are happy—very happy—Stephen is working hard at a new book which will be his best I think." She describes the carriage accident and their trip to Ireland, and notes that they see much of the Frederics and Robert Barr (*C*, 299–300).

19 OCTOBER. The *Westminster Gazette* contains "Queenstown," the first of a series of five "Irish Notes," in which Crane describes his arrival at the port in Cork Harbor now known as Cobh.

22 OCTOBER. "Ballydehob," the second of the "Irish Notes," appears in the *Westminster Gazette.*

29 OCTOBER. Crane writes his brother William a letter, with the return address of William Heinemann in London, in which bravado and apprehension over his increasing financial plight are intermingled. As with his previous letters to Edmund, he makes no mention of a wife:

I have been in England, Ireland, Scotland, Wales France, Turkey and Greece. I have seen Italy but never trod it. Since I have been in England I have been in dreadfully hard luck. I have been here four months and one month I was laid up by the carriage accident. In the working three months I have earned close to 2000 dollars but the sum actually paid in to me has been only £20. 17s. 3d—about 120 dollars. In consequence I have had to borrow and feel very miserable indeed. I am not sure that I am not in trouble over it.

McClures, with security of over 1000 dollars against my liability of four hundred, refuse to advance me any money. And yet they think they are going to be my American publishers.

I am working now on a big novel. It will be much longer than The Red Badge. My next short thing after the novelette (The Monster) was The Bride Comes to Yellow Sky. All my friends come here say it is my very best thing. I am so delighted when I am told by competent people that I have made an advance. You know they said over here in England that The Open Boat (Scribner's) was my best thing. There seem so many of them in America who want to kill, bury and forget me purely out of unkindness and envy and—my unworthiness, if you choose. All the hard things they say of me effect me principally because I think of mine own people—you and Teddie and the families. It is nothing, bless you. Now Dick Davis for instance has come to like the abuse. He accepts it as a tribute to his excellence. But he is a fool. Now I want you to promise to never pay any attention to it, even in your thought. It is too immaterial and foolish. Your little brother is neither braggart or a silent egotist but he knows that he is going on steadily to make his simple little place and he cant be stopped, he cant even be retarded. He is coming. . . .

I am just thinking how easy it would be in my present financial extremity to cable you for a hundred dollars but then by the time this reaches you I will probably be all right again. I believe the sum I usually borrowed was fifteen dollars, wasnt it? Fifteen dollars—fifteen dollars—fifteen dollars. I can remember an interminable row of fifteen dollar requests. (C, 301–302)

[OCTOBER]. Crane begins work on his only short story about the Greco-Turkish War, "Death and the Child." He dictates a draft of it to Cora.

Crane writes an important letter to Reynolds establishing a regular relationship with him as his American literary agent. He does this in part "to get me out of the ardent grasp of the S. S. McClure Co. I owe them about $500, I think, and they seem to calculate on controlling my entire out-put." Crane summarizes the state of his unpublished work. McClure has the manuscripts of "The Monster" and "The Bride Comes to Yellow Sky." He is under contract to write an article ("The Scotch Express") for *McClure's Magazine* about his train ride from

London's Euston Station to Glasgow, from which he had taken the Clyde River steamer to Queenstown, and McClure has an option on his next book, *The Open Boat and Other Tales of Adventure*. He commissions Reynolds to sell "The Monster" to *McClure's*, and if the amount realized substantially discharges his debt, then Reynolds should approach them about "The Bride Comes to Yellow Sky" also. "'The Bride Comes to Yellow Sky' is a daisy and don't let them talk funny about it." Referring to the unsigned "European Letters" published in part by the *New York Press*, Crane comments:

> You might go to Curtis Brown, Sunday Editor of the *Press* and say how-how from me. Then tell him this *in the strictest confidence*, that a lady named Imogene Carter whose work he has been using from time to time is also named Stephen Crane and that I did 'em in about twenty minutes on each Sunday, just dictating to a friend. Of course they are rotten bad. But by your explanation he will understand something of the manner of the articles I mean to write only of course they will be done better. Ask him if he wants them, signed and much better in style, and how much he will give. Then if he says all right you might turn up a little syndicate for every Sunday. You can figure out that I should get about £10 per week out of it. Then—you do the business—I do the writing—I take 65 per cent and you take 35. (*C*, 305–306)

Crane writes to John S. Phillips of the McClure syndicate:

> My dear John: I am in hopes to see the railroad article off early next week. What on earth have you done with *The Monster*? I have written to Reynolds to go to you and get the story. He will offer you this arrangement—that he sells the story and pays the money to you on my a/c—minus his 10% of course. For heaven's sake give the story a chance.
>
> I hope you liked The Bride Comes to Yellow Sky but I could see a slight resemblance to some of your other mistakes if you didnt. I have delivered to you over 25000 words against my debt but I dont see myself any better off than if I had asked you to wait until I got damned good and ready to pay. I have worried poor little Robert for money until he wails and screams like a mandrake when I mention it. Now please tell me where I am at. What has happened? Did I write a story called *The Monster*? Did I deliver it to you? And what happened after that?
>
> My American affairs are all to be now in the hands of Reynolds. (*C*, 307–308)

3 NOVEMBER. Crane sends Reynolds an essay on Harold Frederic, which he wrote at Frederic's request, with a view toward placing it in *Cosmopolitan*, where *Gloria Mundi* is to begin its serial run in January 1898 (*C*, 308, 308n1).

5 NOVEMBER. An "Irish Note" in the *Westminster Gazette*, "The Royal Irish Constabulary," represents the Constabulary as an ostracized occupation army in Ireland.

8 NOVEMBER. Crane writes to his Port Jervis friend Louis Senger, again being careful only to give William Heinemann as a return address (*C*, 309).

9 NOVEMBER. Conrad inscribes a copy of *Almayer's Folly*:

> To Stephen Crane
> with the greatest regard
> and most sincere ad-
> miration from
> Jph. Conrad.
>
> 9th Nov. 1897. (*C*, 309)

11 NOVEMBER. Crane writes to Conrad, who has sent him proofs of *The Nigger of the "Narcissus,"* and invites him to visit Ravensbrook with his wife for lunch the next Sunday, 14 November. He considers the novel "simply great. The simple treatment of the death of Waite is too good, too terrible. I wanted to forget it at once. It caught me very hard. I felt ill over that red thread lining from the corner of the man's mouth to his chin. It was frightful with the weight of a real and present death. By such small means does the real writer suddenly flash out in the sky above those who are always doing rather well" (*C*, 310).

Crane sends an inscribed copy of *The Black Riders* to Henry D. Davray, book reviewer for the *Mercure de France*, with the hopes of having him translate it into French (*C*, 311).

12 NOVEMBER. "A Fishing Village," the best of Crane's "Irish Notes" in the *Westminster Gazette*, is based on the village of Ahakista and contrasts the attitudes of old and young Irishmen in the face of a changing economy.

16 NOVEMBER. Conrad responds to Crane, regretting that he and his wife cannot accept invitations because Jessie Conrad is in advanced pregnancy. He is grateful for Crane's appreciation of *The Nigger of the "Narcissus"* and for his encouragement during their evening walk in London:

> What your appreciation is to me I renounce to explain. The world looks different to me now, since our long powwow. It was good. The memory

of it is good. And now and then (human nature *is* a vile thing) I ask myself whether you meant half of what you said! You must forgive me. The mistrust is not of you—it is of myself: the drop of poison in the cup of life. I am no more vile than my neighbours but this disbelief in oneself is like a taint that spreads on everything one comes in contact with; on men—on things—on the very air one breathes. That's why one sometimes wishes to be a stone breaker. There's no doubt about breaking a stone. But there's doubt, fear—a black horror, in every page one writes. You at any rate will understand and therefore I write to you as though we had been born together before the beginning of things. For what you have done and intend to do I won't even attempt to thank you. I certainly don't know what to say, tho' I am perfectly certain as to what I feel. (*C*, 312–313)

17 NOVEMBER. Harold Frederic writes to the Australian novelist Louis Becke: "Will you come up here Friday of this week? Turn up at midday. We will put you up like a bird, and you will meet Stephen Crane" (Fortenberry, 463).

23 NOVEMBER. The last of the "Irish Notes," "An Old Man Goes Wooing," another contrast between the young and old in Ireland, appears in the *Westminster Gazette.*

25 NOVEMBER. THANKSGIVING DAY. Frederic writes to Judge Alton B. Parker in haste because he is "driving across country to dine with Stephen Crane, and the horses are waiting" (Fortenberry, 464).

28 NOVEMBER. Crane visits Conrad at his home in Stanford-le-Hope, Essex (Karl and Davies, 1: 416). Jessie Conrad recalls:

My first meeting with Stephen Crane came one evening early in November, 1897, a little more than seven weeks before our eldest boy, Borys, was born. My husband, who had met him perhaps twice, had in a way prepared me for someone at once unusual and with a charm peculiarly his own. He must have been then about six and twenty, and appeared to my maternal mind very slight and delicate. He and Joseph Conrad were on the easy terms of complete understanding, I saw at once; his manner to me was slightly nervous and not a little shy. I don't remember much of the evening that followed after that dinner—I left them together and did not see him before he left early the next morning. The most lasting impression I have is of our taking our coffee, when Stephen, balancing himself on his tilted chair, discoursed gravely on the merits of his three dogs, Sponge, Flannel, and Ruby. The former two had the distinction later of being the parents of the dog he insisted on presenting to the baby." (J. Conrad 1926, 134)

1897

1 DECEMBER. Conrad writes to Crane that on the day after his visit to Stanford-le-Hope there was

> a high tide that smashed the sea-wall flooded the marshes and washed away the Rway line. Great excitement.
>
> But *my* great excitement was reading your stories. Garnett is right. "A Man and Some Others" is immense. I can't spin a long yarn about it but I admire it without reserve. It is an amazing bit of biography. I am envious of you—horribly. Confound you—you fill the blamed landscape—you—by all the devils—fill the sea-scape. The boat thing is immensely interesting. I don't use the word in its common sense. It is fundamentally interesting to me. Your temperament makes old things new and new things amazing. I want to swear at you, to bless you—perhaps to shoot you—but I prefer to be your friend.
>
> You are an everlasting surprise to one. You shock—and the next moment you give the perfect artistic satisfaction. Your method is fascinating. You are a complete impressionist. The illusions of life come out of your hand without a flaw. It is not life—which nobody wants—it is art—art for which everyone—the abject and the great hanker—mostly without knowing it. (*C*, 315)

5 DECEMBER. Crane signs and dates the manuscript of "The successful man has thrust himself " (NNC).

Conrad writes to Edward Garnett:

> I had Crane here last Sunday. We talked and smoked half the night. He is strangely hopeless about himself. I like him. The two stories are excellent. Of course *A Man and Some Others* is the best of the two but the boat thing interested me more. His eye is very individual and his expression satisfies me artistically. He certainly is *the* impressionist and his temperament is curiously unique. His thought is concise, connected, never very deep—yet often startling. He is *the only* impressionist and *only* an impressionist. Why is he not immensely popular? With his strength, with his rapidity of action, with that amazing faculty of vision—why is he not? He has outline, he has colour, he has movement, with that he ought to go very far. But—will he? I sometimes think he won't. It is not an opinion—it is a feeling. I could not explain why he disappoints me—why my enthusiasm withers as soon as I close the book. While one reads, of course, he is not to be questioned. He is the master of his reader to the very last line—then—apparently for no reason at all—he seems to let go his hold. It is as if he had gripped you with greased fingers. His grip is strong but while you feel the pressure on your flesh you slip out from his hand—much to your own surprise. That is my stupid impression and I give it to you in confidence. (Karl and Davies, 1: 416)

8 DECEMBER. In the *Daily Telegraph* W. L. Courtney writes: "Mr. Joseph Conrad has chosen Mr. Stephen Crane for his example, and has determined to do for the sea and the sailor what his predecessor had done for war and warriors. The style, though a good deal better than Mr. Crane's, has the same jerky and spasmodic quality; while a spirit of faithful and minute description—even to the verge of the wearisome—is common to both. If we open any page to *The Nigger of the "Narcissus"* we are told with infinite detail what each one was doing, what the ship was doing, and what the sky and sea were doing"(Karl, 409).

9 DECEMBER. Conrad writes a defensive letter to a reviewer of *The Nigger of the "Narcissus,"* probably Courtney, implicitly denying Crane's influence on his novel: "I wrote this short book regardless of any formulas of art, forgetting all the theories of expression. Formulas and theories are dead things, and I wrote straight from the heart— which is alive. I wanted to give a true impression, to present and [*sic*] undefaced image. . . . I wish to disclaim all allegiance to realism, to naturalism and—before all—all leaning toward the ugly. I would not know where to look for it. There is joy and sorrow; there is sunshine and darkness—and all are within the same eternal smile of the inscrutable Maya" (Karl and Davies, 1: 420–421).

[EARLY DECEMBER]. Crane makes a fair copy with some stylistic improvements of his Western story "The Five White Mice," which he attempts to sell to an English magazine (*C*, 317). He begins to compose "The Blue Hotel."

[MID-DECEMBER]. Crane sends "Death and the Child" to Reynolds, cautioning him that "McClure has a call on it," although *McClure's Magazine* rejects both "Death and the Child" and "The Monster." Crane tells Reynolds that the English rights to "Death and the Child" are sold, which would abrogate the exclusive agency rights he had granted him in October. Crane reveals the desperation he feels over his declining financial situation: "For heaven's sake raise me all the money you can and *cable* it, *cable* it sure between Xmas and New Year's. Sell 'The Monster'! Don't forget that—cable me some money this month" (*C*, 320, 321).

17 DECEMBER. Amy Leslie's lawyer, George Mabon, writes to Hawkins addressing him as "Willis Hawkins, Esq., Agent" and threatening

a suit since he has failed to keep an appointment "to arrange for a settlement of the amount held by you in trust for her" (NhD).

[18 DECEMBER]. The San Francisco *Wave* contains "Perverted Tales," a group of parodies by Frank Norris, among which is "The Green Stone of Unrest/By S——N CR——-E," which satirizes *Maggie, The Red Badge,* "The Open Boat," and Crane's poetry. The parody begins:

A Mere Boy stood on a pile of blue stones. His attitude was regardant. The day was seal brown. There was a vermillion valley containing a church. The church's steeple aspired strenuously in a direction tangent to the earth's center. A pale wind mentioned tremendous facts under its breath with certain effort at concealment to seven not-dwarfed poplars on an undistant mauve hilltop.

The Mere Boy was a brilliant blue color. The effect of the scene was not un-kaleidoscopic.

After a certain appreciable duration of time the Mere Boy abandoned his regardant demeanor. The strenuously aspiring church steeple no longer projected itself upon his consciousness. He found means to re-move himself from the pile of blue stones. He set his face valleyward. He proceeded.

The road was raw umber. There were in it wagon ruts. There were in it pebbles, Naples yellow in color. One was green. The Mere Boy allowed the idea of the green pebble to nick itself into the sharp edge of the disk of his Perception.

"Ah," he said, "a green pebble."

20 DECEMBER. Crane sends Reynolds his article, "Concerning the English Academy." He understands the terms offered by Harper's for serial publication of "The Monster" and book publication of *The Monster and Other Stories.* He proposes to flesh out the book by sending stories to be included in the Heinemann edition of *The Open Boat* but not in the Doubleday & McClure American edition, evidently not un-derstanding that international copyright agreements would prevent this. Crane reassures Reynolds, who had apparently protested, "Death and The Child is *not* being sold in England. I am holding it in order to give you a chance with the big fellows." He complains that his Appleton royalties are attached, presumably because of a suit by Amy Leslie to recover $550 of the $800 she allegedly lent him and he did not repay. He adds, "The Blue Hotel will come to you in about two weeks" (*C,* 317–318).

24 DECEMBER. Conrad writes to Crane to convey best wishes of the season. In a postscript he expresses his resentment over W. L.

Courtney's invidious suggestions in the *Daily Telegraph* that he has fallen under Crane's influence:

> Have you seen the Daily Tele: Article by that ass Courtney? He does not understand you—and he does not understand me either. That's a feather in our caps anyhow. It is the most *mean-minded* criticism I've read in my life. Do you think I tried to imitate you? No Sir! I may be a little fool but I know better than to try to imitate the inimitable But here it is. Courtney says it: You are a lost sinner and you have lead me astray. If it was true I would be well content to follow you but it isn't true and the perfidious ass tried to damage us both. Three cheers for the Press! (*C*, 319)

28 DECEMBER. Hawkins decisively rejects Mabon's demands:

> Your letter addressed on the outside to me and on the inside to "Willis B. Hawkins, Esq., Agent", is before me. I do not know of any such person as "Willis B. Hawkins, Agent."
>
> For your personal information, I will say that I did, at one time, more than a year ago, receive a certain sum of money from a friend who wished me to pay it out in certain prescribed manners. I paid it all out in those manners, and I hold receipts for all the items. When that sum was paid out, my connection with the matter ceased.
>
> For your further information, I will say that a long time afterward, I did receive another sum of money from the same friend, but I returned it to him and declined to make any further disbursements for him. I hold a receipt for this sum.
>
> I presume you will agree with me that I do not have to receive and disburse money for my friends if I do not wish to.
>
> I make this explanation to you merely to enable you to d[ecide] whether you desire to proceed further in the direction indicated. (NhD)

31 DECEMBER. Frederic writes to Charles W. Dayton, until 1897 postmaster of New York City, that he is "sitting up tonight with Stephen Crane and Robert Barr—and when we drink in salutation to the New Year, your name shall not be forgotten, dear old friend" (Fortenberry, 465).

[DECEMBER]. Crane sends Hubbard a manuscript of his poem "A little ink more or less" with the injunction "oh, Hubbard, mark this well. Mark it well! If/it is overbalancing your discretion, inform me./S. C." (NSyU). Hubbard does not publish the poem until July 1900, when the manuscript leaf is reproduced in facsimile in the *Fra* under the pretext that Crane had sent it to him a few months before his death, but the poem appeared previously in *War Is Kind*.

*

1898

*

3 JANUARY. In New York State Supreme Court, Mabon obtains a warrant of attachment against Crane's property in the sum of $550, for "a breach of contract, expressed or implied, other than a contract to marry." Copy of the warrant is sent to Willis Brooks Hawkins (NhD).

4 JANUARY. The *New York Times* reports: "Amy Leslie has brought a suit in the Supreme Court to recover $550 from Stephen Crane. On November 1, 1896, according to the plaintiff, she gave him $800 to deposit in the bank. Instead of putting it in her name he placed it to his own credit. Since then he has paid her $250. She sues to recover the remainder."

7 JANUARY. Joseph Conrad writes to R. B. Cunninghame Graham: "Read the *Badge*. It won't hurt you—or only very little. Crane-ibn-Crane el Yankee is all right. The man sees the outside of many things and the inside of some" (Karl and Davies, 2: 4).

11 JANUARY. Henry Mills Alden writes an unsent letter to Reynolds enclosing payment of $450 for magazine rights to "The Monster." The letter is expanded by Harper and Brothers into a draft contract to include book rights: "the exclusive book rights for Great Britain, United States & Canada of the story to belong to us upon the basis, as per agreement, of a royalty of fifteen per cent on the retail price of all copies sold by us, subject to the terms and conditions of our usual agreements with authors, the sum of two hundred fifty dollars to be paid by us to Mr Crane, at the date of the publication of the story in book form. . . . It is further understood that if 'The Monster' is not sufficiently long to make a volume of convenient size, Mr. Crane will supply another short story to be included in this volume, so as to bring it to the required size" (Wertheim Collection).

[12 JANUARY]. Conrad writes to Crane expressing discomfort at Crane's suggestion that they collaborate on a play:

> I am very curious to know your idea; but I feel somehow that collaborating with you would be either cheating or deceiving you. In any case disappointing you. I have no dramatic gift. *You* have the terseness, the clear eye the easy imagination. You have all—and I have only the accursed faculty of dreaming. My ideas fade—yours come out sharp cut as

cameos—they come all living out of your brain and bring images—and bring light. Mine bring only mist in which they are born, and die. I would be only a hindrance to you—I am afraid. And it seems presumptuous of me to think of helping you. You want no help. I have a perfect confidence in your power—and why should you share with me what there may be of profit and fame in the accomplished task? (*C,* 325)

[Edward Garnett later recalls Crane's interest in writing a play with Conrad:

Conrad's moods of gay tenderness could be quite seductive. On the few occasions that I saw him with Stephen Crane he was delightfully sunny, and bantered "poor Steve" in the gentlest, most affectionate style, while the latter sat silent, Indian-like, turning inquiring eyes under his chiseled brow, now and then jumping up suddenly and confiding some new project with intensely electric feeling. At one of these sittings Crane passionately appealed to me to support his idea that Conrad should collaborate with him in a play on the theme of a ship wrecked on an island. I knew it was hopelessly unworkable—this plan—but Crane's brilliant visualization of the scenes was so strong and infectious I had not the heart to declare my own opinion. And Conrad's skeptical answers were couched in the tenderest, most reluctant tone. I can still hear the shades of Crane's poignant friendliness in his cry "Joseph!" And Conrad's delight in Crane's personality glowed in the shining warmth of his brown eyes. (Garnett 1928, 11–12)]

14 JANUARY. Crane writes to Reynolds assuring him that McClure, "that Scotch ass," has no further claim on "The Monster," although he has apparently not yet released it for publication in *Harper's*. Crane complains that "In all the months I have been in England I have never received a cent from America which has not been borrowed. Just read that over twice!" He maintains that "The Five White Mice" is sold in England, but the story does not appear in an English magazine (*C,* 327).

15 JANUARY. Joseph Conrad writes to Edward Garnett: "Crane wrote me . . . a penitent letter for not replying to mine at Xmas. He says he finds it easier to write *about* me than to me. Says he has written about me, but *where* he says not" (Karl and Davies, 2: 18).

16 JANUARY. Conrad writes to Crane to announce the birth of his first son, Borys: "A male infant arrived yesterday and made a devil of a

row. He yelled like an Apache and ever since this morning has been on the war path again. It's a ghastly nuisance" (*C,* 328).

[LAST WEEK IN JANUARY]. Crane writes out a table of contents for the English edition of *The Open Boat* with a dedication for the volume "To/The late William Higgins/and to/Captain Edward Murphy and Steward C. B. Montgomery/of the sunk steamer Commodore." (The same dedication appears in the shorter American edition.) Afterwards, he numbers the two sets of stories in the order they are to appear in the volume (NNC).

25 JANUARY. Conrad writes to Cora Crane accepting an invitation for an extended visit to Ravensbrook with his family beginning 19 February (*C,* 330–331).

29 JANUARY. Crane writes to Hubbard enclosing a typescript of one of his poems:

> My dear Hubbard: I enclose you some lines. Have you yet recieved "*The Blue Battalions*" and "A Man adrift on a slim spar." They are wandering somewhere in America. They were to be sent to you in time. When they arrive let me know.
>
> You sent me two copies of Volume V. I have given one to Harold Frederic. The books are very great feats. Dont forget to mail me continuous Philistines.
>
> The pome enclosed is not the original ms. It is a copy by an outsider.
>
> Go on, brave man, and do well. For my part I am heavy with trouble. (*C,* 331)

31 JANUARY. Crane writes to Reynolds informing him that he has committed "Death and the Child" to McClure for *The Open Boat* volume, although he has allowed Reynolds to sell the story to *Harper's Weekly*, indicating his continuing confusion about the relationship between serial and book publishing rights and the question of international copyright. He intends to mail off "The Blue Hotel" on Saturday and "will keep it open at all ends" so that if it is accepted by *Harper's Monthly*, "they can afterwards put it in the book." Despite his error with "Death and the Child," he seems to understand that Harper and Brothers require both serial and book rights to stories they accept and that publication of "The Blue Hotel" in England would compromise their international rights. He adds, "Of course I see my mistake about their taking some of the stories that Heineman is to use here." He concludes, "I am going to write about a thousand or twelve hundred

more dollars in short stuff and work only on my big book" [*Active Service*] (*C*, 332–333, 333n2).

[JANUARY–FEBRUARY]. Harold Frederic proposes that in order to reduce living expenses he and Kate Lyon and their children share with the Cranes a house at Dunmanus Bay in Ireland lent to Frederic by a wealthy admirer (*C*, 334).

FEBRUARY. "The Bride Comes to Yellow Sky" appears in *McClure's Magazine* in the United States and in *Chapman's Magazine* in England.

"The impact of a dollar upon the heart" is printed on the back wrapper of the *Philistine* under the title "Some Things," with the line "Simpered at by pimpled merchants] substituted for Crane's "Whored by pimping merchants" and other modifications. Hubbard announces that

> Arrangements have been
> Made with
> Stephen Crane
> (There is only one)
> To supply "Lines"
> For the back of every
> Philistine for a decade.
> Stevie has sent me enuff
> Of the Choice Stuff
> To last several lustrums
> (As he may be shipwreckt any time)
> And the matter will be
> Duly printed
> Regardless of
> Cancellations.

1 FEBRUARY. George Mabon serves a summons on Crane to answer to the claim brought against him by Amy Leslie (Copy, NhD).

[2 FEBRUARY]. Conrad writes to Garnett: "The Cranes have invited the lot of us man woman and child to stay with them ten days—from 19th February—and I've accepted for I feel that if there is no break I will go crazy or go out altogether" (Karl and Davies, 2: 32).

3 FEBRUARY. Conrad writes to E. L. Sanderson: "Stephen Crane is worrying me to write a play with him. He won't believe me when I swear by all the gods and all the muses that I have no dramatic gift.

Probably something will be attempted but I would bet nothing shall be done" (Karl and Davies, 2: 34).

4 FEBRUARY. Conrad writes to R. B. Cunninghame Graham: "On the 19th all our tribe man, woman and child shift camp to Oxted to dwell for ten days in the tents of the Beni-Crane. A risky experiment" (Karl and Davies, 2: 36).

5 FEBRUARY. William Howe Crane writes to George Mabon asking "what it will take in cash" to settle Amy Leslie's claim against Crane (Copy, NhD).

Frederic and Cora Crane quarrel about proposed domestic arrangements in the house they are to share at Dunmanus Bay (C, 338).

7 FEBRUARY. Crane writes to Reynolds:

> I am sending you by the Majestic (Wednesday) a new novelette, "The Blue Hotel." To my mind, it is a daisy. I have left every solitary right free—English book, English serial, American book, American serial—so that you can sell the story to *Harper's Magazine* for the volume. You might gently intimate to them that $500 is about the price I am led to expect for a story of ten thousand words. As for "Death and The Child" it is to go in the McClure book. So is "The Five White Mice."
> Besides it would be absurd to conjoin "Death and The Child" with "The Monster." They don't fit. It would be rotten. Now, "The Blue Hotel" goes in neatly with "The Monster" and together they make 32,000. Very little more is needed for a respectably-sized $1.00 book, and that can be readily submitted within the next six weeks.
> If the Harpers take this story, try to get them to produce that £50 which is to be paid for the book rights. I shall need every sou for the next two months. And if it hadn't been for your handsome management of the Harpers I would have been stumped absolutely. As you see, I am buckling down and turning out stuff like a man. If you hold your fine gait it will only be a short time before we are throwing out our chests. (C, 336)

8 FEBRUARY. Crane writes to Reynolds asking him to request early proofs of "The Monster" and "The Blue Hotel" from Harper and Brothers because he notes "many crudities in style" in the manuscripts (C, 338).

Frederic writes to Cora expressing regret over their dispute on Saturday and his realization that since their vacation together in Ireland the previous autumn "Ravensbrook has defined for itself a system and routine of its own—quite distinct, as is natural, from the system of

Homefield—and that an effort to put these two side by side under one roof would necessarily come to grief" (*C*, 339).

9 FEBRUARY. William Howe Crane writes to George D. Mabon: "Yours of the 7th inst showing full claim and costs in Leslie vs Crane is at hand. I have sent copy to my brother and shall be guided by his wishes in the matter. In the meantime an offer of settlement if reasonable will probably be met half way. Kindly let me know if there is a chance for any abatement of these charges" (Copy, NhD).

12 FEBRUARY. Conrad sketches out notes for a novel on the siege and fall of Paris (1870–1871), possibly attempting to find a subject on which he and Crane might successfully collaborate (Sherry, 691).

15 FEBRUARY. George D. Mabon writes to I. Siesfeld, Amy Leslie's brother-in-law, enclosing copies of William Howe Crane's two communications and specifying: "I replied to the first one by sending him claim in full, and to the last one by telling him 'that under the circumstances I did not think that an offer should emanate from the Plaintiff,' but that if he had any offer to make that I would submit it to my client and that it must approximate the full amount of the claim to receive any attention. To this I have no reply" (NhD).
[Amy Leslie's claim was apparently settled out of court since there is no record of adjudication.]

Conrad writes to Crane in anticipation of the Conrad family's visit to Ravensbrook expressing renewed interest in Crane's idea for a play (*C*, 341).

The U.S.S. *Maine* is blown up in Havana Harbor. Whether the explosion was caused by an underwater mine set by Spaniards, by Cubans hoping to bring about American intervention, or by internal combustion in one of the ship's ammunition magazines is never determined.

19 FEBRUARY. Joseph and Jessie Conrad, their infant son, Borys, and Mrs. Conrad's younger sister, Dorothy ("Dolly") George, begin a 10-day visit to Ravensbrook. Jessie Conrad recalls:

> When the boy was two days old I was deeply moved to receive from Stephen's wife Cora a beautiful box of flowers and a warm invitation to spend a week with them in their home Ravensbrook as soon as the baby was old enough to travel. This visit we made when Borys was exactly five weeks old. The royal preparations for the small person's arrival touched

me very much—since we came without a nurse, a huge easy chair was placed by the side of mine at the table for him to lie in. Stephen had brought with him from Greece two brothers, one of whom he retained in his own household as butler. This youth was most assiduous in his attentions on the young gentleman, and would creep into my room when I was bathing the baby if I forgot to lock my door against him. His English amused us not a little on more than one occasion. One day he was sent by Stephen with a message for my husband and this is the form in which he delivered it: "Mr. Conrad, Mr. Stokes, he come, he want you Mr. Crane." I fear that, owing to my inexperience, the baby must have disturbed the peace of the household not a little; his food decidedly disagreed with him and he voiced much of his dissatisfaction in the night, a habit most infants have. However, we spent a very pleasant week and left with a warm invitation to repeat the visit someday soon. (J. Conrad 1926, 134)

21 FEBRUARY. Conrad inscribes an unidentified book, probably *The Nigger of the "Narcissus,"* to Crane (*C*, 342).

26 FEBRUARY. Crane inscribes a copy of *The Little Regiment* to Conrad (*C*, 343).

28 FEBRUARY. Robert Barr joins the Cranes and Conrads at Ravensbrook (*C*, 342–343).

MARCH. Crane's article "Concerning the English 'Academy'" appears in the *Bookman*. While satirizing the attempt of the critical journal the London *Academy* to establish an English equivalent to the French Academy, Crane praises recent works by James and Conrad, who he feels were overlooked by the *Academy* in the first award of its annual prizes for distinction in literature:

Many people suggested that the prizes should be given to Mr. Henry James for his *What Maisie Knew*, and to Mr. Joseph Conrad for his *The Nigger of the "Narcissus"*—a rendering which would have made a genial beginning for an English Academy of letters, since Mr. James is an American and Mr. Conrad was born in Poland. However, these two were the only novelists who figured prominently. They were not puny adversaries. Mr. James's book is alive with all the art which is at the command of that great workman, and as for the new man, Conrad, his novel is a marvel of fine descriptive writing. It is unquestionably the best story of the sea written by a man now alive, and as a matter of fact, one would have to make an extensive search among the tombs before he who has done better could be found. As for the ruck of writers who make the sea their literary domain, Conrad seems in effect simply to warn them off the premises, and tell them to remain silent. He comes nearer to an ownership of the mysterious life on the ocean than anybody who has written in this century. (*Works*, 8: 733–734)

1 MARCH. Crane advises Reynolds that within the week he will send him copies of most of the poems that are to make up *War Is Kind*. Crane has promised Elbert Hubbard "that you will give him the first chance. I think he is quite sure to accept this offer." He asks Reynolds to obtain copy of the title poem, "Do not weep, maiden, for war is kind," from James MacArthur, assistant editor of the *Bookman*, where the poem first appeared in February 1896 (*C*, 343–344).

Reynolds writes to Robert Underwood Johnson of the *Century*: "I send you a story by Stephen Crane entitled 'The Blue Hotel'. Will you kindly read it and please at once. I think it one of the best things Crane has done. I want a good price for it" (NN-Century Collection).

5 MARCH. "Death and the Child" appears in two parts in *Black and White* (London) on 5 and 12 March under the title "The Death and the Child" and in *Harper's Weekly* in New York on 19 and 26 March.

In a letter misdated 5 February Conrad tells Crane that he arrived home the previous evening, having spent a week with Edward Garnett after leaving Ravensbrook. He expresses his concern about Crane's anxieties over his debts and explains the steps he has taken to enlarge Crane's publication opportunities: "I've had letters of thanks from Pearson and Blackwood for inducing you to call on them. The Pearson man writes he hopes they shall be able very soon to do something quite satisfactory to Mr. Crane 'if he gives us an opportunity.' The Blackwood man sends an invite to lunch for the week after next to you and me if you will condescend to accept that invitation through me. It appears old Blackwood is coming to London himself to make your and my acquaintance. He is a good old Scotchman and if you like the idea drop me a line to name the day. It is left to you" (*C*, 335).

13 MARCH. Crane writes to Reynolds, acknowledging his letter telling him that *Scribner's Magazine* is now considering "The Blue Hotel," which the *Century* has rejected (*C*, 345).

Because the Cranes are uncomfortable at Ravensbrook, Edward Garnett writes to Cora, giving her directions to Brede Place, an ancient manor house near Northiam, Sussex, which he assumes may be rented (*C*, 346). Crane had become intrigued by Garnett's description of Brede Place: "Crane, when living at Oxted, was a neighbour of mine, and one day, on my happening to describe to him an ancient

Sussex house, noble and grey with the passage of five hundred years, nothing would satisfy him but that he must become the tenant of Brede Place" (Garnett 1922, 202).

15 MARCH. The *Chap-Book* contains Crane's appreciative essay on the work of Harold Frederic centering upon *In the Sixties* (1897), a reprint of Frederic's *The Copperhead* and *Marsena,* Civil War books that Crane feels were neglected by Americans.

Through David S. Meldrum, head of Blackwood's London office, Conrad arranges for Crane to meet William Blackwood (*C,* 347).

17 MARCH. Crane presents Conrad with the manuscript of "The Five White Mice" "in remembrance of my warm and endless friendship for you." He hopes Conrad will join him and John Scott Stokes, Harold Frederic's literary assistant and secretary, for dinner at the Savage Club Saturday evening (*C,* 347–348).

Crane writes to Reynolds, expressing his regret that he had mistakenly submitted "Death and the Child" to McClure for *The Open Boat and Other Tales of Adventure* when Harper and Company's prior purchase of the story for *Harper's Weekly* gave them the right to publish it in *The Monster and Other Stories* as well (*C,* 349).

19 MARCH. LONDON. Conrad recalls that after dinner at the Savage Club he and Crane

went and sat at Gatti's, I believe; unless it was in a Bodega which existed then in that neighbourhood, and talked. I have a vivid memory of this awful debauch because it was on that evening that Crane told me of a subject for a story—a very exceptional thing for him to do. He called it "The Predecessor." I could not recall now by what capricious turns and odd associations of thought he reached the enthusiastic conclusion that it would make a good play, and that we must do it together. He wanted me to share in a certain success—"a dead sure thing," he said. His was an unrestrainedly generous temperament. But let that pass. I must have been specially predisposed, because I caught the infection at once. There and then we began to build up the masterpiece, interrupting each other eagerly, for, I don't know how it was, the air around us had suddenly grown thick with felicitous suggestions. We carried on this collaboration as far as the railway time-table would let us, and then made a break for the last train. Afterwards we did talk of our collaboration now and then, but no attempt at it was ever made. Crane had other stories to write; I was immersed deeply in "Lord Jim," of which I had to keep up the instalments in "Blackwood"; difficulties in presenting the subject on the stage rose one after another before our experience. The general subject consisted in a man personating his "predecessor" (who had died) in the hope of winning a girl's heart. The scenes were to include a ranch at the foot of the Rocky Mountains, I remember, and the action I fear would have been frankly melodramatic. Crane insisted that one of the situations should present the man and the girl on a boundless plain standing by their dead ponies after a furious ride (a truly Crane touch). I made some objections. A boundless plain in the light of a sunset could be got into a back-cloth, I admitted; but I doubted whether we could induce the management of any London theatre to deposit two stuffed horses on its stage. (Conrad 1923, 29–30)

[At Blackwood Crane gave a prospectus for "The Predecessor," now conceived of as a novel, to the firm's literary adviser George Brown Burgin, author of 90 novels. He preserved Crane's outline and printed it 25 years later in a book of reminiscences, *More Memories (and Some Travels)* (Garner, 99).]

25 MARCH. Crane and Conrad dine with William Blackwood at the Garrick Club (*C*, 350).

26 MARCH. Meldrum writes to Blackwood: "I was so glad you could meet Crane and Conrad—the two foremost of the youngest writers just now, and types of the men we want to get round the firm" (Conrad 1958, 20–21).

30 MARCH. Walter Hines Page writes to Reynolds acknowledging receipt of "The Blue Hotel," which he considers inferior to "The Bride Comes to Yellow Sky": "I look favorably therefore upon the possibility of accepting it for the Atlantic, but not enthusiastically. But the acceptance of a single story by any writer is a matter of little consequence. . . . I prefer, of course—very greatly prefer—to use in the Atlantic only those stories that may be afterwards published in book form by Messrs. Houghton Mifflin & Co., or stories from authors whose books come to us" (ViU).

31 MARCH. The Harpers pay Crane $125, as one half of the advance due on contract for book publication of "'The Monster' and another story, to be published by Harper & Brothers as agreed" (NNC).

APRIL. "The Wise Men," subtitled "A Detail of American Life in Mexico," appears in England in the *Ludgate Monthly* and in the United States, probably seven or eight months afterward, in *The Lanthorn Book*, "Being a Small Collection of Tales and Verses Read at the Sign o' the Lanthorn 126 William Street New York." The edition is limited to 125 copies, most of which are signed by the contributors, except for Willis B. Hawkins, whose signature is in facsimile.

The back cover of the *Philistine* carries "You tell me this is God" under Hubbard's title, "Lines."

In an unsigned overview of contemporary "Novels of American Life" in the *Edinburgh Review*, Stephen L. Gwyne finds little that is commendable in Crane's work, although he considers it among the best that modern American literature has to offer: One finishes The *Red Badge* "and one puts away the book with a sense of relief, feeling as if one had been seeing a curious gymnastic contortion or feat of strength. It is so evident that here is a man straining every nerve to get a certain result, not so much trying to make his readers see as trying to force his own imagination into seeing." *The Little Regiment* is a better book than *The Red Badge*, but unconvincing and inartistic. *Maggie* "does not seem to us to justify its existence." The dialect employed in the novelette "is the most hideous representation of human speech that we have ever met with. . . . Mr. Crane has seen a piece of life in a hard superficial way, and rendered it in the spirit of a caricaturist."

[FIRST WEEK IN APRIL]. On a cloudy afternoon Crane rushes about London with Conrad visiting publishers in an effort to raise funds for Crane's passage across the Atlantic:

> The problem was to find £60 that day, before the sun set, before dinner, before the "six forty" train to Oxted, at once, that instant—lest peace should be declared and the opportunity of seeing a war be missed. I had not £60 to lend him. Sixty shillings was nearer my mark. We tried various offices but had no luck, or rather we had the usual luck of money hunting enterprises. . . . Crane's white-faced excitement frightened me. Finally it occurred to me to take him to Messrs. William Blackwood & Sons' London office. There he was received in a most friendly way. Presently I escorted him to Charing Cross where he took the train for home with the assurance that he would have the means to start "for the war" next day. (Conrad 1923, 32)

3 APRIL. "The Blood of the Martyr," Crane's satiric playlet about German imperialism in China, is published in the *Sunday Magazine* of the *New York Press*.

6 APRIL. Page writes to Reynolds rejecting "The Blue Hotel":

> It seems to me better that I should return Mr. Crane's story to you, because one stray story is hardly worth our while. You told me, I believe, you had the sale of Mr. Crane's whole output in the United States. When

you had one or two longer stories which have a book value as well as a serial value, you took them to the Harpers, with which, of course I have no complaint to make nor any disposition to complain. But after you have taken the really valuable part of Mr. Crane's work to another magazine and another publisher, it hardly seems to me worth while for the *Atlantic* to step in and buy the remnant.

When you have something from Mr. Crane that is of serial as well as book value in hand, you may be sure that it will be a great pleasure to consider it. (Allen, 58–59)

7 APRIL. A draft receipt for £60 from *Blackwood's Magazine*, not in Crane's hand, acknowledges that the advance is made on articles "from the seat of war in the event of a war breaking out" (Levenson 1970, cv n88).

The William Blackwood and Sons cash ledgers disclose an advance to Crane of £40. Another payment of £20 is made to Cora on 16 April and after the last entry is a note "In full, two articles" (Conrad 1958, 21n1). Crane seems to have made an agreement with Blackwood that they would have had first refusal of his war stories. Only "The Price of the Harness" was accepted for *Blackwood's Magazine*.

9 APRIL. Page writes to Reynolds reiterating his attitude toward Crane's work:

I was very much pleased with your spirited letter about Mr. Crane, or really about the Harpers. Of course I care nothing about the Harpers, or about what they publish or do not publish. I spoke of them only because you spoke of them yourself; for you will recall that when you were here you remarked that you had sold two long stories to them. My only point is that a single short story is of hardly sufficient importance for the Atlantic to buy—it ought to give its space and attention to enterprises of more importance. If at any time you have a longer story by Mr. Crane which might make a book, or if you know that he is of a mind to write a suffi-cient number of short stories of the same general kind with their scenes pitched in the same general part of the earth, then there would be some inducement to publish a part of them in the Atlantic. You know, however, that a book of short stories is always less valuable for book publication than a book which contains a long story. (ViU)

10 APRIL. The Sunday supplement of the *New York World* contains an abridged version of "The Five White Mice."

11 APRIL. OXTED. Crane writes a formal acknowledgment for "receipt of £60 (sixty pds) recieved in advance for articles to be contributed to

Blackwoods Magazine from the seat of war in the event of a war breaking out between the United States of America and Spain and undertake to refund the said £60 in case of my failing to reach the seat of war or to supply the said articles. In case of my death, I direct my executors to fulfill this obligation" (Blackwood Papers, National Library of Scotland).

13 APRIL. Crane sails from Liverpool en route to New York aboard the *Germanic*. The passenger list of the ship describes him as "Stephen Crane, age 26, sex male, occupation journalist, citizen of the United States, intended destination New York, port of embarkation Liverpool. He is listed as passenger 797, intending protracted sojourn" (Lyle J. Holverstott to Melvin H. Schoberlin, 17 November 1947, NSyU, and "Official List of Passengers on *Germanic,* National Archives." Copy, NSyU).

14 APRIL. From Queenstown (now Cobh), Ireland, Crane sends a departing telegram to Conrad before the *Germanic* sets sail across the Atlantic (*C*, 357).

18 APRIL. Copyright deposit of *The Open Boat and Other Tales of Adventure* is made in the Library of Congress by Doubleday & Mc-Clure Co. The Heinemann edition, entitled *The Open Boat and Other Stories*, is published simultaneously (Bruccoli and Katz, 279), with deposit made in the British Museum. This volume contains nine New York City stories not included in the American edition under the heading "Midnight Sketches." Two of these, "An Eloquence of Grief" and "The Auction," had not appeared previously. The stories common to both volumes are headed "Minor Conflicts" in the English edition.

19 APRIL. Conrad writes to Cora expressing surprise that she is still at Ravensbrook. Because he mistakenly believes that Crane boarded the *Germanic* in Cobh rather than Liverpool and knew that Cora planned a visit to the Frederics at Ahakista, he assumed that Cora had accompanied Crane to Ireland:

> We thought of asking you to come here at once but on receiving Stephen's wire I imagined you were all in Ireland already. However you will be more entertained and more comfortable at the Frederic's for a time and on your return to England I hope will have the will and the courage to undertake the risky experiment of coming to us with Mrs Ruedy. Moreover I fancy Stephen's absence won't be very prolonged and we may

have the felicity of seeing you all here together. I trust you will let me
know how he fares whenever you hear from him. He is not likely to write
to any one else—if I know the man. (*C,* 357)

20 APRIL. Robert J. Collier expresses interest in "The Blue Hotel" but
asks Reynolds whether Crane will accept less than $400 for the story.
He cautions, "We should probably, at any event, not be able to use it
for four or five months" (ViU).

21 APRIL. The *Germanic* crosses the bar of New York harbor at 11:53
P.M. (*New York Commercial,* 23 April).

22 APRIL. The Atlantic Squadron under command of Admiral William T. Sampson forms off Key West and heads for Havana. In the
afternoon the ships take up formation along the coast of Cuba. The
blockade marks the first major act of belligerence in the war between
the United States and Spain (O'Toole, 173).

[22 APRIL]. Crane contracts with Pulitzer's *New York World,* ostensibly for a fee of $3,000 (Seitz 1933, 137), to report the Cuban War.

23 APRIL. Crane applies for a passport. He lists his permanent address as Hartwood and his occupation as journalist. The application
is witnessed by a member of the *World* staff (National Archives.
Copy, CtU).

[24 APRIL]. Crane leaves New York for Key West. He stops briefly in
Washington to see Lily Brandon Munroe for the last time (*C,* 360).

25 APRIL. Congress declares that a state of war has existed between
the United States and Spain since 21 April (Alger, 6n).

The *New York Journal* prints "The Little Stilettos of the Modern
Navy," an article written earlier in the month about torpedo boats
built in the shipyard of Yarrow.

25 OR 26 APRIL. Crane arrives in Key West, which, like Tampa in the
"rocking chair stage" of the war, is swarming with naval personnel
and reporters eagerly waiting for Admiral William T. Sampson's fleet
blockading the coast of Cuba to intercept the Spanish fleet of Admiral
Pascual Cervera y Topete, making it safe for the navy to transport
troops across the Straits of Florida. Ralph Paine, correspondent for the
Philadelphia Press, recalls:

Correspondents poured in by every steamer from the mainland. Just how they were going to report this war was a matter of hazy conjecture. Later there would be an army to accompany to Cuba, but for a while it was the Navy's affair, and things might happen anywhere over an area of a thousand miles of salt water. Seagoing tugs and yachts were chartered at enormous expense to follow the fleet and serve as dispatch boats. Only a few newspapers could afford such outlay, but the correspondents kept coming to Key West with orders to get the news somehow. Most of them were first-class reporters, assigned to cover this story as they would have been sent to a big fire or a railroad wreck. . . . The Key West Hotel was a bedlam of a place while we waited for the war to begin. And when other diversion failed, you could stroll around the corner to the resort known as the "Eagle Bird" where a gentlemanly gambler, as well-groomed and decorous as Jack Oakhurst, spun the roulette wheel. And there you would be most apt to find Stephen Crane, sometimes bucking the goddess of chance in contented solitude, a genius who burned the candle at both ends and whose spark of life was to be tragically quenched before he was thirty years old. (Paine, 192–193)

26 APRIL. Robert J. Collier writes to Reynolds offering to take "The Blue Hotel" "shortened to seven thousand five hundred (7,500) or eight thousand (8,000) words for Three Hundred Dollars" (ViU).

27 APRIL. Admiral Sampson's flagship, the armored cruiser *New York*, shells Matanzas (O'Toole, 201). Richard Harding Davis is on board the flagship, but Crane misses the bombardment (C. B. Davis, 234).

28 APRIL. Datelined Key West, 27 April, Crane's first known Cuban War dispatch, a telegram headlined "The Terrible Captain of the Captured Panama," dealing with the fear exhibited by the captain of a Spanish steamship captured and brought into Key West, appears in the *New York World*.

29–30 APRIL. Scovel's friendship with Admiral Sampson enables Crane to spend two days aboard the flagship *New York* on an inspection trip to the Bay of Mariel, 35 miles to the west of Havana. He reports this in "Sampson Inspects Harbor at Mariel" (*New York World*, 1 May).

30 APRIL. From the flagship Richard Harding Davis writes to his family: "I have made I think my position here very strong and the admiral is very much my friend as are also his staff. Crane on the

other hand took the place of Paine who was exceedingly popular with every one and it has made it hard for Crane to get into things" (C. B. Davis, 235). "I don't like him myself," Davis adds (Lubow, 158). Crane had replaced Paine, whose sardonic reporting angered the military command, resulting in his being banished from the flagship by an "edict from the Navy Department" (Paine, 202).

[LATE APRIL–EARLY MAY]. Accompanied by Mrs. Ruedy, Adoni Ptolemy, and various dogs, Cora spends two or three weeks with the Frederics at Ahakista, Dunmanus Bay, in County Cork, Ireland (Gilkes 1960, 140).

MAY. "On the desert," entitled "Lines," appears in the *Philistine*. Hubbard warns that "All parties who are unable to digest the Lines of Stephen Crane should cancel subscriptions before next issue," but the promised deluge of Crane poems in the *Philistine* does not materialize.

1 MAY. In the *New York Times* Harold Frederic hails *The Open Boat* as an important literary event and lauds Crane as "a powerful factor . . . in drawing England Westward."

The *New York Press* cautions that "the reader who seeks in fiction only entertainment in pleasant incidents—and none may say definitely that this sort of reader is not right—must be warned away from this volume of stories. They deal with emotions more than with incidents, and, furthermore, with emotions that are not pleasant—generally those of men face to face with death in one form or another. They are fiction that gives no broad full view of human life in general, or even of any one human life in particular. They are simply the work of a remarkable expert along the somewhat narrow line of his specialty. In medicine the specialist now reaps all the honors that used to belong to the general practitioner; but therein doctors and fiction writers are different."

FIRST WEEK IN MAY. Crane asks Reynolds to send him the manuscript of "The Blue Hotel," which he has apparently misplaced. He supposes it is at the Everett House, the hotel on Union Square in which he occasionally stayed when passing through New York (*C*, 359).

4 MAY. Crane is with his bureau chief, Sylvester Scovel, aboard the *World*'s dispatch tug *Triton* on a mission to take the *World* reporter Charles H. Thrall off the gunboat *Wilmington*, which had picked him up on the beach at Guanabocoa a few miles east of Havana the pre-

vious day, to take him back to Key West. Thrall had been in Havana since 13 April and has valuable information about the city's fortifications to communicate to Admiral Sampson. Sampson orders that Thrall be put aboard the *Leyden* for transfer to his flagship, but Crane interviews Thrall while the *Triton* is alongside the *Wilmington* (C. H. Thrall, "Thrilling Adventure of World Scout in Cuba," *New York World*, 8 May).

Hearing that Cervera might be in Puerto Rico, Sampson withdraws most of the larger warships from the blockade and sails to San Juan (O'Toole, 209).

5 MAY. In Key West Crane completes a telegram begun on the *Triton* the previous day deploring the effects of the stalled war on the ships and men of the fleet. "Inaction Deteriorates the Key West Fleet" appears in the *World* on 6 May.

6 MAY. From the dispatch tug *Three Friends*, chartered jointly by arrangement between the *World* and the *Herald* (E. W. McCready to Benjamin J. R. Stolper, 22 January 1934, NNC), Crane boards the *New York* and writes "With the Blockade on Cuban Coast," an account of daily life aboard the flagship as it cruises among the other American ships grouped before Havana, which he completes in Tampa on 8 May and which appears in the *World* the next day.

7 MAY. The *Athenaeum* opines that the stories of *The Open Boat* "show evident signs of that extraordinary ability, amounting to genius, which distinguishes all the prose of Mr. Crane; but we doubt whether they will hit the taste of the public in this country, as they are too sombre and too generally concerned with persons of a somewhat uniform type of white savagery."

The reviewer for *Literature* finds Crane's weakness as well as strength in his impressionistic style. The subjects in *The Open Boat*

are not always interesting; it is his way of presenting them that is everything. In this respect he resembles those painters who care little for the subject but more for the method of their art, and are called, for want of a better term, Impressionists. To this extent, with his carefully-chosen details, his insistence on the main theme, and his avoidance of irrelevance, Mr. Crane is an Impressionist, and not a mere descriptive writer. His book must not be regarded as a collection of short stories. They are incidents rather than stories, and are selected, not for their dramatic interest, which the author apparently wishes to exclude, but as a vehicle for the telling touches in which he paints aspects of nature, or analyses human emotions. (Weatherford, 218)

8 MAY. Crane writes to Reynolds that he cannot cut "The Blue Hotel." "Let Collier's do it themselves" (*C*, 359).

"Stephen Crane's Pen Picture of C. H. Thrall" appears in the *World* on the same page as Thrall's own story.

12 MAY. Failing to find the Spanish fleet at San Juan, Sampson shells the coastal batteries and heads back for Cuba. Almost simultaneously, Cervera's fleet arrives at Martinique (O'Toole, 211).

BEFORE 14 MAY. From Key West Crane, Scovel, and Frank Norris, who is representing *McClure's Magazine*, set forth on a two-day trip in the *Three Friends* to garner what news they can of the stalled war from the American warships blockading the coast of Cuba. They encounter the *Helena, Dolphin, Machias, Mayflower,* and *Hornet,* as well as a number of gunboats. The fastidious Norris, in a dispatch unpublished in his lifetime, "On the Cuban Blockade," characterizes Crane sarcastically as "the Young Personage" and is caustic about his disheveled appearance, which he describes in a pen portrait corresponding with a well-known photograph of Crane taken by Scovel on this cruise:

> The correspondents took themselves off to the cabin and wrote while sitting in their bunks. The Young Personage was wearing a pair of duck trousers grimed and fouled with all manner of pitch and grease and oil. His shirt was guiltless of collar or scarf, and was unbuttoned at the throat. His hair hung in ragged fringes over his eyes, his dress suit-case was across his lap and answered him for a desk. Between his heels he held a bottle of beer against the rolling of the boat, and when he drank was royally independent of a glass. While he was composing his descriptive dispatches which some ten thousand people would read in the morning from the bulletins in New York, I wondered what the fifty thousand who have read his war novel and have held him, no doubt rightly, to be a great genius, would have said and thought could they have seen him at the moment. (*New York Evening Post*, 11 April 1914)

14 MAY. Harry Brown and Ernest W. McCready of the *New York Herald*, Ralph Paine, representing the *Philadelphia Press*, and Crane make their first visit to Haiti aboard the *Three Friends*. They land at Cap-Haitien and attempt to reach the French cable service at Mole St. Nicholas, but they are repeatedly challenged by sentries with the cry of "*Qui vive.*" Paine recalls:

We drifted in the direction of the beach to talk it over. Of the quartet, only Stephen Crane was enjoying the experience. As usual, he refused to take the responsibilities of daily journalism seriously. He had been known to shorten the life of a managing editor. A night in Mole St. Nicholas had its appeal for the artistic temperament.

"It's your move, Crane," said McCready. "Fiction is your long suit. Here it is. Things like this don't happen in real life. Let us have a few remarks from the well-known young author of 'The Red Badge of Courage.'"

"Me?" grinned Crane. "If I caught myself hatching a plot like this, I wouldn't write another line until I had sobered up. Steady, boys, the night is still young, and I have a hunch that there'll be lots more of it. This opening is good."

The correspondents manage to reach the telegraph station after the deck hand who had rowed them ashore learns the password, which sounds like the English "I-am-the-Boss!" The correspondents follow him as he proclaims at each outpost:

"I-AM-THE-BOSS! Salute, you black sons-of-guns."

At his heels marched the four correspondents, chanting in unison: "I-AM-THE-BOSS! Salute, you black sons-of-guns."

The effect was as magical as the astute deck-hand had foretold. The slouching sentinels rolled their eyes and bobbed their heads in recognition of the pass-word. One or two even attempted to present arms, but the result was sketchy. Their hands strayed to their straw hats. A salute was evidently intended. Past them strode the conquering deck-hand and the admiring correspondents. Crane was murmuring aloud:

"I wonder if we could blast the secret out of a French dictionary. Probably not. We shall never know. It is just one of those things." (Paine, 225, 228)

15 MAY. The *Three Friends* anchors at Puerto Plata in the Dominican Republic (San Domingo). According to McCready, in a narrative that seems more likely set in Haiti, Crane "went native" that night and "successfully invited a seduction." He also plotted to rob two drunken men of a "Vast Container of Rum" that was concealed in a barque anchored across the shark-infested harbor:

In the black hills the nigger fires were winking, and the drums gave out that woodeny sound which some one likened to the music produced by a bevy of folk thumping distantly on a flock of wooden piss-pots. Steve went adventuring on this occasion in his bare feet, clothed only by exceedingly soiled blue-striped pajamas, an equally soiled brown beard of a week's well-fertilized herbage—and his circumbient Breath. This last was protection enough for all ordinary purposes. Indeed, it would have

Stephen Crane aboard the *Three Friends,* off the coast
of Cuba, May 1898
(Syracuse University)

sufficed in the still undiscovered stratosphere. But the purposes in view
were very other than ordinary. So he had his due reward." (E. W. Mc-
Cready to Benjamin J. R. Stolper, 31 January 1934, NNC)

The *World* prints "Sayings of the Turret Jacks in Our Blockading
Fleets," a group of fragmentary anecdotes told by sailors.

1898

17–18 MAY. The *Three Friends* anchors in Puerto Rico (*C*, 360).

19 MAY. Believing that Cervera will put in somewhere along the southern coast of Cuba to unload supplies that would then be transported overland to Havana, the Flying Squadron under the command of Commodore Winfield Scott Schley leaves Key West to blockade Cienfuegos. On this same morning Cervera's fleet drops anchor in the harbor of Santiago de Cuba (O'Toole, 212).

[19 MAY]. Returning to Key West, the *Three Friends* is accidentally sideswiped during the night by the gunboat *Machias*, which had first fired a warning shot, as Crane narrates the incident in his dispatch "Narrow Escape of the Three Friends" (*New York World*, 29 May) and later in "War Memories." Paine remembers only being fired at by the *Machias*: "There was a stormy twilight off Cardenas when a suspiciously minded and hasty gunboat, the Machias, concluded that she had sighted an enemy ship. Her gunners aimed a shell which nicked the top of the funnel of the Three Friends and showered all hands with soot, besides spoiling their tempers. Ranging closer, the Machias discovered the error and the officer in charge of the bridge offered a handsome apology" (Paine, 215).

20–25 MAY. The *Three Friends* pursues Admiral Sampson's flagship, the *New York*, as Sampson's fleet maneuvers into position off the Santa Maria Keys on the Cuban coast to prevent the escape of the Spanish fleet from Santiago harbor, where it had arrived on 19 May. Crane's dispatch "How Sampson Closed His Trap" (*New York World*, 27 May) does not reflect its headline since Crane was unaware of Sampson's intentions.

24 MAY. Datelined "Porto Plata, San Domingo, May 15," "Hayti and San Domingo Favor the United States" appears in the *World*. Crane finds "the French and Germans invariably against us; the English and the natives almost invariably with us, and the more clean and modern the people the more they favor us" (*Works*, 9: 118).

26 MAY. In *Life* Robert Bridges praises the title story of *The Open Boat*: "It is easy enough to caricature it, to poke fun at the monotonous repetition of phrases and catchwords, but when you have finished reading it he has indelibly fixed the experience on your mind, and that is the test of a literary artisan" (Hagemann 1968, 350).

Front cover of *The Open Boat and Other Tales
of Adventure*, 1898
(Wertheim Collection)

28 MAY. The Spanish fleet is blockaded in Santiago Harbor by
Schley's Flying Squadron (O'Toole, 212).

29 MAY. Cruising some 160 miles north of Jamaica, the dispatch boat
Somers N. Smith, chartered jointly by the *World* and the *Herald* to
search for Cervera's fleet, is apparently chased by what appears to be
a Spanish warship. Seven correspondents, including Crane, Scovel,
and *Collier's Weekly* photographer Jimmy Hare, are on the boat. The
correspondents prepare for capture, but as the ship swings to star-

board it is seen to be the American auxiliary cruiser *St. Paul.* Crane relates this incident in "Chased by a Big 'Spanish Man-O'-War'" (*New York World*, 3 July).

30 MAY. Crane writes to Reynolds from the *Somers N. Smith*, "Off Havana," that he is sending him "His New Mittens," written on the dispatch boat, "a short story of boy life in Whilomville—the town of The Monster. I think Harpers ought to take it for about £40 and also cough up that other $125 [but Harper's did not pay the second half of the advance on *The Monster* until 6 March 1899 because they did not feel that the book was long enough]. You might send a copy of The Blue Hotel to Blackwood's Magazine London with information as to when Collier's Weekly will publish it" (*C,* 360–361, 361n1).

JUNE. "When a people reach the top of a hill" appears in the *Philistine* under "Lines." The poem is reprinted with the title "The Blue Battalions" in an anthology, *Spanish-American War Songs,* edited by Sidney A. Witherbee (1898), although it is inspired by Crane's experience in the Greco-Turkish War.

1 JUNE. A correspondent on the *Somers N. Smith* reports that "'in the evening we sat in the stern under the awning, spinning yarns, and singing. Sylvester Scovel has a very good tenor voice and an immense repertoire of songs, and Stephen Crane sings a good second'" (*SCraneN* 4, no. 2 [Winter 1969]: 11).

2 JUNE. The *Somers N. Smith* returns to Key West (*Works,* 9: 484).

3 JUNE. Lieutenant Richmond P. Hobson and seven volunteers attempt to carry out Admiral Sampson's plan to sink a large collier, the *Merrimac,* across the narrowest part of the channel at the mouth of Santiago Harbor in order to prevent the escape of Cervera's fleet. The plan miscarries when Spanish shell fire destroys the batteries for detonating all but two of the torpedoes. The *Merrimac* sinks but not in a position to blockade the harbor. Hobson and his men are taken prisoner (O'Toole, 235–237).

4 JUNE. Cora Crane writes to Clara Frewen:

The reason for delay in my writing you about Brede Place, has been because I wanted to hear from Mr. Crane also, to get the architects report on how much it would cost to make the house habitable. I am sending you a copy of his report of things which must be done. I understand from

Mr. Frewen that, say, in about two years time, you are thinking of making extensive additions to the old house. Under these circumstances we would not like to spend too much on the house. I understand that it has rented as a farm house for £14 per year. Now will you accept the following offer? We think that £40. per year, as the house *is*, will be a fair rental. And we will make the repairs named in the architects report. Then I would like priviledge of building a small conservatory. You see it will mean over £120. a year rent.

In a postscript she adds, "The architect has neglected to send estimate of stable, but of course this will be put in order" (Copy, CtU).

[Brede Place was a rambling, decayed country manor, which was partly built in the fourteenth century on the site of a still earlier wooden structure and rebuilt and restored during Tudor and Elizabethan times. Like most old rural houses in late Victorian England, it was devoid of modern plumbing and electricity. Most of the rooms were uninhabitable. Clare Sheridan, whose parents bought Brede Place from her uncle Edward Frewen, recalls that "some inadequate renovation was attempted," but Stephen and his "large managing wife" moved in "before it was the least bit habitable" because he was "bowled over by the sedate grey dignity of this remnant of mediaeval England" (Sheridan, 20). Servants refused to spend the night in the house because of the legend that it was haunted by the spirit of its early sixteenth-century owner, Sir Goddard Oxenbridge, a warlock and an ogre who purportedly ate a child for dinner each night. According to the legend, he was executed by local children who sawed him in half with a wooden saw while he lay in an intoxicated stupor. A contemporary guidebook (Augustus J. C. Hare, *Sussex* [London: George Allen, 1894], pp. 47–48) describes Brede Place as

one of the best existing specimens of the small country-houses of the time of Henry VII, of which Brympton in Somerset is so fine an example. The earlier part of the house was built by Sir Thomas Oxenbridge, who died November 1497, and Sir Goddard, who died in February 1531. It is of stone, with foliated windows, and two fine chimneys with diagonal shafts battlemented. Additions in brick with stone dressings were made under Elizabeth. The entrance was originally in the centre. The house is strangely ill-arranged internally. The hall, which once rose to the whole height of the building, has been subdivided into an upper and lower floor. The present porch leads at once into the principal chamber. South of this is another large but low room, with an arched chimney. Hence a door opens into a chapel, divided by an oak screen. The staircase is dark. The

Place was long a satisfactory resort of smugglers, as the legends attached to Sir Goddard kept people away, and accounted to them for all the strange sounds which were heard there.

Groaning Bridge is pointed out as the spot where Sir Goddard Oxenbridge was sawn in half by the children.

In *The O'Ruddy* (1903) the title character, who has brought a priest, Father Donovan, to Brede with him, is told the legend of Sir Goddard by an elderly caretaker, in a passage written by Robert Barr: "Bullet wouldn't harm him, nor steel cut him, so they sawed him in two with a wooden saw down by the bridge in front. He was a witch of the very worst kind, your honour. You hear him groaning at the bridge every night, and sometimes he walks through the house himself in two halves, and then every body leaves the place. And that is our most serious danger, your honour. When Sir Goddard takes to groaning through these rooms at night, you'll not get a man to stay with you, sir; but as he comes up from the pit by the will of the Devil we expect his Reverence to ward him off" (327–328).]

10 JUNE. Six hundred fifty men of the First Marine Battalion land at Guantánamo Bay from the U.S.S. *Panther*. The purpose of the expedition is to establish a coaling station for the blockading ships that previously had to make the 800-mile voyage to Key West to recoal in port (O'Toole, 248). Crane, McCready and Paine watch the landing from the *Three Friends*. In the evening Crane goes ashore while the other correspondents take the dispatch boat to Port Antonio, Jamaica, to cable their stories (Paine, 243–244).

[Biographical accounts that place the events described in Crane's early dispatches from Guantánamo Bay on 7, 8, and 9 June (See Stallman 1973, 361–364; Bowers 1971, 486; Milton, 303) are inaccurate. According to the official records of the United States Marine Corps and the reports of its officers, the First Battalion commanded by Lieutenant Colonel Robert W. Huntington arrived off Santiago de Cuba aboard the U.S.S. *Panther* on the morning of 10 June. On the same day at 1:00 P.M., the ship dropped anchor in Guantánamo Bay, and the landing began an hour later with no resistance from the enemy. With the exception of a brief skirmish on 12 May between Spanish guerrillas (native-born Cuban irregulars loyal to Spain) and men of the First U.S. Infantry acting as an escort to the steamer *Gussie*, which was landing arms and supplies at Arbolitos Point (Clifford, 23), these were the first American troops on Cuban soil. They were preceded only by a small detachment of Marines from the blockading ships, 20 from the

Marblehead and 40 from the *Oregon*, who reconnoitered the area on the morning of the day the First Battalion landed (Collum, 547–560).]

Cora writes to Moreton Frewen that letters from Crane have been delayed, "but I expect to hear from him any day now that he is satisfied with my arrangements for Brede. I can, however, safely say that we will take it on the terms named in my letter and as soon as I hear from Mr. Crane I will write you a formal letter to that effect" (*C,* 362).

II JUNE. Resistance to the Marine landing intensifies. Captain Henry Bowman McCalla of the *Marblehead* sends in reinforcements. In the fighting three Marines are killed. The Marines establish their headquarters, which they name Camp McCalla, on the high ground above Guantánamo Bay (Collum, 550). That night a large force of Spanish troops and guerrillas attacks the camp. Crane later writes vividly of "The noise; the impenetrable darkness; the knowledge from the sound of the bullets that the enemy was on three sides of the camp; the infrequent bloody stumbling and death of some man with whom, perhaps, one had messed two hours previous; the weariness of the body, and the more terrible weariness of the mind, at the endlessness of the thing, made it wonderful that at least some of the men did not come out of it with their nerves hopelessly in shreds" ("Marines Signaling under Fire at Guantanamo," *McClure's Magazine,* 6 February 1899).

12 JUNE. At 1:00 A.M. Assistant Surgeon John Blair Gibbs, USN, is shot in front of his tent (Collum, 550). Crane reports the casualties in his dispatch, "In the First Land Fight Four of Our Men Are Killed" (*New York World,* 13 June), put together and cabled to the *World* by Ernest McCready from notes dictated by Crane aboard the *Three Friends.* McCready recalls Crane's extreme reluctance to leave the fighting and board the boat waiting to take the correspondents to the cable station at Mole St. Nicholas:

At long last I found Crane—dirty, sleepless from the night attack, bleary from the preliminaries and reviews of his marine hosts, disgusted with life in some aspects, particularly in having smoked the last of his, or their, cigarettes, but somehow gloomily elated over the scenery and the prospect that presently it would be a whole lot worse. The shells from the cruisers were still going over our heads, the marines were still going up the ravines & extending in less rugged but more heavily-brushed ground, and the Spanish rifle fire was evidently slackening. The Americans were pushing up more automatic and 3 inch field pieces.

Crane was sitting on a rock. There was some smoke drifting over and around us from the firing, and while at the moment we did not seem to be directly in line with any bullets from either side, I had already heard some talk about wrongly fused or otherwise ill-directed shells from the cruisers, and was afraid, too, that a shift of the Spanish, or the arrival of their supports would result in the ridge being swift to cripple American runners from the base to the advancing front line. I ignored the artist's gruff greeting—as long since we had dispensed with any but free, frank, & highly colorful forms of conversation, the sky being the limit so far as terms of compliment or complaint were concerned.

Rapidly and perhaps a bit roughly I told him there wasn't a minute to lose, that the dispatch boat was under the hill, that the show was over & complete in the newspaper sense until the after-dark developments, for which I had made arrangements; that he could go to the Mole with me if he liked, and thus get to a cable some hours earlier than by any other course.

"Come on" I said. "Let's hustle like hell down to the boat. It's under the hill, covered from the firing, and we can start her the minute we're aboard!"

He regarded me with visible dislike[.]

"Gimme a cigarette!" he commanded. "Do you think, for God's sake, that I'm going away now on your damned boat, and leave all this?"—and he waved a hand in a sweeping gesture covering the battle picture. I knew what he meant. . . . He'd been in camp with the marines throughout the night attack and seen their dead and wounded, shared their in councils [sic]; loved the picture before him, and saw an artist's profit in it; it was hardening a hundred impressions for his own peculiar treatment, the methods in which he had the most faith—his own. . . . I urged him to forget the scenery & the "effects" and remember that in Broadway and in Park place edition was following special edition, extra following extra, and that he had been the only newspaper man in the show who had means of getting to a cable station.

But Crane was not a newspaper man. He was an artist from crown to heel, temperamental, undisciplined in the narrow sense of the word— careless of any interest that did not march with his own private ones, contemptuous of mere news getting or news reporting; thinking of his World connection as a convenient aid rather than as one imposing sharp and instant responsibility upon him. (E. W. McCready to B. J. R. Stolper, 22 January 1934, NNC)

[Crane's slightly fictionalized account of the Guantánamo fighting in "War Memories" mistakenly places the midnight assault by a party of Spaniards in which Gibbs died, within minutes after being shot in front of his tent, on the third night of the engagement rather than at 1:00 A.M. on 12 June and dramatizes the event:

> On the third night the alarm came early; I went in search of Gibbs, but I soon gave over an active search for the more congenial occupation of lying flat and feeling the hot hiss of the bullets trying to cut my hair. For the moment I was no longer a cynic. I was a child who, in a fit of ignorance, had jumped into the vat of war. I heard somebody dying near me. He was dying hard. Hard. It took him a long time to die. He breathed as all noble machinery breathes when it is making its gallant strife against breaking, breaking. But he was going to break. He was going to break. It seemed to me, this breathing, the noise of a heroic pump which strives to subdue a mud which comes upon it in tons. The darkness was impenetrable. The man was lying in some depression within seven feet of me. Every wave, vibration, of his anguish beat upon my senses. He was long past groaning. There was only the bitter strife for air which pulsed out into the night in a clear penetrating whistle with intervals of terrible silence in which I held my own breath in the common unconscious aspiration to help. I thought this man would never die. I wanted him to die. Ultimately he died. At the moment, the adjutant came bustling along erect amid the spitting bullets. I knew him by his voice. "Where's the doctor? There's some wounded men over there. Where's the doctor?" A man answered briskly: "Just died this minute, sir." It was as if he had said: "Just gone around the corner this minute, sir." Despite the horror of this night's business, the man's mind was somehow influenced by the coincidence of the adjutant's calling aloud for the doctor within a few seconds of the doctor's death. It—what shall I say?—It interested him, this coincidence. (WM, 237–239)]

14 JUNE. Crane accompanies Captain George F. Elliott, commanding a detachment of 160 Marines from his own Company C and from Captain William F. Spicer's Company D and 50 Cubans, on a mission to Cuzco, six miles down the coast from Guantánamo Bay, to destroy a guerrilla encampment guarding the only well in the area (Goode, 294). Crane reports the battle in a dispatch headlined "The Red Badge of Courage Was His Wig-Wag Flag" (*New York World*, 1 July), a reference to Marine Sergeant John H. Quick, whose flag signals directed fire from the *Dolphin* off shore. In "Marines Signaling under Fire at Guantanamo," Crane gives a fuller expression of his admiration for Sergeant Quick's courage:

> Sergeant Quick arose, and announced that he was a signalman. He produced from somewhere a blue polka-dot neckerchief as large as a quilt. He tied it on a long, crooked stick. Then he went to the top of the ridge, and turning his back to the Spanish fire, began to signal to the

"Dolphin." Again we gave a man sole possession of a particular part of the ridge. We didn't want it. He could have it and welcome. If the young sergeant had had the smallpox, the cholera, and the yellow fever, we could not have slid out with more celerity.

As men have said often, it seemed as if there was in this war a God of Battles who held His mighty hand before the Americans. As I looked at Sergeant Quick wig-wagging there against the sky, I would not have given a tin tobacco-tag for his life. Escape for him seemed impossible. It seemed absurd to hope that he would not be hit; I only hoped that he would be hit just a little, little, in the arm, the shoulder, or the leg.

I watched his face, and it was as grave and serene as that of a man writing in his own library. He was the very embodiment of tranquility in occupation. He stood there amid the animal-like babble of the Cubans, the crack of rifles, and the whistling snarl of the bullets, and wig-wagged whatever he had to wig-wag without heeding anything but his business. There was not a single trace of nervousness or haste.

To say the least, a fight at close range is absorbing as a spectacle. No man wants to take his eyes from it until that time comes when he makes up his mind to run away. To deliberately stand up and turn your back to a battle is in itself hard work. To deliberately stand up and turn your back to a battle and hear immediate evidence of the boundless enthusiasm with which a large company of the enemy shoot at you from an adjacent thicket is, to my mind at least, a very great feat. One need not dwell upon the detail of keeping the mind carefully upon a slow spelling of an important code message.

I saw Quick betray only one sign of emotion. As he swung his clumsy flag to and fro, an end of it once caught on a cactus pillar, and he looked sharply over his shoulder to see what had it. He gave the flag an impatient jerk. He looked annoyed. (*McClure's Magazine*, February 1899)

Captain Elliott reports to his battalion commander, Lieutenant Colonel R. W. Huntington, citing Sergeant Quick's bravery—for which he was awarded the Congressional Medal of Honor (Boyd, 410)—and adding, in a supplement to his report dated 18 June (National Archives. Copy, NSyU), "Upon leaving camp you asked me if I wanted an adjutant, I declined to take one, the command being short of officers for duty, but having been notified that a Mr. Stephen Crane would be allowed to accompany the expedition, I requested him to act as an aid if one should be needed. He accepted the duty, and was of material aid during the action, carrying messages to fire volleys, etc., to the different company commanders" (Collum, 559).

[Crane recalls in "Marines Signaling under Fire at Guantanamo" that "it was great joy to lie in the trench with the four signalmen, and understand thoroughly that that night was fully over at last, and that, although the future might have in store other bad nights, that one could never escape from the prison-house which we call the past." The experience in the trench reminds him of that in the dinghy following the *Commodore* disaster, and he later considers fiction-alizing the ordeal. Cora recalls that Stephen eventually wanted to "make an Open Boat story of Cusico (?) Start where Marine went crazy and jumped over cliff killing himself, when the outpost was cut— —off Trumperts called 'Music' Next day the 'music' went to edge of cliff & leeres over, Capt. Short called & said whats that damn red headed music gloating over then he called to him sharply—" (*Works*, 10: 139).]

16 JUNE. Crane's dispatch datelined 14 June via Kingston, Jamaica, concerning the supposed mutilation of the bodies of two Marines killed in the Guantánamo fighting on 11 June appears in the *Boston Globe*. The *World*, which headlined a report on 15 June "Mutilation of Our Marines Too Horrible for Description," does not print Crane's piece, "Only Mutilated by Bullets," which quotes a surgeon who "states positively that the wounds were due to bullets only."

Cora Crane replies to two letters from Moreton Frewen, who has invited the Cranes to visit him at Innishannon in County Cork, Ireland. She has returned from a four-day driving trip with friends that included a visit to Brede Place and to Rye:

> Mr. Crane will be delighted at the idea of camping in your old house. I am so glad that there is a chance of our keeping it longer as I want to take some roses from this place and of course we would have so little good of them in one year.
> We have planned that I shall go to Queenstown with an American lady who is stopping with me [Mrs. Ruedy], to meet Mr. Crane. It will give us great pleasure to come to you for one day. But I fear it will be Sep. or even Oct. before this war business is settled so that Mr. Crane will return. This morning I got cable from Port Antonio that he had been *fighting*. To see what it is really like I suppose. But its very distressing to me. A good book should be written while we are at Brede Place which may please you as adding a wee bit more history to the place. (Copy, CtU)

17 JUNE. Crane, Scovel, and Alexander Kenealy establish *World* headquarters near Santiago. Scovel undertakes a mission to ascertain the deployment of the Spanish fleet in Santiago Harbor, and Crane accompanies him. In the afternoon they swim two Jamaica horses ashore from the *Triton*, and escorted by some insurgents they ascend into the hills overlooking the harbor. Their first stop is an insurgent

camp commanded by a Colonel Cerbreco, where they spend the night ("Hunger Has Made Cubans Fatalists,"*New York World*, 12 July; *Works*, 9: 149).

18 JUNE. Before dawn, accompanied by five insurgents, Crane and Scovel ride to another insurgent camp, where their escort is increased to 15 men. The party makes its way through Spanish lines and laboriously ascends a 2000-foot-high mountain, from the summit of which they can view clearly every ship of the Spanish fleet: "There tranquilly at anchor," Crane relates in "War Memories," "lay the *Oquendo*, the *Maria Theresa*, the *Christobal Colon*, the *Viscaya*, the *Pluton*, the *Furor*. The bay was white in the sun, and the great black-hull armoured cruisers were impressive in a dignity massive yet graceful. We did not know that they were all doomed ships, soon to go out to a swift death. My friend drew maps and things while I devoted myself to complete rest, blinking lazily at the Spanish squadron" (WM, 258). The return trip is a frenzied rush since the correspondents had promised their Cuban escorts, who had eaten nothing but mangoes and the carcass of a lean pony for the past few weeks, some provisions from their dispatch boat, but, "As we breasted the last hillock near the coast we beheld the *Three Friends* standing out to sea, the black smoke rolling from her. We were about one half-hour late. There is nothing in any agony of an ordinary host which could measure our suffering. A faithful escort—thirty-one miles—mangoes—three weeks—*Three Friends*—promises—pledges—oh, horrors" ("Hunger Has Made Cubans Fatalists," *New York World*, 12 July; *Works*, 9: 152). The correspondents leave the coast in a dugout from which they are recovered in time by the *Three Friends* (WM, 261).

[Perhaps as a result of misleading phrasing in Scovel's report, "Cervera's Squadron Discovered by the World" (*New York World*, 20 June), where he states that "the start was made Thursday," which would have been 16 June, the day before the *World* established its headquarters at Cuero, historians have described this adventure as occurring over three (C. H. Brown, 297–298) and even four (Milton, 307–309) days, but the datelines of Scovel's dispatch, "Cuero Cuba, June 18, via Port Antonio Jamaica, June 19," and Crane's detailed narratives in "Hunger Has Made Cubans Fatalists" and "War Memories" demonstrate that the events took place on 17 and 18 June.]

At Key West the first issue of a burlesque newspaper, the *Scorpion*, put together by correspondents with time on their hands, carries on its first page parodies of the war reporting of James Creelman, Scovel, and Crane:

THE PURPLE BUTTON OF FEAR
By Craven Steen
(Stiff Correspondent of the *Scorpion*)

On board the *Scorpion* dispatch boat, *Three Fiends*, off Hoboken, June 17.—This is war but it is not magnificent. I discovered this today. The sea and sky were caressing each other with a sibilant, yellow sound.

On the deck a youth stood and examined his knees, furtively. They wobbled.

"How d'yah like it?" he said.

I bent over and looked into the waters, crystalline, turquoise. A shell whined past. It was a clam shell hurled by the youth. He resumed inspection of his knees. They still wig-wagged unkneesily.

A thought struck me. So did a wave. "This is a shell-game war, any how," I said.

We went on. (C. H. Brown, 271)

20 JUNE. The *World* exults in the accomplishments of its correspondents:

MOLE ST. NICHOLAS, Hayti, June 19.—The New York World is the first newspaper to establish permanent headquarters on Cuban soil. This has been done almost under the guns of Santiago's forts. It was accomplished last Friday, when Sylvester Scovel, Stephen Crane, and Alex. Kenealy, of the World staff of correspondents, landed at Cuero, thirteen miles west of Santiago.

The correspondents, with attendants, signalling apparatus and two horses, were taken to Cuero on the despatch boat Triton. After landing a third horse was purchased from a native. A camp has been set up, over which float the Cuban flag, with The World's banner. From this point constant communication will be kept up by couriers with the Cuban army that guards the mountain passes and approaches to Santiago, and by despatch boats to the fleet and nearest cable stations. . . . After the World camp had been gotten in shape Messrs. Scovel and Crane started up into the mountains, with an escort of Cuban soldiers, to get a view of the harbor of Santiago, where Cervera's warships are anchored. They obtained information which Admiral Sampson particularly wanted. They will be taken on the despatch boat Three Friends to-morrow to the flagship and report. The Three Friends will call at the camp at stated intervals for news, which will be hurried to the nearest cable office. The advantage of this enterprise in news gathering, both to World readers and the naval and military authorities, cannot be over-estimated. (Stallman and Hagemann 1964, 136–137)

Crane and Scovel board the flagship New York and report their sightings of Cervera's fleet to Admiral Sampson, whom Crane considers "the best sea-captain that America has produced since—since Farragut? I don't know. I think—since Hull" (WM, 262).

22 JUNE. At daybreak, 6,000 men commanded by Major General Joseph Wheeler of Major General William R. Shafter's 16,000-man force begins landing at Daiquirí, east of Santiago. Crane reports the disembarkment, uneventful except for the overturning of a boat in the surf in which two men and several horses are killed, in a dispatch headlined "Crane Tells the Story of the Disembarkment" (*New York World*, 7 July). In his fictional treatment of the landing and its aftermath, "God Rest Ye, Merry Gentlemen" (*Saturday Evening Post*, 171 [6 May 1899], 705–707), Crane, in the character of Little Nell, conveys his sense of the undramatic character of the event: "In reality it was the great moment—the moment for which men, ships, islands and continents had been waiting for months—but somehow it did not look it. It was very calm; a certain strip of high green rocky shore was being rapidly populated from boat after boat; that was all. Like many preconceived moments, it refused to be supreme."

Following the landing, Brigadier General Henry Lawton leads two regiments of his Second Division eastward along the jungle trails to Siboney, seven miles down the coast. Arriving shortly after 9:00 A.M., he discovers that the Spanish have evacuated. He reports this to Shafter, and around noon troops also begin landing at Siboney (O'Toole, 269).

23 JUNE. Aboard the *Marblehead* off Santiago, Captain McCalla signs a pass authorizing Crane "to visit the Camp until further orders" (NNC).

Crane, McCready, Edward Marshall of the *New York Journal*, and Burr McIntosh, photographer for *Leslie's Weekly* march to Siboney in the wake of the "mounted infantry," the First Volunteer Cavalry, better known as the Rough Riders, commanded by Colonel Leonard Wood and Lieutenant Colonel Theodore Roosevelt ("Stephen Crane at the Front for the World,"*New York World*, 7 July).

24 JUNE. At dawn the Rough Riders start up the jungle trail from Siboney to Las Guásimas, where there are entrenched Spanish positions, while the main column of regulars marches up the main road. Richard Harding Davis, who joined the march as correspondent for the *New York Herald*, explains that "Guásimas is not a village, nor even a collection of houses; it is the meeting place of two trails which join at the apex of a **V**, three miles from the seaport town of Siboney, and continue merged in a single trail to Santiago" (Davis 1898, 135–136).

Shortly before reaching Las Guásimas the Rough Riders are ambushed. In the fighting Sergeant Hamilton Fish is among those killed, and Edward Marshall is severely wounded. Crane and Davis, near the head of the column, are guided to Marshall by a passing soldier and arrange to have him carried to a field hospital. Crane agrees to file Marshall's dispatches for him ("Stephen Crane at the Front for the World,"*New York World,* 7 July). Marshall recalls:

> On June 23, I was told that a battle would occur the next day. I asked Crane if he intended to go to the front. It was insufferably hot, and we had all learned to distrust rumors. He decided not to go. I was amazed by his apparent indolence. I went to the battle and was badly hurt by a bullet. When I regained consciousness, hours after the fight had ended, one of the first faces I saw was that of Stephen Crane. The day was hot. The thermometer—had there been such an instrument in that God-forsaken and man-invaded wilderness—would have shown a temperature of something like 100 degrees. Yet Stephen Crane—and mind you, he was there in the interest of a rival newspaper—took the dispatch which I managed to write five or six miles to the coast and cabled it for me. He had to walk, for he could get no horse or mule. Then he rushed about in the heat and arranged with a number of men to bring a stretcher up from the coast and carry me back on it. He was probably as tired then as a man could be and still walk. But he trudged back from the coast to the field hospital where I was lying and saw to it that I was properly conveyed to the coast. (Marshall, 71)

[The conclusion of Marshall's account of the Las Guásimas engagement ("A Wounded Correspondent's Recollections of Guasimas,"*Scribner's Magazine,* September 1898) describes an experience at the field hospital that is very similar to the conclusion of Crane's Cuban War story "The Price of the Harness," sent to Reynolds from Havana on 27 September 1898. Crane's story ends ironically with a delirious soldier in a fever tent "wringing from the situation a grim meaning by singing the Star-Spangled banner with all the ardor which could be procured from his fever-stricken body." Marshall, without Crane's irony, portrays about a dozen soldiers lying at the field hospital:

> A continual chorus of moans rose through the tree-branches overhead. The surgeons, with hands and bared arms dripping, and clothes literally saturated, with blood, were straining every nerve to prepare the wounded for the journey down to Siboney. . . . It was a doleful group. Amputation and death stared its members in their gloomy faces.

Suddenly a voice started softly,

> My country, 'tis of thee,
> Sweet land of liberty,
> Of thee I sing.

Other voices took it up:

> Land where my fathers died,
> Land of the Pilgrims' pride—

The quivering, quavering chorus, punctuated by groans and made spasmodic by pain, trembled up from that little group of wounded Americans in the midst of the Cuban solitude—the pluckiest, most heartfelt song that human beings ever sang.

There was one voice that did not quite keep up with the others. It was so weak that I did not hear it until all the rest had finished with the line,

> Let Freedom ring.

Then, halting, struggling, faint, it repeated, slowly,

> Land—of—the—Pilgrims'—pride,
> Let Freedom—

The last word was a woeful cry. One more son had died as died the fathers. (276)

Besides his selflessness toward Marshall, another event during the Cuban War that revealed Crane's concern for others was an incident reported in a "Special Memoir" in the *London Daily Chronicle* (6 June 1900). While in a dispatch boat headed toward the Cuban coast, sailors "began to quarrel, and there was a live prospect of blood being shed. But Crane intervened and before the boat reached land the would-be belligerents had shaken hands and were vowing that the peacemaker was the 'best little fellow alive.'"]

25 JUNE. Crane files his account of the Las Guásimas battle, "Roosevelt's Rough Riders' Loss Due to a Gallant Blunder" (*New York World*, 26 June). While Richard Harding Davis denied the Rough Riders had been ambushed, insisting that "there is a vast difference between blundering into an ambuscade and setting out with a full knowledge that you will find the enemy in ambush, and finding him" (R. H. Davis 1898, 133), Crane takes the more widely accepted view

that the Rough Riders suffered heavy losses "due to the remarkably wrong idea of how the Spaniards bushwack" (*Works*, 9: 146). George Bronson Rea, in a dispatch published on the same page as Crane's, explains, "It is reported that the Cubans warned Col. Wood that there was a Spanish ambuscade, but he refused to heed the warning."

27 JUNE. From Siboney Crane files his dispatch describing the trip into the hills, "Hunger Has Made Cubans Fatalists" (*New York World*, 12 July), in which he first expounds a theme that becomes frequent in his dispatches and stories of the Cuban War, the neglect by the press of the accomplishments of the regular troops in favor of the exploits of the volunteers:

> The gallantry of the First Regular Cavalry has not been particularly mentioned in connection with the first fight. There were five correspondents present under fire and we were all with the Rough Riders. We did not know until after the action that the First Regular Cavalry had been engaged over on the right flank. But when a second sergeant takes out a troop because its captain, lieutenant and first sergeant all go down in the first five minutes' firing there has been considerable trouble.
> In fact, our admiration for our regulars is a peculiar bit of business. We appreciate them heartily but vaguely, without any other medium of expression than the term, "the regulars."
> Thus when it comes down to action no one out of five correspondents thought it important to be with the First Regular Cavalry. And their performance was grand! Oh, but never mind—it was only the regulars. They fought gallantly of course. Why not? Have they ever been known to fail? That is the point. They have never been known to fail. Our confidence in them has come to be a habit. But, good heavens! it must be about time to change all that and heed them somewhat. Even if we have to make some of the volunteers wait a little. (*Works*, 9: 148)

Joseph Conrad writes Cora Crane:

> I was delighted to hear good news of dear Stephen. The life on board that tug of his will set him up in strenght [*sic*] and appetite for years. Have you heard from him since you wrote? I suppose he landed with the army and is in the thick of everything that's going. I've only heard lately he is going to write for Blackwood. They think a lot of him and expect—as well they may—first rate work. Meldrum was here (I suppose you've heard of him? Blackwoods man in London) the other day and spoke of Stephen with real enthusiasm. They are anxious but not impatient. . . . Garnett told me you had secured a house after your own heart. My congratulations on that and still more on the success of American arms espe-

cially on the exploits of Hobson! That was worth all the Manila battle! Magnificent. (*C*, 365)

30 JUNE. In a cable datelined from Playa del Este, "Pando Hurrying to Santiago," Crane reports the widely expressed fear that Spanish general Luis Manuel de Pando y Sanchez is moving to reinforce Santiago with almost 8,500 troops (*New York World,* 1 July).

Crane leads Jimmy Hare on a tour of the Las Guásimas battleground. Hare finds Crane "a charming fellow, fond of a drink and not too fond of work." He maintains that Scovel "usually found it very difficult to get Crane's copy." Crane confides to Jimmy that his only reason for signing up with the *World* was to obtain a military pass so that he might gather material for a novel about the war (Carnes, 60–61).

[In another recollection, Henry N. Cary, who managed the affairs of the *World* field staff in Cuba, characterized Crane as "a drunken, irresponsible and amusing little cuss. He kept me busy trying to get a little work out of him, but I failed in that respect" (Henry N. Cary to Vincent Starrett, 30 March 1922, CtY). However, Crane sent more than 20 dispatches to the *World.*]

1 JULY. Before dawn the American advance begins toward the fortifications of San Juan on the eastern outskirts of Santiago, and the village of El Caney, six miles northeast of the city, where the enemy is entrenched. Crane accompanies Jimmy Hare to the vicinity of El Pozo, where their paths diverge (Carnes, 63). Crane climbs to the vantage point of El Pozo, about two and a half miles south of El Caney, where he can observe the Spanish trenches, the shelling by the battery commanded by Captain Allyn Capron, and the attack of General Lawton's troops on El Caney. Later in the morning he observes an exchange of artillery fire between Captain George S. Grimes's battery and Spanish gunners, which he reports that night in a brief cable, "Artillery Duel Was Fiercely Fought on Both Sides" (*New York World,* 3 July).

With Crane on the hill of El Pozo are Burr McIntosh, Frederic Remington, and Henry J. Whigham of the *Chicago Tribune.* They watch Colonel Joseph E. Maxwell's observation balloon hovering above the Santiago Road. McIntosh feels that "the taking of that balloon down there was one of the most criminally negligent acts of the entire war. Not only were many men killed by the explosion of shells aimed at it, but it also gave those in San Juan a clue to the fact that the road was filled with our men" (McIntosh, 125). The correspondents also observe a lone figure in a Panama hat walking behind the Spanish trenches on the San Juan Heights:

> In truth, there was a man in a Panama hat strolling to and fro behind one of the Spanish trenches, gesticulating at times with a walking stick. A man in a Panama hat, walking with a stick! That was the strangest sight of my life—that symbol, that quaint figure of Mars. The battle, the thunderous row, was his possession. He was the master. He mystified us all with his infernal Panama hat and his wretched walking-stick. From near his feet came volleys and from near his side came roaring shells, but he stood there alone, visible, the one tangible thing. He was a Colossus and he was half as high as a pin, this being. Always somebody would be saying: "Who *can* that fellow be?"
>
> Later, the American guns shelled the trenches and a blockhouse near them, and Mars had vanished. It could not have been death. One cannot kill Mars. But there was one other figure, which arose to symbolic dignity. The balloon of our signal corps had swung over the tops of the jungle's trees toward the Spanish trenches. Whereat the balloon and the man with the Panama hat and with a walking stick—whereat these two waged tremendous battle. (WM, 272–273)

At 11:00 A.M. the 71st New York Volunteer Regiment, "the Gallant Seventy-first," is halted on the Santiago road under heavy fire. There is confusion but no panic or route. Over 400 men are killed or wounded on this trail in an area not longer than a city block (O'Toole, 311–313).

General Lawton's troops are stalled at El Caney, which does not fall until later in the afternoon. At 1:00 P.M. Roosevelt, who has become colonel of the Rough Riders following the promotion of Leonard Wood to brigadier general, leads the volunteer regiment in a charge up Kettle Hill in advance of the regulars. Once at the top Roosevelt's dismounted cavalry gives support fire to regular infantry troops charging the blockhouse on San Juan Hill, about a quarter mile to the southwest of the Rough Riders' position. Crane and the other correspondents are not present at the San Juan action since "nobody had the slightest idea that anything was to occur at San Juan, until General Lawton had finished what he started to accomplish at El Caney" (McIntosh, 125), but they watch the American advance from thickets in the foothills, and Crane later recorded the little he was able to observe in his longest Cuban War dispatch, "Stephen Crane's Vivid Story of the Battle of San Juan" (*New York World*, 14 July):

> One saw a thin line of black figures moving across a field. They disappeared in the forest. The enemy was keeping up a terrific fire. Then suddenly somebody yelled: "By God, there go our boys up the hill!"

There is many a good American who would give an arm to get the thrill of patriotic insanity that coursed through us when we heard that yell.

Yes, they were going up the hill, up the hill. It was the best moment of anybody's life. An officer said to me afterward: "If we had been in that position and the Spaniards had come at us, we would have piled them up so high the last man couldn't have climbed over." But up went the regiments with no music save that ceaseless, fierce crashing of rifles.

The foreign attachés were shocked. "It is very gallant, but very foolish," said one sternly.

"Why, they can't take it, you know. Never in the world," cried another, much agitated. "It is slaughter, absolute slaughter."

The little Japanese shrugged his shoulders. He was one who said nothing. (*Works*, 9: 158)

McIntosh recalls that later in the afternoon,

After remaining for an hour and a half on the hill, where we witnessed the earlier charges, Remington started off alone, while Whigham, Crane, and myself went up the road together, to where the firing was then at its height. As we passed by the ford at the foot of the hill, we saw Scovel sitting under a tree writing rapidly, while a man with a horse stood near, waiting to carry his despatch. As Scovel saw us pass he shouted: "Don't go up there! Sharpshooters!" We stopped and inquired what he meant, and were informed that the trees on both sides of the road were full of sharpshooters, who had been picking off men ever since they started to go up the road. He himself had just returned, having seen much of the famous charging. As we proceeded on our way, the road seemed to be literally strewn with blanket rolls and bits of clothing which had been thrown aside in the rush to get to the front. We met a number of the wounded coming down and saw some really pitiable sights. After proceeding for half a mile, two men were noticed ahead of us, assisting a man who had received a very severe wound in his ankle; he had paused and was bending over to adjust the bandage, when we heard the sharp whir-r-r of a bullet. With a low moan he fell forward. We rushed up to find that his whole left jaw had been shattered. I took a picture of the group as he lay there, but it did not develop. We looked about into the trees, but could not see any sign of life; the smokeless powder rendered detection impossible and we could not judge the direction from the sound. Another two hundred yards or thereabouts were traversed, when suddenly there came the most piercing shriek I ever heard in my life. Looking back some twenty-five feet, toward a spot which we had passed but a few seconds before, we saw a young man bending over and feeling his knee; as he did so, the blood spurted out at both sides. He had been shot directly through the knee-joint. I "snapped" a picture of him, which also was unsuccessful. We all sought to be of any possible service, but he had friends near by who said they would take care of him. We three resumed our march, passing several others, and occasionally a dead body lying by the roadside, when, while in a broad open spot, we heard the whir-r-r of two bullets within a distance of two or three feet in front of us. As we halted, I ventured the remark that it was a little bit warm and getting more so, and that in a very short time we were liable to be targets, in a manner which might be very disagreeable. Consequently, we retraced our steps and returned to near El Poso. Whigham and Crane went back in a few moments, but this for me was a physical impossibility. The fever by this time had taken a very firm hold. (McIntosh, 125–127)

A short time later, Jimmy Hare encounters Crane "mounted on a pinto pony and wearing, of all incredible garments, a gleaming white raincoat. He and the horse made a shining target that fairly cried aloud for the attention of some Spanish marksman; but of the pair, only the horse was showing any trace of nervousness. Crane was cool and unconcerned as if he had been at a garden party. 'Hullo,' he said casually, and raised his chin toward the crest of San Juan Hill. 'I'm going on up. Want to come?'" (Carnes, 70). Crane and Hare proceed along a narrow trail until they come to the dressing station at the "Bloody Bend" of the Aguadores River. Here among the scores of wounded Crane finds his Claverack College classmate Reuben McNab, who in Crane's memory was identified

with the sunny irresponsible days at Claverack, when all the earth was a green field and all the sky was a rainless blue. Then I looked down into a miserable huddle at Bloody Bend, a huddle of hurt men, dying men, dead men. And there I saw Reuben McNab, a corporal in the 71st New York Volunteers, and with a hole through his lung. Also, several holes through his clothing. "Well, they got me," he said in greeting. Usually they said that. There were no long speeches. "Well, they got me." That was sufficient. The duty of the upright, unhurt, man is then difficult. I doubt if many of us learned how to speak to our own wounded. In the first place, one had to play that the wound was nothing; oh, a mere nothing; a casual interference with movement, perhaps, but nothing more; oh, really nothing more. In the second place, one had to show a comrade's appreciation of this sad plight. As a result I think most of us bungled and stammered in the presence of our wounded friends. That's curious, eh? "Well, they got me," said Reuben McNab. I had looked upon five hundred wounded men with stolidity, or with a conscious indifference which filled me with amazement. But the apparition of Reuben McNab, the schoolmate, lying there in the mud, with a hole through his lung, awed me into stutterings, set me trembling with a sense of terrible intimacy with this war which theretofore I could have believed was a dream—almost. Twenty shot men rolled their eyes and looked at me. Only one man paid no heed. He was dying; he had no time. The bullets hummed low over them all. Death, having already struck, still insisted upon raising a venomous crest. "If you're goin' by the hospital, step in and see me," said Reuben McNab. That was all. (WM, 277–279)

At about 3:00 P.M., as Wood supervises the entrenchment of the Rough Riders under still extremely active Spanish fire, Crane walks to the crest of the San Juan Heights. Richard Harding Davis watches as Crane

walked to the crest and stood there as sharply outlined as a semaphore, observing the enemy's lines, and instantly bringing upon himself and us the fire of many Mausers. With every one else, Wood was crouched below the crest and shouted to Crane to lie down. Crane, still standing, as though to get out of ear-shot, moved away, and Wood again ordered him to lie down. "You're drawing the fire on these men," Wood commanded. Although the heat—it was the 1st of July in the tropics—was terrific, Crane wore a long India rubber rain-coat and was smoking a pipe. He appeared as cool as though he were looking down from a box at a theatre. I knew that to Crane, anything that savored of a pose was hateful, so, as I did not want to see him killed, I called, "You're not impressing any one by doing that, Crane." As I hoped he would, he instantly dropped to his knees. When he crawled over to where we lay, I explained, "I knew that would fetch you," and he grinned, and said, "Oh, was that it?" (Davis 1910, 125)

[Langdon Smith of the *New York Journal* also speaks of Crane's calmness under fire: "'Crane was standing under a tree calmly rolling a cigarette . . . some leaves dropped from the trees, cut away by the bullets; two or three men dropped within a few feet. Crane is as thin as a lath. If he had been two or three inches wider or thicker through, he would undoubtedly have been shot. But he calmly finished rolling his cigarette and smoked it without moving away from the spot where the bullets had suddenly become so thick'" ([Arthur Brisbane], "Some Men Who Have Reported This War," *Cosmopolitan* [September 1898]: 537).]

In the evening Crane and Hare assist Davis, who is suffering from sciatica, back to the correspondents' camp near El Pozo, where they spend the night (Davis 1910, 128). "While the victim of sciatica was freshening up in his tent, Jimmy seized the occasion to question Crane. 'Who's this pal of yours we just brought down the hill?' 'Beg pardon, Jimmy, 'said Crane. 'I thought you knew him. That's Richard Harding Davis'" (Carnes, 73). McIntosh remarks that "Crane bunked on a pile of saddles and provender, with a blanket over him, and Scovel, also, slept within a few feet of our camp fire. Davis and I had been told that there were several empty tents which had been pitched by the Rough Riders early that morning. We went in search of them, but without success. Returning to the one covered ruin, we were told by the sentry that there was room for a couple more to lie on the stone floor. Accordingly, we were soon stretching our weary bones upon a blanket, which was the only thing between us and the hardest floor that ever was given to mortal man to lie upon" (McIntosh, 133).

2 JULY. In the morning Crane sits on San Juan Hill and watches Lawton's division return from El Caney and move into position on the San Juan Heights, still under fire. Again, he is impressed with the stolid heroism of the regular soldier, "the spectacle of the common man serenely doing his work, his appointed work" (WM, 281). Later in the day Crane observes Spanish and Cuban guerrilla prisoners in El Caney and the hospital set up in the town church for wounded enemy soldiers (*Works*, 9: 165–166). In the evening he steams past the blockading American fleet on his way to the cable station in Port Antonio, Jamaica (WM, 282).

3 JULY. At 9:30 A.M. Admiral Cervera's fleet attempts to escape from Santiago Harbor and is destroyed by American warships under the command of Commodore Schley (O'Toole, 329). Crane misses the one-sided naval battle, and when he returns in the evening from Port Antonio he is overwhelmed by the ineptness of the Spanish fleet: "One likes to wallop incapacity, but one has mingled emotions over the incapacity which is not so much personal as it is the development of centuries" (WM, 284).

5 JULY. Fearful of an American bombardment, most of the civilian population of Santiago evacuates the city and seeks refuge in El Caney, as Crane reports in "Spanish Deserters Among the Refugees at El Caney" (*New York World*, 8 July). Frank Norris, also exploring the scenes of carnage at the defensive positions in El Caney and in the city itself, reports that "the dead were everywhere; they were in the trenches, in the fields of pineapple, in corners of the blockhouse, and in grisly postures half-way down the slope of the hill. The air was full of smells—the smell of stale powder, of smoke, of a horse's carcass two days unburied, of shattered lime and plaster in the blockhouse, and the strange, acrid salty smell of blood." In the house of a Spanish major Norris comes upon the body of a girl who had been raped and stabbed, but the most horrific sights are in the town square

with its mass of starving people and in the church where American surgeons are treating wounded Spanish prisoners (Wertheim 1991, 55). In "War Memories" Crane, present in the square as well, describes the scene at the church portals metaphorically:

> The church had been turned into a hospital for Spanish wounded who had fallen into American hands. The interior of the church was too cave-like in its gloom for the eyes of the operating surgeons, so they had had the altar-table carried to the doorway, where there was a bright light. Framed then in the black archway was the altar table with the figure of a man upon it. He was naked save for a breech-clout, and so close, so clear was the ecclesiastic suggestion, that one's mind leaped to a phantasy that this thin, pale figure had just been torn down from a cross. The flash of the impression was like light, and for this instant it illumined all the dark recesses of one's remotest idea of sacrilege, ghastly and wanton. I bring this to you merely as an effect, an effect of mental light and shade, if you like; something done in thought similar to that which the French impressionists do in colour; something meaningless and at the same time overwhelming, crushing, monstrous. (WM, 290–291)

6 JULY. From San Juan Hill Crane watches the ceremonial exchange of Lieutenant Hobson and the men of the *Merrimac* for three Spanish officers (WM, 296–299).

7 JULY. In a dispatch datelined from General Shafter's headquarters, "Captured Mausers for Volunteers" (*New York World*, 17 July), Crane urges that Spanish Mausers captured when Santiago falls be given to the volunteers who are using old-fashioned Springfield rifles. He emphasizes that the Mausers with their smokeless powder are superior also to the Krag-Jörgensens of the regulars, which, like Springfields, use black powder that gives away the position of the troops.

8 JULY. Suffering high fever from malaria, Crane is put aboard the transport *City of Washington* at Siboney by George Bronson Rea to return to the United States for medical treatment. On the voyage a medical officer suspects that he has yellow fever and orders him to isolate himself, but this fear turns out to be groundless (Williams, 119; WM, 302–303).

13 JULY. The *City of Washington* arrives at Hampton Roads opposite Old Point Comfort, Virginia, at 10:00 A.M. On board are more than 200 wounded officers and men, most of whom are from the 71st New York Infantry. "Some of the scenes were heartrending, while others aroused to the highest pitch the wildest enthusiasm and cheers min-

gled with sobs. When a trooper, a negro, who had received nine Mauser bullets in his body, was brought ashore on a stretcher borne by four white men the ramparts of Fort Monroe resounded with cheers sent up by soldiers and citizens" (*Richmond Times*, 14 July). Crane is among the first to disembark. From the veranda of the Chamberlain Hotel, he watches the procession of wounded soldiers on their way to the hospital at Fort Monroe (WM, 304–308). In the afternoon he files his dispatch, "Stephen Crane's Vivid Story of the Battle of San Juan."

[Richard Harding Davis comments: "One of the best known of the correspondents, who was on the firing-line at Guantanamo, Guasimas, and San Juan, was sent home, desperately ill with fever, in the same clothes he had been forced to wear for three weeks. He had forded streams in them, slept on the bare ground in them, and sweated in them from the heat and from fever, and when he reached Fortress Monroe he bought himself a complete new outfit at the modest expenditure of twenty-four dollars. For this his paper refused to pay" (R. H. Davis 1899, 947). It has been noted that the character Channing in Davis's story, "The Derelict" (*Scribner's Magazine* 30 [August 1901], 131–152) bears a circumstantial resemblance to Crane. Channing dresses "like an old tramp—like any old beach-comber": he is a chain smoker, is suspected of being a drunkard and an opium eater, and has malaria; his reporting is descriptive and interpretive rather than factual, "Sunday-special stuff, but there's no *news* in it"; he has written a series entitled "Tales of the Tenderloin" and he was with the marines at Guantánamo. Whether or not Davis intended Channing to depict Crane, the portrayal is largely sympathetic. As Davis's most recent biographer has commented, Channing is "irresponsible, but a gentleman; self-destructive, but a charmer; erratic, but a genius. His sins are venial, and his talents are prodigious. There is no bitterness, just a little envy mixed with admiration, in Davis's portrait of his rival" (Lubow, 195).]

Heinemann publishes *Pictures of War* (Bruccoli and Katz, 280), an anthology containing no new material. Included are *The Red Badge of Courage*, "The Little Regiment," "Three Miraculous Soldiers," "A Mystery of Heroism," "An Indiana Campaign," "A Grey Sleeve," and "The Veteran."

[MID-JULY]. Elizabeth Dalton writes in her diary, "Burr Mackintosh & Stephen Crane ill with Malaria" (Wertheim Collection).

16 JULY. *The Publishers' Circular* announces publication of *Pictures of War.*

The *World* prints a brief report by Crane datelined 4 July from Guantánamo, "Night Attacks on the Marines and a Brave Rescue." Among volunteers from Company C who venture into the woods in search of guerrillas the morning following the attack, Crane lists Private Nolan (*Works,* 9: 154), who figures prominently in his dispatch "Regulars Get No Glory" and the short story "The Price of the Harness."

The *World* carries an unsigned front-page story, datelined from Port Antonio on 15 July and probably authored by Sylvester Scovel, which accuses the officers of the 71st New York Volunteer Regiment of cowardice in the incident on the Santiago road on 1 July:

> The following facts are scrupulously gathered: Col. Downs' orders on reaching the road near the hill were to take the regiment as far as possible. This was passed along the line from the Second Cavalry. Downs sent the answer along the line: "I have taken the regiment as far as I can go."
> The Seventy-first at the time had the Second, Ninth, Tenth, Thirteenth and Twenty-fourth Regiments directly behind. The regulars cursed the men of the Seventy-first and called them cowards. They shouted:
> "Let us go ahead then!"
> All this while the Spaniards were pouring in a fire of shell and Mausers.
> The Seventy-first opened its ranks and the regiments above named passed through in a double swing, jeering the Seventy-first, whose men showed good discipline, but were without orders. They were stung by the jeers and boiling to go ahead. The major of the Second Infantry, name unobtainable at present, shouted in passing: "For God's sake, boys, don't let it go back to New York that the Seventy-first didn't do its duty. They need you—need you badly. If officers won't take you," he said, "either go as companies, or go yourselves!"

[Edwin Emerson, correspondent for *Collier's Weekly,* recalls: "At that time . . . Scovel gloried in his scoop about the pusillanimous conduct of the N.Y. 71st Infantry's staff officers in the field. His strictures . . . later were driven home by Theodore Roosevelt's first telling act as Governor of New York, when he demanded and obtained the resignation of those officers from the New York militia" (Edwin Emerson to Ames Williams, 3 and 22 June 1948, DGU.]

17 JULY. The *New York Journal* in an editorial lambasts the *World* for impugning the honor of the 71st Regiment. The *Journal* renews its attacks in articles appearing on the two succeeding days.

At the formal surrender of Santiago, Scovel becomes involved in a scuffle with General Shafter moments before the United States flag is raised over the city at high noon. Accounts differ as to exactly what happens. Scovel follows three American officers to the roof of the governor's palace, where the colors are to be raised, and Shafter orders him down. There is an exchange of words, and Scovel strikes or strikes at Shafter, who strikes back or attempts to. Scovel is placed under arrest, and the incident effectively ends his career as a correspondent (C. H. Brown, 402).

20 JULY. Crane's last dispatch for the *World* (it had appeared in the *Philadelphia Press* and *Boston Globe* the previous day), headlined "Regulars Get No Glory" and datelined from Siboney on 9 July, is a bitter diatribe against the neglect by the press of the commonplace courage of the regular soldier in favor of the exploits of the more aristocratic volunteer: "The public wants to learn of the gallantry of Reginald Marmaduke Maurice Montmorenci Sturtevant, and for goodness sake how the poor old chappy endures that dreadful hard-tack and bacon. Whereas, the name of the regular soldier is probably Michael Nolan and his life-sized portrait was not in the papers in celebration of his enlistment. . . . The ungodly Nolan, the sweating, swearing, overloaded, hungry, thirsty, sleepless Nolan, tearing his breeches on the barbed wire entanglements, wallowing through the muddy fords, pursuing his way through the stiletto-pointed thickets, climbing the fire-crowned hill—Nolan gets shot" (*Works*, 9: 171).

20–25 JULY. In a barrage of articles the *World* denies that it has impugned the courage of the 71st Regiment, calling the charges "malicious and false accusations" (20 July). On the 23d the *World* prints an article headlined "Boys of the 71st Fought Like Devils." On the 24th the *World* announces "New Laurels for the Seventy-first," quoting James Carroll of Company M: "Every officer and man in the Seventy-first did his whole duty at San Juan. Some of the men were so eager to fight that they ran to the regiments which had received orders to attack while the Seventy-first was held in reserve." On the 25th the *World* in a front-page article responds to what is ostensibly a proposal from a reader to establish a fund to erect a memorial to the men of the 71st who have fallen and contributes $1,000 to initiate the fund.

[Ames W. Williams comments: "The *World* at first attempted to stand by its charges, but finally withdrew under the fire of outraged public opinion. In a futile effort to placate the furies which had descended upon him, Mr. Pulitzer offered a plan to raise a monument to the fallen and subscribed a thousand dollars. The readers of the *World* were invited to share its public penance by contributing to the memorial. The total amount of the fund, however, never passed far beyond Mr. Pulitzer's contribution, and this sum, disdainfully rejected by the Seventy-first Regiment, lay unused for many years until it was finally applied to improving the regimental cemetery lot" (Williams, 117–118).]

23 JULY. The *Spectator* concludes that the title story of *The Open Boat* is Crane's finest work to date and that he is "the most striking and irresistible of all the younger American writers."

Meldrum advises William Blackwood to reject "The Blue Hotel" for *Blackwood's Edinburgh Magazine*:

Well, the story is extraordinarily strong: the situations are realized in a really wonderful manner. The characters are pictured so that you would know them if you met them: only the Swede, the central character, you couldn't meet, for he is killed in the end. The transformation of this Swede, by drink, from the coward to the reckless blusterer,—his exhibition of so-called Dutch courage,—is conceived in the best vein of ironic humor; it is very strong stuff, and would make a mark. On the other hand, it is not in *Maga's* line; altogether, it seems to me, too strong and brutal for Maga's readers. I am sorry, for I admire the story greatly and precisely for its strength, but I couldn't take the responsibility of advising its publication. It seems to me to be one of those cases where, greatly against our will, rejection is the wise course. (Conrad 1958, 201–202)

Despite Meldrum's advice, Blackwood considered publishing "The Blue Hotel" because he wanted "stronger stories to wake up people's attention." He did not mind "the brutality if it is not immoral and it is only human nature in low form" (Conrad 1958, 202).

[LATE JULY]. Crane returns to New York City and negotiates with Frederick A. Stokes for publication of a collection of Cuban war stories (*C*, 493, 493 n. 1). He severs his connection with the *World* under circumstances that remain unclear. Don Carlos Seitz, business manager of the *World* at the time, maintained erroneously that Crane "sent only one dispatch of any merit and that, accusing the Seventy-first New York regiment of cowardice at Santiago, imperilled the paper" (Seitz 1924, 241), and that this led to his discharge. Later, Seitz asserted that Crane was discharged from the *World* by the financial manager, John Norris, whom Seitz encountered "coming out of his office, rubbing his hands gleefully" after Crane had visited the *World* building: "'I have just kissed your little friend Stephen Crane good-bye,' he said with a full-face grin. 'He came here asking for another advance. Don't you think you have had enough of Mr. Pulitzer's money without earning it?' I asked. 'Oh, very well,' he said, 'if that is the way you look at it, by-by.' So we're rid of him" (Seitz 1933, 139–140).

Shortly after leaving the *World*, Crane signs with Hearst's *New York Journal* to report the Puerto Rican campaign. Toward the middle of the week he visits Saranac Lake, New York, to consult the eminent lung specialist Dr. Edward Livingston Trudeau, who diagnoses his condition as "not serious" (*C*, 370).

[Despite his physical ailments, Crane apparently had lighthearted moments in his relationship with doctors. W. Pett Ridge recounts an episode with a doctor when Crane was ill at Rye:

> "Now, Mr. Crane," said the doctor breezily, "let us take the question of meals. What is your appetite like in the early morning, eh?"
> "Fine, doc., fine."
> "That's very good to hear. Tell me, what did you have for breakfast this morning?"
> "Double the usual quantity."
> "Oh, splendid!" cried the local man, with something like rapture.
> "I had," Stephen Crane went on, "two brandies and soda instead of one!" (*I Like to Remember* [London: Hodder and Stoughton, 1925], p. 211.)

James Gibbons Huneker recalls a meeting with Crane in the dining room of the Everett House, where Crane usually stayed on brief visits to New York: "The author of The Red Badge of Courage asked me if I had read anything by Joseph Conrad, a friend of his, a Polish sea-captain, who was writing the most wonderful things in English. That was the first time I heard Conrad's name. When I went to see him in England I found a photograph of Stephen Crane on his desk. The Conrads loved the American writer, who had often visited them" (Huneker, 2: 128).

[25 OR 26 JULY]. Crane leaves New York for Pensacola, Florida.

[29 JULY]. Following the surrender of Ponce the previous day, Crane and fellow *Journal* reporter Charles Michelson sail from Pensacola Naval Base for Puerto Rico aboard a tug chartered by the *Journal*. Michelson is struck by Crane's decrepit appearance: "shambling, with hair too long, usually lacking a shave, dressed like any of the deck hands, hollow-cheeked, sallow, destitute of small talk, critical if not fastidious, marked with ill-health—the very antithesis of the conquering male." In an improvised seawater shower Crane reveals "the wreck of an athlete's frame—once square shoulders crowded forward by the concavity of a collapsed chest; great hollows where the once smooth pitching muscles had wasted; legs like pipestems—he looked like a frayed white ribbon, seen through the veil of green as the seas washed over him" (*Work*, 12: xiii-xiv).

[30 OR 31 JULY]. Off San Juan, Michelson recalls,

we found the improvised cruiser *Prairie*, while far inshore a Spanish destroyer was strutting to and fro under the guns of the land batteries trying to decoy the American warship within range of the heavy shore forts. The *Prairie* mentioned to us, hopefully, that if we went in close enough the Spaniard might make a try for us and so give the cruiser an opportunity of cutting her out. Presently we did veer inshore. The chaperon of our war party went to the pilot-house to learn the reason for the turn. There he found Stephen baiting the captain to run in close. Asked why he was doing it, the seaman answered fervently: "You don't think I'm going to let this damned frayed tholepin think he's got more guts than me, do you?"
    Until the joke staled, Stephen was Lord Tholepin. He had taken the Moreton Frewen House, Brede, and had told us something of its spaciousness. Promptly the fiction was created of Stephen as a liverish British squire, with an East Indian background, and the ancestral mansion was christened Mango Chutney. Innumerable variations of the theme were suggested, and Lord Tholepin of Mango Chutney had more fun out of it than anybody else." (*Work*, 12: xvi-xvii)

AUGUST. "The Monster" appears in *Harper's Magazine*, with illustrations by Peter Newell.

[1 AUGUST]. The *Journal* tug arrives at Ponce, and Crane immediately immerses himself in the life of the captured Puerto Rican city. Michelson and the other correspondents "were hardly ashore when we missed him. We found him, where we knew to look for him, in a back-street cantena, with the wastrels of Ponce—drunkards, drabs, and tin-horn gamblers. They did not know a word of his language nor he a word of theirs. Moreover, this was a conquered city and he was one of the invaders. That made no difference. He was accepted into the easy brotherhood of the thriftless without question" (*Work*, 12: xviii).

3 AUGUST. Knowing that Puerto Rican towns along the roads to San Juan were eager to surrender to advancing Americans, Crane, according to Richard Harding Davis, slips past the advance posts and enters Juana Díaz, about nine miles from Ponce:

He approached Juana Dias in a hollow square, smoking a cigarette. His khaki suit, slouched hat and leggings were all that was needed to drive the first man he saw, or rather, the man who first saw him, back upon the town in disorderly retreat. The man aroused the village and ten minutes later the alcaide, endeavoring to still maintain a certain pride of manner in the eyes of his townspeople, and yet one not so proud as to displease the American conqueror, surrendered to him the keys of the cartel. Crane told me that no general in the moment of victory had ever acted in a more generous manner. He shot no one against a wall, looted no churches, levied no "forced loans." Instead, he lined up the male members of the community in the plaza, and organized a joint celebration of conquerors and conquered. He separated the men into two classes, roughly divided between "good fellows" and "suspects." Anyone whose appearance Crane did not approve of, anyone whose necktie did not suit his fancy, was listed as "suspect." The "good" fellows he graciously permitted to act as his hosts and bodyguard. The others he ordered to their homes. From the barred windows they looked out with envy upon the feast of brotherly love that overflowed from the plaza into the by-streets, and lashed itself into a frenzied carnival of rejoicing. It was a long night, and it will be long remembered in Juana Dias. For from that night dates an aristocracy. It is founded on the fact that in the eyes of the conquering American, while some were chosen, many were found wanting. To this day in Juana Dias the hardest rock you can fling at a man is the word "suspect." But the "good fellows" are still the "first families."

In the cold gray dawn, as Crane sat over his coffee in front of the solitary cafe, surrounded by as many of his bodyguards as were able to be about, he saw approaching along the military road from Ponce a solitary American soldier. The man balanced his rifle alertly at the "ready," and was dodging with the skill of an experienced scout from one side to the other of the long white highway. In a moment he was followed by a "point" of five men, who crept close to the bushes, and concealed their advance by the aid of the sheltering palms. Behind them cautiously came the advance guard and then boldly the Colonel himself on horseback and 800 men of his regiment. For six hours he had been creeping forward stealthily in order to take Juana Dias by surprise.

His astonishment at seeing Crane was sincere. His pleasure was no less great. He knew that it did not fall to the lot of every Colonel to have his victories immortalized by the genius who wrote *The Red Badge of Courage.*

"I am glad to see you," he cried eagerly. "Have you been marching with my men?"

Crane shook his head.

"I am sorry," said the Colonel; "I should like you to have seen us take this town."

"*This* town!" said Crane in polite embarrassment. "I am really very sorry, Colonel, but I took this town myself before breakfast yesterday morning." (R. H. Davis 1904 [8–12])

[Michelson tells a somewhat different version of this incident, according to which Crane and a flock of other correspondents were foraging for breakfast along one of the roads leading to San Juan. At Juana Díaz Crane "rode ahead and announced that the American governor of Porto Rico was on his way and ordered breakfast for His Excellency and staff. The most imposing member of the party, fortunately in immaculate whites, took the part of the governor. He gave instructions to advise anybody who appeared that he did not wish to be disturbed during his meal. The preposterous strategy worked." When an American brigadier general and his staff appeared, Crane "went out and greeted the general, and, when the inevitable question came, lied glibly to this effect: 'Governor? Oh, I guess the people here heard us call Jack Mumford governor, he looks so much like one. There's nobody here but a bunch of newspaper correspondents'" (*Work*, 12: xx-xxi).]

In the *Musical Courier* James Huneker parodies Crane's war correspondence:

The American fleet came redly on like a bunch of waving bandana handkerchiefs. The air was full of prunes as a plum pudding. The whitish-green rattle of the rapid-fire guns was exacerbatingly shrill.

The Spanish met the onslaught with a mauve determination. Ecruly they stood at the posts shepherds doggedly.

The two fleets hurtled in a magenta hurtle. They feinted and thrust with a deep canary-yellow vigor. The battle looked like two overturned garbage-cans on a hot night. The shells whistled sealbrownly. The death screams of the Spaniards were full of purplish pink despair. One Spaniard with a cerise voice like the aftermath of an aurora borealis screamed paintingly his desire to kill the Americanos.

Then with a blackish white tremor, strong battleships sank greenly chromely black into the water. A gauntly greenish smell tore the air. The whole thing looked like a German pouring dark wine into a dingy funnel.

Admiral Dewey had won.

Huneker designates the *Buffalo Enquirer* as the source of this parody, but the reference to a previous printing is probably intended as a playful hoax.

4–10 AUGUST. PONCE AND JUANA DIAZ. Crane writes three sketches of the brief American occupation of Ponce and its environs: "A Soldier's Burial That Made a Native Holiday," "Grand Rapids and Ponce," and "The Porto Rican 'Straddle.'" Undistinguished and lacking newsworthiness, they are not published by the *Journal* until 15, 17, and 18 August, respectively.

6 AUGUST. The *Philadelphia American* concludes that the stories of *The Open Boat* strike a false note that may "suit a reader raised and nurtured on milk substitutes extracted through rubber nipples." The book is characterized by "shoddy pathos, sham colloquialisms, and the overdoing of a jerky style, with primary failures in word-painting and hi-falutin description."

12 AUGUST. Crane is in Ponce when a peace protocol is signed in Washington, ending the fighting between the United States and Spain.

12–13 AUGUST. Harold Frederic suffers a stroke that partly paralyzes his right side and stills his writing hand. Cora sends Adoni Ptolemy to Homefield to be his attendant until his death (Weintraub, 129) and takes his three children by Kate Lyon—Helen, Héloïse, and Barry—to live with her at Ravensbrook so that Kate will be relieved of the burden and can devote herself to nursing Frederic (Gilkes 1960, 161).

16 AUGUST. Crane cables Cora that he has returned to Key West (*C*, 371).

[THIRD WEEK IN AUGUST]. Crane returns to Cuba and enters Havana, still under Spanish occupation, illegally but without hindrance. He registers at the Grand Hotel Pasaje, fronting the Prado. "I came into Havana without permission from anybody," he reports in "Stephen Crane Fears No Blanco" (*New York Journal*, 30 August), "I simply came in. I did not even have a passport. I was at a hotel while the Government was firmly imprisoning nine correspondents on a steamer in the harbor. But no one molested me" (*Works*, 9: 188).

22 AUGUST. James B. Pinker, literary agent for Conrad and Henry James, writes Crane: "I have been asked if I could supply a short story

of 3000 words by you, and I shall be very pleased to hear if your engagements will permit you to undertake a commission through me. I do not know what your terms are, but I think I could obtain six guineas per thousand words for the British serial rights of such a story, if those terms would be agreeable to you. There would, of course, be a deduction of 10% from this amount, to cover my commission" (*C,* 367). This letter does not reach Crane until early November, when he begins to deal with Pinker through Cora.

24 AUGUST. William Dean Howells writes Sylvester Baxter: "I missed the August *Harper,* and so have not seen Crane's story. But I have always believed in him, in spite of his poorest and most successful book—the Red Badge" (Howells, 183).

Robert J. Collier writes Reynolds that, as Crane had done previously, he has misplaced the manuscript of "The Blue Hotel": "I had intended to publish it before Christmas, or the week immediately after, but I cannot lay my hands on it at present" (ViU).

25 AUGUST. Crane's first report from Havana, "Havana's Hate Dying, Says Stephen Crane," is filed but does not appear in the *Journal* until 3 September.

28 AUGUST. The *Journal* publishes a cable, "Stephen Crane Sees Free Cuba," which reports general tranquility in Havana but starvation in Matanzas where "the condition of the poor people is simply horrible. Men, women and children lie in the street" (*Works,* 9: 185).

[LATE AUGUST–EARLY SEPTEMBER]. With other correspondents, Crane frequents the American Bar on the corner of the Prado, next door to the Hotel Pasaje. Walter Parker of the *New Orleans Times-Democrat* remembers that "the correspondents began gathering at the American Bar at 10 A.M., and for the most part remained there until 10 P.M. or until a riot broke out. Crane was usually the last to show up in the morning. He drank tropical beer only but consumed many bottles of beer in a day." According to Parker, Crane has a Cuban friend whose life he had saved in the *Commodore* disaster. "This Cuban was an inside figure in the Cuban revolutionary movement, and had real influence and access everywhere, especially to forbidden places. Through him we were able to circumvent the Spanish authorities at nearly every turn." On one occasion Crane's Cuban friend takes the correspondents to a dance, prohibited by the Spanish authorities, to raise money for the insurgents. In the party is an acquaintance of Parker's, a New Orleans journalist who had spent the day in the American Bar consuming too much cognac:

> Down the center of the room there were two lines of chairs, back to back. Our group were assigned seats in one row. Crane's Cuban friend and his lady love, a really beautiful girl, sat in the row just back of us. Our inebriated companion kept tilting his chair which knocked against the back of the chair occupied by the lady. She complained that she was being annoyed.
>
> Up leaped the Cuban, knife in hand, and made for the offender, intending to stab him to the heart.
>
> Crane jumped to the rescue and caught the sharp glittering blade in his right hand. The Cuban dropped to his knees and kissed the hem of Crane's coat. Crane's hand was bleeding. He wrapped it in a handkerchief and thrust it in his coat pocket. We made apologies to the lady through the Cuban and retired.
>
> Next day we shipped the offender back to the United States. Havana was no place for him in those days.
>
> Crane failed to show up in the morning as was his custom. His hotel door was locked and we could get no answer from him. Later we climbed over the half-wall partition and found Crane in high fever, unconscious and with a terrible wound in his hand. The Cuban procured a doctor who gave him treatment. Many days had to pass before Crane's hand was completely cured. Even then he kept his hand in his pocket most of the time as though desirous of hiding it.
>
> He was not the same after the incident, was more reticent and less regular in his habit of joining us every morning. When several days elapsed and he did not turn up, we investigated and found that he had had a personal shock. The affair was wholly personal and the details are nobody's business.
>
> Anyway, he went into complete retirement, and there wrote a poem, "The Ashes of Love," which was the last work of his that we knew of. (Wertheim 1976b, 53–55)

30 AUGUST. Blackwood writes Conrad: "Have you heard anything from Stephen Crane or his Wife—how he has come out of the American & Spanish War. He was to have sent me some articles whenever he got the opportunity but I have heard nothing yet from him" (Conrad 1958, 28).

1 SEPTEMBER. In *Life* Robert Bridges offers a modernistic interpretation of "The Monster" as a synthesis of discontinuous parts:

> There are more kinds of things well done in Stephen Crane's story, *The Monster*, than in any previous work of his. It is really a small novel of

thirty thousand words, though published in a single number of *Harper's*. The motive of it is intensely psychological, and yet there is scarcely a single reflective paragraph in it. It is incident, action, character, in quick succession—and often apparently disjointed and irrelevant. But when the last block is put in place the whole design flashes into an orderly picture—like the landscape painted on six separate boards by a variety artist, and suddenly clapped into a gilt frame.

The adjective which seems best to describe this talent is "dexterity." He always makes you feel a certain dashing confidence behind his work; he is a juggler who is perfectly sure that he will catch the knife by the handle every time. The reader can't escape the suspicion that perhaps Mr. Crane is not juggling with real knives—and if he did catch the wrong end it would not hurt him. All kinds of dexterity are apt to breed a similar skepticism. (Weatherford, 258)

[6–8 SEPTEMBER]. The *Journal* having discontinued his expense account, Crane leaves the Hotel Pasaje, one of the most expensive in Havana, "in arrears for his lodging" (Edwin Emerson to Ames Williams, 3 and 22 June 1948, DGU), although he continues to receive mail there, and takes a room in the boardinghouse of Mary Horan, who had previously harbored Charles H. Thrall. She is depicted in "This Majestic Lie" as "Martha Clancy, born in Ireland, bred in New York, fifteen years married to a Spanish captain, and now a widow, keeping Cuban lodgers" (*New York Herald*, 24 June 1900).

EARLY SEPTEMBER–MID-NOVEMBER. Crane lives a virtually underground existence in Havana, writing his dispatches for the *Journal*, Cuban War stories, and the remainder of the poems that are to make up *War Is Kind*. He communicates regularly with Paul Revere Reynolds, but if he writes letters to his family and to Cora they never reach them, and, from their perspective, he drops out of sight.

[In a covering letter sent to H. L. Mencken with a copy of his reminiscence (2 March 1940), Walter Parker explains the "personal shock" that he believes drove Crane to the seclusion of Mary Horan's boardinghouse:

He found a girl living in Havana, whom he had previously known elsewhere in the world. On her mantel there was a photograph of a handsome Cuban. After some discussion with the girl, Crane left the house and took up his abode with an old woman and lived the life of a complete recluse. He desired to see no one and had no liking for companionship. The old woman took as good care of him as she could. In his place of retirement we never visited him as a group, but now and then would send one of the group to learn how he was making out.

It was in this retirement that he wrote "The Ashes of Love," but would never let us see a copy. I do not know that "The Ashes of Love" was ever published. (Wertheim 1976b, 47–48)

The first of the "Intrigue" poems, a series of bathetically sentimental love poems traditionally assumed to have been written in Havana, is usually associated with Crane's conflict and guilt over his relationship with Cora, a woman of disreputable background, and contains the stanza:

> Thou art my love
> And thou art the ashes of other men's love
> And I bury my face in these ashes
> And I love them
> Woe is me

Parker's disclosure of Crane's disappointment in a love affair of some standing that he attempted to resume in Havana suggests other biographical interpretations for the complex web of longing, disillusionment, and sense of betrayal that permeates the "Intrigue" poems as well as for Crane's self-imposed period of isolation (Wertheim, 1976b, 47).

Fredson Bowers (*Works*, 10: 209–210, 212–214) concludes that the physical evidence of the typescripts at NNC indicates that the earlier "Intrigue" poems (nos. 96–100 in *Works*) were written before Crane sailed for Cuba on 14 April, but it is difficult to reconcile this conclusion with the ideational content of these poems and the accounts of witnesses such as Parker that strongly suggest they were composed in Havana. Furthermore, since Bowers agrees that Crane wrote nos. 101–105 of "Intrigue," none of which is preserved in manuscript, in Havana, it would be mysterious, as Bowers acknowledges, "that of all subjects for poetry in Havana in the autumn of 1898 he would revert to this series and add five more (though briefer) sections, still in the same perfervid vein" (*Works*, 10: 214).

Helen R. Crane provides further details of Crane's underground life in Havana:

It seems that Bertram Marburgh of Leslie's Syndicate had never met the famous author of "The Red Badge," but he had heard he was in town. One day, when all the correspondents foregathered at the American Bar, Matthews and Nicholas of the *American* told Marburgh that Crane was lost, had perhaps been done away with by the people who did not like newspaper publicity. Marburgh immediately sent the news back home.

Now, the attention of the Leslie man had been attracted for weeks before this to a mysterious slight figure in a white suit that used to slink along the street around eleven o'clock every night near the house where he was stopping. He had no idea who the man might be or why he was furtively dodging the lights about the same time every night.

The story soon appeared in print and created a good deal of excitement around Havana. Crane was found, but still Marburgh did not meet him until one evening, when he was sitting in the American Bar, this mysterious white figure came in and sat down alongside of him. They began talking and the Leslie man offered his name. "I'm Stephen Crane," said his new acquaintance. Marburgh apologized for what he had done and Stephen explained that "certain dignified and venerable Ambassadors, not to mention a few Cranes, had been sorely upset by the news."

This Mary Horan, in whose house Stephen was found, was a well-known character in Havana. She was a huge Irishwoman who ran a small boarding-house and bullied the men, and when any of them were ill, nursed them as she would her own children. My uncle shut himself up there in her place for forty days and nights to do a piece of writing. I don't know what it was, but it was something he was anxious to get done and out of the way.

Mary did not approve of his long hours of work, and she used to go in and hover over him with a great tray of food. "I don't want to eat, please go away." "Go away, me eye, you're goin to eat this if I have to feed it to you spoon by spoon!" And Stephen ate. It was she who made him go for a walk every night about eleven. She came into his room, pulled the chair out from under him and drove him bodily into the street. (HRC, 28–29)]

7 SEPTEMBER. "Stephen Crane's Views of Havana," a laconic description of conditions in the city following the landing of the first American troops, half a dozen unarmed men from a relief ship, appears in the *Journal.*

10 SEPTEMBER. The *Florida Times-Union* reports Crane missing: "Stephen Crane, the novelist, also a member of the Journal staff, who entered Havana as a tobacco buyer about ten days ago, and was stopping quietly at the Hotel Pasaje, is missing, and fears for his safety are entertained by his friends. The police had been shadowing him several days before he disappeared" (Gilkes 1960, 151).

14 SEPTEMBER. Crane sends Reynolds the last manuscripts of poems for *War Is Kind,* for which Reynolds has contracted with Stokes, and also his first Cuban War story, "The Lone Charge of William B. Perkins" (*C,* 369). The story is based upon an incident that occurred during the Guantánamo Bay skirmishes when Ralph Paine, caught in crossfire between the Marines and Spaniards, hid in an abandoned sugar boiler until the shooting stopped (Paine, 251–256).

16 SEPTEMBER. Dr. Trudeau responds to an inquiry from Cora: "Your husband had a slight evidence of activity in the trouble in his lungs when he came back here this summer but it was not serious and he has improved steadily I understand since he came. I have only examined him once but he looked very well and told me he was much better last time I saw him" (*C,* 370).

22 SEPTEMBER. LONDON. Crane is elected a member of the Savage Club but never takes up active membership (George Baker to Melvin H. Schoberlin, 6 October 1947, NSyU).

23 SEPTEMBER. The *Journal* prints "The Grocer Blockade," which reflects ironically upon a circumstance of life in blockaded Havana Crane fictionalized later in "This Majestic Lie": "Immediately the blockade was declared the grocers of Havana, stirred by a deep patriotism, arose to the occasion and proceeded to soak the life out of the people. It was a wonder that some sensible person did not go quietly about rearranging matters with an axe, but no one did so, and the grocers throughout the war continued to gracefully pillage the public pockets" (*Works,* 9: 191).

24 SEPTEMBER. Cora Crane writes to John Hay, United States secretary of state: "Knowing you to be a personal friend of my husband, Stephen Crane—I appeal to you to use your influence to find him. News has reached me that he is missing from Havana. He went there for the N.Y. Journal as you doubtless know. And was watched, I understand, by the spanish police. He was stopping quietly at Hotel Pasaje—and disappeared about Sep 8*th.* I am almost distracted with grief and anxiety. I am sure you will personally ask the President to instruct the American commission to demand Mr. Crane from the Havana police" (*C,* 370–371).

25 SEPTEMBER. The *Journal* publishes a diatribe directed at the American public entitled "Memoirs of a Private," purportedly "Dictated to and Taken Down" by Crane, which attacks the competence of the secretary of war, Russell A. Alger. The "private" contends that under normal circumstances nobody knows or cares who holds the position of secretary of war. "Then suddenly there comes on a war, and—behold—you find the chair occupied by a doddering feckless old man who can't even defend himself by remaining silent. You talk about mismanagement! You talk about incompetence and gross criminality! Why, you are to blame! You are the criminals! You have for

years persisted in raising monuments to your own incapacity for knowing anything about the army; for years you have conscientiously and steadfastly ignored every detail of it. What then, in the name of God, did you expect?" (*Works*, 9: 195).

Cora Crane writes to Secretary of War Alger: "If there is any way in which you can communicate the fact of Stephen Cranes disappearance to U.S. authorities at Havana will you do so? He entered Havana about Sep 1*st* as a tobacco buyer. Stopped quietly at Hotel Pasaje and was watched by the police. and was missing about Sep. 6*th* to 8*th*. If you recieve any information about him I beg you will send it to me as I am very much alarmed as to his safety" (*C,* 372). On the same day Cora cables Alger an abbreviated version of this letter.

Cora also expresses her desperation in a letter to Reynolds: "Mr. Crane's affairs here need his attention. I am in *great* need of money. And I fear that we will lose our house here if I cannot get money to pay some pressing debts. . . . This being so helpless in a foreign country together with my fears for Mr. Crane are almost driving me mad. Will you use your influence with Mr. Hearst. He has no right to allow a man like Stephen Crane to be missing for over three weeks without using means to find him" (*C,* 371–372).

[In an unsigned article first printed in the *Omaha Daily Bee* on 17 June 1900, Otto Carmichael, a correspondent for the *Minneapolis Times*, recalls:

The first time I ever met Crane was when General Wade, then chairman of the American Evacuation commission in Havana, asked me to carry word to him that he had a London cablegram for him. I told him in a cafe. He said "Thanks," and it passed out of his mind. The next day General Wade told me he had another cablegram asking if the first had been delivered and would I kindly tell Mr. Crane that the cablegram seemed important and that he should call at the offices of the commission and get it. I delivered the second message at the same place. Crane said:

"Say, didn't you tell me something about a cablegram yesterday?"

"Yes, I told you about one, and this second is an inquiry as to whether the first was delivered."

"Yes, I see. Using the government to find me. Anyway, I'm much obliged."

And again he forgot all about it. Or at least he never paid any attention to my notices. Some time later, after I had become acquainted, I told him that the message was still in Wade's hands.

"Oh, it's some tradesman I owe a bill to, I suppose," and that is the last I ever heard of it, although I saw a great deal of him afterwards. It is not likely that a London tradesman would spend 60 cents a word to find out about a tailor bill, even if Crane did owe one. He was not extravagant, or in the habit of owing large sums. It simply struck him as nothing worth bothering with and he let it go at that.

Carmichael also comments on Crane's desultory existence in Havana:

> He did nothing with regularity. He ate and slept when he could no longer do without these necessary comforts. He would remain in the streets and in the cafes until his friends and chance acquaintances were tired out. He lived with a former filibustering associate in a pair of rooms not far from the downtown hotels and when other places were closed to him he would go there in hopes of finding some stragglers. If he did he would sit and listen to their chatter until they were tired out. Then he would go to work. When I saw him he was doing 600 words a day. This was the only thing he did with regularity. He was very particular about his work. He wrote somewhat slowly and was whimsical about words. He would spend a long time in trying to find what suited him. Inasmuch as he had no dictionary or books of reference, his search for words and information consisted in chewing his pencil and waiting until they came to him.
> When his 600 words were written he would rouse some of his straggling guests—if they would stand for it—and if not he might read or go to bed. To take care of his health never occurred to him. He had the Cuban fashion of drinking light drinks and coffee, but he did not indulge to excess in alcohol. This was somewhat remarkable at a time and place of excessive drinking. This was two years ago and his health then was wretched. There was no chance for him to live unless he mended his ways. (Carmichael, 200–201, 203)]

26 SEPTEMBER. A second article written from the perspective of a private soldier, "The Private's Story," appears in the Journal, depicting scenes from Crane's own arrival at Old Point Comfort, Virginia, on 13 July, some of which are later incorporated into "War Memories."

27 SEPTEMBER. Crane sends Reynolds "The Price of the Harness," his finest Cuban War story. He emphasizes, "Now this is *It*! If you dont touch big money for it I wonder!" He reminds Reynolds that "English copy goes to Blackwood," to whom he owes £60 (*C*, 373).

[27 SEPTEMBER]. Robert Barr responds to Cora's request for aid that would enable her to go to Havana, where the Hearst press had reported that Crane was "hiding" in a rooming house. Cora had also appealed to William Randolph Hearst personally, and Barr had solicited the aid of James Creelman, the *Journal*'s representative in London, who had known Crane in Cuba:

> If what Hurst cables is true, then I should hate to put down in black and white what I think of Stephen Crane. If he has not disappeared, and if he has been drawing money for himself, while leaving you without cash, then that article about his disappearance in the Florida paper is a put-up job, and he does not intend to return. You told me that Frederic had been saying that Stephen was not coming back. What ground had he for making such an assertion? Creelman told me he was certain that some at least of your communications had reached Crane. I am certain that Creelman did everything in his power to get your messages forwarded to Crane. Hurst certainly would not dare cable a lie that he knew would be sent to you, for he would be sure of disgraceful exposure sooner or later. If, in these circumstances, you think it worth while to go after such a man, then there is nothing to do but consider the ways and means.

Barr encloses letters to the German Lloyd and American shipping lines in which he requests passage to New York with deferred payment for Cora. He maintains that Crane has been imprisoned by the Spaniards in Havana and that he will pay for Cora's passage as soon as he is released and returns to New York (*C*, 374–375, 375n3).

29 SEPTEMBER. Cora writes Reynolds: "Will you let me know if Mr. Crane gets my letters and where he is at the time this reaches you. The report that he was 'missing from Havana' caused me great distress" (*C*, 376).

[LATE SEPTEMBER]. Barr attempts to manage Cora's deteriorating financial circumstances as summonses are issued to her for outstanding bills (*C*, 377–378).

[OCTOBER]. Cora visits the Conrads at Ivy Walls. Jessie Conrad recalls that the visit "was marred by her very real anxiety as to [Crane's] whereabouts, and a fierce jealousy as to his possible fancy for someone he might meet. In vain I assured her of my complete conviction that Stephen was deeply attached to her, and that his first thought as soon as he was able to get a letter through would be of her" (J. Conrad 1926, 134–135).
[Both Lillian Gilkes and R. W. Stallman date this visit in August (Gilkes 1960, 150–151; Stallman 1973, 419), but if Cora did not discover that Crane had left the Hotel Pasaje and was "missing" until 22 September (Gilkes 1960, 151) and was concerned about Crane's where-

abouts when she visited the Conrads, the visit probably did not occur until early or mid-October, shortly before the Conrads moved to Pent Farm.]

2 OCTOBER. Datelined 20 September, a *Journal* article, "Stephen Crane Makes Observations in Cuba's Capital," expresses Crane's impatience with the American delay in expelling the Spanish from Cuba and establishing a stable government.

6 OCTOBER. A *Journal* article, "How They Leave Cuba," portrays with uncharacteristic sentiment the separation of a Spanish captain about to sail for home on the *Alfonso XIII* from his Cuban lover and young child, who are watching the ship depart from a boat with a boatman impatient to return to shore: "There is going to be a lot of it; such a hideous lot of it! The attitude of the Cubans will be the attitude of our old boatman: 'Serves them right; why didn't they take up with men of their own people instead of with Spaniards?' But, after all—and after all—and again after all, it is human agony and human agony is not pleasant" (*Works*, 9: 201).

EARLY OCTOBER. Crane sends Reynolds the manuscript of "The Clan of No-Name," which he considers "a *peach*. I love it devotedly. Sell to anybody if the price is grand enough. Otherwise remember that *Blackwood's* have a call on me" (*C*, 379).

9 OCTOBER. The *Journal* prints "Stephen Crane in Havana," a humorous article about sidewalk navigation in the crowded city.

The adjutant general advises Major General J. F. Wade that "the Secretary of War desires inquiry to be made concerning Stephen Crane, and any information that may be learned sent to this office" (National Archives).

10 OCTOBER. Meldrum writes Blackwood: "In a note from Conrad a day or two ago, he says, 'Stephen Crane has been lost, but has turned up. Mrs. Crane had a cable from him yesterday (4th) or the day before. She dropped me word of this good news but did not say when he is coming back. It can't be very long.' I hope Conrad will be spending an afternoon and evening with us this week or next, and I'll hear more of Crane. We must get something of his best out of him. (I am sending you for safekeeping in Edinburgh the receipt for the money which Crane gave me before he went away. I got it stamped

at Somerset House at the time and have had it locked up here.)" (Conrad 1958, 29)

15 OCTOBER. The *Literary Digest* quotes John D. Barry's comment in the *Literary World* (Boston) that it seems odd "that Mr. Crane should have given so slight a literary evidence of his presence at the war. It is true that he wrote a number of articles for *The World*; but they made very little impression, and yet he applied to the fight the method he used so successfully in his famous book; that is, he chose suggestive incidents and treated them realistically. But in *The World* this work seemed insignificant, at times almost puerile. I have heard it said that the articles lost effectiveness by being out of place in *The World*, and that if they had appeared in a more literary medium they would have carried more weight."

17 OCTOBER. Cora Crane insists that doctors, including Dr. Ludwig Freyberger, physician to Friedrich Engels, be called in to attend Harold Frederic, who is being treated by Althie Mills, a Christian Science practitioner (*Times* [London], 19 November).

19 OCTOBER. Harold Frederic dies of "heart disease." The *New York Times*, whose London bureau chief Frederic had been since 1884, reports (20 October) that the death occurred in London, where Frederic maintained his official residence with his wife, Grace, to conceal the fact that he died at Homefield.

General Wade reports to the adjutant general that because of his inquiries among the correspondents in Havana he had learned that Crane "had not been out of the city. After these inquiries Mr. Crane called and expressed regret at having caused so much trouble. I do not know his business or why he has not corresponded with his family" (National Archives).

20 OCTOBER. Crane sends Reynolds "Marines Signaling under Fire at Guantanamo" for *McClure's Magazine* (February 1899) and stipulates that the "Intrigue" poems are for Heinemann (*C*, 380), but Heinemann does not publish Crane's poems and the series entitled "Intrigue" is used to conclude *War Is Kind*.

21 OCTOBER. Crane writes to Reynolds sending him an article, "Stephen Crane on Havana" (*New York Journal*, 6 November), to take to S. S. Chamberlain and stressing that although he is in debt to the *Journal*, he cannot afford to write for twenty dollars a column now

that he no longer has an expense account. He asks for a doubling of that rate and requests Reynolds to try to arrange a syndication for "Cuban letters" with several other newspapers (*C*, 381).

In Kenley a coroner's jury opens an inquest into the death of Harold Frederic:

> Drs. Brown and Friedberger [*sic*], who attended him at one time, declared their belief that he would have recovered if he had had proper treatment. He had rheumatic fever and was paralyzed on one side. Death was due to syncope, sometimes called heart failure.
>
> Mr. Frederic's daughter Ruth testified that her father did not believe in doctors and that it was with his consent, though under the influence of others, that Mrs. Mills, a Christian Scientist, was summoned to attend him.
>
> Kate Lyon, one of the household, testified that Mr. Frederic asked her to call in Mrs. Mills, who came to the house and explained Christian Science. That day Mr. Frederic dismissed his doctors. Most of Mrs. Mills's treatment, the witness said, was what is called "absent treatment." At the request of friends the doctors were recalled, but Mr. Frederic informed them that he had not followed their directions before.
>
> John Stokes, Mr. Frederic's amanuensis, testified that he told Kate Lyon she might be charged with manslaughter if Mr. Frederic died without medical treatment.
>
> The inquiry was adjourned until Wednesday to hear Mrs. Mills. (*New York World*, 22 October)

24 OCTOBER. Crane sends Reynolds the manuscript of "'You Must!'—'We Can't!'" (*New York Journal*, 8 November), again emphasizing that he must change his financial arrangement with the *Journal* since "they originally paid my expenses but that for many weeks they have not, leaving me in fact fastened here in Cuba with a big hotel bill. I am determined to make a clear slate with them—clean out all indebtedness; but at $20 a column, it is simply *awful*." He makes clear that he is not eager to return to England and Cora: "I may stay here all winter if we can get that syndicate going" (*C*, 382).

25 OCTOBER. The *Journal* prints Crane's amusing account of "How They Court in Cuba."

[BETWEEN 25 AND 28 OCTOBER]. Crane sends Reynolds a report headlined "Mr. Crane, of Havana" in the *Journal* (9 November), which deals with how the bumptious behavior of American troops in Santiago is harming the reputation of the United States in Havana. He again emphasizes his desperate need for money, urging Reynolds "in God's name hustle" (*C*, 383).

28 OCTOBER. Conrad replies to Cora's request for help in persuading Crane to return to England and for funds to be donated to a private committee she proposes to set up with John Scott Stokes, who has become Harold Frederic's British executor, in order to provide support for Frederic's children with Kate Lyon:

> Just a word in haste to tell you I shall try to do what I can. Don't build any hopes on it. It is a *most* remote chance—but it's the only thing I can think of. What kind of trouble is Stephen in? You make me very uneasy. Are you sure you can bring him back. I do not doubt your influence mind! but not knowing the circumstances I do not know how far it would be feasible. In Stephen's coming back to England is *salvation* there is no doubt about that.
>
> Will he come? *Can* he come? I am utterly in the dark as to the state of affairs.
>
> We recognize your good heart in your acts. God forbid that we should throw the first—or even the last stone. What the world calls *scandal* does not affect me in the least. My sincere approval and high recognition of the course you've taken is not based on christian grounds. I do not pretend to that name—not from irreverence but from my exalted idea of that faith's morality. I can't pretend to such morality but I hold that those that *do* pretend and boast of it should *carry it out* as the *cost of personal sacrifice,* and in *every respect.* My admiration of your courageous conduct exists side by side with an utter disapproval of those whom you (in *your* own extremity) befriend.

But Conrad regrets that he cannot give more than his empathy since "I've only £8 in the bank and am in debt to publishers so heavily that I can't go to them for more. Or else I would do it, believe me" (*C*, 383–384).

The *New York Times* condemns Mrs. Mills as "a miserable creature . . . stretching out rapacious eyes for the sick man's gold. She got it and Harold Frederic is dead." The *Times* hopes that "she will soon be in a prison, and stay there for a very considerable period. Would that every one of her rivals might bear her company."

NOVEMBER. "His New Mittens" appears in *McClure's Magazine* in the United States and in *Cornhill Magazine* in England.

1 NOVEMBER. Crane sends Reynolds another *Journal* article, "Spaniards Two" (11 November). He asks Reynolds to tell Frederick A. Stokes that he has "completed about 15000 words of Cuban stories

and that he shall have the book for spring." Crane advises Reynolds that English rights to "Marines Signaling under Fire at Guantanamo" should go to Blackwood's, which declined the article, and adds, "I am working like a dog. When—oh, when,—am I to have some money? If you could only witness my poverty!" (*C*, 385).

Conrad writes to Cora telling her that he is attempting to obtain funds from Blackwood through the good offices of David Meldrum and that he has suggested a loan of £50, offering as potential security Crane's future work, Cora's furniture, or his own work should the Cranes be unable to fulfill their obligation (*C*, 386). His letter suggests that Crane is pleading his debts as his excuse for being unable to leave Havana.

3 NOVEMBER. Crane responds to a letter from Reynolds informing him that *Cosmopolitan* editor John Brisben Walker has decided to publish "The Price of the Harness" under the title "The Woof of Thin Red Threads": "Damn Walker. The name of the story is 'The Price of the Harness' because it *is* the price of the harness, the price the men paid for wearing the military harness, Uncle Sam's military harness; and they paid blood, hunger and fever. Let him if he likes conjure some inflammatory secondary title. He is a fool" (*C*, 387).

Conrad writes to Cora, enclosing a letter from Meldrum suggesting conditions for a loan. He asks "Would Stephen come back by himself if written to? Would he tell us *how much* is wanted to enable him to leave Havana? Would he recognize the engagements we would enter into here for means to bring him back? His future is here—I firmly believe—but will he see it?" (*C*, 388).

5 NOVEMBER. In the London *Critic* Michael Neil lauds *Pictures of War* as "the greatest book of its kind that has ever been written. . . . In this book we are shown the sublime exultation, the repulsion and the fascination of human conflict. All the wickedness and wanton waste of war are set forth in masterpieces of phrasing by the hand of a mere youth."

8 NOVEMBER. The coroner's jury at Kenley indicts Kate Lyon and Mrs. Mills for manslaughter in the death of Harold Frederic (*New York Times*, 9 November).

9 NOVEMBER. Cora writes to Reynolds: "It is the opinion of all the men who know, that Stephen's future is in England. No matter what he writes, there is *always* favorable notices in every English paper.

He has a great vogue here and sure he must return if he is ever going to do more great work. A man must have pure wholesome air if he wishes to succeed in art. I beg you will advise Mr. Crane to return to England. He has a great future and a wonderful home awaiting him" (*C*, 388–389).

In a *New York Journal* report datelined 4 November, "Mr. Crane, of Havana," Crane deplores the fact that stories about the misbehavior of American occupation troops in Santiago are reaching Havana.

The lengthy trial of Kate Lyon and Mrs. Mills begins in the Croydon County Police Court. Kate is accompanied to the dock by Cora Crane, Frank Harris, and John Scott Stokes, who take seats in the courtroom (Weintraub, 134).

10 NOVEMBER. James B. Pinker writes to Cora that he does not think it advisable to tell editors that the early New York City sketches Cora is attempting to market were written when Crane was younger since this would be prejudicial and that if Crane "does not think them good enough to stand on their merits, it would be better not to let them go out" (*C*, 389).

William Howe Crane writes to Reynolds that Stephen has telegraphed him requesting a loan: "Can you tell me what the urgency is or whatever you may have to do with it? I shall be greatly obliged. I have written him at Havana, but my letters were returned as uncalled for. Do you know his city address there" (*C*, 390).

12 NOVEMBER. Crane's article in the *Journal*, "In Havana as It Is To-Day," describes visits to insurgent posts near Havana with Walter Parker and another correspondent.

14 NOVEMBER. Pinker writes to Cora acknowledging receipt of two early New York City sketches and "The Reluctant Voyagers," written in the spring of 1893 (*C*, 390–391).

John Scott Stokes informs Cora that he has sent three cables to Crane assuring him that an advance of £50 from Heinemann is being forwarded to him. The last telegram specifies "money shortly through General Wade" (*C*, 391, 391n1).

17 NOVEMBER. The *Journal* prints Crane's last report from Havana, "Our Sad Need of Diplomats," a disjointed article dealing with inter-relationships between the Spanish occupiers of Havana and representatives of the United States government.

24 NOVEMBER. In Havana Crane inscribes a copy of *The Little Regiment* to J. G. Widrig, an officer of the U.S.S. *Scorpion* (*C*, 392).

25 NOVEMBER. A letter from Pinker to Cora and subsequent letters dated 30 November and 1 December indicate that Crane is communicating through her specific terms of sale for a yet unwritten book of short stories or a novel to be offered to an English publisher other than Heinemann, to whom *Active Service* had already been committed (*C*, 392–394).

26 NOVEMBER. Having been rejected by the *Century, Scribner's Magazine*, and the *Atlantic*, "The Blue Hotel" appears uncut in *Collier's Weekly* in two parts on 26 November and 3 December.

Crane inscribes a copy of an 1898 edition of *The Red Badge of Courage* to an unidentified recipient in Havana (*C*, 392).

28 NOVEMBER. In Croydon County Police Court, Cora Crane testifies at the trial of Kate Lyon and Mrs. Mills:

> Mrs. Cora Crane, wife of Mr. Stephen Crane, of Oxted, said she and her husband were old friends of Mr. Frederic's. It was on his return from a tour in Ireland that she first noticed anything wrong with Mr. Frederic, but she did not meet Mrs. Mills until Tuesday, October 11, when she drove to her house in the company of Mr. Frederic. During the last month of his life Mr. Frederic seemed weaker each time she saw him. On the Monday before he died witness went to Homefield to see Miss Lyon. She told her he was not quite so well, and from what she and Miss Sayer said witness, on her own responsibility, telegraphed to Dr. Freyberger. She told Miss Lyon, who said she had every faith in Christian science, but if she thought so and his friends thought so she would consent. She also wished to wait a day or couple of days, saying that it was a critical time then, as it always was in Christian science cases. Correcting herself, witness said Mrs. Mills did not use the word critical; she said deceased was in a state of "chemicalization."
> Did you understand that term was synonymous with dying?—Oh, no. . . . Kate Lyon had treated her husband for a broken nose after a carriage accident. She believed the treatment was purely mental.
> What did she do?—She thought. (Laughter.)
> Did your husband's nose get better under the process?—
> I do not know, it is well now. (Laughter.) (*Times* [London], 29 November)

30 NOVEMBER. Meldrum writes to Blackwood expressing his high opinion of "The Price of the Harness" in the December issue of

Blackwood's but recommending rejection of "The Clan of No-Name." He is not certain of the amount that should be deducted from Crane's debt to Blackwood for "The Price of the Harness":

> I think the question might remain open until he gets back, if ever he does. Let me say again that I should have been very sorry had you advanced money further to the Cranes. I fancy he is far more foolish than you know. I can find no justification for the man, though I can many excuses for one with such a strange and all-on-edge temperament as his. But as I gather from your letter that you object to my personally moving in the matter, I have told Conrad and the Mrs that I can do no more. . . . Some time ago Conrad wrote me that Crane was in deep waters on the other side, and that Mrs Crane wanted to go out to him; and he asked me, if I felt I could, to approach you about a further loan. Conrad himself, he said, had no ready money . . . and all he could offer was to hand over to you as security the book of short stories about which you and he had made a royalty arrangement. Mrs Crane, also, was to offer, as security, a bill of sale on her furniture, and promised that whoever lent her the money should have a story of Crane's one day. A bill of sale is rather a flimsy security, but it is security to some extent. The promise of a story is none; for, apart from the fact that Crane, I know, is tied to Heinemann for his next novel, and is bound to you to offer [the] first free one, Mrs Crane's promise on behalf of her husband is, legally, absolutely worthless. After considering the matter I replied to Conrad that I couldn't put the proposal before you.

Meldrum also advises Blackwood that although he would not advise him to advance the Cranes more money, he has appealed to some of his friends, including London publisher John Macqueen, to do so (Conrad 1958, 31–33).

DECEMBER. "The Price of the Harness" appears in *Cosmopolitan* under the title "The Woof of Thin Red Threads," editorially adopted from the fifth section of the story, where the firing line is described as reminiscent of "a loom, a great grand steel loom, clinking, clanking, plunking, plinking, to weave a woof of thin red threads, the cloth of death." The story is published simultaneously under its proper title in *Blackwood's Edinburgh Magazine*.

"Rumbling, buzzing, turning, whirling Wheels" is printed on the front cover of the *Philistine*.

[DECEMBER]. Cora Crane writes in her Manuscript Book: "My letters are one long inky howl!" (NNC).

2 DECEMBER. Pinker advises Cora that Methuen & Co. has offered an advance of up to £75 as an installment on an advance of £125 and proposed royalty terms for a novel of not less than 70,000 words. "The advance is, of course, not what you anticipated, but I dare say I can persuade them to increase it. But, before negotiating further, can you let me have an assurance from Mr. Crane that he will be able to deliver the ms. of the book by the time specified?" (*C*, 395).

Grant Richards, with whom Cora is also negotiating for Crane's unwritten book, writes her asking why Heinemann has not been approached first, what the terms of Crane's agreement with Heinemann are and what they would be with another publisher, and when the manuscript is likely to be ready. He adds, "If you will let me have an answer to these questions I will at once come to a decision. I should add that the collection of short stories, I confess, has little attraction for me" (*C*, 396).

4 DECEMBER. Conrad writes to Cora expressing his appreciation of "The Price of the Harness," which he considers the best thing Crane has done since *The Red Badge*, "and it has even something that the Red Badge had not—or not so much of. He is maturing. He is expanding. There is more breath and somehow more substance in this war-picture" (*C*, 396).

7 DECEMBER. Pinker informs Cora that *Cornhill Magazine* has accepted "A Self-Made Man," Crane's earlier parody of an Horatio Alger story. He returns the manuscript of another earlier work, the fragmentary "Dan Emmonds," of which he has had a typescript made (*C*, 398).

9 DECEMBER. Pinker writes to Cora: "I have seen Grant Richards, and I told him the terms suggested and that it was absolutely necessary that we should have £100 on the signing of the contract, and £100 on publication. He would not give me an answer on the spot, but he has promised to let me have a decision in a day or two. He said that you had only suggested £75 on publication, and I think it would be better if you did not mention terms if you communicate with any publisher, for fear we should not name the same" (*C*, 399).

11 DECEMBER. Crane is among a group of American newsmen visiting Admiral Sampson's flagship, the *New York*, in Havana harbor (*Havana Advertiser.* Copy, NSyU).

12 DECEMBER. In his burlesque diary, imitating *The Diary of Samuel Pepys*, Edwin Emerson records:

> To the Inglaterra for my daily draught of Xeres wine and there beheld Señor Sanguilly, the Cubano rebel, lately returned, with black ugly looks flashing 'twixt his friends and highly wrathful souldiers of the Spanish King his forsaken army. So lingered until nightfall and after supper back again for trouble was surely brewing.
>
> Of a soddain, we having quaffed our third round of wassail cups, bursts forth an angry quarrell 'twixt Cubanos and Spaniards, and one man striking 'tother in the face, tables be overturned, and flashes of drawn swordes. Anon cometh the loud noyse of a blunderbuss and other souldiers running up, all fall to shooting their arquebuses this way and that, we hiding away into an ingle nook, whilst bullets and broken glass flew hither and thither. The Cubanos flying up the stairway, with Spanish souldiers shooting after them, I out into the square. . . . and anon come upon Stephen Crane, who standeth with both his hands held aloft, lest he be shot for a Cubano, and I accosting him, he did waggishly shake his head and proclaim '*Tis another night of St. Bartholomew.* (Emerson, 148–149)

[This incident involving the pursuit of the Cuban rebel Julio Sanguili (or "Sanguilli"), "whose life had once been spared through banishment and a promise never to return to Cuba so long as the Spaniards were there," is also narrated by Walter Parker (Wertheim 1976b, 54–55). Later, Emerson recalled, "The only civilian I saw on the square was Crane, (or a man whom I took to be Crane), who stood behind the shelter of the central fountain, holding both hands aloft. As I approached him, he warned me to 'look out,' saying whimsically: 'T'is the night of Saint Bartholomew.' . . . In my excitement and in the dark I might well have mistaken another compatriot for Crane, whom I had met but casually before" (Edwin Emerson to Ames Williams, 15 November 1947, DGU).]

Pinker writes to Cora advising her that Richards has apparently refused the terms for Crane's unwritten novel but that he can probably procure an advance of £150 from Methuen (*C*, 400).

13 DECEMBER. Conrad writes to Blackwood that he is greatly impressed with "The Price of the Harness": "The man will develop. I find this story, broader, gentler, less tricky and just as individual as the best of his work. It is the best bit of work he has done since the *Red Badge*. One or two competent men wrote to me about it and they share my opinion" (Karl and Davies, 2: 130).

The Croydon County magistrates withdraw the charges against Kate Lyon and dismiss the charges against Mrs. Mills. In London's Central Criminal Court (Old Bailey) the following day the defendants are found not guilty and discharged (*Times* [London], 15 December).

16 DECEMBER. American troops occupy Havana. Emerson records: "*They have come in the nick of time* quoth Steven Crane, we coming upon him in the midst of the town, for he hateth all Spaniards as they were poison. He most cocksure how more frays and mayhap bloody rebellion must soon follow, and so gave but scant heed when I did bid him go with us to behold them unearth the bones of great Sir Cristopher Columbus in the church of La Habana on the morrow, but in the end gave me a hearty yea" (Emerson, 150).

17 DECEMBER. Edward Garnett's essay in the *Academy*, "Stephen Crane: An Appreciation," concludes that "undoubtedly of the young school of American artists Mr. Crane is the genius—the others have their talents." But Garnett qualifies his praise with an acute awareness of Crane's limitations:

> The rare thing about Mr. Crane's art is that he keeps closer to the surface than any living writer, and, like the great portrait-painters, to a great extent makes the surface betray the depths. But, of course, the written work in the hands of the greatest artist often deals directly with the depths, plunges us into the rich depths of consciousness that cannot be more than hinted at by the surface; and it is precisely here that Mr. Crane's natural limitation must come in. . . . I do not think that Mr. Crane will or can develop further. Again, I do not think he has the building faculty, or that he will ever do better in constructing a perfect whole out of many parts than he has arrived at in *The Red Badge of Courage*. That book was a series of episodic scenes, all melting naturally into one another and forming a just whole; but it was not constructed in any sense of the word. And, further, Mr. Crane does not show any faculty of taking his characters and revealing in them deep mysterious worlds of human nature, of developing fresh riches in them acting under the pressure of circumstance. His imaginative analysis of his own nature on a battlefield is, of course, the one exception. And similarly the great artist's arrangement of complex effects, striking contrasts, exquisite grouping of devices, is lacking in him. His art does not include the necessity for complex arrangements; his sure instinct tells him never to quit the passing moment of life, to hold fast by simple situations, to reproduce the episodic, fragmentary nature of life in such artistic sequence that it stands in place of the architectural masses and co-ordinated structures of the great artists. He is the chief impressionist of this age, as Sterne was the great impressionist, in a different manner, of his age.

1898

In the Book Section of the *New York Times*, John W. De Forest comments on recent developments in American literature:

> One of the most noticeable changes, I think, that have come over the literary field since my time is the multitude of styles of writing and the great range of plot. You have read Stephen Crane's "Red Badge of Courage"? It seems to me to be a really clever book, with a good deal of really first-class work in it. His battle scenes are excellent, though I never saw a battery that could charge at full speed across a meadow. His style is short, sharp, jerky; a style that never would have been tolerated in my day. How different it is from the pure, swinging style of Irving, from Holland, from Mrs. Stowe!

20 DECEMBER. HAVANA. Having watched the cortege bearing what are believed to be the remains of Columbus proceed to the wharf where the casket is transferred to a Spanish warship, Emerson proceeds "home to dinner, deep in meditacion on the vanity of all things, which I seldom am, but tarried at the *Three Friars*, Stephen Crane his chosen tap room, to uprayed him for so light a breach of his solemne promise, but he so far gone in dalliance with two morena damozels and at such losse what to plead in his owne behalfe that he did feign to be too deep in drink to know my face, and so left him, nor knew how to explain his ill manners to my wife, waiting for me below in her hackney coach" (Emerson, 151).

Several London newspapers—the *Daily Chronicle*, the *Daily Graphic*, and the *Daily Mail*—carry a letter signed by a number of prominent persons appealing for money on behalf of Grace Frederic and her children. Among the signatories are Sir Henry Irving, Henry James, A. Conan Doyle, James M. Barrie, A. Quiller Couch, William Heinemann, and W. E. Henley (Bigsby, 80).

21 DECEMBER. Conrad writes to Meldrum: "I don't know whether I've told you that Mrs Crane got the cash and has sent it off to Havana to bring Stephen back. I know you will like to hear that she got over *that* trouble" (Karl and Davies, 2: 133).

23 DECEMBER. Conrad sends Christmas greetings to Cora and thanks her for her gifts to Borys. "I wish you could have given us some news from Stephen. Well, please god you will have your mind and your heart at rest soon" (*C*, 401).

24 DECEMBER. Crane sails from Havana for New York aboard the S.S. *City of Washington* (Passenger Manifest, National Archives. Copy, NSyU).

Stephen and Cora Crane at Ravensbrook, Oxted, Surrey,
1897–1898
(Barrett Collection, University of Virginia)

LATE DECEMBER. Cora Crane writes to Clara Frewen on Brede Place stationery that Crane's return to England is imminent: "I have sent to Brede, over three hundred very choice roses. One in particular which was budded by a very prominent author [Ford Madox Ford], I've had planted against the front of house. I am sure when the time comes that you go into residence we will always be remembered by our rose garden" (*C*, 405).

28 DECEMBER. The *City of Washington* crosses the bar of New York Harbor at 5:00 A.M. (*New York Times*, 29 December). Later in the day Crane meets Hamlin Garland in the offices of S. S. McClure, and in the evening Garland writes in his diary:

> At McClure's I met Stephen Crane the wonderful boy whose early work I saw ~~first~~ and advocated in 1891–2. He is just returned from Havana, and looked dingy and soaked with nicotine but appeared mentally alert and as full of odd turns of thought as ever. He strikes me now as he did in early days as unwholesome physically—not a man of long life. He is now unusually careless in his dress and has acquired an ~~slight~~ English accent in a few of his words—He was not overwhelmed with joy to see me. [Added in Garland's hand but in different pen and ink, possibly much later:] He looked yellow and his gaze was no longer frank. His attitude toward me had changed in some way. (Stronks 1973, 249)

30 DECEMBER. Cora drafts a rejoinder to Alice Creelman, who, in the absence of her husband, had opened Cora's letter appealing for funds on behalf of the children of Harold Frederic and Kate Lyon and had responded indignantly:

> You say your surprised that I should expect anyone to help Miss Lyon with the burden of her children—my surprise is, that people can visit the sins of the parents upon those innocent babies—If self respect can come to mankind by their proving their loathing of sin, (and how can we judge the laws of God—by laws of state or those of our theological brothers?) by not helping these children to bread and shelter—let them so get what comfort they can out the satisfaction that come with the knowledge of their own loved one's warm and fed—I have sheltered these children for five months in my own home and with my own name—and if all the world line themselves up to fight these babes, I will still shelter *them* & God will help me. (*C*, 403).

Robert Barr regrets that he can contribute only £2 to the fund for the Frederic children. He feels compelled to subscribe to the public fund for Grace Frederic and her younger children also (*C*, 404).

31 DECEMBER. Crane sails for England aboard the *Manitou* (*New York Times*, 1 January 1899).

Stephen Crane in 1899
(Barrett Collection, University of Virginia)

CHAPTER SEVEN

England (Brede Place) and Badenweiler

January 1899–June 1900

On returning to England, Crane finds himself besieged by debt. The rent on Ravensbrook has not been paid for a year, and a London department store and local merchants are demanding long-overdue payments. Moreton Frewen directs the Cranes to his own solicitor, Alfred T. Plant, who launches a sustained effort to bring them to a state of solvency, which their increasingly profligate way of life renders all but impossible. When James B. Pinker agrees to act as guarantor for their debts, the Cranes move to Brede Place, Northiam, Sussex, near Hastings, taking with them Mrs. Ruedy, two of Harold Frederic's children by Kate Lyon, and their servant, to whom is added Mack (William MacVittie), Moreton Frewen's former valet-groom, who he insisted remain at Brede Place in charge of the staff that included Vernall, a very drunken cook; Richard Heather, the old butler; and a serving man (Leslie, 159).

Local writers living in the Sussex-Surrey-Kent area—including Henry James, H. G. Wells, Joseph Conrad, Edward Garnett, Edwin Pugh, and A. E. W. Mason—are occasional visitors. Less welcome are a horde of American journalists and adulators, characterized as "lice" and "Indians" by Crane, who descend on Brede for prolonged stays. To support this lavish establishment, Crane, directly and through Cora, bombards Pinker with pleas for payments and advances on Cuban War stories and Whilomville tales, and Pinker forwards small sums to Plant, who wards off creditors with partial payments. In May Crane finishes *Active Service*, begun at Ravensbrook in the winter of 1897 but suspended while he was in Cuba, and *War Is Kind* appears a little later in the month. William Howe Crane's daughter Helen arrives in June for a prolonged visit, and Kate Lyon's niece, Edith Richie, comes to Brede in July as a companion for Helen and stays until January. Near the end of the summer, his financial circumstances worsening, Crane undertakes a series of articles, researched in the British Museum and largely written by Kate Lyon, which are published in *Lippincott's* in 1900 as "Great Battles of the World." He projects a novel about the American Revolution to fulfill his contract with Methuen for an unspecified work of fiction, and secures a contract

Brede Place, Sussex, in 1944
(Syracuse University)

with Frederick A. Stokes for its American publication, but, lacking the leisure and the facilities for the required historical research, he soon abandons the idea by early fall, apparently having written nothing.

In September Crane accompanies Helen to Lausanne, where she is enrolled in the Rosemont-Dézaley school. He begins work on *The O'Ruddy*. *Active Service* is published in October, and at the end of the month or early in November Crane completes the stories begun in Havana for *Wounds in the Rain*. *The Monster and Other Stories* is published in December. The year ends with an elaborate Christmas party at Brede, featuring a farce, "The Ghost," with music taken from Gilbert and Sullivan operettas and dialogue contributed by a number of distinguished writers. After the house party following the performance, Crane has a severe tubercular hemorrhage.

In January 1900 Crane recovers sufficiently to work on *The O'Ruddy*, completing 25 of the 33 chapters. Plans are advanced and abandoned for going to Gibraltar and writing sketches from Saint Helena, site of a Boer prison, as a correspondent on the Boer issue, but at the end of March and in early April he suffers two more massive hemorrhages. A journey to the Black Forest in Germany in search of a cure proves futile, and Crane dies on 5 June at the Villa Eberhardt in Badenweiler. His body remains on view in a London mortuary for a week and then is returned to America, where he is buried in the family plot in Evergreen Cemetery, Union County, New Jersey, on the Elizabeth city line. The area is now incorporated into the town of Hillside. Several books are published posthumously: *Whilomville Stories* (1900), *Wounds in the Rain* (1900), *Great Battles of the World* (1901), *Last Words* (1902), and *The O'Ruddy* (1903), which was completed by Robert Barr.

JANUARY. "The Scotch Express," written for S. S. McClure in the fall of 1897, is published simultaneously in *McClure's Magazine* in the United States and *Cassell's Magazine* in England. The illustrations in *McClure's* are by William L. Sonntag, Jr., who accompanied Crane on the train ride from London to Glasgow.

Munsey's Magazine notes that "the American admirers of Stephen Crane did not know that the young author had taken unto himself a wife, till they learned by cable that it was Mrs. Crane who had persuaded Harold Frederic, a few days before his death, to give up his Christian Science doctor and send for a regular practitioner. During her husband's absence in Cuba, Mrs. Crane remained in England."

2 JANUARY. "The Lone Charge of William B. Perkins" is published in the *Westminster Gazette.*

Sidney Pawling, who had been gathering the fare to pay for Crane's passage home, hedges in responding to a new request for money by Cora: "You don't give me any news about your husband. I thought he would be home by now, as the money was sent some weeks ago. I shall be glad anyhow to have news" (*C,* 411).

George Gissing writes to H. G. Wells in regard to the two Harold Frederic funds: the public one for Frederic's legitimate family and the private subscription, sponsored by Cora Crane and John Scott Stokes, for Kate Lyon and her children:

> On the list of subscribers to the Frederic fund, I saw you down for £5. I fear this represents your final gift in that direction. Yet the fact is that Kate Lyon and her three little children (the eldest seven years old) are in far more serious need than Mrs Frederic and her two grown up daughters and two boys of 10 and 12. They have the brute world against them—and it has shown its bestiality in ways that make me rage up and down the room. Of course no public subscription can be opened for them, but certain people are doing their best, especially Mrs Stephen Crane and the

executor Stokes. The children are away in the country, in good hands, and we want to secure them there for a year or two, till it can be seen what Kate Lyon can do. Of course their identity has to be concealed—else the sweet neighbours would make life impossible for the people who take care of them. (Gettmann, 131–132)

To Cora, Gissing writes:

I feel ashamed to be thanked for that absurd little cheque. I wish I were a popular novelist!—instead of one considerably more talked about than read. . . . I am very glad indeed to know that the poor little children are at present so fortunately placed—excellent for them to be away in the quiet country, away, too, from the incredible brutality of people who would like to make them suffer for their birth. . . . Their mother has my deepest sympathy. More than that; I feel that anyone who has read with understanding & pleasure any of Frederic's recent work owes to *her* a vast debt of gratitude. But for his true companion, his real wife, this work would never have been done. I cannot express the loathing with which I regard any man or woman who speaks slightingly of her. (NNC)

Joseph Conrad writes to David Meldrum: "Mrs Crane still without news. I don't know what to think" (Karl and Davies, 2: 146).

3 JANUARY. John Scott Stokes writes to Cora, asking her and Kate Lyon to provide names for possible contributors to the private fund for the Frederic children: "This—your idea—is excellent and generous. No, Stephen must *not* be saddled with the burden of supporting this young family" (NNC).

Elizabeth Robins writes to Cora, expressing sympathy for Kate Lyon but regretting that she has "already an object for my surplus, that has a prior & most imperative claim" (NNC).

George Gissing writes to H. G. Wells:

There is as yet no printed list, and Mrs Stephen Crane has not yet persuaded her bankers to hold the fund. *She* must be a brick. She had the three little ones for four months, at her own house, during H. F.'s illness, and seems, together with Stokes, to have kept the poor woman alive through all the horrors. Mrs Crane's address is Ravensbrook, Oxted, Surrey, and she will joyfully answer any question. It is Stokes's hope that a very rich man named Lawrence, who lives at Kenley, a friend of H. F.'s, will do something solid for the children, and that another rich man named Barry (after whom the youngest is named) will also help substantially. But rich men are slow.

I seriously doubt whether you ought to give another £5. Indeed, I am sure you ought *not*—quite sure. I wish I had not shared my stupid 4 guineas between the two—but when I decided to do that I had heard only Fisher's story, not Stokes's. Stokes abuses no one; he is a fair man, and says Fisher speaks in honest ignorance. (Gettmann, 133–134)

4 JANUARY. Pinker responds to a letter from Cora announcing Crane's imminent arrival. He has seen Methuen about Crane's yet-unspecified novel: "Of course they are naturally anxious to know what the book will be, the length, theme, and so on, and if we can wait until he arrives and then give them some definite details. I shall be able to get better terms than it would be possible to secure under present circumstances." He has spoken to the editor of *Wide World Magazine* about a projected series of articles by Cora on her experiences as a war correspondent (*C*, 412–413, 413n2).

[FIRST WEEK IN JANUARY]. Cora Crane writes to Edward Garnett, thanking him for sending a clipping of his 17 December 1898 *Academy* essay, "Mr. Stephen Crane: An Appreciation": "I like it very much indeed—one must value a true opinion: but I disagree with you when you say that he may fail when the 'picturesque phases of the environment that nurtured him give out.' The beautiful thoughts in Stephen's mind are simply endless! His great difficulty is the lack of that machine-like application which makes a man work steadily. I hope that the perfect quiet of Brede Place and the freedom from a lot of dear good people, who take his mind from his work, will let him show the world a book that will live" (*C*, 413).

8 JANUARY. McClure syndicates "Stephen Crane in Texas," an article dealing with San Antonio.

[10 JANUARY]. Cora writes to Edward Garnett: "I am, at every moment, expecting a wire saying that the ship which carries my dear one, is sighted. The 'Manitou,' she is due today or tomorrow morning and I shall, if I have time, go to Gravesend to meet Stephen" (*C*, 415).

11 JANUARY. The *Manitou* reaches Gravesend (*Times* [London], 12 January).

Mrs. Julia Field King, Mary Baker Eddy's emissary in London, writes to Cora, enclosing a check for £6 for Kate Lyon's children. She comments: "You must not forget that Miss Lyon was not a Christian Scientist, and that through her claiming to be one, the world at large is justified in believing that Christian Science approves of and upholds

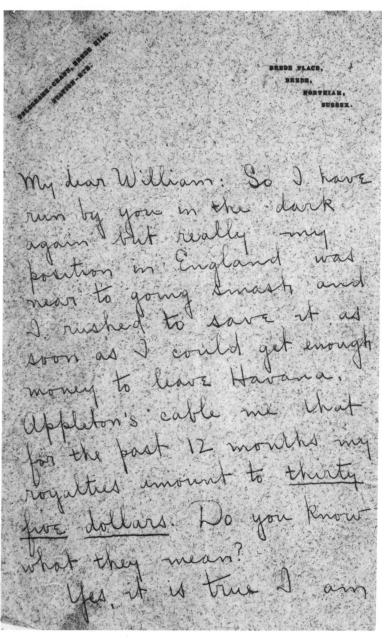

My dear William: So I have run by you in the dark again but really my position in England was near to going smash and I rushed to save it as soon as I could get enough money to leave Havana. Appleton's cable me that for the past 12 months my royalties amount to thirty five dollars. Do you know what they mean? Yes, it is true I am

Stephen Crane to William Howe Crane, mid-January 1899
(Barrett Collection, University of Virginia)

married to an English
lady and through her
connections we have
this beautiful old man-
or but we are beastly
short on ready money
owing to my long illness
and that is why I
want to propose the
five hundred loan. Other-
wise I may go bankrupt
here in February. If you
can do it, cable me
"Crane, care Sunlocks,
London." You need merely
say "Sending." Love to
all from the wayward
brother.
                    Stephen

the breaking of the Ten Commandments *which is not the case*. Had Miss Lyon been a Christian Scientist Mr. Frederic's house hold would have been quite differently constituted" (NNC).

13 JANUARY. Conrad writes to Crane welcoming him home and complimenting him on "The Price of the Harness." He thanks Crane for his telegram congratulating him on the prize of 50 guineas he has won from the *Academy* for his *Tales of Unrest*. He supposes that "the 'Dead Man' story will have to wait till you unload your new experience," revealing that Crane had conceived the germ of "The Upturned Face" before departing for Cuba. Referring to "Heart of Darkness" (*Blackwood's Magazine*, February 1899), Conrad remarks: "I finish a rotten thing I am writing for B'wood. It *is* rotten—and I can't help it. All I write is rotten now" (*C*, 417).

[MID-JANUARY. RAVENSBROOK]. Crane writes to his brother William on Brede Place stationery, acknowledging to his family for the first time that he is "married":

> My dear William: So I have run by you in the dark again but really my position in England was near to going smash and I rushed to save it as soon as I could get enough money to leave Havana. Appleton's cable me that for the past 12 months my royalties amount to *thirty five dollars*. Do you know what they mean?
>
> Yes, it is true I am married to an English lady and through her connections we have this beautiful old manor but we are beastly short on ready money owing to my long illness and that is why I want to propose the five hundred dollar loan. Otherwise I may go bankrupt here in February. If you can do it, cable me "Crane, care Sunlocks, London." You need merely say "Sending." Love to all from the wayward brother. (*C*, 416)

[Crane most likely lied to his family about how and where he met Cora, for the *Port Jervis Union* (5 June 1900) reported in an obituary that they had first met in Greece, not in Jacksonville. In all likelihood, two of Crane's brothers who lived in Port Jervis, William and Edmund, unknowingly supplied the newspaper with the wrong information. The *New York Herald* (6 June) similarly reported that Crane had met Cora "in the East" and married her "at the close of the Greek war."]

16 JANUARY. Hall Caine writes to Cora saying that he would like to postpone contributing to her fund for Kate Lyon's children until he has determined what he can give to the other fund being raised for

the children of Harold Frederic's wife: "What I have to say on Frederic's walk in life, I said to the man himself while he was alive. It would seem to me that the time is gone by for further discussion of that subject. A man's children are his children, and that is all that remains to be said on the subject" (NNC).

17 JANUARY. The Cranes drive to Hastings and spend the afternoon at Brede. Cora writes to Garnett on the 19th that "Stephen was mad over the place. We tramped, later, after a supper of ham & eggs beside the kitchen fire—to a cottage in the village and put up for the night there. Then spent the day at Brede. We are going to move Heaven and Earth to get there. Stephen said that a solemn feeling of work came to him there so I am delighted" (C, 420).

19 JANUARY. Crane writes to Reynolds expressing desperation over his financial plight and urging Reynolds to beg Harper and Brothers for the second $125 (£25) advance for book publication of "The Monster," to which he had promised to add previously unpublished stories to complete the volume. "Ask them why they don't print 'The Blue Hotel' and 'His New Mittens' in one volume with 'The Monster' and then pay up like little men. That would make 36000 words. I fail to see where they get such a hell of a right to decide as to what stories shall be published in a book that bears my name in a damn sight bigger type than it bears their imprint" (C, 418).

24 JANUARY. Pinker informs Crane that Methuen has offered a contract for his projected novel, the subject of which remains undetermined. The royalty terms are unusual: "16 2/3% on the first 3000 copies, 20% on the next 3000, and 25% after—13 copies to be counted as 12—and 3 1/2d per copy on the Colonial edition. The novel to be not less than 70,000 words in length, and the Ms. to be delivered by August 1st next. They agree to pay, on account of royalties, £100 on the signature of the contract and a further £100 on publication" (C, 421).

25 JANUARY. Alfred T. Plant writes to Crane that the solicitors Morrisons and Nightingale have agreed to accept £50 toward payment of the £98.9 owed to Self & Whitely's department store for Cora's piano. The remainder of the debt is to be discharged in six weeks (C, 421–422).

27 JANUARY. Crane sends Reynolds a typescript of "Lynx-Hunting," a Whilomville story in which the aged Henry Fleming of *The Red Badge* appears as a character, and asks him to use it to secure a loan

from McClure. "As to the Harpers, I think that collection of respectable old women has treated us rather badly." He believes that with his burgeoning English market, he should be able to obtain "big money" from the large-circulation American magazines (*C*, 422–423).

31 JANUARY. Crane sends Reynolds a typescript of "The Angel Child" and suggests that he offer this as collateral for a loan from McClure: "I am annoyed with the Harpers and I dont care whether they get their bookful or not. . . . I would again point out to you that my English magazine rights are now going for a sure nine guineas a thousand words, and so it does not behoove me to sell many stories to the three all-over-the places. Indeed, you might point out to some of these people that I can no longer afford to write for either Century, Harper's or Scribner's" (*C*, 424).

FEBRUARY. "Marines Signaling under Fire at Guantanamo" is included in *McClure's Magazine.*

The *Philistine* parodies poem XXIV of *The Black Riders*, "I saw a man pursuing the horizon":

> I saw a man tugging at his Boot-Straps.
> "It is futile," I said,
> "You can never lift yourself that way."
> "You lie!" he cried,
> And tugged on.

1 FEBRUARY. Crane sends James B. Pinker a typescript of "The Angel Child," "which is in the same series with 'Lynx Hunting', 'The Monster', and 'His New Mittens.' We like it a little. Harper's, in one sense has the book-rights to this series but this right is mainly based upon an artistic reason—the fact that I do not think it correct to separate the stories. (Harper's have the rights to the Monster.)" He adds, "You will be glad to know that I am now writing a story with which you can have good game: 'God Rest ye, Merry Gentlemen.' We are sure that you will like it" (*C*, 425).

2 FEBRUARY. David Meldrum writes to William Blackwood to ask how much of Crane's debt of £60, advanced to him by Blackwood, was wiped out by "The Price of the Harness." He reiterates his opinion that "The Clan of No-Name," although good, is not the equal of the earlier story (Conrad 1958, 44–45).

Henry James sends £5 toward the support of Kate Lyon's children: "Greater than I can say is my consideration for those beautiful little children" (NNC).

4 FEBRUARY. In an interview in the *Outlook* headed "Mr. Stephen Crane on the New America," Crane denies that the United States has imperialistic designs upon Cuba.

In a letter to Pinker, Crane reveals that Dominick, the head of the London office of Frederick A. Stokes & Co., has offered to aid him in paying back rent on Ravensbrook, which Morrisons and Nightingale, solicitors for the owner, are attempting to collect and which Crane must pay before he can move to Brede Place. The Stokes agent has asked for a "mortgage" on future royalties from his Appleton books as security. Crane requests that Pinker draw up a letter setting forth this arrangement. He reports that "'God Rest Ye, Merry gentlemen' is coming on finely." Despite his agreement with Harper and Brothers concerning Whilomville stories, he advises, "If you conclude that 'The Angel Child' is not a good opening gun, bury it in the heather i.e. send it to Blackwood. The next story will be a better one" (*C*, 427–428).

6 FEBRUARY. Crane writes to his brother William to say that "because of a certain generosity it wont cost me more than one hundred and sixty five dollars a year" to live in Brede Place. "The taxes are paid for me in advance. We have stables and everything which the usual English country house has attached to it" (*C*, 429).

Crane writes an ingratiating letter to the Reverend Charles J. Little, his former history professor at Syracuse, who after an examination on the French Revolution had warned him that he "was going very wrong indeed." Maintaining that he remains grateful for this advice, Crane self-consciously points out: "It is a little thing to talk about but I have written several little books which have editions in New York, London, Paris, Leipsic, Vienna and in the English colonies" (*C*, 429–430).

7 FEBRUARY. Crane sends Clara Frewen, who as the daughter of Leonard Jerome spent her childhood in New York City, an inscribed copy of *The Open Boat and Other Stories*:

You, with the rest of the world, have herein a further proof of my basic incapacity. However there are some stories of Americans and some stories of America in the book which may remind you of something better but, in any case, allow me to present my esteem

Stephen Crane
February 7, 1899. (*C*, 431)

[7 FEBRUARY]. Cora sends Margery Pease the manuscript of "The Angel Child," which she tells her "comes before Michael's 'story,'" a reference to "The Lover and the Tell-Tale," another Whilomville story, the manuscript of which Crane had given to Mrs. Pease (*C*, 431, 431n2). Both stories feature Jimmie Trescott of "The Monster" and "little Cora." Michael Pease explains:

> As regards the true history behind "The Lover & the Tell-Tale", I played only a minor part. It is, of course, perfectly true that Helen Frederick (subsequently Helen Foreman) was my first flame at the very tender age of eleven—Helen was younger than me, though I forget by how much. I'm afraid the story of the Tell Tale, the fight, and the school mistress was Stephen Crane's romance—or rather, I should say the hero was not me! I was an exceedingly sensitive boy, & had anything of that sort happened to me, it would have burnt itself deeply into my memory. This much however is true of me in the tale. Helen did, to my great distress, leave the Crane household at Oxted & went to live first (I think) in London & then (I feel sure) in Liverpool. What sticks clearly in my memory is that I wrote to her regularly for some months afterwards & that she wrote to me irregularly—two or three times all told. The quotation from the letter may be genuine; I cannot say at this distance & time. Crane may well have been told by my mother, who saw all my letters, & to whom I told all that there was to tell. Mother was my only confidante; I was, however, well aware that the Cranes & the other grown-ups knew what was afoot, though I got the impression that *they* thought I didn't know. (Michael Pease to Melvin H. Schoberlin, 27 November 1948, ViU)

[Cora told the Crane family that "she was the 'Angel Child' of the Whilomville Stories" (Edith Crane to Thomas Beer, 14 January 1934, CtY). Edith Richie Jones recalls that "one day Stephen was talking about his *Whilomville Stories*. He said most of them were founded on stories that Cora had told him of her childhood" (E. R. Jones, 60). Port Jervis was apparently the model for Whilomville, the name suggesting a town that may have existed "once upon a time." From family members, Crane may also have heard of the Whilom drum corps that performed at Peck family reunions until the death of his maternal grandfather, George Peck, in 1876, or he may have read about the corps in his cousin Jonathan K. Peck's book *Luther Peck and His Five Sons*

(1897) (Brown and Hernlund, 116–118). Two copies of this book were in Crane's Brede Place library (Kibler, 237).]

9 FEBRUARY. Crane informs Pinker that Morrisons and Nightingale are willing to defer payment of the rent due on Ravensbrook if Pinker will guarantee that it will eventually be paid. This will enable Crane to move to Brede Place immediately (*C*, 433).

12 FEBRUARY. The Cranes begin their move to Brede Place, where Mrs. Ruedy and Héloïse and Barry Frederic and their governess, Mrs. Lily Burke, are already established, although the back rent on Ravensbrook has not been paid (*C*, 437)

13 FEBRUARY. Crane sends Reynolds a typescript of "'God Rest Ye, Merry Gentlemen,'" a thinly fictionalized account of the experiences of war correspondents during the Daiquirí and Siboney landings and the subsequent action at Guásimas in which he portrays himself as "Little Nell." He mentions that a copy has already been sent to Pinker for the sale of English rights. He inquires about "Lynx-Hunting" and "The Angel Child," acknowledging that they should go to Harper and Brothers since by arrangement with Reynolds *Harper's Magazine* had first refusal on Whilomville stories, but, overestimating what he is being paid by magazines, Crane complains that "the International Magazines are mainly a source of pain and they will jolly well have to wait until my present difficulties are over." He expects to publish two books this year: *Active Service* and the novel for Methuen. Referring to *Active Service*, he adds that it is nearly half finished and "the book-rights belong to Stokes," indicating that the loan he had negotiated with Dominick had become an advance on the novel (*C*, 435–436).

Pinker writes to Crane that Morrisons and Nightingale require the rent on Ravensbrook to be paid at once and also demand that the Cranes make the repairs on the house to which they had agreed. Pinker hesitates to lend Crane the entire sum, but he eventually does so (*C*, 436).

17 FEBRUARY. George F. Elliott, now a major, writes to Crane, commending him for "Marines Signaling under Fire at Guantanamo" and enclosing a copy of a letter to the secretary of the navy that describes Sergeant John H. Quick's heroic actions at Cuzco and recommends him for the Congressional Medal of Honor (*C*, 438–439, 439n2).

18 FEBRUARY. Crane writes to William Morris Colles, of the Author's Syndicate, to which Reynolds had sent a number of his stories, asking whether "The Blue Hotel" has been sold in England (*C*, 439).

19 FEBRUARY. The Cranes move their household permanently to Brede Place (*C*, 440), leaving settlement of their Oxted debts in the hands of their solicitor, Alfred T. Plant (*C*, 441, 444–445, 451–452, 454).

23 FEBRUARY. The Reverend Charles J. Little responds to Crane's letter, denying that he ever admonished him for "'crime'" as a student at Syracuse, except hypothetically:

> For I dealt rather with what might than with what must be. And the "silly books" of which you speak so disparingly and, yet, with proper pride, have not concealed the "might be" altogether. At least so it seems to me who know them slightly. It amuses me, grey-headed fellow that I am, to hear an artist talk of crime. He, of all men, never knows it. He is taken up much with its picturesque aspects. He knows how to use the criminal, actual or potential; but in order to use him, he denaturalizes, derealizes him. . . . And this he does in the *very instant of perception*. In his eagerness to portray, he changes form and color, while he looks, and never sees men and women as they are. It is, I fancy, different with men whose knowledge of crime begins with the sorrow that it causes. (*C*, 442–443)

MARCH. The *Cornhill Magazine* prints "A Self-Made Man," Crane's parody of an Horatio Alger story.

The *Bookman* comments upon Harold Frederic's death and the public fund for Grace Frederic and her children:

> As there may be some persons whose judgment has been obscured regarding the Christian Science complications attending Mr. Frederic's death, and who might be inclined to refuse aid to Mrs. Frederic because she allowed experiments in his last sickness, we should like to make clear the fact that Mr. Frederic died, away from his own home, where his family could not control matters. Anyone who knew him at all knows that the truth of all this twaddle about his belief in Christian Science treatment is simply that he was moved by his consideration for a third person's feelings, and brought himself to submit to everything she proposed sooner than cause her continued anxiety or suffering. There never was any one who was more clear-headed than Mr. Frederic, or who all his life had quicker and saner recourse to physicians in regular standing. It is worth while to dispel the fog that has obscured this point, for it was by no means through any mistake on the part of his wife that the life of this man, beloved by all, ended prematurely at the age of forty-two.

2 MARCH. Crane suggests that Colles offer "The Blue Hotel" to the *Westminster Gazette* for about £15 (*C*, 445), but the story never appears in a newspaper or periodical in England.

Crane sends Reynolds "The Lover and the Tell-Tale," stipulating that he will not offer it for the English market until *Harper's* has refused it. He indicates that he will complete *Active Service* by the end of the month. As he has bypassed Reynolds in selling the book rights of the novel to Stokes, he now wishes to bypass Stokes in selling the serial rights: "Stokes and Co. dont wish me to sell the American serial rights but I think if you tackeled all those news-papers for a big summer serial we could make fifteen hundred dollars out of it. Would a good half of the novel be of any service to you to begin preliminary work with? If so I can send it to you upon reciept of your reply to this letter. On this side of the water Pinker is going to take half of the novel immediately out among the Englishmen." But *Active Service* does not appear serially in England. Crane also acknowledges that Pinker is finding it difficult to sell his Whilomville stories in England (*C*, 447–448).

Crane writes to his brother William: "I forgot to reply to you about the gossip in Port Jervis over 'The Monster.' I suppose that Port Jervis entered my head while I was writing it but I particularly dont wish them to think so because people get very sensitive and I would not scold away freely if I thought the eye of your glorious public was upon me." He boasts about his success in selling recently completed work but cites his immediate financial plight, pressing William once more for the loan of $500 and assuring him that "I hope by this time next year to be fairly rich" (*C*, 446–447).

Crane's brother Edmund writes to him, offering congratulations on his "marriage" and giving news of Hartwood and his horse Peanuts (*C*, 448–449).

5 MARCH. Reynolds cables that he has sold "God Rest Ye, Merry Gentlemen" for $300 (*C*, 450).

6 MARCH. Cora writes to Pinker asking him to withhold "God Rest Ye, Merry Gentlemen" from English sale until she can determine whether Reynolds has sold only the American rights to the story or English rights as well. She complains about the unreceptivity of the English publishers to Crane's recent work:

> I cannot understand what can be the reason for the English publishers refusing such stuff as those children stories and "God Rest Ye." They

seem to fancy themselves as judges of literature but to me they appear to be a good set of idiots to refuse really clever and artistic stuff and to print the rot they do. Mr. Reynolds has pleased us very much by his prompt placing of these stories. We hope that you will be equally successful in placing the serial rights of "Active Service" and in also, perhaps by pointing out to London publishers that Harpers have not only thought "Lynx Hunting" and "The Angel Child" good enough but have asked for *all* the "Whileomville" stories that Mr. Crane may write, that they have a lot to learn and that the firm of Pinker are the people to teach them. It is a good oppertunity for you to let them know that there are others, as we say in America. (*C*, 450–451)

Reynolds signs a receipt for the remaining $125 due from Harper and Brothers for *The Monster and Other Stories*. It is now specified that the volume will include "The Monster," "The Blue Hotel," and "His New Mittens" (NNC).

8 MARCH. Harper and Brothers draw up a final contract for *The Monster and Other Stories* (Levenson 1969, xl).

Judge Alton B. Parker of the New York State Court of Appeals, Harold Frederic's executor and later Democratic nominee for president opposing William Howard Taft, writes to Cora in response to the expressed desire of the Cranes to adopt Barry Frederic under American adoption laws. He advises them that such an adoption may not be carried out in a foreign country, but that he has "drafted an amendment to the statute concerning that deficit and delivered it to Senator Douglas who will press its passage. If it becomes law a legal adoption can be easily accomplished, if such be the desire of your husband and yourself and Miss Lyon" (NNC).

9 MARCH. Pinker responds to Cora's letter of 6 March:

I have withdrawn "God Rest Ye, Merry Gentlemen" until we know the meaning of Mr. Reynold's cable; but I wish we could make some arrangement to prevent the possibility of Mr. Reynold's and my operation overlapping. Editors are not pleased if I go and talk a great deal about a story and ask them to pay special attention to it, and then withdraw it.

In condemning English editors for their want of appreciation, one must remember that Mr. Crane's reputation is not established on this side as it is in the States, so that his name does not carry so much weight with the readers of sixpenny magazines, which are, after all, what one has most to depend on.

I am glad to hear that I may expect the Ms. of the novel soon. I suppose you have arranged so that in the event of my finding a serial opening

Heinemann will hold the novel over. Of course, if it is published serially, Methuen's novel will have to come out first. (*C*, 452–453)

12 MARCH. Crane writes to Moreton Frewen:

We have been in the old house nearly a month and every day it seems more beautiful to us. Each time we catch a new view—notably when walking down from the village—we have new raptures. Our friends are astonished at it and I am now holding delicately in check two rampant students of old English houses and several journalists all of whom wish to burst into articles. I am holding them in check in the opinion that, first, it would be best to have you say how you look upon that sort of thing. For my part, I usually let them bowl away, provided they allow me supervision of all things that are personal matters. For instance, an interviewer once declared of me that in appearance I was very ugly and so when he came again I sent him away in tears. I think if I manage the *career* of the old house it is probable that nothing will be said to annoy any of us aesthetically. My old friends—men like Garnett and others—I should feel quite safe with but the ones I do not know so well, frighten me a little.

The weather here is now delightful; raw-gold sunshine. I am finishing my novel rapidly in the room just over the porch. I wish it were a better novel. I fear that in later years people who wish the house well will be saying that Stephen Crane did *not* write "Active Service" in the room over the porch at Brede Place. (*C*, 453–454)

[FIRST HALF OF MARCH]. Walter Howard, war correspondent in Cuba and Puerto Rico for the *New York Journal*, visits the Cranes; they attend a tea party at the "'Crown and Thistle'" (*C*, 509–510).

15 MARCH. Reynolds sends Crane the contract from Harper and Brothers for *The Monster and Other Stories*. He advises Crane not to surrender dramatization rights, as Harper requires, or to agree to wait four months after royalty statements are issued to receive payment (*C*, 455).

16 MARCH. Crane advises Reynolds that *Active Service* has reached 47,000 words, "and I am going at a clipping gait of some ten thousand words per week." He feels that the book should be finished by the end of the first week in April. He is even more sanguine about serialization than before: "I dont suppose that the Stokes Co. will be pleased to have the story run as a serial in America but the more I look at it the more I feel that we might get even two or three thousand dollars out of newspares [*sic*] like the Sun or the Herald in New York, the Press in Philla. and others" (*C*, 455–456).

[16 MARCH]. Crane renews his effort to obtain a $500 loan from his brother William. As an inducement he offers to undertake temporary care of William's troublesome adolescent daughter Helen at Brede Place (*C,* 456).

17 MARCH. Crane writes to Pinker to inquire "when Mr. Meldrum was kind enough to loosen his talons on the 'Clan of No Name.'" He believes that the *London Illustrated News* or *Black and White* (where the story achieved first English publication in December) are likely prospects. He reports that *Active Service* has reached 48,000 words, "but the English Market seems so stagnant and Reynolds is so successful that I have delayed sending you a copy of the first half of the book in order that I might get a copy off to Reynolds. I am confident that it will be the most successful book that I have ever published" (*C,* 457).

19 MARCH. "The Clan of No-Name" is syndicated in a number of American newspapers.

20 MARCH. Crane advises Pinker that *Black and White* has accepted "The Clan of No-Name" (*C,* 458).

25 MARCH. Crane sends Reynolds 18 chapters of *Active Service* and reiterates that "all my friends like the novel exceedingly and we expect you to make a very successful sale of the American serial rights." He adds, "For your own edification and also for business reasons I think it should be announced that Coleman simply drowns all opposition and marries Marjory" (*C,* 459).

[LATE MARCH]. William Howe Crane sends Crane £100, then the near-equivalent of $500 (Sorrentino 1981, 107).

30 MARCH. Crane sends Reynolds four more chapters of *Active Service* and another Whilomville story, perhaps "Making an Orator" (C, 463).

31 MARCH. Crane returns the Harper and Brothers contract for *The Monster and Other Stories* to Reynolds with the stipulation that he refuse to surrender dramatization rights for the stories:

I recognize the kindness of Harper & Bro's. in accepting our proposal to print "The Monster" "The Blue Hotel" and "His New Mittens" in one volume. But please point out to them that this proposal was made before any other stories of Jimmie Trescott had been written and that at present my idea would be to remove "The Blue Hotel" entirely. It's introduction was in the nature of an expedient to fill up space. I suggest now that the phrase in the contract should read: "The said work is to include stories by the author entitled The Monster, His New Mittens, Lynx Hunting, The Angel Child, The Lover and the Tell-Tale and is also to include other stories of Whilomville which have not yet been named." This to my mind would make a grand book. For my part I would consider it the best book which has yet come from my pen. However I recognize the right of Harper & Bro's. to have the phrase read as it now reads in the contract if they chose because it was originally our proposal. (*C*, 463–464)

8 APRIL. In a *Saturday Evening Post* article entitled "American Brains in London," Robert Barr calls Crane "probably the greatest genius America has produced since Edgar Allan Poe, to whom, I fancy, he bears some resemblance." He reports a story of Crane in Cuba told by George Lynch, war correspondent for the *London Chronicle*, which is reminiscent of events Crane had previously described in "A Mystery of Heroism":

A company under fire was badly in need of water, and water was seven miles away, down hill at that. Stephen collected all the tin canteens he could find and trotted off for the refreshment. Coming wearily back, there was a sharp ping against one of the cans, and it began to leak. Stephen turned up the can and tried to stop the leak. An officer in the woods near by shouted to him:
"Come here, quick! You're in the line of fire!"
"If you've got a knife, cut a plug and bring it to me," replied the young man, and, as he spoke, bang went a bullet against another can.
"Come under cover or you'll lose every can you've got!"
This warning had its effect. The loss of the precious fluid terrified him in a way that danger to himself had failed to do. He finally brought the water up to the thirsty company, and then fainted through exhaustion. (Barr, 649)

10 APRIL. Crane reports a mishap at Brede Place to Moreton Frewen. Mack, who is inclined to tipple, accidentally started a small fire in the room over the porch Crane uses as a study. Little damage is done: "Pray tell Mrs. Frewen that I am fighting nobly with the concluding chapters of my book but that they seem to come with considerable reluctance. If you succeed me here next year, we will depart, at any rate, with a sense of a delightful sojourn. During these late heavy storms the whole house has sung like a harp and all the spouts have been wailing to us. It is rather valkyric. The servants are more im-

pressed than we would like them to be and we have not yet found maids who will sleep in the house" (*C,* 464–465).

As Jessie Conrad recalls,

> Brede Place was supposed to be haunted, and it was impossible to persuade local servants to spend the night there. The only two who would sleep there were the old butler, who fortified himself with liberal potions, and an excellent cook—who did likewise. She had often to be bribed to function in the evening with a bottle of brandy. The chances of dinner—at eight—were often very small, especially when there were many people expected. The cook would appear and announce in the most truculent tone that she was even at that moment departing. Cora Crane, at her wits' end for the moment, would wring her hands and appeal to Stephen. He in turn would give her one glance and solemnly ring the bell. Like clockwork the old butler appeared and handed a bottle of brandy to the thirsty woman, who retired with no further comment to her kitchen, and an hour or so later a perfect dinner would be served, complete in every detail. One night the old butler, who had primed himself a trifle early, knocked over the lamp and set the table alight. (J. Conrad 1935, 73)

11 APRIL. Reynolds writes Crane, telling him that a creditor has sent him a bill incurred by Crane while in Cuba (*C,* 465–466).

17 APRIL. Copyright deposit is made of *War Is Kind.* The book, printed on gray cartridge paper, is lavishly illustrated by Will Bradley.

20 APRIL. Pinker writes to Cora, detailing payments he continues to make to Morrisons and Nightingale on the Cranes' Oxted debts. He makes initial reference to a series of accounts of famous battles proposed by the Philadelphia firm of Lippincott, which Crane is reluctant to undertake: "I am sorry Mr. Crane will not do the battle articles. I think Lippincott would take six, if he would do them; and their representative, to whom I quoted Mr. Crane's objection, says that they would not want elaborate studies of the battles, as it would not be possible in the space contemplated. Perhaps Mr. Crane will think the matter over and write to me again" (*C,* 469).

25 APRIL. Cora sends Pinker the typescript of 22 chapters of *Active Service,* noting that she will send the balance at the end of the week: "Please do your very best to sell serially and give editors to understand that two weeks is the limit to keep Mr Crane's copy. Please make this your fast rule for all Mr Crane's work. Editors have always

subscribed to this for me, when I have been disposing of Mr. Crane's stuff" (*C*, 474).

29 APRIL. An advance copy of the Stokes edition of *War Is Kind* is deposited in the British Museum with a black handstamp "**LON-DON./WILLIAM HEINEMANN**" above the New York imprint. The book is, however, not published in England (*Works*, 10: 215).

[APRIL–MAY]. Crane informs Reynolds that Stokes has been attempting to sell *Active Service* for serialization without his knowledge or permission. "I have told them that I wanted you to conduct that matter and in order to pervent confusion I send you word at the earliest possible moment" (*C*, 475).

MAY. "'God Rest Ye, Merry Gentlemen'" appears in the *Cornhill Magazine* and the *Saturday Evening Post* (6 May).

In *Harper's Magazine*, Richard Harding Davis awards Crane first place among Cuban War correspondents:

The best correspondent is probably the man who by his energy and resource sees more of the war, both afloat and ashore, than do his rivals, and who is able to make the public see what he saw. If that is a good definition, Stephen Crane would seem to have distinctly won the first place among correspondents in the late disturbance. . . . Near the close of the war, a group of correspondents in Puerto Rico made out a list of the events which, in their opinion, were of the greatest news value during the campaign, and a list of the correspondents, with the events each had witnessed credited to his name. Judged from this basis, Mr. Crane easily led all the rest. Of his power to make the public see what he sees it would be impertinent to speak. His story of Nolan, the regular, bleeding to death on the San Juan hills, is, so far as I have read, the most valuable contribution to literature that the war has produced. It is only necessary to imagine how other writers would have handled it, to appreciate that it could not have been better done. His story of the marine at Guantanamo, who stood on the crest of the hill to "wigwag" to the war-ships, and so exposed himself to the fire of the entire Spanish force, is also particularly interesting, as it illustrates that in his devotion to duty, and also in his readiness at the exciting moments of life, Crane is quite as much of a soldier as the man whose courage he described. He tells how the marine stood erect, staring through the dusk with half-closed eyes, and with his lips moving as he counted the answers from the war-ships, while innumerable bullets splashed the sand about him. But it never occurs to Crane that to sit at the man's feet, as he did, close enough to watch his lips move and to be able to make mental notes for a later tribute to the marine's scorn of fear, was equally deserving of praise. (R. H. Davis 1899, 941)

1 MAY. Crane sends Elbert Hubbard copies of two articles from the *Westminster Gazette*, "A Fishing Village" and "An Old Man Goes Wooing," for reprinting in the *Philistine*. He comments on Hubbard's "A Message to Garcia," glorifying the exploits of Andrew Summers Rowan, which had appeared untitled in the March 1899 *Philistine*:

> I have been working up some grievances against you. I object strongly to your paragraphs about Rowan. You are more wrong than is even common on our humble incompetant globe. He didn't do anything worthy at all. He received the praise of the general of the army and got to be made a lieutenant col. for a feat which about forty newspaper correspondents had already performed at the usual price of fifty dollars a week and expenses. Besides he is personally a chump and in Porto Rico where I met him he wore a yachting cap as part of his uniform which was damnable. When you want to monkey with some of our national heroes you had better ask me, because I know and your perspective is almost out of sight. (*C,* 475–476)

8 MAY. Cora invites the American writer and actress Elizabeth Robins to visit her and Stephen for a day (*C,* 479–480).

15 MAY. Crane writes to Clara Frewen: "I am an honest man above all and—according to promise—I must confess to you that on Saturday morning at 11.15—after dismal sorrow and travail—there was born into an unsuspecting world a certain novel called 'Active Service', full and complete in all its shame—79000 words.—which same is now being sent forth to the world to undermine whatever reputation for excellence I may have achieved up to this time and may heaven forgive it for being so bad" (*C,* 480–481).

Crane writes to Moreton Frewen: "If you can stay the night we will be very glad and can put you up comfortably. The ghost has been walking lately but we cannot catch him. Perhaps when the real Frewen sleeps under his roof he may condescend to display himself to all of us" (Leslie, 159).

20 MAY. Publication of *War Is Kind* is announced in *Publishers' Weekly*.

23 MAY. William Howe Crane informs Cora that his daughter Helen will sail for England on 10 June in the company of A. H. Peck and his family, Port Jervis neighbors who may be distant relatives (*C,* 482).

[LATE MAY]. Commander J. C. Colwell, naval attaché of the United States Embassy in London, and his wife are guests of the Cranes.

Crane shows him the manuscript of "The Revenge of the Adolphus" and asks him to correct the naval terminology in the story (*L*, 221n130).

27 MAY. In the *New York Times* Ashley A. Smith characterizes *War Is Kind* as "a collection of impressions, with little of rhyme or rhythm." While the book "shows some of the stronger characteristics of Mr. Crane's earlier prose work, as a poetic production it is closely akin to a genuine disappointment."

Colwell writes to Crane, returning "The Revenge of the Adolphus" with notes making the corrections for which Crane had asked (*C*, 483–485).

31 MAY. Harper and Brothers proposes a contract for a new book of Whilomville stories, adding to the four they have already purchased for *Harper's Magazine* ("Making an Orator,""The Lover and the Tell-Tale," "Lynx-Hunting," and "The Angel Child") the equivalent of 12 more stories to bring the length of the volume to 40,000 words. Conditions include first refusal of the additional stories for *Harper's Magazine*, and "if Mr. Crane fails to supply the available stories, as required, on or before Jan. 1, 1900, we shall be at liberty to include the four Whilomville stories now in our hands in the same volume with 'The Monster', 'His New Mittens', and 'The Blue Hotel', and in that case, the $250. which we propose to advance, together with the $250. which we have already advanced to Mr. Crane on account of royalty upon the volume containing "The Monster," that is to say $500. in all, is to be full payment for the American copyright in this one volume of short stories" (Copy, NhD).

JUNE. The *Book Buyer* finds fault with the design of *War Is Kind*: "Mr. Will H. Bradley has made the book according to the extremity of his fantastic taste, and the result, we think, is lamentable. The paper is so dark a grey that it is difficult to read the not very small type, and the decorative drawings are for the admiration of the few. Mr. Crane's poetry is hard enough reading—some of it—when printed most clearly; it is certainly not fair to throw mechanical difficulties in the way of deciphering it. But if one can manage to spell them out, he will find many poems of singular significance and charm."

Mrs. Ruedy returns to the United States (Gilkes 1960, 220).

1 JUNE. Reynolds responds to Harper and Brothers, indicating that Crane has accepted the conditions proposed for the volume of Whilomville stories: "Will you therefore send me at once a check for

$250.00 as Mr. Crane asked me to cable the money to him and I wish to do so to-day. I should like you to send the check up to me by messenger if you will be so kind." Harpers immediately forwards the check (Copy, NhD).

3 JUNE. Joseph Conrad and his family arrive at Brede Place for an extended visit (*C*, 485–487). Jessie Conrad recalls:

> Our small boy had now attained the age of fifteen months or so, and our next visit to Brede Place was marked by the fact that Borys took his first two or three steps all alone, down the steep bank outside the study window, in full view of his admiring friend and his proud father. The child became a regular rival to those dogs to whom Stephen had become so devoted. Time after time I have seen him raise the thin face bent low over his work and, without the least impatience, open the door for one of those spoiled animals to pass through. Then when he had almost returned to his seat he would have to repeat the performance. Sometimes, when he was too ill and languid to attend to their demands himself, he would request the old servitor (an elderly manservant who had been lent with the house) to do so. Many times I watched the solemn farce, sorely tempted to interfere. The old ruffian, his face set in the most benevolent expression, would escort the dogs to the head of the stone steps and then solemnly kick each one down the steep flight.
>
> Those dogs were the source of much tribulation in the village and were also very destructive to the sheep and lambs in the surrounding park. It happened unfortunately that Stephen either could or would not consent to pay for the damage, and the shepherd more than once threatened dire consequences. All this Stephen disregarded in a somewhat lofty manner. Then one day when we were returning from a long drive (we had been absent two days) we all gasped and held our noses as soon as the horses turned into the drive. A sheep's carcass hung from each of the four or five biggest trees bordering the drive in the park. Stephen's face turned deathly pale with anger while he muttered curses under his breath. The horses shied violently at the ghastly objects swinging on a level with their heads. Next morning when I went out the carcasses had all disappeared, and I never heard that Stephen did more than roundly curse the shepherd. (J. Conrad 1926, 136)

In the *Criterion* Rupert Hughes ("Chelifer") condemns *War Is Kind* under the title "Mr. Crane's Crazyquilting":

> What manner of joke Stephen Crane and his illustrator, Will. Bradley, had in mind when they got up their new book has not leaked out. It is in effect more Mr. Bradley's in the matter of superficies than Mr. Crane's, but Mr. Blank—(an inferential collaborator) has more in the book "War Is

Kind" than either. It is Mr. Crane's purpose to tell us that war is not kind in a thirty-line Walt Whitmian lyric, so why mislead us? To be ironical is all right, but why drive the iron in so far? We all know that war was brutal, that it killed lovers, husbands and sons, but we never thought of telling the sweethearts, wives and mothers that war, therefore, was kind.

Willa Cather makes a similar point in the *Pittsburgh Leader.* "Either Mr. Crane is insulting the public or insulting himself, or he has developed a case of atavism and is chattering the primeval nonsense of the apes. His *Black Riders,* uneven as it was, was a casket of polished masterpieces when compared with *War Is Kind.* And it is not kind at all, Mr. Crane, when it provokes such verses as these—it is all Sherman said it was" (Cather 1970, 701).

19 JUNE. Karl Edwin Harriman, a young editorial writer on the *Detroit Free Press,* introduced to the Cranes by Robert Barr, arrives at Rye Station on the same train with Helen Crane and the Pecks. Harriman confuses Mr. Peck with Wilbur F. Crane, whom he mistakenly identifies as Helen's father (Harriman 1934, 8; Wertheim 1992, 17). Harriman's first impression of Cora is that "she was dumpy, and the dumpiness was enhanced (which is not at all the word but it will do) by the costume she was wearing. This consisted of a plaid skirt and a mandarin blue smock, though in those days they called them middy blouses, I believe. On her feet were some sort of strapped sandals. . . . Her hair was the honeyist I have ever seen, and finer than any floss as real blond hair is likely to be. And Cora Crane's was real—no greenish grey at the roots. Honey all the way down and into her scalp, and through it, and on. Her eyes were just such eyes as her hair demanded. I have seen blue eyes in my time . . . but never such eyes as Cora Crane's" (Harriman 1934, 8–9).

[Harriman spent several weeks at Brede Place. He was one of the "Indians" who, according to Jessie Conrad, gratified Cora's "strange fancy for inviting people in such shoals to visit the house that even Brede Place could not accommodate them each with a bedroom. Cora therefore made the vast rooms into dormitories, and all day long a wagonette, drawn by two horses, plied between Brede Place and Rye Station for the convenience of those friends and acquaintances who might desire to call on the Cranes. I fancy Cora's idea was that this lavish hospitality would bring to Stephen much popularity; and all the while he wrote, feverishly anxious, too anxious to get the best out of himself" (J. Conrad 1926, 136). Ford Madox Ford recalls that "what made the situation really excruciating to James was the raids made by Crane's parasites on Lamb House. No doors could keep them out, nor no butler. They made hideous the still levels of the garden with their cachinations, they poked the Old Man in the ribs before his servants, caricatured his speeches before his guests and extracted from him loans that were almost never refused. There were times when he would hang about in the country outside Rye Walls rather than make such an encounter" (Ford 1931, 30–31). Joseph Conrad comments that Crane "had the misfortune to be, as the French say, *mal entouré*. He was beset by people who understood not the quality of his genius and were antagonistic to the deeper fineness of his nature. . . . I don't think he had any illusions about them himself: yet there was a strain of good-nature and perhaps of weakness in his character which prevented him from shaking himself free from their worthless and patronising attentions, which in those days caused me much secret irritation whenever I stayed with him in either of his English homes" (Conrad 1921, 69–70). At one point Conrad "ventured to say to him, 'You are too good-natured, Stephen.' He gave me one of his quiet smiles, that seemed to hint so poignantly at the vanity of all things, and after a period of silence remarked: 'I am glad those Indians are gone'" (Conrad 1923, 25–26).]

22 JUNE. Harrison S. Morris, editor of *Lippincott's Monthly Magazine*, writes Pinker to ask him to "continue to urge Mr. Crane to do the articles on the Great Battles. I do not believe he appreciates how this would sell here, both in magazine and book form. His name is identified in the American world with war and everybody would want to read and keep such a book" (NhD).

24 JUNE. Crane inscribes a copy of *War Is Kind* to Karl E. Harriman (Wertheim 1992, 17–18).

28 JUNE. Morrisons and Nightingale acknowledge Pinker's check for £37.2 for back payment of rent due on Ravensbrook (NhD).

JULY. "The Lone Charge of William B. Perkins" appears in *McClure's Magazine.*

In the *Bookman* John Curtis Underwood opines that those who admire Crane's war writing will be disappointed in *War Is Kind*:

Technically, the book is in some respects an advance on *The Black Riders*, Mr. Crane's former metrical effort. There is manifested at times, not always, a nice sense of cadence, and the colour effects where we escape from the prevailing fog are fascinating. It is this fogginess, this groping in vagueness of feeling, the natural foe of clear thought, that has doubtless permitted the insertion of such inanities as the lines about the dead knight, such crudities as the description of the successful man. And again this same mystic shadowing has wrought true art in the witchery of the desert serpent charmer.

There is no doubt that Mr. Crane has begun to arrive, but there is grave doubt about his ultimate success along these lines. Evidently he takes himself seriously, in spite of what seems occasional freakishness. There is room for his individuality in fiction—so striking a personality will always find hearers—but in the strait domain of pure poesy he can only win to greatness by a closer regard for the conventionalities of rhyme and reason that the centuries have taught us are the best. The less said of Mr. Bradley's drawings the better.

3 JULY. Cora attends the monthly meeting of the Society of American Women in London, of which she is an honorary member. She meets Lady Randolph Churchill (Gilkes 1960, 201).

[4 JULY]. The Cranes and Helen, along with Karl Harriman, Mabel and Mark Barr, and Mabel's 19-year-old sister, Edith Richie (later Mrs. I. Howland Jones), attend the Henley Regatta (E. R. Jones, 57). Harriman notes that Crane is especially impressed by the figure of "a tiny coxswain, a lad of perhaps ten," urging on the Trinity College oarsmen:

> The veins of his neck were like cords where they were like ropes on the necks of the men he urged. He swore at them like forty pirates. On the bank of Bucks we heard him. We cheered, shouted, screamed for that little coxswain. He never wavered. Curse after curse rang out. Trinity was pulling ahead. In another moment it was all over. Trinity had won. And that little ten-year-old coxswain had made it possible. The big, half-naked fellows knew this. They lifted him up, kissed him, fondled him. He lingered around the lower reach of the course on shore. Crane, taken by his actions while in the boat, sought him out. He found him, a child, buying a little tin rooster, a simple, tinsel toy, from a vender in the street of Henley. The General had become a Boy again. No further oaths fell from his lips, because no further oaths were needed.
>
> And Stephen Crane noted all this, understood the nature, the duality of nature, if you will, in that child. It impressed him. How many of the thousands who had witnessed the race would have learned anything, do you suppose, from seeing a little boy buy a tin, tinsel rooster from a street vender? (Harriman 1900, 86–87)

12 JULY. A new contract is drawn up between Crane and Methuen for the novel Crane is to write that eventually becomes *The O'Ruddy*, "'the title of which has not yet been fixed which shall extend to at

least 70,000 words,'" but, probably because there is no mention of an advance, Crane leaves the contract unsigned (Levenson 1971, xx–xxi).

14 JULY. Harrison S. Morris writes to Pinker:

> Your kind letter of July 3rd. regarding the six papers on Great Battles of the World, by Mr. Stephen Crane, is at hand, and we are pleased to learn that Mr. Crane now looks with favor on the plan. We shall cheerfully supply the books needed, through our London agent, Mr. Joseph Garmeson, 36, Southampton St. Covent Garden, with whom please communicate at once.
>
> It will be quite agreeable to us if Mr. Crane will choose the battles to be treated and we hope he can give us one of the articles in as brief a time as possible. At all events, we should like to have the assurance that they shall be speedily forthcoming, that we may announce them for next year.
>
> The price named by you: $1000. for the six articles, covering English and American magazine rights, is correct. We shall, of course, also wish to arrange for the book rights of these articles and as soon as the first one comes in, thus showing us the general style and treatment, we can then judge better what can be done. There should be no difficulty in a mutual arrangement for these rights which will be thoroughly satisfactory. (NhD)

[MID-JULY]. The Cranes invite their friends from the Henley Regatta and also A. E. W. Mason and George Lynch to a party at Brede Place, and at one point Henry James invites everyone to tea at his house in Rye. Although the party lasts for a few days, the Cranes ask Edith Richie to stay longer; she remains for five months (E. R. Jones, 57).

[Edith Richie Jones recalls that during her stay with the Cranes they frequently visited James, who "would bicycle the seven miles over to Brede at least once a week. One day Mr. James and Stephen were having a discussion about something, and Stephen was getting the better of the argument. Suddenly Mr. James said, 'How old are you?' 'Twenty-seven,' said Stephen. 'Humph,' said Mr. James, 'prattling babe!'" (E. R. Jones, 57)]

THIRD WEEK IN JULY. Crane breaks with Reynolds, and Pinker assumes complete control of his business affairs, becoming Crane's literary agent in England and America (C, 491n2).

21 JULY. Crane sends Pinker copy of "Virtue in War" (C, 490), a story originating in his Cuban War experience. In her notebook, "Things Stephen Says," Cora recalls "Story of Leuitenant of Cavelry asking for,

and insisting upon having a bottle—finally saying he wanted to write the name of his dead pal, on a piece of paper and put it in the bottle—to bury bottle with the body of his friend" (*Works*, 10: 138).

McClure secures copyright for syndication of *Active Service,* the sale probably having been made through Stokes (Bowers 1976, 352, 354).

22 JULY. In the *Saturday Evening Post* prominent essayist Agnes Repplier considers Crane the debased imitator of a decadent Walt Whitman:

> When Walt Whitman gave his Leaves of Grass to a patient and suffering world he could hardly have taken into due consideration the lasting character of bad example. He flung at the public, as the fruits of his genius, a book brimful of every literary sin, of every offense that could well be committed against good taste, good morals and good English; and the public, which is not half so stupid as its teachers would have it believe, recognized, beneath this prodigality of wrong-doing, the broken promise of a poet who missed his place among poets because he despised the beauty of words and the nobility of self-restraint.
>
> Unhappily, the evil we do refuses to descend with us into the grave, and while that which was great in Whitman defied all competition or approach, his riotous absurdities could be reproduced with deadly and destructive ease. It dawned upon eager souls that here was a kind of poetry which anybody could write, and the result of this illumination was the printing of much strange nonsense which does not seem to have been intended as a joke.
>
> Mr. Stephen Crane is the latest aspirant in the field, with a volume of weird compositions, recognizable neither as prose nor verse, and mendaciously entitled War Is Kind. . . . For debility of mind Mr. Crane is without a poetic peer. He is so easily, so utterly prostrated by modest trifles which wouldn't hurt him for the world, that when he assures us his
> "—weak heart sees specters,"
> we surmise that it is but the ghost of a parasol, or a lorgnette, or a filled petticoat which affrights him. Walt Whitman bore himself more stoutly, and squared his shoulders combatively at life. It is only in what may be called Mr. Crane's cosmic moods that he models himself on his master's most objectionable flights. It is only when he becomes intimate and confidential with the universe that we know what influence is at work. . . . There is the same deliberate misuse of words, the same social tone, as of one much at home in the welkin; the same pleasant colloquialisms to emphasize familiarity. "Lord Brougham," said Sidney Smith, "would speak disrespectfully of the equator." Mr. Crane, taught by Walt Whitman, would patronize the spheres.

24 JULY. Lady Randolph Churchill writes to Crane, requesting a contribution "on perhaps your experiences in Crete or Cuba" for her new quarterly miscellany, the *Anglo-Saxon Review* (*C*, 491).

25 JULY. The *London Daily Chronicle* publishes a letter by Crane under the title of "How Americans Make War" in which he criticizes the inability of the American army commander in the Philippines to cope with the realities of guerilla warfare. He comments that "in the meantime, a ray of light has shone through this humiliating fog. We have developed some very gratifying volunteers—and at one time this seemed impossible. The American volunteer was at one time the despair of every man who could distinguish between a good soldier and a mere brave high-minded youth" (*Works*, 9: 231).

[LATE JULY–EARLY AUGUST]. Crane dictates "Plans for New Novel" to Cora:

> Write Stokes full description of project. Ask Will and Stokes to get books on subject Rev. War. Ask Will look in Father's library and send any books devoted to the period of Rev. War. Write sec. N.J. Historical society. Make point joining N.J. historical society. Ask Will about any of Father's papers, recalling to his mind an essay which Father must have written in 1874 called, I think, "The history of an old house." Ask him to borrow the essay for me explaining that it can be typewritten and the original sent home again. Recall to Will's mind a certain book in father's library called, I think, "The N.J. historical collection." Also remind him of the life of Washington, which I believe was the property of our sister Agnes. Write letters to all the men whom I think could help me. This list to include Henry Cabot Lodge, the librarian of Princeton Col., the president of the N.J. branch of the sons of the American rev. etc. Here in England collect the best histories of that time and also learn what British regiments served in America also what officers who served published memoirs; get books if possible. This will be difficult and it will become necessary to write to various people who might know. (*Works*, 10: 158–159)

AUGUST. "The Angel Child" is the first of 13 Whilomville stories to appear in successive issues of *Harper's Magazine,* although "The Lover and the Tell-Tale" was composed first. These stories of boyhood life feature as their central character Jimmie Trescott of "The Monster" and his family and friends. Illustrations are by Peter Newell.

[1 AUGUST]. Now that Pinker is Crane's exclusive agent, Crane brings him up to date on his productions and makes a suggestion for future marketing of short stories:

My short stories are developing in three series.

I. The Whilomville stories. (always to Harpers.)

II. The war tales.

III. Tales of western American life similar to "Twelve O'Clock."

It might be well to remember this. For instance if you could provisionally establish the war tales with one magazine and the western tales with another as the Whilomville yarns are fixed with Harper's, it would be very nice. (*C,* 492)

[*Blackwood's* earlier had English rights to Crane's war stories as a consequence of his pledge made to secure the loan that funded his trip to Cuba. The magazine had published "The Price of the Harness," but had rejected "The Lone Charge of William B. Perkins," "The Clan of No-Name," and "Marines Signaling under Fire at Guantanamo." Consequently, Crane is urging Pinker to find another publisher for his series (Bowers 1970, lxxxix).]

4 AUGUST. Crane advises Pinker that he will begin research on the series of battle articles for Lippincott as soon as he has finished his war stories. "The U.S. book-r'ts of the war-stories were promised to Stokes last year when I was in America. He is to advance $1000." He mentions that Lady Churchill has asked him for a contribution for her review, and he has consented, implying that it will not go through Pinker because "it is not a commercial transaction" (*C,* 493).

Lady Churchill responds: "I have just received your letter & am very glad to think you will write for me. As regards the subject I think I would leave it to you. Would you like to give me a military story of say from 7000 to 10000 words, or if you do not care for fiction some reminiscence war, or a short essay—on a congenial subject—Perhaps you have something by you?" (*C,* 494).

6 AUGUST. Crane sends Pinker "a whacking good Whilomville Story," possibly "The Carriage-Lamps" (*C,* 494).

McClure syndication of *Active Service* begins in the *Chicago Times-Herald.*

8 AUGUST. Lady Randolph Churchill telegraphs: "Hope you will begin article at once would suggest war reminiscences Crete or Cuba six to ten thousand words am telegraphing to save time" (*C,* 495).

10 AUGUST. Crane writes to William that the controversy continues over whether Kate Lyon and the Christian Science practitioner she had called in to treat Harold Frederic contributed to his death:

As I have told you he had enemies. He did not kill himself and if his ladylove killed him she picked out one of those roundabout Sherlock Doyle ways of doing it. It is simply too easy to call a man you don't like a suicide. Mrs. Frederic loved H. maybe. She has taken precious little trouble to put him right with people since May. Neither do I much like Mr. James' manner. He professed to be er, er, er much attached to H. and now he has shut up like a clam. Do you not think that men like Robert and me who were close to H and knew how sane he was should take some trouble to shut this thing up and off? (*C*, 496)

[13 AUGUST]. Crane writes to (Arnold) Henry Sanford Bennett asking to borrow a copy of H. G. Wells's *The Wheels of Chance*. He comments on Ford Madox Ford, who had been rude to Bennett's wife: "You are wrong about Hueffer. I admit he is patronizing. He patronized his family. He patronizes Conrad. He will end up by patronizing God who will have to get used to it and they will be friends" (*C*, 497).

14 AUGUST. William writes to Cora about an indiscretion, probably theft, on the part of Helen. He is apparently under the mistaken impression that Cora is a Roman Catholic: "I have no objection to your bringing influence to bear upon Helen to make her a Catholic. Of course, it would be unfortunate to make a bigot of her. But I do not think there is any danger of that because, for one reason, if you had been a bigot, you would not have married my brother Stephen" (*C*, 500).

[MID-AUGUST]. Crane writes to an unidentified correspondent named "John," perhaps John Scott Stokes: "Please have the kindness to keep your mouth shut about my health in front of Mrs. Crane hereafter. She can do nothing for me and I am too old to be nursed. It is all up with me but I will not have her scared. For some funny woman's reason, she likes me. Mind this" (*C*, 504).

23 AUGUST. A garden party is held in the rectory garden of the Brede village church for the benefit of the parish and the District Nursing Association. Cora's rummage booth is one of the main attractions, and Crane in white flannels and straw hat carries potted plants to the carriages of lady purchasers. Edith Richie in Gipsy costume dispenses love potions and tells fortunes. George Lynch, one of the Cranes' summer guests, snaps photos at sixpence a shot. One he takes of Henry James, squinting with the sun in his eyes while eating one of the doughnuts made by Cora's cook, Vernall, is among a group of

Henry James at the garden party in the rectory
of the Brede village church, 23 August 1899
(*Columbia University*)

photographs she sends him as souvenirs of the occasion (*South Eastern Advertiser*, 26 August; Gilkes 1960, 205). In his letter of thanks (28
August), James quips: "All thanks for the strange images, which I
never expected to behold. They form a precious momento of a romantic hour. But no, surely, it can't be any doughnut of yours that is
making me make such a gruesome grimace. I look as if I had swal-
lowed a wasp, or a penny toy. And I tried to look so beautiful. I tried
too hard doubtless. But don't show it to any one as H. J. trying"
(NNC).

25 AUGUST. George Bernard Shaw sends Cora £5 toward her fund for the Frederic children, although he insists that his "impulse is to repudiate all extra orphans with loud execration" (NNC).

[26 AUGUST]. Crane writes to the secretary of the New Jersey Historical Society: "I am about to attempt a novel upon Revolutionary times in the Province of New Jersey, and I would be very glad if you could tell me the titles of some of the books on the manners and customs of the times in the Province. I am particularly interested in Elizabethtown, and I would be much obliged and gratified if you could give me the title of a good history of that city" (*C*, 505).

27 AUGUST. Conrad writes to Cora, asking whether the Cranes could delay a scheduled visit to Pent Farm until late September because Jessie is suffering from neuralgia. He acknowledges receipt of £15, payment toward Crane's share of a sailboat that he and Crane had bought earlier in the summer from Captain G. F. W. Hope (*C*, 506). Later, Jessie Conrad wrote, "We had bought the boat, *La Reine*, from Mr. Hope on the understanding that Stephen and my husband were to be joint owners, and half the time we kept it in Folkestone and the other half of the time Stephen had her in Rye. But he had never paid his half-share, and his wife's proposition was that she should allow their local wood merchant to take her over in payment for their wood account" (J. Conrad 1935, 74–75).

29 AUGUST. Crane writes to (Arnold) Henry Sanford Bennett:

> The thin man is a Bassett Holmes. He does look like Hueffer. Comes I think from Cornwall somewhere. Met him in a whorehouse in New York when we were kids. The other fellow is a friend of Karl Harriman. Ghost of an idea what he does, is, or goes to. Sorry Miss Bennett was so bored. About Wilde and his troubles a mere stranger and runaway dog like me can't be supposed to care. I met him once. We stood and looked at each other and he bleated like a sheep. With those bad manners that are so awfully much mine I laughed in his face. He tried to borrow money from Dick Davis when he was being tried after insulting Davis all across London. Something pretty poor in him. And I owe my brothers too much money to bother about helping with subscriptions for a mildewed chump like Wilde. Blood, etc. If Harris and the rest of Wilde's friends really want to help him they ought to send him express to Weir Mitchell or some specialist in his kind of malady. Perhaps it is because I lived on borrowed money and ate in lunch-wagons when I was trying to be someone that these magnified sinners in good duds bore me so. That isn't what Conrad

would call a sentiment of generosity but it is mine. If Conrad has any French blood in him I don't know of it. He is, I think, a pure Polish gent.

Tea at James's. My God how does he stand those bores who pester him. Mrs. Humphrey Ward was there. What an old cow! She has no more mind than a president. Nice to us, though. Feeling vile. Am asked to lecture on the 20th. Hoot, mon! Robert says I ought to. All I ought to do right now is pay some of my debts. My charities begin in the right pants pocket. (*C*, 507)

31 AUGUST. Cora writes to Pinker, pleading for money. Crane is hastening to finish the war stories, working on *Active Service*, and finishing a Whilomville story, "The Knife." The local wine dealer threatens a lawsuit if his bill for £35 is not paid immediately. She renews a request to Pinker for an advance of £20 "to enable Mr. Crane to take a few days holiday. This would be to take his niece to Lausanne where she is to go to school and to stay a few days there" (*C*, 508).

SEPTEMBER. "Lynx-Hunting" is published in *Harper's Magazine*.

3 SEPTEMBER. William Howe Crane writes to Cora regarding Helen's proposed schooling at the Rosemont-Dézaley School in Lausanne. He suggests that Cora warn Helen "that an indulgence in her indifference to the property rights of others might possibly land her in the police-court" (*C*, 511).

5 SEPTEMBER. Frederick A. Stokes reacts with indignation to Crane's attempt to cancel his contract for the book of Cuban War stories because Stokes refuses to send an advance royalty before the completed manuscript is received (*C*, 513–514).

6 SEPTEMBER. Henry James inscribes a copy of an unidentified book, probably *The Awkward Age*, to Crane (*C*, 515).

[10 SEPTEMBER]. Crane writes to George Wyndham, asking "what do you know about the Black Forest there? I mean as a health resort? The truth is that Cuba libre just about liberated me from this base blue world. The clockwork is juggling badly. I have had a lot of idiotic company all summer" (*C*, 515).

Conrad renews his plea that the Cranes visit Pent Farm later in the month: "Could you not come? You would make me happy. And will you pardon me for not coming to you. Dear Stephen I am like a damned paralyzed mud turtle. I can't move. I can't write. I can't do anything. But I can be wretched, and, by God! I am!" (*C*, 516). Crane, however, is immersed in writing Whilomville stories and cannot make the visit.

14 SEPTEMBER. Pinker advises Crane that he has sold American serial rights of "The Second Generation" to the *Saturday Evening Post* for £60 (*C*, 517).

[MID-SEPTEMBER]. Crane sets forth to take Helen to Lausanne. They are accompanied by Cora, George Lynch, and Edith Richie. After a party and an overnight stay at Folkestone with Mr. and Mrs. H. G. Wells, they travel to Paris. Edith Richie Jones recalls:

> We four stayed at the old Hôtel Louis le Grand, and Mr. Lynch went off on his own. The first night we were there, after we had all gone to bed, a note arrived from him saying he was going to fight a duel and he wanted Stephen to come at once and be his second. Stephen thought it was just one of George's jokes and refused to go. But early next morning the Wild Irishman appeared, arm in arm with a delightful Frenchman, whose other arm was in a sling!
> Cora and I were alone in Paris for a couple of days while Stephen took Helen to Lausanne. We saw the sights and window-shopped. Stephen returned and immediately did a lot of writing. One morning a page of his manuscript was missing and there was wild excitement in the hotel while chambermaids came into our rooms and emptied wastepaper baskets all over the place to see if the page had been thrown away by accident. It was not found and Stephen had to rewrite it.
> We met various friends in Paris and had a gay time, with lunches, dinners, theaters, cafés-chantants, and sightseeing. We had meant to stay quite a while, but suddenly we all got homesick for Brede and the dogs and decided to go home. All the time we were away, both Cora and Stephen got small pieces of candy from penny-in-the-slot machines and mailed them home to the dogs. (E. R. Jones, 59–60)

With Christmas in the offing, Edith Richie tells the Cranes that she must soon return home: "'No,' said Stephen. 'Let's have a real party. We'll have all your family here and your friends and our friends. It will be your party. We'll have a ball and a play.' 'What play?' asked Cora and I. 'Oh, you two can make up some sort of play and I'll get a lot of friends to send a scene or a sentence or even a word that you can work into it. Then we can say they wrote it.' That was how *The Ghost* was born" (E. R. Jones, 61).

[The decision to center the play on the ghost of Sir Goddard Oxenbridge and his encounter with some tourists at Brede, however, was Crane's, as was most of the writing. He requested nine of his literary friends to participate, if only nominally, in the creation of the farce by contributing a scene, a sentence, a phrase, or even a word.]

Crane dictates to Cora a more detailed outline of his proposed Revolutionary War novel headed "Plans for Story":

> Possible opening chapter, Time 1775—scene an Inn at Elizabeth N.J. People talking over the situation. Their attitude. Strong Tory element. Patriots bitter. Loud words. Their denunciation by old Stephen Crane. . . . Make picture of marching British army as it passed Stephen Crane's house when he lay dying. Battle of Monmouth probably central dramatic scene. Find out if Lord Chatham's speeches were known in colonies soon after deliverance. Read Fenimore Cooper's "Spy." . . . Might have young Howard Crane off to sea with John Paul Jones and let him turn up in last few chapters as a sort of benign influence. Study carefully the mood of the N.J. people with the idea that they were not very keen upon rebellion, showing great influence of Crane family in carrying the revolution through. . . . Read D^r. Weir Mitchell's last book. In describing battle of Monmouth discard the Mollie Pitcher story as being absurd and trivial. . . . Introduce Henry Fleming's grand-father as first farmer. (*Works*, 10: 159–160)

21 SEPTEMBER. Pinker reassures Crane, who had sent a worried telegram, that "Virtue in War," the American serial rights of which were sold to Tillotson's newspaper syndicate, and "The Second Generation" are not different titles for the same story (*C*, 517).

[Crane's confusion between "Virtue in War" and "The Second Generation" reflects his practice of rapid composition at this time, but in part his bewilderment may have been the result of the change of his original title, "The Making of the 307th," to "West Pointer and Volunteer; Or, Virtue in War" for magazine publication. (The story appears simply as "Virtue in War" in *Wounds in the Rain*.) Despite Pinker's reassurance, Crane remained concerned that "Virtue in War" and "The Second Generation" were the same story.]

22 SEPTEMBER. Crane sends Pinker the signed contract with Frederick A. Stokes Company for the American edition of his proposed Revolutionary War novel. He mentions that he has just completed another Whilomville story, "The Stove," and fears that Harper and Brothers have underestimated the length of one of two previous Whilomville stories, "The Carriage-Lamps" or "The Knife," and consequently paid too little for it (*C*, 518–519).

Stephen Crane in his study at Brede Place, September 1899.
The inscription is in Cora's hand
(Barrett Collection, University of Virginia)

23 SEPTEMBER. Frederick A. Stokes writes Crane urging him to expand his book of Cuban War stories in order to make it saleable:

> Of course, you understand clearly that we really did not care for this volume of short stories *in itself* at all, and feel that we shall lose money in its publication,—simply because it *is* a volume of short stories, and will not make a popular volume at best. We rely on you therefore to make the volume as large as possible, and to thus remove one of the obstacles in the way of sales,—on your own account, as well as ours.
>
> We are taking the volume solely because of your agreement to give us

the long novel of the American Revolution and that we are to be your "regular publishers."

Stokes protests Crane's continual demands for advance payments and reluctance to accommodate his books to the requirements of the publishing trade:

> You do not quite seem to appreciate, also, the fact that we have no easy task before us in trying to rehabilitate the commercial standing of your work in book form.
>
> If we should show you quotations from the letters of our traveling salesmen, showing that for some reason or other the leading houses in the trade throughout the country have a strong prejudice against you and your work, you would we think have a little more consideration for us.
>
> We do not care to discuss the reasons for this prejudice, and whether it is just or unjust, except that it is probably due to the comparative failure of your books since "The Red Badge of Courage" and to newspaper attacks on you, with which the writer certainly has no sympathy.
>
> Ever since he met you he has had a desire to become your "Regular Publisher", and to do all within reason to please and satisfy you. He is not discouraged, either, by the circumstances that he has just described, or by your recent cablegrams and letters,—although the latter seem to him to be unjust and unreasonable.
>
> If, however, you do not care to assist him by making your books suited to the demands of the trade in the matter of length, etc., he will be forced to feel that if you can neglect your own interests in this way, he will have to give up the struggle against what will then be altogether too many adverse conditions. (*C*, 523)

In a letter to Cora, A. E. W. Mason responds to Crane's request for a contribution to "The Ghost": "I shall be very pleased to come to you from the 26th to the 30th of December. Also I will certainly do anything for the theatrical entertainment. I will be pleased to write a scene, and act in it if you like and help in any way as regards the stage-management" (NNC). With a subsequent undated letter, Mason sends his conception of the final act of the farce, but the enclosure has not survived, so the extent of Mason's contribution is not known.

[LATE SEPTEMBER]. Cora Crane recalls, "One I said to him, 'Why not write a popular novel for money something that everyone will read?' He turned on me & said: 'I will write for one man & banging his fist on writing table & that man shall be myself etc etc'" (*Works*, 10: 344).

26 SEPTEMBER. Crane writes to Moreton Frewen:

Before I had finished the article for Lady Churchill I was obliged to take my niece to Switzerland to school, and on my return to Brede Place I had a slight attack of Cuban fever and am still seedy. We are getting along happily at dear old Brede; the ghost is behaving himself though the doors open in the same uncanny way.

As to Mack leaving us; the old man found it too much out of the world for him. He missed his usual talk at the tavern we think. We were all very fond of him and he seemed fond of us but when he said that he thought he had better go we did not try to keep him. You see it is impossible for us to keep all beer and drink under lock and key and the old man was tempted two or three times to take a bit too much. With lamps and the open fires it gave me an anxiety for the safety of your old house. You will remember we had one fire though this fact had nothing to do with it; it took place at 7:30 A.M.

You have been very kind to me about rent. I've had a hard year of it settling my affairs which are nearly in shape now. I have taken advantage of your kindness to keep you waiting until almost the last. Next month I can send you a cheque. Will it be convenient for you to wait until then? I hope this next year to do more for the place than I have been able to do this. (*C*, 524)

[The mysterious opening of doors at Brede, especially those to the haunted room, was evidently caused by defective latches. Edith Richie, who slept in the room, describes it as having three doors: "When I went up to dress for dinner, I would carefully close each door. A moment later I would look fearsomely over my left shoulder. Door number one would be open. Then, over my right shoulder, door number two open and, a little further to the right, door number three. I always turned slowly and always had the same spooky feeling. But the doors, I knew, were not really bewitched. They all had old slippery wooden latches which had to be pegged to stay shut" (E. R. Jones, 59). Mark Barr, an American industrial technician whose wife, Mabel, was Edith Richie's sister, also slept in the haunted room. He remembers it as having only one door, and when he slept there he took a scientific approach to the problem: "I noticed that when a strong gust came the latch clicked and the door swung open! On examination I found that the iron rider-piece of the very old latch had been so worn down by the blade that the holding-detent was less than a thirty-second of an inch deep. Also, I found that if unlatched and not held, the door swung open of itself." Barr repaired the latch so that the ghost would walk no more (Wertheim 1976b, 58).]

[FALL–WINTER]. Crane and Mark Barr play a practical joke on Henry James. Barr chemically treats firewood so that James, "seeing colored flames in the ingle-nook fireplace, would think it was ship-timber!" (Wertheim 1976b, 57)

[28 SEPTEMBER]. Crane writes to Pinker, sending the typescript of a Whilomville story, "The Trial, Execution, and Burial of Homer Phelps," and remarking that he is "getting serious" about the possibility of Boer War correspondence. He asks Pinker to see if he can find an assignment for him (*C*, 525).

29 SEPTEMBER. Crane writes to the War Office to apply for a visa as a correspondent to report the Boer War (C, 527, 527n2).

30 SEPTEMBER. Crane writes to Pinker: "I cannot express how worried I am over 'Virtue in War' and 'The Second Generation.' I can only remember writing *one* story and I would almost bet the two titles cover one story. We may be making a hideous blunder. Please find out" (*C*, 526).

Lady Churchill writes to Crane from Scotland that she was in such haste to get his manuscript to London to be set up that she sent it off without reading it. She now hears from her secretary "that owing to some lengthy articles set up in pages—before yours arrived—your article will have to be curtailed some 2000 words" (Copy, Wertheim Collection).

The War Office advises Crane that licenses for war correspondents are granted only to editors of newspapers "who then pass them to the authorised correspondents and are held accountable for their observing the rules; so you had better get your editor to apply on your behalf " (*C*, 527).

The *Saturday Evening Post* prints Crane's story "The Serjeant's Private Mad-House" with an illustration by Howard Chandler Christy.

[30 SEPTEMBER]. Cora thanks Pinker for advising Crane "*not* to go to the Transvaal. His health is not fit for it. He had a return of Cuban fever while we were in Paris and he is in no physical condition to stand a campaign no matter how short it may be." She cautions, "Please dont let Mr. Crane know I've said a word against the Transvaal" (*C*, 527–28).

OCTOBER. "The Lover and the Tell-Tale" appears in *Harper's Magazine*.

Charles Whibley inscribes a copy of *A Book of Scoundrels* to Crane "with the regard of his confrère" (*C*, 551n1).

1 OCTOBER. Crane sends Pinker a typescript of "The Battle of Forty Fort," the first of a series of three posthumously published Wyoming Valley (Pennsylvania) tales dealing with the struggles of settlers against Tories and Indians during the Revolutionary War. The primary source for these stories was George Peck's *Wyoming: Its History, Stirring Incidents and Romantic Adventures* (1858), two copies of which were in Crane's Brede Place library (*C*, 528, 528n1).

2 OCTOBER. Robert Barr writes to Crane analyzing the reasons for the misunderstanding between Crane and Stokes over the advance on *Wounds in the Rain*, for which he believes Crane is at fault, and advises him in the future to leave business communications to Pinker (*C*, 529–532). Crane readily follows this advice.

4 OCTOBER. Robert McClure writes to Pinker to arrange a convenient date for publication of "This Majestic Lie" and two days later proposes a price of £78.15 for the story, although he cannot make payment immediately (NhD). But there is no known serial publication in England, and "This Majestic Lie" is serialized in the United States only posthumously.

[EARLY OCTOBER]. The Cranes and Edith Richie take a short vacation trip to Ireland. After three days in London, where they are entertained by the Frewens and others, they travel from Cork to Ballydehob, Skibbereen, Schull, Bantry, and Glengariff (E. R. Jones, 60). Edith Richie suggests that one purpose of this trip was to gather background material for *The O'Ruddy*, but only the initial two paragraphs of the novel are set in Ireland.

7 OCTOBER. Copyright deposit of *Active Service* is made in the Library of Congress.

9 OCTOBER. Frederick A. Stokes writes to Pinker:

> We have just received instructions from Stephen Crane, Esqr., that our correspondence regarding his affairs with us shall in the future be conducted with you.
> We are very much gratified that this is to be the case.
> We have just made to him an advance payment for a volume of short stories of the Spanish-American War.
> He has promised to send us more copy for this book, and to give us its title, which has not as yet been fixed.
> We have contracted with him for a long novel of the American Revolu-

tion, to follow the short stories above mentioned, and for first offer of following work.

We are to make him advance payments on this novel on the receipt of each instalment.

We mention these details for your guidance, and shall appreciate it very much if you will secure the additional copy and title for the volume of short stories, and send them to us as soon as possible, together with word as to the date of publication of this book.

Undoubtedly you can secure information as to other details connected with the long novel from Mr. Crane, or we shall be pleased to send them to you whenever you wish it.

We regret that our correspondence with Mr. Crane seems to have been mutually unsatisfactory, and we are very glad, for this reason, to deal with you in the matter in the future. (NN-Berg)

A subsequent undated letter specifies: "As to the novel on the American Revolution, we are to pay £200. in installments, as the copy is received, and on receipt of the copy another £100, the £200. being in advance of royalties on the novel alone, and the £100. being chargeable to Mr Crane's account as against royalties in general" (NN-Berg).

10 OCTOBER. Lady Randolph Churchill advises Crane that publication of "War Memories" in the *Anglo-Saxon Review* will be postponed until the December issue (*C*, 533).

14 OCTOBER. *Active Service* is listed in *Publishers' Weekly*. The novel bears a dedication to "E. A.," Eben Alexander.

Robert Barr writes to Cora, declining the invitation to participate in the Cranes' Christmas party and play: "I should like very much to go to your castle, but the more I think of your dramatic house party, the more the frozen horror of the situation comes over me. It is all very well for young people to face either war or the amature drama with equanimity, but for me I have not the courage. I loathe a crowd anyhow, and the only advantage war has over the amature drama is that in a battle you may shoot the amature actors from the other side, while the strict etiquette of cold British society frowns on any attempt to eliminate the heartless, merciless mob who take part in a country house play" (*C*, 534)

15 OCTOBER. An article by Crane dealing with a minor insurgent against the French government, falsely dated 4 October from Paris and headed "France's Would-be Hero," appears in the *New York Journal* and the *San Francisco Examiner*.

[21 OCTOBER]. Cora urges Pinker to continue sending payments for stories to Crane even if he has not himself as yet collected them from the publishers: "Mr. Crane is now sending *everything* he writes to you and so cannot get any money from any other place on account of things written or to be written. It must be painful to you now but in the long run you will benefit as there *is* a market for anything Mr. Crane writes as you know." Summing up various monies due Crane, she mentions that there must be at least £50 due from John Lane, publisher of the *Anglo-Saxon Review,* for "War Memories," forgetting Crane's earlier assurance to Pinker that he was not being paid for the contribution. Pinker is also in possession of the Wyoming stories and the Western story "Moonlight on the Snow," none of which has been sold. Cora encloses the first two chapters of *The O'Ruddy* and suggests that "it will make a popular success & a *good play* (*C,* 537–538).

24 OCTOBER. Pinker acknowledges receipt of "The Fight" and the opening pages of *The O'Ruddy.* He expresses concern over Crane's insistent demands for money: "I confess that you are becoming most alarming. You telegraphed on Friday for £20; Mrs. Crane, on Monday, makes it £50; today comes your letter making it £150, and I very much fear that your agent must be a millionaire if he is to satisfy your necessities a week hence, at this rate. Seriously, you pinch me rather tightly. Mrs. Crane says I have 'probably advanced money to Mr. Crane that I have not myself yet collected.' As a matter of fact, this sum, at present, is £230. I mention this to impress you less with an obligation to me than to yourself. There is a risk of spoiling the market if we have to dump too many short stories on it at once." He urges Crane to write the battle articles for *Lippincott's Magazine* as a way of raising money (*C,* 539–540).

25 OCTOBER. Lady Churchill sends Crane £52.10 in payment for "War Memories" (*C,* 540).

[26 OCTOBER]. Cora writes to Pinker renewing her importunities for money: "Now Mr. Pinker, how could you say to Mr. Crane not to dump too many short stories upon the market for fear of spoiling it? This is a fatal thing to say to a writing man. Particularly to Stephen Crane. And how can you think so with an utterly unspoiled and vast American market? Harpers and the Saturday Evening Post and one story to McClures are the only things sold in America *now* and you could sell a thousand short stories of Mr. Cranes there if you had them." She advises Pinker that he will have the first of the battle articles for *Lippincott's* by 10

November and asks him to inquire if Stokes will accept *The O'Ruddy*, entitled "Romance" at this point, in place of the novel on the American Revolution for which Crane had contracted (*C*, 541–542).

28 OCTOBER. "The Revenge of the *Adolphus*" appears in *Collier's Weekly*. The first English publication in December is Crane's only appearance in the *Strand Magazine*.

[30 OCTOBER]. Cora sends Pinker a typescript of "The City Urchin and the Chaste Villagers" and promises to send another Whilomville story, "A Little Pilgrim," in four days. She comments that one of the *Lippincott's* articles is nearly completed (*C*, 542–543).

NOVEMBER. *Harper's Magazine* publishes another Whilomville story, "Showin' Off," and "Virtue in War" appears in *Frank Leslie's Popular Monthly*.

2 NOVEMBER. The British Museum receives deposit copy of the first English edition of *Active Service*.

4 NOVEMBER. Crane sends Pinker a typescript of "The Upturned Face," which he calls "a double extra special good thing." He is sending a copy to the actor Sir Johnston Forbes-Robertson in the hope that he will be convinced "that in a thirty minute sketch on the stage he could so curdle the blood of the British public that it would be the sensation of the year, of the time." He admonishes Pinker to write him whenever he has made a sale. "For instance the information that you had sold 'The Second Generation' to the Cornhill magazine was conveyed to me when I recieved the proofs. It is only a matter of a few pounds but anyhow it was pleasant to know it and I might have had the pleasure earlier." He concludes, "I have collected about a ton of information on the Battle of New Orleans and the article is now a mere matter of putting together these volumnuous notes in their most dramatic form and this I shall manage within a few days" (*C*, 543–544).

William Howe Crane writes to Cora that included in the funds for Helen's schooling he has mailed to Madame Eytel-Hübbé, the proprietress of the Rosemont-Dézaley school, was the sum of "thirty francs that Stephen borrowed of the Madame, when he took Helen there," referring apparently to money that Helen had extorted from her schoolmistress under the pretext that it was a loan for her uncle Stephen (*C*, 545, 545n1).

7 NOVEMBER. William Howe Crane writes to Stephen and Cora in regard to Helen's schooling and her epistolary flirtation with a young man. He asks, "Will you send to Helen and charge to me a copy of Addison's Spectator? I do not know of any reading that inculcates a love of truth more effectively, unless it may be 'The Deerslayer.'" He has also asked Crane's brother George, who lives in Newark, for a book on the history of New Jersey about which Crane has inquired to aid in his Revolutionary War research (*C,* 546).

11 NOVEMBER. The first English edition of *Active Service* is listed in the *Publishers' Circular.*

The *Athenaeum* criticizes the faulty grammar and use of Americanisms in *Active Service,* but considers the characterizations "admirably sketched and sustained," while the *Spectator* finds the plot of the novel "ingenious and entertaining."

In the *Pittsburgh Leader* Willa Cather disparages *Active Service:* "every page is like the next morning taste of a champagne supper, and is heavy with the smell of stale cigarettes. There is no fresh air in the book and no sunlight, only the 'blinding light shed by the electric globes.' . . . It is a grave matter for a man in good health and with a bank account to have written a book so coarse and dull and charmless as *Active Service.* Compared with this 'War was kind' indeed" (Cather 1970, 704–705).

15 NOVEMBER. Crane solicits a contribution for "The Ghost" from H. B. Marriott-Watson:

Dear Mr Marriott Watson:
   We of Brede Place are giving a free play to the villagers at Christmas time in the school-house and I have written some awful rubbish which our friends will on that night speak out to the parish.
   But to make the thing historic, I have hit upon a plan of making the programmes choice by printing thereon a terrible list of authors of the comedy and to that end I have asked Henry James, Robert Barr, Joseph Conrad, A. E. W. Mason, H. G. Wells, Edwin Pugh, George Gissing, Rider Haggard and yourself to write a mere word—any word "it", "they", "you",—any word and thus identify themselves with this crime.
   Would you be so lenient as to give me the word in your hand writing and thus appear in print on the programme with this distinguished rabble. (*C,* 548–549)

16 NOVEMBER. In an unsigned review in the *Nation* Thomas Wentworth Higginson concludes that his prediction that Crane's poems

subsequent to *The Black Riders* would be merely imitative has been fulfilled.

17 NOVEMBER. Rider Haggard sends Crane a note, "Good luck to your playing!" that is either his contribution to "The Ghost" or a cover to the contribution (*C,* 551).

Charles Whibley declines Crane's invitation to attend the Christmas festivities at Brede Place but acknowledges having just gotten a copy of *Active Service* and looks forward to seeing Crane again to "renew our pleasant talk, & by god we will" (*C,* 551).

18 NOVEMBER. H. B. Marriott-Watson sends Crane a puzzle consisting of five words written on individual pieces of paper pasted on his letter. When deciphered they read, "Most publishers are d——d fools" (*C,* 552, 552n1).

Robert Barr sends Crane a long poem for "The Ghost" entitled "The Tiresome Ghost of Somberly Hall, Sussex," a burlesque of Edwin Markham's poem "The Man with the Hoe" (Crisler, 83–84).

In the *Saturday Evening Post,* Kenneth Herford, a guest at Brede Place, describes the manor, which he believes was built in the thirteenth century:

> It nestles on the side of a hill, covered with ivy and surrounded with flowers. . . . There is the chapel, the tower with the haunted chamber, the falconry, and the great dining-hall where the lord of the manor was one day wont to sit above the salt. All underneath the house run passages pierced with "monk holes" where it was the custom to hide the household priests upon the approach of a party of Cromwell's men. And away up under the roof is the gallows where "hanged so many goodly men and true."
>
> For three hundred years there have been no alterations made in the house. The drawing-room is black oak, carved to the ceiling, and throughout the furniture is in keeping, Mrs. Crane having discovered an old man in Sussex who for years has collected ancient bits of furniture and sold them off again with no appreciation of their value or their beauty.
>
> The dining-room with its great fireplace, thirteen feet in width, bordered with stone brought years ago from France, is strewn with rushes to-day just as it was in years gone by, and dinner there is a sort of genii that carries you backward to another age. It is up in a room in the tower that the stories are written. The table is old, very old, and of black oak. The fire-dogs upon the hearth have seen years and years. On the shelves are piled books to the ceiling. It is interesting to note the authors represented. (Herford, 413)

The *New York Times* reviewer questions "whether the author of 'Active Service' himself really sees anything remarkable in his newspapery hero. One is half inclined to think that all the time Mr. Stephen Crane is laughing at his principal personage, and that the book itself is a satire on current 'yellow journalism.'"

20 NOVEMBER. The *Argonaut* (San Francisco) believes that Crane's best work is that which is purely imaginative, and when he "attempts to make books of the life in which he lives, he becomes uninteresting." In *Active Service* the love affair "is tiresome, through the unreality of the personages. They are all vulgarians masquerading in the guise of their betters. Perhaps Mr. Crane paints people as faithfully as he does inanimate objects, but if that be so, one can not envy him his associates, nor does one care to meet them in his books" (Weatherford, 244).

George Gissing sends Crane his contribution to "The Ghost": "He died of an indignity caught in running after his hat down Piccadilly" (*C*, 554, 554n1).

[Another short contribution, "The Ghost: This is a jolly cold world," is preserved, along with the others, in Cora Crane's "Brede Place Scrapbook" at ViU. It is unsigned, but Cora's note "Joseph Conrad's handwriting" identifies its author. Edwin Pugh sent an ironic comment based upon a familiar proverb: "A bird in the hand *may* be worth two in the bush, but the birds in the bush don't think so" (Crisler, 82, 83n22).]

24 NOVEMBER. The *Westminster Gazette* praises *Active Service*: "The work is of such admirable quality, the incidents are handled with so much skill, the descriptive writing is so clear and vivid and yet so restrained, and on the proper occasion shows such an original humour, that the reader who cares for good literature can only be grateful for what is given him."

[NOVEMBER–DECEMBER]. Elaborate preparations are made for the performance of "The Ghost" and the ball that follows the evening afterward. Edith Richie Jones remembers:

> Cora and I worked like dogs before the party—sending out invitations, hiring extra servants from London. The play had to be written and typed, each of us typing with two fingers. Music had to be copied and new words written for each song. I painted the scenery: the huge fireplace in the hall was the backdrop. Guest rooms had to be arranged for married couples. Erstwhile big empty rooms fixed up as dormitories, one for

men, one for women. An orchestra had to be engaged, cots hired from a local hospital. Cora got the village blacksmith to make dozens of iron brackets, each holding two candles, to hang around the oak-paneled walls of the hall. We made long ropes of holly and greenery and festooned them around the walls. We wrote on cards who-should-take-in-whom to dinner every evening, and put them near each guest's bed. (E. R. Jones, 61)

DECEMBER. "Making an Orator," a Whilomville story with autobiographical overtones, appears in *Harper's Magazine*. Jimmie Trescott struggles unsuccessfully through a school recitation of "The Charge of the Light Brigade," not realizing that "on this day there had been laid for him the foundation of a finished incapacity for public speaking which would be his until he died."

"The Second Generation" is printed in the *Cornhill Magazine* and in the *Saturday Evening Post* (2 December). An abridged version of "War Memories" appears in the *Anglo-Saxon Review*. "Twelve O'Clock," another tale that, like "Moonlight on the Snow," deals with the passing of the Old West, is published in the *Pall Mall Magazine*. "An Episode of War," a Civil War story, appears in the Christmas issue of the *Gentlewoman*.

Book News views Crane as out of his metier in *Active Service*: "A battlefield stands Mr. Crane's descriptive staccato. A newspaper office does not. So far as the reader goes, the result is a story which opens with interest and closes with confused dull talk and incident."

1 DECEMBER. Stokes writes to Pinker, asking for the book title of Crane's Cuban War stories and for the proposed date of publication, but he does not receive the information, prompting him to request it again on 29 December (NhD).

2 DECEMBER. Copyright deposit of *The Monster and Other Stories* is made in the Library of Congress.

5 DECEMBER. Stokes writes to Crane, asking him to write the advertising copy for his volume of Cuban War stories (NhD).

7 DECEMBER. Crane writes to Colles, asking for the return of the manuscript of "A Dark Brown Dog," an early story that he is now attempting to market so that he can revise it (*C*, 556). "A Dark Brown Dog" was published posthumously in *Cosmopolitan* (March 1901).

Cora informs Pinker that Crane has suspended work on *The O'Ruddy* and longer short stories so that he can "return to short stuff which will bring in money at once." She asks "whether there is any one in London who would do an american Military Play," a reference to a two-act play on the Cuban War that Crane has written (*C*, 557, 557n1).

Cora, on behalf of Stephen, writes to Charles Woodruff Woolley, Sr., an elderly Buffalo genealogist, attempting to establish some sort of noble or aristocratic Sussex descent for the Crane family (*C*, 559).

9 DECEMBER. *The Monster and Other Stories* is announced in *Publishers' Weekly*. The English edition, with four previously uncollected stories added, is not published until February 1901.

14 DECEMBER. The *London Morning Post* reviews *Active Service*, describing it as "a cheerful story full of the invincible optimism of America" and "a capital book for a foggy day."

16 DECEMBER. The *Dial* considers Active Service an improvement over "that study in chromatic emotion, *The Red Badge of Courage*, and of the ineffectual pieces of realism by which it was followed. . . . It is, then, with considerable surprise that we find in 'Active Service' a novel which, while not exactly meritorious according to a serious standard, is at least readable and entertaining, by virtue of having a real story to tell, and of telling it with much effectiveness." The *Outlook* concedes that "the novel is clever and brilliant; it is life, more or less, and is full of effective pages. But with all this it is not fine art. The fact is we have learnt to demand more from Mr. Crane than *Active Service* gives us."

[18 DECEMBER]. Cora advises Pinker that "The Storming of Badajoz," the second in the "Great Battles of the World" series, will be sent to him at the end of the week (*C*, 558).

19 DECEMBER. Woolley writes an irritated reply to Crane's request for genealogical information: "We did not know that our Stephen Crane 1*st* was a descendant of Sir George Carteret. . . . We have read of the Townleys having been allied with Royalty, but paid no attention to it, as were not particularly interested in 'Royal Blood'—in 'Coat of Arms', 'Crests' and 'Quarterings'—but our investigations were only for 'family history' and especially that of our ancestors Stephen Crane 1*st* of Essex Co. N.J." (*C*, 559).

22 DECEMBER. William Howe Crane writes to Cora that he has "paid Stephen's debt to Madame Hübbe because she wrote that Stephen had borrowed it through Helen." He does not feel he can afford to

send his daughter Agnes to join her sister at the Rosemont school, which Cora evidently has proposed, and he insists that the Port Jervis schools are adequate. He believes that there is a "false quantity" in some of the letters that Cora has sent to Helen, "when you say to her that Port Jervis could not teach her this or that. The fault is with her, or rather, was with her. The superintendent of our schools is a finished scholar and gentlemen and a scientific educator. But Helen was so indolent in her studies, careless in her choice of associates and so persistent in her ways, that your invitation came as a god-send. She needed a tremendous moral and intellectual awakening and I think she is getting it. I am not defending Port Jervis. I am telling you facts, in order that you may fully understand Helen's case" (*C*, 561–562).

23 DECEMBER. *Literary Digest* finds the title story of *The Monster and Other Stories* "an interesting study in hysteria and sinister terror. It is thought to be one of his [Crane's] strongest and most dramatic efforts."

25 DECEMBER. A traditional American Christmas dinner party is held at Brede Place. The guests include A. E. W. Mason and probably the Mark Barrs and Edith Richie's parents (Gilkes 1960, 223).

26–27 DECEMBER. The cast of "The Ghost" and some of the guests arrive at Brede Place. Despite a horrendous rainstorm and icy roads, which made hard going for the special omnibus Cora had procured from a firm of London carriage makers to transport guests from the railway station, the revelry begins. On the evening of the 27th, a dress rehearsal of "The Ghost" is held for the children of the village in the Brede schoolhouse. H. G. Wells recalls:

> I remember very vividly a marvellous Christmas Party in which Jane and I participated. We were urged to come over and, in a postscript, to bring any bedding and blankets we could spare. We arrived in a heaped-up Sandgate cab, rather in advance of the guests from London. We were given a room over the main gateway in which there was a portcullis and an owl's nest, but at least we got a room. Nobody else did—because although some thirty or forty invitations had been issued, there were not as a matter of fact more than three or four bedrooms available. One of them however was large and its normal furniture had been supplemented by a number of hired truckle-beds and christened the Girls' Dormitory, and in the attic an array of shake-downs was provided for the men. Husbands and wives were torn apart.
>
> Later on we realized that the sanitary equipment of Brede House dated from the seventeenth century, an interesting historical detail, and such as there was indoors, was accessible only through the Girls' Dormitory. Con-

sequently the wintry countryside next morning was dotted with wandering melancholy, preoccupied, men guests.

Anyhow there were good open fires in the great fireplaces and I remember that party as an extraordinary lark—but shot, at the close, with red intimations of a coming tragedy. We danced in a big oak-panelled room downstairs, lit by candles stuck upon iron sconces that Cora Crane had improvised with the help of the Brede blacksmith. Unfortunately she had not improvised grease guards and after a time everybody's back showed a patch of composite candle-wax, like the flash on the coat of a Welsh Fusilier. When we were not dancing or romping we were waxing the floor or rehearsing a play vamped up by A. E. W. Mason, Crane, myself and others. It was a ghost play and very allusive and fragmentary, and we gave it in the School Room at Brede. It amused its authors and cast vastly. What the Brede people made of it is not on record. (Wells 1934, 613–614)

C. Lewis Hind, editor of the *Academy*, found Crane reflective amid the festivities:

Surely there has never been such a house party. The ancient house, in spite of its size, was taxed to the uttermost. There were six men in the vast, bare chamber where I slept, the six iron bedsteads, procured for the occasion, quite lost in the amplitude of the chamber. At the dance, which was held on the evening of our arrival, I was presented to bevies of beautiful American girls in beauteous frocks. I wondered where they came from. All the time, yes, as far as I remember, all the time our host, the author of "The Red Badge of Courage," sat in a corner of the great fireplace in the hall, not unamused, but very silent. He seemed rather bewildered by what had happened to him. (Hind, 72)

28 DECEMBER. The greater number of the guests arrive, and in the evening the principal performance of "The Ghost" is given in the Brede village schoolhouse. There are approximately 50 guests at supper in Brede Place, but more had been invited. A. E. W. Mason later wrote to Vincent Starrett that

there was a tremendous fall of snow, and this being the day before motors, hardly a local resident turned up. This was, perhaps, just as well for H. G. Wells arrived with his wife and he invented a game of racing on broomsticks over the polished floor, which I think would have staggered the local gentry if they had turned up.

Beyond Wells and a man who is now a most important Solicitor and a dramatic critic, I have not one idea of the people who were staying there, but I do remember being greeted by Henry James, who was standing at the gate of his garden at Rye as I drove past him, and being warned by him that I might find an actress or two in the party and should be careful not to get caught. (*L*, 343)

[The printed program for the performance shows that the Ghost was played by A. E. W. Mason. Among the *dramatis personae* are characters from the works of some of the collaborators. Rufus Coleman is taken from the war correspondent in Crane's *Active Service*. Dr. Moreau comes from the mad biologist of H. G. Wells's *Island of Doctor Moreau*, and the doctor's son, Peter Quint Prodmore Moreau, is a hybrid, owing something also to Henry James's *The Turn of the Screw* and perhaps to Joseph Conrad's *The Nigger of the "Narcissus"* or, more likely, Prodmore, the mortgage holder in James's "Covering End." Suburbia may be an oblique reference to Edwin Pugh's *Street in Suburbia* and Tony Drunn to his *Tony Drum, Cockney Boy*. Miranda may derive from A. E. W. Mason's *Miranda of the Balcony* or

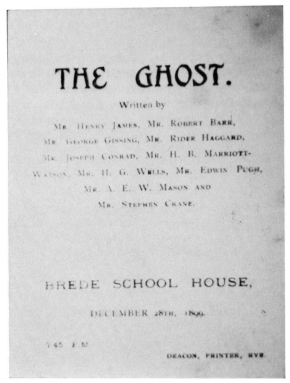

Program for the performance of "The Ghost" in
the Brede school house, 28 December 1899
(*Wertheim Collection*)

H. B. Marriott-Watson's *Heart of Miranda* or perhaps from both. The Three Little Maids from Rye—Holly, Buttercup, and Mistletoe—are allusions to the blousy Buttercup in *H. M. S. Pinafore* and the "three little maids from school" in *The Mikado* (Gordan, 5; Crisler, 107).]

29 DECEMBER. There is a gala ball in the evening. Wells recalls that Crane participated enthusiastically in the events of the three-day celebration, although he seemed "profoundly weary and ill." After the guests had gone to bed, "Mrs. Crane came to us. He had had a haemorrhage from his lungs and he had tried to conceal it from her. He 'didn't want anyone to bother.' Would I help get a doctor? There was a bicycle in the place and my last clear memory of that fantastic Brede House party is riding out of the cold skirts of a wintry night into a drizzling dawn along a wet road to call up a doctor in Rye" (Wells 1934, 614–615). He returns with a local practitioner, Dr. Ernest B. Skinner.

30 DECEMBER. Major Charles L. McCawley, who was quartermaster of the First Marine Battalion at Guantánamo Bay, responds to the Cranes' Christmas greeting: "I, in company with all my brother officers, have always looked back with pleasure and pride upon your service with us in Cuba for you were the only outsider who saw it all and we regard you as an honorary member of the Corps and hope you will always have the same affection for us as we have for you" (*C*, 565).

*

1900

*

JANUARY. "Shame," another Whilomville story, appears in *Harper's Magazine*.

The *Bookman* warns readers of *Active Service* to "concentrate their attention as much as possible on the travel impressions and the few narratives of fighting. The romance of the story has a very anxious side. . . . Mr. Crane shows his usual power of describing scenes he actually knows, whether in college class-rooms, in newspaper offices, or on Grecian roads, in vivid, energetic language. The reader will continue to the end to see whether Marjorie and love crown Coleman at last, or whether he is drowned in champagne and despair by the strong hand of Miss Nora Black; and a book that one must read to the end is not to be sniffed at. But, nevertheless, this one is careless and formless. Mr. Crane has a talent which he should take more seriously."

1 JANUARY. Crane responds to a request by Moreton Frewen's son Hugh for a copy of "The Ghost" for possible subsequent productions or publication:

I am desolated by your request because I fear it is the result of a misunderstanding. It is true that we gave a play in the village school-house but the whole thing was a mere idle string of rubbish made to entertain the villagers and with music frankly stolen from very venerable comic operas such as "The Mikado" and "Pinafore." The whole business was really beneath contempt to serious people and it would be inconsiderate, even unkind, of me to send it you. The names of the authors was more of a joke than anything. Still, we made it genuine by causing all these men really write a mere word or phrase—such as "It's cold" or, in fact anything at all—and in this way we arranged this rather historic little program. (*C*, 569).

Moreton and Clara Frewen made a similar inquiry, causing Cora to send them a detailed explanation of the nature of "The Ghost" and the circumstances of its production (*C*, 570–571).

2 JANUARY. Cora Crane writes to James B. Pinker:

Mr. Crane is ill again—in bed but is still keeping at his work. The pressing of his creditors is so distressing. Now I simply loathe bothering you again, but I can't help it. There is some money, I feel sure, due from Stokes and Co. on "Active Service" Did you ask them for a statement? And is there any news of their wanting the Romance [*The O'Ruddy*]? Of course they want it but I can understand they are dragging things out through the mail to make better terms. If these large sums, which ought to come from Stokes and for the serial rights of story could be gotten in It would put Mr. Crane straight. But as it is we have to keep begging you to put checques in bank all the time. I don't know what Mr. Crane would do without your kind help through these longs days of trying to get straight, but I'm sure you feel that in the long run he will prove his appreciation of your simply saving him from going smash. (*C*, 572)

[Ford Madox Ford recalls visiting Crane on 2 January and found Crane working in a summer house up a bank behind Brede Place, which is unlikely if Crane was ill. According to Ford, Crane was glad that Ford was not the tax collector from whom he was hiding. "He

January 1, 1900

Dear Mr Hugh Frewen: I am desolated by your request because I fear it is the result of a misunderstanding. It is true that we gave a play in the village school-house but the whole thing was a mere idle string of rubbish made to entertain the villagers and with music frankly stolen from very venerable comic operas such as "The Mikado" and "Pinafore." The whole business was really beneath contempt to serious people and it would be inconsiderate, even ~~do do~~ unkind, of me to send it you. The names of the authors was more of a joke than anything. Still, we made it genuine by causing all these men really write a mere word or phrase —— such as "It's cold" or, in fact anything at all —— and

Stephen Crane to Hugh Frewen, 1 January 1900
(Barrett Collection, University of Virginia)

416

in this way we arranged this,
rather historic little program.

Allow me to wish you a
very fine shining 1900.
Yours faithfully
Stephen Crane

had the theory that if, in England, you did not pay your taxes on New Year's Day, you went to prison." Ford assured him that he need not worry about the tax collector for two or three months. As Ford was leaving, Crane suddenly seized his arm and asked "whether I had ever seen him drunk; or drugged; or lecherously inclined; or foul-mouthed; or quarrelsome even." Ford had not heard the rumors being spread about the Cranes by casual acquaintances and curiosity seekers who visited Brede Place but reflected on the certainty that "if you nourish broods of vipers for long periods in your bosom, it is likely that you will be stung" (Ford 1937, 31–33).]

Edith Richie leaves Brede Place (Gilkes 1960, 228).

4 JANUARY. Crane inscribes a copy of *George's Mother* to Thomas Parkin, a local magistrate and bibliophile who lives in nearby Hastings. Parkin grangerizes the book with clippings about Brede Place and the performance of "The Ghost" (*C*, 574, NN-Berg).

Crane inscribes a copy of *The Monster and Other Stories* to Margery Pease (*C*, 574).

5 JANUARY. Crane writes to Pinker: "I *must* have the money. I cant get on without it. If you cant send £50 by the next mail, I will have to find a man who can. I know this is abrupt and unfair but self-preservation forces my game with you precisely as it did with Reynolds" (*C*, 575).

In their reviews of "The Ghost," the *Sussex Express* and the *South Eastern Advertiser* outline the plot of the farce. According to the *Express*,

> The plot of the play was, shortly, as follows:—In the first act the ghost (Mr. A. E. W. Mason), in disguise, is discovered in the empty room in Brede Place in the year 1950; he soliloquises on ghosts and tourists in general, and upon himself and tourists to Brede—"children of Sussex East and West"—in particular. Two of the latter presently appear—Dr. Moreau (Mr. F. L. Bowen) and his son, Peter Quint Prodmore Moreau (Mr. Cunningham)—and converse with him. They are afterwards joined by the caretaker (Miss Bray), an historical story-teller, and the rest of the tourists. Three little maids from Rye—Holly (Mrs. Mark Barr), Buttercup (Miss Bowen), and Mistletoe (Miss Richie)—sing a trio. After this, while the other tourists are conducted off to the dining-room, "but not for lunch," Suburbia (Miss Ethel Bowen) and Miranda (Miss Sylvia Bowen) remain behind to get further information from their unknown companion about the ghost. Suburbia recites and Miranda dances, by way of recompensing the gentleman for his trouble. They learn that the ghost appears at midnight.

In the second act Rufus Coleman (Mr. Cyril Frewer) appears on the scene half an hour too early; he meets Mistletoe, who sings to him, telling how her lover has been the first to enlist in the Sussex volunteers against the Boers. After singing a duet they go out. There appear next in order Tony Drunn (Mr. Ford Richie), who sings the "The Soldiers of the Queen," and Dr. Moreau who, after some business with Tony Drunn, imitates some of the best known denizens of the farmyard and sings "Simon the Cellarer." Holly joins him and sings at his request, and his son Peter makes his appearance. While the father and son are disputing as to who shall look after the young lady, Tony Drunn walks off with the latter. As the hour of midnight approaches the tourists all return, and sing a chorus "We'll be there."

The third act opens with a chorus "Oh, ghost, we're waiting for you to come," sung on the darkened stage. He soon appears and discloses his identity. He tells his story, supported by music, prompted by the caretaker, and helped out by the questions of the tourists. The play ends with a final chorus, in which the company sings the praises of Sir Goddard, their "wicked giant prize."

The songs, most of which were encored, were tastefully accompanied on the piano by Mrs. H. G. Wells. At the close of the performance a vote of thanks to the performers, proposed by Mr. Harvey, in the name of the Rector, who was absent through illness, was carried by acclamation. The audience sang "For they are jolly good people," the original word being changed in consideration of the ladies among those acting.

The *Advertiser* adds: "The inhabitants of Brede have every reason to be thankful to Mr. and Mrs. Stephen Crane, of Brede Place, for providing them with such a treat. . . . No other charge was made for admission, the whole of the expenses being defrayed by Mr. Stephen Crane, including an addition to the stage, which he has since presented to the School."

6 JANUARY. Crane inscribes a copy of *Active Service*:

> To Curtis Brown
> From Stephen Crane
> With the highest assurances of
> regard and esteem, and wishes for
> continual good-luck.
>
> Brede Place
> Sussex
> Jan 6. 1900. (*C*, 576)

The *Academy* reproduces a portion of the title page of the program of "The Ghost" in facsimile. The reviewer comments, "The text of

'The Ghost' will never be printed." The *Academy* evaluates *Active Service* as "a little below Mr. Crane's best. It is mannered, and the mannerisms of a writer with methods so audacious and novel as Mr. Crane's are apt to irritate. But it quite deserves to be called a remarkable book."

In the *Criterion*, Rupert Hughes ("Chelifer") reviews *Active Service* and *The Monster and Other Stories* and offers a spirited summary of Crane's career:

> That Stephen Crane is a genius I have been convinced ever since I read that fatherless yellow-covered book: "Maggie, a Tale of the Streets, by Johnston Smith." To this belief I have clung in spite of many jolts and jars, for the retainer of this author must hang on like the watcher in the crow's nest of a ship, which plows splendidly forward, but with much yawing and buffeting and many a careen.
>
> Mr. Crane's faults are not surreptitiously stowed away; they are carried aboveboard like a defiant figurehead or a pirate's black flag. For instance, there is his grammatical carelessness; he takes the natural liberty of a writer handling so elastic a language as ours and carries it to license, to criminal excess, for which there is no excuse. First you blame the proof-reader; then you realize that no proof-reader could live and let slip the things that get into Mr. Crane's books unless his hands were tied behind him by definite orders. Of all the writers I have ever read with respect, Mr. Crane makes the greatest number of solecisms. Many of them bear the look of absolute illiteracy; they are as inconsistent with his capability for discriminating and *recherché* composition as Wordsworth's off-hours are with his inspirations. That superb work, "The Red Badge of Courage," and the later, "Active Service," fairly bristle with these things.
>
> Then he is wont to take it into his head to send his glorious argosy on some fool's errand of wanton affectation and triviality. Those outlandish junketings marked many, though not all, of his "Black Rider" lines, much of "George's Mother," the general idea (though strangely not the detail) of "The Third Violet," and almost all of that crazy nightmare, "War Is Kind."
>
> Yet, withal, Mr. Crane seems to me to be the most definite and individual of all our book-writers; and I credit him with having written some of the best pages America has contributed to literature, in "Maggie," "The Red Badge," certain of the "Black Rider" lines, "The Open Boat," and in the two books just published from his hand.

[6 JANUARY]. Cora writes to Pinker acknowledging receipt of the typescript Pinker had made of "The Storming of Badajoz" for Crane to correct. She again stresses their financial plight and asks Pinker if he can persuade Methuen to make an advance on the yet untitled *The O'Ruddy*, which she refers to as "The Irish story" (*C*, 577).

7 JANUARY. In "Some Curious Lessons from the Transvaal" (*New York Journal*) Crane protests undue censorship of war correspondents and reflects on losses suffered by crack British regiments in the Boer War.

[7 JANUARY]. Cora assures Pinker that in his letter of 5 January "Mr. Crane intended no threat and will keep all engagements made with you." She mails him the manuscript of "A Dark-Brown Dog" (*C*, 577–578).

9 JANUARY. Paul Revere Reynolds advises Crane that the actor and producer Nat Goodwin has declined his Spanish-American War play (*C*, 582).

[9 JANUARY]. Cora once again assures Pinker that "Mr. Crane says he had no idea of putting any of his work in other hands than yours and cannot understand why you should have recieved any such impression." She also reiterates her request that he urge Methuen to offer an advance on *The O'Ruddy* so that Crane will be able to sign a contract for the novel with them. She stresses that Curtis Brown, who has become a literary agent in London, is eager to buy a Crane book, but she asks if Pinker thinks it would be better for Crane to drop *The O'Ruddy* and write short stories for immediate cash (*C*, 582–583).

13 JANUARY. The *Manchester Guardian* calls "The Ghost" "a remarkable piece of literary patchwork [that] has lately been allowed to waste its sweetness on the Sussex air."

The *Brooklyn Daily Eagle* reviews *The Monster and Other Stories*:

> Stephen Crane's somewhat lengthy "short story," "The Monster," furnishes the caption to a fresh volume of tales from his pen, that have already seen the light in the magazines. This first tale . . . furnishes an excellent example of the author's peculiar powers. It is as grewsome, almost, as anything that Poe ever wrote, and yet it is compounded of very simple materials. . . . It is a picture drawn with a great deal of power, but it is unpleasant reading. It sometimes calls for art of the highest quality to depict the horrible and this art Mr. Crane has employed in this instance, but is it worth while. Is the end served to be commended? The minuteness with which he picked out the details in his "Red Badge of Courage" was the exercise of a striking faculty along justifiable lines and for a worthy purpose. "The Monster" is simply a grewsome story, powerful, if you will, but no one will ever read it a second time; once is enough, it is too creepy. The other short tales in the volume are "The Blue Hotel," and "His New Mittens." Both are examples of Mr. Crane's peculiar faculty and both are interesting only as examples of how much the skillful raconteur, with

a genius for small detail, can make out of the slenderest materials. It may be claimed that it is of such small matters that life is made up. That is true; but the ability to depict them in minute detail does not prove that they are worth the expenditure necessary.

15 JANUARY. Pinker acknowledges receipt of chapters 3 and 4 of *The O'Ruddy*. He presumes Methuen will agree to make an advance on the novel when more manuscript is delivered and urges Crane to send it as quickly as possible (*C*, 585).

19 JANUARY. Conrad compliments R. B. Cunninghame Graham on his stories in the *Saturday Review,* commenting that "they are much more of course than mere Crane-like impressionism" (Karl and Davies, 2: 242).

22 JANUARY. Pinker acknowledges receipt of chapters 6 and 7 of *The O'Ruddy* and advises Crane that he has been unable to secure an assignment for him to write correspondence from Gibraltar (*C*, 586–587, 587n1).

24 JANUARY. Cora writes to Post Wheeler for Crane, who is, she says, too busy to write letters, advising him that Crane has seconded his nomination for the Author's Club and giving him news of Brede Place: "Stephen longs for South Africa but he was really too wretched in health after Cuba to go out so soon again. I pray he may never go again as war-correspondent" (*C*, 588).

28 JANUARY. Cora sends Parkin letters written by contributors to "The Ghost" and forwards the copy of *George's Mother* Crane had inscribed to him on 4 January (*C*, 589).

FEBRUARY. "The Carriage-Lamps" appears in *Harper's Magazine*. "The Kicking Twelfth," the first published of three stories dealing with an imaginary Spitzbergen regiment at war with Rostina, appears in the *Pall Mall Magazine*. The Spitzbergen force is commanded by Major General Richie, named after Edith Richie, and the commander of the 12th Regiment is named Colonel Sponge, after one of Crane's dogs.

In *Book News* Julian Hawthorne condemns "The Monster," with its ambivalent and unresolved ending, as

an outrage on art and humanity; and the splendid descriptive ability of the author, his vividness and veracity, only render it more flagrant. Something is fundamentally out of gear in a mind that can reconcile itself to such a performance. There is abundance of humor in many of the details; but it is an easy thing to be humorous about microscopic things, the essence of humor being in a kindly or amused smile at the weaknesses and absurdities of human nature; but it is one thing to be humorous when writing a history of the French Revolution, like Carlyle; and quite another to be humorous about the tiny trivialities of a New York country town. Anybody can look down on that, and see the fun of it. Crane never gets more than a few feet above the ground, and often falls below even that moderate elevation. Of constructive ability he shows not a vestige. His outfit for literary purposes consists of a microscopic eye, and a keen sense of the queer, the bizarre, the morbid. His minute analysis produces nothing. He is anything but an artist. He has everything belonging to art to learn; and he evinces no disposition or ability to learn it. We all know, nevertheless, how successful he has been; but in these days we are thankful for what we can get, if it be genuine so far as it goes; and Crane's work is no doubt that.

The *Critic* dismisses "The Monster" as "an unpleasant story. . . . There is humor in the telling, but it is humor of a rather grim character."

1 FEBRUARY. Pinker writes to Crane that Stokes's London representative Dominick objects to Crane's subtitle for *Wounds in the Rain*, arguing that "in view of the glut of books on the Cuban war which has appeared in America, it is unwise to proclaim in the title that your book deals with the same subject. Methuens endorse his opinion, and I am therefore, writing to ask if you could suggest another title" (*C*, 591–592).

2 FEBRUARY. Pinker writes to Crane that Lippincott has asked for two additional battle stories to round out the book publication of *Great Battles of the World* (*C*, 592).

A luncheon in Crane's honor is given by Thomas Parkin at Fairseat, his estate in Hastings.
[Crane's biographers usually date this luncheon as occurring in late January (Gilkes 1960, 232; Stallman 1973, 498; *C*, 589n4) because Cora's letter of 28 January to Parkin thanks him for his hospitality on an afternoon spent at his house and stipulates "My husband sends you a copy of 'George's Mother.'" Crane evidently delayed sending the copy because Parkin notes specifically in his grangerized copy of *George's Mother* inscribed by Crane that the party occurred on Friday, 2 February, and that Crane sent the book "a day or so afterwards." A clipping from the *Sussex Express* (16 June 1900) by a correspondent

identified by Parkin as a Miss Bothem-Edwards, who attended the luncheon, reports:

> Already months ago . . . it was easy to see that Stephen Crane's years, if not months, were numbered. In February last I met him at the house of a friend—bibliophile, ornithologist, and amateur artist—living in Hastings. Painful was the contrast between the young author of "The Red Badge of Courage" and the other guests, all of whom were in good health and spirits. Poor Stephen Crane had that white, worn-out, restless look betokening complete nervous exhaustion. He took no tea and did not join in general conversation, but moved about uneasily as if in search of something he could not find. Among the guests present was "that sombre genius," as "Shirley" has called the author of "Mark Rutherford" [William Hale White]. But although the two men spent an hour in each other's company, they did not exchange so much as a syllable! (NN-Berg)]

5 FEBRUARY. Crane writes to Pinker that he "spent two months trying to find an effective title to the book of War Stories. I decided upon '*Wounds in the Rain.*' This seemed to me *very effective.*" He will not change this title, but he is willing to make the subtitle merely "A Collection of War Stories" and he feels that Methuen can adopt the same subtitle (*C*, 595).

[When *Wounds in the Rain* was published in December, the Stokes subtitle was simply "War Stories." Methuen retained what was apparently Crane's first choice, "A Collection of Stories Relating to the Spanish-American War of 1898."]

Crane writes to Elizabeth Jordan, editor of *Harper's Bazaar*, declining an offer to write stories of "little-girl-life." However, if she feels that "'little Cora' of the Magazine stories could be transported to her own New York and there suffer a few experiences—I think I might manage." He refers her to Pinker for terms (*C*, 593–594).

6 FEBRUARY. Pinker responds to Crane's letter of the previous day and agrees that Crane's title for *Wounds in the Rain* is a good one. He inquires whether Crane has yet chosen a title for "the long book," *The O'Ruddy*, and acknowledges receipt of chapter 11 of the novel (*C*, 596–597).

8 FEBRUARY. Pinker acknowledges having received three copies of the typescript of the first 10 chapters of *The O'Ruddy* (*C*, 598).

10 FEBRUARY. In an article on "The New Art of Description in Fiction," the *Literary Digest* identifies Crane as one of the "writers of the

new school" who "in their effort to be vivid and striking, have allowed themselves to be carried away into extremes." A passage from *The Red Badge of Courage* is used to illustrate "striving after effect, and the extravagant use of onomatopoeticism."

11 FEBRUARY. "The Reluctant Voyagers," written in the spring of 1893, is syndicated in two parts, the second appearing on 18 February, in a number of American newspapers.

13 FEBRUARY. Crane lends his gramophone for a concert held at the Brede village school to raise money for the Yeomanry Hospital Fund (*South Eastern Advertiser,* 17 February).

Based on an agreement recently made with Dominick, Stokes sends Pinker an advance of £70 for *The O'Ruddy*: "This payment is, we understand, in advance and on account of royalty for the new, historical romance by Stephen Crane, which is to take the place of the novel of the American Revolution that he was to write for us, the latter being postponed by him" (NhD).

14 FEBRUARY. In an article in the *New York Journal,* "Stephen Crane Says: Watson's Criticisms of England's War Are Not Unpatriotic," Crane applies the ambivalent attitude of a critic of England's policies in the Boer War to his own country: "One has the burning wish for the quick success of the American arms in the Philippines. At the same time, one has a still more burning wish that the Filipinos shall see us as just men, willing, anxious to deal fairly, govern with studious equity; depart, if need be, with honor" (*Works,* 9: 245). In another *Journal* article, "Stephen Crane Says: The British Soldiers Are Not Familiar with the 'Business End' of Modern Rifles," Crane criticizes the British army for ignorance of the destructive effects of firearms.

[20 FEBRUARY]. Cora sends Pinker chapter 14 of *The O'Ruddy* and suggests possible buyers for serial rights to the novel, the Wyoming stories, and the Spitzbergen stories, "The Upturned Face" and "And if He Wills, We Must Die" (*C,* 602–603).

22 FEBRUARY. Frederick L. Bowen, a young technical engineer, agrees to help Cora produce a model of a filter for army canteens that she has designed: "The idea of a flask filter is a good one and should be of great use to an army, particularly in the field, if the volume of the flask is not increased nor its weight or cost much effected" (Frederick L. Bowen to Cora Crane, NNC).

26 FEBRUARY. Pinker advises Crane that Elizabeth Jordan has agreed to his offer to write "little Cora" stories. *Harper's Bazaar* is willing to pay $50 per thousand words for American serial rights (*C*, 603).

27 FEBRUARY. Pinker explains to Cora that *The O'Ruddy* has taken the place of the books Crane contracted to write for Stokes and Methuen: "The terms of the contract with Stokes & Methuen are the terms which had been arranged for the other novel; that is to say, in Stokes' case the Irish romance takes the place of the Revolutionary novel, and in Methuen's case it takes the place of the novel the character of which was not specified" (*C*, 604).

MARCH. Cora inscribes a copy of the June 1899 issue of the *Anglo-Saxon Review* containing Henry James's story "The Great Condition":

> The book was given by Henry James to Stephen Crane.
> and by him to
> Mrˢ Stephen Crane
> Brede Place
> Sussex
> England.
> *March. 1900* (Wertheim 1992, 18)

[A curiosity of this volume is that the leaves containing James's story have been neatly excised, probably by Cora herself. "The Great Condition" concerns a woman who is reputed to have a "past," as James is known to have viewed Cora, "'something or other in her life; some awkward passage, some beastly episode or accident. . . . some chapter in the book difficult to read aloud—some unlucky page she'd like to tear out.'" Resentful of James's dispatch treatment of her following Crane's death, Cora may have removed the offending pages, just as the passage from the story suggested (Wertheim 1992, 19).]

"The Brief Campaign against New Orleans," first written and first printed of the eight articles entitled "Great Battles of the World," appears in *Lippincott's Magazine*. *Harper's Magazine* continues the Whilomville series with "The Knife." "The Upturned Face" is published in *Ainslee's Magazine*.

[8 MARCH]. Crane sends Pinker "Vittoria" for the "Great Battles" series. He is sending chapter 19 of *The O'Ruddy* in a few days but has delayed the typing because the battle articles, which he can send at the rate of one a week, are "sure quick money." He asks Pinker to wire him the next evening, "but state the words rather ambiguously because my post-master is my grocer," who has not been paid (*C*, 605).

[10 MARCH]. Crane sends Pinker chapter 19 of *The O'Ruddy*: "The next battle for Lippincott's is 'Lützen.' It should reach you within ten days. This article will be the one for which £50 is to be paid. Please stretch yourself on Monday. There will £30 due from Stokes on the Romance, £30 from Lippincott on Vittoria which with Lippincotts £100 makes £160. I would like to have £100 on Monday" (*C*, 605–606).

11 MARCH. In an article in the *New York Journal*, "The Talk of London," Crane makes some observations on the effect of the Boer War on the imperialistic ventures of European powers other than England and reports an altercation in the House of Commons involving a member's insulting comments about Irish nationalists.

[MID-MARCH]. Cora writes to Pinker enclosing chapter 21 of *The O'Ruddy*. She reports that Crane declines to write a Christmas story for Tillotson's newspaper syndicate: "He says that he has never written Xmas stories of the kind which seems to be specified and declared that he will not begin now" (*C*, 606), apparently forgetting "A Christmas Dinner Won in Battle."

[18 MARCH]. Crane sends Pinker chapter 22 of *The O'Ruddy*. He asks Pinker to send his solicitor, Alfred T. Plant, £10 for a debt still owed to someone in Oxted (*C*, 607).

20 MARCH. Bowen writes to Cora that the Patent Office has accepted the application with provisional specifications for her canteen filter, but that this does not mean that a patent has been granted, although it does give her some measure of protection. The following day Lafayette Hoyt De Friese sends Cora a copy of her agreement with Bowen to share whatever profits may accrue from her invention (Frederick L. Bowen to Cora Crane, Lafayette Hoyte De Friese to Cora Crane, NNC).

24 MARCH. Crane writes to Pinker:

Please send a checque to A. T. Plant, 18 Bedford Row, Grey's Inn for £22 before Wednesday or a baliff will be here and also deposit £20 to my wife's a/c at Brown Shipley. and send the enclosed wire. This does not include the £15 which I asked from you today. "Lützen" (£50) is finished today but the typing will require tomorrow. It will reach you by special stamps. The XXIV Chapter of the novel is finished but not yet typed. It will reach you on Tuesday.

The novel stands at 61000 but I am extremely doubtful about my prudence in writing it at this time. . . .

I expect the "Romance" to pull me out much more than even. I only question the wisdom of my abandoning my lucrative short story game for this long thing which doesn't pay (much) until the end.

Yours sincerely
S. Crane.

P.S. Cheques to the amount of £16 have been sent back from the bank and I must almost meet my little weekly grocer and butcher bill.

S. C. (C, 607–608)

30 AND 31 MARCH. Kate Lyon writes to Crane about her research and writing in the British Museum on the "Great Battles of the World" series: "Of course all the historians vary about all the things in a war, and I try to piece up a scheme that seems to be the one acknowledged by the most and best authorities" (C, 610).

31 MARCH. Cora leaves for Paris to meet Helen Crane, who has left the Rosemont-Dézaley school, and to shop for clothing. Crane writes to Pinker, sending him chapters 24 and 25 of The O'Ruddy and asking him to send £20 to Cora at the Hotel St. Petersbourg in Paris because she had left with only the money William had sent to buy clothing for Helen. "The poor things may be left high and dry in Paris" (C, 613). But Pinker does not send the check until 2 April (C, 614), and it arrives too late to reach Cora (C, 618). Shortly after writing this letter, Crane has the first of two massive hemorrhages.

Frederick Bowen writes to Crane that he has prepared models of the canteen and hopes to bring them to Brede Place within a few days (C, 614).

The New York Journal prints a satiric essay, "Stephen Crane Says: Edwin Markham Is His First Choice for the American Academy." Crane ridicules the concept of an American academy but speculates that it would be a dignified body "for it is certain that we can show more fine old litterateurs with manes of snow white hair than any country on face of the globe." Crane's sole choice for the American academy would be Edwin Markham, whose didactic poem, "The Man with the Hoe" (1899), inspired by Millet's painting with the same name, had brought him both fame and notoriety: "frame him up; give him a constitution and a set of by-laws; let him convene himself and discuss literary matters. Then we have an American Academy" (Works, 8: 758–759).

APRIL. *Lippincott's* prints "The Storming of Badajoz." "Moonlight on the Snow," another Western story featuring Jack Potter, the town marshal of Yellow Sky, appears in *Frank Leslie's Popular Monthly.* "The Stove," a Whilomville story in *Harper's Magazine,* once again involves Little Cora, "the angel-child."

Reviewing *The Monster and Other Stories,* the *Book Buyer* asserts that in the title story Crane

has spoiled an idea worthy of Poe in the telling. "The Monster" is a weird conception, haunting in its possibilities, but instead of centering his reader's attention, and his own, upon it, he has weakened its force by realistic by-play, or, rather, by the attention to irrelevant detail that is so often mistaken for realism. . . . Of the other two tales the book contains, "His New Mittens" is by far the better one. Mr. Crane has made for himself a distinctive place among the interpreters of child life and the workings of the child mind. He succeeds in awakening dim memories in his readers, in establishing between them and him a sympathy based upon all but forgotten facts and states of mind. It is intuition and observation, not his own memory, that enable him to do this—which means that in this, at least, he is an artist. The remaining story, "The Blue Hotel," deals with a rather shopworn subject.

In the *Literary Review,* under the title "A Romantic Idealist—Mr. Stephen Crane," Karl Harriman presents a fanciful view of Crane at Brede Place that nevertheless reveals the unrelenting drudgery into which his life has degenerated:

Now and again a few friends come down to him for a week, but mostly he is alone. Each morning sees him up in his little study in the tower of Brede House writing, writing. He works methodically, and at the same time by jerks, if the expression is allowable. At present he is toiling upon an Irish romance, having gained the material on the bogs last autumn. But the short stories that have made him famous were all done spasmodically. He goes to his study when he feels the spirit quickening, locks the door and writes, writes, writes, until he has done. Once, to my knowledge, he lingered in that little turret-room three days, and at the end of that time, before lolling upon the divan for a little sleep, he poked out under the door four stories, which Mrs. Crane ran off on the typewriter for him and sent to his agent in London.

In evaluating his own literary performance, Harriman maintains, Crane does not have a high regard for *The Red Badge* but ranks "The Monster" as first among his works and *George's Mother* second. After these come "An Old Man Goes Wooing" and *Maggie.*

3 APRIL. Vernall, Cora's housekeeper and cook, sends a telegram to Paris describing Crane's condition without his knowledge (NNC). Cora telegraphs Lafayette Hoyt De Friese, Moreton Frewen, and William Howe Crane, and she and Helen take the night boat across the channel.

[4 APRIL]. Cora telegraphs the American embassy in London for assistance. The secretary of the embassy, Henry White, arranges for Dr. Thomas J. Maclagen, a well-known physician who had treated Thomas Carlyle, and a nurse to go down to Brede Place immediately (Hagemann 1959, 173, 173n1).

[5 OR 12 APRIL]. S. M. Williams, head of the *New York Journal*'s London office, advises Crane that the *Journal* looks favorably on his proposal to write correspondence from St. Helena and asks for an estimate of expenses so that he can communicate further with management in New York (*C*, 615). The *London Morning Post* later reports that it had arranged to send Crane to St. Helena as a correspondent if his health improved (6 June; Copy, NSyU).

[6 APRIL]. Cora informs Pinker that Crane is ill and that she has had to pay Dr. Maclagen £50 for the consultation. She has "The Battle of Solferino" partly typed (although a letter to Cora from Kate Lyon at this time indicates that the article is not yet completed) and urges him to ask Lippincott for an advance to help defray Dr. Maclagen's bill. "I don't think they will hesitate as it was matter of saving Stephen Crane's life" (*C*, 615–616).

7 APRIL. William writes to Cora that he is alarmed about Crane's condition, but he cannot send any money (*C*, 616).

[7 OR 8 APRIL]. Kate Lyon responds to a confused message from Cora by asking "*What* is the matter with Stephen? I could not tell from your letter." She is still working on "The Battle of Solferino" and offers "to work it up in a *finished* state" if Crane is not well enough to go over what she writes (*C*, 617).

8 APRIL. Cora writes to Pinker asking him to deposit £50 with her bank, Brown, Shipley & Company, to meet the check she has given Dr. Maclagen, who was optimistic about Crane's condition. She has written directly to Lippincott for an advance. "If Mr. Crane should die I have notes of end of novel so it could be finished & no one will lose—if that thought should occur" (*C*, 618).

[11 APRIL]. Cora writes to Clara Frewen: "The last two days have been such anxious one's that I've not been able to write you in answer to your very kind letter from Innishannon. We moved my husband on Monday night downstairs in the oak room. He seems to get weaker every day and my anxiety is very great. There has been no return of hemorrhage but he suffers so horribly from the abscess, which is too deep-seated to open from the outside while he is in such a weak state" (*C*, 620).

To Pinker Cora writes much more optimistically that Crane is better. She urges him to sell English and American serial rights to *The O'Ruddy*. "Ready money is an absolute necessity in illness. I have two nurses who cost £2.4.6 each per week beside their expenses. Then there are medicines and living expenses—so do your best to get serial money in." She again stretches the truth in telling Pinker that the Solferino battle article, which Kate Lyon has not yet finished, is being typed. Pinker has apparently protested Cora's paying £50 to an expensive physician and appealing directly to Lippincott for an advance, and Cora protests: "Now Mr. Pinker, It was a matter of life & death to have the Specialist down. I could not leave any stone unturned. *You* might not have gone to office on Saturday or Friday. I *had* to write to Lippincott at the same time I wrote you. One cannot stand upon ceremony at such a moment, and indeed I was almost distracted. Pray forgive any seeming lack of courtesy to yourself" (*C*, 621–622).

11 APRIL. Cora has also appealed directly to Methuen, who decline to make any further advance on *The O'Ruddy* and tactfully suggest to Cora that "Perhaps as the negotiations were carried on through Mr. Pinker it might be worth your while to write to him on the subject" (*C*, 622).

13 APRIL. William Howe Crane writes to Stephen: "We are very anxious over your sickness. There is in our morning paper every day a London dispatch, giving the latest news from you. We find this unsatisfactory, and we are waiting anxiously for letters. If your trouble is tubercular, we think you ought to leave the English climate and come to America. You and your wife will be welcome at our house, as long as you choose to stay" (*C*, 623).

H. G. Wells writes to Cora: "I have just seen in the *Academy* that Crane is ill. Is this so? And if so how is he?" (Wertheim 1979b, 208).

14 APRIL. The *Academy* expresses regret to hear that Crane "is lying seriously ill at the mediaeval house in Sussex, Brede Place, where he has been living for the past two years."

[15 APRIL]. Cora responds to H. G. Wells: "Stephen was taken with hemorrhages on the 31*st* March, two hours after I had started to go to Paris to meet Miss Crane, who was leaving school. I was recalled on Tuesday the 3*rd* April by wire & crossed that night. I joined him in a very dangerous state when I got here. Sent for trained nurses at once & got the best lung specialist the U.S. Embassy knew about, down from London. He gave us hope. There has been no hemorrhage now since Monday last. The doctors say if he pulls through until next Thursday—ten days—that he will be out of danger. Then the future plans will have to be made. I fear that we shall have to give up Brede Place & go to a more bracing place, on the sea." She adds that Crane seems "much better & very cheerful" (*C*, 623–624).

Cora writes to Pinker that Crane is better in the opinion of the doctors. "Dr. Skinner says that the trouble seems only superficial; not deeply rooted." She and Skinner will take him to London for another consultation as soon as he is strong enough, and then perhaps they will spend a few weeks at a seaside resort (*C*, 624).

[17 APRIL]. Cora writes to Pinker that she is thinking of subleasing Brede Place, apparently with the consent of the Frewens. She does not want Crane to know of this plan (*C*, 625–626).

18 APRIL. The *Sussex Advertiser* reports that Crane is fined 35 shillings for having five dogs without a license. "Mr. Bowen appeared for Mr. Crane, who was very seriously ill at Brede Place. It was an oversight that the licenses had not been taken out." Despite his problems with dogs, Crane told Joseph Conrad that his son "must have a dog, a boy ought to have a dog" (J. Conrad 1926, 135).

19 APRIL. Reynolds advises Crane that his essay "The Great Boer Trek" has been sold to *Cosmopolitan* for $100 after a number of other magazines had declined it (*C*, 626).

Pinker approves of Cora's proposal to sublet Brede Place. "It seems to me it would lift a great deal of responsibility off Mr Crane's shoulders At present he is carrying too much—too much even for a strong man, and it will tell heavily on his health and work" (*C*, 627).

[20 APRIL]. Pinker acknowledges receipt of the typescript of "The Battle of Solferino" (*C*, 627).

21 APRIL. With his attorney Alfred T. Plant and his nurse Charlotte E. Gardner as witnesses, Crane draws up a will to replace the one sent

to William from Jacksonville on 29 November 1896. He names William and Plant as his American and English executors and trustees respectively, directing that they liquidate his real and personal property on both sides of the water and invest the funds remaining after payment of debts in a trust fund in England to be administered by Plant. Cora is named sole beneficiary until her death or remarriage. If Cora remarries, one half of the income is to be held in trust for Edmund's infant son Stephen and the other half divided equally between Edmund and William. In a codicil he exempts from the trust certain personal property, such as "plate linen china glass books pictures prints wines liquors furniture and other household effects watches jewels trinkets personal ornaments and wearing apparel and all my horses carriages harness saddlery and Stable furniture plants and garden tools and implements," which are to be given to "my dear wife Cora Howarth Crane absolutely." Cora is also to receive "during her life or until remarriage," all royalty income from his literary works (Gilkes 1960, 364–367).

William Howe Crane writes to Cora asking if Stephen is willing to go along with a proposal by his brother George to donate Jonathan Townley Crane's theological books to Drew Theological Seminary. He needs Stephen's consent because under the terms of his mother's will Stephen's share in the library is greater than that of the other brothers. William renews his invitation that the Cranes come to live with him in Port Jervis. He will "try to get and send to Stephen a book, written by Dr. Buckley, one of father's old friends, on 'A Consumptive's Struggle for Life.' He had hemorrhages when he was a young man and began the use of Dr. Howe's breathing tube, which Stephen knows about. He recommends it very highly, and also makes some valuable suggestions about climate. Stephen can tell you that I have blown on Dr. Howe's tube over twenty years, and I am sure that it has done me great good" (C, 628).

22 APRIL. H. G. Wells, who suffered from a chronic pulmonary condition that in 1887 was uncertainly diagnosed as tuberculosis, writes Crane:

> I have just heard through Pinker that you are still getting better and I rejoice mightily thereat. I was hugely surprised to hear of your haemorrhaging for you're not at all the hectic sort of person who does that with a serious end in view.
>
> As an expert in haemorrhages I would be prepared to bet you any reasonable sum—I'll bet an even halo only I am afraid of putting you on that high mettle of yours—that haemorrhages aren't the way you will take out of this Terrestrial Tumult.

From any point of view it's a bloody way of dying, and just about when you get thirsty and it bubbles difficult & they inject you with morphia. I know few, more infernally disagreeable.

And confound it! what business have you in the Valley? It isn't midday yet and Your Day's Work handsomely started I admit, is still only practically started. The sooner you come out of that Valley again and stop being absolutely irrelevant to your work, the better! (*C*, 629–630)

[23 APRIL]. Cora sends Pinker the dedication to both the American and English editions of *Wounds in the Rain*:

> To
> Moreton Frewen
> this small token of things
> well remembered by
> his friend
> Stephen Crane.
> Brede Place, Sussex, *April*, 1900. (*C*, 630–631, 631n1).

[24 APRIL]. Cora urges Pinker to secure an advance from Stokes or Methuen in any way he can. The doctors recommend a sea voyage and if some English newspaper will pay expenses for Crane and herself to St. Helena, he can send back some interesting articles and interview General Andrew Cronje, who is in the Boer prison there (C, 631).

25 APRIL. Cora responds to H. G. Wells:

Stephen is not up to letter writing so I am answering your very cheerful letter to him. I am so anxious about him. The lung trouble seems over! The doctor today, after an examination, said that the right lung was entirely unaffected. The trouble is that this dreadful abscess which seems to open from time to time in the bowels—or rectum, makes him suffer the most awful agony. And it takes away his strength in an alarming fashion. The abscess seems to have upset the bowels too. So he is very weak. Then the *fever* (Cuban fever) comes for an hour or two each day. The chills seems to have stopped the past week. And he hopes within three or four weeks to go on a sea voyage. Write to him when you can. Sick people have fancies that their friends neglect them, and wonder at small number of letters etc. Of course, I have up to date read all letters first and there are many which I think best he should not see—you understand. (*C*, 632)

Dr. Maclagen writes to Cora expressing gratification that Crane shows improvement but recommending that he "stay where he is for the present. A change may be advisable later, but I should say not for the next 2 months" (*C,* 632).

[LATE APRIL]. Crane dictates to Cora, and then corrects in his own hand, the draft of a circular advertising a bazaar (NNC), which, according to the printed circular, is "to be held at BREDE PLACE, SUSSEX, on AUGUST 1ST, 1900, (or on AUGUST 2ND if weather on AUGUST 1ST is *wet*), 60 per cent. of the profits to go to assist the FAMILIES of the POOR and NEEDY SOLDIERS who have fought in the TRANSVAAL; 40 per cent. to go to the DISTRICT NURSING FUND" (Wertheim Collection).

30 APRIL. William Howe Crane writes to Cora telling her that he has no objection to Helen's making the trip to St. Helena with the Cranes, providing the expense is not greater than what it would have cost to keep her in school. He sets forth the terms under which Crane tentatively holds a share in the Hartwood property: "Stephen paid me $500 on account of $1250 which he was to pay me for a one-eighth interest in Hartwood. He has no deed and even hasn't a contract—which, however, makes no difference. Now, if he does not wish to complete the transaction, the situation is about like this:—I credit him with $500; I charge him with various items, including the £100 which I sent him in March 1899, and he is still in my debt $155 27/100, at this date." He adds, "Of course, I do not expect him to pay this, until he gets ready. I am merely setting forth the business situation of the Hartwood transaction" (*C,* 634).

MAY. The *Asbury Park Journal* reports that Helen Crane wrote to her father saying that although the Cranes had made plans to spend the summer in St. Helena, the trip has been canceled because Stephen's condition is hopeless. William Howe Crane "will sail for England on the Campania on Saturday" (Copy, NSyU).

"The Siege of Plevna" is published in *Lippincott's Magazine.* A Whilomville story, "The Trial, Execution, and Burial of Homer Phelps," appears in *Harper's Magazine.* A Spitzbergen story, "The Shrapnel of Their Friends," is printed in *Ainslee's Magazine.*

2 MAY. Pinker writes to Cora acknowledging receipt of the last of the "Great Battles" series, "The Storming of Burkersdorf Heights," most likely composed entirely by Kate Lyon. He advises that Tillotson's has declined the terms for serialization of *The O'Ruddy* that he has requested and he will try *McClure's Magazine.* When *McClure's* learned that Stokes already had book rights to *The*

O'Ruddy, they offered only £250, which Pinker rejected, and the novel did not appear serially in America (*C*, 636, 636n2).

4 MAY. Frederick A. Stokes acknowledges the receipt of Pinker's letter of 24 April with the dedication of *Wounds in the Rain*: "We are quite anxious to have some news as to Mr. Crane's condition, as we have heard nothing concerning it for some weeks. In the absence of continued bad news, our hope is that he is recovering. Notwithstanding the friction that we have had with him, we trust you will please tell him of the inquiry that we have made and express our great sympathy with him in his illness,—this entirely apart from any business matters" (NhD).

5 MAY. Cora writes to Pinker:

The doctors say that for Mr. Crane to recover he *must* get out of England. The *Black Forest* first. Now this means, an expensive move within the week. Can you manage an advance in some way? Mr. Crane is no worse & the right lung holds out only, this change must be made without delay. We will go to some small Inn in the Black Forrest. & Rent Brede Place as it stands. I shall have to take nurse & the Doctor will go with us. Its a *very* expensive Journey but its a matter of life or death and it must be done. Please advise me. Can you cable Stokes to advance or get Metheun to advance or How about Serial? Please reply at once. This climate seems simply death to lung Trouble. (*C*, 638)

Conrad writes to John Galsworthy "to say I am going to morrow to stay a week with Stephen Crane. Things aren't very bright. Still!" (Karl and Davies, 2: 266). Because of Crane's condition, this visit is abandoned.

7 MAY. In a circular probably written by Moreton Frewen, Lady Randolph Churchill solicits financial aid for Crane:

The friends of Mr. Stephen Crane will learn with deep regret of the dangerous and it is to be feared, hopeless illness of this accomplished writer. The circumstances are most distressing and pathetic; Mr. Crane when engaged as a special correspondent during the Spanish American War, contracted yellow fever. He was ordered by his doctor a complete and prolonged rest; his straitened circumstances which unhappily he withheld from his friends made this impossible; he has continued and in despite of repeated and positive orders, writing most assiduously until the very moment of collapse; it is but too probable that, not yet thirty, he must pay the penalty with his life.

Mr. Crane is now at Brede Place near Hastings; the Doctors hope that he may recover strength sufficiently to be moved to the Black Forest, and that with great care he may even survive another winter. It is to secure for him, while he still lives, an interval of rest, even though it comes too late that I am permitted to ask the friendly offices of those to whom the pages of The Red Badge of Courage and his other works, have endeared this brilliant young American. (Wertheim 1979a, 31–32)

8 MAY. Cora telegraphs John Hay at the War Department in Washington: "Last hope Stephen Cranes life Blackforest immediately few hundreds need can you help" (*C*, 641). Moreton Frewen appeals to Joseph Pulitzer for funds to help Crane (Wertheim 1979a, 31). He also, perhaps at a later date, approaches J. P. Morgan on Crane's behalf (J. P. Morgan to Moreton Frewen, 18 May 1900, NNC). Walter A. M. Goode, representative of the Associated Press in London, obtains £50 from Andrew Carnegie (W. A. M. Goode to Cora Crane, 7 June 1900, NNC)).

[8 MAY]. Cora writes to Pinker that Crane's life might be saved by the "Nordrach cure," a treatment for consumptives developed by Dr. Otto Walther at Nordrach in the Black Forest. She again outlines the expenses involved and again urges him to find a tenant for Brede Place: "This is a matter of life or death so please do your best. The lung has healed over and he has a chance to get well & live for years if we can get him out of England" (*C*, 641–642, 642n1).

10 MAY. Joseph Conrad writes to Cora expressing his frustration at not being able to provide financial help: "I am a man without connections, without influence and without means. The daily subsistence is a matter of anxious thought for me. What *can* I do?" (*C*, 643).

William Howe Crane writes to Cora reiterating his inability to provide financial help and suggesting means for Helen to return home. He again invites Stephen and Cora to come to Port Jervis or perhaps go to New Mexico (*C*, 644).

[13 MAY]. Conrad responds to a letter from Cora indicating that the doctors have informed her that Crane is dying: "What awful news you are giving me! And yet people given up by the doctors have been known to live for years" (*C*, 645).

14 MAY. Crane dictates a letter to (Arnold) Henry Sanford Bennett:

We are starting for Dover in the morning. My condition is probably known to you. The wine arrived. Many thanks. I want to say something about the Civil List. As I understand it, the fact of having been born outside England does not exclude a man from being taken care of. I have Conrad very much on my mind just now. Garnett does not think it likely that his writing will ever be popular outside the ring of men who write. He is poor and a gentleman and proud. His wife is not strong and they have a kid. If Garnett should ask you to help pull wires for a place on the Civil List for Conrad please do me the last favor of talking about it to that relative of yours who has something to say about these things. I am sure you will. (*C*, 651. This letter is misdated in *Correspondence*.)

15 MAY. The Crane entourage—including Stephen and Cora; their servant, Richard Heather; Dr. Skinner; two nurses, Charlotte Gardner and Annie Taylor; Helen Crane; and the dog Sponge—arrives at the Lord Warden Hotel in Dover, near the Admiralty Pier from which steamers depart for Calais and Ostend three times a day. The hotel is expensive, and, according to Jessie Conrad, "for Poor Cora it was a pitiful business, she had not the means to pay for meals in the 'Lord Warden.' The nurses were fed outside, but I know that the wife often went without" (J. Conrad 1935, 74).

16 MAY. The Conrads go to Dover with their son. While Jessie and Borys remain in their hotel room and comfort Cora (J. Conrad 1926, 137), Conrad visits Crane at the Lord Warden. The following day he writes Galsworthy that he spent 20 minutes with Crane: "Supported move from Brede pretty well. I was awfully shocked of course and had to put on jolly manners. He may yet escape." Conrad mistakenly assumes that the Frewens are paying all of Crane's transit expenses to the Black Forest, "rather more than £100. A doctor friend goes with them. It is a long goodbye to England and Stephen seems to feel it very much. And it may be for ever. He is not *too* hopeful about himself. One lung quite intact at any rate" (Karl and Davies, 2: 270).

17 MAY. John R. Carter, second secretary of the American embassy, writes Cora that although passports are usually only issued at the embassy in London, considering the exceptional circumstances, the consular agent at Dover will take their sworn statements in the Lord Warden and the passports will be mailed to them forthwith (Hagemann 1959, 175).

Robert Barr writes to Cora, proposing that Edward Stewart White, a young American novelist, finish *The O'Ruddy*. He is himself reluctant to do so because of the difference between his style and Crane's: "With pretty near any other man except Kipling and a few others, I would have the cheek to try, but with Stephen, the descrepency would be too marked" (*C*, 647).

BETWEEN 17 AND 20 MAY. H. G. Wells visits Crane at the Lord Warden. He remembers him last

> lying still and comfortably wrapped about, before an open window and the calm and spacious sea. If you would figure him as I saw him, you must think of him as a face of a type very typically American, long and spare, with very straight hair and straight features and long, quiet hands and hollow eyes, moving slowly, smiling and speaking slowly, with that deliberate New Jersey manner he had, and lapsing from speech again into a quiet contemplation of his ancient enemy. For it was the sea that had taken his strength, the same sea that now shone, level waters beyond level waters, with here and there a minute, shining ship, warm and tranquil beneath the tranquil evening sky. Yet I felt scarcely a suspicion then that this was a last meeting. One might have seen it all, perhaps. He was thin and gaunt and wasted, too weak for more than a remembered jest and a greeting and good wishes. It did not seem to me in any way credible that he would reach his refuge in the Black Forest only to die at the journey's end. It will be a long time yet before I can fully realize that he is no longer a contemporary of mine; that the last I saw of him was, indeed, final and complete. (Wells 1900, 233)

18 MAY. F. W. Prescott, an Englishman acting as United States consular agent at Dover, takes Crane's passport application for the purpose of "travelling on the continent of Europe." Cora, Charlotte Gardner, Annie Taylor, and Richard Heather are included in the application as companions. Crane is wrongly described as being 29 years old and 5'10"in height. The passport is issued the following day (Copy, CtU).

19 MAY. Accompanied by Stewart Edward White, Robert Barr visits Crane to read the manuscript and discuss the completion of *The O'Ruddy*. On 8 June, a few days after Crane's death, he writes to an American friend, presumably Karl E. Harriman:

> There was a thin thread of hope that he might recover, but to me he looked like a man already dead. When he spoke, or rather, whispered, there was all the accustomed humor in his sayings. I said to him that I would go over to the Schwarzwald in a few weeks, when he was getting

better, and that we would take some convalescent rambles together. As his wife was listening he said faintly, "I'll look forward to that," but he smiled at me, and winked slowly, as much as to say, "You damned humbug, you know I'll take no more rambles in this world." Then, as if the train of thought suggested what was looked on before as the crisis of his illness, he murmured, "Robert, when you come to the hedge—that we must all go over—it isn't bad. You feel sleepy—and—you don't care. Just a little dreamy curiosity—which world you're really in—that's all." (*New York Herald*, 21 June)

[In 1904, when *The O'Ruddy* was serialized in *The Idler*, Barr recalled other details of his visit to Crane:

Stewart Edward White and I went down to Dover together, and put up at the Lord Warden Hotel, where Stephen was stopping, awaiting a calm day on which to cross the Channel. The doctor would not allow us to see him that night, and Stewart Edward White and I spent the evening reading *The O'Ruddy* in Crane's beautiful handwriting. The jollity of the tale, combined with the fact that its writer lay near us, hopelessly ill, made the evening one which neither the young American writer nor myself are likely to forget. Next day I was urged by both Mrs. Crane and the physician to agree to anything Stephen asked, and this was not a request one could refuse. White and I were shown into the room where the sick man lay by an open window overlooking the blue Channel. Stephen was as humorous as ever, and joked in a whisper. He said I did not look natural, not having a cigarette in my hand, and urged me to light one so that he could have a sniff of it, and condemned his physician. He made me hand him his pipe so that he might caress the bowl of it. All that he could tell me of the story was that he intended to end it at Brede Place, in Sussex, where it had been written, an ancient house which I knew well. I agreed to finish the book, but told him he could not have made a worse choice. He whispered that he was well acquainted with my self-conceit, and did not credit in the least my assumption of incapacity. He said I was merely trying to cloak my cowardice; I was afraid of the critics, so he suggested the splitting of the last sentence he had written and advised me to begin with that.

"They'll all think you began with a new chapter, so you can defy them to point out the junction." (Bradshaw, 176–177)]

20 MAY. Crane's "An Illusion in Red and White," a murder story ostensibly narrated by a correspondent in a dispatch boat during the Cuban blockade, is syndicated through the *New York World*.

[20 MAY]. Cora sends Pinker an inscription in Crane's hand for *The O'Ruddy*: "May—1900/Brede Place/Sussex/England/To/My Wife/Stephen Crane" (*C*, 648). But this dedication does not appear in either the American or English edition of the novel. Cora's covering letter mentions the title of the book for the first time.

Cora writes to H. G. Wells asking him not to come to Dover again because the nurses recommend complete rest for Crane before the Channel crossing (*C*, 649).

21 MAY. Prescott takes Helen Crane's passport application. The passport is issued on 22 May (Copy, CtU).

22 MAY. Stokes writes to Pinker asking if the stories of *Wounds in the Rain* should appear in the order listed by Crane in a memorandum previously sent to them (NhD). The stories appear in the published volume in this order, with Crane's original title "The Making of the 307th" changed to "Virtue in War."

23 MAY. Joseph Conrad visits Crane for the last time. As he recalls, "I saw him for the last time on his last day in England. It was in Dover, in a big hotel, in a bedroom with a large window looking on to the sea. He had been very ill and Mrs. Crane was taking him to some place in Germany, but one glance at that wasted face was enough to tell me that it was the most forlorn of all hopes. The last words he breathed out to me were: 'I am tired. Give my love to your wife and child.' When I stopped at the door for another look I saw that he had turned his head on the pillow and was staring wistfully out of the window at the sails of a cutter yacht that glided slowly across the frame, like a dim shadow against the grey sky" (Conrad 1921, 70–71).

24 MAY. The Crane party crosses the English Channel to Calais. They stop over for two or three days at the Hotel Trois Rois in Basel.

27 MAY. A. E. W. Mason writes to Crane that J. M. Barrie, who is a member of the board of the Royal General Literary Fund, suggests that Crane apply to the fund for assistance, which would no doubt be forthcoming (*C*, 652–653).

28 MAY. The Cranes reach Badenweiler, Baden, a health spa situated on the edge of the Black Forest. They move into Haus Luisenstrasse 44, on the corner of Bergstrasse, also called Villa Eberhardt, owned by Herr Albert Eberhardt. Here Crane is attended by Dr. Albert Fraenkel, himself a victim of tuberculosis (Hagemann 1959, 178).

29 MAY. Cora writes an incoherent letter to Pinker demanding to know what has been done about the sale of serial rights of *The O'Ruddy* and the Wyoming stories: "I simply must have money for Mr. Crane" (*C*, 654).

30 MAY. The Cranes write to Stephen's brother George to say that Stephen has not hemorrhaged for 18 days (*Newark Evening News*, 5 June).

30 MAY–3 JUNE. Despite his weakening condition, Crane continues dictating to Cora fragmentary episodes for the completion of *The O'Ruddy*. Cora makes an effort through Moreton Frewen, who was known for his proclivity to speculate on inventions, to market her canteen filter. In a note to Frewen on the evening of 3 June, Cora concludes "Stephen is not quite clear in his mind tonight" (*C*, 657).

JUNE. "The Battle of Bunker Hill" appears in *Lippincott's Magazine*. "The Great Boer Trek," a derivative essay most likely researched by Kate Lyon, is published in *Cosmopolitan*. "The Fight," a Whilomville story, is in *Harper's Magazine*.

3 JUNE. Cora writes to Moreton Frewen:

I've only sad news to write you. There seems little hope of cure. The fever seems the thing that cannot be conquered. It is not due alone to the lung but is the remains of the yellow fever and the Cuban fever. Dr. Frankel cannot see why the lung trouble was not discovered when Mr. Crane was examined in Dec. He will not take responsibility of Mr. Cranes case alone so I've consented to a consultation tomorrow with Proffessor Brueiler of Frieburg, to whom Dr. Mitchel Bruce wrote & through who's advice we came here. I wired you but have received no reply. There is nothing for me to do but to consent to consultation. Dr. Frankel said that Professor Brueiler would only ask about 125 marks. My husbands brain is never at rest. He lives over everything in dreams & talks aloud constantly. It is too awful to hear him try to change places in the "*open boat*"! I nearly went mad yesterday & the nurse gave me some drug which made me sleep for hours, so I'm fresh again for today. He worries so about his debts and about our not being able to live here. So I told him yesterday that I had £300—cash & since then he has been satisfied. I think it is really worry about my future. so I do everything possible to ease his poor tired mind.

About the book. Mr. Crane said: "There are only two men who could finish 'The O'Ruddy.' One is Kipling & the other is Robert Barr. Kipling would have the style and Robert Barr the humour." So when Robert Barr came to see my husband at Dover, He read the ms. & thought it equal to

"The Three Musketeers." He said: "Kipling is the only man to finish this book" but we said: "no" and so it is that Mr. Barr has the ms. 65000 words. Yesterday when your letter came my husband said: "say to Moreton Frewen that it will ever be my joy to follow his wishes in every way. Tell him that if Robert Barr finishes the O'Ruddy and if Kipling goes over the book, adding to it as he thinks fit I shall be glad. Robert Louis Stevenson left in his will that Quiler Couch was to finish his book [*St. Ives*] and the world calls it *his* book (R. L. S.) and I shall be happy if my book goes through Kiplings hands." (*C*, 655–656)

[The legend of Crane's antipathy to Robert Louis Stevenson originated with Ford Madox Ford and was reinforced by Thomas Beer. One of Ford's "memories" is of hearing Crane, "with his wonderful eyes flashing and his extreme vigor and intonation, comment upon a sentence of Robert Louis Stevenson that he was reading. The sentence was: 'With interjected finger he delayed the motion of the timepiece.' 'By God, poor dear!' Crane exclaimed. 'That man put back the clock of English fiction fifty years'" (Ford 1911, 58). When Ford again alluded to this remark in *Thus to Revisit* (Ford 1921, 17), Beer responded that it was originally made by Harold Frederic and only reiterated by Crane (Beer 1924, iv).]

4 JUNE. William Howe Crane receives a cablegram saying that his brother is near death and that he wishes to be buried in his homeland (*Port Jervis Union*, 5 June). Shortly after 5 June, an unidentified New Jersey newspaper reports, "Mr. Crane had expressed a wish that he be buried in the same lot with his father and mother in Evergreen Cemetery, Elizabeth" (Undated clipping, NSyU).

[Evergreen Cemetery is in Union County in what is now the Township of Hillside, on the Elizabeth city line. The Crane family usually referred to the cemetery as being in Elizabeth, which has caused controversy among Crane's biographers as to exactly where he is buried.]

5 JUNE. Crane dies at 3:00 A.M. in the Villa Eberhardt (Eidson, 149). Cora fears that his end may have been hastened by an improper medical procedure, as the distraught, incoherent jottings in her notebook written shortly afterward reveal:

Write to Dr Skinner about Morphine—
—"Thats what strayed him"—
"You can cut them she cant."
"Little Butcher, I will tell Skinner how he came to Bali & stole me"—
To nurse: "Did you know Dr Bruce never heard of him?" Dr called
June 4th 8 P.M—Gave morphine injection—went at once to heart, I could

Villa Eberhardt, Badenweiler, Germany, the house
in which Stephen Crane died
(Wertheim Collection)

see by muscular contraction Dr. saw too, tried to give champhor injection to revive action of heart. Dr said next day: "Can you forgive me?" What did he mean? don't dare to think. (*Works* 10: 343)

In the morning Cora telegraphs Joseph Hodges Choate, United States ambassador to Great Britain, to arrange for the transportation of Crane's body back to England. Choate contacts Ambassador Andrew Dickson White in Berlin, and he in turn has the secretary of the embassy dispatch a message to E. Theophilous Liefeld, the American consul at Freiburg: "At instance of Ambassador Choate Embassy requests you to facilitate removal to England of remains of Stephen Crane who died at Villa Ebrardt [Eberhardt] Badenweiler" (Hagemann 1959, 178–180).

Henry James writes to Cora:

On the Monday you were at Dover I was on the very point of going over to see you & had arranged for an absence of a day, domestically, the night before, but the a.m. brought with it a mass of proofs to be instantly attended to—I was under much pressure, & I lost the occasion, believing then that you were leaving & leaving with all good omens—on the Tuesday. I learned afterwards that you had waited a day or two longer, but

Skinner expressed doubts of Crane's having been able to see me even if I had gone—& that partly consoled me. . . . I feel that I am not taking too much for granted in believing that you may be in the midst of worries on the money-score which will perhaps make the cheque, for Fifty Pounds, that I enclose, a convenience to you. Please view it as such & dedicate it to whatever service it may best render my stricken young friend. It meagrely represents my tender benediction to him. (*C*, 658–659)

William Howe Crane, who had arranged to travel to Germany, telegraphs "Passage cancelled. Money this afternoon" (NNC).

The *Brooklyn Daily Eagle* announces "Stephen Crane is Dead" and gives a capsule summary of his career: "As an author he had but one notable success, 'The Red Badge of Courage.' He wrote in a slovenly manner, but the incidents which he created were always picturesque, and he paid most careful attention to their minutest detail."

6 JUNE. In its obituary, the *London Daily Chronicle* dwells upon Crane's "genuine pluck":

Before he had reached even the "fatal age" of thirty-five—fatal to so many men of genius—Stephen Crane has passed away, leaving behind him a legacy of brilliant work accomplished, and the promise of more solid and enduring work in the future. He was only thirty, yet he looked more like a boy of eighteen, and, with his fragile physique and shy and sensitive disposition, he was the last man who might be expected to figure in the stress and storm of battle. Yet "little Stevey"—as his friends and colleagues delighted to call him—was possessed of the highest and truest courage, the courage of the man of keen imagination, and he proved it on more than one stricken field.

At the New York Press Club, a special meeting of the Society of the Caribbean, composed of war correspondents in the Cuban and Puerto Rican Campaigns, adopts a memorial resolution:

"Our comrade in the Spanish-American War, Stephen Crane, has just died in a foreign country.
"It is our desire to express our sense of deep personal loss and our own keen sorrow at the untimely end of the brilliant journalist and gifted author, and at the same time to extend our sympathy to his bereaved family.
"We admired his genius and loved him as a man. We shall cherish his memory always." (*New York Journal*, 7 June)

The *New York Sun*'s obituary stresses that in his depictions of battle Crane's imagination exceeded his powers of realistic description:

It has been noted as a curious manifestation of genius that Mr. Crane's imaginative story of a war that was over before he was born should excel his descriptions of the scenes of actual conflict which he witnessed, but it is a fact that his accounts of the wars which he saw were less vigorous and less vivid pictures of strife than those in his works of fiction. He saw the advance of the Rough Riders and the Regulars who were supporting them from Daiquiri and the battle of Las Guasimas, but walking over the trail and the field the next day he was unable to describe the fighting except in a most perfunctory way. "To tell you the truth there was too much going on," he said; "the details escaped me."

7 JUNE. Henry James, who has read of Crane's death in the newspapers, writes: "What a brutal, needless extinction—what an unmitigated unredeemed catastrophe! I think of him with such a sense of possibilities and powers!" (James, 145).

8 JUNE. The funeral entourage superintended by Liefeld arrives in Freiburg, where Crane's body is embalmed by a pathologist. The United States embassy in London makes special arrangements to get Crane's dog, Sponge, back into England (Hagemann 1959, 180–182). Jessie Conrad's anecdote that on the day of Crane's death Cora telegraphed Plant "'God took Stephen at 11.5, make some arrangement for me to get the dog home'" (J. Conrad 1935, 75) is most likely spurious.

William Howe Crane writes a cliché-ridden letter of condolence to Cora:

> Several times I have taken up my pen to write you, but have halted because I could not think of anything to write that would fit the situation. We are simply benumbed by this calamity which has fallen upon you and upon us. I engaged passage upon a steamer sailing yesterday, but canceled it upon the receipt of your telegram. Port Jervis is in mourning.
> So many people here knew him, that the village claimed him as one of her sons and always felt pride in his achievements.
> I suppose Stephen's wish was to be buried in our family plot at Elizabeth, New Jersey. (L, 286)

9 JUNE. Crane's body is conveyed from Calais to Dover. Cora and Helen are met at dockside by Robert Barr (Gilkes 1960, 262).

Edward Garnett lauds Crane's individuality in an unsigned tribute in the *Academy*:

> As a writer he was very modern. He troubled himself little about style or literary art. But—rare gift—he saw for himself, and, like Mr. Steevens,

he knew in a flash just what was essential to bring the picture vividly to the reader. His books are full of images and similes that not only fulfil their purpose of the moment, but live in the memory afterwards. A super-refined literary taste might object to some of his phrases—to such a sentence as this, for example: "By the very last star of truth, it is easier to steal eggs from under a hen than it was to change seats in the dingey," to his colloquialisms, to the slang with which he peppered the talk of his men—but that was the man, who looked at things with his own eyes, and was unafraid of his prepossessions.

10 JUNE. The *New York World*, in an article entitled "Madcap Genius: Stephen Crane," eulogizes Crane and evaluates his career, concluding, as do a number of other obituaries, that he died at 30:

It is a mistake to say that he began life as a reporter. His nature could not brook the drudgery and discipline of reporter's work. He preferred to hover on the ragged edge of starvation, earning a precarious pittance by writing sketches and stories of city life for newspapers.

Although it was not until after years that he developed consumption, he was always more or less delicate. His build was as frail as his stature was small. But so aflame was he with energy, so incessantly did his nervous force goad him into vigorous action that one lost sight of his physical deficiencies. . . .

In speech he was without affectation. He used the vernacular and used it with vigor.

His face expressed both his intellectual strength and his physical weakness. It was an interesting face, lean, sharp-featured, sallow, eager, a mirror of every emotion. The eyes were restless, searching, eloquent and deeply blue.

12 JUNE. Crane's body is moved to a London mortuary at 82 Baker Street (*New York Tribune*, 13 June). Cora goes into residence at Queen Anne's Mansions, St. James Park, a family hotel where the De Frieses, A. E. W. Mason, and other friends reside. From this address, announcement cards for a viewing of the body, handwritten by Helen, are sent out (Gilkes 1960, 262).

14 JUNE. Crane's body is viewed in the Baker Street mortuary. Curtis Brown recalls:

Presently I heard that Crane was dead, and received a card to the effect that his remains could be viewed at an address in Baker Street, just opposite to where Sherlock Holmes was supposed to have lived. I went on the appointed day, and found a small undertaker's shop. The woman in attendance within seemed perplexed when I inquired; but brightened up when my invitation-card was produced, and said: "Outside, under the archway."

I went out, and through the adjoining archway into a large, square stable-yard, surrounded on three sides by covered bays, and with carts piled up in the middle. There were horses in two or three of the bays; but the rest were empty, except one and there was a coffin on trestles, with the face of my old friend exposed through the glass. He looked as if he had suffered greatly. There was no one else about. I stayed for a time, thinking over our talks together; and then went slowly away, with a heavy heart. (C. Brown, 226)

[Jessie Conrad commented that "it was a terrible pity the poor corpse should have to lie in a London mortuary waiting for a passage to America for so long. There was a glass let in the lid of the coffin, and people were allowed to take a last look at poor Stephen, and leave their card at the mortuary" (J. Conrad 1935, 75).]

In a letter to Cora misdated 13 June, H. G. Wells apologizes for not attending the viewing of Crane's body:

I do not know what you will think of my absence from that last sight of Stephen today but indeed if I could have brought myself to see him I would not have failed you. These things however affect me so darkly. I should have found so little comfort & so much distress in this encounter and I have the memory of him in still comfort before that open window & the sea so vividly in my mind, that I do not care to disturb & weaken it by meeting something that was no longer him. The last few days I have been very much with him, with that ample portion of him that will not die, for, at the request of Messrs. Harper I have been writing an impression of his work and of his significance in literature as they appear to English eyes. There I have tried to say without exaggeration & without cant, the essential greatness of his work. (Wertheim 1979b, 210)

15 JUNE. Stokes advises Pinker that the copy of "The Revenge of the Adolphus" sent to them by Crane is incomplete and they are attempting to find the issue of the *Strand* in which the story was printed in England. They have discovered that "The Making of the 307th" and "Virtue in War" on Crane's list "are one and the same story, although in the column for the number of words opposite the titles in this Ms. list he has given the number of 3100 words for the former and 8200 words for the latter" (NhD).

16 JUNE. Moreton Frewen informs Cora that Kipling declines to be involved in the completion of *The O'Ruddy*, stating that "my own opinion is & I hold it very strongly that a man's work is personal to

him, & should remain as he made it or left it. I should have been glad to have done him a kindness, but this is not a thing that a man feeling as I do, can undertake" (NNC).

In *Harper's Weekly* Joseph B. Gilder concludes that Crane's career is "an extraordinary record of literary productivity. To what extent it is a record of growth is another question."

Even in death, the *New York Tribune* continues to denigrate Crane's character and achievement:

> Now that Stephen Crane is dead a good deal is being said about his character as a man. His best attribute seems to have been physical courage, which was conspicuously displayed in Cuba during the Spanish-American War. It is said to have been accompanied by qualities not altogether admirable. In spite of his success and in spite of the five years of hard work following it, Mr. Crane died poor. None of his books had apparently one of those sales that nowadays brings fortunes to their authors. Such success as was obtained by "The Red Badge of Courage" was important to Mr. Crane as given value to his future work, yet the novel that he next published, "George's Mother," proved to be a great failure, in this country at any rate. He had some college training, but it left little impression on him. At the time when he wrote "The Red Badge of Courage" he was a curiously uninformed and ignorant boy. He had not only read little, but he deliberately avoided reading for fear of being influenced by other writers. His friends in New York consisted chiefly of young artists, who, as a class, are not noted for their literary attainments. That they probably influenced him, however, was shown by his extreme fondness for impressionism and for the fantastic in art, then exemplified by Aubrey Beardsley.

17 JUNE. Cora sails with Crane's body from Southampton on the North-German Lloyd liner *Bremen* (*New York Commercial Advertiser,* 27 June). She is accompanied by Helen Crane, Sponge, and another of the Brede Place dogs (Gilkes 1960, 262).

18 JUNE. Alfred T. Plant informs Pinker that Robert Barr has agreed to complete *The O'Ruddy* (NN-Berg).

[Before leaving England Cora made the mistake of giving Frewen's letter stating Kipling's reservations and her own notes for the completion of *The O'Ruddy* to Barr, who, already disturbed by press reports that he would attempt the completion, had second thoughts about his own commitment and suggested that Stewart Edward White or Cora herself finish the novel. H. B. Marriott-Watson briefly considered taking up the task, but in mid-August he declined. David Belasco, who had also considered dramatizing *The Red Badge* (Belasco, 666), contemplated producing *The O'Ruddy* as a play before it appeared as a novel. A. E. W. Mason held the manuscript for almost two years without working on it. Finally, in the autumn of 1902, Pinker and Barr reached a mutually satisfactory understanding, but terms were made final only in June 1903, when Stokes and William Howe Crane signed a contract that referred to Stokes's having arranged with Barr to finish the book. Barr wrote the last 8 of the 33 chapters, and, after considerable wrangling over his payment, the way was finally clear for *The O'Ruddy* to appear. Copyright deposit in the Library of Congress was made on 2 November 1903 and publication announced in *Publishers' Weekly* on 5 December. A variant and shortened version of the novel was serialized in *The Idler* in seven installments in 1904. *The O'Ruddy* was published in book form in England in July (Levenson 1971, liii–lxxii; Bradshaw, 174–175).]

23 JUNE. The *Literary Digest* calls Crane "A 'Wonderful Boy'" but expresses reservations about what his future would have been had he lived: "Whether his fame would ever have reached a higher level is open to doubt, and perhaps critical opinion largely leans to the judgment that his artistic attainment would never have been able to go beyond the extremely clever but impressionistic word-painting of the work already produced by him."

Heinemann publishes *Bowery Tales*, a reprint of *Maggie* and *George's Mother* (Bruccoli and Katz, 281).

24 JUNE. "This Majestic Lie" is syndicated in a small number of American newspapers.

26 JUNE. Stokes writes to Pinker that they have found a copy of the *Strand* containing "The Revenge of the Adolphus." They look forward to Barr's completion of *The O'Ruddy* and "hope that you will prevail upon Mr. Barr not to cut the conclusion of the story too short; as the difficulty of disposing of short novels is greater to-day than at any time in many years past" (NhD).

27 JUNE. The *Bremen* crosses the bar of New York harbor at 9:15 A.M. (*New York Times*, 28 June). Crane's body is transferred to a morgue at 46 Great Jones Street (*Newark Daily Advertiser*, 28 June).

28 JUNE. A funeral service for Crane is held at the Central Metropolitan Temple. Among the pallbearers are Ripley Hitchcock, Willis Brooks Hawkins, and John Kendrick Bangs. The mourners include Cora and Helen Crane; four of Stephen's brothers, William, Edmund,

Wilbur, and George; his surviving sister, Mary Helen Murray-Hamilton; and other members of the Crane family. The sermon is preached by the Reverend James M. Buckley, the editor of the *Christian Advocate*, who had been a friend of Jonathan Townley Crane (*New York Sun*, 29 June).

Wallace Stevens, covering the funeral for the *New York Tribune*, writes in his journal:

> This morning I went to the funeral of Stephen Crane at the Central Metropolitan Temple on Seventh Avenue near Fourteenth Street. The church is a small one and was about [a] third full. Most of the people were of the lower classes and had dropped in apparently to pass away the time. There was a sprinkling of men and women who looked literary, but they were a wretched, rag, tag, and bob-tail. I recognized John Kendrick Bangs. The whole thing was frightful. The prayers were perfunctory, the choir worse than perfunctory with the exception of its hymn "Nearer My God To Thee" which is the only appropriate hymn for funerals I ever heard. The address was absurd. The man kept me tittering from the time he began till the time he ended. He spoke of Gladstone + Goethe. Then—on the line of premature death—he dragged in Shelley; and speaking of the dead man's later work he referred to Hawthorne. Finally came the Judgement day—and all this with most delicate, sweet, and bursal gestures—when the earth and the sea shall give up their dead. A few of the figures to appear that day flashed through my head—and poor Crane looked ridiculous among them. But he lived a brave, aspiring, hardworking life. Certainly he deserved something better than this absolutely common-place, bare, silly service I have just come from. As the hearse rattled up the street over the cobbles, in the stifling heat of the sun, with not a single person paying the least attention to it and with only four or five carriages behind it at a distance I realized much that I had doubtingly suspected before—There are few hero-worshippers.
>
> * * *

Therefore, few heroes. (Stevens, 41)

Sources

Alger	Russell A. Alger. *The Spanish-American War*. New York: Harper, 1901.
Allen	Frederick Lewis Allen. *Paul Revere Reynolds*. New York: Privately printed, 1944.
Allerton	James M. Allerton. *The Civil List of the Town of Deerpark: 1690–1891*. Port Jervis, New York: Gazette Book & Job Print, 1891.
Bacheller (1901)	Anonymous. "Authors' Associations." *Manuscript* 1 (1901): 32–34.
Bacheller (1928)	Irving Bacheller. *Coming up the Road*. Indianapolis: Bobbs-Merrill, 1928.
Bacheller (1933)	———. *From Stores of Memory*. New York: Farrar and Rinehart, 1933.
BAL	*Bibliography of American Literature*.
Barr	Robert Barr. "American Brains in London." *Saturday Evening Post* 171 (8 April 1899): 648–649.
Barry	John D. Barry. "A Note on Stephen Crane." *Bookman* 13 (April 1901): 148.
Beer (1923)	Thomas Beer. *Stephen Crane: A Study in American Letters*. New York: Knopf, 1923.
Beer (1924)	———. "Stephen Crane." *New York Evening Post Literary Review*. 19 July 1924, iv, 910.
Beer (1934)	———. "Mrs. Stephen Crane." *American Mercury* 31 (March 1934): 289–295.
Beer Papers	Thomas Beer Papers, The Beer Family Papers. CtY.
Belasco	David Belasco. "The Genius of Stephen Crane." *Metropolitan Magazine* 12 (1900): 666.
Benfey (1990)	Christopher Benfey. "Stephen Crane's Father and the Holiness Movement." *Courier* 25 (1990): 27–36.
Benfey (1992)	———. *The Double Life of Stephen Crane*. New York: Knopf, 1992
Berryman	John Berryman. *Stephen Crane*. 1950. Reprint. Cleveland: World–Meridian, 1962.

Bigsby

C. W. E. Bigsby. "The 'Christian Science Case': An Account of the Death of Harold Frederic and the Subsequent Inquest and Court Proceedings." *American Literary Realism, 1870–1910* 2 (Spring 1968): 77–83.

Binder

Henry Binder. "*The Red Badge of Courage* Nobody Knows." *Studies in the Novel* 10 (1978): 9–47.

Bowers
(1970)

Fredson Bowers, ed. *Tales of War.* Vol. 6, *The Works of Stephen Crane.* Edited by Fredson Bowers. Charlottesville: University Press of Virginia, 1970.

Bowers
(1971)

———, ed. *Reports of War.* Vol. 9, *The Works of Stephen Crane.* Edited by Fredson Bowers. Charlottesville: University Press of Virginia, 1971.

Bowers
(1975)

———, ed. *The Red Badge of Courage.* Vol. 2, *The Works of Stephen Crane.* Edited by Fredson Bowers. Charlottesville: University Press of Virginia, 1975.

Bowers
(1976)

———, ed. The Third Violet *and* Active Service. Vol. 3, *The Works of Stephen Crane.* Edited by Fredson Bowers. Charlottesville: University Press of Virginia, 1976.

Bowers
(1989)

———. "Regularization and Normalization in Modern Critical Texts." *Studies in Bibliography* 42 (1989): 79–102.

Boyd

Thomas Boyd. "Semper Fidelis: An Interrupted Narrative Regarding Sergeant Major John H. Quick, U.S.M.C." *Bookman* 60 (1924): 409–412.

Bradshaw

James Stanford Bradshaw. "Completing Crane's *O'Ruddy*: A New Note." *ANQ* 3 (1990): 174–178.

C. Brown

Curtis Brown. *Contacts.* London: Cassell, 1935.

C. H. Brown

Charles H. Brown. *The Correspondents' War: Journalists in the Spanish-American War.* New York: Scribner's, 1967.

Brown
and Hernlund

Ellen A. Brown and Patricia Hernlund. "The Source for the Title of Stephen Crane's *Whilomville Stories.*" *American Literature* 50 (1978): 116–118.

Bruccoli
and Katz

Matthew J. Bruccoli and Joseph Katz. "Scholarship and Mere Artifacts: The British and Empire Publications of Stephen Crane." *Studies in Bibliography* 22 (1969): 277–287.

C

The Correspondence of Stephen Crane. Edited by Stanley Wertheim and Paul Sorrentino. 2 vols. New York: Columbia University Press, 1988.

Cady and Wells	Edwin H. Cady and Lester G. Wells, eds. *Stephen Crane's Love Letters to Nellie Crouse.* Syracuse, NY: Syracuse University Press, 1954.
Campbell	Charles A. Campbell. *Traditions of Hartwood.* Winter Park, Florida: Orange Press, 1930.
Carmichael	Otto Carmichael. "Stephen Crane in Havana." *Prairie Schooner* 43 (1969): 200–204.
Carnes	Cecil Carnes. *Jimmy Hare, News Photographer: Half a Century with a Camera.* New York: Macmillan, 1940.
Carroll	William W. Carroll. Untitled Reminiscence, 3 pp. With covering letter to Thomas Beer, 20 March 1924. CtY.
Carruthers	Sharon Carruthers. "'Old Soldiers Never Die': A Note on Col. John L. Burleigh." *Studies in the Novel* 10 (1978): 158–160.
Cather (1900)	Willa Cather [as "Henry Nicklemann"]. "When I Knew Stephen Crane." *Library* (Pittsburgh) 1 (23 June 1900): 17–18. Reprint. *Prairie Schooner* 23 (1949): 231–36.
Cather (1970)	Willa Cather. *The World and the Parish: Willa Cather's Articles and Reviews, 1893–1902.* Edited by William M. Curtin. 2 vols. Lincoln: University of Nebraska Press, 1970.
Cazemajou	Jean Cazemajou. *Stephen Crane (1871–1900): Écrivain Journaliste.* Études Anglaises 35. Paris: Librairie Didier, 1969.
Clifford	John H. Clifford. *History of the First Battalion of U.S. Marines.* N.p.: Privately printed, 1930.
CLSU	University of Southern California, Los Angeles.
Collum	Richard S. Collum, "Services of the First Marine Battalion in Cuba." *The United Service: A Monthly Review of Military and Naval Affairs* 2 (1902): 547–560.
Colvert (1956)	James B. Colvert. "*The Red Badge of Courage* and a Review of Zola's *La Débâcle.*" *Modern Language Notes* 71 (1956): 98–100.
Colvert (1984)	———. *Stephen Crane.* San Diego: Harcourt, 1984.
Colvert (1990)	———. "Crane, Hitchcock, and the Binder Edition of *The Red Badge of Courage.*" *Critical Essays on Stephen Crane's* The Red Badge of Courage. Ed-

ited by Donald Pizer. Boston: G. K. Hall, 1990. Pp. 238–263.

J. Conrad (1926) — Jessie Conrad. "Recollections of Stephen Crane." *Bookman* 63 (April 1926): 134–137.

J. Conrad (1935) — ———. *Joseph Conrad and His Circle*. New York: E. P. Dutton, 1935.

Conrad (1921) — Joseph Conrad. *Notes on Life and Letters*. London: J. M. Dent & Sons, 1921.

Conrad (1923) — ———. Introduction to *Stephen Crane: A Study in American Letters*, by Thomas Beer. New York: Knopf, 1923.

Conrad (1958) — ———. *Letters to William Blackwood and David S. Meldrum*. Edited by William Blackburn. Durham, NC: Duke University Press, 1958.

EBC — Edmund B. Crane. "Notes on the Life of Stephen Crane by His Brother, Edmund B. Crane." 6 pp. Thomas Beer Papers, The Beer Family Papers. CtY.

Mrs. GC — Mrs. George Crane. "Stephen Crane's Boyhood." *New York World*, 10 June 1900. Section E, p. 3.

HRC — Helen R. Crane. "My Uncle, Stephen Crane." *American Mercury* 31 (January 1934): 24–29.

JTC — Jonathan Townley Crane. *Holiness the Birthright of All God's Children*. New York: Nelson & Phillips, 1874

WFC — Wilbur F. Crane. "Reminiscences of Stephen Crane." *Binghamton Chronicle*, 15 December 1900, p. 3. Copy, NSyU.

Crisler — Jesse S. Crisler. "'Christmas Must be Gay': Stephen Crane's *The Ghost*—A Play by Divers Hands." In *Proof: The Yearbook of American Bibliographical and Textual Studies*. Edited by Joseph Katz. Vol. 3. Columbia: University of South Carolina Press, 1973. Pp. 69–120.

CtU — University of Connecticut, Storrs.

CtY — Yale University, New Haven, Connecticut.

Davis — Robert H. Davis. Introduction to *Tales of Two Wars* (1925). Vol. 2, *The Work of Stephen Crane*. Edited by Wilson Follett. 12 vols. New York: Knopf, 1925–1927.

C. B. Davis — Charles Belmont Davis, ed. *Adventures and Letters of Richard Harding Davis*. New York: Scribner's, 1917.

R. H. Davis (1898)	Richard Harding Davis. *The Cuban and Porto Rican Campaigns.* New York: Scribner's, 1898.
R. H. Davis (1899)	———. "Our War Correspondents in Cuba and Puerto Rico." *Harper's Magazine* 98 (1898–1899): 938–948.
R. H. Davis (1904)	———. "How Stephen Crane Took Juana Dias." In *In Many Wars by Many War Correspondents.* Edited by George Lynch and Frederick Palmer. Tokyo: Tokyo Printing Company, 1904. Reprint. La Crosse, Wisconsin: Sumac Press, 1976.
R. H. Davis (1910)	———. *Notes of a War Correspondent.* New York: Scribner's, 1910.
Day	Cyrus Day. "Stephen Crane and the Ten-foot Dinghy." *Studies in English* 3 (Winter 1957): 193–213.
DGU	Georgetown University, Washington, DC.
Dirlam and Simmons	Kenneth Dirlam and Ernest F. Simmons. *Sinners, This Is East Aurora.* New York: Vantage, 1964.
Eidson	John O. Eidson. "The Death Certificate of Stephen Crane." *Notes and Queries* 7 (April 1960): 149–150.
Elconin	Victor A. Elconin. "Stephen Crane at Asbury Park." *American Literature* 20 (1948): 275–289.
Emerson	Edwin Emerson. *Pepys's Ghost.* Boston: Richard G. Badger, 1900.
Ferrara and Dossett	Mark Ferrara and Gordon Dossett. "A Sheaf of Contemporary American Reviews of Stephen Crane." *Studies in the Novel* 10 (1978): 168–182.
Ford (1911)	Ford Madox Hueffer. *Memories and Impressions.* New York: Harper, 1911.
Ford (1921)	Ford Madox Ford. *Thus to Revisit.* London: Chapman and Hall, 1921. Reprint. New York: Octagon Books, 1966.
Ford (1931)	———. *Return to Yesterday.* London: Victor Gollancz, 1931.
Ford (1937)	———. *Portraits from Life.* Boston: Houghton Mifflin, 1937.
Fortenberry	George E. Fortenberry et al., eds. *The Correspondence of Harold Frederic.* Fort Worth: Texas Christian University Press, 1977.
French	Mansfield J. French. "Stephen Crane, Ball Player." *Syracuse University Alumni News* 15 (January 1934): 3–4.
Friedmann (1989)	Elizabeth Friedmann. "Cora Before Crane: The Prologue." Unpublished paper delivered at the Ste-

phen Crane Conference sponsored by Virginia Polytechnic Institute and State University. Blacksburg, Virginia, 29 September, 1989.

Friedmann (1990) ————. "Cora's Travel Notes, 'Dan Emmonds,' and Stephen Crane's Route to the Greek War: A Puzzle Solved." *Studies in Short Fiction* 27 (1990): 264–265.

Fryckstedt Olov W. Fryckstedt. "Stephen Crane in the Tenderloin." *Studia Neophilologica* 34 (1962): 135–163.

Garland (1893a) Hamlin Garland. "The Future of Fiction." *Arena* 7 (1893): 513–524.

Garland (1893b) ————. "An Ambitious French Novel and a Modest American Story." *Arena* 8 (1893): xi–xii.

Garland (1900) ————. "Stephen Crane: A Soldier of Fortune." *Saturday Evening Post* 173 (28 July 1900): 16–17.

Garland (1930) ————. *Roadside Meetings.* New York: Macmillan, (1930).

Garner Stanton Garner. "Stephen Crane's 'The Predecessor': Unwritten Play, Unwritten Novel." *American Literary Realism, 1870–1910* 13 (1980): 97–100.

Garnett (1922) Edward Garnett. *Friday Nights: Literary Criticisms and Appreciations.* London: Jonathan Cape, 1922.

Garnett (1928) ————. ed. *Letters from Joseph Conrad.* Indianapolis: Bobbs-Merrill, 1928.

Gettmann Royal A. Gettmann, ed. *George Gissing and H. G. Wells: Their Friendship and Correspondence.* Urbana: University of Illinois Press, 1961.

Gilkes (1960) Lillian Gilkes. *Cora Crane: A Biography of Mrs. Stephen Crane.* Bloomington: Indiana University Press, 1960.

Gilkes (1969) ————. "Stephen Crane and the Harold Frederics." *Serif* 6 (December 1969): 21–48.

Goode W. A. M. Goode. *With Sampson Through the War.* London: W. Thacker, 1899.

Gordan John D. Gordan. *"The Ghost" at Brede Place.* New York: New York Public Library, 1953.

Greene Nelson Greene. Untitled Reminiscence, 23 pp. With covering letter to Melvin H. Schoberlin, 4 September 1947. NSyU.

Gullason (1957) Thomas A. Gullason. "Additions to the Canon of Stephen Crane." *Nineteenth-Century Fiction* 12 (1957): 157–160.

Gullason (1968a) ———. "The Cranes at Pennington Seminary." *American Literature* 39 (1968): 530–541.

Gullason (1968b) ———. "The First Known Review of Stephen Crane's 1893 *Maggie.*" *English Language Notes* 5 (1968): 300–302.

Gullason (1968c) ———. "The Last Will and Testament of Mrs. Mary Helen Peck Crane." *American Literature* 40 (1968): 232–234.

Gullason (1971) ———. "Stephen Crane and the *Arena*: Three 'Lost' Reviews." *Papers of the Bibliographical Society of America* 65 (1971): 297–299.

Gullason (1972) ———, ed. *Stephen Crane's Career: Perspectives and Evaluations.* New York: New York University Press, 1972.

Gullason (1977) ———. "Stephen Crane's Sister: New Biographical Facts." *American Literature* 49 (1977): 234–238.

Gullason (1986) ———. "A Cache of Short Stories by Stephen Crane's Family." *Studies in Short Fiction* 23 (1986): 71–106.

Hagemann (1959) E. R. Hagemann. "The Death of Stephen Crane." *Proceedings of the New Jersey Historical Society* 77 (1959): 173–184.

Hagemann (1968) ———. "Stephen Crane Faces the Storms of *Life.*" *Journal of Popular Culture* 2 (1968): 347–360.

Harriman (1900) Karl Edwin Harriman. "A Romantic Idealist—Mr. Stephen Crane." *Literary Review* 4 (April 1900): 85–87.

Harriman (1934) ———. "The Last Days of Stephen Crane." *New Hope* 2 (October 1934): 7–9, 19–21.

Herford Kenneth Herford. "Young Blood—Stephen Crane." *Saturday Evening Post* 172 (18 November 1899): 413.

Hind C. Lewis Hind. *Authors and I.* New York: John Lane, 1921.

Hitchcock Ripley Hitchcock. Preface to *The Red Badge of Courage.* New York: Appleton, 1900.

Howells William Dean Howells. *Selected Letters.* Vol. 4, 1892–1901. Edited by Thomas Wortham. Boston: Twayne, 1981.

Hubbard Elbert Hubbard. "As to Stephen Crane." *The Lotos* 9 (1896): 674–678.

Huneker James G. Huneker. *Steeplejack*, 2 vols. New York: Scribner's, 1920.

InU Indiana University, Bloomington.

James — Henry James. *Henry James: Letters*. Vol. 4. Edited by Leon Edel. Cambridge: Harvard University Press, 1984.

Johnson — Willis Fletcher Johnson. "The Launching of Stephen Crane." *Literary Digest International Book Review* 4 (1926): 288–290.

C. Jones — Claude Jones. "Stephen Crane at Syracuse." *American Literature* 7 (1935): 82–84.

E. R. Jones — Edith Richie Jones. "Stephen Crane at Brede." *Atlantic Monthly* 194 (July 1954): 57–61.

Karl — Frederick R. Karl. *Joseph Conrad: The Three Lives*. New York: Farrar, Straus and Giroux, 1979.

Karl and Davies — Frederick R. Karl and Laurence Davies. *The Collected Letters of Joseph Conrad*. Vol. I, 1861–1897. Cambridge: Cambridge University Press, 1983; vol. II, 1898–1902, 1986.

Katz (1964–1965) — Joseph Katz. "Some Light on the Stephen Crane-Amy Leslie Affair." *Mad River Review* 1 (Winter 1964–1965): 43–62.

Katz (1968) — ———. "Stephen Crane: Muckraker." *Columbia Library Columns* 17 (February 1968): 3–7.

Katz (1970) — ———, ed. *Stephen Crane in the West and Mexico*. Kent, Ohio: Kent State University Press, 1970.

Katz (1983a) — ———. "Solving Stephen Crane's *Pike County Puzzle*." *American Literature* 55 (1983): 171–182.

Katz (1983b) — ———. "Stephen Crane: Metropolitan Correspondent." *Kentucky Review* 4 (Spring 1983): 39–51.

Kibler — James E. Kibler, Jr. "The Library of Stephen and Cora Crane." In *Proof: The Yearbook of American Bibliographical and Textual Studies*. Edited by Joseph Katz. Vol. 1. Columbia: University of South Carolina Press, 1971. Pp. 199–246.

L — *Stephen Crane: Letters*. Edited by R. W. Stallman and Lillian Gilkes. New York: New York University Press, 1960.

LaFrance — Marston LaFrance. "A Few Facts about Stephen Crane and 'Holland.'" *American Literature* 37 (1965): 195–202.

LaRocca — Charles LaRocca. "Stephen Crane's Inspiration." *American Heritage* 42 (May–June 1991): 108–109.

Lawrence — Frederic M. Lawrence. *The Real Stephen Crane*. Edited by Joseph Katz. Newark: Newark Public Library, 1980.

| Leslie | Anita Leslie. *Mr. Frewen of England.* London: Hutchinson, 1966. |

Leslie — Anita Leslie. *Mr. Frewen of England.* London: Hutchinson, 1966.

Levenson (1969) — J. C. Levenson. Introduction to *Tales of Whilomville.* (1969) Vol. 7, *The Works of Stephen Crane.* Edited by Fredson Bowers. Charlottesville: University Press of Virginia, 1969.

Levenson (1970) — ———. Introduction to *Tales of Adventure.* Vol. 5, *The Works of Stephen Crane.* Edited by Fredson Bowers. Charlottesville: University Press of Virginia, 1970.

Levenson (1971) — ———. Introduction to *The O'Ruddy.* Vol. 4, *The Works of Stephen Crane.* Edited by Fredson Bowers. Charlottesville: University Press of Virginia, 1971.

Levenson (1975) — ———. Introduction to *The Red Badge of Courage.* Vol. 2, *The Works of Stephen Crane.* Edited by Fredson Bowers. Charlottesville: University Press of Virginia, 1975.

Levenson (1976) — ——— Introduction to *The Third Violet* and *Active Service.* Vol. 3, *The Works of Stephen Crane.* Edited by Fredson Bowers. Charlottesville: University Press of Virginia, 1976.

Linson (1903) — Corwin Knapp Linson. "Little Stories of 'Steve' Crane." *Saturday Evening Post* 175 (11 April 1903): 19–20.

Linson (1958) — ———. *My Stephen Crane.* Edited by Edwin H. Cady. Syracuse: Syracuse University Press, 1958.

Logan — Andy Logan. *Against the Evidence: The Becker-Rosenthal Affair.* New York: McCall, 1970.

Lubow — Arthur Lubow. *The Reporter Who Would Be King: A Biography of Richard Harding Davis.* New York: Scribner's, 1992.

McBride — Henry McBride. "Stephen Crane's Artist Friends." *Art News* 49 (October 1950): 46.

McElrath (1988) — Joseph R. McElrath, Jr. Frank Norris and The Wave: A Bibliography. New York: Garland, 1988.

McElrath (1993) — ———. "Stephen Crane in San Francisco: His Reception in *The Wave.*" *Stephen Crane Studies* 2 (Spring 1993): 2–18.

McIntosh — Burr McIntosh. *The Little I Saw of Cuba.* London: F. Tennyson Neely, 1899.

Marshall   Edward Marshall. "Stories of Stephen Crane." *San Francisco Call.* Reprint. *Literary Life* n. s., no. 24 (December 1900): 71–72.

Martin   Thomas E. Martin. "Stephen Crane: Athlete and Author." *Argot* (Syracuse University) 3 (March 1935): 1–2.

Mayfield (1963)   John S. Mayfield. "Stephen Crane's Bugs." *Courier* 3 (September 1963): 22–31.

Mayfield (1968)   ———. "S. C. at S. U." *Courier* 8 (Spring 1968): 8.

Milton   Joyce Milton. *The Yellow Kids: Foreign Correspondents in the Heyday of Yellow Journalism.* New York: Harper & Row, 1989.

MnU   University of Minnesota, Minneapolis.

Monteiro (1969a)   George Monteiro. "Stephen Crane's 'Dan Emmonds': A Case Reargued." *Serif* 6 (March 1969): 32–36.

Monteiro (1969b)   ———. "*The Illustrated American* and Stephen Crane's Contemporary Reputation." *Serif* 6 (December 1969): 49–54.

Monteiro (1980)   ———. "Addenda to Stallman and Hagemann: Parodies of Stephen Crane's Work." *Papers of the Bibliographical Society of America* 74 (1980): 402–403.

Monteiro (1981–1982)   ———. "Amy Leslie on Stephen Crane's *Maggie.*" *Journal of Modern Literature* 9 (1981–1982): 147–148.

Monteiro and Eppard   George Monteiro and Philip E. Eppard. "Addenda to Bowers and Stallman: Unrecorded Contemporary Appearances of Stephen Crane's Work." *Papers of the Bibliographical Society of America* 74 (1980): 73–75.

Morace (1975)   Robert A. Morace. "A 'New' Review of *The Red Badge of Courage.*" *American Literary Realism, 1870–1910* 8 (1975): 163–165.

Morace (1978)   ———. "'The Merry-Go-Round': An Earlier Version of 'The Pace of Youth.'" *Studies in the Novel* 10 (1978): 146–153.

NhD   Dartmouth College, Hanover, New Hampshire.

NNC   Columbia University, New York City.

Notebook   Donald J. and Ellen B. Greiner, eds. *The Notebook of Stephen Crane.* [Charlottesville]: Bibliographical Society of the University of Virginia, [1969].

Noxon   Frank Noxon. "The Real Stephen Crane." *Step-Ladder* (Chicago) 14 (January 1928): 4–9.

NSyU   Syracuse University, New York.

O'Donnell   Thomas F. O'Donnell. "John B. Van Petten: Stephen Crane's History Teacher." *American Literature* 27 (1955): 196–202.

Oliver   Arthur Oliver. "Jersey Memories—Stephen Crane." *Proceedings of the New Jersey Historical Society* 16 (1931): 454–463.

Osborn   Scott C. Osborn. "The 'Rivalry-Chivalry' of Richard Harding Davis and Stephen Crane." *American Literature* 28 (1956): 50–61.

O'Toole   G. J. A. O'Toole. *The Spanish War: An American Epic.* New York: Norton, 1984.

OU   Ohio State University, Columbus.

Paine   Ralph D. Paine. *Roads of Adventure.* Boston: Houghton Mifflin, 1922.

Parker   Hershel Parker. "Getting Used to the 'Original Form' of *The Red Badge of Courage.*" *New Essays on* The Red Badge of Courage. Edited by Lee Clark Mitchell. Cambridge: Cambridge University Press, 1986.

Peaslee   Clarence Loomis Peaslee. "Stephen Crane's College Days." *Monthly Illustrator* 13 (August 1896): 27–30.

Peck   Jesse T. Peck. *What Must I Do to Be Saved?* New York: Carlton and Porter, 1858.

Pizer (1960)   Donald Pizer. "The Garland–Crane Relationship." *Huntington Library Quarterly* 24 (November 1960): 75–82.

Pizer (1979)   ———. "*The Red Badge of Courage* Nobody Knows: A Brief Rejoinder." *Studies in the Novel* 11 (1979): 77–81.

Poems   Joseph Katz, ed. *The Poems of Stephen Crane: A Critical Edition.* Revised edition. New York: Cooper Square, 1971.

Pratt (1939a)   Lyndon Upson Pratt. "The Formal Education of Stephen Crane." *American Literature* 10 (1939): 460–471.

Pratt (1939b)   ———. "A Possible Source of *The Red Badge of Courage.*" *American Literature* 11 (1939): 1–10.

Price — Carl F. Price. "Stephen Crane: A Genius Born in a Methodist Parsonage." *Christian Advocate* (New York) 98: 866–867.

Randel — William Randel. "From Slate to Emerald Green: More Light on Crane's Jacksonville Visit." *Nineteenth-Century Fiction* 19 (1965): 357–368.

Robertson — Michael Robertson. *Stephen Crane at Lafayette.* Easton, Pa.: The Friends of Skillman Library, 1990.

Roosevelt — Theodore Roosevelt. *The Letters of Theodore Roosevelt.* Vol. 1. Edited by Elting T. Morison. Cambridge: Harvard University Press, 1951.

Rubens — Horatio S. Rubens. *Liberty: The Story of Cuba.* New York: Brewer, Warren & Putnam, 1932. Reprint. New York: Arno Press & The New York Times, 1970.

Schoberlin — Melvin H. Schoberlin. "Flagon of Despair: Stephen Crane." Unpublished manuscript, NSyU.

SCraneN — *Stephen Crane Newsletter.*

Seitz (1924) — Don Carlos Seitz. *Joseph Pulitzer: His Life and Letters.* New York: Simon & Schuster, 1924.

Seitz (1933) — ———. "Stephen Crane: War Correspondent." *Bookman* 76 (February 1933): 137–140.

Sheridan — Clare Sheridan. *Naked Truth.* New York: Harper, 1928.

Sherry — Norman Sherry. "A Conrad Manuscript." *Times Literary Supplement,* 25 June 1970, p. 691.

Sidbury — Edna Crane Sidbury. "My Uncle, Stephen Crane, as I Knew Him." *Literary Digest International Book Review* 4 (1926): 248–250.

Sloane — David E. E. Sloane. "Stephen Crane at Lafayette." *Resources for American Literary Study* 2 (1972): 102–105.

Slote — Bernice Slote. "Stephen Crane in Nebraska." *Prairie Schooner* 43 (1969): 192–199.

E. G. Smith — Ernest G. Smith. [Comments and Queries]. *Lafayette Alumnus* 2 (February 1932): 6.

H. B. Smith — Harry B. Smith. *First Nights and First Editions.* Boston: Little, Brown, 1931.

Sorrentino (1981) — Paul Sorrentino. "Stephen Crane and William Howe Crane: A Loan and Its Aftermath." *Resources for American Literary Study* 11 (1981): 101–108.

Sorrentino (1984)	———. "Stephen Crane's Sale of 'An Episode of War' to *The Youth's Companion.*" *Studies in Bibliography* 37 (1984): 243–248.
Sorrentino (1985)	———. "New Evidence on Stephen Crane at Syracuse." *Resources for American Literary Study* 15 (1985): 179–185.
Sorrentino (1986)	———. "Newly Discovered Writings of Mary Helen Peck Crane and Agnes Elizabeth Crane." *Courier* 21 (1986): 103–134.
Stallman (1972)	R. W. Stallman. *Stephen Crane: A Critical Bibliography.* Ames: Iowa State University Press, 1972.
Stallman (1973)	———. *Stephen Crane: A Biography.* Revised edition. New York: Braziller, 1973.
Stallman and Hagemann (1964)	R. W. Stallman and E. R. Hagemann, eds. *The War Dispatches of Stephen Crane.* New York: New York University Press, 1964.
Stallman and Hagemann (1966)	———, eds. *The New York City Sketches of Stephen Crane.* New York: New York University Press, 1966.
Starrett (1921)	Vincent Starrett. "Stephen Crane: An Estimate." *Men, Women and Boats.* New York: Boni and Liveright, 1921.
Starrett (1923)	———. *Stephen Crane: A Bibliography.* Philadelphia: Centaur Book Shop, 1923.
Stevens	Wallace Stevens. *Letters of Wallace Stevens.* Edited by Holly Stevens. New York: Knopf, 1966.
Stronks (1963)	James B. Stronks. "Stephen Crane's English Years: The Legend Corrected." *Papers of the Bibliographical Society of America* 57 (1963): 340–349.
Stronks (1973)	———. "Garland's Private View of Crane in 1898 (With a Postscript)." *American Literary Realism, 1870–1910* 6 (1973): 249–250.
ViU	University of Virginia, Charlottesville.
Vosburgh	R. G. Vosburgh. "The Darkest Hour in the Life of Stephen Crane." *Criterion,* n.s. 1 (February 1901): 26–27.
Weatherford	Richard M. Weatherford, ed. *Stephen Crane: The Critical Heritage.* London: Routledge & Kegan Paul, 1973.
Weintraub	Stanley Weintraub. *The London Yankees: Portraits of American Writers and Artists in England, 1894–1914.* New York: Harcourt Brace Jovanovich, 1979.

Wells (1900)	H. G. Wells. "Stephen Crane from an English Standpoint." *North American Review* 171 (August 1900): 233–242.
Wells (1934)	———. *Experiment in Autobiography.* 2 vols. London: Victor Gollancz, 1934.
Wertheim (1970)	Stanley Wertheim, ed. *The Merrill Studies in* Maggie *and* George's Mother. Columbus, Ohio: Merrill, 1970.
Wertheim (1976a)	———. "Stephen Crane's 'Battalion Notes.'" *Resources for American Literary Study* 6 (1976): 79–80.
Wertheim (1976b)	———. "Stephen Crane Remembered." *Studies in American Fiction* 4 (1976): 45–64.
Wertheim (1979a)	———. "The Stephen Crane Testimonial Fund." *Resources for American Literary Study* 9 (1979): 31–32.
Wertheim (1979b)	———. "H. G. Wells to Cora Crane: Some Letters and Corrections." *Resources for American Literary Study* 9 (1979): 207–212.
Wertheim (1983)	———. "Stephen Crane in the Shadow of the Parthenon." *Columbia Library Columns* 32 (May 1983): 3–13.
Wertheim (1991)	———. "Frank Norris and Stephen Crane: Conviction and Uncertainty." *American Literary Realism, 1870–1910* 24 (Fall 1991): 54–62.
Wertheim (1992)	———. "New Stephen Crane Letters and Inscriptions." *Stephen Crane Studies* 1 (Spring 1992): 15–20.
Wertheim (1993)	———. "Another Diary of the Reverend Jonathan Townley Crane." *Resources for American Literary Study* 19 (1993): 35–49.
Wertheim Collection	Collection of Stanley and Mary Wertheim, New York City.
Wheeler and Rives	Post Wheeler and Hallie E. Rives. *Dome of Many-Coloured Glass.* Garden City, N.Y.: Doubleday, 1955.
Wickham	Harvey Wickham. "Stephen Crane at College." *American Mercury* 7 (March 1926): 291–297.
Williams	Ames W. Williams. "Stephen Crane: War Correspondent." *New Colophon* 1 (April 1948): 113–123.
WM	"War Memories." *Wounds in the Rain.* New York: Frederick A. Stokes, 1900.

Work   Wilson Follett, ed. *The Work of Stephen Crane.* 12 vols. New York: Knopf, 1925–1927.

Works   Fredson Bowers, ed. *The Works of Stephen Crane.* 10 vols. Charlottesville: University Press of Virginia, 1969–1976.

Index

INDEX

Index

Index

INDEX

INDEX

Index

INDEX

INDEX

Index

INDEX

Index

INDEX

M

Mabon, George D., 274, 282–83
  Hawkins and, 284
  suit against Crane, 285, 288, 289, 290
MacArthur, James, 292
McBride, Henry, 135–36
McCalla, Henry Bowman, 310, 317
McCauley, Fannie G., 13
  See also Crane, Fannie McCauley
McCawley, Charles L., 414
McClure, Robert, 274, 402
McClure, Samuel S., xli–xlii, 155, 246, 274
  and coal mine article, 108–9, 110
  Garland and, 95–96
  letter from Crane, 167
  and *The Red Badge of Courage*, 69, 104, 116
McClure's Magazine, xli–xlii, xliv, 282
  and *The O'Ruddy*, 435–36
  pieces by Crane, 161, 186, 198, 272, 288, 349,
    363, 370, 386
McClure syndicate, xli, 115, 191, 198, 199, 200,
    214–15, 277–78, 287
  Active Service, 389, 391
  and Civil War series, 161, 162
  Greek war dispatches, 250, 255, 258
  "Opium's Varied Dreams," 184
  "Stephen Crane in Texas," 365
  The Third Violet, 216–17
  war correspondent contract, 221
  "With Greek and Turk" series, 262–63
McClurg, Alexander C., 179
McCready, Ernest W., 302–3, 309, 317
  on Crane, 310–11
McCumber, Thomas, xix
McDermott (New York Police Sergeant), 206
Mace, Frances L., *Under Pine and Palm*, 54
McGonegal, Henry G., 212
Machias (gunboat), 305
McIntosh, Burr, xlii, 317, 321, 328
  and San Juan battle, 323–26
McIntosh, William, 148
  "The Philistines at Dinner," 155
Maclagen, Thomas J., 430, 434–35
McMahon, Lena, 71
McNab, Reuben, 324–25
McNeil, Hammond, xxxi
Macqueen, John, 353
Macracken, John, 54
McTeague: A Story of San Francisco, Norris,
    xlii–xliii
MacVittie, William (Mack), 361, 379, 400
Maggie: A Girl of the Streets, Crane, xxi, 68, 69, 82,
    160, 184, 187
  Barry's view of, 88
  British editions, 204, 207
  copyright application, 83, 185

drafts of, 62–63, 64, 80
  expurgated version, 122
  Howells and, 99, 134–35, 193
  inscription to Lemperly, 202
  manuscript of, xlii
  preface to, 177
  private printing, 69, 83, 84
  reprint, 450
  reviews, 85, 89, 91, 99–100, 123, 131, 141, 171,
    185–86, 188, 189–93, 196, 198, 199, 202–3,
    208–9, 215–16, 229–30, 234, 295
  revisions, xli, 81, 169–70, 171, 175
Maine (hospital ship), xxix–xxx
Maine (United States warship), sinking of, 290
Main-Travelled Roads, Garland, xxxv
"Making an Orator," Crane, 43, 378, 383, 409
"The Making of the 307th," Crane, 441, 449
Malaria, Crane ill with, 328
Male prostitute, 105
"A Man adrift on a slim spar," Crane, 287
"A Man and Some Others," Crane, 137, 188, 204,
    209, 215, 243
  changes in, 231
  Conrad's view of, 281
"A man builded a bugle for the storms to blow,"
    Crane, 181
Manchester Guardian, review of "The Ghost," 421
A Man Could Stand Up, Ford, xxxiv
"The Man in the White Hat," Crane, 250–51
Manitou (ship), 359, 365
"A Man said: 'Thou tree!," Crane, 181
Manuscripts, excerpts from, xxiii
"The Man with the Hoe," Markham, 428
Marburgh, Bertram, 341
Mardi Gras, New Orleans, 128
"Marines Signaling under Fire at Guantanamo,"
    Crane, 310, 312–14, 347, 370, 373
  Blackwood's and, 390
  English rights, 350
The Market Place, Frederic, xxxv
Markham, Edwin, "The Man with the Hoe," 428
Marriott-Watson, H. B., 406, 407, 449
  and *The Red Badge of Courage*, 152
Marsena, Frederic, 293
Marshall, Edward, xlii, 114, 132, 317–18
  interview with Howells, 99–100
  reviews of Crane's works, 143, 193
  "A Wounded Correspondent's Recollections of
    Guasimas," 318–19
Martin, Thomas E., 62
Mason, A. E. W., 361, 388, 399, 411, 413
  on Christmas party at Brede Place, 412–13
  and Crane's Christmas play, 406
  and Crane's illness, 441
  and *The O'Ruddy*, 450
Matanzas, Cuba, 299, 337
"Mathilde" (companion of Cora), 262

Index

INDEX

INDEX

INDEX

INDEX

INDEX

INDEX

INDEX

INDEX

INDEX

INDEX